The Ukrainians

Andrew Wilson is Professor of Ukrainian Studies at University College London and a senior policy fellow at the European Council on Foreign Relations. He is the author of numerous books, including *Belarus: The Last European Dictatorship* and *Ukraine Crisis: What It Means for the West.*

The Ukrainians
The Story of How a People Became a Nation

New Edition

Andrew Wilson

Yale University Press
New Haven and London

To Ella and Alfie

First published in 2000
Second edition published in 2002
Third edition published in 2009
Fourth edition published in 2015
This edition published in 2022

For information about this and other Yale University Press publications, please contact:
U.S. office   sales.press@yale.edu   www.yalebooks.com
Europe office   sales@yaleup.co.uk   www.yalebooks.co.uk

Set in Sabon by Fakenham Photosetting, Norfolk and IDS (UK) Data Connection
Printed in Great Britain by Clays Ltd, Elcograf S.p.A

Library of Congress Catalog Control Number: 2022943778

ISBN 978-0-300-26940-6 (new edn pbk)

A catalogue record for this book is available from the British Library.

10 9 8 7 6 5 4 3 2 1

Contents

Illustrations

Black and white plates

Preface to the New Edition

In earlier editions, this book was subtitled the 'unexpected nation'. Modern Ukraine has been founded four times; each time with an element of surprise. The emergence of an independent Ukrainian state in 1991 was certainly unexpected in the chancelleries, universities and boardrooms of the West, all of which underestimated the centrifugal forces leading to the USSR's collapse, and then struggled to adapt to the reality of independent Ukraine. This new Ukraine was also considered by many to be an unlikely candidate as a new nation, given its pronounced patterns of ethnic, linguistic, religious and regional diversity. However, an unexpected nation is still a nation – no more and no less than many others. The elite of Putin's Russia clearly thought otherwise (as outlined in chapter thirteen). To them, Ukraine simply does not exist, or Ukrainians and Russians are one nation, or its 'Russian-lite' parts should be sub-divided from the rest. The invasion in February 2022 was designed to impose these beliefs, regardless of what Ukrainians actually thought. But the new post-Soviet Ukraine had already been refounded with two revolutions. First with the 'Orange Revolution' in 2004 (chapter fourteen); then with the 'Revolution of Dignity' in 2013–14 (chapter fifteen). The second was more radical than the first; and more explicitly anti-colonial. This cumulative reinvention accelerated in 2022 (chapters sixteen and seventeen), with Ukraine proving the historical principle that war is a great nation-builder. At the time of rewriting, Putin seemed to have failed on this key existential question at least. Ukraine was more united after the invasion than before. Militarily, the outcome of the war also partly depended on this identity question: patriotic Ukrainians were prepared to fight Russians who were sent to war on a lie. The strategic factors shaping the outcome of the war – sanctions, Western response, effective arms supply, Russian resolve – were harder to predict.

Nationalists tend to see their nation as eternal, as a historical entity since the earliest times. Their history is written as the story of the nation's trials and triumphs. In reality nations are formed by circumstance and chance. Ukrainians like to talk about the 'national idea'. Precisely so. Concepts such as 'nation' really belong to the realm of political and cultural imaginations. The approach of this book, to use another ugly but fashionable term, is therefore deconstructivist. Nations are cultural constructs and this is how I have tried to present 'Ukraine' – as the product of various imaginations, both Ukrainian and other. Alongside the more obvious narrative of political and social change, I have therefore included representations of Ukraine in literature and the arts and, in the chapter on geopolitics, cartographers' images.

I have also tried to deconstruct, in the sense of debunk, some of the myths about Ukraine and its past – both Ukrainian nationalists' flights of fancy and Russian and other rival nationalists' attempts to belittle or deny Ukraine. This should not be taken as an attempt to undermine the 'Ukrainian idea', just to build it on more secure foundations. The Ukrainians may now be becoming a nation before our very eyes, but this does not mean that they were always Ukrainians or that they were always destined to become such. Often the inhabitants of what is now Ukraine would have been better described as rebellious peasants, members of a particular faith, or left-wing activists. Often they thought in terms of a local identity; often they saw themselves as part of other communities, some still existing, some long disappeared. The process whereby they became Ukrainians could have unfolded in different ways. The book therefore also tries to be counterfactual. History would have been very different if Russia had absorbed what subsequently became the nationalist stronghold of western Ukraine in 1772 or 1815 rather than 1945. Modern Ukraine might then have been more like modern Belarus, with a much weaker sense of national identity. Conversely, if Kyiv had not been sacked by the Mongols in 1240, it might have developed into a rival centre of power to the fledgling state in the north that eventually became first Muscovy and then Russia. This book aims to capture the fact that history is always pregnant with possibility.

The approach is also, where necessary, *re*constructivist. Significant aspects of the past are often now overlooked and need to be written back into the picture. Above all, this concerns the Ukrainian experience of empire, which has been a more or less ever-present factor in Ukrainian life since the sixteenth century at least. Many Ukrainians were quite willing citizens of the Polish Commonwealth and the Habsburg, Romanov and Soviet empires, and this should not be wished away by, ironically, taking too deconstructivist an approach to the history of these lost worlds and disassembling them out of the Ukrainian experience. I have begun my study in the time of the early medieval kingdom of Kyivan Rus, but that history is one that is shared with Russians and Belarusians. Ukrainian Cossacks created an independent 'Hetmanate' in 1648, but, again, it could not create the trappings of a modern state. Various Ukrainian governments emerged in 1917–20 after the collapse of the Romanov and Habsburg empires, but they were always precarious and many Ukrainians supported the rival Soviet project. On the whole, therefore, Ukrainian identity has had to be developed in other peoples' states – until now. The period since 1991 is in many ways Ukraine's first period of consolidated statehood.

The reader will, I hope, forgive what is historically arguably an over-concentration on Ukraine's last imperial relationship, that with tsarist then Soviet then independent Russia. Ukraine's long linkage with Poland features heavily in the earlier historical chapters, but less so in those on the present day.

Ukraine has not always been defined by its relationship with Russia, but it certainly is today, particularly given the legacy of the Soviet period, which continues to exert a huge influence on Ukrainian identity, politics, economics and even religion. It is no exaggeration to say that the management of this relationship is the key to the future of the whole of Eastern Europe. It is also an association without obvious analogies. Even more so than the Scots and the English, the Slovaks and the Czechs, the Ukrainians and Russians have long been both friends and rivals, and on extremely intimate terms. But the crisis that began with covert invasion in 2014 and then full-scale invasion in 2022 is definitvely driving the two apart.

Finally, the book seeks to challenge stereotypes about Ukraine's place in the wider world. Like the Balkans,[1] Ukraine is neither as incontrovertibly 'other' nor as 'non-European' (or just 'non-visible') as many have seen it as being in the past; nor is it as incontrovertibly 'European' as Ukrainian nationalists would have it in the present. Ukraine has always stood at a crossroads of cultural influences – at times a key part of a Europe that has itself been constantly redefined, at others not. Ukraine's foreign policy has often vacillated between Russia and the West. In 2004, 2014 and 2022 it attempted to choose the West, and Russia attempted to stop it. The subsequent struggle will profoundly affect the future of Russia and Europe, not just Ukraine.

In none of this are the Ukrainians unique. As Ernest Renan famously remarked, history is as much about forgetting as it is about remembering: 'getting history wrong is part of being a nation.'[2] All nations tell a version of their histories that is shaped by present circumstances. One of Ukraine's best young historians, Yaroslav Hrytsak, has argued that Ukrainian history is just as 'normal' as that of any other nation.[3] Indeed so, but part of that normalcy consists in being prepared to be less fetishistic about the past. One warning is necessary, however. A book of this size cannot be a *complete* history of Ukraine, both past and present. The same is true of the chronology that follows. I have included most main events, but concentrated on the times and places that feature in the text. Readers can look elsewhere (perhaps starting with the bibliographical essay at the end) for every fact and detail, but can proceed with the assurance that I have tried to include enough information to make the story comprehensible and have assumed only a minimal amount of prior knowledge. The amount of necessary information has, however, varied with how I have chosen to tell the story.

A word or two about technical aspects. Given what I have said so far, it would perhaps have made more sense to render names of individuals and places in all the various ways they have been used in the past, rather than impose present-day categorisations and spellings. The city of Lviv (the current Ukrainian spelling), for example, has also been known as Lvov (Russian), Lwów (Polish) and Lemberg (German). Rather than burden the reader with two or three versions of the same name, however, I have used modern Ukrainian versions throughout. Nevertheless, sometimes it has made sense to refer to the same place or person in different fashions. The twelfth-century text *The Lay of Ihor's Host* (Ukrainian 'h') is therefore also the nineteenth-century opera *Prince Igor* (Russian 'g'). The great tenth-century prince of Rus is both Volodymyr (Ukrainian version) and Vladimir (Russian version). After all, in a sense Volodymyr, according to the Ukrainian tradition the founder of Ukraine-Rus, and Vladimir, according to Russian history the founder of Russia, are different people.

I have tried to avoid using the adjective 'Ukrainian' or the place-name 'Ukraine' (or indeed 'Russian' or 'Russia') before the seventeenth and eighteenth centuries, when the beginnings of modern national identities make them appropriate. Sometimes, however, this is just grammatically impossible. Also, it is difficult to avoid situating very early periods with modern place-names; but this is not meant to undermine the general thesis that national identities are relatively recent creations.

To make things easier for the reader I have used an adapted Library of Congress system for transliteration, keeping diacritical marks and distinctive lettering (Pochaïv not Pochaiv), but ignoring soft signs (therefore Khmelnytskyi not Khmel'nyts'kyi and Viacheslav not V"iacheslav), although I have kept them in the footnotes for reference purposes. In the first four editions, certain Anglicisms were retained: most notably Kiev, not Kyiv. But the rest of the world has been using the Ukrainian transliteration since 2022, so chapters sixteen and seventeen shift to Kiev, as do the captions for plates 46–53. Otherwise, modern Ukrainian place-names have been used. I have tried to keep footnotes to a minimum, apart from cases of direct quotation. Compensation is provided in the bibliographical essay of mainly English-language material at the end of the book.

My thanks go to the many friends and colleagues who have helped in the preparation of the book, including Jonathan Aves and the two anonymous readers for their comments on the first draft of the text. My good friend Graham Smith helped me to liven up chapter thirteen. Graham died in 1999 and is sorely missed by all of his many family, friends and colleagues. Thanks in Kyiv go to the Petrus family, Valentin Yakushik, Valerii Khmelko, Yevgeniia Tesliuk and Oleksii Haran. Catherine Pyke of UCL helped prepare the historical maps. Thanks to Hans Petter Midttun for his photo. Grants from the ESRC and Leverhulme Trust helped my research. At Yale I am especially grateful to Joanna Godfrey, Katie Urquhart, Meg Pettit, Robert Baldock, Candida Brazil, Tami Halliday, Katie Harris, Heather Nathan, Elizabeth Pelton and Maha Moushabeck for all their patience and hard work. None of the above is of course to blame for my own judgments. Warmest thanks as always are due to my wife, Helen, this time also for producing Ella and Alfie and most of the better photographs in the book.

Chronology

	Politics/History		Culture
980–1015	Reign of Volodymyr (Vladimir) 'the Great'		
988	Baptism of Rus		
1019–54	Reign of Yaroslav 'the Wise'	1037–44	Building of St Sofiia's
1051–4	Ilarion serves as first native metropolitan	1048–9	Ilarion, *Sermon on Law and Grace*
1054	Catholic-Orthodox schism	late C11?	*Angel with the Golden Hair*
		1073–84	Building of the Assumption cathedral,
1108	Foundation of Vladimir		Pechersk
1113–25	Reign of Volodymyr Monomakh	1134	*Lady of Vyshhorod/Vladimir*
		early C12	*Virgin Oranta*
1147–55	Klymentii Smoliatych serves as metropolitan	C12	*The Tale of Bygone Years*
1169	Andrei Bogoliubskii's armies sack Kiev	1187	*The Lay of Ihor's Host*
1199–1205	Reign of Roman of Halych		
1237–64	Reign of Danylo of Halych		
1240	Mongols sack Kiev		
1246–7	Danylo's 'union' with Rome		
1299	Kiev hierarchs move to Vladimir		
1349	Poland occupies Galicia	C14	*Icon of Volhynia Mother of God*
1362	Battle of the Blue Waters, Lithuanians advance through Kiev		
1439	Union of Florence		
1448	Moscow establishes metropolitanate		
1453	Fall of Constantinople		
1458	Election of Gregorii, Kievan Church stabilised to 1596		
1569	Union of Lublin	1581	Ostrih Bible
1596	Union of Brest, creation of Uniate (Greek Catholic) Church		
1620–32	Restoration of Kievan Orthodox Church	1621	Boretskyi, *Protestation*
		1621–2	Kopystenskyi, *Palinodiia*
1632–47	Petro Mohyla metropolitan of Kiev	1640–3	Mohyla, *Orthodox Confession of Faith*

	Politics/History		Culture
1648	Great Rebellion, establishment of Hetmanate		
1654	Treaty of Pereiaslav		
1657	Death of Khmelnytskyi		
1658	Treaty of Hadiach		
1667	Treaty of Andrusovo	1672–3	Sofonovych, *Kroinika*
		1674	Gizel, *Sinopsis*
1685–6	Kievan Church dissolved		
1687–1709	Mazepa serves as Hetman	1690–3	St Nicholas's church
		1690–1707	Baroque additions to St Sofiia's
		late C17	Icon of the *Holy Protectress*
		1698	All Saints' church, Pechersk
1709	Battle of Poltava		
1720	Synod of Zamość	1720	Velychko, *Tales of the Cossack W.*
		1731–44	Bell tower, Pechersk
		1740s	Icon of *SS Juliana and Anastasia*
1772	Habsburgs occupy Galicia		
1774	Habsburgs occupy Bukovyna		
1775	Destruction of Zaporozhian Sich		
1783	Russia annexes Crimea		
1785	Abolition of Hetmanate		
1793–5	Russia occupies Right Bank, Volhynia	1790s	Bortnianskyi, Choral Works
		1831–2	Gogol, *Village Evenings*, *Taras Bu.*
		1836	Gogol, *The Government Inspector*
		1837	Shashkevych et al., *Nymph of the Dniester*
		1840	Shevchenko, *Kobzar*
1845–7	Cyrylo-Methodian Society	1846	*History of the Rus*
1848	Revolution in Austria		
		1861	Kostomarov, *Two Rus Nationaliti…*
1863	Valuiev circular	1863	Hulak-Artemovskyi, *Zaporozhian beyond the Danube*
1867	Ausgleich: creation of Austria-Hungary		
		1874	Nechui-Levytskyi, *The Clouds*
1876	Ems Ukaz	1876	Myrnyi, *Lover of the People*
1890	First Ukrainian political party established	1892–3	Hrinchenko and Drahomanov, *Dialogues*
1894	Hrushevskyi moves to Lviv		
1905–6	Russian Revolution	1908	*Link* exhibition, Kiev
1911	Stolypin shot in Kiev	1910	Ukraïnka, *The Noble Woman*
1914	Outbreak of World War I		
1914–15	Bobrinskii's occupation of Galicia	1914	Maksymovych, *The Kiss*
		1914	Semenko burns the *Kobzar*
1917 (Feb)	Russian Revolution	1917	Boichuk becomes professor of Ukrainian Academy of Arts
1917 (Mar)	Ukrainian Central Council set up		
1917 (Nov)	It becomes the Ukrainian People's Republic (UNR)		

	Politics/History	Culture
1917 (Dec)	First Soviet Ukrainian government set up	
1918 (Jan)	UNR declares independence	
1918 (Apr)	Skoropadskyi's Hetmanate	
1918 (Nov)	West Ukrainian People's Republic established	
1918 (Dec)	Petliura, Vynnynchenko lead Directorate	
1919	Bukovyna awarded to Romania	
1919	Transcarpathia awarded to Czechoslovakia	
1921	Ukrainian SSR stabilised	
1921–30	Ukrainian Autocephalous Orthodox Church	1921 Burliuk, *Carousel*
1922	Polish control of Galicia, Volhynia confirmed	
1922	Ukrainian SSR joins USSR	
1923–33	Ukrainianisation campaign	1926 Khvylovyi, *Ukraine or Little Russia?*
		1926 Dontsov, *Nationalism*
		1928 Kulish, *The People's Malakhii*
1929	Formation of the OUN	1928 Petrov/Ilf, *Twelve Chairs*
		1928 Petrytskyi, *Turandot*
1930	First purges in Soviet Ukraine	1930 Dovzhenko, *The Earth*
1932–3	Great Famine	1932 Dovzhenko, *Ivan*
		1934 Tychyna, *The Party Leads*
		1935 Yanovskyi, *Horseriders*
1939–41	First Soviet occupation of western Ukraine	1938 Korniichuk, *Bohdan Khmelnytskyi*
1941	German invasion of USSR, OUN declare independence	
1943–54	UPA Insurgency	
1944–5	Second Soviet occupation of western Ukraine	1944 Sosiura, *Love Ukraine!*
1954	Crimea transferred to Ukrainian SSR	1954 Khmelko, *Pereiaslav Council*
		1961 Ivanov, *Two Things at Once*
1963–72	Shelest Soviet Ukrainian leader	1965 Paradzhanov, *Shadows of our Forgotten Ancestors*
		1968 Honchar, *Sobor*
1972–89	Shcherbytskyi Soviet Ukrainian leader	1980 Kostenko, *Marusia Churai*
		1983 Shevchuk, *House on the Hill*
1989	First Rukh congress	
1990	First Ukrainian elections	
1991 (Mar)	Referendum on preservation of USSR	
1991 (Aug)	Failed Moscow coup, Ukraine declares independence	
1991 (Dec)	Referendum confirms independence, Kravchuk elected president	
1992–3	Orthodox Church splits in three	1992 Andrukhovych, *Recreations*
1993	Donbas miners' strikes	1993 Andrukhovych, *Moskoviada*

	Politics/History		Culture
1994	(Mar) Parliamentary elections		
1994	(July) Kravchuk loses presidential election to Kuchma		
1994	(Oct) Launch of economic reform		
1995	Funeral of Patriarch Volodymyr, Filaret succeeds		
1996	New constitution	1996	Zabuzhko, *Field Notes on Ukrainian Sex*
1996	Introduction of hryvnia		
1997	Friendship Treaty with Russia, Partnership Charter with NATO	1997	Andrukhovych, *Perversion*
1998	Parliamentary elections	1998	St Michael's monastery rebuilt
1999	Presidential election, Kuchma reelected, Zaseev-Rudenko, *Black Council*	1999	
	Yushchenko appointed prime minister		
2000 (Apr)	Constitutional Referendum	2000	Completion of the Assumption Cathedral
2000 (Sep)	Gongadze disappears		
2000 (Nov)	Kuchma accused of complicity		
2001 (Apr)	Fall of Yushchenko government	2001	Illienko, *Mazepa*
2001 (June)	Papal visit to Ukraine		
2002 (Mar)	Parliamentary elections: Initial success for Yushchenko and Tymoshenko		
2004	Presidential election prompts 'Orange Revolution'	2004	Ruslana, *Wild Dances* wins Eurovision
2005 (Jan)	Yushchenko inaugurated as president	2005	Zhadan, *Anarchy in the UKR*
2005 (Sep)	Collapse of first Orange government		
2006 (Jan)	Constitutional changes enacted		
2006 (Mar)	Parliamentary elections		
2006 (Aug)	Yanukovych prime minister		
2007 (Sep)	New elections, new Orange government in December		
2008 (Oct)	Economic crisis hits, IMF loan		
2009 (Jan)	Gas crisis		
2010 (Feb)	Yanukovych elected president		
2010 (Mar)	Tymoshenko ousted as PM		
2010 (Oct)	Constitution restored		
2011 (Oct)	Tymoshenko sentenced		
2012 (Oct)	Parliamentary elections	2012	Ukraine and Poland host 2012 European Championship finals
2013 (Aug)	Russia begins trade war	2013	Akhtem Seitablaiev, *Haytarma* (a Crimean Tatar film)
2013 (Nov)	Ukraine rejects EU trade deal, 'Euromaidan' protests begin		
2014 (Feb)	Climax of protests, one hundred killed in Kiev, Yanukovych flees	2014	'Revolution of Dignity', Leninopad – removal of Lenin monuments

Politics/History		Culture	
2014 (Feb–Mar)	Coup in Crimea		
2014 (Apr)	War in Donbas		
2014 (May)	Poroshenko elected president		
2014 (Aug)	Russian offensive at Ilovaisk	2015 (May)	De-communisation laws
2014 (Sep)	First Minsk agreement	2015–19	*Servant of the People* TV series
2014 (Oct)	Parliamentary elections	2016	Jamala, *1944* wins Eurovision
2015 (Feb)	Second Minsk agreement	2016	DakhaBrakha play Glastonbury
2019 (Jan)	Tomos granted to Orthodox Church of Ukraine	2017	Seitablaiev, *Cyborgs*
2019 (Mar–Apr)	Zelenskyi wins presidency		
2019 (July)	Servant of the People party wins parliamentary elections		
2019 (Dec)	First Trump impeachment		
2022 (24 Feb)	Russia invades Ukraine	2022	Kalush Orchestra, *Stefania* wins Eurovision

1

Contesting National Origins: Lays of Ancient Rus

> So let us begin, brothers,
> this tale –
> from Volodymyr of yore
> to nowadays Ihor,
> who girded his mind
> with fortitude, .
> and sharpened his heart
> with manliness;
> imbued with the spirit of arms,
> he led his brave troops
> against the land of the Polovtsians
> in the name of the land of Rus.

The Lay of Ihor's Host (1187)[1]

The 'land of Rus' that Prince Ihor of Chernihiv set out to defend in 1185 was the early medieval kingdom of Kievan Rus,[2] the dominant power in Eastern Europe between the ninth and thirteenth centuries AD. Its territory covered most of modern-day western and central Ukraine, nearly all of modern Belarus and the western parts of what is now Russia (see the map on page 3). *The Lay of Ihor's Host* is the great narrative epic of the period, the equivalent of *Beowulf* for the Anglo-Saxons or *Táin Bó Cuailnge* for the Celts. It depicts Ihor's heroic campaign against the Polovtsians, a pagan tribe from the eastern steppes who were a constant thorn in the side of the Rus. Unfortunately, Rus was already in decline by 1185 and Ihor's campaign ended in spectacular defeat. *The Lay of Ihor's Host* is therefore more of a lament than a celebration.

The poem was supposedly written immediately after the event, but disappeared until its rediscovery in the 1790s by a certain Count Musin-Pushkin, a collector of antiquities in the service of Catherine the Great. The original copy was destroyed along with Musin-Pushkin's house during the great Moscow fire that preceded Napoleon's occupation in

1812, leading some to cast doubt on the saga's authenticity – especially as it seemed to evoke rather than merely describe a sense of Rus patriotism, thereby fitting rather too conveniently the tsarist ideology of the time. However, the discovery in 1852 of another (fourteenth-century) chronicle, the *Zadonshchina*, which drew much of its inspiration and material from *The Lay of Ihor's Host*, has led most experts to accept that the latter was genuine.

On the other hand, there is little agreement as to who the Rus actually were. Linguistic imprecision and, unfortunately, Russocentrism have too often led to the assumption that the 'Rus' were simply early medieval 'Russians'. Many translations of *The Lay of Ihor's Host*, including the 1961 version by Vladimir Nabokov from which the above quotation is adapted, render the 'land of Rus' (*Ruskaia zemlia*) as 'the Russian land'. Tsarist and Soviet historians, and many of their Western rivals, have too often abused the idea of east Slavic common origin in an 'ancient Rus nation' to deny Ukrainians (and Belarusians) any separate identity at all. Ukrainian historians, on the other hand, have tended to argue that the Russians and Ukrainians, or at least their ancestors, have always pursued separate historical paths. Two distinct Ukrainian views exist: either Rus was only ever a loose agglomeration of peoples; or the opposite – Rus was a relatively united early Ukrainian state, dubbed Ukraine-Rus, from which the Russian nation emerged as a later offshoot.

It is also possible to argue that all the eastern Slavs (Ukrainians, Russians and Belarusians) are descended from the Rus, a once-united people amongst whom fundamental differences emerged only after the time of Prince Ihor. In this case, the fact that a common identity may have existed in the twelfth century is not at all the same thing as saying that Ukrainians and Belarusians are just 'Russians' today. 'Rus' was what came before all three, at a time when collective identities were extremely loose and modern 'nations' as such did not really exist.

Why does any of this matter? Russians are still brought up on the idea of a single ancient Rus/Russian nation and still have great difficulty adjusting to the idea not just of a separate Ukrainian state, but of the Ukrainians' separate origin as a people. Ukrainian historians have often swung to the opposite extreme and, by claiming the unity of Rus as their own (Rus was a Kievan and therefore a Ukrainian state), have sought to deny the Russians their traditional theory of national origin. Or they have rewritten the history of Rus as one of ethnic conflict between the three east Slavic nations already formed – the first stage in a more or less permanent struggle that has continued ever since. Neither approach is capable of explaining subsequent history. The former cannot comprehend why Ukrainians have ever pursued a path of separate development, the latter cannot do justice to Ukraine's long history of partnership and cooperation with Russia. Simply put, the origins of many current arguments lie in

Map 1. Rus in the Twelfth Century

perceptions of the past. We therefore begin our story with Rus, as an investigation into the origins of the Ukrainian nation and of Ukrainian identity.

Theories of Unity

The Lay of Ihor's Host seems to support the views of those historians who regard the Rus as a single people. First and foremost, 'the Rus' are referred to throughout as a single entity (although in other sources there are references to travelling, for example, from Novgorod in the north 'to Rus' in the south – that is, to the heartlands around Kiev).[3] This common name for the previously separate and individually named east Slavic tribes can be found as early as the 860s in local chronicles and in documents recording negotiations with foreign powers, such as those with Byzantium in 911 and 944.[4]

Second, the willingness of the Rus to fight against common enemies such as the Polovtsians (also known as the Cumans) indicates that internal differences could be subsumed and that the main line between 'us' and 'them' lay on the outside. *The Lay of Ihor's Host* describes how Ihor assembled his army from all over Rus; from Kiev and Pereiaslav in the south, from Halych in the west and from Smolensk in the north. The chronicle records how Ihor's departure was celebrated throughout the land:

> steeds neigh beyond the Sula
> glory rings in Kiev
> trumpets blare in Novgorod
> banners are raised in Putivl.[5]

The description of the consequences of Ihor's defeat leaves little doubt as to the perceived difference between the Rus 'we' and the Polovtsian 'they',[6] nor as to the fact that the relationship was (at least then) fairly antagonistic. After the key battle

> in the field unknown, midst the
> Polovtsian land,
> the black sod under hooves
> was sown with bones
> and irrigated with gore.[7]

Although the princes of Rus fought each other on occasion – especially after central authority grew weaker in the wake of the death of the last great Rus rulers, Volodymyr Monomakh (1125) and his son Mstyslav (1132) – they tended to fight over the entire patrimony of the state, so long as Kiev remained its most prestigious and prosperous part (by the time a failed attempt was made to establish a capital at Vladimir in the late twelfth century, Kiev was losing this preeminence). The system of political succession, whereby princes were rotated amongst the provinces, was designed to prevent hereditary lines and closed fiefdoms forming in (most of) the principalities, although in practice it had an unfortunate tendency to encourage fratricidal competition amongst the princes. However, Volodymyr Monomakh's warning to his children in his *Testament* (1117) regarding the dangers of internecine strife showed that the idea of Rus as a united patrimony remained strong.[8]

The lack of natural internal borders in Rus facilitated the movement of people and the dissemination of homogenising cultural influences, although the sheer size of its territory somewhat limited this effect. The river Dnieper, then the main East European trade route 'from the Varangians [Scandinavia] to the Greeks', was the central geopolitical fact in Rus and the key image in foreign and domestic representations of its inhabitants. 'This great waterway', one Russian historian has argued, 'was able to overrule all the local centres of crystallisation and to unite the various Slavonic tribes ... into a single state'.[9] It also contributed to the view of the Rus as a single trading nation adopted by outsiders who were less familiar with the Dnieper's hinterlands.

The Lay of Ihor's Host makes clear that, although Ihor's army may have had mercenary motives –

> With their vermilion shields
> the sons of Rus have barred the great steppe
> seeking for themselves honour
> and for their prince glory –

they nonetheless saw themselves as

> princes and knights
> fighting for the Christians
> against the pagan troops.[10]

The Christianity brought to Rus from Byzantium in AD988 was a powerful unifying factor, both in itself and because it provided a more monolithic official ideology that helped to underpin princely authority. Indeed, this may have been Volodymyr the Great's (ruled 980–1015) primary motive in accepting the new faith. Before 988 he had been an equally enthusiastic promoter of the cult of the pagan god Perun as a means of uniting his diverse realm. Unquestionably, however, Rus became a more unified entity after the Baptism in 988 as the culture that was spawned by Christianity spread throughout the land.[11] The new religion also created a new style of public space. The architecture of churches in more northerly towns such as Vladimir and Novgorod echoed that of Kiev, based, usually, on the model of the Cathedral of the Assumption (built 1073–84) in the Pechersk monastery complex, which was itself based on Constantinople originals. (The Assumption was dynamited by retreating Soviet troops in 1941, most probably in the hope of engulfing visiting German dignitaries; rebuilding began in 1998.) Churches were in the Middle Byzantine rather than the Western Gothic style, with a central turriform structure topped by golden cross-domes and a main tower with a circle of windows at its base, supported by tall apses over a compact, centripetal core, usually in the shape of a cross. Internal decoration was similarly elaborate, with painted walls, rich mosaics and ornate iconostases separating the (standing) congregation in the knave from the sanctuary, the privileged domain of the priests.

This common style can be seen in the illustrations (see plates 1 and 2) of St Sofiia's in Novgorod, the Dmitrievskii church in Vladimir and the church of SS Borys and Hlib in Chernihiv. As the Assumption was demolished by the Soviets and the earlier church of the Tithes by the Mongols, the closest example of the type still standing in Kiev is probably St Cyril's (1146). In a similar but more compact style is the Pyrohoshcha church of the Virgin, built in Kiev's lower town of Podil in 1135, destroyed in 1935 and carefully restored in the original style in 1998. Kiev's main church, St Sofiia's, was built by Yaroslav the Wise (ruled 1019–54) in 1037–44. Its original five apses and 13 cupolas (symbolising Christ and the 12 apostles) were first arranged in a flatter domed style more obviously derived from the Hagia Sophia in Constantinople, before later Baroque additions gave the church its current appearance (see also pages 68–9).

A common liturgy was used in all the new churches, and by the thirteenth century the simplified Christian canon of saints and apostles had (largely) displaced the many and varied gods of the pre-Christian era.[12] The adoption of local saints such as Borys and Hlib, Volodymyr's martyred sons, and the veneration of Volodymyr himself as the 'founder-saint' of Rus, as with St Stephen of Hungary or Arthur of England or Clovis of France, further strengthened the unity of the local version of Christianity. The preeminent symbol of the new religion, the icon, introduced another new constant into the life of Rus. Icon-painting and mosaic work supposedly demonstrated a common local style developed from Byzantium, with at least those icons produced in Novgorod (if less so those in Vladimir) following the Kievan style. The twelfth-century *Annunciation of Ustiug* and the *Angel with the Golden Hair* (see plates 3 and 17) were probably produced in Novgorod, although the fact that some authors have attributed one or the other to Kiev indicates that definitive judgment is difficult and emphasises the point about the diffusion of a common style (Ustiug is in the north).[13] The golden braid on the head of the angel and on the figure of Gabriel on the left of the *Annunciation* is one possible indication of an incipient local 'school'.[14]

The advocates of a relatively united Rus have also argued that its inhabitants probably spoke a common language of sorts.[15] As written sources are thin on the ground no definitive judgment can be made, but constant commercial and military intercourse and the fact that rival princes attended one another's courts and assemblies without the need for translators is taken as evidence of a common tongue. Moreover, it has been claimed, books 'circulated widely, from Halych to Suzdal'.[16] One source asserts somewhat implausibly that there were 140,000 books in circulation by the end of the eleventh century – if true, certainly a literary tradition well in advance of states such as Poland.[17] One eleventh-century text refers to the Rus as a people 'feasted to fulfillment on the sweetness of books'.[18] The chronicles themselves, constantly retold and rewritten, were a powerful unifying force, both symbolically and linguistically, although, as indicated above, they were no doubt themselves in advance of cultural developments on the ground, promoting as much as reflecting the idea of Rus cultural unity.

Admittedly, 'the literary language was a little elevated over the popular, but this is a common occurrence for all languages';[19] prince could communicate with prince, armies could operate a common chain of command and congregations could understand their priests. On the other hand, the liturgical language was actually Church Slavonic. Although this 'was close to the literary language of Rus',[20] the literate high culture of Rus was therefore not exclusively local and was shared with fellow Slavs in neighbouring states such as Bulgaria and Moravia. Rus was also something of a diglossia. Communication on an elite level may have been possible, but differences at the level of local popular dialect were probably considerable.

The Rus also had a common system of customary law, codified in the eleventh-century 'Law of Rus' (*Ruska Pravda*). The large number of extant copies suggests it was in wide use. The code was notable for its relative humanity, with fines more common than capital or corporal punishment. Women also received surprisingly equitable treatment, at least in terms of tort and family law, if not of inheritance. On the other hand, there was very little in the way of administrative structure to implement this law: Rus was not a modern state and in this respect was less developed than the Carolingian or Holy Roman empire in the West.

In other words, the Rus possessed substantial attributes of ethnic unity – a common name, common enemies, a sense of territorial unity and elements of a common culture, although how much of this extended beyond the elite to the lower orders is hard to tell. The Rus were not a modern 'nation', but they were not too dissimilar to the 'English' or 'French' of the twelfth century.[21] Like the Angles and Saxons, Aquitainians and Burgundians, they often quarrelled amongst themselves and made occasional deals with outsiders and heathens. Prince Oleh Sviatoslavych (c1050–1115) sought the help of the Polovtsians to recover his throne at Chernihiv in 1078; several notables defected before the 1223 Battle of Kalka: but this was normally a result of personal ambition or outsiders' deeper pockets. A crusade was always likely to raise more troops than a vendetta.

Theories of Difference

This picture of relative unity is disputed by many Ukrainian and Belarusian historians, for whom Rus was no more than a 'union of monarchs', a loose collection of warring principalities, a federal entity at best. The nineteenth-century Ukrainian historian Mykola Kostomarov (1817–85) identified six separate peoples amongst its inhabitants. In addition to the Ukrainians or 'Southern Rus', the 'Northerners', the 'Great Russians', and the Belarusians or 'White Rus', there were the inhabitants of the city-states of Pskov and Novgorod. The name of 'Rus' was sometimes applied to the collective east Slavic whole, but it also had a narrower meaning, referring only to the southern heartland, around Kiev, Chernihiv and Pereiaslav. Byzantine emperors such as Constantine VII Porphyrogenitus (ruled 913–20 and 944–59) referred in a similar fashion to 'Internal' and 'External' Rus. The ninth-century Arab writer Al-Jayhani listed three groups of Rus: the Kuiavii, the Slavii and the Artanii (see page 31).

Kostomarov also stressed the factors that brought these disparate peoples together (the fruitful marriage of the southern love of liberty with the northerners' 'state-building' preference for autocracy), but other Ukrainian historians have depicted the various subgroups as more or less constantly at war. Particular attention is paid to the supposed north–south conflict, which in 1169 led to the sack of Kiev, the main principality in the north-east, by armies loyal to Andrei Bogoliubskii, Prince of Vladimir (ruled 1157–75). According to one account:

> They plundered the whole town for two days – Podil and the hills, the monasteries, St Sofiia's, the Virgin of the Tithes. No one was shown mercy by anyone, churches were burnt, Christians were slaughtered, and others taken prisoner, women led into captivity, forcibly separated from their husbands, children wept looking at their mothers. The plunderers took countless booty, churches were stripped of icons and books and vestments, and bells were all taken down ... and all things sacred were carried away.[22]

Others have argued that such attacks were fairly common occurrences. Prince Riuryk Rostyslavych and the princes of Chernihiv sacked the main Kievan monastery complex at Pechersk in 1203. The Ukrainian historian Petro Tolochko has pointed out that Bogoliubskii's armies were assembled from all points of the compass, so their 'destruction' of Kiev, which in any case was only partial, could not be considered an act of one part of Rus against another.[23] The long-running feud between the princes of Kiev and those of nearby Chernihiv was as deadly as any between north and south.

Belarusian historians have also sought to deconstruct the idea of a single Rus state. Unable to claim Kievan Rus as their own and anxious to play up the autonomy of their own north-western region – the 'city-state' of Polatsk – they have attacked the notion that Kievan Rus was ever a truly unified entity. 'The name – Kievan Rus', they claim, 'is not to be found in any of the chronicles. Secondly, this "state" was a patchwork, not long-lasting, united [only] by armed force.'[24] Rus was 'a loose union of principalities, which only ever achieved a form of union in the 70 years between Volodymyr the Great and Yaroslav the Wise.'[25] The idea that Rus was only a confederation of city-states, 'a union of unions', with a monarch of limited authority and administrative capacity balanced by the power of local assemblies (*viche*) and militias (*druzhyna*), even began to creep into Russian historiography in the late Soviet period, particularly in the writings of Igor Froianov.[26]

However, for Ukrainian historians such as Volodymyr Antonovych (1834–1908), Mykhailo Hrushevskyi (1866–1934) and modern successors such as Yaroslav Dashkevych, the difference between the various city-states was caused by more than mere geography or local dynastic loyalties. There was already an *ethnic* difference, at least between the lands around Kiev and those around Vladimir-Suzdal. Hrushevskyi dated the difference to the emergence of the Antes tribal federation in the fourth century AD, others have gone as far back as the Bronze Age. Chapter two discusses these theories. Others have accepted that a relatively united east Slavic mass existed until the seventh century AD, when it divided into early Ukrainian tribes (the Polianians, the Volhynians) and their Belarusian (the Krivichians and Drehovichians) and Russian equivalents (the Viatychians and Slovenians). Furthermore, the 'Russian' group mixed with local Finno-Ugric elements and the 'Belarusian' group with local Balts to increase these embryonic differences, while the Ukrainians had a strong tradition of Iranian and Ural-Altai influence. Some Ukrainians have even argued that the Russians are not proper Slavs at all, but a bastard mixture of Finnic and Mongol elements. Vladimir-Suzdal, the basis of 'future Russia', is therefore depicted as a highly marginal outpost of Rus, a frontier melting pot of all sorts of ethnic flotsam, including Bulgarians and Volga Tatars.

In one favourite passage from the main Rus chronicle, *The Tale of Bygone Years* (also known as the *Primary Chronicle*), several versions of which exist from the eleventh century and after, the behaviour of the civilised Polianians is contrasted with that of the tribes to the north, particularly the Derevlianians, who existed in bestial fashion, and lived like cattle. They killed one another, ate every impure thing, and there was no marriage among them, but instead they seized upon maidens by capture. The Radmichians, Viatychians and Severians had the same customs ... They spoke obscenely before their fathers and their daughters-in-law. There were no marriages among them, but simply festivals among the villages. When the people gathered together for games, for dancing, and for all other devilish amusements, the men on these occasions carried off wives for themselves ... [for] they did not know the law of God, but made a law unto themselves.[27]

Whereas settled agriculture and even manufacture had long been practised in the south, life in the north was supposedly barbaric, peripatetic and short. It is even claimed that the north-east was barely occupied in this period, or at least was beyond the reach of civilisation. Viking chronicles, for example, refer constantly to Kiev, 'the best realm in all Rus', Polatsk, Novgorod, Perm and Smolensk, the area known collectively as Gårdarike, or 'Greater Sweden', the 'World of the Gods' as opposed to the 'World of Men'; but, like the geographer Ptolemy, the Vikings thought this world ended at the river Don (then known as the Tanais), and the north-east in general was off the edge of their known world.[28] The rise of the principality of Vladimir came relatively late, in the twelfth century, when Rus was already in decline. The Ukrainian geographer Stepan Rudnytskyi (see pages 280–1), claimed that the 'wide [forest] zone, difficult of passage, separat[ed] the East Slavic tribes of the south from those of the north and west ... the centers in which the Muscovite nation later developed bore the name of *Salissye* (land behind the forest).'[29]

The eleventh-century *Yngvar Saga* (written in the thirteenth) places the north-east firmly in the land of magic rather than the land of civilisation. The hero ventures on a journey to find the source of the greatest of 'the three rivers flowing through Rus from the east' and encounters rampant paganism, giants, a flying dragon known as the Jakulus, 'unpleasant pirates' and troll-women who attempt to seduce Yngvar's men with 'devilish witchcraft'. To protect his men from this particular 'heathen practice', the saga records, Yngvar grew 'so enraged, he drew out a knife and stabbed [the leading troll] in the private parts'. In another incident, Yngvar's men kill a giant with footprints 'eight feet long', 'with a large number of men dangling from his belt', 'so fearsome and ugly they thought it must be the Devil himself'. The giant's severed leg comes in useful further upriver, when the Vikings need a bait to lure another dragon away from the cave where he guards a glittering hoard of gold so vast that they had to use 'their axes to hack off a piece that alone was worth a fortune'.[30]

Many Ukrainian historians, such as Dmytro Doroshenko (1882–

1951), have therefore sought to displace the Russians or their ancestors from the picture altogether, arguing that the Russian nation only began to develop after Andrei Bogoliubskii severed ties with Kiev in the late twelfth century.[31] 'Ukraine-Rus', as they term it, was relatively unified before that date, but was simply an old Ukrainian state. 'Difference' was not so much within Rus but between the Ukrainians and the Russians, who developed outside or after Rus. (Some Ukrainians have argued that Novgorod in the north, unlike Vladimir in the north-east, was culturally close to Kiev until it was sacked by Moscow in 1478; it has even been claimed that Novgorod established Kiev, rather than vice versa,[32] although how this fits with the idea of a distinctive southern ethnicity and geography is hard to grasp.)

Kulturkampf?

These differences between north and south can allegedly be seen in all aspects of life, most importantly in language and religion, then the main manifestations of cultural difference. According to Ivan Yushchuk, a leading member of the contemporary Prosvita Ukrainian language society:

> The Russian [people and] language as such began to form on the territory of modern Russia from the eleventh century onwards, as a result of the [relatively late] colonisation of these lands by the Kievan Rus. Rus boyars ... and militia [*druzhyna*], ruling over local Finno-Ugric tribes (Chud, Meria, Ves, Muroma, Mordva, Perm, Pechora and so on), brought there their own mixture of Church Slavonic and Rus: just as, for example, also happened with the formation of the English and French languages, that is as a result of the mixing of the language of the conquerors with local dialects.
>
> In Kievan Rus [proper] the dominant language until the adoption of Christianity was the Rus language, which, as many facts demonstrate, sounded closer to the modern Ukrainian language and already possessed the majority of its grammatical and phonetic characteristics.[33]

'Old Ukrainian' only gradually became a 'peasant language' because the ruling Rus elite adopted Church Slavonic after 988 and drifted away from their original traditions. Most scholars, however, would not accept the equation of the Rus and 'Old Ukrainian' languages. The three modern east Slavic tongues only began to form as separate entities in the thirteenth and fourteenth centuries, that is once the Rus themselves had been politically divided.[34]

Ukrainian historians have also tried, with somewhat more success, to undermine the idea of a unified Rus Church. The first step in their argument is to deny that the Kievan Church was a creature of Byzantium.

From the time of the Baptism, claims one author, 'the attempts of Byzantium to influence Rus politics through the Church met with resistance',[35] in part because of the strong local traditions that had already developed before 988 (see pages 33–7). 'Volodymyr sought to be subordinate neither to the Constantinople patriarchate, nor to the Roman curia, but to continue the process begun in Moravia by Cyril and Methodius of building a Slavic version of Christianity.'[36] According to Yevhen Sverstiuk, editor of the main Ukrainian Orthodox paper, *Nasha Vira* ('Our Faith'), 'there were no great barriers between Rus and Rome or Rus and Byzantium because Rus had few links with either.'[37] Rus and Byzantium were after all at war between 1043 and 1046, and it has been argued that the 'uncanonical' baptism of the inhabitants of Kiev in the river Dnieper is evidence that no Byzantine envoys were present.[38]

Second, it is argued that in the three centuries after the Baptism there was a constant struggle between the 'patriotic-evangelical' and 'messianic-Caesaropapist' wings of the Rus Church. Instead of an argument between Rus and Byzantium, this opposition is presented as a further manifestation of north–south division, as it is argued that hierarchs from the north tended to support the Byzantine, that is 'Caesaropapist', position against the Kievan 'patriots'. The latter were supposedly closer to the Greek aspects of Byzantine culture and the northerners to the Roman (sic).[39] Whereas the southern Rus supported a 'theological rationalism [that] opposed itself to Byzantium's aggressive attitude to ancient philosophy, to philosophy and reason in general [and] to its tendency to irrationalism', the latter 'became the characteristic feature of Muscovite Orthodoxy'. 'The Kievan Church', on the other hand, was characterised by 'Christian universalism, tolerance towards different religious centres ... an authentic early Christian orientation, patriotism, evangelism and Paulism', so that 'the cross-pollinated fruit of the Eastern variant of Christianity with the Western on the basis of pre-Christian Slavic culture' created 'a tolerant open relationship to East and West'.[40]

This nationalisation of the Church and its embryonic 'Kievan ecumenism' can supposedly be seen in the key text of the period, the *Sermon on Law and Grace* written by Ilarion, the first native Rus metropolitan to head the local Church (probably served 1051–4). In the *Sermon*, Ilarion argues that all (Gentile) nations and Churches are equal in the sight of God, thus being by implication even-handed towards Rome and Byzantium ('the Jews' justification was grudging and jealous for Judea alone, not extending to the nations; but the Christians' salvation is generous and beneficent, extending to all corners of the earth,' he argues). Ilarion's eulogy to Volodymyr, described as 'a likeness of Constantine the Great: of like wisdom, of like love for Christ', and of Yaroslav the Wise, called 'Solomon' to Volodymyr's 'David', can also be seen as a step towards justifying the Rus Church as an institution in its own right.[41]

Rumblings in favour of autocephaly, that is formal independence for the Rus Church, were initially heard in the eleventh century. A first sign was the desire of Kiev to establish its own saints (Volodymyr, his grandmother Olha and the martyrs Borys and Hlib), although Constantinople refused to recognise their canonisation until the thirteenth century. By the sixteenth, there was a total of 148 Rus saints.[42] A second sign was the emergence of native metropolitans. The first, Ilarion, had only a limited localising agenda, of which Constantinople was in any case extremely wary at the time of the schism of 1054. After Ilarion, Greek metropolitans, such as Nikephoros (served 1104–21) and Michael I (1130–45), reimposed Byzantine control and tried to stir up hostility to Latin Christendom.

Ukrainian historians have argued that a second, more serious attempt to establish autocephaly was made at the synod of 1147, when Prince Iziaslav Mstyslavych (ruled in Kiev 1146–54) ensured the election of Klymentii Smoliatych as metropolitan (served 1147–55). Iziaslav's early death cut the attempt short, and a rival, more 'northerly' and pro-Byzantine party led by Niphont of Novgorod and Yurii Dolgorukii, the founder of Moscow (ruled 1149–57), was then able to settle accounts with the 'autonomists'. Significantly, however, a trend had been set. The 'northern' party again clashed with the 'southern' when Andrei Bogoliubskii attempted to appoint his protégé Feodor as metropolitan of Vladimir and effectively split the Rus Church in two. The attempt failed – Feodor was taken to Kiev in 1169 and executed. The severity of his fate indicated the seriousness with which the idea of a united Church was still taken: '[Kievan] Metropolitan Constantine charged him [Feodor] with all his transgressions and ordered him to be taken to the dog's island. And there they maimed him and cut out his tongue, as fitting for an evil heretic, and they cut off his right hand and gouged out his eyes, because he said abusive [things] about the Holy Mother of God.'[43] Nevertheless, there were many signs of the 'northerners' developing an ideology and identity of their own under Bogoliubskii. Of particular importance was the cult of *Our Lady of Vladimir*. Originally imported from Constantinople in 1134 and known as the *Virgin of Vyshhorod* (a town near Kiev), the icon was one of the central symbols of the divine authority of the princes of Kiev (see plate 18). Its capture in dubious circumstances by Bogoliubskii and transfer to the north therefore symbolised his attempt to usurp the city's power. In 1395 the icon was transported to the Moscow Kremlin, where it supposedly deterred Timur (Tamerlane) from attacking the city. To this day it is used as a symbol of the continuity of Russia and Rus.[44] Bogoliubskii also established new feast days and local saints and embarked on a grandiose scheme of church-building so that Vladimir could pose as a serious rival to Kiev. His scribes elaborated the idea that Vladimir had been founded and Christianised by Volodymyr (the normal date for its foundation is, in fact, 1108, by Vladimir Monomakh, not Vladimir the Great), making it the second city of Rus and eventual successor to Kiev, both lands blessed by God – Bogoliubskii means 'lover of God'. The sack of Kiev in 1169 was supposedly therefore a deeply symbolic act, deliberately designed to undermine the city's sacred status.[45]

Other historians have argued that the Church remained relatively united and that the idea of Kievan autocephaly is a fantasy invented to serve later political purposes. Petro Tolochko continues to suggest that the Church, or at least its hierarchs, 'was the most consistent supporter of all-Rus-ian unity'.[46] The good offices of the Church were the most likely means of keeping the peace between warring princes, and the ideology of the unity of Christ's realm in Rus remained a strong unifying force even after the arrival of the Mongols in 1240.

According to the Ukrainian art historian Dmytro Stepovyk, the embryonic cultural difference between north and south can also be observed in forms of artistic expression, icon-painting in particular. In attempting to deconstruct the idea of a common Rus style, he has argued that 'the Byzantine notion of sacred art discarding all kinds of outside influence ... was only a starting point for developing the Ukrainian national templeal art', which drew on earlier pagan traditions and European influences to create a unique local style. Whereas Muscovy supposedly remained a slavish imitator of the Byzantine style of the twelfth-century Komnenos dynasty until as late as the eighteenth century, Kiev artists simply 'took what they needed' to form their 'own original school'.[47]

In contrast to the northern school in Vladimir, Pskov, Smolensk and eventually Moscow, with its 'plain use of space, regulated localisation of colour, [use of] reverse perspective, severe linearity' and 'excessively brilliant gilded pale-coloured shading', the Kievan school was characterised by its 'more reserved use of gold, localised on the aureole [halo] and with shading not of pale, but of deep red-brown gold'.[48] In other words, whereas 'Muscovite' art actually exaggerated the Byzantine tradition – repetition of standardised and etiolated versions of the human form, flatness of colour and formalistic representations of the material world as a means of concentrating on the image of the divine – Kievan art was more naturalistic, humanistic and more 'organically' in touch with local tradition. In short, it had more colour and life. The widespread use of elaborate mosaics in a similar style supposedly attests to the artistic unity of the 'Kievan school' and to the wealth and growing cultural solidity of the south. However, the Russian art historian Igor Grabar argued more or less the opposite, namely that the national style developed in the north and was exported south to wean Kiev off its Byzantism.[49] Others have rejected altogether the idea of sub-Rus-ian local 'styles'.

The monk Alempius (Alimpyi) is held to have been the leading exponent of this 'Kievan' school of icon-painting and mosaic art. The most spectacular example of his style (although actual authorship of the work is uncertain) is held to be the great mosaic of the *Virgin Oranta* above the altar of St Sofiia's (see plate 20). The Virgin is depicted in a local version of one of the three classic Byzantine poses, standing alone with her arms proffered outwards in prayer. Her serenity and transcendent calm, matched in the simple colours of the local stone, is one of the greatest achievements of Kievan art. At the same time, the Virgin is also a powerful symbol of the new Rus state, dressed in the clothes of an empress extending her protection, as the inscription above states, to Kiev, 'the Holy City, the Holy House of the Eternal. God is within and this house is unshakable'.

In the same style is the *St Demetrius* mosaic, while the depiction of the Virgin is remarkably similar to the icon of the *Orans (Panagia) Virgin*, which some scholars have also attributed to Alempius, others to artists from Yaroslavl, especially in terms of line and silhouette.[50] Both works are now in the Tretiakov Gallery in Moscow (see plate 4). Other icons attributed to Alempius or his school include the *St Nicholas*, while other works, such as the mosaics for the Cathedral of the Assumption in Pechersk, have unfortunately been lost. One other surviving example of local Rus art is the twelfth-century *Angel Rolling Up the Sky* in Kiev's St Cyril church, with its beautifully delicate blue and cream (artist unknown).

Ukrainian historians have also argued that Kievan architecture was in an adapted Byzantine style, strongly influenced by local 'indigenous' traditions. Kiev's St Sofiia's, for example, is not only modelled on the earlier church of the Tithes, it is argued, but on even more ancient predecessors.[51] Moreover, it is claimed that Kievan architects had already mastered the use of stone, contrary to the normal assertion that before invited Byzantine masters introduced the practice all Rus buildings were made of wood. The configuration of St Sofiia's, in particular the proliferation of apses, naves and galleries, has no direct analogy in Constantinople. It has even been argued that St Sofiia's demonstrates elements of the Western European Romanesque style, as in the great cathedrals of Trier (1047) and Worms (1110–1200) – built after St Sofiia's. Most important, however, is the internal decoration, whose 'native' style is discussed on page 36. In the north of Rus, in contrast, the Kievan style was supposedly first copied and then forgotten, as Moscow developed its own architectural culture with a pronounced eastern influence, the most obvious example of which is St Basil's in Red Square.[52] Other local architectural schools appeared in Vladimir, Chernihiv, Halych (Galicia) and elsewhere as Kiev's authority began to diminish in the twelfth century.

Further alleged differences are found in political culture. Forms of government varied between the principalities. The *viche* system (gatherings of nobles) was more prominent in Novgorod, Pskov and Polatsk, whereas princely autocracy was the norm in Vladimir and Rostov-Suzdal, though also in Halych.[53] In Vladimir, Andrei Bogoliubskii began to compare himself to the Byzantine emperors, even to Solomon, although Ukrainian historians have cast doubt on the line of succession

Ill. 1. Andrei Bogoliubskii taking the Vyshhorod/Vladimir Icon

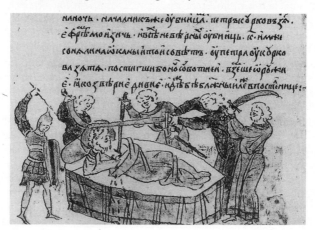

Ill. 2. The Assassination of Bogoliubskii, 1175

to the north-east, through Yurii Dolgorukii to Andrei Bogoliubskii, as Dolgorukii was only a junior son of Volodymyr Monomakh, born to a concubine (like many would-be autocrats, Bogoliubskii came to a sticky end, savagely murdered by assassins in 1175 – the illustrations above show him obtaining the *Vladimir* icon and the ultimate consequences of the act.) Bogoliubskii's successor, Vsevolod III (ruled 1176–1212), was the first to style himself 'Grand Prince' – of Vladimir, not Kiev. The autocratic Byzantine idea of the ruler as Christ's prince on earth was therefore first copied in Vladimir rather than in Kiev, before being passed on to the tsars of Muscovy. The practice had not been original to Rus. When the early chronicles of Vladimir and Moscow referred to Volodymyr as 'tsar' they were attempting to justify their own practices by inventing a title he himself had never claimed.

The Fall of Rus

The Mongols sacked Kiev in 1240. Although this event is commonly taken to mark the formal end of Rus, it need not necessarily have been the case. One prince, Danylo of Halych (ruled 1237–64), attempted to rebuild Rus from the west. If he had been more successful in resisting the Mongols and in creating a link between Halych and Kiev, and if Poland, Hungary and Serbia had joined a promised crusade in his support, then the main successor state to Rus might have looked more like modern Ukraine than modern Russia. Alternatively, embryonic Ukrainian and Russian polities might have developed in parallel, one in the south under Danylo and one in the north under Andrei Bogoliubskii's grandson Alexander Nevskii (ruled 1252–63) in Novgorod–Pskov and/or Vladimir–Suzdal. Even in the north there were rival centres of power. Novgorod's mercantile democracy could have triumphed over Muscovite absolutism in the fifteenth century, rather than vice versa. North and south might have cooperated, as with the brief alliance against the Mongols between Danylo and Alexander Nevskii's brother Andrei in the 1250s, or they might have moved further apart.

The *translatio imperii* theory (according to which Moscow, via Vladimir, was regarded as the direct and only successor of Kiev and Byzantium) much beloved of future Russian historians, was certainly not the only possibility. The others were closed off by circumstance rather than destiny. Rus could not be rebuilt in the south, as two-thirds of the territory of modern Ukraine was lost to the Mongols. The 'northern' option won out, temporarily at least, but the north enjoyed no mon-opoly. The Kingdom of Galicia and Volhynia enjoyed a century's after-life after 1240, until Galicia was occupied by Poland in 1349. Indeed, for Ukrainian 'Occidentalists' such as the historian Stefan Tomashivskyi (1875–1930), Galicia–Volhynia was the first true 'national Ukrainian state'.[54] Whereas Rus was a multinational agglomeration like the Frankish empire in the west, too much under the influence of Byzantium, Tomashivskyi's school argued that Galicia–Volhynia was an ethnically distinct entity moving rapidly away from Vladimir–Suzdal in the north. Galicia, he argued, was also more unambiguously in the European cul-tural sphere. Under Roman (ruled 1199–1205), Danylo and Lev I (1264–1301), Galicia–Volhynia interacted on equal terms with its neighbours Poland and Hungary in joint defence of Europe against the Mongols, and developed a social structure and conception of royal authority that were more typically feudal than the patrimonial system of Rus. Latin culture penetrated the Galician court and economic ties were mainly with the Baltic and Danube river basins rather than the Volga and Ladoga systems around which Vladimir now based its trade (the once-shared Dnieper system, the 'route from the Varangians to the Greeks', being in serious decline).

Tomashivskyi's school have also argued that Galicia–Volhynia was also more 'European' in its geography and economy. They have therefore sought to exempt themselves from the agro-cultural determinism propagated by Richard Pipes and others, which argues that the infertile territory of Russia proper is unable to support an accumulative, city-based culture, and in the absence of urban civil society has historically been forced into collective social life and authoritarian state power as the only means of maintaining order.[55] Muscovite Russia has been unable to sit still and husband its own meagre resources and has always been an aggressive power coveting its neighbours' territory. Galicia and Volhynia, however, along with the Kievan heartland when it was not under foreign threat, supposedly provided a fertile forest-protected haven where towns and civic culture were able to develop – an important point in keeping western Ukraine at the centre of the Ukrainian national myth (the steppe zone of south-east Ukraine was at this time still a no-man's-land). Whereas Vladimir and then Muscovy were natural prey to the Golden Horde and soon came to ape its patrimonial authoritarianism, Ukrainian historians have argued, Kiev and Galicia developed a more 'European' political culture.[56] Ukrainians point out with pride that it is Kiev, not Moscow, that contains a statue celebrating the Magdeburg law (city self-government) which persisted in Ukraine until 1835 – its abolition coming unfortunately not long after the monument was erected in 1802–3 (the monument now has the word 'Independence' graffitoed on it – in Russian).

Danylo floated the idea of a more formal link with the Catholic West as a means of resisting the Golden Horde, to whom Moscow was already paying tribute. Ukrainian historians have claimed that his representatives accepted a papal crown in 1253, and even that his negotiations with Innocent IV led to his 'conversion' and a form of 'union' with Rome in 1246–7, Danylo's predecessor Roman having first considered a similar proposal in 1204.[57] Danylo was supposedly recognised as 'King of Rus', underlying Halych's potential supremacy over Vladimir in the north. Significantly, this claim was codified in local historicist mythology, with the main Galician chronicle, the *Hypatian Codex*, formulating the idea that Halych, not Vladimir, was the real successor to Kiev.

Other Ukrainians, including the doyen of historical studies, Mykhailo Hrushevskyi, have seen the Galician-Volhynian experience as transitory. Without a secure hold on Kiev they do not see how it could have been a true Ukrainian state.[58] Whatever the case, Poland sought to eradicate all links to Rus in Galicia relatively quickly after it occupied the region in 1349. Further to the east, on the other hand, elements of Rus statehood survived in the Grand Duchy of Lithuania, Rus and Samogitia founded in the fourteenth century (often misrepresented in Western historiography as the 'Kingdom of Lithuania'), and even in the Principality of Moldavia (see pages 45–6). Kiev, after all, was also a successor to Kiev. Ukrainian historians reject Russian suggestions that little of significance remained in the former capital after 1240.

Conclusions

It is vital to begin our story with an honest assessment of the Ukrainians' and Russians' common past. The balance of argument supports the claim that the Rus possessed a unity of sorts, at least in terms of the embryonic higher culture that sat above the various tribal cultures. The Orthodox of southern Rus were already different in many respects from their cousins in the north-east, and subsequent events meant their fates would diverge yet further, but as yet there was no well-developed contemporary ideology of difference between the northern and southern Rus. The idea of Rus unity was admittedly only partially developed, but that of two (or more) Ruses was hardly developed at all and is largely a projection of later historians. Internal quarrels tended to pit prince against prince rather than one ethnic group against another. Significantly, it has been easier for Ukrainian historians to take the whole history of Rus and change its subject from 'the Rus' or 'the Russians' to that of 'the Ukrainians' than to write a general history of discord between north and south – in other words to write the Russians out of the picture.

The point of the argument that Rus was a Ukrainian or proto-Ukrainian state is obviously to provide the Ukrainians with a myth of their emergence as a separate nation – as with the Slovak claim that the Great Moravian empire (833–907) was an early Slovak state rather than the original common homeland of both the Czechs and Slovaks, or the Norwegian historians who have portrayed rulers such as Olaf (1015–30) and Håkon IV (1217–63) as definitively independent of Denmark. However, it is perfectly possible to argue that the Rus were a single people, or a pre-national unit, and that the embryonic differences that already existed in 1240 became much greater as a result of the fall of Rus,[59] leading to the formation of a truly separate Ukrainian identity by the seventeenth century (see chapters three and four). This is not to subsume the history of one people under that of the other: Rus was simply that which existed before the modern Ukrainian and Russian nations developed. Still less is it to deny the Ukrainians a proper beginning to their history.

Nor would it deny the Russians a proper beginning to their history.

True, for most Russians the idea of Kiev as the 'mother of Russian cities' is still central to their understanding of their origins as a nation. Moreover, Ukrainian historians have hardly made it easy for Russians to accept the idea of their descent from Andrei Bogoliubskii by lacing their account of Russian 'ethnogenesis' with overtones of miscegenation. However, other possibilities do exist. The 'Eurasianist' and mystic philosopher Lev Gumilev (1912–92),[60] whose views on other questions if not on this particular issue have been highly influential on Russian nationalism in the 1990s, has dated the emergence of the Russian 'superethnos' to the post-thirteenth-century synthesis of Rus, Finno-Ugric and Mongol influences. In theory, this approach could allow the Ukrainians to enjoy a separate history of their own, although it tends to be assumed that the Mongol influence affected all the Rus equally.[61] Other alternative theories of Russian origin could date their 'ethnogenesis' to a direct influence from Byzantium unmediated by Kiev, to the democratic traditions of Novgorod, to 'the formation of the Moscow state' or to the 'indigenous' traditions developed after the fall of Byzantium in 1453.[62] Once again, any of these alternative myths of origin could in principle allow the Ukrainians to be disentangled from Russian history. In practice, none of these approaches is yet common.

This is not just an academic problem. Until the equation of 'Rus' and 'Russia' is no longer universal, modern-day Russians are bound to suffer an existential blackout whenever they are confronted with Ukrainian historiography. They will also have a distorted understanding of their own national origins. Most importantly, however, they will continue to find it difficult to engage with the political reality of an independent Ukrainian state.

2

The Armies of Gog and Magog: Myths of Ukrainian Antiquity

What came before Rus? In a period where there is very little written evidence and archaeological sources are open to a variety of interpretations, it would be foolish to say too much. The Rus themselves, or at least their chroniclers, had little real sense of what preceded them.[1] Nevertheless, many Ukrainian historians date the beginnings of the Ukrainian nation to as far back as the end of the last ice age, and the Ukrainian view that Kievan Rus was in essence a 'Ukrainian state' cannot be fully understood without knowing something of their view as to what came before. A second reason why modern Ukrainians dig so deep into the past is that the geography of pre-Rus civilisations are a closer fit to modern Ukraine than medieval Rus. Most were concentrated on the river Dnieper rather than any further north, and most made a more definitive occupation of south-eastern Ukraine and Crimea than Rus ever did – a fact of paramount importance should these vulnerable borders ever be seriously disputed. The current focus on the ancient era is also a product of the Soviet period, both psychologically (much of the hyperbole is a natural reaction to the Soviet denigration, even denial, of the Ukrainian past) and methodologically. Soviet theory assumed ethnicity was an objective given: the task of historians was therefore to describe 'ethnogenesis', identifying various ancient cultures as one's ancestors. Moreover, much of the research that was undertaken in the Stalinist period to prove the ancient roots of the Russian/Slavic people concentrated on the area around the river Dnieper and has therefore been lifted wholesale by the Ukrainians and given a local spin. The reader will perhaps therefore not mind if we backtrack slightly, thereby avoiding a chronological approach which serves to perpetuate the existential fallacy that there has always been a Ukrainian or Russian nation and the teleological assumption that Rus was some kind of continuation of earlier polities. Some of the wilder flights of historical fancy provide entertainment at least.

Japheth's Seed

'Who we are' depends crucially on 'where we came from'. Even mainstream Ukrainian historians now tend to argue that Ukrainians and their ancestors have lived on their present territory for thousands of years. Nevertheless, around this central theory of descent are woven versions of history that combine the respectable and the frankly bizarre. Moreover, the further back we go, the more bizarre things tend to get. Since independence, a variety of way-out theories have been popularised by writers such as Yurii Kanyhin and Yurii Shylov, the 1970s dissident Oles Berdnyk and the émigré mystic Lev Sylenko. Many, if not all, mainstream historians steer clear of such arguments,[2] but Kanyhin and the others are not just a fringe. One of Kanyhin's central texts is endorsed with an enthusiastic foreword by ex-president Leonid Kravchuk; another was summarised in the *Bulletin of the Academy of Sciences* in 1995; Oleksii Bratko-Kutynskyi's mystical book *The Phenomenon of Ukraine* was published by *Vechirnii Kyïv*, Kiev's traditional evening paper.[3] The leitmotif of the 'ancient origin' of the Ukrainians is a central feature of Ukrainian nationalism.

Many of these works are downright incomprehensible, but three key elements tend to be present in varying degrees: recycled biblical mythology; the claim that Ukraine was the original homeland of all the Indo-European peoples; and a peculiar form of Ukrainian Aryanism. Yurii Kanyhin claims that the Bible mentions the Ukrainians at least five times, once for each link in a chain of descent from earliest times to the 'Ukrainians' of Kievan Rus. According to Kanyhin, as we 'read the Bible – the first [reference] was [to] Homer (the Cimmerians), then to Magog (the Scythians), the Madai (the Sarmatians), Tiras (the Slovenes), and finally Tuval/Tubal (the Galician-Ukrainians)'.[4] In this particular school of biblical interpretation, the Ukrainians are claimed to be the descendants of Cain, via Lamech, who before the Flood had three sons. As the Bible records (Genesis 10: 5): 'of these were the isles of nations divided, in their lands, every one after his tongue; after their families, in their nations.' As the myth has it, the descendants of the first son, Jabal, peopled the Middle East; those of the second, Jubal, Greece. The Slavs are descended from the third son, Tubal-Cain and his sister Naamah, via Magog and Tiras, sons of Japheth. The tongue of the sons of Japheth was the original Slavonic.

According to Kanyhin, Ukraine was first known as Tubal (Tuval) or Tiras (Firas), supposedly the country in 'the far recesses of the north' mentioned in Ezekiel 38:2; 15.[5] The Ukrainians' ancestors were therefore the people named by the Bible as the Magog, whose divinely ordained mission was to oppose the armies of Gog, 'the dark forces of Asia',[6] and lead the 'White' peoples against the 'Black'. According to the authors of one popular text: 'our ancestors were the illustrious Magog, who through the ages fought to the death in battle against the rapacious Gogs of the steppe, and shielded Western (Christian) civilisation from fatal inroads and invasions. The history of early Ukraine and Ukraine itself has, it can be said, a clear and explicit "Anti-Gog" character.'[7] One of the key Ukrainian national myths, the image of Ukraine as the frontier of European civilisation against the encroachment of barbarian Asia, thus has a very early beginning indeed. As eloquently argued by Neal Ascherson in his book *Black Sea*, the lands to the north of Asia Minor have often been depicted as the beginning of the barbarian world, and the steppe zone characterised as the preserve of warrior-nomads.[8] A quick glance at any popular map of the ancient world confirms a blank space or warning 'there be monsters' in this spot. Eccentric as the likes of Kanyhin may be, Ukrainians therefore have an obvious interest in counteracting such stereotypes by shifting the historical boundaries of 'civilisation' sufficiently far to the east.

The idea that the Ukrainians were the 'Magog', however, is confusing to say the least. Ezekiel in fact refers to 'Gog, the prince of Rosh [supposedly the Rus], Meshech and Tubal, in the land of Magog' (38: 1–2). As Gog is 'prince of' the Magog, the two are presumably one and the same. Moreover, they are both on the wrong side of the divide between chaos and civilisation. It is the armies of 'Gog *and* Magog' that Revelation (20: 8–9) prophesies will be unleashed against the Lord's Kingdom on Judgment Day, and they have become jointly synonymous with the threat of apocalypse. It is surprising that the Ukrainians would want to be associated with either. The English artist John Martin (1789–1854), for example, in his monumental painting *The Last Judgment* (1853) puts as clear a divide as possible between the righteous (assembled on the left) and the damned (being cast into utter darkness on the right), with the armies of Gog and Magog being repulsed from the Holy City of Jerusalem the most prominent part of the latter (see plate 19).[9]

Nevertheless, the idea that the Ukrainians, or indeed all the Slavs, are descended from Japheth has a long pedigree. It appears in the main Rus chronicle *The Tale of Bygone Years*, which states that, 'after the flood, the sons of Noah (Shem, Ham and Japheth) divided the earth among them ... to the lot of Japheth fell the northern and western sectors (including the land of Rus).'[10] Japheth's sons are often claimed to have been the first inhabitants of Kiev. The myth was still common in the seventeenth century, in texts such as Metropolitan Iov Boretskyi's *Protestation* (1621), which describes the Ukrainian Cossacks as 'the tribe of the glorious Rus nation of Japheth's seed',[11] and in the old Russian myth that Moscow was founded by Mosokh, the sixth son of Japheth. The Polish nobility of the sixteenth and seventeenth centuries believed they were descended from Japheth, while their peasants were the sons and daughters of Ham.[12] The idea is even to be found in the work of the Soviet linguist Nikolai Marr (1864/5–1934), who argued that all the Slavs could be grouped in a single 'Japhetic' language family, from whose original root other 'ancient' languages such as Hebrew and Etruscan are descended. Georgian nationalists, in particular the ill-fated president Zviad Gamsakhurdia, have also made use of the myth, arguing that all the 'Japhetic' languages are descended from the original Georgian *Ursprache* (universal language).[13]

The second element in this peculiar melange of ideas is the notion that Ukraine was the original homeland (*Urheimat*) of all the Indo-European peoples. The myth of a common mother culture for all the Indo-Europeans has proved remarkably persistent, as have attempts to pin it down geographically and to identify an original *Ursprache* as its mother-tongue.[14] The Ukrainian version is that the original homeland was around the lower Dnieper in the fourth to third millennium BC. Moreover, it is claimed that the Ukrainians were the first speakers of Sanskrit, since the nineteenth century the favourite candidate for an *Ursprache*. 'Ukrainian/Sanskrit' is therefore the mother of all the Indo-European languages,[15] and it was the ancient Ukrainians who first exported the secrets of the Hindu Veda to India. The Ukrainian language, 'the language of the world aristocracy', is therefore as much as 25,000 years old.[16]

Some of this is not as barmy as it seems. Several mainstream scholars have also placed the Indo-European 'homeland' on the Ukrainian steppe, rather than in Asia or elsewhere.[17] Colin Renfrew has placed it nearby, in Anatolia.[18] The philosopher Leibnitz (1646–1716) thought that all the European languages originated from 'Scythia' (that is modern Ukraine – see pages 28–30).

The Ukrainian Indo-European theory is, however, tarnished by its association with the belief that the Ukrainians were also the original Aryans. Although Aryanism in general – the myth of an original White race – has been discredited in most people's eyes by its adoption by the Nazis, it is enjoying a rather dubious afterlife in Ukraine. Ukrainian scholars have argued in their defence that theirs is a linguistic, not a racial conception.[19] According to Kanyhin and others, an Aryan is supposedly a 'tiller of the soil' (*khliborob*) or 'ploughman' (*orach*), and therefore an archetypal Ukrainian.[20] The word *orach* is supposedly derived from the ancient Ukrainian god Ora, hence *orii* or *arii*, meaning 'Aryan' in Ukrainian. The Ukrainian Aryans are therefore more properly labelled *Oriiany*.[21] In the Ukrainian version of Aryanism, the Aryans first appeared in north-western Europe around 20,000 years ago, roaming the steppe from the Carpathian mountains to Tibet and the Hindu Kush, but eventually made their home in what is now Ukraine, whose 'boundless steppes are the Aryan Golgotha'.[22] The ancient name for this homeland was Oriiana, which is depicted on the cover of one of Sylenko's books (*Guest from the Tomb of our Forefathers*) as the centre of the ancient world.

Ill. 3. Lev Sylenko, 'Guest from the Tomb of our Forefathers', showing early Ukraine or Oriiana *as the centre of the ancient world and of ancient agriculture*

Without much in the way of concrete archaeological evidence, the case for Ukraine's Aryan heritage tends to focus on the alleged antiquity of certain Ukrainian 'national' particularities. For example, the trident of Prince Volodymyr, now the official symbol of the state, was supposedly in use long before the time of Rus, as was the sign of the sun, the eight-pointed star and various forms of the swastika, such as that now used by nationalist groups like the sinister paramilitary Ukrainian People's Self-Defence Force (UNSO).[23] The Aryan belief-system that centred around the worship of sun gods seems to have persisted in Ukrainian popular religion up to the time of Rus and beyond. The argument of racial descent is, however, also made, in glossy publications that can be bought in Kiev's main square.[24] On the other hand, much of this mythology echoes, or just copies, Russian neo-pagan theories, such as the obvious forgery produced in the Brezhnev era by Valerii Skurlatov, *The Book of Vlas* – the 'Vlas' being the original Russian Aryans. The ideologues of the Russian New Right are just as prone as their Ukrainian equivalents to mystical speculations about obscure pagan symbols and the links between Rus, Atlantis and Egypt.[25]

The Trypillians

The Aryan line has been traced throughout Ukrainian history. According to Kanyhin, 'the Cimmerians, Scythians, Sarmatians, Antes, Tavrians [Crimeans], "White" Huns, Slovenes, Polovtsians, Kipchaks, and, eventually, the Rusych-Ukrainians [all] belonged to the Aryanised peoples, who played a huge creative and civilising role [throughout the ancient world], and who received the biblical name Magog.'[26] The first proper 'Aryan' civilisation in Ukraine is held to have been the Trypillian (or Tripolye) archaeological culture, named after the village below Kiev on the river Dnieper, where painted pottery, clay figurines and farming implements were discovered by the Czech archaeologist Vikentii Chvojka (Khvoika) in the 1890s. Belief in the Trypillian origin of the Ukrainian nation spreads far beyond the ranks of Ukrainian 'Aryanists' and is a relatively mainstream nationalist idea, having been popularised by the archaeologist Viktor Petrov (1894–1969).[27]

The Trypillian culture is normally dated to the late Neolithic or Eneolithic (Copper) eras, sometime between 4000 and 2700BC, although some Ukrainians would place its origins as early as the sixth millennium BC. It was not necessarily unique to Ukraine: similar remains have been found at the Cucuteni site in Romania (more than 100 sites exist in total). Other archaeologists have therefore supported the theory of the Thraco-Phrygian origin of the Trypillian culture – it may have had little to do with the Indo-Europeans, let alone the early Slavs. Nevertheless, Ukrainian archaeologists such as Vadym Shcherbakivskyi, Oleh Kandyba and Yaroslav Pasternak have claimed that it provides evidence of an early Ukrainian civilisation,[28] even bizarrely a 'state' known as Arrata, 'which in the period of its development embraced the territory of what are now Poltava, Cherkasy and Kiev oblasts (for Ukraine's modern territorial divisions; see the map on p. 173), and further to the west the whole of the region up to the Dniester and the Danube.'[29]

The claims made for Arrata-Trypillia are astonishing, but reveal much about the perceived need to anchor Ukrainian identity in a more prestigious past. Ukrainians have claimed for example that Arrata was 'the first post-Diluvian civilisation on the planet, which gave mankind "modern" agricultural technology', 'before Egyptian or Sumerian civilisation' even existed.[30] 'The horse and cart – the first human transport – was invented in Ukraine', the Trypillians having been the first people properly to domesticate the horse.[31] The highly talented Trypillians, the world's oldest metallurgists,[32] also made copper farming implements and used harnessed oxen. They were able to create a grain-exporting civilisation at a time when life further north (that is, in modern Russia) was still primitive and precarious. It seems that the ancient Egyptians had to buy their bread from Trypillia.[33]

Thus another key component of the Ukrainian self-image takes root, the idea of themselves as a uniquely productive agricultural people, even as the fathers of world agriculture. Ukrainians, it is pointed out, occupy almost 'two-thirds' of the world's 'best land', including not only

Ukraine's own 'black earth' but the land settled by Ukrainian émigrés in the American and Canadian prairies, the Argentinian pampas and the Australian outback. Ukrainians have always sought out the best land, in natural symbiosis with the fertile territory beside the river Dnieper, which has therefore provided the ecological 'genesis of indigenism' in Ukraine.[34] In other words, the local people have a long history of staying put in order to enjoy its riches. The lost Arcadian golden age referred to in Greek legend is even meant to have taken place in Ukraine, thanks to 'its warm climate, fertile black earth, flat fecund steppe, the clean waters of its rivers and its masses of wild animals'.[35] To the writer Yevhen Malaniuk (1897–1968) Ukraine was the 'Hellas of the Steppe'.

Arrata-Trypillia had all the other attributes of a developed civilisation, with 'towns' of 500 inhabitants or more, two-storey buildings and long defensive 'anti-barbarian' walls, long before the building of the Great Wall of China.[36] The population so protected thrived to the point where 'the number of inhabitants in the region from the Dnieper to the Carpathians and the Dniester reached two million'.[37] Sadly, concrete evidence of these achievements has not been found. Nevertheless, this has not prevented Ukrainian publicists from making even more outlandish claims, such as 'modern literacy in Europe comes not from Egypt or Mesopotamia, but from Arrata. [The Trypillians possessed] a written alphabet, which the Phoenicians merely spread.'[38] The Trypillians' 'written symbols'[39] were passed on in adapted form to the Greeks via the Cimmerians, and to the Romans via 'the Etruscans, [who were] also émigrés from Arrata' (the Etrus-cans, none too obviously, bear the Ukrainians' later proper name, the Rus).[40] Wandering Trypillians founded the Sumerian (building the ziggurats) and Hittite civilisations, and settled in Palestine (leading to the particularly bizarre claim that Christ's ancestors were from Galicia).[41] Budda and Zarathustra were Trypillians/Ukrainians. The Typillians/Ukrainians invented the calendar,[42] and their craftsmen even helped to build Stonehenge, which, just to complete the impression of careful historical research, is described in one source as 'a temple in Scotland'.[43]

The Horsemen of Herodotus

After the Trypillians came the little-known Cimmerians. Homer's *Odyssey* refers fleetingly to

> the land and city of the Cimmerians,
> shrouded in mist and cloud, and never does the shining sun
> look down on them with his rays.[44]

Many Ukrainian scholars argue that the Cimmerians were the direct descendants of the Trypillians, other archaeologists that they were once again probably of Thraco-Phrygian origin. Their art and implements have much in common with the finds at Hallstatt in Austria, with its Celtic and Danubian influences – a sign to some of Ukraine's early and close connection with the West, evidence for others of just how inappropriate it is to attach ethnic labels to pottery collections.

After the Cimmerians came the Scythians, probably sometime in the seventh century BC. Most scholars argue that they emerged from the eastern steppe, but Ukrainian nationalists have claimed that they were locals, the direct descendants of the original Aryans, whose three founding 'tsars' (Lipoksai, Arpoksai and Kolaksai, lords of the mountains, sea and sun) were the sons of Magog, son of Japheth.[45] As with the Trypillian myth therefore, history is often mixed with fantasy. Much more, however, is known about the Scythians.

In the Ukrainian version of events, by the sixth century BC the Scythians 'had created a great state from the Dniester to the Don', which developed from a mere 'union of tribes into a single people, united under the leadership' of the tsar Ateas in the fourth century BC.[46] The Scythians were also fearsome warriors. Some Ukrainians have claimed that the prophet Jeremiah's warning to the Israelites refers to the Scythians, the people later called the Magog, who laid waste to large parts of the Near East in the seventh century BC: 'Behold, a people cometh from the north country; and a great nation shall be stirred up from the uttermost parts of the earth. They lay hand on bow and spear; they are cruel, and have no mercy; their voices roar like the sea and they ride upon horses, every one set in array, as men to the battle against thee, O daughter of Zion' (Jeremiah 6: 22–3; see also 5: 15–17).

The Scythians are also described in the *Histories* of Herodotus (c485–425BC). Herodotus is credited by Ukrainian historians with distinguishing between the Scythian ruling elite, the 'Royal Scythians', and the 'Neuri', the 'Scythian *orachi*' or ploughmen, who were in fact the more properly proto-Ukrainian indigenous inhabitants, descendants, once again, of the Trypillians.[47] Some have also claimed that Herodotus' description of the 'Budini', 'a great and numerous nation ... native to the soil', with a great 'city built of wood, called Gelonus', whose walls were '30 furlongs in length on each side of the city', refers to the Ukrainians and that Gelonus, 'the largest city of the then world', was Kiev – or possibly the town of Bilske, just north of what is now Poltava. Herodotus also refers to 'the Black-Coats' and 'the Man-Eaters', who lived beyond the borders of Scythia and off the edge of the civilised world – presumably the ancestors of today's Russians.[48]

The Royal Scythians, with their 'semi-Asiatic' and semi-nomadic form of statehood, engaged in the Scythians' main business – war – and oversaw some nomadic cattle-breeding, while the Budini continued to develop their habits of settled agriculture (a system of private property in livestock was by now supposedly well established). Scythia also combined cultural influences. The ruling elite brought a further eastern element to Ukraine. Their language probably belonged to the north-eastern Iranian group, remnants of which survive in modern Ossetian speech. The names of local rivers, the Dnieper, Dniester, Donets and Danube, are probably derived from the Iranian root *danu*. Relics found in Scythian graves also suggest an Iranian or Assyro-Babylonian provenance, in particular the animal motifs of their ornamentation. Scythian gods such as Khors, the sun god, Simarhl, the god of the underworld, Ares, the god of war, and Tabiti, the spirit of the hearth, were also probably of eastern origin. At the same time, the influence of the Hellenic world was increasingly making itself felt through the Greek colonies on the Black Sea coast. However, the local Trypillian culture was still extant and gradually led the Scythians to 'go native' amongst the locals and be absorbed into their culture.

Like 'Arrata' at its height, the Scythian empire was an advanced state of some '12 million inhabitants',[49] which according to Lev Sylenko enjoyed its golden age 'before Socrates, or any democrat lived in Athens. Only centuries later were [the Greeks] closer to knowing the truths taught to them by the Scythians.'[50] Southern Ukraine is still dotted with Scythian burial-graves (*kurhany*) that once were up to 60 or 70 feet tall, such as the *Tovsta Mohyla* (literally 'Fat Grave') in Dnipropetrovsk. The sumptuous gold ornaments found in such graves are taken to be evidence of the Scythians' developed culture and manufacturing habits – or merely of their wealth, as many of them were bought from the Greeks. They are certainly too valuable to display in poorly guarded Ukrainian museums nowadays (an exhibition 'Gold of the Nomads: Scythian Treasures from Ancient Ukraine' travelled across the USA in 2000).

What Herodotus actually says about the Scythians is rather different from what some Ukrainian historians would have us believe. It is clear that he saw few of what to him were the normal signs of 'civilisation', declaring 'as to marvels, there are none in the land'. Although there were some 'farming Scythians', he writes, most were 'not tillers of the soil, but wandering grazers'. 'Having no stabilised cities or fortresses', true temples, 'towns or planted lands', the Scythians were mainly 'house-bearers and mounted archers, living not by tilling the soil but by cattle-rearing and carrying their dwellings on wagons'.[51] They were certainly a martial nation:

> As to war, these are their customs. A Scythian drinks of the blood of the first man whom he has overthrown. He carries to the king the heads of all whom he has slain in battle; for he receives a share of the booty taken if he brings a head, but not otherwise ... each saws off the part beneath the eyebrows, and cleanses the rest. If he be a poor man, then he does but cover the outside with a piece of raw hide, and so makes use of it; but if he be rich, he covers the head with the raw

hide, and gilds the inside of it and so uses it as a drinking cup. Such cups a man makes also of the head of his own kinsman with whom he has been at feud, and whom he has vanquished in single combat before the king; and if guests whom he honours visit him he will serve them with these heads, and show how the dead were his kinsfolk who made war upon him and were worsted by him; this they call manly valour.

Moreover once in every year each governor of a province brews a bowl of wine in his own province, whereof those Scythians drink who have slain enemies; those who have not achieved this taste not this wine but sit apart dishonoured; and this they count as a very great disgrace; but as many as have slain not one but many enemies, they have each two cups and so drink of them both.[52]

Their treatment of captured enemies was particularly enlightened: 'They pour wine on the men's heads and cut their throats over a vessel; they then carry the blood up on the pile of sticks and pour it on the scimitar. So they carry the blood aloft, but below by the sacred pile they cut off all the slain men's right arms and hands and throw these in the air.'[53] The Roman poet Ovid was equally scathing: '[The Scythians] are scarcely worthy of the name [of men]; they have more of cruel savagery than wolves. They fear not laws; right gives way to force, and justice has been conquered by the aggressive sword.'[54]

There is a long tradition of equating the Scythian with the Asiatic and the 'barbarian': either negatively, as with the fiendish devil-worshippers Walter Scott's Crusader confronts in Constantinople in *Count Robert of Paris* (1832), or positively, as in the Russian writer Aleksandr Blok's famous 1918 poem *The Scythians* ('We're Scythians and Asians, too, from coasts/That breed squint eyes, bespeaking greed').[55] Nevertheless, contemporary Ukrainians continue to make use of the Scythian myth, such as the poet Lina Kostenko in her *Scythian Odyssey*, whilst, unlike Blok, reappropriating their ancestors as defenders of the European littoral. After all, the region north of the Black Sea continued to be referred to as 'Scythia' until well into the Middle Ages.

Sarmatians, Roxolanians, Rus

After the Scythians came the Sarmatians (third century BC to third century AD). Until fairly recently, they occupied a much more central place in local mythology than the Scythians. The idea of descent from the Sarmatians was particularly popular during the time of the Polish Commonwealth in the sixteenth and seventeenth centuries. Several versions of this myth existed, however (see also chapters three and four). The Commonwealth's aristocracy and gentry liked to argue that their class was descended from the Sarmatians, irrespective of whether a noble was a Pole or a Ukrainian, much as the Spanish nobility claimed to be descended from the Visigoths. An alternative idea was that the Ukrainians were descended from the Roxolanian branch of the Sarmatians, the name 'Roxolani' supposedly being derived from 'Ruskolani', meaning 'the plains inhabited by the Rus', or from 'Rhos', the Iranian word for 'light', and that this in turn was the root of the name 'Rus' (the well-travelled Roxolanians also gave their name to Roussillon in southern France). The Poles on the other hand were descended from a different Sarmatian tribe, the Alanians. The seventeenth-century Cossack leader Bohdan Khmelnytskyi called himself 'prince of the Sarmatians', and the name was still being used a century later by chroniclers such as Samiilo Velychko.[56]

The Greek cartographer Ptolemy (c90–168AD) defined Sarmatia as the edge of Europe, just as his predecessor Herodotus had placed Scythia on the edge of the civilised world. To be precise, Ptolemy distinguished between European Sarmatia, the region between the Vistula and the Don (more or less the territory of modern Ukraine), and Asian Sarmatia, east of the Don and the Sea of Azov. He saw little of significance to the north or north-east. To the south, Sarmatia had some contact with, but remained independent of, the Roman world.

The next link in the Ukrainian myth of descent is the Antes tribal federation, established as early as the second century AD and identified by Ukrainian archaeologists with the Cherniakhivska culture (which others identify with the Goths). According to many historians, the Antes established the first recognisably east Slavic culture, but the Ukrainian historian Mykhailo Hrushevskyi narrowed its provenance and suggested it was the original progenitor of Ukrainian civilisation.[57] The central element in the Antes federation was the Polianian tribe, under the leadership of the semi-mythical princes Bozh, Ardahast and Pyrahost. The Byzantine historian Procopius is quoted as claiming that while the Antes were consolidating the various east Slavic tribes in the south, the 'Veneti' were doing the same in the north-west and the 'Slovenes' or 'Sclavenes' in the south-west. From this is perhaps derived the Arabic legend of three ninth-century proto-states amongst the eastern Slavs; Kuiava, which is presumed to be Kiev; Slava, later to be Novgorod; and Arta, perhaps the site of the city of Tmutorokan, on the Black Sea coast.[58] Ukrainians certainly take this as a harbinger of future divisions.

Ukrainian historians reject the idea that the Antes were temporarily overthrown by a Goth 'state', the so-called 'empire of Ermanaric' (ruled 350–75), which the historian Jordanes describes in his *De origine actibusque Getarum* (551) as dominating the northern Black Sea coast (the Ostrogoths between the Kuban and the Dniester and the Visigoths from the Dniester to the Danube), between the end of the Sarmatian period in the third century and the arrival of the Huns in the fourth. The

Goth incursion is depicted as a passing phenomenon, swept away by the Huns who forced the Goths to flee to the west.[59] The Antes federation was therefore able to survive until AD602, when, after another wave of invaders arrived from the east, the Avars, it is presumed to have dissolved into its constituent tribes, most of whom fell under the authority of the Khazar Kaganate until the middle of the ninth century (the Khazars were Turkic-speaking nomads from the east). However, the most dynamic of the tribes, the Polianians, who inhabited the area around the middle Dnieper, mainly on the Right Bank, were able in the ninth century to reestablish the Antes federation as Rus (one source claims that 'Polianska Rus' was established as early as AD560).[60]

Kiev first became a recognisable city under the Antes, although some Ukrainians point to Ptolemy's earlier references to the Sarmatians' capital 'on the Dnieper' as proof of the fact that Kiev, or 'Gelonus' before it, is 'an "eternal" city, like Jerusalem, Rome or Lhasa',[61] which has been occupied since the late Stone Age and was the capital of the Trypillians and Scythians (Herodotus in fact describes how the Scythians melted away before Darius's invading Persian armies in 514–512BC, having no primate city to defend). The normal date given for the foundation of Kiev is, however, AD482, or at least this was the excuse for the fifteen hundredth anniversary celebrations in 1982. The three brothers Kyi, Shchek and Khoryv and their sister, Lybid, who according to the legend repeated in *The Tale of Bygone Years* were the founders of Kiev (Kiev being spelt Kyïv or Kyyiv in Ukrainian), were therefore local Polianian princes. The arrival of Scandinavian overlords (the Riurykovych) to rule in Kiev in the ninth century was therefore, in theory, only a 'dynastic revolution, which led not to the formation of Kievan Rus, but to a change of ruling dynasty'.[62] Here Ukrainian historians finally share something with their Russian counterparts. Both reject the 'Normanist theory', according to which it required Viking intervention to defeat the Khazars and establish a state amongst the Rus. The first Viking ruler of Rus may have been Oleh (Helgi) of Novgorod, who arrived as late as 882.

Ukrainian historians have been keen to stress the vitality of early Rus culture. Literacy, even a 'pre-Rus-ian' alphabet, supposedly existed before Volodymyr's baptism in 988 – even before Cyril and Methodius codified an alphabet for the Slavs in 863. It is even claimed that St Cyril saw the Psalms 'written in Ruthenian [i.e. Rus-ian] letters in the city of Chersonesus' in Crimea some century and a half before 988 and that he therefore derived much of his alphabet from early Ukrainian.[63] Traces of this 'pre-Cyrillic' alphabet, 'a transitional variant from the Greek alphabet to the Cyrillic',[64] are on show in the exhibition in Kiev's St Sofiia Museum. Armenian chronicles record correspondence with Kiev as early as the sixth century, and agreements with Byzantium were supposedly written in the respective languages of the two sides.[65] It has been suggested that the Rus wrote several chronicles in the pre-Baptism period, which helps to explain the rapid spread of literate culture after 988; but examples of such have never been found.

Christianisation

Culture in the first millennium AD meant religion above all. Tradition has it that the whole of Rus was baptised into the Christian faith by Prince Volodymyr of Kiev in AD988. The celebration of the millennium in 1988 was one of the milestones of Gorbachev's glasnost, although the Ukrainians were not allocated any special role in the commemorations, which were held in Moscow. For Ukrainian nationalists this was doubly galling, as they consider that Volodymyr's subjects were Ukrainian, not Russian. It also sits ill with their argument that Ukraine is a core European state that Christianity should have come relatively late to Kiev, compared to around 700 for Croatia and Serbia, 864 for Bulgaria under Boris I and the 960s for Poland under Mieszko I, and that it was something of a hand-me-down from Byzantium.

Ukrainians have therefore tried to prove that their Christianity is as old as that of Constantinople and that the Ukrainian Church was always a national Church, independent in many respects from Byzantium, Moscow or Rome.[66] At the same time, emphasis is also placed on local pre-Christian traditions to argue that their preservation after 988 and partial synthesis with Christianity were a key reason for the development of Ukraine's unique brand of national religion (once again much of this pre-Baptism mythology is shared with Russian nationalists, although put to different uses).

Supposedly, Christianity has enjoyed an unbroken presence in Ukraine since apostolic times. According to one persistent legend, Ukraine's first contact with Christianity came with the mission of St Andrew, the 'first-called', to Kiev in AD55. Andrew's importance as the supposed founder of the Church in Constantinople has led to rival claims that he also visited Georgia and Poland; *The Tale of Bygone Years* refers to him venturing further north to the future Novgorod, but Ukrainian scholars have denied that he ever visited what was to become Russia.[67] The churches founded by the apostle were unfortunately swept away by the Gothic invasion in the third century, although it is claimed that 'the head of the Scythian bishopric' was present at the First Ecumenical Council in Nicaea in AD325 (probably in fact Bishop Cadmus from the kingdom of the Bosphorus).[68] The myth of Andrew's 'mission to the Scythians' began to develop in the eleventh century and was widespread by the Middle Ages – a Church Sobor (council) held in Kiev in 1621 declared him the 'Rus apostle'. The St Andrew's Church that was erected in Kiev in 1086 is no longer standing, but the eighteenth-century Baroque extravaganza bearing his name can still be seen on the hill above the Dnieper where Andrew is meant to have raised his cross (see also page 226), as depicted on one of the keynote paintings inside the church, *The Sermon of Andrew the Apostle to the Scythians* by Platon Boryspilets (1847). The myth that Andrew gave his privileged blessing to the Ukrainian soil is a central tenet of the modern Ukrainian Church – even the Pope gave it favourable mention during his visit in 2001.

Christianity also came to Ukraine via Crimea. Pope Clement IV was exiled to the Greek city of Chersonesus, whose ruins are near the modern town of Sevastopil, in AD92–101. His relics were used to bless the enthronement of Klymentii Smoliatych in 1147. Christianity grew rapidly amongst the neighbouring city-states, especially after the sixth and seventh centuries, when Byzantium began to strengthen its links with the northern Black Sea coast, and the Ostrogoths who remained after the Hun invasion established a metropolitanate at Dorus in northern Crimea in around AD400 under the authority of Constantinople. The new faith allegedly penetrated the hinterland from its Crimean bridgeheads, reaching the Antes, who lived in direct contact with Byzantium until the Bulgarians interjected themselves by settling south of the Danube in the seventh century (the Antes also had some contacts with Rome).[69] The southerly location of the main 'proto-Ukrainian' tribes, it is claimed, meant that the Polianians in particular were therefore well acquainted with the new faith from 'the Age of the Apostles' onwards, whereas 'the other east Slavic tribes [i.e. the ancestors of the Russians] . . . definitely did not know Christianity in the pre-historic period'.[70] Even after the Baptism in 988, it is claimed that paganism, superstition and witchcraft remained more widespread north of Kiev, the new faith only reaching Vladimir in 1108 and Moscow on its foundation in 1147, although it is hard to see how this could relate to ethnic differences, rather than simple geographical remoteness or a more likely distinction between elites and masses.

Rus had contacts with Constantinople long before 988. A series of missions from Rus to Byzantium is said to have led to a 'First Christianisation' of Rus, or at least of its upper classes, either in 839 or under the princes Askold and Dir, baptised in Constantinople sometime after 860. For 20 years (862–82) the two headed a 'Christian party' at the Kievan court. Some have even argued that Askold established a local metropolitanate and complete hierarchy for the Church. One of the encyclicals of the Byzantine patriarch Photius in 867 refers to the Rus having 'exchanged their heathen teaching ... for the pure faith' and accepted 'a bishop and a pastor'.[71] A Christian church of St Elijah existed in Kiev by around 900, after the example of the church of the same name used by the Rus in Constantinople. However, the 'pagan party' remained dominant. Oleh of Novgorod (ruled 882–912) attempted to snuff out the new religion and had Askold murdered in 882 (the monument marking his 'grave' can be seen in Kiev's Botanical Gardens on Uhorska Hill). The Greeks were expelled from the city.[72] Nevertheless, *The Tale of Bygone Years* refers to the treaty between Rus and Byzantium in 945 (other sources date it to AD944) being signed by both 'the baptised' and 'the unbaptised Ruses'.[73] There is stronger evidence that Olha, regent of Rus from 947 to 957 (and periodically thereafter until her death in 969), was received into the Christian Church in Constantinople sometime around AD946 with the blessing of the emperor and patriarch, and received the Christian name Helen.

As with other Christian missions, such as those of St Augustine to Canterbury in 596 and St Patrick to fifth-century Ireland, Byzantium's aim in 988 was therefore probably as much to consolidate as to establish Christianity. Two bishoprics already existed at the margins of Rus territory: one on the Black Sea coast opposite Crimea in Tmutorokan founded 120 years before the Baptism, and the other in Peremyshl (now in eastern Poland) founded in 906 as a result of Cyril and Methodius's Christianisation of Moravia (the 'Ukrainian' White Croat tribe was then part of the Moravian empire), whose authority extended as far as Halych and Kholm. As a consequence of this long pre-history, many Ukrainian historians have refused to accept that the Kievan Church established in 988 was a mere creature of Byzantium. According to one myth, the first metropolitan of Kiev was the Slav Mykhail (served 988–92), brought by Volodymyr from Chersonesus. According to another, the Church was under the Bulgarian patriarchate at Ohrid. Some take the reference in *The Tale of Bygone Years* to Yaroslav the Wise having 'founded the Metropolitanate in 1037' as evidence that no Greek hierarchs were appointed before that date and that a local, independent Church was already in existence in Kiev.[74] Others take it as a reference to the founding of St Sofiia's as the 'metropolitan', that is primary, church in 1037. Most likely, however, the first head of the Rus Church after 988 was the Byzantine envoy, Feofilakt.

Paganism and Neo-Paganism

On the other hand, the argument that the Kievan Church, like the Catholic Church in Latin America, was decisively shaped by its pre-Christian inheritance is also a vital means of establishing its 'Ukrainian' character. According to scholars such as Ivan Ohiienko, later Metropolitan Ilarion (1882–1972), the specifically Ukrainian version of Christianity developed as a natural outgrowth of the religion of the Trypillians, Scythians, Antes and Polianians, whose forms of worship (pantheism tending towards monotheism) provided fertile ground for the later development of the Christian faith.[75] The Russian historian Boris Rybakov has argued that paganism and Christianity coexisted in a system of *dvoeverie* ('dual faith') throughout Rus until at least the thirteenth century,[76] others that it has persisted right up to the present day. Western historians have raised as an open question whether Rus 'became a co-inheritor of Byzantium's Graeco-Roman culture; or whether Kievan Rus was isolated by language, the recipient only of the ecclesiastical component of that culture which was available in Slavonic translation'.[77] After all, 'unlike the Balkan Slavic states, Kievan Rus lay not only beyond the existing border of the Byzantine empire but also outside the boundaries of the old Roman empire. It was therefore removed from the Greek and Roman classical foundations of Byzantine culture.'[78]

Ukrainian historians and mystics have pointed to the signs and 'pagan forms' on the walls of Kiev's St Sofiia's as evidence of the strong nativist influence on the original religion of Rus. The inside of the church is indeed beautiful and intriguing. The interior layout, it has been claimed,

embodies the Indo-European idea of the garden of paradise, manifested in the pillars and columns, which symbolise the trunks of trees. This depiction of the tree of life, in which is metaphorically encoded the model of the Cosmos, finds its reflection in the symbolic division of the space of the church into three spheres: the higher for the divine, the middle for the world of men and the lower the kingdom of the underworld [the traditional Byzantine pattern].[79]

Evidence of pagan influence includes the symbols on the ceiling and walls (often in the national colours of blue and yellow), 'the swastikas decorating the altar' (just below the twin images of Christ dispensing bread and wine), 'going both clockwise [from the material to the spiritual worlds] and anti-clockwise [vice-versa]', 'the six-pointed stars we see on its marble friezes, on the floor slabs, on the iron-bound doors, the tridents that stand on many of the crosses, the discs with sun rays garlanding the dome of the church structures'.[80] It is even possible to find trident-like images on the external walls, on Volodymyr's sarcophagus and on the shields of some of the saints depicted inside. Some have claimed to see in the spectacular figure of the *Virgin Oranta* that dominates the wall behind the main altar echoes of Mokosha, the ancient Rus fertility goddess (see plate 20), in a pose similar to that of many Scythian statuettes (her rounded face and figure) and Trypillian figurines (her raised hands).[81] All this is taken as evidence of the early provenance of Ukrainian culture and national symbols. There are indeed swastika-like images on the altar, painted 900 years before the Nazis came to power in Germany. However, for all that it has its origins in Sanskrit (from *swasti* or 'inner peace') and Hittite culture, the swastika is not necessarily the first thing to embrace with enthusiasm if you are looking for national symbols for a new state.

In truth, little is known of the pre-Christian religion of Rus, let alone that of earlier periods. According to Lev Sylenko and others, the local naturalistic-animistic-agrarian religion had developed on Ukrainian soil for thousands of years before Rus. Sylenko identifies the main Rus god as Dazhboh, the god of abundance, a benevolent sun god like Brahma or Yahweh, who was supposedly the original god of the Trypillians, the god of Arrata, 9,000 years before Christ.[82] Dazhboh was venerated in turn by the Polianians (the god Khors was perhaps the Roxolanian equivalent of Dazhboh), which is why *The Lay of Ihor's Host* refers to the Rus as 'the children of Dazhboh'.[83] To Sylenko and others of a like mind, the Christianisation of Rus in 988 was therefore a disaster, as it alienated the Ukrainians from their real 'native faith' and forced them to worship other peoples' gods.[84] Sylenko therefore established his own religion in 1968, which he called RUNVira, or the 'Native Ukrainian Popular Faith', based around the worship of Dazhboh – first in North America, but after 1991 also in Ukraine, where 35 branches had been established by 1998.

Some Rus gods may in reality have been of Scandinavian origin. The deity dethroned by Volodymyr in 988, Perun, the maker of thunder and lightning, may have been modelled on Thor and/or Odin, especially as he seems to have replaced a similar deity, Rod, as god the father and creator and the god of war sometime in the ninth century AD. Rod may therefore have been an earlier, more 'indigenous' god – it is certainly significant that Scandinavian gods were not imported wholesale. Once again, some Ukrainian historians have argued that Perun or Rod was worshipped by the Antes and perhaps even their predecessors.[85] However, images of Perun have also been found in Poland, Lithuania (Perkunas) and the Balkans (Pirun or Pir). Other gods may have come from the east, such as Svaroh, god of the sky, whose name is most probably derived from the Sanskrit *swarga* ('sky'). Svaroh was also a god of fire, sun and thunder and perhaps also the god of war and, in some interpretations, the father of Dazhboh. Khors, another sun god and the source of righteousness, was also possibly of Iranian origin.[86]

Much of the symbolism and ritual surrounding such gods transferred into the Christian pantheon. The festival of Perun became that of the prophet Elijah, master of the elements; Mokosha became St Parasceve; harvest and midsummer festivals became the Christian celebrations of Nativity and the birth of St John the Baptist (the latter being originally the festival of Kupala, the god of summer). The idea of pagan persistence is symbolised by the story that, when Volodymyr had Kiev's main statue to Perun thrown into the river Dnieper in 988, it stubbornly emerged downriver, near the site where the Vydubytskyi monastery now stands, its name being derived from the Ukrainian for 'arise!' (*vydybai!*). Lesser deities, such as water nymphs and forest spirits, remain part of Ukrainian folk mythology to this day, helping to define Ukrainian religion by its popular character.

Attila the Ukrainian

Some rather more fantastical beliefs about Ukrainian pre-history ought perhaps to be mentioned. Among them is the idea that Ukraine was the centre of the ancient empire of U-Hor, which stretched from the Atlantic to the Pacific and passed on its culture to the later empire of Atlantis – which is why the gods Poseidon and Neptune were also associated with the sign of the trident.[87] Another is the suggestion that the Amazons were a Ukrainian tribe that lived between the Don and the Danube delta, rather than 'beyond the Don' where they are traditionally placed. Some have argued that the Amazons were in fact the Sarmatians or Scythians, given their tradition of women serving as warriors before marriage, although Herodotus gives a long account of a meeting between the Amazons and Scythians as clearly separate peoples.[88]

Some have claimed that Troy was a Ukrainian city, at or near the site of the later Greek city of Olbia or Olviia, near the mouth of the southern Buh river in what is now Mykolaïv oblast. Alternatively, Troy may have been near Tenedos, now the Tenderivska spit in the estuary of the Buh and Dnieper. The grave of Achilles is therefore also to be found some-where on a small Black Sea island in the Buh delta, although it has escaped the attentions of archaeologists to date.[89] Most fantastically, it has been claimed that Troy was Herodotus' city of Gelonus, the future Kiev.

Equally bizarre is the idea that Attila the Hun was in fact Attila the Ukrainian. Supposedly he came not from the far steppe, but was born in what is now Kiev in AD401. He ruled there from 433 until his death in 453, the city serving as the capital of his empire, which stretched 'from the Atlantic to the Pacific, from the Baltic to the Mediterranean'.[90] His palace was built on the site of the old Scythian fortress of Gelonus, ruined by Darius I of Persia in 512BC, in what is now the south-west part of the city. The Huns, like the Scythians, were therefore a 'super-ethnos', with elements of foreign leadership perhaps, but containing a substan-tial segment from the indigenous 'Ukrainian' population and becoming increasingly subject to its influence. For the advocates of a Ukrainian Attila, Kyi, the legendary founder of Kiev, was one of Attila's compan-ions-in-arms: it has even been argued that Attila was Kyi.[91]

It is perhaps worth mentioning that Attila reportedly took great offence at a mural in Milan depicting the princes of Scythia paying homage to the Roman empire.[92] The consequences of his wrath are not recorded.

Conclusions

The Ukrainians are not uniquely guilty of historical embellishment. It is perfectly normal to mix the 'facts' of chroniclers and archaeologists with the 'fictions' of artists and poets. The Irish, led by W.B. Yeats, idealised pre-Christian Tara, the Victorian English embraced the idea of King Arthur's Avalon and many Jacobean Protestants sincerely believed they were descended from the 'lost tribe of Israel'. Under Nicolae Ceauşescu, Romanians were encouraged to add to the traditional myth of descent from Roman legionaries, itself somewhat shaky, the even hazier notion of an indigenous 2,000-year old 'Dacian' state, founded by a certain King Burebista two centuries before the arrival of the Romans.

It is important, however, to point out degrees of plausibility and obviously controversial artifice. In the words of Anthony Smith, 'the better documented and more securely attested the golden age, the more it can bear the weight of emotion placed upon it, and withstand processes of demythologisation.'[93] In the Ukrainian case, Russian nationalists will always make hay with the more implausible myths.

A second problem is how much of this pre-history is solely 'Ukrainian'. Much of it can serve equally well as the foundation for generalised theories of the origins of all the east Slavic peoples. That is, once the story has progressed as far as Rus, it can simply be given a different ending. Many Russian historians have indeed treated it as such, as have Russian artists and composers (see p. 85). The nineteenth-century Slavophile Aleksei Khomiakov (1804–60) argued that the Huns were a special type of 'old Russian Cossack'; the *fin-de-siècle* 'Scythian' movement looked to the 'early Slavs' for myths of Russia's pre-Christian origins; and 'neo-paganism' is alive and well in modern Russia, using the same symbols and celebrating many of the same gods as its Ukrainian variant. Stripped of the more eccentric mythology, there is much that can be salvaged from Ukraine's pre-Christian history. But the dilemma remains. The more 'Ukrainian' the presentation, the less catholic its appeal.

On the other hand, a nation with a partially mythologised past is no less a nation. As one Ukrainian nationalist, Dmytro Korchynskyi, rabidly extreme in most other respects, has pointed out: 'even if the Ukrainians are descended not from the Trypillians, but from Symon Petliura [the nationalist general in 1918–20] and are worthy, they can and should in the very near future begin to dictate to everyone in politics, science, in economics, and in art.'[94] If the latter part of the statement was changed to read 'live a normal life as a normal state', then why not? Ukrainians have a perfectly serviceable history from later periods and can easily concentrate on that.

3

Neither Fish Nor Fowl:
Between Poland and Russia

'Neither meat nor fish' (*ni miaso, ni ryba*), or, in the normal English idiom 'neither fish nor fowl', was how Paul I, tsar of Russia from 1796 to 1801, characterised the west Ukrainian Greek Catholics. The description, however, could apply equally well to all Ukrainians, and indeed Belarusians. To the Romanov authorities, their Western subjects were either Orthodox or Catholic, Russian or Pole. Apart from special categories (Jewish, Baltic Protestant), they simply could not conceive of anything existing in between – which is why Paul I simply assumed that Ukrainians of the Orthodox faith were 'Russian'. However, existing 'in between' is precisely what the Ukrainians did do between the fourteenth and twentieth centuries, carving a niche for themselves between Russia and Poland – the main powers in Eastern Europe after the fall of Rus. In fact, Ukraine's entire history could be written in terms of its oscillation between the two sides, with the Russians decisively surpassing the Poles in importance only in the nineteenth and twentieth centuries.

Without a tradition of statehood, however, Ukraine's niche has been a difficult one to occupy. The very concept of 'Ukrainian' was developed at a time when political conditions encouraged its target group to identify with whatever state or nationality offered the greatest political, economic and/or cultural advantages. Moreover, Ukraine's niche has rarely been equidistant between Poland and Russia. At most times Ukrainians have allied with one against the other, encouraging affinities to develop with the friend of the time. Maintaining or promoting a sense of separateness has therefore been difficult, but not impossible.

Byzantium or Rome?

First, a word or two ought to be said about how the relationship with Poland and Russia symbolises Ukraine's general position at the borders of Western and Eastern 'civilisation'. Polish rule did not begin the European influence on Ukraine *ex nihilo* in the fourteenth century. For all that Rus was firmly in the Byzantine cultural orbit, it remained open to Central and even Western European influences, although these have been somewhat exaggerated by Ukrainian historians seeking to demonstrate Ukraine's manifest destiny in Europe.

Rus took its Christianity from the Byzantine 'East', just after Poland joined the Catholic 'West', but Ukrainian historians have tended to deny that this was in any way a definitive civilisational choice.[1] Some have even retrospectively depicted the preference for Byzantium over Rome as a national tragedy, as Western Europe was the civilisation of the future and the Byzantine faith would tie Kiev too closely to Moscow.[2] Either way, Rus (or, as Ukrainian historians would have it, Ukraine–Rus) was always open to the possibility of a link with the Roman West, just as many of its neighbours, such as Bulgaria and Bohemia, were initially under the influence of both Byzantium and Rome. The Rus chronicles and Roman sources record that Kiev received a total of 12 missions from the papacy.[3] Moreover, one Ukrainian historian has claimed that 'the chronicles were subject to frequent reediting ... under the influence of Greek clergy, who, being hostile to Rome, made a habit of eliding all references to Kiev's relations with Rome.'[4] Olha's mission to Constantinople in 946 was followed by the despatch of envoys to Otto I of Germany in 959 and the ill-fated trip of Adalbert, archbishop of Magdeburg, to Rus in 961. According to some Ukrainian historians, Adalbert actually established himself in Kiev for a short time before being expelled by the 'pagan party' led by Prince Sviatoslav (ruled 944–73). His departure was fairly ignominious – most of his entourage were killed on the way home. It has also been claimed that a mission from Pope Benedict VII in 979 established a 'Latin eparchy' in Kiev before it was expelled by Volodymyr, in his original pagan incarnation.[5]

Legend and the account of the Baptism of Rus in *The Tale of Bygone Years* both suggest that Prince Volodymyr sent delegations to research all the great religions before making his choice of faith. He rejected the Muslim option, as 'he was fond of women and indulgence, regarding which he [listened] with pleasure. But circumcision and abstinence from pork were disagreeable to him. "Drinking", said he, "is the joy of the Rus. We cannot exist without that pleasure."'[6] The chronicle also records that Volodymyr considered the claims of the Volga Bulgars, the Germans, the Pope and the Jews, with the latter probably based in Khazaria, perhaps in Crimea. The Byzantine option won out because of the strength of previous links, practical geopolitics and the prestige of Byzantium, which was at the zenith of its power after the end of the iconoclastic controversies (*The Tale of Bygone Years* quaintly records that the Rus were in considerable awe of the culture and architecture of Constantinople, including presumably the mechanical birds and mobile thrones deployed for the benefit of more impressionable visitors).[7] Significantly, the Jewish option was rejected for reasons of realpolitik, as

Volodymyr considered their statelessness to be a divine punishment and had no wish to be similarly afflicted. The chronicle records his dismissive comment – 'If God loved you and your faith, you would not be thus dispersed in foreign lands. Do you expect us to accept that fate also?'[8]

The link with Byzantium did not exclude other contacts. Intermarriage between Volodymyr's Riurikid dynasty and the crown heads of Central and even Western Europe was common, including three sisters and three daughters of Yaroslav the Wise, earning him the epithet of the 'father-in-law of Europe'. When Yaroslav's daughter Anna married Henry I of France, she brought with her a lavish Slavonic Gospel, subsequently used at French coronations. She could read it, he could not. Volodymyr Monomakh married the daughter of Harold Hardrada, defeated at the Battle of Stamford Bridge in 1066. Exiles from other European courts, such as the widow and sons of England's King Edmund Ironside and Harold's older daughter Gytha, sojourned in Kiev.[9] Traffic also passed in the other direction. The exiled Rus prince Iziaslav Yaroslavych (1024–78) promised 'due fealty' to Pope Gregory VII in the 1070s in return for papal intercession in his struggle to retain his lands, as well as doling out vast quantities of gold at various German courts to promote his cause.

Danylo of Halych's alleged 'conversion' to Rome in the 1240s was mentioned in chapter one. The tale is not as fanciful as it may seem. 'Conversion' from east to west was a common and not even particularly dramatic occurrence before divisions between Byzantium and Rome began to harden in the fifteenth century. Although Bohemia moved decisively into the Latin orbit after the reign of Wenceslaus (900–29), its initial contacts were with Byzantium, as were those of Hungary, until the Battle of Lechfeld in 955 established the preeminent influence of the Germanic Church. However, there is much nationalist wishful thinking in the idea of a Catholic Rus or even a Catholic Galicia. If the southern Rus had indeed moved close to Rome they would probably in time have also moved closer to their neighbours the Poles, whom, *The Tale of Bygone Years* records, they already referred to as 'Liakhs' – Catholic and already 'other' (the chronicle also records how the devil appeared in the 1070s disguised as a Pole). Although a Catholic Ukraine would have been more sharply distinguished against Russia in the east, the boundary between Polish and Ukrainian identities in the west would, conversely, have been harder to draw. In any case, although a more ecumenical version of Orthodoxy was able to develop amongst the southern Rus, it is highly unlikely that they would have taken to the unfamiliar Latin liturgy.

As a matter of historical fact, of course, Byzantium was a logical choice at the time and the Rus *were* Orthodox, so the above scenario was reversed. From the fourteenth century onwards, the southern Rus lived in closer contact with Poland. In terms of religion it was clear they were not Poles, although in periods when it was politically and culturally advantageous to assimilate to a Polish identity, many of them did so. The blurred boundary was in the east.

Religion and Identity

By the late fourteenth century, the division of Rus lands was well established. Moscow and the north-east were under the Golden Horde; Galicia went to Poland in the 1340s, followed by Podillia in the 1360s; Transcarpathia was under the Hungarian crown and Bukovyna under first the Moldovans and then the Ottomans; Kiev and Volhynia were absorbed by the new Grand Duchy of Lithuania. For two centuries, therefore, the majority of the southern Rus were under Lithuania or Poland, although at a time when the two states were moving closer together after the establishment of a common crown at the Union of Krevo in 1385.

The main element in Rus identity was still religion (until the Counter-Reformation in the sixteenth century the Polish-Lithuanian Commonwealth was more or less tolerant of its Orthodox subjects).[10] Other possible props, such as myths of historical descent, were underdeveloped until the seventeenth century, in part because the local Orthodox came under the influence of the Byzantine Hesychastic movement, a form of quietism that sought salvation through a life of divine contemplation and distance from such earthly concerns as the recorded past. Linguistic trends also inhibited the strengthening of a local identity, as the turn towards religious formalism led to the adoption of the more stylised Euthymian version of Church Slavonic, reversing the trend towards the gradual interpenetration of Church Slavonic and local vernaculars that had been apparent since the tenth century. Moreover, after the fall of Constantinople to the Ottomans in 1453 the southern Rus Church was in a pretty parlous state, deprived of wealth and resources and its traditional protector, unable even to tend to the basic needs of its flock.

The future development of the Rus religious community now depended on a complicated quadrilateral relationship between the divided Orthodox (the northern and southern Rus), the latter's Catholic overlords and the spiritual authorities in Constantinople. In time the southern Rus began to acquire the proper name 'Ruthenian', implying a culture community related to, but distinct from, the Orthodox of Muscovy, but this was not the only possibility. For the moment, the local Orthodox were still aware of a common bond with the northern Rus. The original Church of Volodymyr was in disarray, however.[11] On the one hand, many of its hierarchs had moved first to Vladimir (1299) and then to Moscow (1325). The more powerful northern metropolitans, in particular Feognost (served 1328–53), Kiprian, a Bulgarian, (served c1381–1406) and Foty (1408–31), fought hard to assert unified authority over the Church and tended to be backed by Constantinople, which considered Moscow's secular power the most likely means of preserving a united Church.[12] Kiprian was probably responsible for *The Trinity Chronicle* (c1406–8), which first gave formal expression to the idea of the Moscow Church as Kiev's direct successor. Although sometimes accused of neglecting Kiev and the south, Moscow prelates still resided there on occasion and conducted pastoral tours away from their home base. Foty's peregrinations in 1421–2, for example, took him through Novaharadok, Halych, Lviv and Kiev. Moreover, southern prelates were often active in the north. A bishop from Halych buried Petr, metropolitan of Moscow, in 1326; and Kiprian was originally a metropolitan of 'Halych and Lithuania'. Petr (served 1308–26), who organised the move to Moscow, and Aleksii (1354–78) were originally from the south.

On the other hand, Moscow's claims were resented by many, and not just the rulers of Poland and Lithuania, especially as the north was to an extent complicit with the *Pax Mongolica*. A Halych metropolitanate was established by Yurii of Galicia-Volhynia in 1303; although its first metropolitan, Nifont, was deposed by Moscow after only two years and attempts to revive a separate hierarchy in the 1330s and 1340s were frustrated by Feognost. Nevertheless, Constantinople recognised a metropolitan, Antony, in 1372–5 after Kazimierz the Great of Poland occupied Halych and threatened to Latinise all its inhabitants (the opposite possibility of converting all of the as yet pagan Lithuanians to the eastern faith was the one factor encouraging Constantinople periodically to favour the south).[13] Although the Moscow-based Kiprian may have been the nominal head of the Halych Church in the 1380s, Jagiełło II appointed a certain Ioann in 1391 and it is unclear whether Kiprian managed to supplant him.

Lithuania's rulers also tried to establish metropolitanates for their Orthodox subjects. The first was probably established at Novaharadok in 1300 and seems to have lasted until 1330. The little-known Feodorit served briefly as metropolitan in 1352 and was succeeded by Roman (1354–62), who is known to have resided in Kiev. In 1355 Roman and Aleksii of Moscow journeyed to Constantinople, where they accepted a territorial division of sorts, with Roman having authority over all of southern and western Rus. Vitautas, Grand Duke of Lithuania from 1392 to 1430, reacted angrily to the election of Foty in Moscow and installed Hryhorii Tsamblak in Kiev as a rival between 1415 and 1419.

Competing hierarchies were therefore often in existence, although they were rarely as well established in the south as in Moscow. Southern metropolitans were often forced to reside in Vilna/Vilnius or Novaharadok rather than Kiev. One who braved Tatar raids, St Makarii I (served 1495–7), was murdered on his way to Kiev in 1497. Regular residence in Kiev was always difficult until the time of Metropolitan Rahoza (1588–99). Historians also dispute whether the rival bodies emerged because of new political boundaries or because of the growing sense of separateness between north and south. In favour of the latter theory is the fact that, while Moscow began to develop the myth of itself as the 'third Rome', Kievan metropolitans continued to develop the contacts with the Latin West first cultivated by Roman and Danylo of Halych in the thirteenth century, attending the Councils of Lyons in 1245 and Constance in 1418. Different reactions to the abortive Union of Florence in 1439 further demonstrated the growing divide (the Union sought to reunite the Orthodox and Latin Churches, largely on the latter's terms). There is some controversy over how much direct effect the Union had in the southern lands. One Kiev metropolitan, Gregory the Bulgarian (served 1458–72), was supposedly a 'Florentine'. At the least, the Union does not seem to have been actively opposed – if only because Kiev's comparative isolation had left it relatively ignorant of post-1054 disputes.[14] In Moscow, by contrast, Metropolitan Isidore was imprisoned and forced to flee when he attempted to conduct a sermon in the cathedral of the Assumption under a Latin cross and with the name of the pope before that of the patriarch.

Between 1448 and 1458 the division of the old Kievan metropolitanate in two was consolidated, after Constantinople's final fall in 1453 left the rival branches of the Church freer to go their own way. With the Turks at the gates of Constantinople, Moscow jumped the gun by declaring autocephaly in 1448, and electing its own metropolitan, who claimed to head the Church of 'Moscow and all Rus'. In 1589 the metropolitanate was elevated to a patriarchate. In 1458 Gregory (Hryhorii) was elected as a rival southern metropolitan (of 'Kiev, Halych and all Rus') for the Grand Duchy of Lithuania and the Kingdom of Poland. Apart from a break between 1596 and 1620, the southern Rus Church now enjoyed a continuous existence until 1686. Moreover, whereas Greeks were prominent in the two Churches until the fifteenth century, both were now 'nationalised'. Nearly all heads of the Moscow Church were Russian and those of the southern Church Ruthenian. A further consequence was that the original 'eastern' influence on the culture of southern Rus began to fade. Whereas Moscow clung to the original Greek faith and reinvented itself as the 'third Rome', the Kievan territories came under the influence of the three great European cultural revolutions of the next two centuries: the Renaissance, Reformation and Counter-Reformation.

A Lithuanian Rus?

The southern Rus were themselves divided between Poland and Lithuania; although between 1362, when the Lithuanian armies' victory against the Golden Horde at the Battle of the Blue Waters led to their advance through Kiev to the south, and the Union of Lublin in 1569 the majority were under Lithuanian rule. In fact, for these two centuries it seemed more likely that Lithuania would be the main successor state to Rus, as Moscow was preoccupied with freeing itself from the 'Tatar yoke' and Poland controlled only the westernmost territories around Halych. Indeed, if Lithuania had not met a serious reverse at the Battle of Vorksla River (1399), it could have consolidated its hold long before Moscow made any serious claim to the region. In the three Moscow campaigns, of 1368, 1370 and 1372, Lithuania even briefly contemplated unifying the whole of the former Rus under its authority, until the advance of the Teutonic Knights in the west forced it to scale down its ambitions in the east.

Lithuania's designs on Rus were in many ways just as plausible as Moscow's. The proper title of Lithuania was in fact the Grand Duchy of Lithuania, Rus and Samogitia and its rulers styled themselves *Lethewindorum et Ruthenorum rex* ('King of the Lithuanians and Ruthenians'). Although ruled by the Catholic (before 1386, pagan) Gediminas dynasty, their Orthodox subjects were left largely undisturbed. In fact, the ruling elite 'went native'. The old Kievan principality was only abolished in 1471; the official language of law and administration was 'chancellery Ruthenian' (a mixed form of Belarusian-Ukrainian, closest to the dialects around Vilna) rather than Lithuanian; and the legal code, the Lithuanian Statutes of 1529, 1566 and 1588, which survived in adapted form in Ukraine west of the Dnieper until 1840, was a direct descendant of the *Ruska Pravda*. Some have even claimed that the Lithuanians and Rus were kith and kin, as the Lithuanians were descended from the 'Oriiany' – hence the supposed closeness of their language to Sanskrit.[15] The peculiar hybrid polity that was 'Lithuania and Rus' therefore served to bridge the gap between the end of the Galician-Volhynian kingdom in the 1340s and the Orthodox revival of the seventeenth century, ensuring that something of local Rus culture was preserved in between. A partially similar situation existed in the Romance state of Moldova, originally under strong Galician influence. Even after a separate metropolitan see was established at Suceava in 1401 and Ottoman rule was consolidated in 1512, Church Slavonic continued to be used until the eighteenth century.

At this point a lengthy digression is necessary on the relations between the peoples who later became the 'Belarusians' in the north and the 'Ukrainians' in the south. At the time, both were more properly collectively 'Ruthenians', the Orthodox subjects of the Lithuanian state – that part of the former nation of Rus under local rule. The two halves of this Ruthenian 'nation' shared the same chancellery language and were normally under the same church hierarchy in common rivalry to Moscow. Churchmen and nobles could move from Vilna to Novaharadok to Kiev without any great sense of crossing a cultural boundary. The cultural revolution of the sixteenth and seventeenth centuries actually began in 'Belarusian' Ruthenia, before moving south to 'Ukraine'. The programme of religious modernisation promoted by southern magnates such as Kostiantyn Ostrozkyi and Petro Mohyla was begun by the great Belarusian writer Francis Skaryna (1490–1552), who produced a Belarusian/Ruthenian translation of the Bible (the *Bibliia Ruska*) in 1517–19. The great contribution of the future Belarusian lands to southern Ruthenia was therefore to provide a haven for cultural regeneration in the extremely difficult years between 1453 and 1596.

According to some authors, it was only the events of 1648 and after that crystallised the differences between the embryonic 'Ukrainian' and 'Belarusian' nations. According to others, the historical-mythical innovations made by Kiev intellectuals in the 1620s and 1630s had already done the job (see pages 54–5). In neither case were earlier differences fundamental. Furthermore, elements of a common identity remained. As late as 1811, the Belarusian count Mikhal Kleafas Ahinski (1765–1833) proposed to Alexander I the restoration of the medieval Grand Duchy of Lithuania (with one of the Tsar's brothers as prince), along what were in essence the borders of old Ruthenia (Galicia excepted), stretching from Vilna in the north to Podillia, Ternopil and Kiev in the south. One possible author of the anonymous history that ignited the nineteenth-century Ukrainian national movement, *History of the Rus* (*Istoriia Rusov*), was the Belarusian archbishop Heorhii Konyskyi. From a southern perspective, the chronicler Samiilo Velychko's definition of the lands of the Cossack nation in the 1710s could still include Vitebsk, Vilna and Polatsk in the north (and Smolensk, now in Russia), as well as more obvious territories such as Kiev and Galicia.[16]

The possibility of the eventual emergence of a united Ruthenian nation is more than just a matter for abstract speculation, as a joint Belarusian-Ukrainian front would historically have had much more weight in relations with Russia and Poland. It may even have made it more difficult for Russia to view the two as simply 'Russian'. This missed historical opportunity is also a useful reminder that the potential Russian-Belarusian alignment 'against' Ukraine that many feared was emerging after the election of Belarusian president Aliaksandr Lukashenka in 1994 is only one of several possible models for relations between the three peoples.

Old Ruthenia was becoming more differentiated by the sixteenth century, however, and the influence of Lithuania was fading. The Union of Lublin in 1569 separated the south and north. What is now Belarus remained in loose union with Lithuania, while Kiev and Lviv were united under Polish rule. The political chain reaction created by the seventeenth-century Cossack revolts had no real counterpart in the north. Moreover, they created a social class in southern Ruthenia, the Cossack gentry, who had a vital interest in defending and promoting local rights and privileges, and indeed in creating the very idea of 'locality'. In northern Ruthenia no such class emerged. The long social decline after the golden age before the Union of Lublin left only a generalised nostalgia for Ruthenia, but no well-articulated sense of local distinction until very late in the nineteenth century, even, arguably, as late as 1905. In the crucial nineteenth century this meant that there was no real Belarusian movement as such that it was worth the Ukrainians allying with.

Options under Poland

The Tale of Bygone Years records a first meeting between Rus and Poles when Volodymyr led a campaign against the Liakhs (Poles) in 981. However, in practice Ukraine's long and ambiguous relationship with Poland began with the latter's occupation of Galician Rus (also known as 'Red Ruthenia') in the 1340s. It was an inauspicious start, as Polish rule snuffed out any chance of the Galician-Volhynian kingdom becoming the nucleus of a future Ukrainian state along the lines of Vladimir-Suzdal for the Russians. Conflict then continued intermittently until World War II. Relations with Muscovy/Russia, on the other hand, were initially at least geographically distant.

Poland became the main power in the region after the Union of Lublin transferred Volhynia and Kiev to the newly created Polish Commonwealth (Rzeczpospolita) in 1569. Like the other contender powers (Galicia, Lithuania and Moscow), Poland sought to present itself as the legitimate successor of Rus, but its claim was undoubtedly the weakest of the four. Poland could assert that western parts of Rus (Pidlachia, even perhaps Volhynia) had once been part of Mazovian Poland, but elsewhere links were tenuous. Poland was left to claim a 'right of conquest' dating back to Bolesław the Valiant's campaign against Kiev in 1018, or to rely on the vagaries of the 'Sarmatian myth' (see page 49). Few Ruthenians were likely to be taken in by this claim. Moreover, unlike virtually all other European states, the Polish Commonwealth had no ruling dynasty around which projects of cultural centralisation could be based. Instead it had elected kings, an anarchic form of democracy for the nobility and a somewhat *laissez-faire* attitude towards the non-gentry majority. With no incentive to identify with a nation defined socially as a noble democracy, the peasantry remained in their largely self-contained communities of faith.

On the other hand, Poland won control of southern Rus at the very moment when it was abandoning its liberal pre-Lublin traditions in favour of Jesuit-inspired policies of Catholicisation and Polonisation. After 1569, the comparative weight of Poland's new post-Renaissance and Counter-Reformation culture began to provide a new pole of attraction for

Ruthenian elites (Lithuania's culture having been Ruthenian-biased). The higher nobility were particularly vulnerable to Polonisation, given the opportunities for political participation and self-enrichment now opening up under the Polish Commonwealth (during a boom in the European grain market). A typical and notorious example was that of the Wiśniowiecki family, whose vast wealth and private armies were frequently mobilised against the Ruthenian Cossacks in the seventeenth century, but who were in origin from old Ruthenian stock, the Vyshnevetskyis.

In 1606, of the 29 Ruthenian members of the Commonwealth senate, only one was Orthodox, compared to seven Protestants and 21 Catholics.[17] In 1605 or 1606 one Ruthenian writer bemoaned

how Poles have settled in the Rus dominions, how they became friends with them [the Ruthenians], how they gave their daughters in marriage to Ruthenians, and how they implanted their refined norms and their learning through their daughters, so that the Ruthenians, in fraternising with them, began to imitate their language and their learning. Not having any learning of their own, they began to send their children to receive Roman instruction, and these children learned not only the instruction, but the [Latin] faith as well. And so, step by step, by their learning they enticed all the Rus lords into the Roman faith so that the descendants of the Rus princes were rebaptised from the Orthodox faith into the Roman one, and changed their family names and their Christian names as if they had never been descendants of their pious forebears. As a result, Greek Orthodoxy lost its fervour and was scorned and neglected, because people obtaining superior status in life, despising their own Orthodoxy, stopped seeking ecclesiastical offices, and installed mediocrities in these offices just to satisfy the needs of those who were of low birth.[18]

The Ukrainian historian Viacheslav Lypynskyi (1882–1931) argued that, without the later revolt of 1648, direct and indirect Polonisation might well have led to the eventual disappearance of the Ruthenian nation. Significantly, in 1569 the question of Ruthenian input into the newly created united Commonwealth was not even discussed. Not surprisingly, other Ukrainian historians have disputed the extent to which the nobility were Polonised, the middle and lower ranks in particular.[19] Some have argued that conversion was only half-way. This is normally expressed in the formulation *gente Ruthenus natione Polonus* ('of Ruthenian race and Polish nation'), but in fact this label covers several possible relationships between 'race' and nation. In the sixteenth and seventeenth centuries many Polish nobles believed fervently in the Sarmatian myth, the idea that the noble estate (not the population as a whole) was descended from the ancient Sarmatians (see pages 30–1). Many assimilating Ruthenian nobles bought into this myth wholesale and accepted that it created a common bond between them and their Polish counterparts. As one contemporary lament had it, 'Grieve O God for the unhappy hour when the Sarmatians' sons were fighting each other'.[20] Gradually, however, this myth came to be put to subtly different uses. According to one magnificently named belletrist from Peremyshl, Stanislav Orikhovskyi-Roksolan (1513–66): 'I am from the tribe of the Scythians, from the Rusyn nation; that is I am also myself a Sarmatian, because Rus, my fatherland, is to be found in European Sarmatia.'[21] This was a position that contained the seed of later ideas that would underpin Ruthenian separatism (see page 63).

The second option for the Ruthenians was compromise. Growing estrangement from Constantinople, the tradition of Kievan ecumenicism (or at least relative indifference to post-1054 divergence between Catholic and Orthodox) and the desire to preserve the traditional faith from the excesses of local Protestantism and Counter-Reformation Catholicism led many Ruthenians to seek the alternative protection of the Pope, resulting in the creation of the Uniate or Greek Catholic Church at the Union of Brest in 1596.[22] The Ruthenian bishops saw the Uniate compromise as the best deal obtainable and could in many ways present it as a reprise of the ecumenical aims of the Union of Florence and earlier contacts between the Rus and Rome. Yosafat Kuntsevych (c1580–1623), archbishop of Polatsk, even died for it. His murder by an enraged Orthodox mob (he was hacked to death with an axe) led to his beatification by the Vatican in 1642 and canonisation in 1867, making him the first Eastern-rite saint of the Catholic Church.[23]

The new Church was under the authority of the Pope, but initially only in matters of faith and morals. The Ruthenians retained a separate synodal administration until 1720. They also continued to use the adapted local version of Church Slavonic and the traditional rite, including the old Divine Liturgy of St John Chrysostom, with its reference to the faithful as the 'Orthodox'. Some have argued that Uniatism, as originally conceived, was a stable identity option in itself, indeed that it was a means of resisting the advance of Catholicism, Protestantism and other heresies; others that it was a halfway house to eventual Catholicisation and/or Polonisation.[24] Historians have also disputed how many Ruthenians accepted the Union in the early seventeenth century – it seems initially to have been more popular in the north-west, that is in the later Belarusian lands.[25] Certainly, the new Church divided Ruthenians amongst themselves. Six out of eight local Orthodox bishops originally supported the Union, but many, perhaps most, middle and lower clergy were bitterly opposed, despite the fact that between 1596 and 1620 the Poles supported it as the only legal Ruthenian Church. In fact, the struggle against the Union was a key factor promoting the Orthodox revival of the seventeenth century. It was only two centuries later, after Poland had disappeared from the map and the Habsburgs ruled in western Ukraine, that the new Church would come to be seen as a specifically Ukrainian institution.

It should be pointed out that many Ruthenians also adopted the new Protestant faith (more, again, in the 'Belarusian' north), particularly before the Counter-Reformation gathered pace in the Polish Commonwealth. Significantly, however, the great cultural achievement of the period, the 1581 Ostrih Bible produced by Ivan Fedorov (c1525–83), was written in Church Slavonic, rather than in the local vernacular favoured by most Protestant reformers.[26] The Ostrih Bible was therefore in many ways common property for all the eastern Slavs. The text drew heavily on the 1499 Bible sponsored by Archbishop Gennadii of Novgorod, albeit supplemented by many other sources, and, with small phonetic changes, formed the basis of subsequent editions in Moscow (1663) and St Petersburg (1751).[27] Resistance to vernacularisation was common enough in the Orthodox world, but this meant that the new text failed to establish sharp boundary-markers between Ukrainians and their neighbours in the manner of other great popular Bibles, such as the 1611 King James Bible (approved by England's Scottish King, which had a great homogenising influence on his two sets of subjects), the Welsh Bible of 1588, Luther's 1539 and 1545 German Bibles, the Catalan Bible of 1478 or even the (Counter-Reformation) Polish Leopolita Bible of 1561.[28]

The increasing influence of Polish Latin and Baroque culture on the Ruthenian Church moved it away from the Muscovite tradition, which sought to preserve Church Slavonic as the only suitable means of expressing an exclusively religious Truth, but didn't move it far enough. The development of a secular culture that valued language in itself was therefore hampered. Even the Kievan Mohyla Academy in the seventeenth and eighteenth centuries did not develop a Ukrainian literary language (see pages 54–5). Eastern Orthodoxy was not really a religion of the book. The Ukrainians had to wait until 1903 for a full vernacular translation of the Bible.

Options in the North

For those who sought to preserve Orthodoxy from Catholic and/or Uniate pressure there were two main options. One was defensive self-organisation (see pages 53–6). The other was to seek the patronage of Moscow, the course favoured by Iov Boretskyi, the first metropolitan of the restored Orthodox hierarchy in Kiev (served 1620–31), who appealed to the tsar for protection against Polish persecution in 1624. He was supported by polemical prelates such as Ivan Vyshenskyi (c1550–1620) and Zakhariia Kopystenskyi (d.1627), archimandrite of Pechersk, who attacked the 'Westernising' influence of the Union of

Brest and rejected the 'modernising' idea of secular education as inherently pagan. Kopystenskyi, who came from Galicia, was also notable for developing some of the elements of an early theory of east Slavic unity in works such as a *Book on the True Unity of Orthodox Christians* (1623) and, written in local Ruthenian, *Palinodiia, or a Book in Defence of the Eastern Church* (1621–2). The *Hustyn Chronicle*, written sometime in the 1620s, says of Kiev and Moscow that 'although the names of the lands are different, it is well known that all of [their people] are of the same blood and line, and even now all of them are called by the very same name, Rus',[29] although it treats their recent histories as separate. Feelings of religious and cultural solidarity with the north still existed, despite the latter-day Ukrainian nationalist argument that it was only Polish pressure that pushed the Ruthenians towards Moscow. As Ihor Ševčenko has argued, in the early seventeenth century 'a few nobles, the more prosperous townsfolk, some prelates, ordinary priests, and the Cossacks collectively became more intensively aware of their "otherness" *vis-à-vis* the Poles', but it was exactly this heightened sense of Orthodoxy that also risked driving them into the hands of Moscow.[30]

Moscow's attitude was still somewhat ambiguous, however. Since the reign of Ivan III (1462–1505), its rulers had claimed to be the sovereigns 'of all Rus'. This was also an invented tradition, albeit one that could trace its roots back to Bogoliubskii's appropriation of the symbolism of the icon of Vladimir/Vyshhorod, and to the first attempts by Simeon the Proud, grand prince of Moscow from 1341 to 1353, to assert control over the entire Church of Rus. The creation of the new myth was a function of several factors: Moscow's growing ambitions after the fall of Byzantium; the final casting off of 'the Tatar yoke' in 1480 (Ivan's military campaigns against Novgorod had already doubled the size of the state, making it a serious European player for the first time); and the growing ability of secular power to impose its historiographical needs on church chroniclers after the local appointment of metropolitans began in 1448. Ivan's claim was duly backed up by texts such as Metropolitan Spiridon's *The Tale of the Princes of Vladimir* (c1505), which depicted the grand princes of Muscovy as the main progeny of Volodymyr/Vladimir and sought to trace their descent from the Roman emperor Augustus. Later works such as the *Book of Degrees of the Imperial Genealogy* (*Stepennaia kniga*, 1560s) sought to promote the myth of Moscow as Constantinople's equal and natural successor – most famously formulated in Filofei of Pskov's notion of Moscow as the 'third Rome' (1511).[31] In a more poetic fashion, the *Tale of the White Cowl* (late fifteenth century) records how the holy shroud was originally given by the Emperor Constantine to the Roman pontiff to represent the purity of Christian belief, but the apostate Latins lost it to Byzantium, who in turn bequeathed it to Novgorod and then Moscow as the ultimate symbol of the Resurrection and the True Faith.

Some authors have skipped over these claims;[32] many Ukrainian historians have seen them as largely fictional retrospective inventions by Moscow's ambitious rulers;[33] others have argued that they were a natural extension of previous chronicles (usually literally, with discussions of more recent periods being added on to reproductions of *The Tale of Bygone Years* or other Kievan works).[34] Whatever the case, it is entirely possible that Moscow could have gained control of southern Rus during the long Lithuanian wars of the fifteenth and sixteenth centuries, before the Ruthenian 'cultural revolution' of the seventeenth century greatly increased the differences between the two peoples. Their 'union' or 'reunion' might then have taken place on contrasting terms. Alternatively, others – Lithuania, Poland, even the princely house of Chernihiv, once a serious contender – could have got there first, or the local southern Rus could have developed a serious national programme at an earlier date, or Moscow could have collapsed during the 'Time of Troubles' (1604–13).

As it was, by the 1600s the gap between Moscow and Kiev seems to have widened again. In particular, the Muscovites were extremely suspicious of the Ruthenians' religious innovations, even to the extent of banning all their books in 1627. Still, as David Frick has argued, when Ruthenians like Simiaon Polacki (the tsarevich's Belarusian tutor) and Epifanii Slavynetskyi (Nikon's 'authenticator') travelled north to Moscow, there 'was an encounter quite definitely across some sorts of borders that were cultural, confessional and political, in which, nonetheless, participants could at times and in an atmosphere of mutual distrust, pretend for a variety of reasons that no borders had been crossed, that "we are all Rus".'[35] These borders were pliable and negotiable. There was no manifest destiny drawing the southern Rus back towards Moscow, or existential incompatibility preventing them from being so drawn. Much depended on events.

The Ruthenian Revival

Given the ambivalent relations between the two types of Orthodox Rus, the final option for resisting Polish pressure was the revival of the local Church. On the back of this religious movement a powerful local Ruthenian option began to develop in the late sixteenth and early seventeenth centuries. So powerful, in fact, that by the 1620s and 1630s the Ruthenians were beginning to develop many of the key elements of a truly national ideology. Not, to be sure, the mobilising nationalism of the nineteenth and twentieth centuries, but nevertheless a potent historical and religious mythology that justified the claims of the local elite, much, indeed, like any other seventeenth century nationalism.[36]

At first, the Ruthenian programme was fairly limited. Its priority was defence against the Uniate advance and the restoration of the Orthodox Church, which was achieved *de facto* in 1620 and *de jure* in 1632. The Ruthenians were fortunate in that Poland was losing strength after the failure of its campaign to take advantage of Moscow's 'time of troubles'. As this perception grew, it began to seem possible that the Ruthenians could go further and 'turn the Commonwealth of two nations into a Commonwealth of three nations; instead of a Commonwealth of Poles and Lithuanians there would be a Commonwealth of Poles, Lithuanians and Rus.'[37] One Polish historian has argued, rather optimistically, that the Ruthenians could have achieved some kind of autonomy within a remodelled Commonwealth as early as 1632 or 1638,[38] along the lines of the abortive Hadiach treaty in 1658, which would have created a kind of tripartite Commonwealth (see page 65), but by then the Cossack revolt of 1648 had intervened and a third, very different strategy of outright independence emerged.

The key figure in the second stage of the process was Petro Mohyla (1597–1647), who served as Kievan metropolitan from 1632 until 1647 and founded the academy that bore his name as the major centre of learning in the eastern Orthodox world until it was forcibly converted into first a seminary and then a naval academy in 1817 (the academy was reopened with considerable fanfare in 1991 and is now the main independent university in Kiev). Significantly perhaps, Mohyla (Petru Movilă) was something of an outsider – Moldovan by origin, and the 'majority' of his school were Red Ruthenians from Galicia.[39] Mohyla organised a programme of religious modernisation designed to reverse the inroads that Protestantism and Counter-Reformation Catholicism had made into Ruthenian culture since 1500, largely by adopting their methods in self-defence. He therefore organised the standardisation and 'updating' of the liturgy, activated a passive and often corrupt clergy by imposing obligations of pastoral care and revolutionised the system of religious education, now based on the post-Reformation disciplines of grammar, poetics, rhetoric, arithmetic, geometry, astronomy and music (using as the approved text his own *Orthodox Confession of Faith*, 1640–3). He also promoted the use of Latin and Greek as a means of restoring traditional teaching. Although aiming at 'original orthodoxy', Mohyla therefore imported many Roman practices. His 1646 *Euchologion* ('Book of Ritual'), for example, contained several passages copied wholesale from the *Ritual* of Pope Paul V. Other innovations included the Reformation practice of lay involvement in church life, which was regarded as uncanonical by the Muscovites.

Mohyla's critics characterised his plans as 'Latinisation'. Their ranks included not only many Orthodox hierarchs and nobles, but also substantial numbers from the lower orders and the Cossacks, who reportedly 'intended to stuff the sturgeons of the Dnieper with the teachers of [Mohyla's] school'.[40] Mohyla's elite project of cultural reform was difficult for the masses to grasp. On the whole they preferred the more sim-plistic solution of allying with the neighbouring Orthodox power (Moscow). The Metropolitan's critics also suspected, unfairly, that he was plotting to perfect the 1596 Union with Rome, whereas in fact he sought broader ecumenical reconciliation between all the Christian faiths, as he formally proposed to a deaf papacy in 1644–5.[41]

Moyhla's programme offered the possibility of an expanded middle ground where Ruthenian culture might survive and flourish. He was greatly assisted by the first stirrings of a historical mythology promoting the idea of the Ruthenians' separate origin and descent, as local scholars began to lay the foundations of a distinct local patriotism – if only as a defensive reaction against Polish pressure. The key period here was the 1620s and 1630s, when texts such as Kasiian Sakovych's *Verses* (1622), on the death of the Cossack leader Petro Sahaidachnyi (see the cover illus-tration), even Iov Boretskyi's *Protestation* (1621), and later works such as Archimandrite Feodosii Sofonovych's *Chronicle* (1672–3), began to reconnect the Ruthenians to Kievan Rus, describing them as 'true Orthodox Christians', 'the remnants of the Rus of old', 'the warlike race … who with Volodymyr, the sainted king of Rus, conquered Greece, Macedonia and Illyria' (something of an exaggeration), whilst also pro-moting the idea of the Rus as a chosen people and Kiev as the 'new Jerusalem' (in contrast to the myth that Moscow was the 'third Rome'), a city blessed by God.[42]

This historiographical project was in its early stages, however. It helped to make it clearer that the Ruthenians were not Poles, but unfor-tunately it was too easily usurped by the Muscovites, as their newly invented tradition sought to anchor itself in the same historical begin-nings. In Ihor Ševčenko's words, later academics and churchmen 'used history to promote the notion of all-Russian oneness as much as their predecessors had used it to foster local patriotism'.[43] Local myth-making now had to compete with Moscow's alternative ideas of imag-ined community. Some of the new Muscovite mythology, moreover, originated in the south. The most widely copied Kievan text of the period, the 1674 *Sinopsis*, probably written by Innokentii Gizel (c1600–83), spoke explicitly of the common heritage of the Ruthenians and Muscovites, both members of a single 'Slaveno-Rusian' nation or *pravoslavnyi Rossiiskii narod* ('Orthodox all-Rus-ian nation', *Rossiia* being the Hellenic version of Rus now fashionable amongst Ruthenian intellectuals), the sons of first Japheth and then Volodymyr. The *Sinopsis* praised the 1654 Pereiaslav treaty between Kiev and Moscow (see page 64). Before there was disunion and decay, after its signing 'Kiev returned to its former condition and ancient imperial dignity' and what was previously divided was again made whole.[44] Although origi-nating in the south, the *Sinopsis* was therefore used as a main school text throughout the Russian empire until the nineteenth century. In fact, it was the *only* history of 'Russia' until the 1760s.

Critics have attacked Mohyla for forcing the pace of modernisation and maintaining or even deepening the splits in Ruthenian society. The nineteenth-century writer Mykhailo Drahamanov liked to refer to the period as Ukraine's 'interrupted Reformation'. Russians have continued to depict Mohyla as a Catholic stooge.[45] However, he undoubtedly did much to 'Europeanise' Ruthenia and inject new vigour into local Orthodoxy. Given time, the programme of 'Westernising' change could have been even more radical. Ruthenian Orthodoxy was certainly now very different from its Russian equivalent, which, in a word, was still much more orthodox. Lindsey Hughes records Moscow's Patriarch Joachim (served 1674–80) fulminating in his *Testament*: 'May our Sovereigns never allow any Orthodox Christians in their realm to entertain any close friendly relations with heretics and dissenters – with the Latins, Lutherans, Calvinists and godless Tatars (whom our Lord abominates and the Church of God damns for their God-abhorred guile); but let them be avoided as enemies of God and the defamers of the Church.'[46] Arguably, the great schism in the Russian Church in 1667 was provoked by the attempt to export the new practices to the north. Even the Russian mystic nationalist Lev Gumilev has argued that 'when speaking of the history of the Russian Church's schism, we can be sure that it was a conflict of the Great Russian [Muscovite] and Ukrainian Orthodox traditions.'[47]

Conclusions

In the late sixteenth century, the local Ruthenian elite in Poland lived at the interface of four languages and cultures: Polish, Church Slavonic, Ruthenian and Latin. Religion was the main badge of identity; less so language, as many individuals could easily use all four of the above. Even the most self-consciously Ruthenian of individuals, such as Sylvestr Kosiv, metropolitan of Kiev between 1647 and 1657, and Atanasii Kalnofoiskyi (dates unknown), often wrote in Polish. When Ruthenian was used it was often heavily Polonised.[48] 'Ruthenian' was in any case still an amalgam of Middle Ukrainian and Middle Belarusian. A 'conflict of identities' would be one way of describing the period, but it would be more exact to say that identities themselves were not fully formed; it was more a question of Ruthenians moving back and forth along a cultural continuum.

Sometimes particular individuals took opposing sides, sometimes they embodied the period's complexities themselves. A typical example of the latter was Meletii Smotrytskyi (1577–1633), the archbishop of Polatsk, who led the defence of the restored Orthodox hierarchy in 1620, defected to the Uniates in 1627–8, made a failed attempt to renegotiate the terms of the Union and ended his life proposing to Pope Urban VIII and the Polish king Sigismund III the forcible unification of all the Orthodox subjects of the Rzeczpospolita.[49] Another characteristic figure was Adam Kysil (1580–1653), a conservative Ruthenian noble who served as the Polish authorities' main negotiator with the rebel Cossacks after 1648, but whose attempts to preserve a noble-dominated Commonwealth of both Orthodox and Catholic hue served *de facto* to promote the Ruthenian cause.[50]

Nevertheless, from unpromising beginnings in 1569, when Ruthenian voices had been almost totally silent during the negotiations that led to the Union of Lublin, a Ruthenian society of growing strength and distinctiveness was beginning to emerge from the 1620s onwards. None of this was inevitable. The Uniates could have consolidated their strength to a greater degree. Even more radically, if the Counter-Reformation had not swept Poland, the local Protestant influence might have survived and prospered. Alternatively, if Poland had stayed stronger for longer, the Catholic influence may have grown. Poland, after all, had sought to conquer *all* of Rus in 1603–6. Jesuit schools survived in Kiev (Podil) until 1648. Alternatively, the Ruthenian revival could have been more free-ranging and all-encompassing. A more definitively Ruthenian Church might have emerged from a proposed Uniate–Kievan Orthodox (re)merger in 1629 – vetoed by the Cossacks. The revival that had begun, however, had yet to decide many aspects of its fundamental orientation and would be blown somewhat off course by the gathering storm that burst in 1648.

4

The Cossacks: Defenders of the Wild Field, Defenders of the Faith

The other major element in the turbulent identity politics of the late medieval east Slavic world was the Cossacks. To modern Ukrainian historians, they played the key role in the seventeenth-century 'Ukrainian revolution', which has been seen, like the Dutch revolt of the same period, as a national uprising that led to the creation of a 'Ukrainian Cossack state' in 1648.[1] The period was undoubtedly of crucial importance to the development of Ukrainian national identity. However, there are several myths here that need disentangling. First, how 'Ukrainian' was this revolution? The Cossacks were at least in part defined by their religion and their social status, rather than their ethnicity. The idea of a 'Ukrainian' identity was in any case still in the making. Second, how complete was this 'revolution'? Third, can its end-product plausibly be described as a 'state'?

Free Men, Wild Field

The Cossacks were (from the Turkic *qazaq*) 'free men', who took advantage of the 'wild field' (*dike pole*), the no-man's-land in the open steppe, to establish autonomous farming and raiding communities beyond the reach of the formal authority of the main regional powers – the Polish Commonwealth, Muscovy and the Crimean Tatars and Ottoman Turks. Most early Cossacks were originally fleeing serfdom or religious persecution, but eventually the free-booting lifestyle became an attraction in itself.

Cossacks came from both Muscovy and from Ruthenia. It was often hard to tell what separated the 'Russian' Cossacks from the north, centred on the river Don, and the 'Ukrainian' Cossacks from the south and west, centred 'beyond the rapids' (hence, in Ukrainian *Za-porozhian*) on the river Dnieper. At times, the two groups were in sharp conflict, fighting each other with particular ferocity between 1648 and 1654. At other times, Cossacks would move back and forth between the two 'camps'

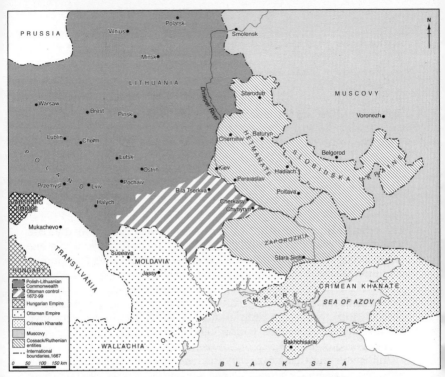

Map 2. The Seventeenth Century: Ruthenia, Poland, Muscovy, Zaporozhia

and join forces to fight against their normal mutual enemy, the Crimean Tatars and Ottoman Turks.[2] The Orthodox faith was after all what brought the Cossacks together in the first place, between the twin pressures of slave-trading Islam and Counter-Reformation Catholicism. On the other hand, it has also been argued that the Cossacks absorbed the residual influences of Iranian and Turkophone culture on the open steppe and were in many ways similar to their Islamic enemies in dress, vocabulary and methods of military organisation.[3] The very nature of Cossack life often meant that they would hire themselves out to all-comers.

Neither Cossack group was properly speaking an ethnic community. The 'Ukrainian' Zaporozhian Cossacks were defined by their Orthodoxy and their democratic/demotic political culture (the Cossacks elected their leaders, who were known by the title of Hetman), and welcomed recruits from far and wide. Moldovans, such as the celebrated Ioan Nicoară Potcoavă (Ivan Pidkova, died 1578), Poles, Jews, Greeks and even renegade Tatars were to be found in their ranks. There is a statue to Pidkova in Lviv (see plate 5), although it has been tampered with. Someone took exception to the wording on the plinth erected in

Soviet times that described his leadership of bands of 'Ukrainians, Russians and Moldovans'. The reference to the Russians has been painted over in white, but the rest of the list remains multi-ethnic.

Not many Cossacks came from Lviv, however. Basic facts of geography meant that, after the Unions of Lublin and Brest increased the pressures of serfdom and Catholicisation on the Ruthenians, it was easier to escape from the edges of the Polish Commonwealth (the palatinates of Kiev, Bratslav and Podillia) than from Galicia in the west or the Belarusian north. The Cossack 'nation' was therefore not the same as 'Ruthenia', either geographically or socially. Most Cossacks were men of humble origins (women did not play an active part in Cossack society). Cossack heroes were outlaws or warriors like Severyn Nalyvaiko (c1560–97), a craftsman's son who led a rebellion in 1594–6 that stretched from Bratslav to Belarus, only to be captured by the Poles and, like *Braveheart*'s William Wallace, tortured, quartered and beheaded in Warsaw.[4] Nalyvaiko's world was far-removed from that of the increasingly Polonised Ruthenian nobility. Landowners such as Jeremiasz Wiśniowiecki (1612–51) and Stanisław Koniecpolski (c1590–1646), with vast estates and private armies, were a law unto themselves. Wiśniowiecki, whose son became king of Poland in 1669, owned a staggering 38,000 households with 230,000 serfs in the Kiev palatinate; Koniecpolski owned 18,548 out of the 64,811 households in Bratslav.[5]

Ruthenian and Cossack society did overlap and interpenetrate, however. The Cossacks' anarchic democracy did not necessarily mesh well with the noble Ruthenian culture of the Commonwealth, but their willingness to fight for the hard-pressed Orthodox faith did. Their frequent rebellions slowed the progress of the Union of Brest after 1596, and by the 1620s the Cossacks were acting as the *de facto* defenders of the restored Orthodox hierarchy. The real consummation of the relationship, however, came with the biggest of all the Cossack revolts, in 1648.

The Khmelnytskyi Revolt

The 1648 uprising differed from its predecessors in several crucial respects. It was led by a disaffected noble, Bohdan Khmelnytskyi (1595–1657), and as it progressed it managed to attract many more to its cause. At the same time, and only in partial contradiction, the uprising's early successes snowballed rapidly by feeding off an upswing of socio-economic discontent and mass peasant action against landlords and Jews in the central Ruthenian regions. Third, the uprising came at a time of relative Polish weakness after the ravages of the Thirty Years War (the Polish king Władysław IV died in the middle of the fighting). Fourth, the Orthodox Church had stabilised its position under Mohyla (served 1632–47), and his successor Sylvestr Kosiv (1647–57) sought to

link the Cossacks and the Church together in a common ideological programme. In Kiev Kosiv hailed Khmelnytskyi as 'the new Moses', the 'gift
of God' (the literal Ukrainian meaning of 'Boh-dan'), the 'Prince of
Sarmatia', the deliverer of his people from foreign domination, and
encouraged him to pose as the defender of Orthodoxy.[6] Polish sources
record the conversion of Khmelnytskyi – 'formerly I was struggling to
rectify my own hurt and harm; now I shall liberate all the Ruthenian
nation from servitude to the Poles'[7] – although since his mythology and
political programme were largely fashioned for him by others (both then
and now), his aims are often unclear.

By 1649 Khmelnytskyi had taken control of most of the Kiev, Bratslav
and Chernihiv palatinates, despite Wiśniowiecki raising a private army
against him, and had installed himself in Kiev as Hetman. The liberated
territories were christened the 'Hetmanate'; Khmelnytskyi and his successors were now in charge of an embryonic administrative structure
rather than merely leading bands of peripatetic Cossacks. Significantly,
however, the Hetman's war aims were limited. Although it is common
in Ukrainian historiography to refer to 1648 as 'a war of national liberation', Khmelnytskyi's uprising was not a war of the whole Ruthenian
'nation', either geographically, socially, politically or ideologically.

Geographically, Ukrainian historians have argued that Khmelnytskyi
aimed to control all of Ruthenia, only to be frustrated by circumstance.
The nature of his ambitions in the west remains controversial, however;
in particular the question of why he failed to press his campaign in Galicia
when it seemed his for the taking in late 1648. Whatever his intentions,
the relative recovery of Polish power by the early 1650s meant that Red
Ruthenia could not be added to the Hetmanate, which, by the time of the
Treaty of Andrusovo in 1667, controlled little territory west of Kiev.
With regard to the north, it has been argued that Khmelnytskyi coveted
'Belarusian' Ruthenia and that the agreements signed near Prypiat in June
1657 to place Berestia/Brest and Turov under the Hetmanate amounted
to 'an announcement of the union of Belarus with Ukraine'.[8] Once again,
Khmelnytskyi was supposedly only frustrated by circumstance, this time
the presence of tsarist armies in the north and his own untimely death. In
the south, the Black Sea coast remained disputed territory.

Socially, the seventeenth-century Ruthenians were hardly a united
nation – although neither were the thirteenth-century Scots, even as portrayed by Mel Gibson. Huge differences existed between magnates,
lesser nobility, black (monks from whose ranks the hierarchy was
chosen) and white (parish) clergy, Cossacks and peasants. Even amongst
the Cossacks, social differences began to emerge over time – between
'registered' and 'unregistered' Cossacks, between various regional sub-
groupings and between aspirants to the nobility and the rank and file.
Nineteenth-century Ukrainians like the poet Taras Shevchenko mythologised 'two Cossack worlds': the 'real' Cossacks who continued to

struggle against Polish rule on the Right (Western) Bank of the Dnieper river and their would-be aristocratic brethren on the Left. Shifting allegiances were common. The generations of Soviet historians who depicted the rebellion solely as a peasant revolt had a point when they emphasised the vast social gulf between a noble like Wiśniowiecki and a Cossack like Nalyvaiko (significantly, it is Nalyvaiko, not Wiśniowiecki, who is the subject of popular novels in today's Ukraine).[9] The 1648 revolt was as much a 'Jacquerie' as it was a 'national uprising'.

Politically, there is the question of Cossack 'statehood'. Although modern Ukrainian historians like to refer to 'the Ukrainian Cossack state' supposedly established in 1648, many of their predecessors, such as Panteleimon Kulish, Volodymyr Antonoych and Viacheslav Lypynskyi, criticised the Cossacks precisely for having failed to achieve real statehood. There were actually three political entities after 1648: the Hetmanate, the Zaporozhian 'Sich' (the traditional Dnieper base of the Cossack army) and the new territories of 'Slobidska (Free) Ukraine'. None was a true state as such, with fixed boundaries, widespread international recognition and aspects of sovereignty such as a common currency, bureaucracy or legal system (though the development of the latter at least produced the 1743 Code of Law). They did provide a political space for the consolidation of a new identity, but the Cossacks had only a limited state-building elite. As Khmelnytskyi declined to establish a hereditary Hetmanate, his successors concentrated on fighting amongst themselves (the period after Khmelnytskyi's death in 1657 is known as 'the Ruin').

One way of examining these contrasting views of the Cossacks is to compare their representation in the work of two famous nineteenth-century artists (see plates 21 and 22). The first is Ilia Repin's (1844–1930) epic painting *Zaporozhian Cossacks Writing a Mocking Letter to the Turkish Sultan* (1891), an enormous canvas that took 12 years to complete. Repin's Cossacks are revelling in their disrespect for authority and clearly bow to no man. Inner repose and confidence shine from their faces, full of enjoyment of the vigours of the life of free men.[10] These are the Cossacks celebrated in nineteenth-century poetry (see pages 90–5), and criticised by Kulish for their destructive anarchism.

Second is Mykola Ivasiuk's (1865–1936) equally grandiose painting of *Khmelnytskyi's Entry into Kiev, 1649,* finished in 1912 (Repin's painting hangs in the Russian Museum, St Petersburg; Ivasiuk's in Kiev's State Museum of Ukrainian Art, where it covers an entire wall). In contrast to Repin's celebration of the Cossacks' sturdy individualism, Ivasiuk evokes the birth of a nation. His emphasis is much more on elites. Ordinary Cossacks can be seen on the left of the painting, but Khmelnytskyi himself takes centre-stage on a white charger, where he is being hailed by the leaders of the Kievan Church in front of St Sofiia's as the 'new Moses' (there are even echoes here of Palm Sunday) – Ivasiuk's intention being to stress that the religious and social movements of the time were animated by the same national spirit. Khmelnytskyi is depicted as the saviour of a nation reborn rather than the mere leader of a social revolt.[11]

Ivasiuk therefore concentrates on the historical mythology; Repin, normally thought of as an 'imperial' painter, on the idealisation of popular liberty, despite the richness of his ethnographic detail. Nevertheless, Ukrainian nationalists have sought to claim him as one of their own (he was born in Chuhuiv, near Kharkiv), making much of the presence of one furled blue and yellow flag in the right of this picture (other flags are red) and the blue and yellow hat worn by one of the Cossacks at the back of the main group – these being the colours of the national flag, banned in Repin's time (see page 86). Stalin, reportedly a big fan of the painting, obviously missed this supposed coded nationalism.[12] A second irony lies in the fact that Repin was in fact evoking the spirit of the 1877–8 Russo-Turkish war.

Roxolania

On the level of ideology and identity, in many ways the 1648 revolt produced a break with the traditions that were developing in the 1620s and 1630s, particularly after these were usurped by Moscow and its local supporters in the 1670s. Instead of the Christian myth of the Rus as the chosen people, the new Cossack elite tended to rely more on a version of the Sarmatian idea, which came increasingly to resemble the Polish nobility's justification of its own power,[13] and explained the Cossacks origins as a class, rather than as representatives of the nation. This was the myth that the Cossack elite was descended from the Roxolanian Sarmatians, just as the Polish nobility was descended from the Sarmatians' Alanian branch (see page 31). Increasingly, this served as an argument for normalising the Cossacks' status on a par with other elites rather than as a means of legitimising separatist aspirations. On the other hand, the Roxolanian myth helped the Cossacks to go beyond the somewhat vague notion of *Slavia Orthodoxa* by adding a geographical element to their identity. Given the common idea at that time that Europe ended at the Don (Ptolemy's border between *Sarmatia Europea* and *Sarmatia Asiatica*), the Cossacks could locate themselves in the space in between the Catholic world and the river that also marked the edge of the *antemurale Christianitatis*.[14] It was largely left to nineteenth-century Ukrainian historians to rediscover the idea of descent from Rus.

In terms of cultural affinity and geopolitics, Ukrainians continued to look both east and west. Mohyla's Europeanising mission was cut short, and internationally there were too many options for real consensus to be built. Khmelnytskyi tried alternate alliances with all of the Hetmanate's

Ill. 4. Cartoons of the Rukh movement: 'Two Sovereigns, 1654' (left) and 'Two Sovereignties, 1990'

neighbours, even including the traditional enemy, the Crimean Tatars. One of these was the Pereiaslav treaty agreed with the Russian tsar in 1654. Russian and Soviet historians have traditionally depicted the agreement at Pereiaslav as the logical end of a process of discarding other unrealistic alternatives and as an affirmation of east Slavic 'reunion' rather than as foreign policy realpolitik – ignoring the fact that only one part of 'Ukraine' was subject to the treaty. They have also tended to stress its final, definitive nature. Ukrainian historians, on the other hand, view it as simply one choice amongst many, a 'confeder- ational alliance directed against an external enemy',[15] and as a contract not an act of fealty.[16] That contract was then judged to have been vio- lated, as depicted in the 1990 cartoon reprinted above. The first picture shows 'Two Sovereigns, 1654', with Ukraine and Russia as equal part- ners; the second, 'Two Sovereignties, 1990', how the Ukrainians were reduced to penury by the tsars' progressive abolition of the Hetmanate's autonomy and the 'colonial' status that followed.

Clearly, there was something special about the treaty. The Cossacks inevitably regarded the potential protection of an Orthodox tsar in a completely different fashion from a tactical alliance with Transylvania or the Crimean Tatars. As Khmelnytskyi himself wrote to the tsar in May 1649: 'We petition Your Tsarist Majesty: Do not banish us from your favour; and we pray to God that Your Tsarist Majesty, as a faith- ful Orthodox sovereign, may rule over us as tsar and autocrat. In such a unification of all the Orthodox lies our hope under God that any enemy will utterly perish.'[17] On the other hand, the Pereiaslav treaty did not lead neatly and simply to the union of the Hetmanate with Russia. Other possibilities existed. Hetman Petro Doroshenko (ruled 1665–76) and Khmelnytskyi's son Yurii (1677–81) preferred an alliance with the Crimean Tatars and Ottoman Turks. Ivan Vyhovskyi (1657–9) turned back towards Poland and signed the Hadiach (in Polish Hadziacz) treaty in 1658 – one of the great 'What ifs?' of Ukrainian and East European history. If it had been successfully implemented, the Commonwealth would finally have become a loose confederation of Poles, Lithuanians and Ruthenians. The missing Ukrainian buffer state would have come into being as the Commonwealth's eastern pillar. Russian expansion might have been checked and Poland spared the agonies of the Partitions or, perhaps just as likely, it might have struggled on longer as the 'Sick Man of Europe'. Many historians, however, have argued that the Hadiach treaty was only a gentry project, involving the pursuit of privilege rather than a change in the Hetmanate's geopolitical orientation and that there was too much social opposition for it to succeed. Most of the Zaporozhian rank and file still looked to Moscow.[18] The treaty was never implemented.

Coda

As well as the Hadiach possibility, there was the rebellion of Ivan Mazepa, the Hetman (ruled 1687–1709) eulogised by Byron in the 1819 poem bearing his name:

> of all our band,
> Though firm of head and strong of hand,
> In skirmish, march, or forage, none
> Can less have said or more have done
> Than thee, Mazeppa! On the earth
> So fit a pair had never birth,
> Since Alexander's days till now,
> As thy Bucephalus and thou,
> All Scythia's fame to thine should yield
> For pricking on o'er flood and field.[19]

Mazepa also managed to inspire three operas, a tone poem by Liszt, a tribute by Victor Hugo, paintings by Géricault and Delacroix, and numerous novels.[20] Why? The romance of heroic failure was one reason, but so was the mythology of a great lost national leader. Mazepa was originally a favourite of Peter the Great. As such, he had an impressive record of church-building and cultural achievement in the Hetmanate (see page 68). Many Ukrainian historians have therefore seen him as a man of destiny manœuvring for the opportunity to inherit the mantle of Khmelnytskyi, and have interpreted his heroic failure against Peter at the Battle of Poltava in 1709 (when Mazepa catastrophically sided with

Charles XII of Sweden in the decisive act of the Great Northern War) as the last gasp of Cossack separatism. Mazepa, after all, had not been the first of Khmelnytskyi's successors to rebel. Ivan Vyhovskyi had defeated the Russians at the Battle of Konotop in 1659, but had failed to press home the advantage. Others have seen Mazepa as the quintessential opportunist, whose self-interested rebellion failed to win the support of the majority of Cossacks, only some 4,000 of whom were persuaded to fight on his side (five out of eight Cossack regiments remained loyal to the tsar).[21] Russia and complicitous locals subsequently created a dichotomous myth of treasonous 'Mazepists' and loyal 'Bohdanites' – in some ways the origin of the cult of Khmelnytskyi.[22] The actual battle was a disaster – 22,000 to 28,000 Swedes and Cossacks were defeated by 40,000 Muscovites and their loyal Cossacks. Mazepa died in exile three months later. The rebellion did nothing but damage to the Ukrainians' long-term interests, as the mistrust it engendered set in motion the events that led to the dissolution of Slobidska Ukraine in 1765, the Zaporozhian Sich in 1775 and finally the Hetmanate itself in 1785.

Mazepa's defeat at Poltava brought the Ruthenian-Cossack experiment in quasi-statehood to an end. It was no small irony therefore that the 1648 rebellion also began the process whereby Poland was to disappear from the map. In the territorial rearrangements resulting from the three Partitions of the Commonwealth (1772, 1793 and 1795), Romanov Russia took another stride westwards by occupying Volhynia and central Ukraine west of the river Dnieper (the Right Bank). On the other hand, Russia failed to obtain Galicia. Kiev and Lviv remained in different states, but the ruling power in the west was now the Habsburgs, who added Galicia and Bukovyna to their long-standing possession of Transcarpathia – although the Polish or Polonised nobility were to remain the dominant social force in most areas west of the Dnieper for another century and a half.

Cultural Europe

The beginnings of a distinct 'Ukrainian' society in the sixteenth and seventeenth centuries can also be observed in terms of accelerating patterns of cultural change. As in earlier periods, this mainly manifested itself in the religious sphere, although part of the effect of Renaissance and Reformation influences was to lay the foundations of a new secular tradition in arts and literature. Political boundaries (and shorter distances) meant that Ruthenia was much more affected by these changes than Muscovy, as did the fact that the towns and monasteries of western Ruthenia, as a peripheral part of the European city-space, were able to serve as incubators of cultural diffusion. Muscovite artists remained under the strict authority of the Church, while Ruthenian masters were employed under the much-looser regime of the urban stauropygial Brotherhoods, formed to protect the Orthodox faith and seeking the direct authority of Constantinople ('stauropygial', from the Greek, means 'bishop-approved').

A typical example of the changing nature of Ruthenian culture can be seen in the preeminent local art of icon-painting. By the sixteenth century the adapted Byzantine style, with its aestheticism and its highly formalised concentration on the divine image, was ceding ground in Ruthenia, at least in western regions such as Lviv and Peremyshl,[23] where Renaissance influences were increasingly predominant in the work of local masters such as Fedir Senkovych (died 1631) and Mykola Petrakhnovych (died c1666). Icons from Galicia and neighbouring areas were also notable for the use of local folk influences, one very early example of which is the fourteenth-century *Volhynia Mother of God*, whose sad countenance is supposedly a reflection of the misfortunes that befell Rus after the Mongol invasion in 1240. In Ruthenia greater realism and a willingness to embrace all of God's creation led to bolder lines, a more rounded portrayal of figures and the use of colourful local landscapes as background, rather than the previously invariable stylised rocks or church outlines. Colour contrast became less sharp, and oil paints were introduced alongside tempera. As Dmytro Stepovyk records, 'icons with a rural background appeared, with planned distant or linear perspective', depicting 'mountains, buildings, trees, shrubs, grass ... like rough sketches, on decorative wood'. Figures became less formal, with a 'white skin colour, smaller cut eyes, moderate lips, and ruddy cheeks ... becoming the norm.' In effect, because painting now drew on local landscapes, architecture and costume, it became increasingly 'Ukrainianised'.[24]

Ruthenia (both Ukraine and Belarus) and Serbia were supposedly the only parts of the Orthodox world that were then receptive to such influences. Belarusian art historians make similar claims that local icon-painting 'merged Orthodox iconography with the novel technical and stylistic methods of European Renaissance painting', such as depth of perspective, light and shadow, greater naturalism and the use of fretted ornamentation in backgrounds, in the Italian style.[25] Good examples would be the sixteenth-century *St Paraskeva* and *Christ Pantocrator*. Russian art on the other hand, like Russian society, was supposedly conservative and static. This point of view rather ignores the stylistic innovations of Muscovite masters such as Dionysii (c1440–1503) and Andrei Rublev (c1370–1430), whose icon of the Holy Trinity exemplified his softer and more simplified style and has been called 'a Greek hymn upon a Slavonic tongue'.[26] Nevertheless, Moscow remained closer to the Byzantine tradition, rejecting the new use of perspective in the Western style and the preference for oil over tempera. In sharp contrast to the stauropygial liberalism further south, the *Stoglavov* ('One Hundred Headings') council in 1551 set strict limits on artistic freedom of expression. One modern author has argued that as late as the seventeenth century the work of the great Simon Ushakov (1626–86), although notable for adopting some naturalistic post-Renaissance traits, was marked by 'the utter absence of any traces of the Baroque'.[27] Self-isolation was, after all, the central principle of Muscovite cultural policy.

In the fifteenth and sixteenth centuries, therefore, the new Ruthenian school centred in Galicia began to produce an increasingly secularised form of art that was still largely foreign to Moscow. Typical of the era were *The Transfiguration of Christ* from the Lviv region, dated to the 1580s, *Christ's Passion* from the village of Velyke and the *Annunciation* from near Peremyshl. In the seventeenth century the revival of icon-painting spread to Kiev, Chernihiv and other centres of the Hetmanate and came under the further influence of the Baroque style and its luxurious celebration of earthly glory. The new Cossack elite provided an expanding market of artistic patrons, whose tastes inclined towards realism and the display of worldly wealth.[28] Famous examples of this new Kiev school include the *Holy Protectress* (where Khmelnytskyi can be seen in the right foreground – see plate 24) and the *Zaporozhian Protectress* – both from the late seventeenth century. Particularly stunning are the iconostases of Pechersk, Kiev – especially in the church of the Trinity Gate (1734) and the Rococo extravaganza in the church of the Exaltation of the Cross (1769). The reconstructed Cathedral of the Assumption was to include copies of its original interior after external work was finished in 2000.

The new Ruthenian or Cossack Baroque style probably made its most decisive mark in architecture (see plates 6 and 7, 41 and 43), although the decorative flamboyance typical of Western European Baroque was somewhat more subdued in Ukraine, where the local style was simpler in form, more reserved in ornamentation and softened by traditional naturalistic images.[29] Nevertheless, the sheer quantity of church-building, in particular under Mazepa's Hetmanate, is evidence of the importance of the new cultural project. Good examples of the genre are St Catherine's in Chernihiv (1715) and, in the Pechersk complex, the 1730s entrance of the remodelled Trinity Gate, the bell tower, on which Mazepa lavished 74,000 gold ducats (finished 1745), and All Saints' (1698). St Sofiia's received a remodelled Baroque exterior between 1690 and 1707, when the glorious azure bell tower and distinctive gilded cupolas were added to give the church its present appearance Also substantially reworked were the nearby twelfth-century monastery of St Michael of the Golden Domes, which was painstakingly rebuilt in 1998 as it was when demolished by the Communists in 1935–6, and the cathedral of the Assumption in Pechersk

The grandest new church of the period was St Nicholas's, built thanks to Mazepa's patronage in 1690–3, which had a seven-tier iconostasis that was almost 50 feet high and 90 feet across and originally bore Mazepa's coat of arms on the façade. Tragically it too was demolished by the Communists in 1934 (the murky image in plate 7 is a computer reconstruction). In Lviv there is St Yurii's (1738–58), by the Galician-

Italian architect Bernard Merettini, notable for its stepped style, ornate sculpture and spectacular golden interior, which is now the headquarters of the Greek Catholic Church. Also in the Baroque style are the exuberant St Andrew's church above the river Dnieper (1747–53) in Kiev and the chocolate-box Mariinskyi Palace (1752–5), now the official residence of the president of Ukraine. Both were designed by the Italian Bartolomeo Rastrelli, but there is little that is specifically Ukrainian about them. Rastrelli was working for all-Russian masters, as with his famous contributions to the Winter Palace in St Petersburg and the Catherine Palace in Tsarskoe Selo.

Russia, on the other hand, had originally rejected the Baroque style as decadent and a means of covert Catholicisation. Its belated adoption in the eighteenth century was closely associated with the state-directed 'Westernisation' programme. It is striking, therefore, that at the crucial moment of contact in the seventeenth century, Ruthenian and Muscovite culture were both distinct and diverging. According to some, it was Ruthenia, not Muscovy, that had changed. In the words of the Ukrainian historian Petro Tolochko: 'Ukraine drifted away from the traditions of Rus after 1240 because of the Polish influence on Ukrainian culture in architecture, icon-painting and in language. Even the word "Hetman" comes from the Polish. It was the second position in the Polish elite after the king. The melody of the language of Rus is closer to the Russian of today than it is to Ukrainian.'[30] The theory that Ukrainian culture and language is nothing but Polonised Russian is still widespread amongst Ukrainians of a certain age and/or politics as well as amongst Russians.[31] According to one seventeenth-century source: 'notwithstanding that they received their monastic rule from the holy mountain, the people of Kiev, owing to the neighbourhood of the Poles, have changed their humility into haughtiness in dress as well as in behaviour and habits, in the manner of the Latins.'[32] According to others, it was the Muscovite culture in development since the time of Andrei Bogoliubskii that departed from the original traditions of Rus, and it was Ruthenia-Ukraine that remained closer to the latter's more ecumenical and 'European' traditions.[33] The 'Europeanisation' of the sixteenth and seventeenth centuries took root because it built on that which had come before. The debate has obvious contemporary relevance, as the period is central to Ukraine's claim to be 'returning' to Europe after a long enforced absence, whereas many Russians still cling to the myth that Ruthenianism was but an artificial and temporary aberration.

Conclusions

In the end, the striking thing about the seventeenth-century Ukrainian 'revolution' is its incompleteness. Some ambiguities were resolved by the

1648 revolt, but others remained. The Cossacks' quasi-military society and the academic church culture of Kiev overlapped and interpenetrated but never completely fused. There were too many rival pressures on the Ukrainians in the seventeenth century for any single orientation to win out. The separatist option never became hegemonic. Geography meant that Ukraine was profoundly affected by the great European upheavals of the Renaissance, Reformation and Counter-Reformation, but also, after Pereiaslav, that the eighteenth-century Englightenment had much less impact. However, the new Ukraine was already sufficiently different from Russia to ensure that Romanov rule did not produce total assimilation. Nevertheless, the period also demonstrated that identity markers in the west, against Catholic Poland, remained sharper than those in the east, against Orthodox Russia.

This is not to say that the seventeenth century did not make an enormous difference. It created the foundations of the modern Ukrainian identity. Before 1648, the Ruthenians were really the southern Rus, sharing much in common with the Belarusians, even the Litwino-Polacy or 'Lithuanian-Poles'; after 1648 the partial marriage of Mohyla's new Orthodoxy with the new Cossack culture created a more distinctly 'Ukrainian' society. The Uniate Church was effectively eradicated east of Kiev and a distinct local Orthodoxy emerged. The Ukrainians even had a new name: Cossacks, or Little Russians (*malorosy* – 'Russian' in the sense of the 'all-Rus-ian' state, *Rossiia*). Although the latter epithet was used in the nineteenth century to relegate Ukrainians to the position of the Russians' 'younger brothers', Ukrainian historians would argue that it amounted to a rediscovery of the idea that Kiev was the original centre of Rus. 'Little Russia' and 'Great Russia' stand in the same relation of core to periphery as *Grecia Minor* to *Grecia Major*. The term 'Ukraine' also became increasingly current in this period, at first in reference to the Kiev palatinate and then to the newly consolidated territories around the Hetmanate. Popular use of the term diminished with the political decline of the Hetmanate in the eighteenth century, but it would be revived and refashioned (to refer to all 'ethnographic' Ukraine) in the nineteenth century.

Finally, the mere fact of the establishment of a Cossack polity in 1648 was also important for moving the mythopoeia of 'liberty' to centre-stage in Ruthenian society. The Don Cossacks were a more marginal element in Russia, and in any case their ideology was built around the idea of service to the tsar. The Cossacks who were unleashed on Jews and subversives with whips and swords in the Romanovs' later years were hardly guardians of liberty. The Ukrainian Cossack identity, however, added something more. It might even be possible to argue, although I would not push the point here, that modern Ukrainian identity was actually founded on an idea – Cossack liberty as opposed to tsarist autocracy – rather than on ethnicity or religion alone.

There are three periods when it is possible to speak of the emergence of a Ukrainian 'nation'. As argued in chapter one, the era of Kievan Rus is problematic because so much of its heritage is shared with Russians and Belarusians. Chapter two, on the other hand, argued that there are too many lacunae and simple eccentricities in the mythology of the period before the Baptism of Rus in 988. The seventeenth-century is when a distinct local culture really emerged. Preserving it was to be another thing entirely.

5

Ukraine, Russia and Rossiia

Between 1654 and 1795 what are now Ukrainian lands were progressively absorbed into the newly dominant dynastic empires of Eastern Europe. In the climate of the time, this was not abnormal. The imperial principle held sway over the national; multinational empire was the standard form of statehood east of the Rhine. The Poles were similarly divided, as, at various times, were the Serbs and Romanians. For our purposes, it is important to understand that empire was a viable project in the eighteenth and nineteenth centuries, and that it was perfectly natural for subject populations to identify with its basic principles. Empires, like nation-states, can also be successful 'imagined communities', particularly in eras when 'empire' is perceived more in terms of international might and cultural prestige than the potential repression of subject nations. Indeed, historians who perhaps overconcentrate on the available evidence of texts produced by intellectuals, may well neglect the thousands of ordinary folk who identified with empire out of basically pecuniary or status motives. Many Ukrainians accommodated themselves quite happily to the new arrangements, helped by the fact that Ukrainians and Russians were culturally close, if not necessarily convergent.

On the other hand, the nineteenth and twentieth centuries were also the era of national 'awakenings' at the sub-state level, (Finns, Czechs, Romanians, Serbs), as well as of attempts by existing empires or nation-states to embed themselves more securely in new networks of cultural loyalties. Once European multinational states began to acquire the resources and the ambition to attempt to 'nationalise' their populations, this was likely to produce both assimilation and defensive counter-mobilisation. It was natural that Ukrainians would take part in one or more of these projects, either their own or someone else's. In order for it to be their own, however, a successful division of labour had to be established – the Habsburg Ukrainians had to distinguish themselves from, mainly, the Poles, and the Romanov Ukrainians had to distinguish themselves (which, on the whole, they did with less success) from the

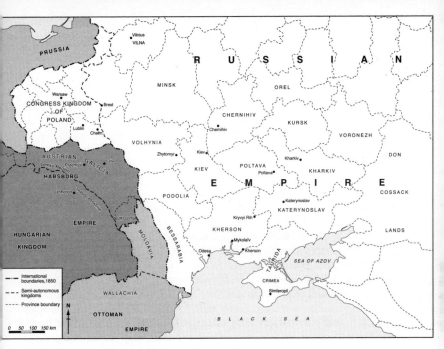

Map 3. *Ukraine in the Nineteenth Century*

Russians. Other options had to be closed off, and the two halves of the Ukrainian 'people' had to be persuaded they were a whole.[1] The observer should therefore always be aware of the dangers of writing history as 'parallelism': the teleological fallacy contained in the assumption that the histories of the Romanov 'Little Russians' and the Habsburg 'Ruthenians' were necessarily proceeding along separate but coordinated paths towards the same destination.

Ukrainians and Scots

Can any analogies be drawn between the Ukrainians and other peoples in similar multi-ethnic states? One potential comparison is with the Scots, not least because the 1707 Act of Union between Scotland and England was signed a mere two years before Mazepa's defeat at the Battle of Poltava ended lingering hopes of Ukrainian statehood.[2] At first glance, however, there appear to be more differences than similarities. Neither 'Ukraine' nor 'Russia' was yet fully formed as a nation; Scotland and England largely were. Scottish and English history had often over-lapped, but there was no Ukrainian equivalent of the 1320 Declaration of Arbroath to provide a clear, if somewhat programmatic, statement of separate identity. Institutional differences had existed for centuries. It was after all a Scottish king who ascended the English throne in 1603, not the other way around. England and Scotland, already nations, had to create a third overarching identity (Britishness); Ukraine and Russia, both essentially pre-national, had the possibility of merging or blurring their own indistinct identities.

The Act of Union was a voluntary decision of two parliaments, albeit ones with only limited franchises. Key Scottish institutions were preserved in a manner that allowed Scottish identity to remain intact at the sub-state level. After 1707 the Scots retained a national Church and separate legal and educational systems, preserving a local middle class in the three institutions most vital to nurturing a sense of national identity. The British army had Scottish regiments and a Scottish Office was established in 1885. In Wales, by contrast, which was institutionally and administratively integrated with England in 1536, nationalism has tended to be a more narrowly cultural phenomenon, concentrated in Welsh-speaking areas of the north and west.

The Ukrainian experience was very different. Britain was a democracy of sorts, Russia was not. Although Cossack leaders and historians argued that the Pereiaslav treaty bound Tsar Aleksei Mikhailovich and his successors to respect their privileges, this was never accepted by Russia's autocratic rulers. Consequently, whereas Scotland kept separate institutions and elites, all the structures of the Hetmanate were progressively abolished in the eighteenth century, and the vestiges of Ruthenian law disappeared in the nineteenth. Ukrainian elites were therefore extremely vulnerable to assimilation at the very moment when the Scots were making their greatest contribution to the British imperial synthesis. Russia's adoption of a distinctly anti-Ukrainian policy in the later nineteenth century, moreover, was made all the easier by the fact that the state was still an autocracy.

A further key point relates to the idea of synthesis, in particular the cultural consequences of union. Relations between Scotland and England remained distant, even difficult, up to and obviously during the Jacobite rebellion in 1746. Thereafter, however, the two nations did begin to develop a genuine overarching 'British' identity of sorts, based on a common religion, shared hostility to the French and the expanding opportunities of trade and empire.[3] Here, parallels with the early Ukrainian experience are stronger. Elements of Ukrainian culture were used to create a new imperial identity in eighteenth-century Romanov Russia.[4] First and foremost, the Ukrainian influence on the post-Nikon Church was immense. In the first half of the eighteenth century, a massive 70% of the upper levels of the Church hierarchy were from Ukraine or Belarus, men such as Stefan Yavorskyi (1658–1722), first president of the Holy Synod, and scholar-churchmen like Simeon Polotskyi (1629–80) and Teofan Prokopovych (1681–1736).[5] Ukrainians could be found on both sides of the great debate that animated the Church after the 1667 schism. Yavorskyi was a leading conservative, Prokopovych was one of the main ideologues of both Petrine absolutism and religious 'enlightenment'. Significantly, when Peter visited Kiev in 1706, Prokopovych welcomed him as the saviour of the 'new Jerusalem' – just as Kosiv had greeted Khmelnytskyi in 1648.[6]

Ukrainians like the writer Hryhorii Poletyka (1725–84) also made a disproportionate contribution to the initial phases of the empire's language-building project in the second half of the eighteenth century. Russian grammarians and lexicographers such as Trediakovskii and Lomonosov were in any case building on the earlier work of seventeenth-century Ruthenians such as Meletii Smotrytskyi and Lavrentii Zyzanii (?1550s–1634), author of the Orthodox catechism. Ukrainian nationalists have, perhaps predictably, exaggerated this point, claiming rather less plausibly that contemporary Russian is descended from Old Ukrainian.[7]

In other fields, Ukrainian musicians such as Dmytro Bortnianskyi (1751–1825), dubbed the 'Russian (sic) Mozart', and Maksym Berezovskyi (1745–77) who studied with Mozart, began the gradual introduction of the European idea of music as art (both had spent their formative years in Italy) to a country that had previously only known the highly stylised plain chant (monody) of the Russian Orthodox service. Significantly perhaps, the newer, more polyphonic style, particularly, the concerto in 'parts' (*partesnyi*) – alternating choral groups with up to 48 voices – failed to spread much beyond the level of the royal court and noble salons before nineteenth-century composers such as Glinka and Musorgskii tried to restore ethnic Russian nativist traditions.[8] It was rejected by Stravinskii in 1926/7. In art, icon and portrait painters such as Dmytro Levytskyi (1735–1822) and Volodymyr Borovykovskyi (1757–1825) encouraged the export of the more naturalistic Ukrainian style to the north (portraiture being itself a tradition that arrived via Ukraine). Ukrainian writers were instrumental in encouraging the growing popularity of secular literature; theatres were established by patrons such as Yavorskyi, where historical pieces like Prokopovych's eulogy *Vladymyr* (1705) were to be found alongside more traditional morality plays.

There was, in other words, the possibility of developing an *Überkultur* ('elite culture'), to which both Russians and Ukrainians had contributed, and which might have been more properly labelled *Rossiiskaia* (after the name of the state – hence the Ukranians' alternative name of, literally, 'Little, [state] Russians') than *russkaia* (after the Russian people), just as British, Ottoman or Hindi identities were also to an extent synthetic. In Russia a genuinely 'national' identity was in any case only in the very beginnings of development in the eighteenth century, in the sense of 'society' gradually conceiving of itself as autonomous from the patrimonial service state.

Significantly, many of the organisers of the 1825 Decembrist uprising were attracted to Ukrainian Cossack ideas of liberty that might have made it more easy for them to build a 'nation' more distinct from the state, in particular the poet Kondratii Ryleev (1795–1826), one of the initial leaders of the revolt. Ryleev's poems *Voinarovskii* (1823–5) on Mazepa's martyred nephew and the unfinished *Nalivaiko* (1824–5) sought inspirational parallels for the nineteenth-century struggle of the 'people' against the 'autocracy' in the two Ukrainian folk heroes (Ryleev's Dedication to *Voinarovskii* famously declared 'I am not a poet, I am a citizen').[9] Nalyvaiko was one thing, but siding with Peter the Great's would-be nemesis Mazepa was another. Ryleev provoked Pushkin to write his version of events in the epic *Poltava* (1829), which depicted Mazepa as a scheming and deceitful traitor – the view held by most Russians to this day (for centuries Mazepa was the subject of an annual Easter Anethema in the Russian Orthodox Church).

Nikolai Trubetskoi (1890–1938), one of the founders of the 'Eurasian' school of the 1920s, even argued that the new synthesis was overly Ukraine-biased and portrayed Patriarch Nikon and Peter the Great's 'modernising' project as nothing less than the forcible 'Ukrainianisation' of the old traditional 'Great Russian, Muscovite culture'.[10] However, Trubetskoi also recognised that this was a state-directed project imposed to serve the interests of St Petersburg. Ukraine's window on Europe was used by Nikon and Peter to kick-start the 'modernisation' process, but the direct import of French and Italian models soon took over. There was no long-term Russian-Ukrainian synthesis or fundamental cultural *rapprochement*. Indeed, it follows from Trubetskoi's argument that the distinctive Ukrainian culture of the seventeenth century was largely destroyed by its absorption into the Russian one. Because their identity relied strongly on the distinct local brand of Orthodoxy, the Ukrainians were less able to influence the increasingly predominant imperial secular culture after the Kievan Church was absorbed into the Muscovite Church in 1685–6 and Peter subordinated Church to state by abolishing the patriarchate in 1721 (he also banned the printing of Ukrainian ecclesiastical works in 1720). The very fact of the original influence from Kiev to Moscow and St Petersburg left Ukrainians more vulnerable to subsequent 'Russification'. By the first half of the nineteenth century, Ukraine had been more or less sucked dry, leaving it a cultural backwater.

This effect was compounded by a conscious state strategy to integrate Ukrainian elites. Until the late nineteenth century the Romanov autocracy governed through a multi-ethnic service bureaucracy in which Ukrainians were able to rise to the very top, albeit on all-Russian terms. Romanov Russia remained an essentially dynastic empire, in which political loyalty counted for more than (most types of) ethnic origin. The particularly oleaginous Count Kankrin (who was of German descent), minister of finance from 1823 to 1844, fulsomely declared:

if we consider the matter thoroughly, then, in justice, we must be called not *Russians*, but *Petrovians* [after Peter the Great] ... Everything: glory, power, prosperity and enlightenment, we owe to the Romanov family; and, out of gratitude, we should change our general tribal name of *Slavs* to the name of the creator of the empire and its well-being. Russia should be called *Petrovia*, and we *Petrovians*; or the empire should be named *Romanovia*, and we-*Romanovites* [other suggestions included *Nikolaevia*, after Tsar Nicholas I].[11]

The imperial elite were a caste, but there were always Ukrainians, Baltic Germans, Georgians and Tatars in the caste. Ukrainians at St Petersburg, such as Oleksandr Bezborodko (1747–99), imperial chancellor and one of the architects of Catherine the Great's 'southern strategy', or Petro Zavadovskyi (1738–1812), Russia's first minister of education, preserved a certain regional patriotism and a desire to promote Ukrainian interests where possible, or more exactly the interests of the new Ukrainian nobility. Bezborodko helped finally to secure the Black Sea coast from the Tatars and Ottomans, a long-standing aim of both Ukrainians and Russians; Zavadovskyi to found the university at Kharkiv in 1805. However, such men (hardly ever women) lacked institutional channels for their efforts. The bulk of their lives was spent in imperial administration and they grew used to thinking in all-Russian terms. As David Saunders has remarked, 'Ukrainian ministers ... did not manage significantly to alter the balance or change the pace of imperial policies.'[12]

Other Ukrainians, such as Viktor Kochubei (1768–1834), who ended his imperial service with seven years under the arch-conservative Nicholas I as chairman of the State Council and Committee of Ministers, assimilated almost completely, to the extent of becoming *plus royaliste que le roi*. Kochubei spent as little time as possible on his Ukrainian estates and claimed to be 'more Russian than any in my principles, my circumstances and my manners', even declaring that he dreaded the prospect of ending his life 'vegetating in Ukraine'.[13]

Some Ukrainian magnates, such as the semi-secret Novhorod–Siverskyi circle, campaigned in the 1780s and 1790s for a restoration of the Hetmanate's autonomy. The writer Vasyl Kapnist made a mysterious trip to Berlin in 1791 to plead unsuccessfully for Prussian support for the Ukrainian cause. But on the whole there was much less scope for ambiguous identities or dual loyalties for Ukrainians in Russian imperial service than there was in Victorian Scotland or, indeed, in seventeenth-century Kiev. This is not to say that all Ukrainians were completely assimilated. Ukrainian identity could still be nurtured at the margins of public life and in the private sphere. Myth has it that Bezborodko was the secret author of the *History of the Rus* (*Istoriia Rusov*), a popular proto-nationalist tract that circulated in manuscript in the early nineteenth century. But as an empire Russia was more centralised and more autocratic than most.

Economic interests also favoured the integration of the Ukrainian elite, especially after Catherine II's 1785 Charter of the Nobility granted, or offered the possibility of granting, noble status to Cossack officers. Two years previously, serfdom had been universalised in Russia's Ukrainian lands and the newly created Noble Bank was available to disburse cheap loans. St Petersburg was soon full of the kind of careerist Ukrainians satirised by Gogol in his *St Petersburg Tales* of the 1830s, as the Ukrainian Cossack elite came increasingly to resemble its former Polish counterpart. Odd vestiges remained (the Poltava noblewoman Yelysaveta Myloradovych [1832–90], although of Serbian origin, was one of the biggest sponsors of Ukrainophile causes, including donating 20,000 Austrian crowns to the Shevchenko Society in Lviv), but in the main by the mid-nineteenth century all that was left of a potential multilayered nation was a Russified nobility and an impoverished peasant mass. 'Ukrainian' meant the countryside, with a residual folk tradition, but no high culture; the cities were dominated by Russians, Jews and Poles. Therefore, to many nineteenth-century Ukrainian historians (especially Volodymyr Antonovych) the Cossacks had betrayed their birthright.

Building the Russian Nation

In the early nineteenth century, the Ukrainians seemed fully integrated. There was no specifically Ukrainian programme in, or in response to, the Decembrist revolt in 1825 (the plotters' 'Southern Society', despite its name, having a strongly anti-federal platform). The Ukrainians did not join with the Poles in their 1830–1 rebellion. In fact, they took much pleasure from the Poles' defeat. It seemed possible that the Ukrainians would become as integrated as the Bavarians in Germany or Provençals in France. However, the very gradation of identities that had helped encourage Ukrainians into varying degrees of accommodation with empire was also potentially the means of undoing this adaptation. The nineteenth-century Russian 'nation-building' project also had many weaknesses that prevented the Ukrainians from becoming as fully integrated or assimilated as they might otherwise have been.[14]

Only under the last two tsars, Alexander III (ruled 1881–94) and Nicholas II (1894–1917), was there a serious attempt to Russify the Romanovs' subjects.[15] The first flaw in the Russian nation-building project was therefore that it began so late. Nascent peripheral nationalisms were bound to react defensively to any new Russian nationalism emanating from the centre. Indeed, some nationalisms were already fully formed. The Poles in particular proved indigestible and disruptive,

arguably at the cost of the whole project, which may have had more success had it not overreached itself by targeting the empire's most rebellious subjects.[16] The reactive vigour of Polish nationalism also helped
ignite the nationalism of others – the Jews and Lithuanians as well as the
Ukrainians.

A second problem was that the Russian state lacked sufficient means
to promote the cultural homogenisation of its subjects. As Ernest Gellner
and others have emphasised, resources such as schools and mass media
are of central importance in promoting a common culture.[17] The
Russian state was poorly equipped in all such means of social communication. Most Ukrainians, almost 80% of whom were still peasants,
were illiterate (87% in 1897) and even basic primary schooling was
extremely patchy.[18] In part, this was a result of the sheer size of the
empire and the weakness of its infrastructure in comparison to the states
it was trying to emulate (Britain, France, Germany), but it also reflected
deliberate policy. The authorities were well aware of the dangers of
allowing teaching in Ukrainian. A plea by the St Petersburg Literacy
Committee to create Ukrainian elementary schools was rejected in 1862;
a petition by 37 Ukrainian deputies on the same lines was decisively
rejected by the Third Duma in 1908. The restrictions imposed on the use
of Ukrainian in 1863 and 1876 were specifically designed to prevent the
Ukrainian intelligentsia establishing institutionalised channels of communication with the peasantry.

However, Ukrainian peasants were not taught in Russian either. Nor,
for that matter, were Russian peasants. The authorities' more general
problem was their mistrust of the so-called 'third element', the would-be
teachers, who were all viewed as potential subversives, regardless of
their national origin (plans to introduce universal elementary education
before the war came to naught). The fear was perfectly justified – many
non-Russians who assimilated did so to the 'other', revolutionary
Russia.[19] Unlike the paradigmatic case of modernising nationalism,
Third Republic France, the peasant-dominated countryside in both
Ukraine and Russia proper remained largely untouched by the march of
modernity even as late as 1914.[20] To put it another way, a key weakness
of the Russian nation-building project was the assumption that the
Ukrainians were already Russians, whereas in fact most possessed a
parochial or pre-national identity – as, indeed, did many Russians.

These assumptions can be seen in the ethnic names used in the nineteenth century. Ukrainians were never *inorodtsy* ('those of different kin')
like Jews or Muslims. Under the last two tsars there was a (far from
complete) change of emphasis, with less frequent reference to *rossiiskie*
(most subjects of the state) and a greater use of *russkie*. The latter is
usually considered to be an ethnonym referring to Russians alone, but it
would in fact be better described as a politonym or historonym, that is
a name implying the idea of descent from Rus and of the essential unity

of the three branches of its people: the Great Russians *(veliko-russkie)*, the 'White' or 'Belo-' Russians *(belo-russkie)* and the 'Little Russians' *(malo-russkie* now, rather than *malorusy* or *malorosy)* or Ukrainians. It was therefore impossible to refer to 'Russians' without implicitly including Ukrainians (and Belarusians). Only some Ukrainians were excluded from this naming process – political separatists could be labelled *Mazepintsy* ('Mazepists') and the cultureless masses *khokhly* (a derogatory term for 'hicks', which probably originally referred to the Cossacks' tufted hairstyles).[21] A common name did not of itself create a common people, however.

The Orthodox Church ought perhaps to have played a bigger role in cementing a common identity, but since the time of Peter the Great it had been a broken reed, too much the creature of the state to shape hearts and minds in the manner of the Church of England or the Catholic Church in France (in any case the Russian Orthodox Church was not the kind of institution that supported or encouraged the growth of ancillary civil society). Ritual still took precedence over sermon, and the widespread use of Church Slavonic until the late nineteenth century meant that the liturgy was hard for many peasants (even Russian peasants) to understand. Once again, the attempt to promote a greater use of Russian under the last two tsars came somewhat late in the day and led to the backlash that resulted in the formation of the Ukrainian Autocephalous Orthodox Church in 1921.

Significantly, there was a degree of confusion as to what 'Russification' policies were in fact supposed to be promoting, reflecting the fact that Russians themselves did not yet agree on what constituted their national identity and had no well-developed theory of an imperial 'mission'. Administratively, language was increasingly important, but to conservatives like Konstantin Pobedonostsev, Procurator of the Holy Synod, it was the imposition of Orthodoxy that was all-important. Ukrainians themselves have disagreed as to what they were actually subject to. Many have objected to the traditional Ukrainian term for Russification – *Rusyfikatsiia* – as Kievan Rus (one 's') originally belonged to the Ukrainians. In any case, Ukraine supposedly lost more than language. Some Ukrainians have therefore preferred the term *rosiishchennia* for 'Russification', to emphasise the change of identities at the imperial level, or even *moskovshchennia* – 'Muscovisation'. On the other hand, as Moscow, later the USSR, was supposedly a cultural void in comparison with Ukraine, some Ukrainians have preferred to emphasise only the negative, talking of 'deculturation' or 'denationalisation'.[22]

Many Ukrainians have, however, rejected the premise of compulsion. The use of Russian reflected cultural closeness, the natural emergence of a *lingua franca* and the attractiveness of the imperial culture as much as it did artificial administrative pressure.[23] There were indeed many factors still encouraging Ukrainians to become Russians, both in the broader (*rossiiskii*) and even the more narrowly ethnic (*russkii*) senses. The power and prestige of the empire were one, although, crucially, its relative decline in the late nineteenth century meant that its pulling power on the periphery was diminishing, in comparison to Victorian Britain or Third Republican France. The existence of common enemies was another. The outpouring of all-Russian and anti-German patriotism in cities such as Kiev, Odesa and Kharkiv in 1914 was genuine enough and might have become a more powerful factor if the war had been prosecuted more successfully.[24] After all, it was only World War I that finally turned Occitanian or Provençal peasants into Frenchmen.[25] Shared antipathy to the Poles and the continuing struggle with the Ottoman Turks were also important. Common Orthodoxy was of immense importance in an era when religious affiliations remained a primary factor in determining identities. It was still possible, at least in Volhynia and parts of Right Bank Ukraine, to convince Ukrainian peasants that their real enemy was not ethnic Russians in general, but Polish landlords and Jewish middlemen.[26] Throughout the nineteenth century, there were always elements in the imperial administration who wanted to bolster a limited (folkloric) Ukrainian consciousness as a bulwark against the Poles.[27] The new territories of southern Ukraine and the industrial Donbas were in a very real sense a multi-ethnic melting pot for all the peoples of the empire. They were therefore called *Novorossiia* ('New Russia' in the broader sense), but also 'New Europe' or the 'European California'.[28] Moreover, rapid urbanisation of these regions in the nineteenth and twentieth centuries reversed the traditional pattern of Ukrainian settlement – a central and western core and a south-eastern periphery. By the 1920s, most of the major urban centres in Ukraine were in the south-east and their culture was Russian.

The key problem, however, was that the terms the empire offered to the Ukrainians were bound to repel as well as attract. Although a genuine Ukrainian-Russian synthesis had at times seemed possible in the eighteenth century, the terms of engagement were radically changed around the middle of the nineteenth, becoming much more unilateral. Thereafter, Ukrainians were faced with an increasingly direct choice between assimilation and resistance, as the possibilities for mutual influence began to fade dramatically. Whereas an earlier generation of Russian intellectuals such as Vissarion Belinskii (1811–48) simply couldn't comprehend why anybody would want to try to develop the Ukrainian language or culture, a milieu that would have such a limited subject matter and audience,[29] after the Polish rebellion in 1861–3 leading figures such as Mikhail Katkov (1818–87) turned violently anti-Ukrainian, arguing that the Ukrainophiles were artificially dividing the Russian nation and seeking to deliver half to the Poles. The growing imperial weakness that made the Ukrainians more likely to 'defect' was also what made such defection seem like treachery to the Russians.

Katkov's political arguments were supported by intellectual developments, which were projected onto a much-expanded audience as a mass press began to develop in the 1860s. After Pushkin, nineteenth century literary Russian broke with the embryonic eighteenth-century tradition and was much less of a north–south synthesis. Historians like Pogodin and Kliuchevskii developed the mythopoeic basis for a more Russocentric Russia by fine-tuning the *translatio imperii* or *translatio auctoritatis* theory according to which Russia, in re-creating the lost unity of Rus, was not only reuniting that which had been unnaturally divided, but re-exporting to the south the traditions that had only survived in the north. (It is perhaps significant that, while the Ukrainians added to the empire in 1654 had shared a common religion with Moscow, those acquired in 1793–5 were often Uniate Catholics – though not for long, as the Church was abolished in 1839. Myths of a common past rather than a common religion now assumed greater importance.) The new attitude produced the repressive measures of 1863 and 1876 (severe restrictions on the use of the Ukrainian language, harassment of even semi-private Ukrainian organisations), at the very moment when modernisation was taking off, making it very difficult for Ukrainians to participate in urban, literate culture on their own terms.

Consequently, conscious Ukrainophilism was very difficult to express in the 1870s and 1880s. Nevertheless, it never completely disappeared and was able to revive from the 1890s onwards, for three key reasons. First, painful though it may be for modern Ukrainians to admit, the authorities' anti-Ukrainian measures were not that repressive. They were certainly harsh in the context of the time, but were not radical enough to destroy the Ukrainian movement root and branch. The tsarist authorities simply did not have the repressive capacity that Lenin or Stalin would later develop. And of course, when political repression holds down but does not destroy a movement, it can often give it added strength in the long run. It also made it more difficult to occupy the middle ground. Indeed, some imperial officials continued to believe that a softer line would encourage more voluntary 'Russification'.[30] Second, the repressive measures were imposed at a time when the Ukrainian movement was gaining strength in Habsburg Galicia (see pages 101–18), and the cross-border fertilisation of activists, inspiration and ideas helped to sustain the Ukrainian movement in the Romanov empire through its low ebb. Third, Katkov and his circle were promoting policies that were based on a serious misinterpretation of the past. The unilinear *translatio imperii* theory ignored at least four centuries of separate development and over two centuries of subsequent Ukrainian–Russian interaction, and imposed on both nations a distorted view of their origins.

Why, however, did Russia turn on Ukraine so quickly? An explanation might perhaps be sought in Russia's fixation on its struggle with the West. In the great nineteenth-century debate between Slavophiles and Westernisers, neither side could allow for any complexity on the home side of the boundary-markers between *Rossiia* and the West.[31] Nor could Russia afford the geopolitical and numerical loss of the Ukrainians in that struggle. At the same time, the crudity of Russia's nationalising model largely derived from the fact that it was borrowed in ideal–typical form from the West. Most fundamentally, however, as noted by the Russian nationalist A.I. Savenko (who had a Ukrainian surname!) 'the Polish, Armenian, Finnish, and other problems are peripheral, i.e. secondary problems [but the] Mazepist injures Russia at the origins of its existence as a great power ... Poland, Finland, and other borderlands did not give Russia her greatness.' Ukraine did.[32]

Russian Images of Ukraine

The inability of Russians to come to terms with Ukraine can also be observed in the way in which Ukrainian themes are dealt with in Russian art and literature of the time. Whereas in the early nineteenth century Ryleev could see in Ukraine idealised values of liberty and democracy, by the late nineteenth century Russians tended to see only themselves. They used Ukrainian elements with no acknowledgment whatsoever (or no acknowledgment of the need for acknowledgment), reflecting how automatic the assumption that 'Ukraine' was just 'Russia' had become. There was certainly little real engagement with key Ukrainian themes on their own terms. Nor, in contrast to (some) English views of the Scottish Enlightenment, was there any longer much sense of what *value*, other than ethnographic colour, the Ukrainians had to contribute towards the 'Union'. To most Russians, 'Little Russia' was synonymous with the gentry culture of the Hetmanate. Once it assimilated, Ukraine simply disappeared off their horizons.

In music, Russian composers were seeking to combine classical styles with native traditions, just like their contemporaries in Bohemia (Dvořák) or England (Elgar, Vaughan Williams); but their definition of 'native' was rather more expansive. Tchaikovskii, for example, when using folk themes in his Second Symphony, nicknamed the 'Little Russian' (first drafted 1872, rewritten 1879–80), juxtaposes a Ukrainian song, 'The Crane' (the symphony's original title), with a Ukrainianised version of 'Down by Mother Volga'. He assumes that both are part of the same common cultural fundament for the particular version of Russian nationalism he is trying to project. Similar folkish elements of Ukrainian origin can be heard in Tchaikovskii's First Piano Concerto (1875), but without significantly altering the 'Russian' character of the work. Prokofiev, who was born in Ukraine to Russian parents and spent his childhood in a village near Donetsk, was arguably more successful in using Ukrainian themes on their own terms. A good later example would be the famous melody at the opening of his Second Violin Concerto (1935), which is after the style of a Ukrainian *duma* (epic songs recited from memory by blind bandura players).

Nor is there any mistaking the triumphalist Russian nationalism of Musorgskii's finale to *Pictures at an Exhibition* (1874), despite, or rather because of, its title, 'The Great Gate of Kiev'. Musorgskii combines exuberant rhythm, snatches of Russian hymns and pealing bells to celebrate Alexander II surviving an assassination attempt in the city in 1866, but once again his projection of Kiev as 'the mother of all Russian cities' is simply unthinking (at a time when the 1874 Kiev census recorded only 7.7% of the population as 'Great Russian').[33] Musorgskii, it has to be said, also penned an unfinished opera, *Sorochyntsi Fair*, which drew sympathetically on Gogol's Ukrainian folk-humour. Two of Rimskii-Korsakov's operas, *May Night* (1878–9) and *Christmas Eve* (1894–5), are also based on Ukrainian stories by Gogol, but the latter's celebration of Ukrainian daily life is sanitised by shifting the action into a distant and fantastical past, and the former was catcalled by Kiev audiences in the 1880s.[34]

Often Ukraine features in a barely registered fashion. When Chekhov's heroine Liuba Ranievskaia exclaims 'God, how I love my own country!' in *The Cherry Orchard* (1903), the action is actually taking place in Ukraine, near Kharkiv.[35] However, the country Chekhov has in mind is obviously Russia, not Ukraine, although the dramatist was born in Taganrog (Tahanrih), then considered by Ukrainophiles to be part of 'ethnographic Ukraine'. Even less would Chekhov have thought of adding a Ukrainian aspect to any of his stories set in Crimea, such as *The Lady with a Lapdog* (1899).

Historical works by modern Russian writers, such as Irina Ratushinskaia's novel *The Odessans* (1996), have maintained this tradition. Ratushinskaia's protagonists undergo a spiritual journey from the patriotic fervour of 1905 and 1914 to opposite sides of the civil war after 1917, but the Ukrainian hinterland rarely affects their lives. One of the characters, the well-to-do Anna, takes a dislike to Gogol's novel about the seventeenth-century Cossack hero Taras Bulba. 'Why had he [Pavel, her would-be protector] never noticed what a cruel book it was? Of course, all that the Ukrainians and Poles ever did in it was to go round killing one another, and, really, what sort of stuff was that for a girl from a family like this?'[36] The classic of glasnost cinema, *Little Vera* (1988), with its mini-skirted heroine rebelling against the grim realities of Soviet urban life, was also set in Ukraine, along the coast from Odesa (Mariupol, on the Sea of Azov); but nobody noticed.

Ukrainian history was also subsumed into 'all-Russian' history when Russian artists evoked the more distant past. A classic example is Borodin's reworking of *The Lay of Ihor's Host* in his opera *Prince Igor* (first performed in 1890, three years after his death).[37] Borodin's version of the story is a morality play in which the fate of the Rus depends on the ability of its warring princes to unite against the Polovtsians – at least Igor's ultimate defeat is portrayed as a noble moral victory. Although Borodin is promoting the idea of the oneness of Rus, there is no hint whatsoever that its princes could be divided by anything other than ambition. The key struggle is still between the Rus and the Polovtsian 'outsiders', certainly not between northern and southern Rus – although the opera's celebrated Polovtsian Dances present an ambiguously inviting picture of the cultural other. (Borodin was in many respects an early 'Eurasian', keen to celebrate the synthesis of European and Asian culture that many latter-day nationalists have argued is the basis of Russia's greatness.)

The myths and symbols of even earlier periods were also used in a way that completely bypassed Ukraine, as in the work of the 'Scythian' movement in the Russian arts, which looked to the pre-Christian era for inspiration. A prime example is Stravinskii's *Rite of Spring*, given a first performance in Paris in 1913, which famously provoked a near-riot. Stravinskii's designer Nicholas Roerich wryly remarked that 'this wild primitivism [of the audience's reaction] had nothing in common with the refined primitivism of our ancestors'.[38] Stravinskii, in his 'atonal' music, and Roerich, in the vivid colours of his set and costume designs, saw no problem in appropriating the southerly Scythians for their nativist and 'eastern' imagery (Roerich's designs for *Prince Igor* also drew on Russia's 'Asian' and pre-Christian past – see plate 26). Once again, they would not have regarded this as an act of appropriation (Stravinskii was born in Lomonosov, Roerich in St Petersburg). They just assumed that the Scythian period was the beginnings of all-Russian history, as does Prokofiev in his *Scythian Suite* (1916), which simultaneously looks back to a world of pre-Christian sun gods and demons and forwards to the arrival of revolutionary modernity. There was, in other words, nothing any the less Russian about 'the south'.

The same equation of Ukraine and Russia can be seen in the spectacular paintings of Rus saints by the Russian artist Viktor Vasnetsov that adorn Kiev's St Vladimir cathedral. The two keynote works over the main entrance, *The Baptism of Saint Prince Vladimir* and *The Baptism of the Kievites* (see plate 25), were commissioned to celebrate the nine hundredth anniversary of the Baptism in specifically all-Russian terms, as was the cathedral itself. Vasnetsov's paintings, completed in 1895, are a glorious example of the 'neo-Russian' style, which sought to anchor itself in a rediscovered Byzantine tradition, combined with a nativist Russian aesthetic – as can be seen in the use of both traditional gold and modern silver haloes. The evocation of 'a thousand years of Russian history' can also be seen in the parade of saints and princes adorning the nave, leading through Olga and Vladimir to Andrei Bogoliubskii, Alexander Nevskii and beyond. The cathedral's architecture also echoes, somewhat eclectically, the eleventh-century Rus style, with its vertical apses standing in sharp contrast to the Western-leaning Neoclassicism popular earlier in the century. In a similar fashion, Mikhail Vrubel's sadly rather faded 1885 additions to Kiev's twelfth-century church of St Cyril were also commissioned to celebrate the glorious ancestors of nineteenth-century tsars. Both churches, it is worth repeating, are in Kiev. It is more than a little ironic that St Vladimir's is now St Volodymyr's, the principal Kievan cathedral of the more nationalist branch of the Ukrainian Orthodox Church.

Other 'Russian' artists had a more ambiguous attitude to Ukraine, particularly Ilia Repin. Chapter four discussed his painting *Zaporozhian Cossacks* and the attempt by Ukrainian nationalists to reclaim him as one of their own. Some Ukrainian critics have also pointed to the supposed coded message in *They Did Not Expect Him* (1884–88), which depicts the return of a political exile to his family, who have a portrait of the national poet Shevchenko hanging on the wall. However, as Repin also painted specifically Russian themes, such as Kuzma Minin's call to the people of Nizhnii-Novgorod to resist the Polish invaders in 1613 (1876, 1915) and, most famously, the *Russian State Council* (1903), he is perhaps best seen as a figure combining local ethnography with *rossiiskii* patriotism.

When Ukraine appeared in Russian works as a landscape or as ethnographic background, it could be presented in neutral or positive terms (the 'Russian Italy'), but attitudes to 'political' Ukraine were uniformly hostile. A classic example is Mikhail Bulgakov's play *The White Guard* (1925). Bulgakov (1891–1940) was born and grew up in Kiev at a time when the Russian intelligentsia thought of the city as its own. The play is set in late 1918, with the godless Bolsheviks installed in Moscow and Petrograd, and the Ukrainian nobleman Pavlo Skoropadskyi ruling in Kiev as a self-styled 'Hetman', presiding over a loose coalition of Ukrainophiles, White monarchists and occupying German forces. As his regime collapses, the city is threatened by the Ukrainian peasant armies of Symon Petliura (see also pages 126–7).

To Bulgakov, city and civilisation are equated with Russian culture, or just culture *per se*, whereas 'Mr. Dostoevskii's dear, simple, bloody God-fearing peasants', represent anarchy and the abyss that is about to engulf his version of 'Russia'.[39] In the play the Ukrainian language is reserved for Petliura's troops, the 'dark forces' massed outside the city and depicted by Bulgakov in acts of wanton violence and petty bullying. They are likely to take the city, but are shown to be incapable of governing it. Bulgakov has the play's protagonist, Alexei, a White-leaning artillery officer, declaim: 'Do you know who this Petliura is? He's a myth, a black fog. He doesn't exist. Look out of the window and see what's there. A snow-storm, shadows, that's all ... there are only two real forces in Russia, gentlemen: the Bolsheviks and us ... We shan't stop Petliura. But he won't stay for long. And after him the Bolsheviks will come.'[40] It is significant that Bulgakov was able to put on such a play so soon after the Revolution (for the Moscow Art Theatre). The authorities were more worried by its sympathetic portrayal of the Whites than by its Ukrainophobia. Bulgakov's Kiev would, however, be swept away by the purges of the 1930s, although his house still stands on the city's most picturesque shopping street, Andriivskii Uzviz.

Ukrainian Versions: Language and Identity

There was a much greater variety of possibilities on the Ukrainian side of nineteenth-century *Rossiia*. Indeed, Ukrainian identity was defined in part by its very plurality of possibility.[41] As in the seventeenth-century Polish Commonwealth, there were many ways of living with the possibilities of being *gente Ukrainus, natione Russus* or, conversely, of rejecting the idea that to be Ukrainian one had also to be partly Russian. Without much in the way of a political movement until after 1906, one has to look mainly at writers, artists and historians to examine these varieties of representation. In fact, because overtly political expressions of Ukrainian identity were difficult, in a way the Ukrainian national movement *was* the movement in arts and literature. In any case, the issue of language was at the heart of what it meant to be a Ukrainian at this time.

Many Ukrainian writers continued to think of Ukraine and Russia as regional societies within a bi-cultural state and accepted that this meant a common identity of sorts.[42] The idea central to later Ukrainian (and Russian) nationalism that a single people should naturally speak a single language was not yet common. Patterns of language use were defined as much by social as by ethnic milieu. According to Mykhailo Drahomanov (1841–95), for example, nineteenth-century 'Russia' (*Rossiia*) could be seen as comprising one state, two languages and three literatures. The state was a bi-ethnic unity, while the two languages (Ukrainian and Russian) had produced a common 'all-Russian' (*vserossiis'ka*) and two popular, 'national' (Ukrainian and Russian) literatures. To a significant extent, both the Ukrainian and the Russian intelligentsia could share the 'all-Russian' literature.[43] Works such as Gogol's *Dead Souls* belonged to the 'all-Russian sphere', as, in Drahomanov's opinion, did writers such as 'Pushkin, Ryleev, Griboedov and Lermontov [who] in their lyrical dramas and poetic monologues expressed the thoughts and feelings which were in the heads and hearts not just of the inhabitants of Moscow and Nizhegorod, but also those of Poltava, Kiev and Katerynoslav [now Dnipropetrovsk]'.[44] The 'national Ukrainian' literature was represented by populist writers from Kotliarevskyi to Kulish, the 'national Russian' literature by Pushkin in his more nationalistic moments and writers like Ostrovskii and Nekrasov. In a similar fashion, Mykola Markevych (1804–60) distinguished between simultaneous loyalties to Ukraine as his native land (*rodina*) and Russia as his fatherland (*otechestvo*); and the writer and historian Ivan Novytskyi (1844–90) contrasted ethnic (*narodnyi*) and state-national (*natsionalnyi*) identities. Even one of the great founding fathers of Ukrainian history and literature, Mykola Kostomarov (1817–85) argued that the Ukrainian language should be developed primarily for what his critics dubbed 'home use'. As Ukrainian was the language of 'the people', it had to be accessible to the people. High culture might come to them in time, but forcing the pace would only serve to alienate them from Ukrainian as an embryonic literary language. In his history writing Kostomarov combined the argument that Ukrainians and Russians were culturally distinct with an acceptance of the fact that they were fated to live together as 'Two Rus Nationalities', or, as his more conservative colleague Panteleimon Kulish (1819–97) put it, a 'Two-in-one Rus nation' (*dvoiedynyi ruskyi narod*).[45]

These were not at all unusual arguments for stateless East Europeans in the nineteenth century. Early Slovak writers such as Pavel Josef Šafárik (1795–1861) and Jan Kollár (1793–1852) sought to combine local patriotism with a broader pan-Slavism. Croat intellectuals such as Ljudevit Gaj (1814–72) originally promoted the 'Illyrian' idea of a common Serb–Croat identity. On the other hand, the fact that early Czech and Estonian activists wrote their anti-German tracts in German didn't make them much less anti-German.

Gogol

No one embodies the complex nature of nineteenth-century Ukrainian identity better than the writer Mykola Hohol, better known to the world by the Russian version of his name, Nikolai Gogol (1809–52). Scholars have long debated the question of whether he should be seen as a Ukrainian or a Russian writer. Some Ukrainian critics, such as Yevhen Malaniuk and Serhii Yefremov,[46] have attacked him for his indifference to the Ukrainian 'question' and the depoliticised nostalgia of works such as *Evenings on a Village Farm near Dikanka* (1831–2); others, including Pavlo Fylypovych, Volodymyr Doroshenko and a host of Ukrainian scholars since 1991, have sought to reclaim the neglected Ukrainian elements in his work.[47] The Canadian Ukrainian scholar George Luckyj, on the other hand, has steered a sensible middle course.[48]

As Gogol himself wrote in a letter in 1844:

I myself do not know whether my soul is Ukrainian [*khokhlatskaia*] or Russian [*russkaia*]. I know only that on no account would I give priority to the Little Russian [*malorossiianinu*] before the Russian [*russkim*], or to the Russian before the Little Russian. Both natures are too richly endowed by God, and, as if by design, each of them separately contains within itself what the other lacks – a sure sign that they complement one another.[49]

Gogol was born in Ukraine and used Ukrainian themes, drawing particularly on the baroque humour of Ukrainian folk theatre (*vertep*), but he wrote in Russian. He sought a niche within Russian literature promoting naturalism and a concern for the common people, besides, as Kulish famously argued, trying to educate Russians about Ukraine and its charms.[50] Moreover, by importing huge numbers of Ukrainianisms into Russian, Gogol helped (temporarily) narrow the gap between the two languages.

Is *The Government Inspector* (1836) a Ukrainian play? Is *Dead Souls* (1842) a Ukrainian book? The answer in both cases would have to be no, if for slightly different reasons. As George Luckyj has argued, 'the substratum of Gogol's art and philosophy was Ukrainian. His humour' – his delight in poking fun at authority and petty social climbing – 'were the products of his native soil',[51] as was the disdain for conformity and social regimentation and love of the free spirit that underlies *The Government Inspector*. The protagonist, Klestakov, a man with little authority even over his own affairs, does after all get away with the money. Gogol's general purpose, however, was always to strive for broader meanings, to reach beyond even 'all-Russian' literature and culture to explore the universal themes that have made him so enduringly popular. The lampooning of corruption and petty bureaucracy in *The Government Inspector* is perfectly comprehensible in all the many locations and styles into which it has been translated and set (including an English Klestakov amongst local Scots). In the climate of the 1830s, when Gogol was at his most productive, it was possible, even normal, to argue that the Russian language was simply the broader medium. According to Luckyj, Gogol thought that 'great literature in the Ukraine could be written only in Russian, the language of the educated classes. Writing in Ukrainian [as his father had done], in Gogol's opinion, led automatically to certain themes and styles which were not of universal significance.'[52]

Dead Souls, however (*pace* Drahomanov), with its over-quoted passages on the nature of Russian (*Russkii*) identity (the closing image in part one of Russia as a runaway troika and as 'a land that cares not for jokes, but sweeps smoothly and evenly over half the world'), is more specifically Russian,[53] just as *Evenings on a Village Farm near Dikanka* is more specifically Ukrainian. Gogol set his works in both Ukraine and St Petersburg, but the two are not mythological opposites as they are in Shevchenko's work (see below). The alienated individuals of Gogol's *St Petersburg Tales* (1830s) are not alienated because they are cultural foreigners; their anomie is universal and affected Gogol himself, who was in many ways an outsider in both worlds, caught between the metropol and periphery – a common archetype for new subjects of empire. Gogol's Ukraine is a gentler world of spirits and folk magic and young girls seeing the faces of future lovers in the mirror of the stream, but in St Petersburg a man can turn into a nose. Ukraine is a repository of humour, folk wisdom and spiritual refreshment, but it is not idealised. The Cossack past depicted in *Taras Bulba* is often barbaric – although the first (1835) edition is more 'Ukrainian' in terms of the object of its patriotism than the second (1842) – and in stories such as *Evenings on a Village Farm near Dikanka* it is a past that has gone for good, a backdrop to the gentle decline of the present.

If Gogol had been born at a later date, he might have revised his opinion of Ukrainian language and literature, as the literary face-workers of the later nineteenth century strove to provide them with the depth and capacity that Gogol had judged lacking. As it was, in the words of Mykhailo Hrushevskyi's later assessment, Gogol was 'a part of old Ukraine ... he enveloped her grave with the scent of poetry without suspecting her close resurrection'.[54] He was a typical man of his time.

Shevchenko and the Cossack Myth

The other great Ukrainian writer of the nineteenth century was Taras Shevchenko (1814–61), the son of a serf who was eventually to be canonised as Ukraine's national bard. Shevchenko and Gogol could hardly be more different. First and foremost, Shevchenko wrote in Ukrainian, where his very talent validated the use of the language and constructed its modern form. Second, and just as importantly, the images, symbols and myths of his poetry helped to create the foundations of an alternative conceptual universe to the 'Little Russia' of men like Kochubei or Bezborodko, Kostomarov or Gogol.[55]

For Shevchenko, Ukrainian, Russian and Polish identities were mutually exclusive and fundamentally hostile. According to the writer Oksana Zabuzhko, he was therefore the first true 'national intellectual', who dealt with the traditional problem of 'Ukrainian dualism' by counterposing a new myth of Ukraine to the imperial myth of St Petersburg and providing 'a radical new paradigm for the coexistence of the Ukrainian individual with the empire'.[56] In modern terms, he was the first Ukrainian radically to deconstruct that idea of empire, whose temptations had proved so great for many of his contemporaries. Like other nineteenth-century national poets such as Adam Mickiewicz for the Poles and Vuk Karadžić for the Serbs, his tools were those of a Romantic and a Herderian nationalist. The central theme of his poetry is Ukraine's loss of freedom, which stands in stark contrast to its glorious past:

> Once there was the Hetmanate –
> It passed beyond recall;
> Once, it was, we ruled ourselves,

But we shall rule no more ...
Yet we shall never forget the Cossack fame of yore![57]

Why with the Poles did we once fight?
Engage the Hordes with slashing knives?
Why did we harry with our pikes
Muscovite ribs? There [Chyhyryn, the Hetmanate capital] once we sowed,
And well we watered with red blood,
With sabres harrowed what was sown.
But in that field what crop has grown?
Rue, rue has grown,
And choked our freedom down.[58]

As with other prophets of national revival, Shevchenko evokes a dormant patriotic spirit. Ukraine has 'fallen asleep, mould-grown, covered in weeds',[59] but Shevchenko confidently predicts that

that glory will revive,
The glory of Ukraine,
And a clear light, not a twilight,
Will shine forth anew.[60]

Shevchenko's call to his fellow-countrymen to reject the lure of empire and take power in their native land preempts the Irish slogan of 'ourselves alone' in 1916.

In one's own house, – one's own truth,
One's own might and freedom.[61]

What was 'one's own' and what was 'other' is defined by Shevchenko in explicitly national terms – one of his most frequently used terms was *chuzhyi*, meaning 'foreign', 'alien' or 'strange'. One of his poems is called *Ne hriie sontse na chuzhyni* (1847) – 'The Sun Does Not Shine on a Foreign Land'. The Cossacks' traditional enemies, the Poles, figure prominently throughout his work, but so do the Russians, whom Shevchenko usually characterises as *Moskaly* ('Muscovites', but the sense is pejorative), as well as the Jews and Germans (Shevchenko's master was a local German called Engelhart). Moreover, Shevchenko presents Muscovy and Ukraine as cultural and political antitheses. Whereas the Cossack land is depicted as one of simple Christian brotherhood, Shevchenko's Muscovy is full of

Palaces and churches,
Pot-bellied worthies,
Nowhere a *simple* house emerges![62]

Russia's tsars, moreover, are 'executioners, cannibals!' In his poem *The Dream* (1844), in many ways a parody of the St Petersburg depicted by Pushkin in *The Bronze Horseman* (1833), Shevchenko courted the censor's wrath by describing Peter the Great as

> thou evil tsar!
> Accursed Tsar, insatiate,
> Perfidious serpent, what
> Have you done, then, with the Cossacks?
> You have filled the swamps
> With their noble bones! And then
> Built the capital [St Petersburg]
> On their tortured corpses.

He continues:

> It was [Peter] the First who crucified
> Unfortunate Ukraine,
> and [Catherine] the Second – she who finished off
> Whatever yet remained. [63]

The idea of empire was therefore radically undermined. The imperial capital, a place to seek wealth and opportunity for many of his fellow-countrymen (and where Shevchenko himself went to university), was inverted into a symbol of Ukraine's oppression. Other images Shevchenko chooses for Russia include the imperial 'Black Eagle', turned from the double-headed symbol of righteous might into a bird of prey hovering 'high above' the river Dnieper, the 'warder' of Ukraine's imprisonment. In *The Great Vault* (1845) Poland and Russia are characterised as twin crows, comparing notes on how to pillage the land.[64] One of the greatest of Shevchenko's poems, *The Caucasus* (1845), is a long indictment of Russian imperialism in its rawest form, which was revisited with relish by modern Ukrainian authors in the wake of Russia's 1990s Chechen wars.[65] Russians, finally, are dubious partners in any enterprise. In the great allegorical poem *Kateryna* (1838) Shevchenko warns his heroine who, like Ukraine itself, accepts the fateful Muscovite embrace:

> O lovely maidens, fall in love,
> But not with Moskaly
> For Moskaly are foreign [*chuzhi*] folk,
> They do not treat you right.
> A Moskal will love for sport,
> And laughing depart.[66]

Shevchenko even attacks the Cossack hero Khmelnytskyi for signing the fateful Pereiaslav treaty with Russia:

Bohdan, O my little Bohdan!
Had I known, in the cradle
I'd have choked you, in my sleep
I'd have overlain you.
Now my steppes have all been sold,
In Jews' and Germans' hands;
And my sons at foreign toil,
Far in foreign lands;
My brother, Dnieper, now runs dry
And is deserting me;
And my dear graves the Moskal
Is plundering utterly.[67]

Shevchenko's view of the world, therefore, revived but also subtly readapted the embryonic Cossack myths of the eighteenth century. Shevchenko's version of 'imagined Ukraine' was basically the space between the Catholic world in the west and Muscovite autocracy in the east. The western boundary was clear enough. A similar anti-Catholic mythology can be found in Gogol's historical novel *Taras Bulba*, and indeed in modern works such as Lina Kostenko's *Marusia Churai* (1980). However, because Shevchenko constructed his notion of Ukrainian kinship around constant references to Orthodox brotherhood and Ukraine's descent from the Cossack past, he tended to exclude the west Ukrainians from the picture. Shevchenko was capable of bracketing together the

Poles and Uniates, like jackdaws
Covering the plain[68]

as all 'Catholics' and therefore all the enemies of Ukraine. The opening lines of his short poem *To the Poles* (1850?) evoke an era when

We were still Cossacks,
And of the Union [of Brest in 1596] we hardly heard,
How jolly life was then![69]

Shevchenko's epic poem *Haidamaki* (1841) on the eighteenth-century peasant rebellions in Right Bank Ukraine (then still a part of Poland), describes the slaughter of Catholics with particular relish. One of the Haidamak leaders, Ivan Honta (died 1768), even kills his own Catholic sons and refuses them burial. Shevchenko excuses the act:

sons of Slavs like beasts
Got drunk with blood. Who was to blame?
The Jesuits, the priests![70]

It was left to others, primarily the historian Mykhailo Hrushevskyi, to sidestep the Uniate problem and construct a broader and more ecumenical national myth.

On the other hand, Shevchenko gives a much clearer answer to the question of who is a Ukrainian and who is a Russian. The eastern boundary of Ukraine was now not just the river Don and the geographical 'Asia' that lay beyond. The difference between Russia and Ukraine was above all cultural and political – a love of liberty for one's own against the imperialist's desire to rule all others in chains. A similar line was taken by the historian Mykola Kostomarov, whose juxtaposition of the egalitarian traditions of the Ukrainian people against the authoritarian collectivism of the Russians produced a powerful combination of ethnic and cultural boundary-markers that laid the basis for a later, more nativist nationalism.[71] Ukrainians' natural affinity was for popular democracy, whereas the Poles' natural preference was aristocracy and the Muscovites' autocracy. The twentieth-century historian Viacheslav Lypynskyi, a Ukrainian of Polish origin, agreed that

> the basic difference between Ukraine and Muscovy is not the language, nor the tribe, nor the faith, nor the appetite of the peasant for the lord's estate ... but a different political system which had evolved over the centuries, a different ... method of organising the ruling elite, a different relationship between the upper and lower classes, between the state and society – between those who rule and those who are ruled.[72]

Religion in the west and the myth of national personality in the east now provided a much clearer space for imagined Ukraine. The ideal of Cossack liberty that took the central role in Shevchenko's poetry therefore became the leitmotif of the nineteenth-century Ukrainian national movement. At this time, significantly, little use was made of the alternative myth of Rus, which was too closely associated with the new imperial Russian myth of origin. In any case, a rich reservoir of material on the Cossack era was available in the form of eighteenth-century chronicles and the popular culture of Ukrainian *dumy*.[73]

The idea of freedom as the defining quality of Cossack identity can also be found in the classic opera buffa *Zaporozhian beyond the Danube* (1863), by Semen Hulak-Artemovskyi (1813–73). The work's central theme is the homelessness of the Zaporozhian Cossacks after the destruction of the Sich in 1775 has forced them to settle under the Turkish sultan. The message is hidden beneath a comedy of resourceful drunks, nagging wives and shrill-voiced eunuchs, but the pain of the Cossacks' lament for their lost homeland and the justice and nobility of their cause is clear enough, as is the sense of triumph on their eventual departure. Audiences would also have been aware that it was Catherine II who originally expelled the Zaporozhians. The piece also strained at the limits of the permissible by gently pointing out that the opening of the Black Sea coast was more of a Ukrainian than a Russian affair. The two other operas in the limited repertoire of the time, *Natalka Potalka* (1889) and *Taras Bulba* (1891) by Mykola Lysenko (1842–1912), carry basically the same message – and in a medium striving towards the creation of a proper Ukainian 'grand opera'. *Taras Bulba*, however, was not performed until after World War I, largely because Lysenko refused to allow the libretto to be translated into Russian (in the early 1990s the opposition movement Rukh liked to use the merry 'Zaporozhian March' to open its political meetings).

Shevchenko, heavily censored, was still published in Soviet times, when he was reinvented as a prophet of social revolution. It is possible with hindsight to criticise the poet for his limited subject range of the noble Ukrainian peasant struggling against his oppressors and his blurring of the national with the social issue, but ultimately this was precisely his importance. To Shevchenko, autocracy and liberty were opposites, but so were the Russian and Ukrainian cultures. One could not oppose the one without opposing the other. In this, Shevchenko spoke to the climate of the times. The overlap between national and class messages was characteristic of the Ukrainian movement through the 1917 revolution and beyond. Until the 1920s almost all Ukrainian activists would also have called themselves 'Socialists' or 'progressives'. As the Ukrainian historian Ivan Lysiak-Rudnytskyi (1919–84) once remarked, at the turn of the century Ukraine was full of earnest young men with 'Marx's *Communist Manifesto* in one pocket and Shevchenko's collected poems *Kobzar* in the other'.[74] The overlap also meant, however, that the line between the 'Ukrainian' and the 'Bolshevik' revolutions after 1917 was not as clear-cut as is often argued, and the former would lose vital strength to the latter. Historians still argue about what Ukrainian peasants were actually fighting for in 1917.

Young Ukraine

The other great theme of the nineteenth-century Ukrainian national movement was a typical struggle between 'fathers and sons'. Whereas the older generation – Drahomanov, Markevych and others – could absorb Shevchenko's poetry without losing their faith in a joint Russo–Ukrainian community of fate, by the end of the century Shevchenko's Cossack nativism was beginning to be used by the younger Ukrainians in more political forms and in a manner that asserted the impossibility of multiple identities. At a time when many Ukrainians were still assimilating to Russian culture, a specifically and militantly anti-Russian nationalism began to develop.

The paradox is real, but superficial, as it was largely the former trend that produced the latter. In the latter half of the nineteenth century, many self-conscious Ukrainians began to fear that the Russian embrace could smother Ukrainian culture for good. To the younger generation, what they saw as the self-abnegating posture of their own side made them complicit in this process, though the extremity of their attack is best explained as, quite literally, a phobia, a fear of the very real continuing attraction that the empire still had for many Ukrainians. To the present day, Ukrainians have therefore spent as much time criticising their own 'cosmopolitan' brethren as the Russian enemy. For the young radicals, anyone who wrote or even spoke in Russian betrayed their own people. According to Borys Hrinchenko (1863–1910), for example, 'anyone who brings even the slightest Muscovitism to our people (whether by word of mouth or through the written word) does them harm because it separates them from [their] national soil'.[75]

Kostomarov's theory of literature for 'home use' came to be strongly opposed by the younger generation of writers such as Hrinchenko and Ivan Nechui-Levytskyi (1838–1918). The latter claimed rather bluntly that 'Russian literature is useless for Ukraine', the former that if the Ukrainian movement was ever 'to create from the Ukrainian nation [*natsiia*] one nationally self-conscious educated community' it would have to be a community united by the use of its own native language at all levels. According to Hrinchenko, the idea of a restricted function for Ukrainian was simply absurd. 'History knows no "subliterature", no literature "for home use", no literature specially about the lord or specially about the peasant, but knows [only] *plain literatures*, which in essence are the manifestations of the intellectual life of one or another people as a whole, both for the lords and for the peasants'.[76]

Whereas the majority of Ukrainian activists still thought in terms of accommodation with Russia, the younger generation developed Shevchenko's radical deconstructivist attack on the empire to new levels. Instead of images of common cultural achievement and the power and prestige of empire, the new radicals counterposed the ideas of Russia as a predator, Russia as 'Asia', Russia as Europe's last and greatest autocracy, Russia as the enemy of all the free peoples of Europe. Many of these themes, and the conflicts within Ukrainian culture, can be observed in the play by Lesia Ukraïnka (1871–1913) *The Noble Woman*. Set in the later seventeenth century during the time of Hetman Petro Doroshenko (1665–76), but obviously also to be read as a commentary on the situation in 1910, when it was written, the play concerns the marriage of Stepan and Oksana, two scions of the Cossack nobility. Stepan embodies all the key characteristics of the 'Little Russian' – he defends his father for signing the Pereiaslav treaty, characterised as 'the Devil's temptation' by Oksana's brother Ivan: 'My poor father did not go to Moscow to seek fur coats or money from the Exchequer! He did not want to serve a foreign [i.e. Polish] lord in his native land, he just wanted to serve his native faith abroad [i.e. in Muscovy] – to help his oppressed brothers albeit from afar, and gain for them the grace of the tsar.'[77] Stepan has a similarly naïve faith in the tsar and his respect for Ukraine's Pereiaslav 'rights'. He believes that Moscow and Ukraine are united by a common faith and condemns Doroshenko's rebellion for bringing about 'fratricidal' strife between Ukraine and Russia, which he compares to that between Cain and Abel. He dismisses the idea of a 'free' Ukraine. When Ivan expresses the hope that one day Ukrainians will no longer have to 'lick the boots of Poles or Muscovites' and can stand on their own two feet, he replies sarcastically, 'And were there many who stood independently then [in 1648]?' Doroshenko has also sinned by siding with the Ukrainians' and Russians' real common enemy – the heathen Tatars and Turks – and 'paying them with Christian slaves' (Doroshenko indeed negotiated an alliance of sorts in his attempt to overturn Pereiaslav). Finally, despite what he says about his father's motives in 'obtaining a position', it is also pretty obvious that Stepan likes living the good life in Moscow. After taking his father's advice to 'marry in his native land', Stepan persuades his new wife to overcome her doubts and join him in Moscow, reassuring her that 'nothing will be foreign there in our own wee house – will it?'[78]

Oksana, however, is the antithesis of Stepan, the nostalgic patriot to his 'Little Russian'. Her initial doubts are soon confirmed in 'alien' Moscow (like Shevchenko, Ukraïnka repeatedly uses the word *chuzhyi*, that is, 'foreign' or 'other'), despite her mother-in-law's advice to copy the locals' strange language and 'harsh customs'. 'We are outsiders here,' she tells her, 'when you live with wolves, you learn to howl like a wolf' (ironically a common Russian saying). The people are only superficially of the same faith – 'they are not afraid of sin: in God's own church people buzz in conversation instead of keeping silence, yet people boast of being more faithful than us ... there is something about the service I do not recognise.' Their manners are coarse (courtiers have to drink prodigiously to keep pace with the tsar), and their attitude to women, who are forced to wear the veil and sit idly at home waiting for matchmakers to arrange their marriages, is 'Asian' – 'men are not used to spending time to converse with womenfolk'. The Russians, in short, are just as 'Tatar' as the Tatars themselves.

Their clothes are dowdy in comparison to the traditional Ukrainian head-dress, corset and tunic Oksana prefers. She even objects to the Russification of her name to Aksynia or Aksiusha. 'There is something unpleasant about it,' she says, 'Oksana would be better.' She fears ending up like Stepan's sister Hanna, who has forgotten her religion and 'remembers little about Ukraine'. Ultimately, Oksana sides with an unnamed 'guest' from Doroshenko's Ukraine and his attacks on Moscow's unilateral betrayal of the Pereiaslav 'oath' (there are undertones here of her own marriage contract) and the despoiling of their native land by 'Muscovite beadles'. As homesickness causes Oksana to lose strength, the audience is left in no doubt as to whose views were originally correct. When Stepan suggests returning to the peace and calm of Ukraine, Oksana erupts: 'What are you saying? Calm? Ukraine's will is broken, she is prostrate under Moscow's feet, is this your world – this Ruin? [the historical name for Ukraine's post-Khmelnytskyi decline]. I too would rapidly become *calm* in a coffin.'[79] Significantly, this was Ukraïnka's one play that went unperformed, both under the tsars and the Soviets (it was, not too surprisingly, popular in the diaspora). However, similar themes can be found in her other works, for example the play *Captives of Babylon* (1902), which, as well as providing an obvious allegory for subject Ukraine, contains a not particularly oblique attack on

> those, who in captivity,
> Have learned to use the language of our foes.
> How shall such understand their native song,
> And how can it be sung in alien speech ...
> To suffer chains is shame unspeakable,
> But to forget them is far worse disgrace.[80]

Slavophilia

The creation of the idea of 'Asian' Russia can also be seen in Ukraine's position in the nineteenth-century between Slavophiles and Westernisers. Like Russia, Ukraine had its fair share of both, but the two were not in strict opposition as they were in Russia. Industrialisation, the first stirrings of Russian capitalism and the confrontation with the West also produced social tensions in Ukraine, but, as the modern Ukrainian writer Mykola Riabchuk has argued: 'Ukrainian nativists felt threatened by [and were reacting against] Russification more than Westernization ... because the discourse of Russian dominance was mostly nativist and anti-Western, Ukrainian "emancipational" discourse became pro-Western and anti-nativist ... while their separatism was centrifugal in regard to Russia, it had to be centripetal in regard to Europe.'[81] In the late nineteenth century, therefore, the myth of Europe began to play an increasingly important part in the Ukrainian self-image. Not unproblematically. Shevchenko's deconstructive attack on imperial St Petersburg had helped produce a certain inward focus. Ivan Nechui-Levytskyi and others argued that the essence of Ukrainian literature and culture was its popular base (*narodnist* and *natsionalnist*), as opposed to Russian 'cosmopolitanism'.[82] Although many Ukrainians objected to Russian influence because they saw themselves as European, for many other Ukrainians Europeanism followed from opposition to Russification, and was fairly skin-deep. According to Riabchuk again, taking the example of Hrushevskyi, '[his] Westernism was more the obverse of his anti-

Russianism than proof of his commitment to modernity.'[83] In Lesia Ukraïnka's *Little-Russian Writers in Ukraine* (1899), the adoption of Western ideas is specifically and candidly presented as a means of avoiding assimilation to the Russian cultural sphere, with its relatively ambiguous attitude to Europe – although, as Drahomanov was fond of pointing out, 'the new European ideas of democracy and liberalism' came to Ukraine through St Petersburg: 'they appeared in Ukraine for the first time not in Ukrainian attire, not in the Ukrainian language, but in the Russian.'[84]

Most Ukrainian 'Europeans' still didn't really know the West. It was left to Drahomanov and others, such as the Galician writer Ivan Franko (1856–1916), to appreciate the idea of Europe for its own sake and attack the 'poison' of 'Ukrainian *Khomiakovism*' – by which Drahomanov meant the anti-Western Russian Slavophilia of writers like Aleksei Khomiakov.[85] Riabchuk argues against misinterpreting the fact that most nineteenth-century Ukrainians called themselves Slavophiles. Local Slavophilism was a practical means of giving sufficient space to all the varieties of Ukrainian identity, to both Little Russianism and Ukrainophilism, rather than an indication of general Russophilism, although this was another of the tendencies it encompassed. The Cyrylo-Methodian Society of the 1840s, for example (which included Kostomarov, Kulish and, indirectly, Shevchenko), called itself pan-Slavist. But one of its number, Heorhii Andruzkyi (born 1827), drew up a proposal for a Slavic union that would have had seven members: 'Ukraine, including the Black Sea, Galicia and Crimea', 'Poland with Poznan and Lithuania', 'Bessarabia with Moldavia and Wallachia', 'the Eastern Sea, Serbia, Bulgaria and the Don' – but no Russia.[86]

It might also be pointed out that the Ukrainians developed their own version of the Polish myth of the nation as 'suffering Christ' – except that, unlike Poland or Russia, Ukraine's unique position astride the Catholic and Orthodox worlds would make it the redeemer of *all* the Christian peoples of the Earth, not just the (eastern) Slavs.[87] To others, the link with Russia was an important part of their identity. The idea that Ukraine was 'European' was not universally accepted. Gogol, for example, in his essay *A Look at the Making of Little Russia* (1832), argued that Cossack identity in fact emerged through the constant struggle with Asia. The very traits beloved of nineteenth-century Ukrainian Romantics – individualism, courage and a martial culture – had developed because the Ukrainians had been forced to 'turn the Tatars' own methods of warfare against them'. Ukraine's open geography had also encouraged this effect: in contrast to those hiding in the forests of the north, only 'a warlike people could unite in' the steppe.[88] Whether through origin or mimicry, the Cossacks' 'Asian' character was therefore obvious in their dress, physiognomy and methods of warfare.

Ukraine's lack of obvious geographical borders (compare chapter thirteen) also forced it to look to the north-east and seek the assistance of Russia. Gogol remarked that 'if there had been a natural border from mountains or the sea on [just] one side, then the people who settled here would have held on to their own political way of life and would have formed a separate state' from the Russians and Poles – but historically (sic) they did not (unfortunately Gogol was too lazy to complete the history of Ukraine he once planned to write).[89] Nevertheless, the myth that the divide between Ukrainian and Russian culture mirrors that between the 'European' and the 'Asian' survives to the present day.

Conclusions

The various choices open to nineteenth-century Ukrainians in Romanov Russia were only partially resolved by 1914. Even individual families could be divided. Amongst the Shulhins, scions of Poltava Cossack stock, for example, Yakiv (1851–1911), the historian, and his son Oleksandr (1889–1960), who became the minister of foreign affairs in the short-lived independent Ukrainian state created after 1917, were famous Ukrainophiles; amongst their distant relations, Vitalii Shulgin (1882–78), the founder of the Kiev paper *Kievlianin*, and his son Vasilii (1878–1978), a leading White publicist, were Russian monarchists and notorious Ukrainophobes.[90] Within the Ukrainian movement, radical nationalism coexisted with moderate populism and empire loyalism, but the latter predominated. As of 1914 rather more Ukrainians were cast in the mould of Lesia Ukraïnka's Stepan than in that of her Oksana.

Russia, on the other hand, remained frozen in postures of denial.[91] As the distinguished British academic R.W. Seton-Watson remarked in 1917, 'never even in the history of national movements was there a more perverse example of a government kindling, by its stupid intolerance, centrifugal tendencies among a population which might easily have been appeased with a tithe of what it afterwards came to demand.'[92] It could also be argued that, after the appearance of radical 'Young Ukrainian' nationalism, the Russian authorities feared that this would be the eventual 'Mazepist' destination of all Ukrainian activists. A policy of reasoned concession may have only served to stoke the fire. From either perspective, a policy promoting cultural distinction was but the first step on the road to national separatism.[93] Whatever their motivation, however, for the late tsarist regime, Ukraine was an obvious blind spot compared to Poland or Finland.

6

The Habsburg Alternative

Identities were also fluid amongst the Ukrainians who lived under the Habsburgs, although, in Galicia at least, a more decisive resolution of possibilities was achieved by 1914 (in the Habsburg empire the Ukrainians were known as 'Rusyns' or, in the English version, 'Ruthenians' until the 1890s).[1] As in Romanov Russia, the Ruthenians were part of a multi-ethnic empire, subject to the twin pressures of national revival (their own and others') and assimilation to the imperial culture. However, in the Habsburg empire arguments over identity were more than just the concern of small groups of intellectuals. Elementary schooling had been compulsory since 1781,[2] largely in the vernacular, and the choice of what that vernacular would be, as Ernest Gellner and others have argued, would have a massive effect on the development of identities as the pace of social development began to quicken in the nineteenth century. Also crucial was the question of which language and culture would take precedence at a higher level and determine the criteria for entry into 'developed' society. The two issues dominated the politics of the nineteenth century.

Rusyns, Austrians or Poles?

Between the annexation of Galicia in 1772 and the 'springtime of nations' in 1848 local Ruthenian society was split more or less in three. Rus patriots coexisted with Polonophiles and 'Austrians', although boundaries between the three groups were neither precise nor mutually exclusive. The language of primary education was either Polish or, after 1818, the old-fashioned clerical 'Slaveno-Rusyn' of the Rus patriots, but the only languages of higher education were Polish and German. It was therefore still the case that many Ruthenians would adopt a Polish identity if they wished to move in a 'higher' culture. Indeed, Roman Szporluk has argued that 'the enormous attractiveness of the Polish national project to "Ruthenians"' even under Austrian rule meant that 'there was more Polonization ... after 1795 than there had been in the four centuries between 1370 and 1772'.[3] Significantly, the attempt to establish a Studium Ruthenum in Lviv failed in 1809 because Ruthenian students themselves preferred an education in Polish or German.[4] In the 'alphabet controversy' of the 1830s, many conservative Ruthenians advocated the adoption of the Latin alphabet and Polish orthography as a means of broadening literacy and cultural access (had they succeeded, Galician and Dnieper Ukrainians would have drifted even further apart). The 'high' culture of Polish literature that had been in development since at least the sixteenth century as yet had no real local Ruthenian rival. Until one was created, the mere fact of education could make a Ruthenian a Pole.

On the other hand, although social and cultural conditions encouraged the Ruthenian elite to Polonise, that elite was still small, and there was much less chance of the mass of Ruthenian peasants ever becoming Polonised. Social conditions in Galicia were such that it is fair to say that, if a Ruthenian was not a cleric or an artisan, he or she would be a peasant (in status and income many lower clergy were in any case barely elevated above their peasant flock). Not all Poles were nobles, but nearly all nobles were Poles. This created a gulf too vast to cross. Galician peasants were notorious for sticking pitchforks in the hated Polish landlords whenever they got the chance, as in the particularly violent disturbances of 1846. Polonisation of the Ruthenian elite made little impact on this basic social fact. There would therefore always be a reservoir of support for the explicitly anti-Polish versions of Ruthenian identity, both Ukrainophile and Russophile, that began to develop in the later nineteenth century. Anti-noble populism explains the otherwise surprising centrality of the Cossack myth in Ruthenian identity – as the Galicians played only a marginal role in the historical Cossack movement (though the Galicians were closer to their spiritual successors, the *haidamaky* of Right Bank Ukraine who led peasant revolts in the eighteenth century). The Uniate clergy was also fairly resistant to Polonisation.

Furthermore, the social changes induced by Joseph II's reforms were gradually equalising the terms of competition between Ruthenians and Poles. The previously unbridled social power of Polish landlords was now restrained by Austrian law. The more repressive aspects of serfdom were removed in 1781 and the institution itself abolished in 1848. Education reform led to the gradual emergence of a local intelligentsia and strengthened the Ruthenian presence in the major towns. The Habsburgs also gave the Uniate Church (now usually called the Greek Catholic Church) equal status with the Roman Catholics. The Church had been in a pretty parlous condition in 1772, with its ill-educated clergy and feeble hierarchy unable to provide an effective defence against Polonisation. By the early nineteenth century, it was the main national institution – a remarkable transformation from the situation in

1596–1620. Having once been seen by many Orthodox as a threat to Ruthenian identity, it was now the best means of preserving it from outright Polonisation. Austrian rule also consolidated boundaries by making it extremely difficult to move from one faith to another. That said, the Austrians also did the Ruthenians a disservice by lumping together the old Rus palatinate (eastern Galicia) with western Galicia (Kraków and Sandomierz) to form a unified Galician province in which the Poles predominated, thanks to strength of numbers in the west and dominance of the upper social strata in the east. It is interesting to speculate what might have happened if the old division had remained. Significantly, the call to reestablish it rose to the top of the Ruthenians' political agenda very early in the nineteenth century (1848).

The changing nature of Polish society and Polish nationalism was also a factor exercising both pull and push on the Ruthenians. During the 1830–1 Polish uprising the Poles alienated the Ruthenians with their unthinking assumption that they would back the Polish cause narrowly defined both ethnically and socially; i.e. a revolt led by Polish aristocrats. In fact, the uprising had the opposite effect, encouraging the Ruthenians to copy Polish tactics and develop their own countervailing nationalism in the 1830s and 1840s. For a brief period after 1831 there was some possibility of *rapprochement* as many Poles switched to the idea of reviving a commonwealth of four nations (Poles, Ukrainians, Belarusians and Lithuanians) and adopted a more radical social agenda. Based on the 'modernising', anti-feudal Polish nationalism that had been emerging since 1795, this 'Young Poland' had considerable emancipatory appeal to radical Ruthenian democrats like Kasper Cięglewicz (1807–86). During the 'springtime of nations' in 1848 the Ruthenians set up both an anti-Polish Supreme Ruthenian Council (*Holovna Ruska Rada*) and a Polonophile Ruthenian Assembly (*Ruskii Sobor*). Young Ruthenians often backed the Poles and 'revolution', generally defined, whenever there seemed a danger of the Supreme Ruthenian Council siding with the conservative Austrian authorities.

After the second revolt in 1863, however, most Poles reverted to a more narrowly Polish agenda, and the rising tide of Polonising ethnonationalism typified by Roman Dmowski and the slogan of '*Polak-Katolik*' (Polishness and Roman Catholicism being now assumed to be synonymous) drove the two communities definitively apart.[5] In the new Polish national mythology, in the life-and-death struggle with Russia in which Poland was seen as the *antemurale Christianitatis* and the suffering 'Christ of nations', there was no room for the Ruthenians. Most Poles saw 'Ruthenianism' as a schismatic and self-interested conspiracy of the local Greek Catholic clergy or, ironically given that many Russians regarded it as a Polish conceit, considered it an invention of Russia or the local Austrian authorities seeking to counterbalance their local dominance.[6] By the late nineteenth century Polish and Ruthenian society only overlapped in some rural backwaters, such as the Lemko region, and amongst the *Latynnyky*, the small number of Roman Catholic Ruthenians. The Ruthenians became increasingly vocal in their demands for political boundaries to protect culural divisions, calling for the division of Galicia into Polish and Ruthenian halves.[7]

In the early part of the century there had been a 'Ukrainian school' in Polish literature. Writers like Seweryn Goszczyński (1801–76) had peddled a romanticised view of a tolerant and diverse Commonwealth before the seventeenth-century 'Deluge', often delivered through the mouth of the semi-mythical Cossack prophet Zvenihora (Mojsej Wernyhora). More typical of the later nineteenth century, however, were the historical novels of Henryk Sienkiewicz (1846–1916): the trilogy *With Fire and Sword*, *The Deluge* and *Fire in the Steppe*. Sienkiewicz's epics which helped win him the Nobel Prize for Literature in 1905, are rollercoaster rides of adventure, valour and romance in the style of Walter Scott or Alexander Dumas, but, put simply, the Ukrainians are always the bad guys. *With Fire and Sword* (1883) in particular presents a dichotomised view of the 1648 revolt that is the complete reverse of the Ukrainian perspective – Prince Wiśniowiecki is the hero and defender of civilisation; Khmelnytskyi its enemy, exploiting a tide of anarchic anger amongst the Cossacks, described as 'those wild restless masses that fret on the land' (not that Sienkiewicz knew Ukraine well – the banks of his river Dnieper are crawling with the alligators he saw on the Mississippi during a trip to America). Sienkiewicz's depiction of Cossack revels left a lasting impression on generations of Polish schoolchildren:

Vodka splashed out of open barrels in which dancing Cossacks dipped their steaming heads and other nightmare shapes reeled about in alcoholic frenzy. Huge bonfires burned in the streets and in the town square where whole carcasses roasted on the spits, and flaming casks of pitch cast a lurid glow on the shuttered windows. The scarlet shadows of reflected fires that leaped about along the tiled rooftops made it seem as if the town was already burning. Nothing seemed human in that savage mass, wild as a storm at sea. Its sound was crazed laughter, the bellowing of slaughtered animals, and wild howls and brays that would have been more natural if they'd come from wolves. In all that frightful chaos, shrill Tatar whistles piped a hellish music while blind men, the wandering soothsayers of the Ukraine, kept time for mournful Cossacks ditties with their lyres, fiddles and rattles made out of hollow bones.

One glance at this scene was enough to tell that a single inflammatory spark thrown on this powder keg would turn the Ukraine into a funeral pyre and let loose a holocaust of murder such as the country had never seen before.[8]

Some of these stereotypes were revived in 1999 when Jerzy Hoffman's lavish film version of Sienkiewicz's epic debuted as the most expensive ($8.5m) and probably most popular Polish film ever made (330,000 people went to see it on its opening weekend). Hoffman discussed the project at length with old Ukrainian contacts and actually toned down the Ukrainophobia of the original novel – with Wiśniowiecki portrayed as something of a dissolute and Khmelnytskyi, played by the Ukrainian theatre favourite Bohdan Stupka, not necessarily the anti-hero. Still, the film attracted some criticism in Ukraine. It would have to have been completely reinvented not to.

The Tyrol of the East

A second option for many Ruthenians was to become so-called 'political Austrians', in response not only to the cultural and material opportunities offered by the new dominant power, but also to the periodic relative favour granted by the Austrians to the Ruthenians as a counterweight to the Poles. Large numbers of Ruthenians were *Kaisertreue* (loyal to the Crown) – even in the 1990s one could still find pictures of Emperor Franz Joseph in west Ukrainian homes.

On the other hand, Habsburg Austria never sought to become a 'nationalising state', even in the limited manner of Romanov Russia. The serious attempt to weld the Habsburgs' disparate possessions into something resembling a homogeneous *Kulturnation* with a common identity or *Staatsidee* lasted barely a century after the accession of Maria Theresa and the shock of the loss of Silesia to Prussia in 1740. The limited success of Joseph II's Germanising reforms in 1780–90 demonstrated that the German-speaking minority was spread too thinly across the empire (as of 1910, the German element made up only 24% of the population; even in the Austrian half of the empire it constituted only 36%). In the relative backwater of Galicia, German language and culture were attractive to some. A good example would be the writer Leopold von Sacher-Masoch (1836–95), whose German-language tales of rural idiocy and sexual peccadilloes gave rise to the term 'masochism'. Austrian bureaucrats and state resources were especially thin on the ground, however. 'Nation-building' therefore had to be rethought as an indirect project involving the cooption of local elites.

The aftermath of the 1848 revolution and the military defeats of 1859 (Italy) and 1866 (Prussia) forced the Habsburgs to abandon any serious 'nationalising' ambitions.[9] After the 1860s, political power and, just as importantly, control over the key resources of school and seminary were shared between Vienna and the peripheral nationalities. On the one hand, this decentralisation after the creation of a dual monarchy in 1867 allowed Hungary to become rather more of a paradigmatic nationalising state, insofar as the limited resources of the late nineteenth century permitted (see page 113). In Galicia, on the other hand, indirect rule through Polish satraps was Vienna's preferred option. Polish separatism, however, was another matter entirely. The Ruthenians were not left to their own devices, but granted key institutional and social resources in an attempt to contain Polish ambition within channels that served Habsburg interests.

The Ruthenians were also fortunate that the events of 1867 came a generation after the revolution of 1848. A local 'Rus patriotism' already existed. This was not yet a fully fledged nationalism as such, more of a bridge to (both) later Russophilism and Ukrainophilism. Nor was it necessarily incompatible with Austrianism or even Polonism. Rus patriotism was above all a defensive preference for the traditional Greek Catholic faith and its historical foundations in the Church of 'Kiev, Halych and all Rus'. Its ranks were dominated by conservative clergymen, who did not think a Ruthenian 'high culture' possible. A local vernacular literature was beginning to develop, most notably the folkloric almanac *The Nymph of the Dniester* (1837) by the 'Ruthenian Triad' of Markiian Shashkevych (1811–43), Ivan Vahylevych (1811–66) and Yakiv Holovatskyi (1814–88), but most Ruthenians continued to use the *yazychie* (macaroni), a hotchpotch language with no formal grammar. The Triad had little lasting impact. Shashkevych died young, Vahylevych switched to promoting the idea of a Polish-Ruthenian union under Polish leadership after 1848 and Holovatskyi ended up a Russophile.

The most important limitation, however, was that in the 1830s and 1840s the Ruthenians were only just becoming aware of the idea that they might share a common bond with their brethren in the Romanov empire. The Supreme Ruthenian Council's famous declaration during the 1848 revolution that they were 'part of a great Ruthenian people that speaks the same language and numbers 15 million, of whom two and a half million live in Galicia' was in fact a late substitution for the formula 'we belong to the Galician-Rus people, who number two and a half million'.[10] The former idea had yet to fully displace the latter.

Moscowphiles and Ukrainophiles

After 1848, Ruthenian society began to differentiate further, especially as the revival of Polonising pressure in the 1860s necessitated a more effective response than the conservative Rus patriots could provide. When the Polish count Agenor Gołuchowski, three times the Habsburg viceroy in Galicia between 1849 and 1875, attempted, as he saw it, to 're-Polonise' the region, Ruthenian society was already strong enough to resist. When he revived Latinisation proposals in 1859, the possibilities of the 1830s had dissipated and the reaction was almost uniformly hostile. Nevertheless, the Ruthenians increasingly felt the need to posit a high culture to counter that of the Poles, and they were learning from the advances of their Slavic neighbours the Czechs, Slovaks and Slovenians that broad sectors of the population had to be mobilised to create an effective national movement. However, as vernacularising reformers sought to narrow the gap between the literary/clerical language and popular dialect, Slaveno-Rusyn came increasingly to be seen as an unsuitable instrument. Its admixtures were difficult to codify and a long way removed from the many local Galician dialects. The 'Old Ruthenians' therefore came to be seen as increasingly out of touch with the demands of the modern age.

A second option was the use of Russian. Slaveno-Rusyn was close to Church Slavonic and linguistic borrowings could bring it closer to nineteenth-century literary Russian (the first Russophiles or 'Moscowphiles' used a joint Galician-Russian recension of Church Slavonic). There were obvious reasons for this. Russian culture was entering the 'golden age' of Pushkin, Tolstoy and Lermontov. Russia was a powerful and prestigious empire, and if the Ruthenians were to join a new imagined community stretching from the 'Carpathians to the Urals' (or the Pacific) the mathematics of their long-standing struggle with the Poles would be transformed. Some Ruthenians, such as Ivan Naumovych (1862–91), argued that Russian was derived from 'Little Russian' anyway and that it was simply being 'readopted'. Indeed, according to the modern Lviv historian Yaroslav Hrytsak, 'the Muscovite orientation became dominant in the political and social life of Galician Ukrainians between the 1860s and 1880s.'[11] Many local peasants clung to the naïve belief in the saviour tsar who would 'devour the Jews, chastise the Poles, seize the land from the lords and dispense it to the local peasants'.[12]

Russian patronage, however, implied the adoption of Orthodoxy. Some Ruthenians were happy to convert, but to others the Greek Catholic Church remained the foundation of their identity, and locals were aware that the Romanovs had banned the Church on their own territory in 1839 (the Right Bank) and 1875 (Kholm). A second problem for the Russophiles was their increasing preference for standard literary Russian, and the Russian language after Pushkin had moved a long way from local Galician dialect. By the 1890s the Russophiles had effectively opted for a minority 'high' culture. Their 'top-down' efforts were never likely to be as effective as the 'bottom-up' strategy of the Ukrainophiles (see page 108). Geopolitics also played a part. Russia provided increasing financial and material support for the Russophiles after the Congress of Berlin in 1878 and the Bosnia crisis of 1908 caused it to seek ways of restraining Habsburg ambition in the Balkans and to revive its claim to the remnants of Rus. Vienna's countervailing reaction, strengthened by the Vatican's hostility to the spread of Orthodoxy, led to a major treason trial of Russophile leaders in 1882, and more than negated Russia's efforts. Potential Russophiles were also likely to be disillusioned by the Russian autocracy's heavy-handed behaviour in Dnieper Ukraine, especially the restrictions of 1863 and 1876, about which the numerous émigrés from the east kept the Galicians well informed. Russophilism was in serious decline by 1914. In the 1907 elections to the Vienna parliament the Russophiles won only five seats.[13]

The Ukrainophiles, by contrast, won 22 seats. The Ukrainophiles also promised inclusion in a wider community, which in their version stretched 'from the Carpathians to the Caucasus'. Although smaller than imperial Russia, this alternative eastern fraternity also had much to offer. Despite the later adoption by the Galicians of the 'Piedmont' theory (see page 118) leading to a strong influence passing from west to east, the initial flow was the other way around. Above all, the standardisation of Ukrainian by Panteleimon Kulish provided a medium of east Ukrainian origin that was capable of bridging the gap between the many Galician dialects in a way the Russophiles could not. The Galicians would certainly have found this task difficult on their own since the majority of all Ukrainian dialects are in the hills, mountains and river valleys of the west. Self-generated consensus was unlikely in such circumstances. In 1893 the Austrian authorities recognised the use of Kulish's version of Ukrainian in the schools, thereby granting *de facto* supremacy to the Ukrainophiles.

Other factors sealed the victory of the Ukrainophiles. Their populist Socialism was well suited to the increasingly impoverished countryside, whereas the Russophiles were tied to the most conservative regime in Europe. By the 1900s the Ukrainophiles had created a whole civil society of peasant cooperatives, land banks, reading rooms, scholarly societies and political parties. The Russophiles could only offer pale imitations. Last but not least, between the 1860s and 1900s Austria had transformed itself into a constitutional monarchy, with both a national and local parliaments (diets) elected by universal suffrage. The Galicians grew used to organising their own affairs. By 1914 they were even able to negotiate a new arrangement with Vienna. Galicia would not be formally divided, but there would be separate boards of education and separate Polish and Ukrainian chambers in the local diet. The possibility of a proper Ukrainian university was to be investigated. Only the outbreak of war prevented the changes being implemented.

The Mythic Structure of Galician Ukrainophilism

In the Russian empire there were many Ukrainians who were working towards establishing a sense of separate Ukrainian identity, but in the main they were trying to deconstruct the idea of a common Russo-

Ukrainian identity from within basically fraternal assumptions. The historian Mykola Kostomarov, for example, argued that separate east Slavic peoples had emerged as a result of geography and diverse political traditions, working to differentiate a common ethnolinguistic and even cultural base.[14] In Galicia, however, the Ukrainophiles developed a more radical version of national identity that placed Ukrainians and Russians on separate sides of much sharper divides. This Galician version also took on a harder edge by aping the style of the radical Polish movement with which it was forced to compete.

In this constant rivalry with the Poles, the Galician Moscowphiles defined the Ruthenians as part of 'Russia' (*Rossiia*) and therefore as a self-sustaining civilisation, an 'other' power to European Poland. The Ukrainophiles' alternative imaginative strategy was to redefine the European family of nations. As the Poles' own *antemurale* myth either ignored the Ruthenians or marginalised them as part of the 'east', it was imperative to shift that boundary outward, adopting and adapting the Polish myth and adding Ruthenian elements. It made more sense for the Galicians to argue that all Ruthenians/Ukrainians were 'European', than to argue that the European and Habsburg frontiers were one and the same. This strategy had its roots in the Cossacks' version of the Sarmatian idea – *Sarmatia Europea* and *Sarmatia Asiatica*, with the frontier of the latter beginning on the Don. In the nineteenth century this myth began to take on new forms, with the Ruthenians taking up its reworking by the Right Bank Pole Franciszek Duchiński (1816–93), who proposed a much broader dualism – Europe as a whole versus the alien and threatening 'Turanian' (i.e. pan-Turkic) world of Russia, which he defined as originating with the Severianians (the most easterly of the southern Rus tribes who lived near what is now Chernihiv) and stretching to the Pacific.[15]

The central role in creating the new Galician ideology, however, was played by native historians, in particular Mykhailo Hrushevskyi (1866–1934) during his tenure of the first-ever chair in Ukrainian History at Lviv University from 1894 to 1914.[16] Although Hrushevskyi built on the works of predecessors such as Kostomarov and Antonovych, his rediscovery of the myth of Rus and the exclusion of Russia from that myth (see pages 1–20) had a revolutionary effect on both Ukrainian historiography and national identity.[17] By renaming Rus as 'Ukraine-Rus', the Ukrainians no longer had to rely on the antiquarian romanticism of the Cossack myth as the main foundation of their identity. After Hrushevskyi, they could invert prevailing stereotypes and claim that their culture was older than Russia's – insofar as Russia was cultured at all, it was only so in virtue of having stolen Ukraine's birthright. (Stefan Tomashivskyi [1875–1930] performed a similar service for the local history of Galicia but the myth of Ukraine-Rus now provided a more secure link between the two halves of the Ruthenian nation.[18]) Russia was redefined as

Muscovy, a natural outsider in the European concord of states. Free from its influence, Ukraine would be a natural part of the European order.

The most obvious sign of this shift in psychology was a change of name. By 1900 the Galician Ruthenians tended to call themselves and their brethren across the border 'Ukrainians' (the terminological change drew on seventeenth-century precedents and had first been introduced in Kharkiv in the early nineteenth century, before being popularised by Shevchenko).[19] This did not mean abandoning the claim of descent from Rus implied by the older name Ruthenian or Rus-yn (*rusyny*); exactly the opposite. 'Rusyn' was too easily confused with 'Russian'. 'Ukrainian' was therefore a means of sidestepping Russia's linguistic and historiographical monopolisation of Rus – and of making sure that the Ukrainians would no longer be confused with the Russians.

Other elements in the new Galician 'Occidentalism' included the idea of a distinct and distinctly European Ukrainian 'space' promoted by geographers like Stepan Rudnytskyi (see pages 280–4). Anthropologists like Khvedir Vovk (1847–1918), who was born in Poltava but conducted much of his research in Galicia, argued that not only were there clear 'racial' differences between the Ukrainians and the Russians, but also that the Ukrainians were more closely related to the Danubian southern Slavs than to their northern neighbours.[20] In the arts, the writers of the 'Young Muse' movement rejected the traditional realist and populist approach in favour of what was fashionably West European. In architecture, official Habsburg styles coexisted with many fine Secessionist buildings in turn-of-the-century Lviv, with local architects such as Ivan Levynskyi (1851–1919) producing a unique combination of Art Nouveau and local folk influences, particularly in the detail of public façades, decorative metalwork, ceramics and stained glass.[21]

Not that such ideas were absent in Russian-ruled Ukraine: they were implicit in the incipient nationalism of Kostomarov and fairly explicit in the writing of Borys Hrinchenko and Lesia Ukraïnka, and of course in Shevchenko's poetry. There was increasing contact between west and east and Galician ideas began to filter back over the border. However, the overall paradigms of nationalist thought in Galicia and in Dnieper Ukraine were very different. There was a radical fringe in Dnieper Ukraine, but not a radical mainstream. Galician Ukrainians were prepared to think 'Beyond the Limits of the Possible' (the title of a 1900 essay by Ivan Franko) in a way that most Dnieper Ukrainians were not. In 1900 most of the latter still believed in some kind of federal link with Russia and a day-to-day concentration on apolitical 'cultural work'. The Galicians on the other hand had a concrete political programme, expressed by Yuliian Bachynskyi (1870–1940) and others in the slogan of a 'Ukrainian, Independent, United State' stretching 'from the Sian [river] to the Caucasus'. No longer were their ambitions confined to just Galician autonomy, but the unity of all Ukrainian lands in a single independent entity.

Transcarpathia: 'Over' or 'Under' the Carpathians?

The Galicians were not the only west Ukrainians, however; nor was Galician Ukrainianism the only possible future for all west Ukrainians. Although the new national identity was well established by the eve of World War I in the core territories around Lviv and Stanyslaviv (now Ivano-Frankivsk), in periphery regions where would-be Ukrainians mingled with (would-be) Poles, Belarusians and Slovaks, *tuteshni* ('local', from *tut* meaning 'here') and overlapping identities still predominated. Nor was a Ukrainian identity preordained. Areas like Brest/Berestia or the Lemko region were specific targets of Ukrainian nationalism in the nineteenth century but were lost in the twentieth. Przemyśl/Peremyshl might at one time have been a rival to Lviv, but the local Polish movement eclipsed its Ukrainian rival after 1863. In Chełm/Kholm, once a leading centre of Greek Catholic culture but after 1795 located over the border in Russia, the local Ukrainian movement faded quickly after the Church was abolished in 1875. A potential *Orthodox* west Ukrainian identity almost developed when Chełm became part of interwar Poland, but was snuffed out by the Roman Catholic Church in the 1930s and the population exchanges of the 1940s.[22] In Volhynia, however, it survived, thanks to the region becoming the last stronghold of the Ukrainian Autocephalous Orthodox Church (see page 139). Berestia is now in Belarus, the other three regions in south-eastern Poland. Only Volhynia is part of modern Ukraine.

The case of Carpathian or Hungarian Ruthenia (*Uhorska Rus*) provides the most interesting counterpoint to Galicia (an 'alternative to the alternative', as it were) and is both interesting in itself and an excellent illustration of the dangers of assuming that a given national identity is ever fixed or final. As in neighbouring Galicia, rival Ukrainophile and Russophile movements appeared in the nineteenth century, but the belief in local exceptionalism, the idea that the local Slavs were a separate 'Rusyn' nationality, went much deeper than Rus patriotism in Galicia. Moreover, Carpathian Ruthenia demonstrated how vulnerable potential Ukrainians were to a nineteenth-century 'nationalising' regime, whose nationalism (Hungarian) was more powerful than Austria's and which, unlike its Polish equivalent, was backed by the resources of the state. Local Ruthenian and Slovak identities also overlapped; particularly amongst the more westerly dialectal groups it was difficult to distinguish between the two. Consequently, identities remained fluid up to and beyond 1914, and a much greater proportion of would-be Ukrainians assimilated to the dominant imperial culture. Even the very name of the territory was disputed. From the point of view of Lviv, Kiev or St Petersburg, the region was 'Trans-carpathia', *beyond* the Carpathians, whereas to Budapest or the local Rusyn movement it made more sense to describe it as *Pidkarpatska Rus* 'Sub-Carpathia', *below* and to the west of the mountain ridges that marked the border with Galicia. To Hungarian nationalists it is simply *Felvidek* (the uplands).

In most eastern Slavic versions of the history of Carpathian Ruthenia, it is claimed that the area was occupied by the Slavs several centuries before the Hungarians arrived in 896 (Hungarian historiography tends to argue that the local Slavs arrived in the thirteenth century as a result of a Hungarian invitation to settle their unprotected mountain borders). In both the Ukrainophile and Russophile versions it is argued that the Slavs (mainly the White Croat tribe) had strong links with Kievan Rus; in the local Rusyn version it is argued that a separate local kingdom or *Ruska Kraina* existed until the time of its last independent ruler, Prince Fedir Koriiatovych (1393–1414).[23] It is also asserted that the local population belonged to a separate Mukachevo eparchy centred on the Basilian monastery at Chernecha Hora since the time of the mission of SS Cyril and Methodius to Moravia in 862 (long before Kiev's Baptism in 988), and that this contributed to the strong Orthodox influence on the early Hungarian Church.[24] Rusyn activists therefore also claim that a distinct local identity emerged because 'Rusyn culture [was formed and] is continuing to form itself through the contact of two Slavic civilisations – the eastern and the western' – or, more baldly, that the Rusyn mentality and culture are definitively western in a way that general Ukrainian identity is not.[25]

It is not disputed that in the eleventh century the region came under the Hungarian crown of St Stephen. Hungarian culture was established in the foothill towns of Mukachevo and Uzhhorod, but the Slavic population in the valleys and mountains beyond was left largely undisturbed in its rural backwater. Its identity was above all religious, which after the Union of Uzhhorod in 1646 meant the local branch of the Uniate Church established in Mukachevo. Increasingly, however, the locals came under Catholic pressure to undermine the original terms of the Union and fully subordinate the diocese to the Hungarian Roman Catholic bishop of Eger. Salvation was provided by the more even-handed religious policy of Empress Maria Theresa, who feared that crude Catholicising pressure might drive the locals back to Orthodoxy and restored the Mukachevo diocese in 1771 (subsequently moved to Uzhhorod in 1777). These new institutional underpinnings and the development of a regional historicism to legitimise the status of the Church led to the first stirrings of a local national movement under Bishop Andrei Bachynskyi (served 1773–1809), who petitioned for the Uzhhorod diocese to be joined to the Galician Church in 1774 and 1807.

The education policies of Maria Theresa and Joseph II led to the appearance of some 300 schools in the region by 1806.[26] Education, however, meant assimilation to the dominant Hungarian culture. Despite a brief period after the suppression of the Hungarian uprising in 1849, when Vienna intervened more directly in local affairs to the benefit of the minorities, this was even more true once Hungarian direct rule was imposed following the creation of the Dual Monarchy in 1867. After the *Ausgleich* the Magyar plurality was more decisive than the German in Austria and grew from an estimated 41% in 1843 to 48% in 1910. Just as importantly, Hungarian nationalists behaved as if the whole eastern half of the Dual Monarchy was *Magyarország* ('Hungarian land') and sought to bolster their position through assimilation policies that were particularly attractive to the Carpathian Slavs (the 1868 nationality law allowed anyone to become a Magyar). As a consequence, the local Carpathian intelligentsia was overwhelmingly Hungarian-speaking right through to 1914, the only argument being about degrees of assimilation. The peasantry in the mountains were relatively unaffected, but the authorities in Budapest had more contact with them than their counterparts in St Petersburg had with their peasants. School networks were expanded, but Magyarised. There were 479 schools using variants of Ruthenian in 1874, but after the passing of particularly centralising school laws in 1902 and 1907 all were converted to Hungarian,[27] as were the lycées and universities. The political system was gerrymandered. Budapest refused to copy Austria's introduction of direct universal suffrage in 1907 and a curial system was used to ensure underrepresentation of the minorities.

Not surprisingly, alternatives to Magyar identity were at a much more embryonic stage before 1914.[28] Ukrainophilism was unable to build on the few beginnings made by Bachynskyi and the creation of a short-lived 'Uzhhorod District' in 1848–9 in response to the pleas of the Supreme Ruthenian Council in Lviv for the unification of Transcarpathia and Galicia. As in Galicia, Russophilism periodically made more sense than Ukrainophilism. At the crucial juncture of the late eighteenth and early nineteenth centuries, when local clerics and scholars began to use the idea of a local Slavic identity to defend themselves against Catholicisation, pan-Slavists tended to look to Russia. Activists such as Adolf Dobrianskyi (1817–1901) had often spent time at Russian universities and were impressed by the Russian army that passed through the Carpathians in 1848 on its way to suppress the revolution in Hungary (Dobrianskyi provided practical assistance). As in Galicia, however, Russophiles and Orthodox converts were increasingly seen as politically subversive, with a famous treason trial being brought in 1913–14.

The importance of the political factor and of the dissemination of culture through the education system was further demonstrated in the interwar period, when Transcarpathia became part of the new Czechoslovak state. The Prague authorities had good reason to fear Magyar irredentism and Russophilism was now associated with support for the USSR; but they had less reason to choose between Ukrainophilism and Rusynism. A general 'east Slavic' civil society – cultural organisations and political parties supported by a new school network – developed rapidly from a very low ebb, but the language they used (Ukrainian,

Russian or 'Rusyn') often depended on circumstance or a local teacher's preference. The main Ukrainian party (the Christian People's Party) was able symbolically to declare independence for 'Carpatho-Ukraine' as the Czechoslovak state was dismembered in 1939, but the extent of its popular support is often questioned (Ukrainian parties won 93% of the vote in elections held in February 1939, but participation was restricted). The region was joined to Ukraine by the Soviet-Czechoslovak treaty of 1945 and more thoroughly Ukrainianised, if only on the surface; but both a Rusyn and a Magyar movement have revived since 1991.

Support for Ukrainian nationalism in the region remains low. Local politicians have flirted with the idea of regional autonomy (78% of voters backed the idea of a 'special self-governing administrative territory' in a 1991 referendum), but not with outright separatism. Ukrainian independence may be encouraging locals to commit more wholeheartedly to an idea that required a degree of force to win support in 1945 or a new Slavic nation may be forming before our very eyes. It is probably too soon to tell.

Bukovyna: Gateway to the Carpathians

The other Habsburg Ruthenian province of Bukovyna (in German Bukowina, in Romanian Bucovina) has long been disputed territory, occupying a key frontier role in rival national mythologies. To Romanian historians such as Grigore Nandriş, Bukovyna, like neighbouring Moldova (Bukovyna was supposedly an integral part of Moldova from 1359 to 1774; many Romanians would argue that it is simply 'North Moldova'), was a 'Trojan Horse for Russian [i.e. east Slavic] colonial expansion to the Mediterranean'. As a key 'point of entry into the Carpathian chain' for 'the invaders of the east', it defined Romania's historical destiny as one of the guardian 'pillars of the entry gates towards Western Europe' and the route to Constantinople. The monastery at Suceava was the font of local Christianity – the site were a 'neo-Byzantine culture, unique in the Orthodox Christian community' was able to develop. Furthermore, according to Nandriş, 'before the annexation of Bukovyna by the Habsburgs between 1774 and 1777 there is no mention of the Slavo-Ruthenes of Bukovyna in any historical documents.' The Ukrainian element supposedly arrived after 1777 from Galicia in the north.[29]

For the Habsburgs, Bukovyna was a site for resisting such advances and also a model ethnic melting pot; for the local Jews the site of the unique 1909 electoral reform that gave then guaranteed nationality representation.[30] The Ukrainian point of view, represented by the historian Arkadii Zhukovskyi (born 1922) and others is that Bukovyna is the natural hinterland of the Ukrainian Carpathians. Long before the Moldovan period it was occupied by the Antes, and between 885 and 1340 was an integral part of first Rus and then the Kingdom of Galicia–Volhynia. The Moldovan period (the Romanians first crossed the Carpathians in numbers only at the end of the twelfth century) only lasted from 1359 (in southern Bukovyna) or (in the north) from the late fifteenth century until 1514. The local 'Shypynska Territory' was in any case as much a Ukrainian as a Romanian or Moldovan phenomenon. The local Orthodox Church was part of the Rus Church, then the Galician, then the 'Ukrainian-Moldovan' Church, even after the establishment of the metropolitanate at Suceava (Suchav) in 1401 – until 1781. From 1514 until 1775, Bukovyna was in any case under the Ottomans, but an indigenous Ukrainian majority survived and still numbered 68% at the onset of the Habsburg period.[31]

The prospects for the development of Ukrainophilism in Habsburg Bukovyna were better than in Transcarpathia but not as good as in Galicia. Austria was the governing power, but 'political Austrianism' was more influential than in Galicia, as it had the support of the numerically more significant German element and many local Jews, while the equivalent of the Poles in Galicia were the locally dominant Romanians – and the emergence of an independent Romanian state in 1858 gave a powerful boost to the alternative Romanian national project in the region. Unlike in Galicia, the rival nationalities, Ruthenians and Romanians, both belonged to the same, Orthodox, Church (which was dominated by the Romanians), although the linguistic distance between the two groups was much greater than in Galicia. A network of Ruthenian schools existed, but appeared fairly late – after 1848, alongside Ruthenian departments at the University of Chernivtsi (Cernăuți or Czernowitz) in 1875 and 1899.

Ukrainian and Romanian movements therefore competed in 1918, with the issue being settled by Romania's ability to commit the armed forces the Ukrainian Peoples Republic (see pages 119–51) could not. In the interwar period, the Ukrainophile movement regressed dramatically once relatively benign Austrian rule had been replaced by a Romanian state (and Romanian Orthodox Church) committed to the idea that all local Ukrainians were simply Romanians who had 'forgotten' their nationality and native tongue (all Ukrainian elementary schools were closed by 1926).[32] However, Romania overreached itself in its wartime alliance with Hitler, and the balance of arms was reversed. Bukovyna and southern Bessarabia (the region west of Odesa to the Danube, which now cuts off Moldova from the sea) were joined to Soviet Ukraine, first by the Molotov-Ribbentrop Pact in 1940 and then permanently in 1945.

With the return of open politics in the 1990s, the historical Ukrainian tradition has revived; but the modern oblast of Chernivtsi is a gerry-mandered entity, in which one (northern) half of Bukovyna is sandwiched together with the traditionally Romanian areas of Hertsa and Hotin (Khotyn). Unlike Transcarpathia, whose loose identity tends to make it stand aside from national politics, Chernivtsi is the one part of Ukraine where Ukrainian nationalism and a strong minority nationalism coexist. Romanian nationalists have continued to question the legal status of the region, pointing to the fact that other aspects of the Molotov–Ribbentrop Pact (the annexation of the Baltic states) were never accepted by international opinion and even questioning whether the 1991 referendum on Ukrainian independence could legitimately be held in the affected regions. The then-strong possibility of an invitation to join NATO trumped nationalist uncertainties and encouraged Bucharest to accept current borders in the 1997 state treaty with Ukraine, but doubts remain on the political fringes.

Other Alternatives: The Ukrainian Diasporas

The abolition of serfdom in the Habsburg empire, the continuing poverty of Galicia and the relative freedom of travel to the New World led to the creation of yet another Ukraine – the Ukrainian diaspora. From the mid-century onwards Ruthenian émigrés spread far and wide: to Australia, Argentina and Brazil, but the greatest numbers went to North America. Official statistics record 740,803 persons of Ukrainian origin in the USA (as of 1990) and 1,054,300 in Canada (1991).[33] As with many diasporas, these new Ukrainian communities helped to preserve a sense of national identity when this was under pressure at home, providing a refuge for ideas and organisations as well as individuals, such as the Ukrainian Churches and the Organisation of Ukrainian Nationalists (see pages 131–4). This function was strengthened by the fact that by the late nineteenth century Habsburg Ruthenians had a much higher level of national consciousness than other potential Ukrainians.[34]

This also meant, however, that the North American diaspora was doubly removed from the homeland. As well as the physical distance of the Atlantic, there was the psychological distance between their Galician origins and the rest of Ukraine (there were also many differences within the diaspora between those of Galician, Lemko or Transcarpathian origin). This distinction became even more pronounced after the redivision of homeland territories after 1920 and the traumas of World War II, which led to a new outflow of émigrés, but again, from western Ukraine only. Distance was of course also compounded by diasporisation, as émigrés adapted to their host states in varying degrees. The version of Ukrainian identity that developed in North America was therefore simultaneously both more 'traditional' and more 'modern' than that in Dnieper Ukraine. The Ukrainian language, for example, was not forced to adapt to the pressures of Soviet rule. Diaspora Ukrainians, however, particularly those of the second generation, did adapt to twentieth-century North America, becoming computer-literate and just as at home with the Rolling Stones as with Shevchenko. Many did not recognise the land they returned to after 1991.

There was also considerable out-migration from the Ukrainian territories in the Russian empire, but it was of a very different character.[35] First, because it was in the opposite direction – eastwards to agricultural territories in the Kuban and North Caucasus (which Ukrainians call *Malynovyi Klyn* or 'The Painted Wedge'), to Southern Siberia (*Siryi Klyn*, 'Grey Wedge') and even the Far East (*Zelenyi Klyn*, 'Green Wedge'), given the popularity of the sea route from Odesa; then to the new melting-pot cities in the Soviet period. Numerically, this was a larger movement than that to the New World, at its peak between the abolition of serfdom in 1861 and Khrushchev's 'Virgin Lands' campaign in the 1950s (which encouraged Slavic settlement in the 'virgin' Kazakh steppe). The last Soviet census in 1989 recorded 6.8 million Ukrainians resident in the USSR outside Ukraine, though Ukrainian sources go as high as ten to 12 or even 20 million.

Those leaving were not yet Ukrainians, however, but first Orthodox peasants and then Soviet settlers. The communities they helped to create were as much east Slavic or Soviet-Russian as they were Ukrainian. Those who left Ukraine brought with them dialect and folk memory, but they lacked the resources to create truly national communities. Things could have been different in the 1920s. Ukrainian Communist leaders like Mykola Skrypnyk patronised the eastern diaspora and sponsored the creation of Ukrainian schools and cultural institutions in neighbouring Russian territory (the eastern parts of Slobidska Ukraine that ended up in Voronezh, Kursk and Belgorod oblasts), in the Kuban and even the Far East. The experiment came to an abrupt end in 1932, because a successful Ukrainianisation was incompatible with the new Stalinist nationalism. Thereafter Ukrainians were extremely vulnerable to assimilation to the new Soviet-Russian culture, especially in third-party environments such as Central Asia or the Baltic republics.

Diaspora influence on the Ukrainian homeland therefore comes from two opposite directions. North American Ukrainians are often strongly nationalist but somewhat alien in their 'homeland'. The eastern diaspora, on the other hand, represents the other extreme – an identity that is more Soviet than Ukrainian.

Conclusions

By the turn of the century, the Galicians had developed a strong local nationalism that defined their identity against the Poles and others, but it was as yet unclear how they would relate to the rest of *Ukraina irredenta* (the title of a 1895 work by Yuliian Bachynskyi). In an article written in 1906 significantly entitled 'Galicia *and* Ukraine', Mykhailo Hrushevskyi expressed the fear that the divided Ukrainian territories might go their separate ways. The Ukrainians, 'like the Serbs and the Croats', would then form 'two nationalities on one ethnographic base'.[36] According to the Ukrainian historian Ihor Ševčenko, this did not happen because, despite the division of territories between the Romanov and Habsburg empire,

> three factors contributed to the preservation of Ukrainian national unity: first, the long period of [previous] time during which the major part of Ukrainian territory remained under the sway of one state, that is, the Polish-Lithuanian Commonwealth; second, the relatively short period of time during which this same territory was ruled by several states (1772–1945); third, the absence of complete Catholicisation in the western Ukrainian lands.[37]

The Croats and Serbs by contrast 'were divided by faith and frontiers from the eleventh century on'.[38] The two Ukraines were seemingly convergent in the early twentieth century, but nevertheless represented very different models of national identity. It was significant that, in the title of another article by Hrushevskyi, Galicia by the 1900s saw itself as the 'Ukrainian Piedmont'[39] – not only, following the model of Italian unification in 1860, the potential agent of national unity, but also the keeper of the true faith on behalf of the rest of Ukraine. Its nationalism was proselytising rather than inward-looking. Dnieper Ukraine did not necessarily yet accept this vision, however. In Kiev a nascent national movement still coexisted with empire loyalism. Hrushevskyi was, moreover, writing in the period before World War I, when it was far from clear how the two Ukraines could ever be brought together.

7

The Twentieth Century: Peasants into Ukrainians?

It is now something of a cliché in Ukrainian scholarship to claim, following the title of the benchmark 1996 history by the Lviv historian Yaroslav Hrtysak, that the twentieth century completed 'the formation of a modern Ukrainian nation'.[1] Even the controversial 'alternative' history by a group with supposed 'Eurasian' sympathies close to President Kuchma (his original chief of staff Dmytro Tabachnyk and others) claims that 'the central theme of the twentieth century is the uprising of the Ukrainian nation, the transformation of an ethnic community into a conscious political and cultural community'.[2] Clearly the independent Ukraine of 1991 was very different from the Ukraine, or several Ukraines, of 1914. However, this chapter will try to avoid the manifest destiny approach. The creation of the Ukrainian nation in its present form was far from inevitable. The fluctuating balance of power in Eastern Europe in the twentieth century has offered Ukraine a variety of possible futures. The main ones are discussed below.

Bobrinskii's Galician Project

World War I was not of Ukraine's doing, nor was it at all clear at the outset that it would serve Ukrainian interests. The philosopher and historian Viacheslav Lypynskyi saw only three possible outcomes, none of which was likely to benefit Ukraine. A Russian victory would lead to the occupation of Galicia and the destruction of the local Ukrainian movement; any Habsburg advance to the east would only lead to the export of the post-1867 'Galician model' of Polish-dominated administration to Right Bank Ukraine; while a draw, or Habsburg successes in the Balkans, would mean material Ukrainian losses on both sides and a further deflection of attention away from the 'Ukrainian question'.[3] On the Romanov side of the border, many Ukrainians were swept along with the patriotic mood of 1914 (or were browbeaten into going along with it), and leading figures such as Dmytro Doroshenko, Andrii Viazlov and

Andrii Nikovskyi joined the All-Russian Union of Zemstvos and Towns to assist in the war effort.[4] In Kiev there was even a Carpatho-Russian Liberation Committee, established in 1913, which supported the full integration of Galicia into the Russian empire. It was dominated by Russian nationalists and Russophile émigrés from Galicia, but also included many Ukrainians.

The first of Lypynskyi's three possibilities therefore seemed the most likely at first. Russia's initial war aim, as with the Habsburg attack on Serbia, was to try and take out *Ukraina irridenta*. As Austro-Hungarian armies marched towards Belgrade, Russia's marched into Lviv. Most of Galicia and Bukovyna was occupied between September 1914 and June 1915, and placed under the authority of Count Georgii Bobrinskii, a prominent Russian nationalist whose cousin Vladimir had established the Galician-Russian Benevolent Society in 1907 – a precursor of the Carpatho-Russian Liberation Committee. Bobrinskii immediately sought to Russify the region after the Russian minister of foreign affairs Sergei Sazonov proudly declared that 'now is an opportune moment to get rid of the Ukrainian movement once and for all'.[5]

It is significant that many Russians have expressed regret that Russia failed to seize Galicia on previous occasions, either in 1772, when Austria annexed the region after the first Partition of Poland, or in 1813–15, when Alexander I attempted to secure it before and during the Congress of Vienna. It is even possible that Russia might have secured Galicia during the diplomatic manœuvrings at the Congress of Berlin in 1878.[6] The first two at least were real possibilities; Russian armies occupied Lviv in 1769–72 and part of Ternopil was temporarily annexed between 1809 and 1815. No less a figure than Aleksandr Solzhenitsyn has criticised Alexander I for failing to press home Russia's decisive advantage after the defeat of Napoleon in 1812:

Was [Alexander] seeking territorial rewards for Russia after such a bloody and victorious war? No, he did not put forward any pre-conditions whatsoever for aiding Austria and Prussia in 1813. The single wise move he could have made was to return Galicia to Russia, thus uniting the Eastern Slavs (and from what disastrous problems would he have rid our future history!). Austria was not particularly bent on retaining Galicia at the time, seeking rather to regain Silesia, annex Belgrade and Moldo-Wallachia – thus stretching herself between the Black and Adriatic Seas. But Alexander did not make use of this opportunity, although it was then easily within his grasp.[7]

According to Solzhenitsyn, Alexander only compounded the mistake by seeking instead the 'poisoned gift', the 'rebellious nest' of Poland (i.e. the Grand Duchy of Warsaw), 'not seeing, if only through Austria's example, how harmful it is for the dominant nation in a state to create a multiethnic empire'.[8] (It says everything about Solzhenitsyn's point of view that in his eyes the 'return' of Galicia rather than Grand Duchy Poland would not have made Russia more 'multiethnic'.)

Counterfactually, it is interesting to speculate what might then have happened. Solzhenitsyn's prediction that all of Russia's 'disastrous problems' with Ukraine would have been avoided assumes there were no significant differences to eradicate in 1815. In truth, the differences were already considerable. Nevertheless, with nearly all significant Ukrainian territory under Russian control, Ukraine might have been in the same situation as Belarus and any nineteenth-century Ukrainian national 'revival' might have looked more like its much weaker north-western counterpart. The Greek Catholic Church would have been almost completely, rather than only partially, abolished in 1839, apart from some tiny remnants (assuming its other outpost in Transcarpathia was also under Russian control). On the other hand, in the Ukrainian territories already under the tsars, the Left Bank in particular, there was already a much stronger national tradition than in Belarus. The nineteenth-century Ukrainian national movement began in Kharkiv. It would have had to stay there rather than transfer to Galicia, so it would have developed differently. But it would still have existed.

Bobrinskii's attempt, moreover, came after a century of profound change. What might have been conceivable in 1815 would have been much more difficult in 1878 and was more or less impossible to achieve in nine months in 1914–15 (Russia briefly reoccupied the eastern half of the region during the Brusilov offensive in 1916–17). The Galician Russophiles were a declining force, fatally weakened by political measures after 1882, revived when Austria interned many of their number at Thalerhof in 1914. Bobrinskii in turn relied too much on coercion, imprisoning thousands of Ukrainophiles, closing down their organisations and making threatening gestures against the Greek Catholic Church, but against a movement on the crest of so many recent successes such methods were only likely to produce a stronger backlash. Even if Russia had fought a better war and occupied Galicia for longer, Dnieper Ukraine might have initially accepted 'reunification' on tsarist terms (though Galicia would not have), but in the longer term would itself have been influenced by the higher level of Ukrainian consciousness in the West, as indeed was to happen after Galicia was finally absorbed in 1945. The first geopolitical project that Ukrainians were subject to after 1914 was therefore the first to end in failure.

The Populist Project

There was considerable irony in the fact that the second project to get off the ground was that of the relatively weak intelligentsia movement in

Map 4. Ukraine, 1917–20

Romanov Ukraine. The fall of the dynasty in February 1917 allowed the populists to set up an assembly in Kiev, which styled itself the Ukrainian People's Council, later the Ukrainian People's Republic (UNR). Ukrainian historians have traditionally taken 'the Ukrainian revolution' as their central subject for the long years of upheaval that followed, but this misrepresents the situation in key respects. The 'Ukrainian people' did not yet exist and could not act as single entity. There were plenty of other dramas unfolding on Ukrainian territory at the time – 'revolution' did not necessarily have a Ukrainian adjective in front of it. Finally, it tends to be assumed that the various attempts to establish a Ukrainian state in 1917–20 were the (only) inevitable product of the nineteenth-century 'national revival'. In reality, many outcomes were feasible. Fewer were still on the agenda after 1920, but a plurality of possibilities remained. The period was therefore not a 'revolution lost', just a revolution that came too early.

The Kievan project grew out of nineteenth-century populist assumptions. The intelligentsia claimed to represent the people, but a crucial weakness of the UNR was that it was not elected (nor, of course, were the Bolsheviks). Many of its delegates emerged from a series of congresses of peasants, soldiers and soviets in the summer of 1917, but this was no substitute for the legitimacy that a Ukrainian general election would have provided. One was planned for January 1918, but a

Bolshevik assault on Kiev disrupted the preparations. German armies were occupying Ukraine by March and were not exactly interested in experiments with the ballot box. The founders of the UNR also initially assumed that a free Ukraine would be built in federation with a democratised Russia. The weakness of the Provisional Government in Petrograd and the Bolshevik coup in October quickly radicalised the Ukrainians, and they were fast-forwarded through five 'Universals' (meaning 'decrees', a term revived from the days of the Cossack Hetmanate). The First Universal in June 1917 proclaimed Ukrainian autonomy within a federated Russia, but the Provisional Government only recognised its authority in five central *guberniyas* or territorial divisions (Kiev, Chernihiv, Poltava, Podillia and Volhynia). The Fourth Universal of 25 January 1918 declared independence for a Ukraine that would occupy nine *guberniyas* (the earlier five plus Kharkiv, Katerynoslav, Kherson and Taurida – basically modern Ukraine minus the Habsburg territories and Crimea); but the Ukrainians were ill-prepared for the speed with which they moved from step one to step four. Nor did they get much time to consolidate thereafter. The Bolsheviks forced the Republic's leadership out of Kiev by February 1918. The Germans temporarily restored the UNR in March within the boundaries agreed by the Treaty of Brest-Litovsk (the expanded nine *guberniyas*, plus Chełm/Kholm, now in Poland, and southern Minsk and Grodno, now in Belarus), but replaced it with a conservative 'Hetmanate' in April. The UNR briefly restored itself as the 'Directory' after the Hetmanate collapsed in December, but its second coming, although protracted, was less glorious than the first.

The historian Mykhailo Hrushevskyi, elected president of the Republic by the Ukrainian People's Council in March 1917, put in place many of the prerequisites of a new nation. The UNR had no real army or state administration (its idealist leaders favoured the creation of 'people's militias'), but it had a currency, the hryvnia (originally silver coinage at the time of Rus), a crest (the trident, the coat of arms of the Riurykovych dynasty, although some Ukrainians date it back to the Trypillian period) and a flag (azure over yellow – sky over corn, evoking the Ukrainian fertility myth). All were designed to relate the new Ukraine to the Rus and Cossack eras, as was the national anthem 'Ukraine Has Not Yet Died', by Mykhailo Verbytskyi and Pavlo Chubynskyi (first published in 1863): a stirring celebration of the spirit of Cossack fraternity and liberty, albeit inspired by the rival Polish hymn. The new nation the populists sought to bring into being was therefore defined by Hrushevskyi's historical mythology and by nineteenth-century assumptions about a community of descent determined by 'native tongue'. Dmytro Doroshenko, minister of foreign affairs in 1918 recalled how

in their eyes, anyone who didn't know or use the literary Ukrainian language, belong to the Ukrainian national parties and was a member of Prosvita – was also not a Ukrainian; in the understanding of these people the Ukrainian world [*Ukraïnstvo*] ended outside of the ranks of the Social Federalist, Social Revolutionary and Social Democratic parties [the main populist forces] and was limited to a few hundred or few thousand intelligentsia, grouped in these parties.[9]

The Ukrainophile intelligentsia was therefore unable to escape from a double bind. Based in the towns, its members had quickly to forge the links to the countryside that the tsarist authorities had, quite sensibly from their point of view, prevented them from developing before 1917. Because the Republic was unable and unwilling to relate to the peasantry on the crucial land question, they largely failed to do so. As in most ways with the Bolsheviks, the key Ukrainian parties favoured the socialisation of land, the creation of a Land Reserve and large model state farms rather than simple distribution to the peasants.[10] The Ukrainian movement was also unable to build a broader political base in the towns, where they were a small minority, compared to Russian monarchist, Russian radical and even Jewish and Polish forces. In the all-Russian Constituent Assembly elections in 1917 the Ukrainian parties won almost 68% of the vote in Ukraine as a whole, but in the earlier municipal elections they won only 12.6% in the towns (populations between 15,000 and 50,000) and a mere 9.5% in the cities (over 50,000).[11] Kharkiv and the Donbas were controlled either by the Bolsheviks or by local workers' militias. Kiev was invaded by the Bolsheviks three times, with considerable assistance from workers inside the city. In the absence of any outside forces, this was too narrow a base on which to build the new Ukrainian nation. The leaders of the UNR, such as Volodymyr Vynnychenko (1880–1951), celebrated the 'bourgeoislessness' of Ukrainian society, as they thought this would help them construct their utopian vision of a socialist future,[12] but it was this very factor that hindered the construction of a stable new order – even before the UNR was overwhelmed by superior force.

In a sense, the UNR was a 'virtual republic'. Its existence was brief, its boundaries variable and its power limited, but it still left a durable mythology behind it, (its flag, crest, anthem and currency were all readopted after 1991). The Bolsheviks were forced to replace it with an ersatz substitute – the Ukrainian Soviet Socialist Republic. As well as the structure, they conceded the name, Ukrainian, which in many ways was half the battle. It was also significant that statehood, however illusory, was achieved by the Dnieper Ukrainians. It is an obvious irony that by the time the better organised Habsburg Ukrainians joined the fray in November 1918 the experiment was already faltering, but if the timing had been reversed and the Habsburg empire had collapsed before the Romanov (or if the Romanov empire had survived) it is difficult to imagine the Galicians matching the UNR's brief success in such all-Ukrainian dimensions.

Peasants and Pitchforks, Intellectuals and Inorodtsy

The key problem for the UNR was undoubtedly the vagaries of peasant support. One should, however, be wary of the assumption in 'national awakening' models that peasants are always latent nationalists. Peasants had their own priorities – basically they wanted their land. As one local assembly put it, 'the land must be transferred to the people without compensation. The land is God's, the people reaped and protected it for thousands of years.'[13] The problem is defining what 'their land' meant. In the narrow sense, it obviously meant the land the peasants tilled, and as order collapsed they grabbed it. But there was also a broader sense in which peasants sought to define the land as belonging to their group and to deny it to outsiders. Does this mean they possessed an embryonic 'national' identity?

Arthur Adams referred to the period as the 'Great Ukrainian *Jacquerie*', with lawless and bloodthirsty peasants taking whatever justification they could for sticking pitchforks into their landlords – and their neighbours if they coveted the same land.[14] Like the everyman hero in Jaroslav Hašek's classic Czech short story *The Good Soldier Švejk* (1911), Ukrainian peasants tended to think that the enemy was just as likely to be the leaders of 'their' side and devoted most of their energies to keeping their heads down and looking after their own. Each village or region kept to itself and made pragmatic deals with whatever force came by. As the UNR struggled to assert itself against the Bolsheviks, Whites and Poles (even temporarily against French forces in the south), 'in a real sense, it was the peasantry, or more precisely the various peasant armies, who by the Summer of 1919 controlled most of Dnieper Ukraine.'[15] 'Control' was of course not collective – 'various peasant armies' came and went in different regions. The largest individual force was the self-proclaimed anarchists led by Nestor Makhno (1884–1934), who for long periods dominated the south of Ukraine. Makhno earned a certain notoriety in the West, in part for the glorious gesture of issuing his own money but printing it with a disclaimer offering anybody permission to forge it, but ended his days in poverty in Paris. He was, however, only the most famous of a thousand self-proclaimed Hetmans or *otamany* who patrolled the countryside elsewhere.

Recent research has suggested that the situation in the countryside was reasonably calm until early 1919, and that peasants were amenable to intelligentsia propaganda so long as it came to them in a language and with a message they could understand,[16] as demonstrated by the large peasant vote for the Ukrainian parties in the Constituent Assembly elections. Peasant hostility to the *chuzhi* (aliens), particularly Jews and Polish and Russian landlords, was considerable. Nevertheless, although local peasants might identify agitators from the city intelligentsia as their 'own', there was little sense as yet that their cultural stake in the populist project was sufficient to motivate them to action beyond the strictly economic. Illiterate peasants could have little interest in Ukrainian literature (except when it was read to them). The Ukrainian language was neither a passport nor a stumbling block to employment so long as peasants remained on the land. A potential coincidence of interests was aided by the relative familiarity of the outsider voices, but as yet no more.[17]

Skoropadskyi's Project

Pavlo Skoropadskyi (1873–1945), who led the Ukrainian 'Hetmanate' government in 1918 between the two manifestations of the UNR, has often been dismissed in Ukrainian historiography as a triple stooge – as a front for conservative landowners, German occupiers and the anti-Bolshevik Whites (including both those long resident in Kiev and those fleeing the 'Red Terror' in Moscow and St Petersburg after the attempt on Lenin's life in August 1918). Skoropadskyi has also been mocked as an aristocrat out of his time, a descendant of the Ivan Skoropadskyi who tidied up after Mazepa as Hetman from 1709 to 1722 (he was also Yelysaveta Myloradovych's nephew).

Of these various sins, Bulgakov might only have classed Skoropadskyi's Germanophilia as reprehensible, but his play *The White Guard* has helped to shape the Hetman's image as a comic-opera figure, strutting around in 'a gorgeous Circassian tunic with silver cartridge pockets, wide magenta-coloured trousers, heel-less Caucasian boots without spurs [and] glittering General's epaulettes', and half-heartedly promoting an 'absurd comedy of Ukrainianisation' before he eventually takes flight with the retreating Germans).[18] Bulgakov invents the following exchange:

> HETMAN: For a long time I've been meaning to remind you and the other officers of my staff that you are supposed to speak Ukrainian. It's disgraceful! Not a single one of my officers can speak the language of the country, and this makes the worst possible impression on the Ukrainian troops. Please speak Ukrainian.
> SHERVINSKII [his aide-de-camp]: Very Good, Your Highness. (*Aside.*) God, what is 'prince' in Ukrainian? (*Aloud.*) Er . . .
> HETMAN: Oh, talk Russian, man![19]

Ten out of 15 members of Skoropadskyi's 1918 Cabinet 'adhered to a Russian orientation' and many were members of all-Russian parties such as the Kadets and Oktobrists.[20] In the final days of its existence (November 1918), the Hetmanate's last throw of the dice was to propose a federated union with Russia. However, Yaroslav Hrytsak has pointed out that Skoropadskyi's achievements in Ukrainianising education and creating an army of 65,000 far outstripped those of the short-lived and ineffective UNR – in part because he raised fewer alarms by basing his policies on a new version of Ukrainian identity. 'Skoropadskyi built neither a Ukrainian, nor a Russian national state,' Hrytsak argues, 'the Hetmanate regime tried to introduce a new conception of the Ukrainian nation, founded not on knowledge of the Ukrainian language, but on loyalty to the Ukrainian state.'[21] In his memoirs Skoropadskyi wrote: 'the difference between myself and Ukrainian leaders is the following: in loving Ukraine they hate Russia. I do not have such hate. In all the oppression that was so harshly displayed by Russia in relation to all things Ukrainian, it is impossible to accuse the Russian people, it was the system of government; the people took no part.'[22] These ideas would be more fully developed in the 1920s by the historian and philosopher Viacheslav Lypynskyi amongst a Ukrainian émigré movement centred in Prague, when Skoropadskyi himself moved to endorse more unambiguously the idea of Ukrainian independence. They would return to centre-stage in the 1990s. Skoropadskyi therefore deserves a more conspicuous place in the history of the period. If Germany had won the war, which was not inconceivable in the spring of 1918, Ukraine would have received the third-party assistance it desperately needed, and this would most definitely have gone to the conservative Hetmanate rather than the leftist UNR (although the Austrian Archduke Eugen also quite fancied a Ukrainian throne). Skoropadskyi himself had counted on German backing until at least 1919.[23] His particular bind, however, was that German occupation policy – grain requisitions in particular – prevented him from acquiring a broader social base. The UNR in opposition was already gathering peasant armies to overthrow him before the Germans withdrew.[24] It is certainly conceivable that the Hetmanate might have enjoyed a longer life; its success, however, was not preordained.

The West Ukrainian Project

After the fall of the Habsburg empire in November 1918 the west Ukrainians established a third Ukrainian state, named the West Ukrainian People's Republic (commonly known by its Ukrainian acronym of ZUNR). It claimed sovereignty over eastern Galicia, Bukovyna and Transcarpathia, plus what are now the Polish territories of Peremyshyl, Kholm, Pidlachia and the Lemko region (a maximum definition of ethnographic Ukraine).[25] The ZUNR's effective life was, however, even shorter than that of the UNR. With Habsburg sponsorship the western Ukrainians might have been able to achieve some form of autonomy, but in a straight fight between the three and a half million local Ukrainians and the 18 million Poles who simultaneously declared independence in November 1918 the Poles won an easy victory by July

1919. Even this brief half-life suggested several interesting possibilities, however.

A west Ukrainian version of Ukraine would have had a more solid base in the civil society developed by the Habsburg Ukrainian parties – in contrast to the *bunt* (social explosion) by now engulfing the east. Plans to hold the elections that would have given a Ukrainian government a more solid mandate were more advanced than in Kiev. A West Ukrainian Republic would also have had closer links with the Central European powers, old and new, although it was created at the very moment (November 1918) when Austria–Hungary had already collapsed and Germany was losing the war in the west. Instead of Vienna cooperating with a Ukraine they more or less recognised (the pre-1914 Galician 'crownland' model), Berlin was forced to work with a Ukraine it did not (the Hetmanate in Kiev). In any case, Habsburg interest in Ukraine had faded over the course of the war (an independent Ukraine was simply too large for the Habsburgs to swallow, it would have vastly increased the 'zone of confrontation' with Russia, and a border with Poland would have been nigh impossible to draw).[26] A putative link with withdrawing German forces, however, was also no longer on the cards. In any case, it would have made a possible further difference more problematical, namely the western Ukrainians' greater willingness to resort to armed force in comparison to the idealistic leaders of the UNR. Galician 'Sich Rifelmen' had been in service since 1914 and one of their offshoots provided the closest thing that the Ukrainians had to a regular military force. Finally, it is extremely doubtful that a Ukrainian government more in the image of the conservative ZUNR would have been any better at understanding or leading peasants from Dnieper Ukraine.

Different approaches meant difficult relations between the ZUNR and the various governments in Kiev. Skoropadskyi's Hetmanate collapsed just as the ZUNR was established – it is interesting to speculate how the more conservative west Ukrainian politicians, already used to court and chancellery politics under the Habsburgs, might have cooperated with him. Instead, the ZUNR had to work with the second coming of the leftist UNR, whose leaders were not always as fraternal as they might have been. The union of the two states proclaimed in January 1919 existed only on paper. The secret clauses of the Brest–Litovsk treaty in March 1918 allegedly envisaged a Ukraine without Galicia, albeit with possible autonomy under the Habsburgs; the alliance of convenience between Symon Petliura, the last head of the UNR, and Poland in 1919–21 left the Galicians more definitively in the lurch.[27] The ZUNR, on the other hand, flirted with Denikin. A final irony is that the failure of the ZUNR somewhat discredited the conservative approach. The opportunity for moderate Ukrainian nationalism to make a success of actual government had been missed.

West Ukraine between the Wars: Ethnonationalism Refined

If the ZUNR had offered an alternative concept of Ukrainian identity with a stronger civic base and a more obviously European orientation, the redivision of Ukrainian lands in 1918–22 (Galicia and Volhynia went to the new Polish state, Transcarpathia to Czechoslovakia, Bukovyna to Romania; the Ukrainian Soviet Socialist Republic took most of the rest, minus Crimea, which was a separate Autonomous Republic) led to the development in the western territories of a radical ethnonationalist alternative that was as much anti-Russian as anti-Polish. When Ukrainian lands were therefore finally united in 1945, this would be on rather different terms than had briefly seemed possible in 1919.

This development was not inevitable. Poland was the main occupying power and, with the Habsburg ringmaster having quit the stage, Polish-Ukrainian antagonism was exposed as never before. Moscow's backing for an anti-Polish Ukrainian nationalism was not impossible to imagine geopolitically. In a kind of reverse 'Piedmont effect', one reason why the Bolsheviks had originally sanctioned the creation of the westerly Soviet republics was to target irredenta populations in the new Central European states (the Ukrainian and Belorussian SSRs were aimed at Poland, the Karelian SSR at Finland, the Moldovian SSR at Romania). As late as the 1920s Ukrainian nationalist leaders such as Yevhen Petrushevych, former leader of the ZUNR, and even emissaries of Yevhen Konovalets, head of the ultra-nationalist paramilitary Ukrainian Military Organisation, made secret pilgrimages to Soviet Ukraine to seek support.[28] The new Communist Party of Western Ukraine and the remnants of the Galician Russophiles also looked to Moscow. Any orientation towards the USSR was, however, necessarily predicated on a better deal for Ukrainians under Soviet rule. The dashed hopes of the Ukrainianisation programme, the Famine of 1932–3 and the Purges of the 1930s (see pages 144–6) strengthened the perception that Russia was a factor hindering the development of a Ukrainian nation rather than a potential ally, even before the renewed experience of occupation in 1939–41 reminded western Ukrainians of 1914–15 and the defeats of 1918–20. Moreover, after 1930 Soviet policy towards western Ukraine was wholly decided in Moscow rather than Kiev or Kharkiv, which was never subtle enough to build on residual east-Slavic sentiment.

Instead, the western Ukrainians built on the incipient ethnonationalism of the 1890s and 1900s to develop a version of Ukrainian national identity that sought to stand alone between the twin evils of Polish and Russian nationalism. This did not mean equidistance. To the main ideologist of the new identity, Dmytro Dontsov (1883–1973), Poland was Ukraine's oppressor, but Russia was its existential antithesis, just as it was that of Europe as a whole. 'The conflict between Europe and Russia'

Map 5. *Ukraine Between the Wars*

he saw as 'a conflict of two civilisations, two political, social and cultural-religious ideals'. Because 'the amorphous Russian mass could only be led by absolutism' in all these spheres, Russia's rulers had always seen the European social order as the opposite of their own – and sought to destroy it. Bolshevism was just tsarist absolutism by another name.[29] Ukraine's historical destiny, argued Dontsov, was therefore to save Europe from Russia – and save itself by such opposition. The intensity of its anti-Russian stance would have to exceed all others in consequence of its front-line position and its special need to overcome the inroads of centuries of Russian influence. Ukraine would become a new type of *Antemurale* – defending the rest of Europe from the scourge of Bolshevism.

Dontsov therefore devoted much of his venom to the internal consequences of the 'Russian complex' of the Ukrainian intelligentsia; namely, the 'spiritual lameness' and 'provincialism', produced by the phenomenon he dubbed 'national Hermaphroditism' and 'Ukrainian Provençalism' – a fixation on minor literary achievements, rather than a real movement for political revival. Fellow writer Yevhen Malaniuk joined the attack on 'the self-repudiation', 'national defeatism' and 'national lameness' inherent in Ukraine's 'historic disease' of 'Little Russianism', and lambasted each and every Ukrainian '-philism' (Moscowphilism, Polonophilism, Austro-philism) as obstacles to the development of a real national self. All of these inferiority complexes, he argued, would have to be expurgated from the national psyche if Ukraine was ever to develop as a historical subject in its own right.[30]

Dontsov preached 'the twilight of the gods to whom the nineteenth century prayed' and proposed in their stead a Nietzschean 'revaluation of values'. In place of 'reason, evolution and cosmopolitanism', 'the broken table of commandments' of the era before 1914 and the mawkish populism of the older generation (the 'Brotherhood of SS. Cyril and Methodius and Drahomanov'), he advocated 'the fire of fanatical commitment' and 'the iron force of enthusiasm'. Only the latter was capable of asserting the 'national Eros', 'the gathering of millions of wills around one common ideal, the ideal of the rule by one ethnic group over a territory, which it received as a legacy from its parents and which, perhaps a little enlarged, it will bequeath to its children.' To Dontsov, the basic rule of life was Heraclitus' 'law of struggle', 'the law of eternal antagonism between nations'. On both an individual and a collective level, the new order could only be created by 'voluntarism', the 'strong man', the 'creative force' and 'initiative of the minority'. The nation, he continued, was 'the most beautiful emanation of the will to struggle and the fight for freedom', but only those nations that had 'the psychology of a masterful and dominant people' would succeed in that struggle. If Ukraine 'does not take [its chance], someone else will. Nature abhors a vacuum.' 'Ukraine does not yet exist,' he lamented, 'but we can create it in our souls.' 'A nation needs no objective preconditions in order to wrest from history its claim to be a state', just the 'subjective' valour of a few men. The soft-hearted 'anti-fanaticism of Drahomanov' would be replaced by those who realised that the existing order could not be overthrown by utopian anarchism, but only by 'the organisation of a new violence' to take its place. Dontsov therefore named his doctrine *chynnyi natsionalizm* – the 'nationalism of the deed'.[31]

I have quoted Dontsov at some length to give a flavour of his highly eclectic neo-Fascist ideology and of the political turmoil of the time. The *Sturm und Drang* of his philosophy also helps to give a better understanding of the milieu inhabited by the party that came to dominate the era, the Organisation of Ukrainian Nationalists (OUN), founded in Vienna in 1929. The OUN declared itself to be based on his principles of 'social voluntarism', 'the idealism of the deed', *natsiokratiia* – the power of the nation in the state' and – during 'the time of struggle and the transitional periods of Ukrainian state-building – the dictatorship of the Chief (*Vozhd*) of the nation'. (The OUN's first such charismatic leader was Yevhen Konovalets, commander of the Sich Riflemen that backed the Hetmanate in 1918, until he was assassinated by a Soviet bomb in a box of chocolates in Rotterdam in 1938.) The OUN anticipated little need for political pluralism when it came to power. Declaring itself above the particularisms of party and class, it would form 'the basis of the state order', and 'all social levels' would be organised by the OUN into corporate bodies serving the state. Its 'attitude to national minorities would depend on their attitude to the liberation efforts of the Ukrainian people and their statehood'.[32] At its Kraków congress in 1941 the OUN promised to 'vanquish' the Jews from Ukraine, as they were 'the most loyal prop of the ruling Bolshevik regime and the avant-garde of Muscovite imperialism in Ukraine'.[33]

Dontsov and the OUN were obviously not bleeding-heart liberals. On the other hand, their politics were fairly typical of the region and the time (though this was of course precisely what made the west Ukrainian and Soviet Ukrainian experiences so different). Equally characteristic was the fact that ideological sympathy and practical geopolitics increasingly drew the OUN into seeking the support of Germany, both Weimar and Nazi, contacts having been established as far back as the early 1920s.[34] Croatia had the Ustashe, Slovakia the clerico-Fascist People's Party with its paramilitary wing, Rodobrana, Romania had Carneliu Codreanu's Legion of the Archangel Michael, Lithuania the Iron Wolves.[35] Also fairly typical (as in Weimar Germany and truncated Hungary) was the development of a culture of humiliation focusing on the defeats in 1918–20, the predominance of ex-combatants in the right-wing rank and file and a developing obsession with the lack of national 'will' rather than *force majeure* as the cause of the Ukrainians' misfortunes.[36] That said, the OUN were not the only political force in western Ukraine. The civil society values of prewar nationalism were still represented by the Ukrainian National-Democratic Organisation (UNDO). However, constitutional politics offered few practical benefits in interwar Poland and by the mid-1930s the UNDO was losing members to the radicals, who found ready recruits amongst disaffected youth and the rural poor after the Great Depression hit the region with particular severity.

The OUN sought to actualise the 'nationalism of the deed' with a campaign of terror and assassination against the Poles and 'collaborationist' elements in Ukrainian society. Its controversial methods were therefore condemned by the local Greek Catholic Church. And by the mid-1930s they were hardly 'uniting the social organism'. However, new opportunities for the OUN began to open up after the Soviet occupation of eastern Poland/western Ukraine in 1939–41 brought a definitive end to constitutional politics, and the German invasion of the USSR in 1941 the real possibility of displacing Soviet power. Once the OUN actually started fighting, it became more widely popular. Its units raced to Lviv, where they symbolically declared national independence on 30 June 1941, and promised that 'the revived Ukrainian state will cooperate closely with National-Socialist Great Germany ... the Ukrainian National Revolutionary Army, to be formed on Ukrainian soil, will henceforth fight along with the Allied German Army against Muscovite occupation for a Sovereign United Ukrainian State and a new order in the whole world.'[37]

Despite these entreaties, the Germans were distinctly unimpressed and promptly arrested the leader of the more radical OUN faction, Stepan Bandera (1909–59), Konovalets' successor as *Vozhd*, and his associates. The OUN had placed its hopes on German *Geopolitik*, in other words the expectation that Germany would support the creation of a network of East European buffer states as it had in 1918. This was not an unreasonable assumption. Some of Hitler's advisers, Alfred Rosenberg in particular,[38] along with elements in the Abwehr and German High Command, were indeed entertaining such a possibility. But they lost out to Hitler's racial vision, in which the Ukrainians were no more than *Üntermenschen* – the people suitable for slave labour, the land for German colonisation (Hitler had Galicia and Crimea particularly in mind). A possible future in which Germany defeated the USSR would not have been good for Ukraine (see also page 286).

The OUN continued to agitate for a 'Ukrainian, Independent, United State', but had to rethink its tactics. It also had to adjust to the fact that its support base was confined to the west. Small expeditionary groups (*pokhidni hrupy*) reached some central and even east Ukrainian areas, but reported back that Dontsovite ultra-nationalism was unpopular, even incomprehensible in the cities and towns of Dnieper Ukraine, where Soviet culture had already begun to take root. The planned 'Ukrainian National Revolutionary Army' therefore took flesh in the form of the less ideological Ukrainian Insurgent Army, established in 1943 and known by its Ukrainian acronym, UPA. At a special congress in 1943 the OUN made sweeping changes to its ideology, embracing, at least on the surface, ethnic pluralism and Soviet welfare Socialism. After July 1944, the OUN began to operate through a multi-party front, the Ukrainian Supreme Liberation Council. The Dontsovite project therefore reached a dead-end even before the war's conclusion, although it left a lasting, and differentiating impact on the political culture of western Ukraine.

At its peak, roughly between 1944 and 1947, the UPA had as many as 90,000 men under arms – nearly all in western Ukraine.[39] A difficult three-cornered fight against Germans, Soviets and Poles was sustainable so long as there was some hope that the geopolitical situation might change to the Ukrainians' advantage (the OUN hoped the war would continue, as the 'Anglo-Saxon bloc' would 'always oppose the strongest state in Europe', now 'Bolshevik Russia').[40] Once the Cold War set in, however, Ukraine was isolated way behind the frontline – materials and men were parachuted in by MI6 and the CIA, but Kim Philby betrayed the operation – and the lonely struggle petered out as the weight of reprisals began to outweigh any likely benefit. Nevertheless, the last units were only defeated in the mid-1950s.

The complicated history of the OUN-UPA is not well remembered. The fact that the OUN and UPA were able to fight at all is what is now celebrated in western Ukraine. The Soviet propaganda caricature of the movement before 1943 – its initial reliance on the invading Germans and the claim that opponents in the Red Army were largely kith and kin – prevails elsewhere. There is no more divisive symbol in modern Ukraine.

Peasants into Ukrainians: Ukrainian Modernism

As the OUN themselves came to recognise, the extreme Russophobia of west Ukrainian nationalists did not easily translate to the rest of Ukraine. Back in 1913 the publicist and UNR activist Mykola Zalizniak (1888–1950) had penned a powerful critique of Dontsov, arguing that Ukrainians could appreciate Russian culture not 'in order to denationalise or assimilate themselves, but in order to fix its value and draw from it [what they needed] for their own activity'.[41] The events of 1917–20 demonstrated that the Dnieper Ukrainians had been influenced both by the official 'nation-building' project of tsarist Russia and by the rival project of their own intelligentsia, but that neither had been completed by 1917. The various attempts to establish an independent Ukrainian state after that date were in themselves a defining event, but much remained to be resolved when tsarist Ukraine, minus Volhynia, was incorporated into the new unified Soviet state established in 1922. The ongoing struggle over the nature of Ukrainian identity became particularly intense in the 1920s, as debate raged as to the successes and failures of 1917–20 and how Ukraine might take the next steps forward.

A critique of Ukrainian populism had actually been developing since the 1890s, arguing for a modernisation of Ukrainian culture to transcend the passivity and provincialism of folklorism. Two novels captured the spirit of the nineteenth-century movement. In the first, Ivan Nechui-Levytskyi's *The Clouds* (1874), a radical student expresses the essence of populism:

> We, father, wear the *svyta* [peasant's overcoat], for we are populists, we side with the people, we are nationals! We protest through our *svyta* against the despotism which is oppressing our literature, our life. We protest in this way against any kind of despotism and side with our people, defending them from the landowners, and moreover, foreign landowners, from the influence of alien languages, alien religion, from the influence of all the devils and fiends who have dared to put their hostile hand on our property and on our people.[42]

The revolutionary hero Orel in the second novel, Panas Myrnyi's (1849–1920) *Lover of the People* (1876) defined the simplistic solution, 'to establish justice on earth ... it only remains to go to the people, to help them get rid of their wretched fate, to give them our strength and vigour and desire'.[43]

By the 1900s younger Ukrainians were beginning to criticise the 'peasantomania' or 'homestead philosophy' of the old guard – the narrowness of vision that the writer Mykola Khvylovyi would later satirise as *khokhlandia* (*khokhol* being a derogatory term for bumpkin Ukrainians, though also used by Gogol to describe himself).[44] The local peasants were potential Ukrainians, but many, even most, still possessed only a parochial identity. Populism's desire simply to reflect peasant culture would only perpetuate this situation. What began as an artistic and literary debate was therefore also about the changing nature of Ukrainian identity as a whole, and whether is was to remain mired in ethnokitsch or was to develop a new dynamism. The Canadian scholar Oleh Ilnytzkyj has argued that younger Ukrainians were labouring

> against their own peculiar variant of cultural stagnation ... [and trying to develop] a new national cultural norm, the main principle of which rested on a denial of populism and provincialism (stigmas of Ukraine's colonial position in the empire), and the recognition of Europe – primarily in its traditional and classical guise – as the pre-eminent cultural model.[45]

As elsewhere in Eastern Europe, there was a turn away from Romanticism and Realism towards a new aesthetic in the arts, towards 'art for art's sake' and immersion in the growing plurality of styles emanating from Europe, France in particular. As Steven Mansbach has argued, Modernism in all of its guises penetrated the whole of Eastern Europe to a much greater extent than has often been credited, at the same time as being subject to a variety of metamorphoses through marriage with local styles.[46] Indeed, the revolutionary artistic changes of the early twentieth century arguably began on the European 'periphery', in the Habsburg Secession, and the Russian 'World of Art' (Modernist) and 'Blue Rose' (avant-garde) movements.[47] Between the 1900s and the 1920s there was an extraordinary explosion of artistic talent in Ukraine.[48] Many artists commonly classed as 'Russian' were in fact from Ukraine. Indeed, Ukrainian historians have argued not only that 'Ukraine was a primary source for Russian avant-garde art [but that] it [also] became its last refuge' when repression began in the late 1920s.[49] Kandinsky grew up in Odesa and was supposedly influenced by local folk motifs and the traditional bright colours of Ukrainian art. Malevich was born in Kiev and supposedly 'rediscovered' his Ukrainian roots on his return to the city in 1926. The Futurist Burliuk came from Sumy.

There were also artists who were not just from Ukraine, but were more tangibly Ukrainian in style and mentality. Most noteworthy were the self-styled Modernists in and around the 'Young Muse' movement established in 1906 (see plate 27). Oleksandr Murashko (1875–1919), Fedir Krychevskyi (1879–1947) and Vsevolod Maksymovych (1894–1918), sought to embrace and adapt European styles as a means of shaking up Ukraine's provincial torpor. All were notable for their celebration of both the autonomy of the artist and the inspiration of local culture. Maksymovych in particular, dubbed 'the Ukrainian Klimt' (because he painted his own version of Klimt's *The Kiss* in 1914 – a closer parallel would be Aubrey Beardsley), has gained considerable popularity in recent years. His appeal is assisted in no inconsiderable part by his early suicide in his twenties and by his narcissistic self-portraits and decadent depictions of sexual languor (see plate 28).[50]

Beginning with the 1908 'Link' exhibition in Kiev, a new generation of the Ukrainian avant-garde – artists such as Oleksandr Bohomazov (1880–1930) and Oleksandra Ekster/Exter (1882–1949) – began to challenge the Modernist aesthetic with a new formalism of line, colour, style and surface. In time, this produced the specific local schools of (1910s) Cubo-Futurism and (1920s) Constructivism, although the Ukrainian avant-garde overlapped with the Russian (and the European) to a greater extent than its Modernist predecessor. Myroslav Popovych has argued that 'the Ukrainian avant-garde belonged to the marginal Ukrainian-Russian culture of general-imperial character, which it is impossible to attribute one-sidedly'.[51] There were notable exceptions, however (see plates 29–31). One was Oleksandr Arkhypenko/Archipenko (1887–1964), who drew on pagan Trypillian artefacts, Scythian 'earth-mothers' and the mosaics of St Sofiia's as inspiration for his sculpture – as during his later career in New York. Another was Mykhailo Boichuk (1882–?1937) and his circle, including Maria Syniakova (1890–1984) and Burliuk's brother David (1882–1967), which developed a rather different style, combining a highly colourful (the 'national' colours of yellow, bright blues, greens and reds) and often burlesque 'neo-Primitivism' with a neo-Byzantine monumentalism, specialising in huge frescoes of peasant scenes in the style of Diego Rivera (most of which were sadly destroyed in the 1930s).

The young Ukrainians eventually subdivided into several movements – Futurists, Cubists, Expressionists, Constructivists and so on. In literature at least they developed their own ideology of 'Panfuturism', which, it was argued, 'embraces all "isms", considering them all partial elements of a single organism'.[52] In art the neo-Primitivists took their own path, but the Cubo-Futurists and Constructivists were united by their desire to transcend the essentially static populist version of national identity and drag Ukraine into the modern age. As with Italian Futurists such as Marinetti, the young Ukrainians embraced the developmental symbols of modernity: speed, technology, science, the urban over the rural, the rational over the instinctive, believing that they held the key to transforming what they now considered was Ukraine's 'backward' culture. All could therefore be termed more or less modernists (with a small 'm'). A classic example is the racing tram in Bohomazov's famous *Lviv Street, Kiev (1914)*; nearly always classed as 'Russian' avant-garde.

The new generation argued that not only had the populists produced a lot of bad art by insisting that art's primary purpose was to 'serve the people', but they had made it more difficult for urban elements to identify with Ukrainian culture. Novels such as *Fata Morgana* (1903–10) by Mykhailo Kotsiubynskyi (1864–1913) now depicted peasant life as a potential dead end, albeit still with the hope of transcendence through social revolution. The *enfant terrible* of the new generation, Mykhailo Semenko (1892–1938), even attacked the 'cult' of Shevchenko as a dead weight on the development of Ukrainian identity, famously and provocatively burning a copy of *Kobzar* as other Ukrainians struggled to circumvent an official ban on celebrations of the centenary of the poet's birth in 1914. The new generation of artists, such as Ostap Lutskyi (1883–1941), argued that art should be 'neither a nurse nor a propagandist',[53] but in truth they also had a cause to promote. The 'progressive' proletariat, the hitherto foreign cities, would be the new audience for their art. The Ukrainian movement would then be able to move beyond its obsession with the peasant question and create a modern nation.

The new artists and writers therefore developed a more urban message. The playwright Mykola Kulish (1892–1937) produced a triptych of dramas, *The People's Malakhii* (1928), *Myna Mazailo* (1929) and *Pathetic Sonata* (1931), that were notable for their daring criticisms of the new Soviet Ukraine – NEPmen, the new bureaucrats, the Council of People's Commissars, sarcastically described as 'the Olympus of proletarian wisdom and strength' – albeit voiced through the device of a madman's ravings.[54] His colleague Les Kurbas (1887–1937) revolutionised the art of theatrical performance, developing Expressionist techniques of stage image, visual device and audience interaction, and a stylised repertoire of gesture in many ways the forerunner of modern 'method acting'. The designer Anatolii Petrytskyi (1895–1964) produced stunningly vivid sets and costumes to accompany the new school of theatre. A notable example are his sketches for a 1928 performance of *Turandot*.

Not surprisingly, the new generation attracted the wrath of the old. As early as 1902 the populist writer Serhii Yefremov (1876–1939) attacked the self-serving 'hashish' of the Modernist extreme, arguing that the primary function of the Ukrainian arts still had to be the 'enlightenment' of the Ukrainian people. Only the native, Yefremov argued, could be authentic. All the various currents of 'Ukrainian' Modernism were therefore mere copies of (mainly) French or German originals; only Populism was a true expression of indigenous values. Another writer, Yurii Mezhenko (1892–1969), complained that the iconoclasm of the young was a tad premature – 'since, after all, [in Ukraine] there really is nothing to destroy'.[55] The line between Modernism and Populism was in any case an artificial one, as the basic project of the latter, the construction of an idealised peasant nation, was still far from complete. In most respects, therefore, the modernists were unable to break away fully from their populist predecessors.[56]

Nevertheless, after 1920 the tide was at least temporarily with the younger generation. According to the writer Mykola Zerov (1890–?1938):

> The old idea of Ukraine died after the battles of 1917–20 ... an image of a bright peasant paradise, a free community without peasants or lords, of private homesteads wreathed in flowers. This was the picture of Ukraine inherited from folklore; this was how Shevchenko raised it onto the pedestal of an almost religious purity and greatness; it was for this Ukraine that the peasants and intelligentsia fought at Kruty [where Kiev students fought the advancing Bolsheviks in January 1918], and in the army of the UNR, and in Makhno's regiments and even some in the Red Army ... However, when the war was over and the rifle salvoes of insurgents grew less frequent, it finally became clear that such a Ukraine was impossible ... the generation of the twenties finally parted with this Ukraine. Sometimes with tears, sometimes with the scorn of a disenchanted hope.[57]

The modernist alternative was leadership. Instead of a system that made 'epigones out of talents', the talents would point the way forward. The key figure in this movement was the writer Mykola Khvylovyi (1893–1933). Khvylovyi was both a Communist and a nationalist, but in both respects something of an elitist. One of his short stories was called simply 'I', and he often veered dangerously close to the kind of Nietzschean voluntarism that was more explicit in west Ukrainian writers like Dontsov and Malaniuk. What Ukraine desperately needed, Khvylovyi argued, was a new elite, intellectuals of the ideal European type (Voltaire, Goethe, representatives of the 'Faustian culture'), 'living individual[s] with thoughts, will and aptitudes', who were capable of dragging Ukraine out of its provincialism and forging a real *national* identity. Another echo of Dontsov could be heard in Khvylovyi's famous slogan 'Away from Moscow!' and his argument that provincialism and dependency on 'imperial' culture were two sides of the same coin. Ukrainians were forced to relate to world culture through Moscow and St Petersburg, but it was this very dependency, 'the slavish nature that had always worshipped the northern culture', that perpetuated their provincialism (Khvylovyi's most famous work asked the question 'Ukraine or Little Russia?'). Khvylovyi implied that Ukraine could break out of this cycle of dependency by a simple act of will, once Ukrainian intellectuals had embraced what he called '*psychological* Europe'.[58]

Khvylovyi's rejection of 'empire' and all its works was prefigured by Shevchenko, but whereas for Shevchenko this meant a certain inward focus, for Khvylovyi the result would be the liberation of Ukrainians to join the world community. Khvylovyi's cultural model for this new Ukrainian identity was classical Greece and Rome and post-Renaissance Western Europe, not Shevchenko's idealised Cossack world, still less Muscovite Byzantism or even the original culture of Rus.[59] Significantly, artists like Boichuk cited Cimabue and Giotto, respectively often said to be forerunner and founder of the Renaissance, as models for Ukrainians to emulate. Like Spengler, however, Khvylovyi believed that the West, having created first feudal and then bourgeois civilisation, had exhausted itself. Russian-Asian patriarchal culture was also exhausted. It therefore fell to the 'young nations', the newly created non-Russian republics of the USSR, to lead the next, proletarian phase of civilisation. Ukraine was particularly well placed to be at the head, not just of this 'young' Europe, but of an 'Asiatic Renaissance' as well.

Once again, the new Ukraine would be built in the cities, amongst the new working class (Khvylovyi invented the term 'non-Paris' for the generically provincial traditional Ukrainian town). Khvylovyi's writers' group was therefore known as VAPLITE, the 'Free Academy of Proletarian Literature', in opposition to the official Soviet organisations Proletkult and RAPP, the 'Revolutionary Academy of Proletarian Writers'. In art the 'Boichukist' group ARMU ('The Association of Revolutionary Artists of Ukraine') opposed the Association of Artists of Red Ukraine, which had strong all-Soviet links.

Another aspect of Ukrainian modernisation in the 1920s was religion, although the activists who established the Ukrainian Autocephalous Orthodox Church in 1921 very much saw themselves as restoring the original Kievan Church abolished in 1685–6 (autocephalous is Greek for 'self-governing'). The founders of the new Church, such as its first head, Vasyl Lypkivskyi (1864–1937), and its chief intellectual, Volodymyr Chekhivskyi (1876–?), had little in common with Khvylovyi or the Panfuturists, or the atheistic culture of Soviet Ukrainianism, but they contributed just as much to the developing ideology of cultural difference between the Russian and Ukrainian nations and their respective faiths.[60] The Ukrainian Autocephalous advocated a strict separation of Church and state, a decentralised and democratised conciliar system in which key decisions were taken not by a hierarchy of bishops but by local Sobors with a strong element of lay participation, an elected and married episcopate, the Ukrainianisation of the rite and the use of folk art and music in church – in particular the rich harmony, folk lyricism and vocal polyphony of composers such as Kyrylo Stetsenko (1882–1922) and Mykola Leontovych (1877–1921), developing the tradition of eighteenth-century masters such as Bortnianskyi and Berezovskyi. At its peak in the mid-1920s, the new Autocephalous Church, centred on its 'ancient home' of St Sofiia's in Kiev, had an estimated six million faithful.

In all their efforts, the Ukrainian 'modernisers' were greatly assisted by political developments, namely the brief Ukrainianisation campaign that lasted from the mid–1920s to the early 1930s. The campaign was sponsored by Communist Party leaders like Mykola Skrpynyk (1872–1933) and Oleksandr Shumskyi (1890–1946) for their own ends – the official party term of *korenizatsiia* implied an elite party 'putting down roots' by making itself more indigenous – although nationalist pressure helped get the policy off the ground (counterfactually, that pressure would have been much stronger if a united Ukraine had emerged in the period 1917–20). The party itself was the first to be Ukrainianised, but this was soon followed by the schools and the mass media; initial steps were even made to Ukrainianise the trade unions. In the last decade of Ukraine's 30-year artistic 'golden age', the Ukrainian intelligentsia was therefore able for the first time to exercise a real influence on the Ukrainian peasantry, as economic recovery and Soviet development encouraged it to move into the new cities and become the new Ukrainian working class.

This is precisely what Khvylovyi had wanted and Moscow conservatives had feared. Stalin's consolidation of power in Moscow brought a swift end to Ukrainianisation and the embryonic Ukrainian modernisation project. Its leading advocates were shot or imprisoned. Khvylovyi and Skrypnyk committed suicide in 1933. Zerov and Chekhivskyi disappeared in the camps. Boichuk, Kulish and Kurbas were shot. The Autocephalous Church was destroyed and forced into exile. Thereafter, the Soviet version of modernisation would predominate, although the 1920s had many lingering effects. Precisely because the decade's debates were artificially terminated, many of their key themes resurfaced in the 1990s.

Peasants into Soviets

Unfortunately for the young Ukrainians, their attempt simultaneously to modernise and Europeanise Ukrainian identity and culture met with more than political obstacles. Transnational identities still exercised a considerable attraction over many Ukrainians. Indeed, they received a new lease of life from the hopes invested in the Revolution – hopes that were shared by many Ukrainian modernists. Under the new regime Ukrainians were encouraged to identify with the 'imperial' identity, but also not to think of it as imperial. As argued in chapter five, it was perfectly normal for many non-titular subjects of a powerful and prestigious empire to identify with the 'imperial idea', especially when it was associated with a utopian project of such wide-ranging social, cultural and international ambition. And lest it be forgotten, until the 1970s at least, the Soviet Union was relatively successful in both international competition and in providing a rising standard of living and an expanding welfare system at home. As historians such as Mark Mazower and Ronald Sumy have sought to reassert, East European Communist parties were, initially at least, successful agents of a version of modernisation.[61] The fact that most Dnieper Ukrainians were Orthodox peasants with as yet only a limited sense of a broader identity undoubtedly helped.

Nor should it be forgotten that the Soviet state made considerable efforts to mobilise popular loyalties in the cultural sphere. Soviet Ukrainian intelletuals now tend to be dismissed as hacks prostituting their art to the Soviet state.[62] This may well be true, but much of their work nonetheless resonated on the popular level.[63] Their work also illustrated the considerable overlap between the native Ukrainian and Soviet versions of modernisation (Khvylovyi's partially excepted). One small example is the modernist paintings from the 1920s such as Bohomazov's *The Sawyers* (1929) and Ivan Pashchyn's *The Smiths* (1930), which celebrate the joys of proletarian labour in a distinctively lively and colourful Ukrainian style (see plate 33). In any case, the same overlap can be observed in the work of more celebrated 'national' artists, such as Mykola Kulish. His plays, especially the civil war drama *Pathetic Sonata*, are clearly rooted in the new Soviet national identity; its targets include outdated populist Ukrainian nationalism just as much as Russian chauvinism and the contorted self-restrictions of the 'Little Russian' mentality.

The work of the noted Ukrainian film-director Oleksandr Dovzhenko (1894–1956) is also a case in point, especially his acclaimed masterpiece *The Earth* (1930).[64] The film celebrates the simple beauties of Ukrainian peasant existence as well as the arrival through collectivisation of the technology (in the form of a tractor) that is about to transform their lives (in Eisenstein's alternative 1929 vision of collectivisation, *The General Line*, the tractors actually perform a waltz to mark the coming of modernity). Dovzhenko's version of traditional village life is often idyllic, but neither static nor free of conflict. Images of the natural rhythms of rural life – the opening shot of a hillside of corn waving under a lowering sky, the peaceful death of an old man in an orchard full of ripening fruit, the repose after the harvest with young couples' sexuality echoing the fertility of the land – are set alongside a melodrama of the triumph of the new village collective over kulak 'saboteurs'. Collectivisation is presented as a means of developing the natural order – the film looks backwards and forwards at the same time. The traditional is married to the modern. At the funeral of the young Vasyl, killed by the kulak Khoma as he dances home from the successful harvest, the entire village crane their necks to track the wonder of a plane passing overhead: 'The fame of Vasyl' will fly throughout the world – like that Bolshevik airplane of ours up there!'

The Earth is not a simple propaganda piece. It is difficult to imagine it being produced either by a traditional Ukrainian populist or a later Socialist Realist. However, it appeared at a time when rather different and decidedly more forceful means of collectivisation were beginning to be used. Moreover, the end of Ukrainianisation meant that the peasants who were now being driven off the land and into the rapidly expanding cities, particularly in the new lands of eastern and southern Ukraine, would be exposed to a more specifically Soviet symbolism.

Eulogies to the building of Socialism such as Volodymyr Sosiura's (1898–1965) *The Dnieper Dam* (1932) undoubtedly played a part in building Ukrainian loyalties to the new Soviet state. Dovzhenko's first sound film, *Ivan* (1932), returns to the theme of industrialisation, and its 'unheroic hero' can be taken as symbolic of the period. Ivan the everyman is an uneducated peasant who is recruited from his native village and converted into a Soviet shock worker on the Dnieper hydroelectric project. As usual, Dovzhenko's approach is far from clichéd. Ivan has trouble adjusting to the new working conditions and is initially reluctant to accept the value of education as a means to social progress, while Dovzhenko treats his counterpart, Stepan Guba, the project slacker, with sympathy (ironically or not, 'Guba-ism' entered the Soviet lexicon as a synonym for indiscipline at work). Dovzhenko also portrays many of the negative consequences of the industrialisation drive: the sublimation of the individual, the anomie of the lives of the new workers, the exploitation of the countryside they left behind. Nevertheless, there is no mistaking the central message as Ivan struggles to redefine himself through labour for the common Soviet good.

Many Ukrainians were also receptive to the idea of the new Soviet community being built around an east Slavic core. Traditional tsarist myths of the common endeavour of Russians and Ukrainians were temporarily challenged in the 1920s by historians such as Matvii Yavorskyi (1884–1937) and by Hrushevskyi, who returned to Kiev in 1924 and was temporarily fêted by the authorities. Significantly, however, the mythology of east Slavic identity was already being refashioned. Dovzhenko's civil war films *Arsenal* (1925) and *Shchors* (1939), as with *The Earth* and, in rather more fratricidal terms, the immensely popular novel by Yurii Yanovskyi *Horseriders* (1935), weave a rich ethnographic portrait of Ukraine, but this is a Ukraine in joint social struggle with revolutionary Russia, in which Ukrainian nationalists are depicted as the outsiders – an alien and alien-backed counter-revolutionary force. This type of Soviet propaganda went into overdrive during World War II, although it vacillated in an interesting fashion, sometimes appealing to the new Soviet patriotism as a factor in itself, sometimes making concessions to Ukrainian particularities, sometimes looking to the solidarity of the eastern Slavs against the common enemy. Classic examples are the war poems of the former Symbolist Pavlo Tychyna (1891–1967),[65] or Dovzhenko's monumental and rabidly anti-German film *The Battle for our Soviet Ukraine* (1943), which used 24 camera crews to provide a theatrical panorama of every aspect of the front.[66] 'Ukraine' is the object of their patriotism, but this is a patriotism that moves seamlessly back and forth across the triptych Ukraine-Soviet Ukraine-Soviet Union. Both men were careful to stress how the Soviet cause benefited Ukraine. The poster reproduced in plate 39 demonstrates one of the more important advantages. Written in Ukrainian, it shows a Soviet soldier liberating 'free Ukraine', with the west Ukrainian territories conquered in 1939–40 in the background. Works that were too 'one-sided' in praising the Ukrainians only, such as Volodymyr Sosiura's *Love Ukraine!* (1944), were soon denounced.

Outside of western Ukraine, such propaganda effectively marginalised the OUN's rival version of wartime nationalism. The Soviet World War II myth undoubtedly resonated on a popular level (two million Ukrainians fought in the Red Army, including Marshal Yeromenko at Stalingrad; no more than 90,000 in the UPA),[67] at the very time when Ukrainians as well as Russians were playing a key role in developing the pan-Slavic myth of the 1654 'reunion' of Ukraine and Russia, focusing in particular on a renewed cult of Khmelnytskyi. The other two wartime posters shown on plates 37 and 38, illustrate this point, appealing to 'the brave successors of Bohdan [Khmelnytskyi]' and urging 'To Battle, O Slavs!' Stalin created a special Order of Khmelnytskyi in 1943: this of course represented a particular version of Khmelnytskyi – the reunifier of Rus rather than the Ukrainian nation-builder. Concentrating on the former and ignoring the latter was not always easy. The play *Bohdan Khmelnytskyi* (1938) and subsequent film version (1941), by the long-term head of the Writers' Union of Ukraine Oleksandr Korniichuk (1905–72), seemed to fit the bill initially, but both were ultimately criticised for not being enthusiastically one-sided enough. The theme of Russian 'fraternal assistance' to Ukraine was much stronger in Korniichuk's civil war play *Pravda* (1937). Without it, the embryonic 'Soviet Slavic' nation-building project would have had a much greater chance of success.

An emblematic view of Khmelnytskyi the reunifier can be seen in Mykhailo Khmelko's painting *Eternal Unity* (finished 1954), which provides a sharp contrast to Mykola Ivasiuk's or even Ilia Repin's view of the Cossack era (see plate 36). In this painting the signing of the Treaty of Pereiaslav itself is placed centre-stage, as with Repin's vision of the Cossacks' mocking letter to the sultan; here, however, the Cossacks are seen to be celebrating their new destiny with Russia rather than sharing in the pleasure of their humorous despatch. The Cossacks are united before their leaders, hats in the air and swords held high, but this is a far cry from Ivasiuk's birth of a nation. The light shining on the church in the background hints at the role of outside forces (i.e. Moscow) in saving their Orthodox faith – in sharp contrast to Ivasiuk's self-contained group portrait. Not surprisingly, it is Ivasiuk's painting that now has pride of place in the Kiev National Museum of Fine Art; Khmelko's version of events is no longer fashionable and has disappeared from the Museum of National History. The 'riot of national costume' in this and other sketches of the painting somewhat undermines the effect,[68] but

Khmelko's enthusiasm for official Soviet nationalism is evident. He was a great stalwart of the 'giganticist' school of Socialist Realism. His other works include *To the Great Russian People* (1946), depicting Stalin's notorious 1945 victory toast, *The Triumph of the Conquering People* (1949), a monumental sweep of the postwar victory parade in Red Square with the massed Soviet troops tossing captured Nazi banners at Stalin's feet (see plate 35), and *The Motherland Greets a Hero*, another huge canvas depicting Khrushchev welcoming the quintessential Soviet hero Yurii Gagarin (1961). However, Khmelko was a Ukrainian, more Ukrainian than Repin or Malevich.

On the other hand, even in the work of loyalist artists like Khmelko, Ukrainian Socialist Realism had some key differences from its Russian counterpart. Many Ukrainians painted in the Soviet-Russian style, as with Oleksandr Maksymenko's *Masters of the Land* (1947), with its starkness of vision echoing the style of the nineteenth-century Itinerant movement – the new arrivals are clearly themselves itinerants. There was of course no separate Ukrainian 'school', but other Soviet Ukrainian painters were notable for their greater variety of style and more vivid use of colour.[69] Good examples would be Konstantin Lomykin's *Peasant Women with a Watermelon* (late 1950s), Viktor Zaretskyi's *Girls* (1963), Tetiana Holembiievska's *Harvest Festival* (1982) and, in particular, the work of Tetiana Yablonska, such as *Bread* (1949), *Young Mother* (1964) and *Morning* (1954), (see plate 40). The influence of Ukrainian Modernists such as Oleksandr Murashko and Mykola Kuznetsov (1850–1930) was also apparent. Whereas in the official Soviet canon Impressionism was equated with 'cosmopolitanism' and 'Zionism', its influence can clearly be seen in works such as Petro Slota's *Khreshchatyk: A Study* (1957).

Two great shadows threatened the mythology of 'Socialist achievement', however. One was the bloody Purges of the 1930s. The other was the Great Famine, which engulfed Soviet Ukraine in 1932–3 and which is now accepted to have left up to seven million dead, in addition to those who died in two other famines in 1921–3 and 1946 (hence a certain poignancy in Yablonska's *Bread* – the predominance of female labour in 1949 would not have been just a matter of custom).[70] Whole villages were wiped out, people ate domestic pets, grass, even next year's corn (notoriously defined as 'the theft of Socialist property' and made punishable by death), and cannibalism was widespread. Internal passports were introduced to prevent the starving leaving their villages in search of food. Kasimir Malevich's haunting *The Running Man* (1933–4), showing a peasant fleeing across a deserted landscape, is eloquent testimony to the disaster (see plate 34).[71]

Many Ukrainians have sought to characterise the Famine as an act of genocide. According to Ivan Drach, 'in essence the Famine of 1932–3 was not an accidental or unique episode in the fate of the Ukrainian people ... just one stage in the planned eradication of the Ukrainian nation ... almost a third of our peasants died 60 years ago just because they were and wanted to remain Ukrainians.'[72] According to James Mace, 'enemy number one for Stalin and his circle was not the Ukrainian peasant nor the Ukrainian intelligentsia. The enemy was Ukraine itself.'[73] Nevertheless, even after 1991, despite official commemorations of the sixtieth anniversary in 1993, the Great Famine has not moved to centre-stage in official or even nationalist rhetoric in the manner that might have been expected. This is not necessarily surprising. Ireland too seemed prepared to practise a form of collective amnesia about its own Famine of the 1840s until fairly recently, despite the best efforts of nationalists and others to keep the issue alive.[74] Moreover, in Ukraine the nationalist stronghold of Galicia, then under Poland, did not experience the Famine directly, and in Soviet Ukraine it segued with a succession of other tragedies – the Purges and World War II. The Famine was obviously not mentioned in official Soviet discourse, but even in popular memory the sheer trauma of the event seems to have repressed it. The seamless official rhetoric of Soviet success and the reality of recalled experience do not seem to have conflicted in the way they should.[75]

In any case, the Great Famine was only partly a 'national' tragedy. Other areas, notably the lower Volga and the Kuban, also suffered terribly.[76] The Famine was deliberate and brutal, but part of an ideological rather than a national war. It pitted town against countryside (it was of course unnatural that the countryside starved and the cities survived), proletarian against peasant, poor peasant against 'rich' peasant, young against old, as much as Russian against Ukrainian. Many ethnic Ukrainians participated in the grain-requisition bands that descended on the villages, just as many Irish exploited their fellow-countrymen in the 1840s. Nevertheless, the key cause of the famine was Stalin's 44% increase in Ukraine's grain procurement quota in 1932. Guards were posted on the Ukrainian–Russian border. It would be fair to say that the small-holding, 'rich peasant' (kulak, or *kurkul* in Ukrainian) culture that Stalin sought to destroy was disproportionately concentrated in Ukraine and that the Ukrainian population was therefore particularly vulnerable. If Gennadii Ziuganov is right to claim that there is a natural affinity between (specifically) Russian peasant culture and Socialism via the tradition of the land commune (and if Stalin thought the same way), the implications for Ukraine are clear.[77]

The Ukrainian Famine certainly had great practical effects – another reason why it was suppressed in the popular memory. It all but destroyed the social and cultural reservoir of Ukrainian identity in the countryside and left traditional populist Ukrainian nationalism stranded without a target constituency. It accelerated the move to the cities; and therefore altered the balance of forces under which the new urbanites would be exposed to Soviet-Russian culture; it left the Ukrainian intelligentsia even more isolated than before. Significantly, the upsurge in Ukrainian nationalism when German forces occupied Dnieper Ukraine for a second time in 1941–3 was but a pale shadow of that in 1917–20.

By then the intelligentsia, both the old populists and their younger rivals, had also suffered tremendously in the other great 'unmentionable' of the Soviet era – the Purges. These hit Ukraine particularly hard and were longer and more thorough-going than elsewhere. Up to '80%' of the Ukrainian intelligentsia were killed or disappeared or sent to the camps; the party was completely purged twice, in 1932–4 and 1937–8.[78] Once again, however, the Purges did not necessarily discredit the regime, at least not at the time, until the 'blank spots' in Soviet Ukrainian history began to receive proper publicity in the late 1980s. In part this was simply because the Purges were brutally effective. It was also because they provided 'evidence in blood'. As Andrei Sakharov confessed in his memoirs, it was easier to believe that so much sacrifice had a higher purpose.[79] It was also true that many Ukrainians benefited from the Purges, namely the so-called 'newly promoted' (*vydvizhentsy*) – hundreds of thousands of upwardly mobile proletarians and former peasants in the mould of Dovzhenko's Ivan, who filled the dead men's boots of the old intelligentsia.

Solzhenitsyn characterised the *vydvizhentsy* as a Soviet quasi-intelligentsia – the product of semi-education (*obrazovanshchina*), with an imbalance of 'technical' over 'creative' elements. They were little more than state functionaries, unable to provide independent social leadership and, in the words of a Ukrainian historian, 'barely connected with former cultural traditions which they were taught to abhor'.[80] In Russia elements of the old intelligentsia survived, whereas Ukraine was subject to the continued haemorrhage of its best and brightest to Moscow and Leningrad. Ukraine was increasingly governed by a nominally national but basically comprador elite, although that new elite was itself a further factor underpinning Soviet power in Ukraine. Many of Ukraine's leaders after 1991 were classic *vydvizhentsy*. Presidents Kravchuk and Kuchma were both sons of the village; prime minister Lazarenko's first job was as a driver on a collective farm.

Ukraine's Split Personality

Notwithstanding the 'hyperreality' of many aspects of official Soviet culture,[81] and, like its tsarist predecessors, its crucial failure to build an adequate support base in a civic society, its core elements were absorbed by many Ukrainians. The new Soviet cultural symbolism was of course also important for confirming Russian myths of Ukrainians as 'really' Russian but it is also true that the Soviet identity was attractive to those Ukrainians who located their sense of self in myths of common east Slavic origin. Moreover, unlike Romanov Russia, the USSR quickly acquired the resources of a serious nationalising state, creating a network of schools and mass media that was beyond the dreams and indeed the desires of tsarist bureaucrats. In terms of the nationality policy promoted through these institutions, however, the USSR was as contradictory and ambivalent as its tsarist predecessor, albeit in different ways.

Differences were most apparent on the political level. Whereas tsarist Russia had abolished all local institutional peculiarities in Ukraine, the Soviet Union was formally a federal state. Before 1991, many Western commentators dismissed Soviet federalism as a sham. It was certainly true that local power was more apparent than real and that the federalisation of the state was counterbalanced by the highly centralised Communist Party. However, formal federalism made a real difference, and not just because sleeping institutions were finally invested with real power after Gorbachev's reforms led to democratic elections in all the republics in 1990. Even before then, the territorialisation of Ukraine in the Ukrainian SSR, the existence of a Ukrainian 'parliament', a Ukrainian cabinet of ministers, a Ukrainian version of the Soviet flag, even separate Ukrainian membership of the United Nations, all provided important consolidation points for Ukrainian national identity.

Another consolidating factor was Kiev, which was much more Ukrainian in 1991 than it had been in Bulgakov's time (the *White Guard* was set in 1918). Again, this was an unintended by-product of Soviet policy. The original capital of the Ukrainian SSR was Kharkiv. It was moved to Kiev in 1934, not so much to control a Ukrainianisation campaign that was already defeated as because the authorities were confident they could create a model proletarian Soviet city in the heart of Ukraine and proselytise its Soviet Ukrainian identity westwards.[82] Nevertheless, the capital generated an Academy of Sciences, institutes and libraries, which in turn bred a new postwar intelligentsia, who exercised a certain Ukrainianising influence on the former peasants moving into the city (which was 72% Ukrainian by 1989) after 1945. Despite the intentions of the Soviet authorities, the cultural and civilisational symbolism of a Kievan Ukraine was of course also very different from that of a Ukraine based in Kharkiv, on the edge of the great Eurasian steppe, where even Khvylovyi had looked to an 'Asiatic Renaissance'.

One great similarity between the Soviet and the late tsarist states, however, was that the official Soviet culture was centred around (a particular version of) Russian culture. The Soviet empire-building project was also a type of Russian nation-building project. Whereas this was deeply alienating for Estonians or Chechens, for the Ukrainians (as under the Romanovs) the privileging of Russian was both attractive and repellent. It helped some to identify more easily with the new 'imperial' culture, while for others the very insidiousness of this temptation produced a backlash against the dangers of 'Russification'. As the USSR's official culture readopted and readapted many of the tactical blind-spots and downright Ukrainophobias of its tsarist predecessor, Ukrainians continued to be subject to both push and pull.

From the late 1950s onwards this split identity was increasingly regionalised, with schools, universities, media and other cultural institutions in urban areas of eastern and southern Ukraine converting wholesale to the official Soviet-Russian hybrid. By 1989, when the ethnic balance of the population was 73% Ukrainian and 22% Russian, 47.5% of schoolchildren studied in Ukrainian language schools, with 47% in their Soviet-Russian counterparts. In Galicia the number in Ukrainian language schools was around 90%, in the Donbas it was less than 10% and in Crimea zero.[83] The conflict of identities was in part a struggle between the 'all-Soviet' and Ukrainian republican levels, but it was also a struggle at the lower level, between different versions of what it meant to be Ukrainian. Kenneth Farmer has defined this as the opposition between the myth of 'national moral patrimony' and the myth of 'proletarian internationalism' in Ukraine; Ilya Prizel has written of the 'Central European' version of Ukrainian identity versus the 'national Slavic' concept; Oleksandr Hrytsenko has contrasted the 'sacred' nineteenth-century populist and 'profane' (Soviet) versions of Ukrainian identity.[84] Then there was the opposition between 'high' and 'low' culture, perhaps best symbolised by the popular post-war comedians Shtepsel and Tarapunka. Shtepsel spoke mostly Russian, Tarapunka Ukrainian. Tarapunka expressed the folk wisdom of the village, but was usually the butt of his more 'sophisticated' partner. These oppositions are not identical. Nevertheless, Ukrainian nationalism and the idea of a 'Central European' Ukrainian identity now had to compete with a Soviet Ukrainian identity that largely coincided with the east Slavic idea after the Ukrainianisation and internationalist possibilities of the 1920s faded away and High Stalinism turned inwards.

For Ukrainians under the USSR, therefore, the semiotics of 'nation-building' was once again operating on two levels. All-Soviet institutions worked in parallel with those of the Ukrainain SSR. Many Ukrainians developed a stronger sense of their Ukrainian identity under the USSR; many others were caught up in the Soviet project. To test which was the stronger would have required the kind of sociological inquiry that was hardly a feasible option at the time, and retrospective surveys would be unreliable. It is significant, however, that Ukrainian (and Russian) peasants entering the cities after the 1930s were the prime target of the new Soviet symbolism. Soviet identities have proved remarkably persistent since 1991 in the very places where one would expect, in the new urban centres of eastern and southern Ukraine.[85] Another telling piece of evidence is that Russification (better, 'Sovietisation') is exactly what Ukrainian dissidents of the 1960s and 1970s thought was happening (see page 152). The very same Ukrainians who hailed the independence of 'eternal' Ukraine in 1991 were worried about its possible disappearance only a decade before. At the time it was assumed that Russia's Ukrainian 'younger brothers' would assimilate;[86] after 1991 it tended to be forgotten that the creation of *homo Sovieticus* had ever been a viable project at all.

The Soviet project still had to deal with western Ukraine, however, annexed to the Ukrainian SSR at first temporarily in 1939–41 and then permanently in 1944–5 (western Ukraine here means the four regions of Galicia, Volhynia, Bukovyna and Transcarpathia – Berestia went to Belarus, Peremyshl and Kholm to Poland, the Lemko region to Poland and Czechoslovakia). Stalin's policy in western Ukraine was based on the assumption that he could succeed where Bobrinskii had failed. Although it is tempting to say that he might have done so if Sovietisation policies had been applied with greater force, it is hard to see how these could have been more repressive than they actually were. Hundreds of thousands of west Ukrainians were killed or deported in the late 1940s, and an undeclared state of war existed between the Soviet authorities and the OUN-UPA until the early 1950s. All Ukrainian institutions were suppressed, including the Greek Catholic Church, forcibly dissolved into the Russian Orthodox Church at a staged unity 'Sobor' (council) in 1946. (The 'Sobor' was completely uncanonical. The real Church hierarchy was in prison; delegates were chosen by the KGB and were in any case 'fortified at breakfast with a hundred grams of vodka and two hundred grams of wine'.)[87] Until the early 1990s the region was policed with particular severity by the KGB to prevent any resurgence of nationalism.

The only respect in which Soviet policy could perhaps have been even more brutal was that Galicia was not 'ethnically cleansed'. Many Galicians were deported, but there was no large-scale Russian resettlement of the region, apart from a one-off influx of party officials in the late 1940s. Khrushchev claimed in his secret speech to the 1956 Soviet Party Congress that 'the Ukrainians avoided meeting this fate [the mass deportation of other nationalities] only because there were too many of them and there was no place to which to deport them. Otherwise, [Stalin] would have deported them also. (Laughter and animation in the hall.)'[88] He must have been referring only to the west Ukrainians and to the worse fate that might have befallen them; but who knows? There was in fact 'cleansing' of minorities, but the near-disappearance of the prewar Jewish population and the flight and expulsion of an estimated 1.3 million Poles in 1944–8 only served to increase Ukrainian dominance of the region (some 520,000 Ukrainians were expelled from Poland).[89] Expulsion of Poles from Volhynia was in fact begun by the UPA, and in the euphemistic and inappropriate modern terminology would indeed qualify as 'ethnic cleansing'. So would many actions of the Polish Home Army and the destruction by the Communist security forces of centuries of Ukrainian history in areas such as Peremyshl and Kholm in 'Operation Visla' in 1947.[90] Nevertheless, the definitive end to the long historical struggle with the Poles helped to consolidate the new

Ukraine and would in the long run undermine a key reason for Ukrainian solidarity with Moscow.

Stalin was unable to extirpate west Ukrainian nationalism, however. In part, this was because Soviet policy elsewhere dictated restraint. Poland's new borders and the Ukrainianisation of newly annexed Transcarpathia were justified on an ethnic basis. On the whole, however, the simplest answer is the most plausible. As in the Baltic states, national identity was now simply too strong to eradicate by force. At this point, another counterfactual suggests itself. What if Stalin had not annexed western Ukraine in 1945? Might the balance of political forces in Soviet Ukraine have been more manageable, especially as the rest of Ukraine would not then have been so directly subject to the west Ukrainian 'contagion effect'? More broadly, did Stalin not obviously overextend the USSR by absorbing rebellious western regions such as Galicia and the Baltic states, without whom there might have been no 'demonstration' or 'domino' effect to encourage the other Soviet republics to break away in 1990–1? Could the USSR have survived as a more compact unit?

To look at the question in another way, what would an unabsorbed western Ukraine have looked like? It is difficult to imagine it as a rump state on its own; it would in any case have been fiercely irredentist. Renewed Polish control was never a serious possibility. The situation had changed radically since Galicia was awarded to Poland in 1922–3, and holding down a long postwar Ukrainian *intafada* would have seriously weakened the new Poland. An unresolved 'west Ukrainian' problem would have reopened the 'Polish problem' and even the 'German problem', undermining the postwar deal whereby Poland was encouraged to shift itself bodily westwards and become more of a homogeneous nation-state. Nor was a 'two Ukraine' solution at all likely (as with Moldova and Romania). The western half would have to have been led by the Communist Party of western Ukraine, which Stalin had eliminated in 1938. The Western powers at least were therefore perfectly happy with Stalin's option.[91] Unless, as many Ukrainians then hoped, the geopolitical situation had been transformed by the Cold War suddenly becoming Hot, an independent Ukrainian, even a west Ukrainian, state was not a serious possibility.

The USSR was therefore forced to create a hybrid it ultimately could not control. *Sobornist* (Ukrainian national unity) may have been achieved by Soviet power, but would help undermine it in the end. A rather different effect was achieved by the one other piece in the territorial jigsaw – Crimea. Having been an 'autonomous republic' between 1921 and 1945, the peninsula was transferred from the Russian SFSR to the Ukrainian SSR to mark the three hundredth anniversary of the Treaty of Pereiaslav in 1954. Once again, different motives were enmeshed. To most Russians and Soviet leaders the legal niceties were immaterial. For economic reasons and to help build Ukrainian loyalty to the Union, Crimea was placed in Ukraine but not of it. Ironically, Russian nationalists have been loudly questioning the 'legality' of the decision since 1991 – as if matters of constitutional procedure were always the USSR's number one priority (they are certainly important now – Crimea belongs to Ukraine). On the other hand, Ukrainians like Hrushevskyi and others had long argued that Ukraine was geopolitically 'incomplete' without Crimea.[92] Crimea also occupies very different places in different national mythologies. To the Ukrainians it was the Cossacks' outlet to the sea; to the Russians it was the jewel in the crown of empire and a site of military glory – or at least glorious defeat, the most emotive symbol in all of the former Soviet territory that Moscow lost in 1991. To the Crimean Tatars, it is their historical homeland.

The timing, if not the legality, of the transfer was certainly important. Regardless of previous history,[93] in 1954 the peninsula was almost *terra incognita*. The Slav population was but a fraction of prewar levels, and the Crimean Tatars had been deported *en masse* in 1944. The total population was a mere 228,000 in 1945. Most of the new in-migrants would be Russian. Crucially, moreover, Crimea had missed out on the Ukrainianisation of the 1920s. Whereas in eastern Ukraine Ukrainian cultural institutions were in postwar decline, in Crimea they simply did not exist. If Soviet–Russian culture put deep roots down in the Donbas, in Crimea the dominant culture would be better described as Russo-Soviet. Nor was there a Ukrainian hinterland to which new settlers might partly adapt, as in eastern Ukraine. Crimeans were therefore acculturated according to the Russian nationalist version of the peninsula's mythology, as they were never exposed to any other. The Russian majority that inhabited Crimea in 1991 (67% of the total local population were ethnic Russian, 81% were Russophone) was a relatively recent phenomenon, but it was a reality independent Ukraine would have to live with.

Conclusions

Many have taken the fact that Ukraine achieved independence in 1991 as vindication of the theory that the twentieth century saw the development and universalisation of a modern Ukrainian national consciousness. Clearly, Ukrainian national identity was stronger in 1991 than it had been in 1917. However, this new national identity was not uniform and had been profoundly transformed, in many ways *created*, during the Soviet era. Independence was delivered as much by chance and circumstance as by the teleological progress of some kind of Hegelian national spirit. These factors will be examined in chapter eight. In reality, many Ukrainians accommodated themselves to the conditions of the time. The period after independence cannot be understood without realistic remembrance of the complex influences to which Ukrainians were subject to throughout the Soviet period. Modern Ukraine has been shaped as much by the Soviet experience as by the legacy of the national idea of 1917–20.

8

Independence: Gained or Gifted?

There was a real fear amongst Ukrainian dissidents in the 1960s and 1970s that they were losing the battle. Just as Ukrainian culture had effectively been eradicated from territories beyond the Ukrainian SSR in the 1930s (such as the Kuban, the refuge of many Zaporozhian Cossacks in the 1790s) and eastern Poland in the late 1940s, they feared it would soon disappear in Soviet Ukraine itself. One samizdat document from 1980 claimed that 'for 60 years the so-called government of Ukraine has been imposing the practice of national genocide ... every day Ukraine remains a part of the USSR brings our national destruction closer.'[1] The mechanism was clear. According to the writer Yurii Badzo, in his samizdat epic *The Right to Live* confiscated by the police in 1979 but eventually rewritten and published in the 1990s, 'the route to the creation of a "single Soviet nation", that is to deepening the Russian nation [by absorbing] the other ethnoses of the USSR' was through the increasing predominance of Russian as the so-called ' "inter-national language of communication". A change of language will sooner or later lead to a change in ethnic consciousness,' he predicted.[2] Language was not the only aspect of acculturation, but it was certainly the most obvious. The Soviet-Russian culture had clearly put deep roots down by the 1980s, especially in the big cities of the east and south of Ukraine.[3]

Badzo's statement came in a section entitled 'The Future, or a Prediction of National Death'. The pressure on Ukrainian language and culture was perhaps real enough to justify his prophecy. If Andropov had survived longer as Soviet leader after Brezhnev, or if Gorbachev had stuck to his original moderate path of system-preserving reformism, an extra generation of Soviet rule might indeed have had the effect Ukrainian dissidents feared. Ukraine was already a country of two languages and cultures, with the Ukrainian half in retreat. Like their counterparts in the nineteenth century and in countless national movements elsewhere in the world, Ukrainian nationalists therefore had a difficult circle to square – 'to maintain the position that a traditional culture had been [or was being] destroyed while making the integrity of that culture a claim for political independence'.[4]

The 1960s: A Prelude or a Coda?

Ukrainian dissidents in the 1960s and 1970s therefore saw themselves as conducting a life-and-death 'defensive movement' (*rukh oporu*) against the threat of assimilation to the Soviet-Russian culture. Significantly, Ukraine had probably the largest national dissident movement in the USSR, and not just because of the size of the republic. Russia was even larger, but had fewer 'national' dissidents. The Ukrainian 'movement' never numbered more than a thousand individuals (one survey counted exactly 942),[5] but it was at least embedded within a broader culture seeking national rehabilitation and revival. The KGB paid the Ukrainians the compliment of policing them with particular severity – an estimated 50% of all political prisoners in the USSR in the 1960s were Ukrainian.[6]

The dissident movement that arose during the Khrushchev 'thaw' (in Ukrainian the 'generation of the 1960s' or *shistdesiatnyky*) was, however, very much a product of its times. The armed insurrection tactics of the 1940s were abandoned as both impractical and, in the changed circumstances of a consolidated Soviet regime, counterproductive. The majority of dissidents operated within the existing legal framework, not just to avoid arrest, but also in the attempt to force the authorities to live up to their own formal commitment to 'Leninist Nationality Policy'.[7] Although this might seem like a lonely exercise in irony, it was precisely by animating these paper rights (Article 72 of the 1977 Soviet constitution gave the republics the right to secede) that Ukraine eventually won its independence in 1991. Most dissidents recognised other aspects of regime consolidation by speaking the language of Soviet welfarism, remaining within the parameters of a Socialist project that was still assumed to be viable and popular. Ukrainian autonomy or independence was not now promoted as a value in itself. It was promised instead that it would 'secure an incomparably high standard of living' for all.[8]

Another difference was that the centre of the 1960s movement was in Kiev rather than in Lviv, and the new Soviet Ukrainian intelligentsia at its heart were the intellectual heirs of Kostomarov and Drahomanov rather than Malaniuk and Dontsov. The explicit ethnonationalism that the OUN-UPA had itself begun to question in the later years of the war was subsumed in a rhetoric of Leninist 'internationalism'. Even in Lviv, the programme of the underground Ukrainian Worker-Peasants' Union declared that 'the struggle for an independent Ukraine is not a struggle for privileges for our nation at the expense of other nations, it is a struggle for equal rights ... the enemies of the Ukrainian people have been Russian governments, not the Russian people.'[9] (This did not stop the authorities arresting the group's leader, Levko Lukianenko, in 1961 and imprisoning him for 27 years in the camps.) As, again, parts of the Ukrainian underground of the 1940s had already recognised, the *shistdesiatnyky* accepted that in order to win its independence Ukraine would now have to distinguish between 'Russian imperialists' and the 'Russian people' and make contact and common cause with the latter. As one author had argued in 1943, 'in the destruction of the empire, the Russian people must [also] play out their historical role.'[10] The Ukrainians therefore adopted the Polish slogan of 'for your freedom and ours', although there was as yet little reciprocal interest from Russia.[11] This strategic alliance was not pursued as actively as might have been expected until Ukrainians began to build links with the Democratic Russia movement in the Soviet parliament elected in 1989.

Ukrainian dissidents also embedded their appeals in the language of universal human rights. According to Yaroslav Hrytsak, the watchwords of the *shistdesiatnyky* were therefore simultaneously 'the rights of the individual and the [rights of the] nation'.[12] In the words of the iconic poet Vasyl Stus, who died in the Gulag in 1985, his 'generation of young Ukrainian intelligentsia, turned [involuntarily] into a generation of political prisoners, were brought up on the ideas of humanism, justice and freedom'.[13] As a consequence, Ukrainian dissidents had some success in building a broader geographical base for their rebranded nationalism. The above-mentioned survey recorded that 25% of dissidents came from Lviv and 38% from Kiev (the latter representing a considerable revival after the repressions of the 1930s) and the rest from further afield – still geographically lopsided, but more evenly spread than in the past.[14]

The new rhetoric helped to reassure, if not to recruit, Russians and Russophones in Ukraine. However, what was true of the mainstream was less true of the extremes. Groups operating in the spirit of the OUN, such as the Ukrainian National Front, two different versions of which spanned the 1960s and 1970s, continued to appear. One of the more celebrated dissidents, Valentyn Moroz, by calling for a 'noble frenzy' of anti-Soviet heroism, echoed none too subtly the excitable prose of Dontsov.[15] (Moroz was forced into exile but reemerged in Lviv in 1992 as a figurehead of local ultranationalists.) The promotion of 'national revival', in particular the call for a defensive renationalisation of the schools and mass media, in any case inherently involved some elements of ethnonationalism. It also meant a certain parochialism. Kiev writers and artists were concerned to protect their milieu,[16] but this was a long way removed from that of the highly Sovietised working class and indeed of most Russophones in Ukraine. In the big cities of the east and south there were few active dissidents, and even they rarely concerned themselves with the national question, the one notable exception being Ivan Dziuba from Donetsk (where Vasyl Stus also spent his childhood). The Ukrainian dissidents were unfortunate that an era of relative liberalisation was also one of perceived prosperity for the apolitical majority.

Nevertheless, the *shistdesiatnyky* ensured by their civic rhetoric and innovative tactics that they were more popular and harder to isolate than a narrowly ethnonationalist movement would have been. It took three waves of arrests to bring a final end to their protests – in 1965–6, 1972–3 and 1976–80 – but many of the same individuals would return to the forefront of the national movement under Gorbachev. The much weaker Belarusian Popular Front, in contrast, had only a handful of former dissidents (in essence one, Zianon Pazniak) to lead it. As well as the same individuals, the same tactics would also reappear, as would the label 'national-democrat'.

The 1960s and 1970s were less innovative culturally. There was little real sense of cultural ferment preparing the ground for the eventual political breakthrough in 1991, as in the Russian empire before 1917 or Poland before 1980. Ukrainian dissidents put immense energy into reviving old cultural icons and cultural styles (and even this was difficult by the mid-1970s), but the conceptual bases of the 'national idea' were never renewed. For once, the Ukrainian diaspora, in the shape of the 'New York' writers' group of the 1960s and 1970s, was more innovative, in part because it was obviously closer to Western trends and fashions.[17] A typical example is Oles Honchar's (1918–94) 1968 novel *Sobor* ('The Cathedral'), about a small east Ukrainian town whose residents struggle to preserve a local Cossack church. The fact that the tale was controversial enough to cause a furore says a lot about the limits of official Soviet Ukrainian identity, but as a novel it broke no new ground. Most of the key poets and writers of the era, with the exception of unusual talents like Vasyl Symonenko (1935–63), followed a familiar recipe of folklorism mixed with a revived cult of Shevchenko and the Cossack myth, while Ivan Drach (born 1936) and others revisited the modernism of the 1920s. Reviving, recycling and restarting the unfinished projects of the past were natural priorities for a new generation that felt itself to be beginning again almost *ex nihilo*, in the year zero of the new Soviet order circa 1958. Undercurrents of Western influence were reaching Ukraine by the early 1960s – especially in music (the Beatles) and the visual arts, but by the 1970s artistic rebellion was limited to rock music played in basement cafés and the 'new lyricism' or 'quiet painting' style of artists like Yevhen Volobuiev (born 1912) and Zoia Lerman (born 1934) – issuing no open challenge to official canons, but still staking out a limited sphere of private expression.[18] More radical artists, such as Feodosii Humeniuk (born 1941), a follower of Boichuk, found themselves living abroad. Two exhibitions of non-conformist Ukrainian art were held in 1975 and 1976, but the venue on both occasions was a private apartment – in Moscow. Many intellectuals turned inwards, or, like the Lviv group based around the samizdat journal *The Chest,* sought solace in Oriental mysticism or obscure musings about the Trypillian past.

Still, occasional works could slip through the censor's fingers, such as Lina Kostenko's 1980 verse novel, a popular reclamation of the

Khmelnytskyi period through the eyes of the semi-mythical poetess *Marusia Churai*. More subtly, Valerii Shevchuk's novels *Dim na hori* ('House on the Hill', 1983) and *Try lystky za viknom* ('Three Leaves outside the Window', 1986) were notable for their subversive rebranding of Gogol's 'provincial prose' and reworking of Hryhorii Skovoroda's eighteenth-century philosophy of Stoic endurance into a theme of passive resistance to the Leviathan of empire.[19] An Aesopian opposition to Sovietisation was also provided by the music of Volodymyr Ivasiuk, whose most famous Ukrainian-language song *Chervona ruta* ('Red Rue', 1969) was later taken as the name of the biannual Ukrainian music festival, established in 1989. Ivasiuk was found hanged in mysterious circumstances in 1978. Most of the reported 10,000 people who turned up to his funeral knew to point the finger at the KGB. The 1970s were also the time, however, when the new Soviet TV culture was making huge inroads in Ukraine. Alla Pugacheva, a sort of Soviet cross between Barbra Streisand, Joni Mitchell and Elizabeth Taylor (at least as far as her tortured love life was concerned), was just as popular as Ivasiuk.

The most innovative cultural product of the era was Serhii Paradzhanov's acclaimed film *Shadows of our Forgotten Ancestors* (1965, based on the 1911 novel by Mykhailo Kotsiubynskyi). The film is set in a nineteenth-century Carpathian village, and its bizarre kaleidoscopic techniques, atonal score and non-naturalistic use of colour evoke an atmosphere and lifestyle where Ukraine's pre-Christian traditions are still a part of everyday life. The film's central characters are star-struck lovers, Carparthian Montagues and Capulets, except that Romeo (played by Ivan Mykolaichuk, to whom the director gives an ethereal countenance supposedly reminiscent of the twelfth-century icon the *Angel with the Golden Hair*),[20] having fallen in love with the daughter of the man who had his father murdered, in the end marries a local witch. The film's real significance, however, was its radical subversion of the official canon of Socialist Realism and a suggestion of a rival discourse of Ukrainian magic realism. But most nationalist intellectuals, for perfectly good reasons, remained stuck in a romantic, revivalist mode. Paradzhanov was an outsider, originally born in Georgia to Armenian parents.

Rukh

Apart from a tiny handful of radical dissidents, real hope of independence survived only in the Ukrainian diaspora when Mikhail Gorbachev succeeded Konstantin Chernenko as General Secretary of the CPSU in 1985. Ukraine was still run by Brezhnev's long-time crony Volodymyr Shcherbytskyi, who managed another four years in power until September 1989, during which time Ukraine lagged behind events elsewhere. In the late 1980s as glasnost gripped Moscow and the attention of foreign jour-nalists, it was still possible for Ukrainian dissidents to be arrested on trumped-up 'rape' charges and for demonstrators to be pummelled with truncheons, if they managed to demonstrate at all. Embryonic opposition groups were infiltrated by the KGB's notorious local 'Third Department', and *agent provocateurs* fomented internal disunity and helped create an 'extremist' image.[21] The Ukrainian Politburo archives reveal that this was still conscious policy.[22] Shcherbytskyi continued to talk of building the Soviet nation and 'strengthening the feeling of Soviet general-national pride'.[23] Nevertheless, movement 'from under the rubble' began in 1987.

The subsequent period is now often depicted in dualistic, even moralistic, terms, with the new opposition 'slaying the dragon' of the Communist Party, but in fact at least four potential 'oppositions' emerged in Ukraine at this time. First to appear were the 'informal' ginger groups such as the Ukrainian Helsinki Union (1988), dominated by highly motivated former political prisoners. Later (1989), and somewhat belatedly by the standard of other Soviet republics and COMECOM states, came the Ukrainian 'Popular Front', the hybrid organisation called the 'Popular Movement in Support of Perestroika' (Rukh), the natural home of the mainstream of former *shistde-siatnyky*. As with the embryonic civil society of the 1960s, both groups mainly focused on the national question. The third potential opposition was the Democratic Platform (1990) within the local Communist Party, which had some crossover with Rukh, but saw itself as more of a 'general democ-ratic' movement. The fourth came in the form of the independent trade unions that emerged after the miners' strikes in the Donbas in 1989.

To begin with the last, the miners were largely a negative force. They undermined the Communist Party's claim to represent the working class and reminded the authorities that the Donbas had a long history of reject-ing all outside authority.[24] However, despite the opinion of one author,[25] there is little evidence that the contacts established between Ukrainian nationalists and working-class activists in 1989–91 were anything more than ephemeral. A confidential report to the Ukrainian Politburo in July 1991 estimated with somewhat mystifying precision that only '8%' of the workforce was under nationalist influence. 'More than 50%' was res-olutely apolitical.[26] Rukh and the miners enjoyed a temporary coincidence of interests and of anti-centrist ideology – an important factor in neutralising some potential east Ukrainian opposition to independence in 1989–91 – but there was no sign of any real meeting of minds. A key weakness of the Ukrainian opposition was that there was no local equivalent of Poland's Solidarity, or even KOR, the dissident-worker contact group.

The history of the Democratic Platform in Ukraine has received less attention, but is also instructive. Unlike Rukh, it emphasised the goals of democratisation and, after it left the Communist Party in mid-1990, de-Communisation and market reform. As with Skoropadskyi in 1918, spokesmen such as the sociologist Valerii Khmelko hoped to build a new multi-ethnic Ukrainian democracy and appeal across ethnolinguistic and regional divides, and that parallel democratisation in all the Soviet republics would allow them to coexist in some form of loose confederation. Significantly, however, the Democratic Platform failed to find any common agenda with Rukh. The terms 'general democratic' and 'cosmopolitan' were actually insults in Ukrainian nationalist circles where national independence always had to come first. Nor was the Platform ever able to establish itself as a real rival to Rukh. Rukh had its own problems, but a clearer support base; the Democratic Platform had little success in mobilising the population across ethnolinguistic lines. By aiming at the centre ground between Ukrainian and Soviet nationalism, the 'general democrats' targeted the floating vote of the soft middle, Ukrainians with vague or multiple identities who were difficult to motivate out of their armchairs. A key lesson in modern Ukrainian politics has been that the silent majority usually stays silent. A second lesson was the discovery that between the extremes of nationalism and orthodox Communism there were too few Ukrainians prepared to lobby for democratisation and market reform as ends in themselves – hence the difficulty in pushing both these issues after 1991. It is significant that the existing Communist elite eventually decided the Democratic Platform's anti-Communist agenda was more of a threat to their own survival in power than Rukh. Nevertheless, the Platform had one major achievement to its name. At a conference in Kharkiv in January 1991, of likeminded groups from throughout the Soviet Union, they devised the formula that would eventually replace that union: a 'Commonwealth of Independent States'.

Ukrainian nationalism on the other hand had a more emotive appeal to its particular constituency. Initially, the pace of events was therefore set by the first two of Ukraine's potential 'oppositions' – Rukh and its penumbra of 'informal' groups. Rukh was originally a broad church. Its first leaders were the establishment intellectuals and former *shistdesiatnyky* who had managed in the main to avoid arrest in the 1960s and 1970s, flanked on the one side by former political prisoners and on the other by reform Communists attempting to control the movement from within. Official control tactics were common enough in the Communist bloc, but so was the difficulty of maintaining the basic triangle of reformist officials and moderate and radical opposition. Moreover, in Ukraine the number of former prisoners was exceptionally high and regional pressures more telling – west Ukrainians preferred an alliance of the two oppositions, east Ukrainians moderates and reform Communists. Although Rukh initially tried to marry the two strategies, Ukraine's lopsided political geography meant that it was always likely to lose more support through competition with radicals in the west than it could gain through moderation in the east. Under pressure from the Ukrainian Helsinki Union, which in April 1990 reconstituted itself as modern Ukraine's first proper political party, the Ukrainian Republican Party, and with its vision of the possible radically broadened by the domino-like collapse of Central European Communism in late 1989, Rukh transformed itself between its first and second congresses (in September 1989 and October 1990). It dispensed with the initial tutelage of the Communist Party and came out 'in opposition to the CPSU and the totalitarian state-party system' and unambiguously for 'the state independence of Ukraine'.[27]

Rukh's leadership, in the main intellectuals like Ivan Drach and Dmytro Pavlychko, tended to concentrate on cultural politics, spearheading a 'writers' renaissance' – the revival of the national language, myths and symbols of which they saw themselves as the guardians.[28] Rukh's guiding political principle was the 1960s model of a 'simultaneous national revival' of the Ukrainians and all local national minorities. But the latter were still deemed to be minorities. Rukh spokesmen constantly referred to Ukrainians' 'special status' on their 'native land' or assumed there was no zero-sum game – Ukrainian national revival need not harm the interests of Ukrainian Russians or Russophone Ukrainians. Although it described itself in its original programme as acting 'according to the principles of humanism, democracy, social justice and [the key Soviet code word] internationalism, proceeding from the interests of all citizens of the republic, regardless of nationality ... Rukh considers the propaganda of racial and national exclusivity and chauvinistic and nationalistic views to be incompatible with its principles', it was nonetheless capable of gross insensitivity to Russophones, as when it appealed to them to return to their 'maternal tongue ... your choice [of language] is weak-willed (*malodushnyi*) and mistaken'.[29]

Russophone activists, liberal centrists and social democrats therefore drifted away. In Ukraine's bifurcated society, Rukh increasingly only represented one half of the population at most. A poll of delegates to the first Rukh congress in 1989 revealed the gap: 73% gave as their top priority 'supporting the development of Ukrainian culture and language', and 46% the 'solving of pressing economic problems'. Amongst the general population priorities were the other way around – 44% opting for economic problems and only 12% for 'the development of Ukrainian culture and language'.[30] At the 1990 congress, a massive 95% of delegates were Ukrainian (73% in the general population), and 57% came from either Galicia or Kiev (19%).[31] Copying the tactics of the Baltic Popular Fronts, from whom the Ukrainians learnt much, Rukh mobilised an impressive human chain to symbolise national unity in January 1990 (the anniversary of the UNR–ZUNR 'union' in 1919). Over a million people linked hands from Lviv to Kiev but, equally significantly, no further. Unlike in the Baltic republics, however, excluding the 'Soviet' half of the population from the political process was not a practical possibility. Nor did the Baltic republics' 'Citizens' Congress' tactics – rejecting all manifestations of Soviet power and seeking to restore pre-Soviet authorities – transfer easily to Ukraine. In 1990–1 a new group to the right of Rukh, the Interparty Assembly, backed by the émigré OUN, attempted to organise a petition campaign to register citizens of a restored Ukrainian People's Republic, possibly within broader 'ethnographic' borders. One source accepts a figure of 729,000 signatures, collected mainly in western Ukraine of course, but this was a pale shadow of the Baltic movements.[32] Significantly, most Ukrainians, and most Ukrainian nationalists, automatically thought within the limits of Soviet Ukraine. This was not true of the Ukrainian diaspora, and its richer members in North America helped Rukh considerably with financial and moral support. However, unlike its equivalents in Armenia and the Baltic republics,[33] it was unable to add decisive political weight in the domestic arena. It did help to steer Rukh away from initial Communist Party control, but in the Ukrainian context a more radical agenda was always a mixed blessing.

A Minority Faith

The decisive moment in the Gorbachev era in Ukraine came with the March 1990 elections to the Ukrainian Supreme Soviet. Thereafter politics was no longer a simple struggle between the unelected Communist Party apparatus and romantic nationalists claiming the right to speak for an undifferentiated 'people'. Real democratic representation made all the difference. A 'national-democratic' opposition (Rukh) now existed for the first time in a Supreme Soviet that had suddenly become a real parliament; and the Communist Party was forced bewilderedly into forging real rather than ascribed relations with the people it claimed to represent (and it *did* still represent many). However, the elections also showed the historical divisions between nationalist and Soviet Ukraine were still strong.

In 1989–90, as its counterparts collapsed throughout the Warsaw Pact states, a seriously rattled Communist Party had feared that Rukh might sweep all before it. In fact, it won only a quarter of the seats, compared to up to 80% for similar popular fronts in the Baltic republics, Transcaucasia and Moldova. Rukh won almost every seat in Galicia and performed strongly in Volhynia, Kiev and some other urban areas of central Ukraine, but picked up only a handful of seats in the southeast.[34] In the far west, Transcarpathia kept to its own ways, electing neither Communists nor national-democrats. Rukh did not do as well as expected in Chernivtsi (Bukovyna), although widespread fraud was alleged. In total, Rukh had 108 seats to the Communist Party's 239 (the parliament had 450 seats – 385 were in fact originally elected as Communists, but defections began almost immediately). The Democratic Platform had 28 deputies; the rest were independents.

The elections confirmed that Ukraine was still a highly regionalised country. The population remained divided by ethnic, linguistic and religious differences and by the variety of historical experiences of the regions in which they lived. Towards the end of the twentieth century it was clear that both Ukrainian and Soviet-Russian culture had made inroads on the basically parochial identities that had predominated at its beginning. Since 1991 it has become possible to carry out opinion surveys which have confirmed these impressions. One poll taken by Democratic Initiatives in 1996 recorded only 34% of the population as identifying primarily with Ukraine (mainly in the west, the centre and the countryside), 3% with Russia and 17% with the USSR or CIS (mainly in the urban east and south), as compared to 37% with their own town, village or region.[35]

The elections also revealed partial, but not widespread, disillusionment with the Soviet system. Many elites were aware that the Soviet modernisation project was running out of steam – hence the launch of perestroika – but it was unclear how far this had filtered down to a popular level. Real economic growth probably stopped sometime in the 1970s. The limited shelf life of Soviet 'welfare state authoritarianism' was apparent to those Soviet leaders who had simultaneously to subsidise international superpower competition, the appeasement of so many post-Stalinist interest groups and a rising domestic standard of living, but it was precisely these subsidies that disguised economic slowdown for the general population.[36] It was a masterpiece of Gorbachev's rhetoric to characterise the Brezhnev era as the 'time of stagnation', but to most it represented the period when their standard of living caught up with the sacrifices made in the 1930s and 1940s. After almost a half-century of constant traumas since 1914, the peace and (relative) prosperity of the 1960s and 1970s were undoubtedly attractive to many Ukrainians.[37]

Roman Szporluk and others have raised the question of whether the USSR might have survived the end of Communism if Soviet culture had proved to be more durable than Soviet economics.[38] If, as of 1990, there was considerable confusion as to the extent of the system's economic failure, its culture was clearly extant in many parts of the urban east and south. The national-democratic movement was clearly making little impact in this regard. Ukraine as a whole therefore lacked the clear trajectory of the Baltic republics towards separation from the USSR. Yet, on 24 August 1991 the parliament chose national independence by 346 votes to one, and this was confirmed by 90.3% of voters in a referendum on 1 December 1991. How did such a transformation come about? How real a transformation was it?

Ukrainian Communism: National and Soviet

Unlike the 'popular fronts' in the Baltic republics, Moldova or Transcaucasia, Rukh did not have the strength to win independence on its own. This required two more elements – the support of so-called 'national Communists' like Leonid Kravchuk and the collapse of central authority in Moscow.

In 1989 the Communist Party had 3,302,221 members in Ukraine (Rukh had 280,000), more than 6% of the total population. Its monopoly on public political life was constitutionally enshrined by the notorious Article Six which guaranteed its 'leading role' in society. Nevertheless, it was far from a monolithic entity. Nor could it act with real independence from Moscow. The party was riven by a number of divisions, with Moscow-based politics interacting with regional groups in Ukraine, especially the three 'clans' of Dnipropetrovsk, Kharkiv and Donetsk. A Kiev group had also grown in importance since the transfer of the capital in 1934 and was relatively close to the sensitivities of the cultural intelligentsia. The party in western Ukraine on the other hand was always suspect – either outsiders or locals who were unlikely to be allowed to make a career elsewhere were in charge.

'National Communist' was the term used in Ukraine to describe party stalwarts who were prepared to back the national cause. There were, however, many possible types of *gente Ruthenus, natione Sovieticus*. In the 1920s party leaders like Skrypnyk and Shumskyi were both enthusiastic Communists and Ukrainianisers; in the 1960s Petro Shelest (1963–72) exhibited some tolerance for Ukrainian dissent whilst being able to take a hard line during the 1968 Czechoslovak crisis. Shelest was probably the quintessential Soviet Ukrainian, seeing the combination of the two identities as perfectly natural.[39] Volodymyr Shcherbytskyi, (party leader from 1972 to 1989), on the other hand, subordinated the local to the Soviet. Under his rule, the party seemed devoid of all internal life, although the speed with which internal debates surfaced in 1989–91 showed that this was an illusion (his aide Vitalii Vrublevskyi published a memoir in 1993 that rather implausibly sought to emphasise his defence of local interests whenever circumstances permitted).[40] The Ukrainian party therefore had both a national Communist and a Soviet loyalist tradition. The former helped to make a difference in comparison to, say, Belarus, where the professed role model of rogue Belarusian president Lukashenka has been the tough but 'incorruptible' former partisan Petr Masheraŭ, who headed the Belarusian Communist Party between 1965 and 1980. Ukrainian Communists on the other hand could hark back either to Skrypnyk and Shelest or the 'loyal Leninist' tradition dating from the 'Yekaterinoslav [Donbas] faction' in the 1920s, which defined the party's past for its more orthodox members.

As elsewhere in the USSR, with the partial exception of the Baltic republics, the Ukrainian Communists were struggling to orient themselves towards the new electoral politics introduced by Gorbachev in 1989–90. Shcherbytskyi's successor, Volodymyr Ivashko (1989–90), began the process of political adaptation, speaking with little fluency the new language of local rights and sovereignties, but the limits of his approach were revealed at the twenty-eighth Ukrainian Party Congress in June 1990. Twin movements for the internal democratisation and nationalisation of the Communist Party were defeated and their respective supporters left its ranks. In 1991 Oleksandr Moroz, leader of the Communist group in parliament, renewed the demand for the party to declare itself independent in the manner of the Lithuanian Communists under Algirdas Brazauskas, but once again the plea fell on deaf ears.[41] Ivashko moved on to Moscow as Gorbachev's deputy and was replaced by the dour Stanislav Hurenko (1990–1), Ivashko's more orthodox opponent in September 1989, and a man with strong links to Gorbachev's hardline opponents in Moscow. Gorbachev would have been better advised to leave Ivashko's 'Kharkiv group' in charge. A Ukraine led from the former Soviet capital in the east would have had a very different trajectory in 1990–1.

Formal renovation proved impossible, but not all Communists were beholden to the party apparatus. In parliament different dynamics were at work, personified by Leonid Kravchuk, who was elected its chairman after Ivashko in the summer of 1990. Kravchuk had a redoubtable past as a cultural policeman and scourge of the dissidents, but he understood the logic of his former opponents and the power of his new position as head of an elected institution. Nevertheless, like Gorbachev in Moscow, he always took a measured political course, trying to maintain support to both his left and right. Kravchuk, in no small part because of his former role as Ideology Secretary, was well attuned to the political sensitivities of the 'other Ukraine' – the Soviet Ukrainian identity for which the slogan of 'friendship of the peoples' was not empty rhetoric but a synonym for social accord and an aversion to political experimentation. After so much turbulence in the twentieth century, Kravchuk perhaps understood this better than the national-democrats.[42] He never plunged into nationalism wholesale, and tacked and trimmed where necessary – as during the winter of 1990–1, when it seemed that Moscow conservatives were in the ascendance – until the botched assault on the Baltic republics in January 1991 allowed him to resume a course towards building Ukrainian sovereignty and promoting himself as its main guarantor. By spring 1991 he was beginning to appropriate the language and the symbolism of Rukh and, in the words of Hurenko's complaint to a closed party meeting, 'belonged only nominally to the party'.[43]

In contrast, Ukraine's Soviet loyalists were bewildered. They raged against their internal enemies – 'Galician Messianism', 'Galician ideological aggression' and 'Uniate fanatics', as well as the turncoat Kravchuk and, worst of all, Gorbachev, the author of all their troubles – but were short on ideas as to how to oppose them,[44] once the traditional police tactics had been deemed politically unacceptable (though there is evidence that Shcherbytskyi contemplated stifling Rukh at birth on several occasions in 1989).[45] Passive support for the Union amongst

Ukrainians was still strong, as was hostility to Ukrainian nationalism. It was possible to exploit these sentiments at election time, but outside the voting booth Soviet nationalism proved itself a powerful but lumbering old heavyweight, while Ukrainian nationalism was organised and motivated to punch way above its weight. A series of Soviet loyalist organisations – the Fatherland Forum, the Union of Workers of Ukraine for Socialist Perestroika, Unity – were set up in eastern Ukraine, but made little impact. Unlike Rukh, they could put few people on the streets when it mattered. The fact that Ukrainian nationalists were unlikely to win power on their own in Kiev meant that it wasn't worth getting too worked up in opposition to them. There seemed to be no clear and imminent danger of a development of an importance to match Baltic independence or the proposed Moldovan union with Romania. Some Communists toyed with the idea of linking up with pan-Slavic intellectuals 'to create a left-centre block', but the Communist Party leadership was never flexible or imaginative enough to embrace the idea.[46]

Nor was empowering local separatisms the logical way of opposing Ukrainian nationalism. In the one place where Russo-Soviet nationalism was a powerful force, Crimea, a local autonomy movement successfully organised a referendum in January 1991, in which 93% of local voters backed the idea of creating a separate 'Crimean Republic'. Kiev acceded to the demand within two months. Nevertheless, even Crimean nationalism was only superficially centrifugal. The referendum backed the idea of autonomy for Crimea 'as a subject of the Soviet Union and a party to the Union Treaty'. The logic of the 'other Ukraine' was that it saw itself as part of a broader but diffuse imagined community. To conservatives, the idea of cordoning off or repressing Galicia was a common enough piece of wishful thinking; the idea of splitting the country in two was not.

Nevertheless, the orthodox Communists, posing as the 'party of national accord', were still a political force, if increasingly only a negative one, in the sense of blocking the path to full independence, although their counterattack on Rukh's suposed 'national extremism' scored several hits in 1990–1. Rukh's desire for a wholesale revamp of the local political system through a rewrite of the Ukrainian constitution was also impossible without Communist consent. Hurenko's one big apparent success was the March 1991 referendum called by Gorbachev to help gather support for his proposed new version of the 1922 Union Treaty. In answer to the question 'Do you consider it necessary to preserve the USSR as a renewed federation of equal sovereign republics, in which human rights and the freedom of all nationalities will be fully guaranteed?' (actually at least three questions in one), 70.5% of Ukrainian voters said 'yes' (turnout was high at 83%). Ukrainian Communists have always regarded the dissolution of the USSR within a mere nine months of the vote as a flagrant betrayal of the popular will. On every subsequent 17 March there have been demonstrations in favour of a restored Union.

Plate 1. Rus architecture: the recently restored Pyrohoshcha church of the Virgin, Kiev.

Plate 2. St Sofiia's in Novgorod, now Russia.

Plate 5. Statue of the Cossack leader Ivan Pidkova, Lviv.

facing page

Plate 3. Rus art: the *Annunciation of Ustiug* – probably a Novgorod copy of Kievan style.

Plate 4. The *Virgin Oranta*, attributed by some to Alempius (Alimpyi) of Kiev.

Plate 6. Ukrainian Baroque: the Cathedral of the Assumption, Pechersk, Kiev in its eighteenth-century style. The cathedral was dynamited by Soviet forces in the hope of blowing up visiting German generals in 1941. It underwent final reconstruction in 2000.

Plate 7. 'Mazepa's church': St Nicholas', Kiev (built 1690–3), one of the first churches to be destroyed by the Soviet authorities in 1934.

Plate 8. Socialist Realist sculpture, Kiev.

Plate 9. The colossal twin statues to the 'Eternal Unity' of the Ukrainian and Russian peoples, erected by the Soviet authorities in Kiev to celebrate the 300th anniversary of the Pereiaslav treaty in 1954.

Plate 10. Celebrating popular culture: Holokhvastov making entreaties, Kiev.

Plate 11. Panikovskyi – Ilf and Petrov's great
Soviet survivor.

Plate 12. Memorial to the Great Famine of 1932–3, Kiev, where Bill Clinton laid a wreath in June 2000.

Plate 13. Nationalising Rus: the new statue to Mykhailo Hrushevskyi in Kiev implies acceptance of his Kievocentric view of the past – a similar version now stands in Lviv.

Plate 14 (*above left*). Statue of the Archangel Michael, Kiev.

Plate 15 (*above right*). A more explicitly national pantheon: statue of Taras Shevchenko, Lviv.

Plate 16. Cartoon mocking the supposedly archetypal materialist 'Soviet Ukrainian'.

Plate 17. The *Virgin of Vyshhorod/Vladimir*,
Andrei Bogoliubskii's controversial symbol.

Plate 18. *The Angel with the Golden Hair*, artist unknown,
but the style is more clearly 'post-Byzantine' than in the above.

Plate 19. The fate of the armies of Gog and Magog: John Martin's *The Last Judgement*, 1853.

Plate 20. Pagan progenitor of Ukrainian art?: the great figure of the *Virgin Oranta*, above the altar in St Sofiia's, Kiev.

Plate 21. Ilia Repin's celebrated *Zaporozhian Cossacks Writing a Mocking Letter to the Turkish Sultan*, 1891.

Plate 22. Mykola Ivasiuk, *Khmelnytskyi's Entry into Kiev, 1649*, 1912.

Plate 25. A Russian version of Rus: Viktor Vasnetsov's
Baptism of the Kievites, 1895.

facing page

Plate 23. Icons of the Ukrainian Baroque:
SS Anastasia and Juliana, mid-eighteenth century, Konotop.

Plate 24. The *Holy Protectress* or *Intercession of the Mother of God*,
late seventeenth century. Khmelnytskyi can be seen on the right,
holding his Hetman's mace.

Plate 26 (*above*). Russian 'Scythianism': Nicholas Roerich's costume designs for Stravinskii's 'The Rite of Spring'.

Plate 27. Ukrainïan Modernism: Oleksandr Murashko's *Annunciation*, 1907–8.

The success was, however, only apparent. Once again, the Communists were unable to make full and practical use of their support. Hurenko soon found himself outmanœuvred by the other two votes held on the same day. In Galicia only a vote on complete Ukrainian independence received 88% local support. More importantly, Kravchuk inserted a rival question on Gorbachev's ballot throughout Ukraine – 'Do you agree that Ukraine should be a part of a Union of Sovereign States on the basis of the Declaration of State Sovereignty of Ukraine?' (passed the previous July) – to which 80.2% said 'yes'. What was the difference between the two main questions? To many Ukrainians, none or very little. The language of 'sovereignty' and its cognates was much debased in Soviet discourse; Ukraine had after all been described as a 'state' since 1921. There seems to have been considerable confusion, with many people voting 'yes' to both questions. Nevertheless, they were designed and interpreted very differently. Kravchuk, and it was now his responsibility as chairman of parliament to negotiate with Moscow, insisted that Gorbachev's proposed 'Federation of Sovereign Republics' would have to be replaced by a loose 'Union of Sovereign States', and only on the basis of Ukraine's own law. Whereas Gorbachev talked of '9+1' as a possible formula for a new Union (willing republics plus the centre), Kravchuk preferred '9+0' (no centre), or even left the first number unspecified (that is, teasing Moscow as to whether Ukraine would be a party to it at all). Although some nationalists held out for complete independence, at the time the ballot formulation was enough to win the support of most of Rukh. Kravchuk was therefore able to build a political base that was wide enough to drive local politics forwards towards 'sovereignty', if not yet sufficiently so to persuade a majority to leave the Union. Between March and August 1991 the sovereignty issue was still the limit of most political imaginations.

The Centre That Could Not Hold

The other factor in the equation was Moscow, to whom Ukraine's orthodox Communists looked to preserve the USSR more or less intact. Could the centre have maintained the old version of the Union and kept Ukraine in it, by force if necessary? In 1987 or 1988 perhaps yes, by the time of the Moscow coup in August 1991 almost certainly no, at least not without the kind of bloodshed that the junta was unable seriously to contemplate. As they could not even win control of Moscow, the question of how much violence might have been required in Ukraine hardly arose. Western Ukraine would certainly have resisted any crackdown, especially with the inevitable disorder in the Baltic states, and the atmosphere in Kiev would have been difficult, although the rest of the country would probably not have needed much 'pacification'. The junta's emissary in Kiev, General Varennikov, quietly suggested to Kravchuk that he declare a state of emergency in Galicia. Varennikov's own memoirs record Kravchuk, although evasive on this issue, as being more or less cooperative.[47] Nationalist Ukrainian parties were already preparing to go underground.[48] An embryonic 'committee' under deputy prime minister Kostiantyn Masyk and local KGB chief Yevhen Marchuk (later prime minister in 1995–6!) already existed to do the junta's bidding in Kiev.[49] The Western powers would have been unlikely to intervene, given that President Mitterrand was already referring to 'the new Soviet authorities', although how long it would have been before trouble flared again is another matter.

Temporarily at least, the majority of Ukrainian leaders, Kravchuk probably included, might well have fallen in with who ever emerged victorious in Moscow. Hurenko's support was hardly surprising, if private. In two letters sent on 19 August, authorized with his signature, the central leadership of the Communist Party called on local party leaders to 'rally all patriotic forces, standing up for the preservation of the unity and integrity of the USSR ... to preserve calm everywhere ... all demonstrations, meetings, rallies and strikes must be prevented.'[50] Then there were Kravchuk's two notoriously ambivalent TV broadcasts on the first day of the coup, Monday 19 August. Even in the less controversial broadcast on Ukrainian TV Kravchuk stressed that 'our position – is a position of deliberation and once again deliberation'. He balanced his phrases with well-practised care:

> in such extraordinarily serious political circumstances we mustn't make haste with judgments ... in a law[-based] state everything must take place on the basis of the law ... I call on you, dear comrades, to [show] calm and moderation ... the legally elected and established organs of state power and administration are [still] working throughout the whole of the republic ... in Ukraine no emergency situation has been declared ... all [politicians], leaders of political parties [must] avoid destabilising the situation ... we will act in order to avoid spilling innocent blood.[51]

On Soviet TV Kravchuk stated that 'what has happened was bound to happen', although he later claimed his remarks were 'censored'.[52] Leading national-democrats also accused Kravchuk of stifling discussion at two meetings of the parliamentary presidium on 19 and 20 August and stonewalling on demands for a full recall of the assembly.[53] Finally, the former party archives in Kiev contain an interesting document listing Kravchuk as present and 'taking part in discussion' at the last meeting of the Ukrainian Politburo on Thursday 22 August, although Kravchuk would in time assert that he had left the party on the Monday morning, and the coup was effectively over by the Wednesday.[54]

Unfortunately, the official record of the meeting reveals little about what was actually discussed.[55]

The balance of his public statements clearly shows that Kravchuk was prepared to tack back in Moscow's direction to an extent. Not completely – he said enough about 'sovereignty' to indicate that it would have been difficult for him fully to abandon the course he had been following since March. Most probably, Kravchuk would have waited for the junta to reveal its weaknesses. The key question would then have been the extent of the damage done to his alliance with local nationalists. Potential weaknesses were many. In a historical perspective, the most striking was the junta's inability to play the Russian nationalist card against Ukraine. A new Russian nationalism – the dog that didn't bark – was on the rise, but was not a natural ally of the Soviet centre. In part because it was struggling to assert its identity within Soviet nationalism, in part because it was anti-Soviet. The fact that the latter strain, represented by Boris Yeltsin's Democratic Russia, now usefully courted by Rukh, saw Ukrainian elites as natural allies in their attempt to displace central power, was a dramatic contrast to the situation in 1905–17. An equally important contrast was the absence of any powerful ideologue of imperial/Russian national unity. Coup leader Yanaev's trembling hands were no match for Stolypin's iron fist, or the haughty imperialism of Pobedonostsev or Suslov.

Putting things another way, would Ukraine have declared independence without the failure of the August coup? It is impossible to tell. Kravchuk had carefully manœuvred to ensure that Ukraine was not due to attend the signing ceremony for Gorbachev's Union Treaty on Monday 19 August that provoked the coup in the first place. In June the Ukrainian parliament had reserved the right to consider its position again in September. Ukraine was already taking practical measures to underpin its sovereignty before August; in July two laws had created a national bank and a presidency. First elections for the latter were scheduled for 1 December 1991. Events were moving at a faster pace in Kiev than seemed obvious in Moscow, especially to the Western correspondents who rarely set foot down south. However, it is unlikely that Kravchuk would have abandoned his characteristic middle path, and in September 1991 orthodox Communists would still have been a powerful force resisting outright independence. Creeping autonomy was a more likely scenario, although the events of August 1991 demonstrated that this was not a possibility that Moscow conservatives would have countenanced with any patience. A prolonged period of quasi-statehood, however, would have required greater compromises with 'Soviet Ukrainianism' than were necessary after 1991. Before August, Kravchuk was, for example, promoting the idea of a hybrid blue and yellow (UNR) and crimson (Soviet) flag.

As it was, Ukraine's orthodox Communists were disabled by the events of August – at least temporarily. Rukh feared that its window of opportunity might still close relatively quickly and kept up the pressure for a speedy decision on independence. As Levko Lukianenko later remarked, 'Kravchuk was now leaning to our side, but [who knew] where he would be leaning in a week or two?'[56] Rukh considered it especially vital that the Ukrainian parliament should take matters into its own hands and assemble before the USSR Supreme Soviet was due to meet on 26 August (Kravchuk had originally proposed a meeting after the 26th), and gathered the 150 signatures necessary to call for a special sitting on Saturday 24 August. The Communist group met in caucus and, conscious that it had lost its majority (given that 20 deputies had already resigned from the 'Group of 239') and in the absence of any alternative, decided to throw in its lot with the pro-independence forces. Many Communists considered this would be the best way of isolating themselves from the apparent 'de–Communisation' wave engulfing Russia, the ultimate extent of which no one could yet predict.

The vote on the Declaration of Independence was 346 to one.[57] The Communists could not prevent the decision to ban the party on 31 August, despite a last-minute effort to cut their ties with Moscow (an attempt to force a reconsideration of the ban on 4 September received 54 votes against 204),[58] but they were able to prevent any real de-Communisation. As well as an informal understanding with the opposition that the existing elite would remain in power (see next chapter), the ex-Communist majority was able to recover its wits sufficiently to defeat proposals to 'de-partify' all state organs and prevent the hasty destruction of state documents. The Communists felt confident that most national-democrats' priorities lay elsewhere.

During the debate, deputy chairman of parliament Volodymyr Hrynov objected (speaking in Russian):

> I am not against the independence of Ukraine. But I see a terrible danger today if we pass this Act on its own. Without a decision on the problem of the decommunisation of Ukraine, this Act will just be a piece of paper [*pustym mestom*]. We are building a totalitarian Communist society in Ukraine. I propose that we pass this Act only as part of a package together with [other] measures by which the totalitarian society in Ukraine will be demolished.[59]

But his and a handful of other voices were drowned out in the rush.

A referendum to confirm the vote for independence was now scheduled for 1 December 1991. Some nationalists were nervous about obtaining the necessary majority and argued that the parliament's vote was sufficient. The national 'will' had already been expressed.[60] Fortunately, wiser voices prevailed – given the obvious need for a mandate in the south and east of Ukraine (if Belarus had held such a referendum in 1991, then Lukashenka's drive towards 'reunion' with Russia would have been considerably more difficult after 1994). In any case, it was understood that the left would not campaign against independence. Moroz was allowed to found a Socialist Party of Ukraine as early as October, but only on the condition that it too fell into line. With no real (public) political force urging a 'no' vote and the mass media converting *en masse*, and with Kravchuk skilfully broadening the issue by brazenly coopting the wildest predictions of future Ukrainian prosperity outside the Union, a hugely impressive 90% voted 'yes' on a high turnout of 84%. Every oblast voted 'yes', even Crimea with 54%. On the same day Kravchuk was elected president with 62% of the vote, comfortably beating Rukh's main candidate, Viacheslav Chornovil, who won 23%. No one opposed Kravchuk from the left.

'What, Even the Donbass Voted Yes?'

The referendum was only the penultimate act in the drama, however. Moscow still had to be reconciled, which meant both Yeltsin as representative of resurgent Russia and Gorbachev, who was still clinging to the vestiges of Soviet power. Famously therefore Kravchuk, Yeltsin and the Belarusian leader Stanislaŭ Shushkevich secretly arranged to settle matters at a historic meeting in Brezhnev's old dacha in the forests of western Belarus on 7–8 December.[61]

In Kravchuk's words, 'the meeting in Belovezhkaia Pushcha was not for people with weak nerves'. After arriving on the evening of the 7th, the participants at first studiously avoided discussing the matter at hand. According to Kravchuk again, we 'partied till very late ... drained our glasses [*charkuvaly*], chatted ... there was conversation, toasts, joking and laughter' – which presumably means most were as drunk as they were reported to have been.[62] The next morning they met 'without advisers', but possibly with hangovers. Yeltsin had brought with him from Gorbachev a draft treaty for a new union, which resembled a 'federation with elements of a confederation', and to which he was apparently prepared to give serious consideration. Kravchuk's blanket refusal even to discuss it took Yeltsin somewhat by surprise, but seemed to suit his purposes (i.e. ditching Gorbachev). According to Kravchuk, Yeltsin said simply, 'then we must find another way out ...', accepting and emphasising 'without Ukraine there is no Union'. On the other hand, Kravchuk later claimed that Yeltsin was unaware of the exact results of the 1 December referendum, asking him somewhat increduously, 'What, even the Donbass voted yes?' Kravchuk's response was to take great pleasure in pedantically reading out the results from each oblast one by one.[63]

The referendum had of course changed everything. Significantly, however, both Yeltsin and Kravchuk accepted that 'if we go to the people and announce that there is no Union and propose nothing in its place – there will be an inevitable explosion. [Some] variant is necessary. Transitional.'[64] Many Ukrainians (and even more Russians) still assumed that 'independence' was compatible with some sort of residual linkage. The Ukrainian delegation was also aware that George Bush had promised to recognise Ukrainian independence 'expeditiously', within 'weeks', but the USA, having also talked of 'delayed [conditional] recognition', would be much more comfortable with some overarching structures in place, particularly if they could help clear up ambiguous nuclear and security issues.[65]

Different possibilities were discussed by Yeltsin and Kravchuk (Kravchuk does not record Shushkevich as saying much), including a 'Union of Sovereign Republics, then a Union of Sovereign States', before the two men finally hit on the formula originally devised in Kharkiv in January – a 'Commonwealth of Independent States' – the point being to avoid the awkward connotations of the term 'Union'. Even then, according to Kravchuk, 'Boris Mikhailovich [i.e. Nikolaievich], as it seemed to me, understood by independence something different: each republic would have sovereignty, but we would all remain together.'[66] Kravchuk by contrast understood a 'commonwealth of independent states' to be precisely that – the former republics were now independent states and the 'commonwealth' would have no separate status other than that voluntarily delegated to it by the participants. An element of ambiguity therefore remained – presumably necessarily – and was increased when the Ukrainian parliament created its own version of the treaty by adding 13 amendments which watered down the agreement. Nevertheless, it was Ukraine's opposition that had prevented the possibility of the USSR being resurrected 'under new management'.

The legal basis claimed by the three men for dissolving the Union was that 'our very states – Belarus, Russia, Ukraine – were the original founders of the Union [by signing the original Union Treaty in 1922]. Therefore they can also begin its disassembly.'[67] This was a half-truth. None of the three was even geographically the same entity it had been in 1922, and of course the Union had expanded considerably since then. The position of the Central Asian states remained especially unclear (unless Russia was to be considered in its borders of 1922 which included the then Turkestan), until they were also admitted to the CIS at the second summit at Alma-Ata on 21 December – efforts to contact Nazarbaev of Kazakhstan having been foiled by the fact that he was mid-flight to Moscow.[68] Nor was it clear how the idea of Russia as the formal successor to the USSR would fit in with the idea of a vanished Union.

Nevertheless, the deed was done. Neither Kravchuk nor Yeltsin was prepared to phone Gorbachev with the bad news, passing the buck to Shushkevich as host. Gorbachev hit the roof when he learnt that Yeltsin had phoned president Bush first. Kravchuk returned to Kiev 'afraid that violent methods might be used against Ukraine ... from the side of the Union. There existed a very real threat, as all power structures – the ministry of defence, the KGB, the ministry of the interior – were [then] under the authority of the Union centre.'[69] Only once that threat had passed, and once Kravchuk had faced down Gorbachev's angry summons to an emergency summit in Moscow, would-be preservers of the empire presumably feeling unable to reprise the task that had failed them in August, was an independent Ukraine finally up and running.

Conclusions

Independence was won without any real fireworks. The dissident movement of the 1960s and 1970s had produced many martyrs, but no lives were lost in 1989–91. Demonstrations had been periodically important, but there was no large-scale street violence or revolutionary protest (student hunger strikes had temporarily forced the regime to the negotiating table in October 1990, but they could not be renewed when the concessions made were subsequently withdrawn). In fact, the word 'revolution' hardly fits at all. Events had been enormously accelerated between 1989 and 1991, but then choices made in haste can quickly be set in stone. There was only a limited transcendence of the historical divisions between the Ukraine represented by Rukh and a deeply disoriented Soviet Ukraine. As such there was little momentum to carry forward after 1991, and no all-powerful independence movement like the Vietcong, capable of shaping the new state in its image. The old guard were still in charge, a little dazed perhaps, but still perfectly capable of looking after their own interests.

9

Politics: Developing the Rules of the Game

Ukrainian independence arrived as much by accident as design, and largely as a result of events occurring elsewhere. A specifically Ukrainian politics therefore existed only in embryonic form in December 1991. Political parties, state institutions, the very shape of the polity were all in very early stages of development. Our discussion therefore focuses on general trends and patterns, although of course these patterns are very much determined by Ukraine's recent history as a cultural palimpsest with pronounced divergences of ethno-linguistic, regional, confessional and economic interest. It is precisely these underlying differences, moreover, which have made the construction of a post-Communist reform project in Ukraine unusually difficult.

If Ukrainian politics is classified in terms of a conventional left, right and centre, then the best organised group is the right – the Ukrainian nationalists. The big advantage of the nationalist camp is that voters in Galicia and in parts of central Ukraine will back it come what may. Its big disadvantage is that this guaranteed support represents a maximum of only 20–25% of the electorate. At the opposite extreme are the parties of the left, whose political base is in the still highly Sovietised population in the laager cities of the east and south. Like the right, the left represents a minority, but a bigger one – approximately 40% of voters backed it in the elections of 1994 and 1998. The third key group is obviously the centre, but in Ukraine the centre is something of a 'black hole', a 'quagmire' – to use just two of the metaphors that have been coined. Ukrainian nationalism is a powerful rallying cry in Galicia. Russian nationalism in Crimea and Soviet nostalgia in the big cities of eastern Ukraine can put fewer people on the streets but are still mobilising forces. Crucially, however, there is little in between – most of Ukraine does not really vote on ethnonationalist lines. The middle ground has therefore tended to be 'non-party', but in practice is dominated by corporate lobbies and local barons. Their pursuit of self-interest has known few bounds – the middle ground has rarely been common ground.

Map 6. Independent Ukraine after 1991

Since 1991 Ukraine has been governed by an informal coalition. The Ukrainian nationalists, uncomfortably aware of their own minority status, have supported non-party, supposedly 'centrist' corporate government from the outside (with a few key ministries for themselves), so long as it has been sufficiently 'Ukrainian', while the left has made hay in noisy opposition. Kravchuk's loss of office in the 1994 presidential election at first seemed likely to disrupt this arrangement, but in retrospect it only resulted in a shift from one corporate group to another. This permanent government of the corporate centre is paradoxically the result both of the weakness of the right and the strength of the left. The right cannot govern alone. The left, however, might. It was artificially weak between 1991 and 1993 when the Communist Party was banned, but since its reemergence in 1993–4 the left has assumed a powerful role as a 'destructive opposition'. Ukraine has found itself in the same position as postwar Italy and Japan (and to some extent neighbouring Russia), with an 'illegitimate' left opposition not regarded as a safe custodian of state power. As yet there is no exact Ukrainian equivalent of Italy's Christian Democrats or Japan's Liberal Democrats – the party thereby granted a permanent monopoly in office – but the lack of changeover and the opaque centrist 'non-party' nature of Ukrainian government has produced a similar recipe for stagnation, corruption and the growing abuse of the power of the state. Whereas Western observers have expected Ukraine to be 'transitional', it has made slow progress in key aspects of democratisation, marketisation and globalisation. Unfortunately, unlike postwar Japan or Fourth Republic France there is no technocratic/bureaucratic class able to run the country behind the façade of venal politicians' public quarrels.

Where might a break in the political logjam come from? For the foreseeable future the right is unlikely to transcend its minority status. In any case, it has begun to lose momentum, as its political agenda has seemingly been implemented by centrist proxy in the decade since independence. The centre will not find coherence and purpose overnight, although, after the experience of the Yushchenko government (1999–2001) – see below, there were signs that a genuine reform party was finally beginning to emerge, albeit extremely late in the day. A third possible catalyst might come from internal struggles within the left camp. As in Fifth Republic France, the main protagonists are the Socialists and Communists. 'The Long March of the French Left' – the 15-year struggle of François Mitterrand's *Parti Socialiste* before 1981 to replace the Communists as the main opposition force and make the left as a whole electable – has its parallels in Ukraine.[1] The Ukrainian Communists stand unequivocally against market reform, for the preservation of the Soviet identity and the restoration of the Soviet state – the hatred between them and the Ukrainian nationalists remains visceral. The Socialist Party, created with a degree of official connivance in October 1991, has tried to carve a niche for itself as a more social democratic and 'national leftist' alternative. There was a real prospect that the left parties might win the 1999 presidential election, but, by failing to unite around the latter ideas and the candidacy of the Socialist leader Oleksandr Moroz, the opportunity was lost although the way forward was clear. The main contours of Ukrainian politics are therefore reasonably well established. This chapter will look in turn at Ukraine's right, centre and left, as well as the country's two presidents since independence, Leonid Kravchuk (1991–4) and Leonid Kuchma (1994–).

The Right's 'Grand Bargain'

As argued in the last chapter, the inherited historical weaknesses of Ukrainian ethnonationalism meant that the opposition (Rukh) was unable to take power on its own in 1989–91. Rukh was perfectly aware of this fact, and since mid-1990 had been groping towards a 'Grand Bargain' – national Communist elites would be allowed to stay in power so long as they supported independence and that support remained firm. In return, Rukh would no longer be a strictly oppositional force. In one sense this strategy was a success. As the veteran dissident Levko Lukianenko put it in May 1992, the twin victories of

24 August and 1 December 1991 'became possible because both nationalists and [national] Communists agitated for independence'.[2] However, the nationalists had been forced to deal with the Devil to a much greater degree than in most other post-Communist states. The lack of leverage over the former Communists once they were left in power would store up problems for the future.

For a majority of the Rukh elite, the most important argument in favour of this historic compromise was the one again made by Lukianenko: 'since 24 August we no longer have an occupying administration, but a Ukrainian state. If before 24 August we were prepared to attack it from the bunker, then after 24 August we must raise ourselves to the same level [as the state], cooperate with it, defend it against external enemies and fifth columns.'[3] Periodic crises in relations with Russia, real and imagined, would keep reinforcing the argument about 'external enemies'. In other words, the national Communists, for whatever motives, had delivered the independence the national-democrats craved but had been unable to achieve through their own efforts alone. The situation had historical precedents, or at least this was the argument made by Larysa Skoryk in 1992, quoting Viacheslav Lypynskyi on the reasons for the failure of 'the Ukrainian revolution' in 1917–20:

a Ukrainian state can only be established when the stronger, better-organised and more united part of the old ruling elite is prepared to struggle for it, [those] who until that time have ruled Ukraine in the name of and with the assistance of the metropol. Without such support Ukraine will not separate from the metropol and will remain a colony – an *okraina* or *kresy*, organically linked with the metropol through its elites . . . [Only then will] the new ruling elite be able to deliver Ukraine from its tragic situation between Poland and Moscow, so that in breaking away from Warsaw we do not drown in Moscow, and breaking away from Moscow we do not drown in Warsaw.[4]

The former 'metropolitan' elite was of course Kravchuk's national Communists, the equivalent of the former imperial bureaucrats who had served the UNR in 1917 and the Hetmanate in 1918. If anything, however, the choice was now even more restricted. As Yurii Badzo pointed out, his own intelligentsia class had been decimated in the 1930s:

Ukraine's historical good fortune in the 1990s is that when the imperial-totalitarian [system] simply collapsed from shock (the antistate revolt), power [had to] be given to someone. It is completely natural that it should fall into the hands of the 'nomenklatura'. We simply did not and for the moment do not have any other social and political milieu which is sufficiently advanced in both quantity and quality, and therefore capable of building a state.[5]

In essence, this amounted to an admission that the poets, writers, historians and philologists who dominated the leadership of Rukh were unable to govern on their own.

The 'Grand Bargain' did not go unchallenged. The case against was made by Viacheslav Chornovil during the presidential campaign of late 1991 (see also the quotation from Volodymyr Hrynov on page 168). Chornovil argued that only a 'thorough de-Communisation of Ukrainian society' to remove 'the repainted party nomenklatura which has entrenched itself in all levels of the organs of power' could create a Ukraine that was both independent and democratic. The latter aim could not be sacrificed to the former; the two could only be achieved together. Moreover, real economic reform would only be possible if the self-interested and venal old elite were levered out of power.[6] Chornovil was left to rue in his 1998 election literature that

> the only post-Communist states to have moved far ahead, compared with Ukraine, and secured the well-being of their citizens, are those in which their own popular movements came to power in 1990–91 – Solidarity in Poland, the popular fronts in the Baltic States, the democratic forces in the [now] Czech Republic. Today we have tens of thousands of poor Ukrainians travelling to the Czech Republic in search of wages . . .[7]

Chornovil and his supporters worried that the 'Grand Bargain' was simply too unconditional. The dangers of 'predatory privatisation by the Communist party-state Mafia' were all too obvious if it remained in power unelected.[8] As Levko Lukianenko predicted in May 1992, 'they [the former Communists] will, without a doubt, try to privatise state property into their own pockets'.[9] With barely a touch of irony, the new parties of the populist left were soon speaking in much the same terms, but the right added the argument that there were too many 'cosmopolitan' elements in power, that is non-Ukrainians and even Russophone Ukrainians who could not be considered trusty custodians of a state for which they felt little affection, even affinity. The 1995 'Manifesto of the Ukrainian Intelligentsia', for example, berated 'Ukrainian international careerists' for organising 'the export abroad of valuable products at unfavourable prices' and 'the sale of large enterprises and branches of industry that form the basis of our economy at very cheap rates to Russian capital and to other foreigners'.[10] Ukraine was not the only country to face the problem of elites plundering state assets – a problem with deep roots in Soviet history – but Ukraine had few countervailing resources with which to resist it.

Back in the 1920s the above-mentioned Lypynskyi had in fact also considered this very possibility – that members of the old elite might defect for basically mercenary motives. He therefore argued that it

would be necessary for 'the Ukrainian intelligentsia to support that separatist part of the old local ruling elite with all its influence over the
people. Without such support, this separatist part will not take up the
people's language and unite with the people into one cultural-national
unity, and will not be able to struggle with that part [of the old elite]
which will [continue to] support the metropol.'[11] In other words, the
national Communists had to be encouraged to 'rediscover' their national
roots by the intelligentsia and resist the siren call of imperial nostalgists.
The poet Dmytro Pavlychko even argued that Kravchuk had 'genetically
inherited' his Ukrainian essence and 'the reason or wisdom [of the
Ukrainian people] by which the pen is valued more highly than the
sword'.[12] This role suited Rukh – close to, but not actually in, power.
Many of its leaders thought rather naïvely that the careerism and 'slip-
periness' (a term frequently applied to Kravchuk) of the national
Communists, their lack of any real ideology of their own, were the very
things that would force them to rely on the prophets of national revival
for their script (in one interview Kravchuk had specifically encouraged
Rukh to provide 'the ideological basis of the New Ukraine').[13] It soon
became clear, however, that the hoped-for alliance was not working as
planned. Kravchuk's behaviour during the coup had been a salutary
warning. The intelligentsia's hope that the national Communists would
act under its direction were misguided. Rather, the script was read –
Kravchuk could deliver beautiful eulogies to Hrushevskyi and
Shevchenko on formal occasions – but the ruling elites' real interests lay
elsewhere (in Soviet times, diaspora Ukrainians liked to use the radish
metaphor – Soviet leaders were red on the outside but white, that is
Russian nationalist, on the inside; what, the nonsensical joke now had
it, was blue and yellow on the outside, but red on the inside?).
Increasingly disunited and preoccupied with self-interest, the old guard
were incapable of providing a solid centre that could work with the right
to promote much-needed economic, political and social reform.

Was there an alternative? Chornovil's arguments against the likely
effects of the 'Grand Bargain' may be persuasive, but there was never
any real possibility that Rukh might come to power and govern on its
own. It had certainly punched above its weight since winning a quarter
of the seats in the 1990 elections. The tide of events was in its favour and
it managed to use greater discipline and force of argument to persuade
many Communists and former Communists to travel in its wake. The
idea of a Rukh government, on the other hand, was another thing
entirely. Chornovil once retrospectively argued that 'if elections had
been held in 1992 we would have had an absolute democratic majority
in parliament',[14] but it is doubtful that the historical divisions in
Ukrainian society that were the real reason for Rukh's limited showing
in 1990–1 had suddenly disappeared in 1992, even though the
Communist *Party* had been temporarily removed from the scene (they

were certainly apparent at the next elections in 1994 and 1998). Such is Ukraine's historical misfortune. Ukraine was also unfortunate that the local Communist Party was so dominant until 1990–1. Russia did not have its own Communist Party until 1990, which quickly became a radical and, more importantly, oppositional force. There was therefore a relative vacuum of power in Moscow for reformers temporarily to exploit.

The Right Breaks Up

It is unlikely that even Chornovil and his supporters could have torpedoed the 'Grand Bargain'. The one occasion when they might conceivably have done so was the benchmark (third) Rukh congress in February–March 1992. The assembly was a truly Ruritanian occasion. The opening day was carefully stage-managed around Kravchuk's address. The new president played his audience well, first flattering them that 'for justice, for history, it needs to be said that Rukh did most to achieve [independence]', and then offering an obvious olive branch – 'I believe that the idea of Ukrainian statehood will be the consolidating factor which will unite the strengths of the president and Rukh'.[15] The second day, by contrast, was dominated by non-stop internal argument and orchestrated personal abuse. When it appeared that Chornovil's supporters would win the day, the advocates of the 'Grand Bargain' tried to engineer a split, circulating a declaration stressing that they, the former *shistdesiatnyky*, 'the best representatives of the creative and scientific-technical intelligentsia, who had openly opposed the existing totalitarian-Communist regime' and where necessary 'spent the best years of their lives in prisons and camps', were the ones who 'had established Rukh' and were not about to allow it 'to assume the role of an opposition at this most crucial moment for Ukrainian independence'.

Ivan Drach mounted the podium and called on all those who thought the same way to assemble the following morning at 11am in the Writers' Union building and establish a redefined pro-presidential Rukh – his supporters having first pulled the cable on TV transmission in case anyone might think he was actually being disloyal. Not surprisingly, all hell broke loose.[16] A recess was called, during which militia guarded the platform and Rukh's émigré backers brokered a deal whereby Drach and his ally Mykhailo Horyn would share power with Chornovil. The announcement was greeted with near-ecstatic relief by the rank-and-file, seemingly oblivious to the fact that the right to elect the leadership had just been taken away from them. The new leadership 'troika' lasted barely four months. By the time it split up (Chornovil controlled the largest faction and kept the name 'Rukh'), the damage had been done and Kravchuk was hardly likely to risk his political future by formalising an alliance with such a weak and unstable movement.

An outright victory for Chornovil at the congress would certainly have created a stronger right-wing opposition to Kravchuk, but it is difficult to see what exactly Rukh could have done to change the fundamental balance of power in Ukraine. Its limited mobilising powers were revealed in autumn 1992, when it was only able to collect 1.2 million signatures in a campaign to force early elections (parliament had established an impossibly high barrier of three million signatures for issues to be put to a national referendum). The key problems motivating the 'Grand Bargain' have in essence operated ever since. Given the narrowness of their support-base (most of western Ukraine, the central Ukrainian intelligentsia), the national-democrats have been forced to support governments from the outside, despite a few fig-leaf ministries typically being thrown in their direction (normally education and culture, usually the key economic ministry responsible for negotiating with the IMF). Successive governments have coopted the surface outlines of their programme, but the nationalist counterpoint has always been kept alive by the lack of any Ukrainianisation of the state or society *en profondeur*. Even Chornovil was ultimately ensnared by the dilemma he described in 1991–2. He remained in control of the Rukh apparatus, but was being criticised by his own rank and file for excessive intimacy with new president Kuchma before his untimely death in a road accident in February 1999.

The right was never able to build any momentum. Despite the hope constantly expressed that it could expand in the key target area of central Ukraine and build on pockets of support in the east and south, the results of parliamentary elections in 1994 and 1998 showed that it could not, with support for the national-democrats never rising above 20–25% and even falling in some places.[17] Unable to break out of its traditional strongholds, the right began to turn in on itself. The relative unity of the late 1980s was soon lost, with the formal division in mid-1992 being only the first of many (the first splinter parties from Rukh had in fact appeared as early as 1990). Many political parties and groupings have appeared since, but underlying these no doubt ephemeral divisions are three basic types of nationalism. The mainstream 'national-democratic' camp, including the remnants of Rukh, is still shaped by the 1960s, both in terms of the life experience of its leading figures and the ideological mélange inherited from that key transitional decade. The label 'civic nationalism' is often used, but 'national-democrats' is more accurate. The hyphen is all-important: 'nation' and 'democracy' are seen as equal values and as mutually dependent phenomena. In an oft-repeated phrase of questionable value, 'there can be no individual rights without national rights.'[18] The ideas inherited from the 1960s – the rejection of revolutionary struggle, the emphasis on minority rights and

Ukrainian Nationalist Cartooons.

Ill. 5. (above left) *Imagining imperialist Russia – a ruddy-faced Yeltsin, placing Belarus in his sack and casting an eye on Ukraine, says 'Look! Once again immemorial Rusian land.'*

Ill. 6. (above right) *Yeltsin as an octopus, interfering in Ukraine, Crimea.*

Ill. 7. (right) *Communism depicted as an alien force, being manfully returned by a Ukrainian nationalist to the Kremlin from where it came.*

working within a rule of law – are still intact, but so is the conceptual framework of what is best termed national revival politics: the unthinking existential assumption that a 'nation' has a collective interest in the promotion of its language and culture. Like the *shistdesiatnyky*, the national-democrats also derive much of the mythology underpinning their sense of national identity from earlier periods, in particular Hrushevskyi's ethnocentric view of history, the 'Occidentalist' critique of Russia as an inherently 'Asian' and imperialist power, and the myth of Communism as a purely external, Russian-imposed force (see the cartoons above). In the Ukrainian context, however, it is questionable how many of the more than half the population, including so many Ukrainians, who tend to speak Russian wish to give up their language or their 'Soviet' or 'Ukraino-Russian' identity. The national-democratic view that such people are suffering from a form of false consciousness is a familiar solipsism often employed by other movements that claim to know individuals' interests better than the individuals themselves. This proselytising attitude has narrowed the national-democrats' support base to a regional sub-set of even the Ukrainophone electorate.

The national-democrats therefore still share many things in common with the second stream of modern Ukrainian nationalism, which, loosely speaking, seeks to revive the politics and mythology of the 1930s and early 1940s. The OUN itself returned to active political life in Ukraine in 1992, thinly disguised as the 'Congress of Ukrainian Nationalists' (or KUN), although it has sought to remodel itself as a democratic, civic party. In practice, however, it still feeds off the reputation of its Banderite (that is, pre-1943) past in the only region where it has anything of a political base – Galicia – and is still prone to racist musings about the 'national genotype' and reinventing the pre-war myth of Ukraine as an anti-Bolshevik vanguard.[19] The founding programme of the congress called for

the building of a national, unitary and orderly state, which will occupy all Ukrainian ethnic territory, in which the source of power will be the sovereign [ethnic] Ukrainian people . . . guaranteeing national minorities the right to the free development of their national-cultural individuality, on the basis of a loyal attitude to the Ukrainian state . . . the eradication of all the consequences of Russification [*Rosiishchennia*] and Bolshevik anti-culture – all the remnants of the years of domination of Ukraine by Russia.[20]

In Galicia there is a plethora of rival groups claiming to represent the true spirit of the OUN, and plenty of youths earnestly reading reprints of Dontsov. In this milieu the ideas that the Ukrainian authorities were still 'an occupying force' even after 1991 and that the Act of Independence was only 'a miserable slip of paper' are still commonly expressed.[21] The OUN has pointedly not directly reestablished itself as a normal political party. As a direct electoral force, however, the far right is currently marginal, winning only 2–3% of the vote in the 1994 and 1998 elections. It has an effect on the political atmosphere, however. So long as the national-democrats have little chance of expanding their support in the political centre, they are forced to compete on their home turf with the far right and its slogan for the 1998 elections of (ethnic) 'Ukrainian power in the Ukrainian state!'

The third stream of modern Ukrainian nationalism is no less politically extreme, but more ideologically innovative. In September 1991 a group of former student activists succeeded in converting the old Interparty Assembly into the Ukrainian National Assembly (UNA) and providing it with a paramilitary wing, the Ukrainian National Self-Defence Force (in Ukrainian UNSO). The UNA–UNSO has deliberately rejected both the 'parliamentary cretinism' of the national-democrats and the 'outdated' ideology of the OUN. It has not sought to base itself on a particular region (Galicia), language or ethnic group, but on the power of the state and a rebranded historical mythology combining neo-paganism and the idealisation of Kievan Rus as the past and future centre of Slavdom and world Orthodoxy. Unlike the national-democrats or the modern OUN, the UNA–UNSO recognises that Ukraine is divided internally and that a new national idea, other than 'divisive' linguistic nationalism, is necessary to unite the new state and project its influence in the region (though the UNA–UNSO's ideology creates problems for the Greek Catholics). The UNA–UNSO's formal position is therefore 'pan-Slavism', but a 'united Slav state with its centre in Kiev' rather than Moscow. Aryan mysticism and a martialised Cossack mythology also find their way into this heady ideological brew.

The younger generation of UNA–UNSO leaders felt themselves, like Zhirinovskii in Russia, to be better attuned than the *shistdesiatnyky* to the populist core of post-Soviet culture. Their publications are full of sexually explicit jokes and proudly crude slogans. One of their appeals to the workers of Ukraine declared 'If the air conditioning in the factory toilets doesn't work – sleep in the Director's flat!'; their 1994 election slogan was 'Our people are used to living in a great state [by implication both Rus and/or the Russian empire/USSR]. We will make Ukraine a great state once again, so that people don't have to change their habits.'[22] The authorities clamped down hard on the UNA–UNSO after its participation in the violence surrounding the funeral of Patriarch Volodymyr in 1995 (see page 236), but its subculture is likely to survive and its ideas possibly to resurface.[23]

Leonid Kravchuk's Dance of the Seven Veils

The other side of the original 'Grand Bargain' was of course the national Communist camp under Kravchuk. Always a consummate opportunist, Kravchuk became Ukraine's preeminent figure in the build-up to independence by skilfully constructing a public persona that was most things to most people. As president, he sought to delay any final act of self-definition for as long as possible by maintaining the broadest possible consensus amongst elites. However, after December 1991 he was gradually forced to strip himself of his layers of ambiguity until he stood revealed as an unabashed nationalist in pursuit of reelection in 1994. By the end of his term of office, therefore, national Communism had largely lost its unique selling point, and the need for a proper organisation of the political centre became more clearly apparent.

There is no space here to discuss Kravchuk's presidency in detail.[24] However, it should be noted that Kravchuk never seriously contemplated dissolving parliament and holding early elections immediately after his twin triumph in December 1991. To his way of thinking, this would have required identifying himself with a particular party and narrowing his political base unnecessarily. He was also aware that new elections might revive the centrifugal tendencies suppressed in December 1991. The same caution explains Kravchuk's failure to press for more fundamental reform during the window of opportunity provided by the Communist Party's absence from the political scene between August 1991 and June 1993. Without either attempt to break the deadlock, however, Kravchuk was lumbered with the parliament elected in March 1990 and soon found himself trapped in the very position of narrowing support he had sought to avoid. He was also stymied by his original mandate. In the 1991 election he had been unable or unwilling to campaign on a real reform agenda, seeing his main tasks as maximising the vote for independence and mobilising the anti-nationalist electorate to defeat the Rukh candidate, Chornovil. Although Kravchuk won a massive 62% of the vote, the core of his support was essentially the same people who had voted for the Communists in 1990. Kravchuk was not forced to remain chastely beholden to the left-wing electorate of the east and south, but he had no real mandate for change and the revivified left would scream 'betrayal' at every tiny step towards reform. He also had no real means of challenging the entrenched position of the thousands of apparatchiks whose motives for supporting independence were even more cynical than his own. This is the only charitable explanation for Kravchuk's fatal failure to make any real beginning in the crucial area of economic reform. By 1993, the old guard were recovering in confidence, thus reducing still further Kravchuk's room for manoeuvre.

Kravchuk remained wedded to a very Soviet style of politics – clientelism, government as compromise between elites, divide and rule, the *kompromat* of opponents and an aversion to viewing either the state or political parties as arenas of public accountability rather than a battleground for personal or group interests. The 'Grand Bargain' therefore delivered Kravchuk's steadfast support for independence in the foreign policy sphere and the creeping bureaucratic Ukrainianisation of national symbols, education, culture and government documentation; but it was unable to bring about any kind of parliamentary activism or more deep-rooted programme of political and/or cultural change. The national Communists did not manage to establish a real political party after 1991 and most ran in the next (1994) parliamentary elections as individuals. As well as their failure to organise the centre properly, Kravchuk and his supporters were unable to hold the line against the left and prevent the Communist Party from re-forming in June 1993. By the time new elections were finally held in March 1994, the rejuvenated left won 145 out of 338 seats (a bizarre election law left 112 seats empty; despite some unfortunates being asked to vote six or more times, 36 seats were still empty by the time of the next elections in 1998).[25] Reform prospects were little better in the new parliament than in the old.

National-democrats won 80 seats (with Rukh on 27); the far right, including KUN and the UNA-UNSO, won twelve. One hundred and seventy members of the new parliament were non-party, but once again this potential centre had its mind on things other than reform. The national Communists established a 'Centre' faction in parliament, later the 'Constitutional Centre', but it was unable to impose, or even articulate, a reform agenda. The original 'Grand Bargain' therefore reached its logical end during the early presidential election in summer 1994, which Kravchuk had been forced to concede when protests at the slow pace of change and at the consequences of 'reform' had ironically coincided a year earlier. Kravchuk had no real economic record on which to campaign and felt unable to launch any significant reforms in the face of the new parliament, so he stood on his achievements in 'state-building'. Conveniently, his main opponent was former prime minister Leonid Kuchma, an archetypal Russophone Ukrainian, whom Kravchuk and his nationalist coterie sought to portray as a dangerous Russophile. Kravchuk's chosen strategy inevitably resulted in an election polarised around the national issue.

It's not that economic concerns weren't at the forefront of voters' priorities. They were. The very fact that Ukraine's growing economic difficulties (see pages 253–5) topped almost everybody's list of priorities, cannot explain the division of votes, unless voters perceived either Kravchuk or Kuchma as more capable of delivering salvation – which they didn't. Rather, Kuchma's measured defence of the rights of Russophones coincided with the hope of most eastern and southern voters that the way out of the economic quagmire was to rebuild links with Russia, while Kravchuk's essentially nationalist message appealed intrinsically to Ukrainophones and to their hopes of economic revival through linkage with Europe. Voters were also sharply divided on the merits of even Kravchuk's half-hearted nationalising policies. Ukrainian nationalists rejoiced in what they saw as their potential for rolling back the process of Russification. Ethnic Russians and Ukraine's many Sovietised Russophones felt no need for such change. The election therefore highlighted the conflict between the nationalist and the Soviet versions of Ukrainian identity, as much as that between ethnic Ukrainians (73% of the population) and the Russian minority (22%).[26]

This is why Kravchuk lost, with 45.1% of the vote to Kuchma's 52.1%. The result left the right in shock and the old national Communists in even greater disarray.

Ukraine's Missing Liberals

There were several reasons why the domestic side of Kravchuk's presidency ran aground – his own natural caution, the unconditional nature of most of his support on the right, the eventual revival of the left – but also crucial was the absence of a real reform lobby in the political centre. Herein lies another long-term problem for Ukrainian politics. If the nationalist right is a minority force and the left is to be excluded from government, the centre is the key to any potential majority, but it has never had much of an identity of its own. Ukraine has suffered particularly from the absence of an effective party of liberal reform, like the Democratic Union in Poland or even Václav Klaus's Civic Union in the Czech Republic or Yabloko in Russia (Ukraine does have a 'Liberal Party', but it is actually the party of the Donetsk business elite). In its absence, the political centre has been occupied by virtual politics, a shifting kaleidoscope of clan groups, shadowy business and old nomenklatura interests. These have dominated every Ukrainian government since 1991, but have never imposed any coherent strategy for change.

The first problem for Ukraine's would-be centre parties is the amorphous nature of the potential common ground between Ukraine's extreme diversities of region, ethnicity, language, religion and economic interest. Even when Ukrainian centrists might agree about the importance of economic reform, they have too often argued about other things. An instructive example is the fate of the first candidate for the position of a Ukrainian centre party, the New Ukraine movement established on the basis of the Party of Democratic Revival in 1992 (itself an offshoot of the Democratic Platform, set up within the Communist Party of old in 1990). New Ukraine sought a power-base in the intelligentsia and amongst new capital, with little success in either endeavour. The intelligentsia was still divided between Ukrainophones and Russophones. The former were still captivated by the 'Grand Bargain', while the latter, according to national-democrats like Yurii Badzo, 'placed one-sided emphasis on liberal reform in the economy, and not enough on the strengthening of Ukrainian statehood'.[27] By way of contrast, New Ukraine were wary of Rukh's 'obsession' with the national question, and the two wasted most of the period 1992–4 in mutual distrust, just as Rukh had originally failed to cooperate with the Democratic Platform in 1990. Although Chornovil later claimed that if the two 'had consolidated' as a single block they could have swept all before them,[28] he should really have been expressing his regret that cooperation, let alone consolidation, was never really on the agenda. New Ukraine ultimately fell between several stools. By trying to be all things to all men, it missed a real opportunity to create a powerful left-liberal or social-democratic movement while the Communist Party was still banned.[29]

These divisions have plagued the Ukrainian centre ever since. In the 1994–8 parliament Ukrainophone liberals formed the 'Reforms' group, but their Russophone equivalents preferred the company of the east Ukrainian managerial class in the 'Unity' and 'Interregional' factions. Even worse, in the 1998 election Reforms' main successor party,

'Reforms and Order', was opposed by the almost identical 'Forward Ukraine!', leading to a split in the limited Ukrainophone liberal vote and the failure of either party to get into parliament. New Ukraine leader Volodymyr Hrynov, on the other hand, was sidetracked into Russian minority politics when forming his Social-Liberal Union (SLOn) and won less than 1% of the vote.

A second problem was that new capital was slow to appear so long as economic reform remained stalled. Most 'new business' was really old business operating through the clan politics of a semi-privatised economy, with no interest in promoting liberal ideas *per se*. Significantly, a genuine liberal party failed to emerge even after new president Kuchma belatedly launched Ukraine's first real economic reform programme in October 1994. Kuchma continued Kravchuk's habit of placing liberals in one or two key economic ministries, but left most of the old guard undisturbed elsewhere. Jokes about the only real party of reform in Ukraine taking the form of the periodic IMF visitations were not far off the mark, but the IMF's external pressure, though now real enough (see pages 262–3), was no substitute for a proper domestic impetus to reform. The main 'party of power', the National Democratic Party (set up in 1996), had a liberal faction, but this became increasingly disillusioned by the party's excessive closeness to government.

The next set of elections, in 1998, brought about renewed attempts to consolidate the political centre, but once again they were only partially successful. The introduction of a semi-proportional electoral system forced the shadowy elite groups that had governed the country since 1991, if not out into the open, then at least to work through new or already existing political parties. These parties were therefore often little more than fronts for business interests and governing cliques (see also pages 270–2). The spectacular rise and fall of the catch-all National Democratic Party, a cranky coalition of regional and producer groups, like New Ukraine before it, once again demonstrated the difficulty of creating a truly transcendent *Volkspartei* in Ukraine. It won a derisory 5% of the vote and only 29 seats – a shocking result for a party with the sitting prime minister (Valerii Pustovoitenko) at the top of its electoral list. Equally shockingly, by the time arms had been twisted and palms greased in the new parliament the National Democrats ended up (temporarily) with an astonishing 93 out of 450 seats. The party was a large but fragile beast and split into several factions within less than a year.

For the 1998 elections many old national Communists, including Kravchuk and former premier Yevhen Marchuk, joined the United Social Democratic Party, which won 17 (eventually 25) seats, in part by concentrating its campaigning out in the sticks of rural Transcarpathia, where votes were easily bought. The Social Democrats also did well in Kiev, as they had strong links with the Dynamo Kiev football team, itself backed by the Slavutych oil and gas trading concern. The big surprise of the elections was the Green Party, which won 24 seats; the surprise being the fact that the pony-tailed Vitalii Kononov, the party's leader since 1992, was the only genuine environmentalist amongst the crowd of businessmen and bankers that had bought the other places on the party's list.

The not particularly green Greens and the not particularly social democratic Social Democrats were basically satellite parties of the new corporate state. A more serious rival, because it had an independent economic power-base, was Hromada, the party of former prime minister Pavlo Lazarenko and his United Energy Systems company (40 seats). Hromada's relative early success demonstrated how faction and self-interest still divided the centre as much as ideology. Ukraine now had three centre parties headed by current or former prime ministers. Kuchma's supporters spent most of 1998 trying to destroy it. Even after the 1998 elections, the political centre was still a quagmire of fractious and self-serving elites, and the non-left majority was hardly more united than before. In December 1998 the Constitutional Court made a disastrous ruling that deputies were no longer constrained to membership of the eight parties elected in the March elections. The National Democrats and Hromada promptly split, as did Rukh and the left-wing bloc of the Socialist and Village parties. By spring 1999 there were 14 factions in parliament. A Bulgarian or Romanian scenario – the belated discovery of political unity in opposition to the left – still seemed unlikely in Ukraine. The 'New Majority' announced in January 2000, as in Bulgaria and Romania, proved an artificial alliance, collapsing within a year.

After the elections there were rumours that Ukraine's new generation of younger businessmen were plotting to launch a 'real' liberal party to rival the National Democrats, possibly to be led by the reformers' new Great White Hope, the chairman of the Central Bank, Viktor Yushchenko, but he was under enormous pressure not to 'rock the boat' (the contract shooting in 1998 of his predecessor Vadym Hetman in the lift outside his flat was widely assumed to be such a warning). It was also true that president Kuchma did not want the embarrassment of having his reform credentials seriously questioned in an election year. Without such a party, however, it was difficult to see how Ukraine would sustain a much-needed new impetus to reform. Yushchenko was appointed prime minister in December 1999, but whether this made it more or less likely that the centre would eventually consolidate, only time would tell.

Ukraine's Resurgent Left

Just as the centre parties are relatively weak in Ukraine, so the various Communist successor parties are relatively strong, winning around 40% of the seats at both the 1994 and 1998 elections – never enough to take

Ukrainian Leftist Cartoons: The West, not Russia, depicted as the force unnaturally dividing Ukraine.

Ill. 8 (above). *Uncle Sam behind the division of the USSR.*

Ill. 9 (right). *Artificial attempts to divide the Soviet family.*

Ill. 10 (below). *Kuchma (with Cossack moustache) and Yeltsin, depicted as US stooges, divide the Black Sea fleet.*

Ill. 11 (left). Ukrainian nationalism, not communism, depicted as the alien force. With one suitor, 'Pan Democrat', disappearing out the window, the bride ('Ukraine') declares 'My [Soviet] Husband has returned!'

Ill. 12 (below). A Communist cartoon demands (in Ukrainian) 'No to NATO troops on the territory of Ukraine!'

power, but sufficient on both occasions to create a blocking minority in parliament.[30] Unlike its counterparts who have returned to power in Poland, Lithuania or Hungary, however, the Ukrainian left is extremely conservative and derives much of its strength from its anti-national agenda. In fact, the Ukrainian Communists are even more unreformed than their Russian counterparts. But, whereas Soviet nostalgia culture makes Ziuganov's Communists natural allies of the Russian right, in Ukraine right and left are bitter enemies and the left has gained extra strength from being the main *de facto* vehicle for Russophone protest at 'nationalising' policies in Ukraine.

The Ukrainian left still inhabits the Soviet version of Ukrainian identity (see the cartoons above). Ukraine to them should be a bilingual state, 'purged of the imposed language of the diaspora' and the artificial influence of Ukrainian nationalism.[31] It should of course have strong links with Russia – the Communists simply believe in reunion, with no ifs or buts, others favour various forms of voluntary association. The left is also united by its deeply entrenched opposition to all aspects of economic reform. The relatively moderate Socialist Party accepts that Ukrainians might open their own stall or run their own café; ('all forms of private property have the right to exist, if they have the character of labour' for the individual's own benefit),[32] but all the leftist parties oppose 'large-scale' privatisation, which to them is nothing less than the 'genocide of the people' by the 'bandit class' in power.[33] For most of the left, the period since 1991 has only served to confirm the importance of traditional Marxist tools of analysis: class struggle, historical materialism, the labour theory of value. As soon as our café owner took on employees, he or she would be deemed to have joined the exploiter class.

The impulse towards reform is explained away via the corrupting influences of 'liberals' and Western, usually American, interests. Whereas nationalists see the main threat to national independence coming from Russia, the left sees it coming from Western monopoly capitalism bent on dismantling former Soviet economic might. In the view of Oleksandr Moroz, leader of the Socialists and chairman of parliament from 1994 to 1998, 'Ukraine, as with Russia, is rapidly finding itself dependent on the world financial oligarchy and is building a capitalism of a colonial type.'[34] According to the Progressive Socialist Party, a far-left splinter group, 'we have warned since 1991 that reforms carried out to the prescriptions of the IMF have as their end-goal the peaceful colonisation of Ukraine.'[35] The left therefore sees itself not as 'anti-national', but as defenders of the Soviet Ukrainian identity. It is 'national-fascist' Galicians and their Western puppet-masters who are not just anti-Soviet, but actually 'anti-Ukrainian', rather than the other way around. According to Moroz again: 'do we, in standing up against unjustified economic illusions, against the unprecedented, uncontrolled profiteering of Western monopolies in the economical and spiritual space of Ukraine, against the collapse of [our] national economy and national culture, not defend the real sovereignty of our state just the same [as the nationalist right]?'[36]

That said, there is an incipient political and cultural division within the Ukrainian left. The self-styled 'Leninist Communist Party of Ukraine' is still both the biggest party on the left and the biggest party in Ukraine, winning 95 out of 338 seats in the 1994 elections (six were 'loaned' to other leftist parties) and 122 out of 450 in 1998. It also remains one of the most left-wing parties in the post-Soviet world. Unlike other Communist successor parties, such as Poland's Democratic Left Alliance or Romania's Party of Social Democracy, the Ukrainian Communists have never even contemplated a name-change. 'Communist' is still actually an advantage when it comes to gathering in the nostalgia vote. In 1998 the party programme called unabashedly for the 'restoration of state and workers' control . . . a savage war against shadow [sic] business', the elevation of Russian to a second state language and, in a carefully formulated standard phrase, 'the voluntary creation of an equal Union of fraternal peoples' 'on the territory of the former USSR'.[37]

A flavour of the Communist Party's culture can be gained from leader Petro Symonenko's eulogy on the occasion of Lenin's 128th birthday in 1998:

> Great October, the Union of Soviet Socialist Republics, our victory over Fascism, our grandiose [achievements of] Socialist construction, our assistance to the development of tens of the countries of the world, our multinational, free and educated Soviet people, the flourishing of Soviet Ukraine, as with the life of every one of us, whose destiny was set by Soviet power – all of this [really happened], all of it is true, all of it is the idea and work of Lenin![38]

Whereas Ziuganov has subtly transformed the ideology of the Russian Communist Party to create a mélange of national Bolshevism, 'Eurasianism' and Russian Messianism, allowing him to subsume the party's identity in the 'People's Patriotic Union' formed for the 1996 presidential contest with Yeltsin, the Ukrainian Communists are in essence still Soviet nationalists.[39] The party's core constituency is little interested, as yet, in other ideas (pan-Slavism, pure Russian nationalism), though their time may come.[40] 'National Communists' like Borys Oliinyk, a populist pan-Slavist (and one of the original leaders of Rukh) who nevertheless believes that the Communists could fulfil that role as 'a party of Ukrainian statehood', remain thin on the ground. The *Theses on the Eightieth Anniversary of the Communist Party of Ukraine*, prepared by the party in 1998, were notable for their complete lack of interest in relocating the party in a more 'national' myth and continued fidelity to all the key myths of the Soviet era.[41]

Waiting in the wings, however, is the Socialist Party, until now junior partners to the Communists, which has increasingly flirted with the idea of creating a more social democratic and 'patriotic' left – 'a normal national left'.[42] Moroz's pragmatic adjustment to Ukrainian independence stands in sharp contrast to Symonenko's Soviet patriotism. In 1992 Moroz declared: 'every nation has the historical right to self-determination. Ukraine is now going through the same period of growing national consciousness and the formation of national statehood that the countries of Western Europe went through in the seventeenth to nineteenth centuries. This is an objective process. Therefore a natural return to the USSR in its old, that is ruthlessly centralised, form is impossible.'[43] Moroz was also fond of the soundbite 'Anybody who does not regret the collapse of the USSR has no heart; anybody who wants to restore the Union today has no head.'[44] Moreover, unlike their would-be Russian equivalents, the Ukrainian Socialists can claim to be the inheritors of a relatively pragmatic tradition of national leftism dating back to the 1920s, and of the rival Ukrainian non-Bolshevik left-ist parties of 1918–25 (the *Borotbisti* and *Ukapisti*) and even the pre-Revolutionary national movement, which was in many ways as much Socialist as it was nationalist. Significantly, many national-democrats were comfortable with the idea of a Moroz presidency, which is precisely what earned him such opprobrium amongst the parties further to his left.

Moroz also liked to talk of the left taking a 'Polish route' to power in Ukraine, copying the tactics that led to the victory of the Democratic Left Alliance in 1993 and Aleksander Kwaśniewski's capture of the presidency from Lech Wałęsa in 1995. Kwaśniewski's 'Polish route', however, came about after a profound transformation in the main Communist successor party and his consequent ability to construct a genuine left-centre alliance. In Ukraine, the latter would always be difficult so long as the former had still to occur. A possible alliance between the left and Hromada would have been a giant step towards the realisation of Moroz's plans, which is another reason why Kuchma sought to destroy his former prime minister's party in 1998–9. Moroz found few alternative centrist (and moderate Communist) allies for his campaign for the 1999 presidential election. The 'Polish route' was also partly blocked by internal divisions within the Socialists' ranks between Moroz's pragmatists and 'nostalgic ballast',[45] who engineered a split as he tried to move to the centre in 1996. In the 1998 elections the new Progressive Socialist Party actually took a position to the left of the Communists. The populist diatribes of party leader Nataliia Vitrenko against 'national liberalism' and the IMF won the party 4.05% of the vote and 16 seats at his party's post-election parliament. Although some Ukrainian commentators referred to Moroz's formal adoption of a more social democratic 'New Course' in 1998 congress as a 'Ukrainian Bad Godesberg',[46] it was clear that the course of left politics had yet to change as fundamentally as it did in Germany in 1959 (and it took the German SPD another seven years to gain power after the changes it made at the Godesberg congress).

Paradoxically, the 'modernisation' of the Ukrainian left was more likely to occur if it took on the burdens of government. As a permanent opposition, it was never likely to be under the same pressure to change and adapt, nor would it be easy for the Socialists to displace the Communists. It is possible that the predominance of the Communists on the left might diminish in time as the party's elderly support base passes on. An alternative possibility is that the Communists' nostalgia for the Soviet era will continue to appeal to Ukraine's mixed-identity popu-lation, who as yet lack any other obvious label for themselves (see pages 217–18). In practice, however, the left already has its own version of the 'Grand Bargain'. The Ukrainian Communists have close links with

Gennadii Ziuganov's Russian Communist Party and were even more enthusiastic members of the umbrella 'Union of Communist Parties-CPSU' than their Russian 'cousins' (the Socialists had their own Eurasian Socialist Congress established in 1995);[47] the leader of the Ukrainian Communists, Petro Symonenko, habitually talks as if the 'Soviet people' still exist. Nevertheless, the party in fact operates within a national framework – its leaders are happy to be bigger fishes in a smaller pool. During the clamour of protest against the Communist Party's revival in 1993, few noticed that it had actually purged its ranks of its more radical supporters – members of the Union of Communists of Ukraine – who had urged the party to declare itself the legal and institutional, not just the ideological, successor to the Communist Party of old and act as if they still formed a part of the CPSU. Nonconstructive opposition to the government in Kiev is actually a position of considerable psychological comfort to the Communists. Symonenko seemed genuinely surprised when Kuchma defused a left-sponsored no-confidence vote in October 1998 with the simple suggestion that he would appoint one of their rank as prime minister.

The Ukrainian Communists also had their fair share of new *biznesmeni* in their ranks. Some were old apparatchiks turned wheeler-dealers (Stanislav Hurenko, of all people, was deputy general director of the metals trading joint venture Navasko); others were outsiders buying their way onto the party list. After all, the Communists were the most popular party in Ukraine and represented too good an opportunity to miss. Such matters are understood, if perhaps never spelt out.

Leonid Kuchma: The Wrong Mandate

The left had ironically supported Kuchma back in 1994, as they felt ill-prepared to enter the contest directly.[48] Kuchma's first term of office was shaped by this original sin and, of course, by the other factors that won him the election. It needs to be restated that ethnolinguistic and geopolitical factors and not economic issues decided the 1994 presidential contest. One only has to look at the map – Kuchma won every oblast to the east of Poltava in the exact centre of Ukraine, Kravchuk every oblast to the west. It is impossible to understand Kuchma's later difficulties without realising that he was elected on one programme, namely opposition to Kravchuk's perceived 'nationalising' policies in 1991–4, and then sought to govern on another, economic reform, without having a strong mandate for the latter (the cartoon reproduced overleaf criticises the about-turn). This also helps to explain why Kuchma suffered a partial loss of nerve very early on in the reform period, watering the programme down in mid-1995 *before* electoral pressures began to accumulate in advance of the parliamentary elections in 1998 and the presidential poll

Ill. 13. Kuchma attacked for abandoning the policy he was elected on in 1994 and becoming a puppet of the IMF by 1998.

in 1999. Kuchma also owed his win to the support of business interests. Kravchuk had tried to build bridges with Ukraine's so-called 'red directors'; but after the Donbas miners' strikes of summer 1993 had made the mistake of investing too heavily in one group to control that particular situation – the local Donetsk clan, led by the man he made acting prime minister, former coal boss Yukhym Zviahilskyi. Kuchma, on the other hand, headed the powerful Ukrainian Union of Industrialists and Enterprise Bosses, and his election inaugurated a virtual corporate takeover of the state from the ideology apparatchiks and cultural intelligentsia who had been close to Kravchuk. This was a general trend, but it was also a regional one. Kuchma soon gained notoriety for showering appointments and favours on his home region of Dnipropetrovsk. Most worrying, however, were some of the shadowy interests that stood in the background of Kuchma's campaign, in particular the two companies Seabeco ('Seabeco International' and 'Seabeco Moldova') and Nordex, with an unsavoury reputation for links with organised crime and exporting arms to rogue regimes like Iran and North Korea. Seabeco was controlled by Boris Birshtein, partner of Sergei Mikhailov, alleged head of the notorious Russian Solntsevskaia crime syndicate. Some reports claim that Birshtein headed a meeting in Tel Aviv in 1995, 'the subject of [which] was the sharing of interests in Ukraine'.[49] It was of course unclear how far such groups had managed to progress from the margins of Ukrainian political and economic life to the centre. They were, however, not that different from the new type of former Communist who now dominated the political mainstream – eastern/Soviet Ukrainian industrialists who were just beginning to realise the new Ukrainian state could make them very rich indeed. In time the national-democrats would have to deal with them too, but the Grand Bargain had now become a lot less grand.

Kuchma's first presidency was also marked by the same forces that characterised the late Kravchuk era: a weak right, a resurgent left and a divided centre. Like Kravchuk, Kuchma spent more time on disabling his opponents than on building up a party or parties that might have given him a more positive support base. Paradoxically or not, the proliferation of relatively weak parties that made it difficult for the president or his government to devise and carry through a coherent policy agenda was at least in part the result of behind-the-scenes machinations by the president's own staff. Like Kravchuk, however, Kuchma was more interested in the retention of power. Kuchma was, however, a more ruthless practitioner of the art of *kompromat*, allegedly orchestrated by Minister of Information Zinovii Kulyk and a shadowy 'Centre for Political Analysis and Planning' under the presidential administration, not too dissimilar in style and structure from the Ukrainian KGB's old Third Department. The methods he chose increasingly resembled the creeping authoritarianism of Yeltsin's regime in Russia or even Mečiar's in Slovakia: the formal and informal presidentialisation of state power, tight control of the media, increasing reliance on control (if not reform) of the economy through decree, politically motivated prosecution and ultra-vires harassment of political opponents. Kuchma was, however, temperamentally more inclined than Kravchuk towards activist government, at least on the rhetorical level. His problem was less likely to be failing to initiate than failing to deliver.

Kuchma's controversial inauguration speech reiterated many of his campaign themes. After swearing his oath on the sixteenth-century Peresopnytsia gospel, he declared that 'Ukraine is historically part of the Eurasian economic and cultural space' and that 'the self-isolation of Ukraine [under Kravchuk] and its voluntary refusal to promote its own interests actively in the Eurasian space were a serious mistake, causing colossal damage to our national economy'.[50] It soon became clear, however, that acting on these beliefs would force him to court the Communists, who loudly applauded his speech, whilst economic reform would need the support of the nationalists, who jeered and left. The need for international support settled the issue and the 'Eurasian' theme was soft-pedalled thereafter. Ukrainianisation was quietly forgotten, but not reversed – even promoted in some areas if it coincided with

Kuchma's vision of *raison d'état*, such as building up a Ukrainian TV network under his control. Nothing was done to raise the official status of Russian, however, which made a gift of the issue to the Communists.

With the national issue on the backburner, Kuchma's first term as president was dominated by four issues: the belated launch of an economic reform programme, the growth of corruption, constitutional reform and, earlier than was strictly necessary, his struggle for reelection. Economic reform is dealt with in greater detail in chapter twelve – the main political point is that necessary first steps were taken after the launch of a 'Systemic Transformation' programme in 1994, culminating in the introduction of a new national currency in September 1996, but that the follow-through was disappointing. None of Kuchma's first-term governments (Vitalii Masol to February 1995; Yevhen Marchuk, March 1995 to May 1996; Pavlo Lazarenko, May 1996 to July 1997; and Valerii Pustovoitenko, July 1997 to December 1999) could be considered 'reformist' in the sense of having the collective will of, say, the Balcerowicz administration in Poland, Václav Klaus in the Czech Republic or even Sergei Kirienko's short-lived 1998 Russian government. The Ukrainian governments did not really have any collective identity at all. Particular clans looked after their particular interests and the reform project gradually lost impetus. Kuchma blamed the obstruction of the left-wing 'majority' in parliament, which indeed complained bitterly that Kuchma had betrayed his original mandate and adopted the programme of the IMF (see the cartoon shown on page 194), but after 1996 he was equipped with the power to enact economic reform by decree but chose not to use it. Western observers got used to Kuchma's lengthy descriptions of the contents of his back pocket – the decrees that were prepared for when the time was right, but that always seemed to remain firmly in his trousers. A second spurt of economic measures followed in summer 1998, as the incipient Russian crisis threatened to engulf Ukraine. They were enough to allow Ukraine to weather the storm slightly better than its neighbour, but not enough to restart the reform process before pre-election politics set in once again.

Kuchma also scored an initial victory by succeeding where Kravchuk had failed and persuading the Rada (parliament) finally to adopt a new post-Soviet constitution (Ukraine was the last Soviet successor state to do so) – once the possibility of a Communist victory in the 1996 Russian elections had helped to concentrate most deputies' minds sufficiently. Not surprisingly, the constitution was a compromise text: the right got most of what it wanted in terms of the constitutional expression of the 'national idea' (see pages 208–9), Kuchma got most of what he wanted in terms of state structures and the balance of constitutional powers, while the left got most of what it wanted in terms of generous promises of welfare provision and emphasis on the 'social character' of the state. On paper, the constitution reflects Ukraine's 'European' traditions by enshrining key principles of the rule of law and the separation of powers. In practice, power is concentrated in the hands of the presidency, the state bureaucracy is still highly politicised, judicial independence is as yet unestablished and significant hangovers from the Soviet era persist. Follow-up was in any case once again minimal and many of the aspects of the new political order exist only on paper.

Kompromat

After 1996, Kuchma achieved little in terms of domestic policy. Like most domestically inactive leaders, he therefore made a lot of compensatory noise on the world stage (see pages 279–310). The year 1997 was particularly successful, with Kuchma securing key agreements with Russia, NATO and Romania. Even in this sphere, however, there was something of a tailing-off in the second half of Kuchma's term. By 1998–9, it seemed that Kuchma's main goal was simply staying in office. Whereas the 1994 presidential election occurred before real economic reform had begun, the 1999 vote would take place in the middle of a hesitant and state-directed privatisation process, and the stakes involved in the retention of power to influence its outcome were correspondingly higher. It was unlikely that Kuchma would surrender power as readily as Kravchuk had in 1994.

On the contrary, he showed every sign of seeking to entrench himself by whatever method he could. Kuchma sought and won a considerable expansion of his constitutional competence in 1995–6. The president now dominated the executive, provided he had a pliant prime minister. Parliament was weak and fractious. The presidential administration, symbolically located in Bankivska Street in the old headquarters of the Communist Party Central Committee, increasingly began to act like its predecessor.

Significantly, the one serious challenge to Kuchma's power came not from the right or left opposition, but when a rival from his own home turf in Dnipropetrovsk briefly seemed capable of manipulating the post-Soviet system even better than he could. Pavlo Lazarenko was appointed prime minister in 1996, and rapidly exploited the one area where Kuchma had yet to establish control – the economy. Within a year, by using 'administrative resources' to the full, a staggering 50% of Ukraine's (fast-declining) GDP – and some $700 million – had fallen under the sway of business structures under his direct or indirect control. Corruption seemed to enter a new dimension. Lazarenko may have acted alone, he and Kuchma may have at least initially been in cahoots. Either way, the systematic destruction of Lazarenko and his Hromada party in 1997–8 set a precedent for how future challengers would be treated. Kuchma would also pay more attention to the monetary base of his power in the future. Half a dozen other leading members were arrested, one only two days after opening an office to organise a campaign for Kuchma's impeachment. Sympathetic papers were closed by Kulyk. *Kiev News* was evicted from its offices because they were deemed a 'fire hazard'. Along with its sister paper, *All-Ukrainian News*, it was crippled by huge 'libel' damages of over $1.5 million in suits brought by the chairman of Dynamo Kiev Hryhorii Surkis and the interior minister, Yurii Kravchenko. *Truth of Ukraine* was accused of violating the electoral law by offering free subscriptions to readers. Other 'non-players' were also subject to ultra-vires pressure. In the currency crisis of August–September 1998, the main bank to be 'renationalised' (taken under state security control) was Ukraïna, the bank which had contributed least to Kuchma's reelection coffers. This anomaly was soon rectified (drained by political loans, the bank collapsed in 2001). Previous Kuchma ally Vadym Rabinovych was excluded from the country in 1999 and was left with the impression that increased campaign funding was the way to get back in.

News coverage in the official state media is not exactly catholic. The OSCE report on the 1998 elections concluded that 'state television was clearly under the control of the government, which used both state channels for the promotion of the party of power'.[51] This was even more true in 1999. The rival STB channel was particularly harassed. Opposition candidates' TV appearances were book-ended by comedians who mocked their performance. Kuchma also benefited from the manipulation of two other hangovers from the Soviet era: the wide-ranging constitutional principle of parliamentary immunity; and the inappropriately politicised office of the state prosecutor. The former, by effectively granting sitting deputies freedom from any type of prosecution, criminalised a large percentage of the political class. Many very shady politicians continued to enjoy protection.

In Ukraine the state prosecutor conducts criminal investigations, orders arrests, decides on prosecutions and acts as state attorney in court – a vast array of powers that are strictly divided in archetypal Western liberal systems. Most of Kuchma's appointees have been hired guns. One, Oleh Lytvak, pursued Kuchma's political opponents with such over-enthusiasm in 1997–8 that parliament refused to confirm his appointment. Others have been more circumspect, but there was no doubt as to the identity of their master's voice. The 'transitional provisions' attached to the 1996 constitution promised that the office of prosecutor would only be retained for a limited period, but Kuchma made no move towards its abolition. The same provisions also declared that an independent judicial system would be introduced within five years, with elected and 'professional' judges enjoying security of tenure. Once again, this promise was undermined by the provision that all existing Soviet-era appointees should remain in office during the transitional period.

Whereas awkward parties were harassed, the potentially useful were given discreet support. The National Democratic Party, with its spectacular growth from 29 to 93 seats in 1998, was obviously built on state money and patronage. Informal channels existed to the Social Democrats and the Greens, even Rukh. In the 1998 elections Kuchma's administration reportedly supported the Progressive Socialists and a host of other new fringe leftist groups like Working Ukraine, the Party of Defenders of the Fatherland and the All-Ukrainian Workers' Party, in order to siphon off votes (some 12% of the national total) from the mainstream left. It was, shall we say, 'convenient' for Kuchma that Communist leader Symonenko was likely to run against Moroz in 1999. Kuchma money and 'administrative resources' were used to split Hromada from within in late 1998, even to the extent of temporarily supporting Yuliia Tymoshenko, famous to most people as one of Kuchma's most vociferous critics. Nataliia Vitrenko, the Progressive Socialist leader, was also loud in her public opposition, but compromised by her private complicities. In a similar fashion, the huge number of splits amongst the parties of the right could not all have been accidental. One nationalist deputy, Mykola Porovskyi, helped to split both Rukh in 1992 and the Republican Party in 1997;[52] right-wing firebrand Serhii Zhyzhko cut a swathe through Memorial, the Ukrainian Helsinki Union, the Republican Party, the Ukrainian National Assembly, Statehood and Independence for Ukraine and the Congress of Ukrainian Nationalists. Such men were either *agents provocateurs* or just plain provocative. Support also meant obligation, and favours were called in from politicians and their backers as the 1999 campaign began in earnest.

Democratisation was always likely to be difficult for independent Ukraine, given its twin burdens of the post-Soviet legacy and its own internal divisions. Nationalists have always claimed that Ukrainian political culture is more democratic, tolerant and pluralistic than in Russia, where the autocratic reflex and the habit of deference towards the 'strong leader' are still strong.[53] Unfortunately, there is no real evidence to back up this myth.[54] Certainly, there has been no equivalent in Ukraine of the bombing of the Moscow White House in October 1993, and Ukraine achieved the kind of peaceful transfer of power in 1994 that Russian elites never seriously contemplated in 1996. On the other hand, the common Soviet heritage has led to similar patterns in the exercise of power emerging in both states. In fact, without a strong 'national idea' to hold it together, Ukraine may be even more prone to the authoritarian rule of the former Soviet bureaucratic elite. Pessimists might also point out that civil society remains weak and that wealth and economic power are not sufficiently dispersed to create a true polyarchy. Ukraine may be a weak state, but the state still exercises disproportionate control over the resources that do exist and controls them in a partisan manner.

By 1998, public confidence in Ukraine's new political institutions had seemingly reached rock bottom. Corruption was on a truly Olympian scale, both in its excess and its extent (see pages 265–6). On the other hand, Ukrainians still turned out to vote, 70.8% in the 1998 elections and 74.9% in 1999, so popular cynicism was perhaps more apparent than real.

The 1999 Election

One important advantage for Kuchma as he prepared to face reelection was the provision in the 1996 constitution that protected him against the constant campaigning for early elections that had plagued Kravchuk. The next presidential election was fixed for 1999. In fact, the agreement gave him an extra three months in office by setting the date in October rather than July. Kuchma therefore had plenty of time to prepare his strategy, although in fact he decided soon after Yeltsin's victory in Russia in 1996 that his best option would be to plan a repeat performance – once the March 1998 elections to the Ukrainian Rada convinced him that it was safe to run on the centre-right with the familiar slogan of *après moi, le déluge* against the spectre of a 'red *revanche*'.

His first priority was to ensure that he had no enemies to his right. As with his predecessor in 1994, the vast majority of national-democrats took the bait and sold their support relatively cheaply.[55] Just to make sure, yet another split in Rukh was engineered in early 1999. Second, Kuchma obviously preferred to face a real ogre on the left – either, as in Russia in 1996, the Communists, or Ukraine's home-grown bugbear, the 'Konotop Witch', Nataliia Vitrenko of the Progressive Socialist Party (the casual sexism, sadly possible in Ukraine, was a reference both to her parliamentary constituency and to a 1837 short story by Hryhorii Kvitka-Osnovianenko, in which the wicked witch of the north tries to lead astray the good Cossacks of the south). Vitrenko played her allotted role of local firebrand with populist aplomb. Calling herself Ukraine's 'one true Marxist' (the Soviet Union having, she argued, betrayed its one true period of Marxism when it abandoned War Communism in 1921), she promised to outdo Pakistan's Pervez Musharraf by closing all borders and foreign accounts the day she was elected president, kicking out the IMF, and sending 'reformers' and 'the bandit class' to Siberia.[56] This was of course popular with many, but the implication that she would return Ukraine to the 1930s was not.

Both Vitrenko and Symonenko, leader of the Communists, were discreetly supported as alternatives to the potentially more threatening 'Ukrainian Kwaśniewski', Oleksandr Moroz. The promotion of general disunity on the left was obviously also to the administration's advantage. Finally, the left had to be kept in its ghetto. Any potential breakout to the centre had to be headed off. For a time, the most potent danger to the administration was the threat of an alliance between

Moroz and former prime minister Pavlo Lazarenko. Moroz had potential broad-church popularity, Lazarenko very deep pockets. Several papers published a supposed plan of action from Horbulin to Kuchma calling for the tax authorities, police and public prosecutor to be used for the coordinated destruction of Lazarenko's Hromada party.[57] As mentioned above, corruption charges were brought against Lazarenko, leading to his flight to the USA once his parliamentary immunity was lifted in February 1999. Meanwhile Moroz, who had usefully discredited himself by being the only major politician not to vote against Lazarenko, was subjected to systematic media and economic harassment. The president's supporters paralysed parliament for almost four months after the 1998 elections in their determination to prevent Moroz regaining his post as chairman of parliament. It took 19 rounds of voting to elect an alternative successor – Oleksandr Tkachenko of the Village Party, widely assumed to be in the president's debt after the authorities wrote off a $70 million loan to his Land and People agricultural concern that had mysteriously disappeared – but the job was done. Thereafter, Moroz found it hard to remain in the public view.

As Moroz faded in the opinion polls in early 1999, Vitrenko actually led. This was obviously more than Kuchma's strategists had intended – until a bizarre incident in October 1999 left her looking like the patsy she undoubtedly was. A small bomb was thrown at a meeting of her supporters in Dnipropetrovsk. The state media immediately blamed Serhii Ivanchenko, local organiser of the Moroz campaign (it was true that the two party leaders had not parted on good terms in 1995). The alleged perpetrators then surfaced in Russia, claiming they had been paid by Vitrenko. At the same time the media heat was turned on her candidacy, with state TV now giving full publicity to some of her wilder statements. Her support fell back to a relatively modest 11% in the final election, just behind Moroz's equally disappointing 11.3%. Two birds with one stone for the administration, whether they had originally planned the incident in Dnipropetrovsk or not. As his leftist rivals faded away, Communist leader Petro Symonenko was left with a relatively clear run, and headed the challenger field in the first round with 22.2% (Kuchma led with 36.5%). He was easy meat in the second – once his comparatively low profile in the official media was suddenly overcome by a blitz of propaganda blackening the Soviet era – losing by 56.2% to 37.8%.[58]

As well as his successful negative tactics, Kuchma also benefited from an overwhelming imbalance of political resources in his favour. The 1999 election was a much dirtier affair than 1994 or even 1991 or 1990. It is only a small exaggeration to say that in previous elections the issue at stake had been only independence, or the form that independence should take. Now it was about money. Kuchma's allies raised huge sums as down-payments on future income streams. Laughable official figures reported a mere 1.7 million *hrivnia* ($372,000) at Kuchma's disposal.[59] In reality, the shadowy 'Social Protection Fund', controlled by Oleksandr Volkov, may have had over $1.5 billion to spend. Russian mogul Boris Berezovskii reportedly pledged $150 million at Volkov's birthday party to protect his investments in Ukraine (surely his interests in Ukraine couldn't be worth that much?).[60] Attention began to focus on the rather hazy line between public and private sources of finance for the Kuchma campaign, on the nature of his backers, and on the original source of their wealth.

As in Russia, the Kuchma 'family' contained both blood relatives and close political allies. His wife Liudmilla was criticised for her involvement in the highly expensive redevelopment of the Ukraïna concert hall in Kiev and the somewhat opaque financing arrangements of her organisation 'From the Wife of the President – to the Children of Ukraine'. His daughter Yelena has secured a privileged role for her mobile phone company Kievstar, and since 1999 has been living with one of Ukraine's more notorious oligarchs, Viktor Pinchuk. Kuchma's former in-laws, the Franchuk clan in Crimea, have been linked to Sergei Voronkov, head of the local Seleim crime syndicate, and to rumours of the disappearance of business opponents. In September 1999 parliament passed separate resolutions calling for criminal investigations against both Volkov and Pinchuk. The former was accused of operating a string of shadowy accounts throughout Western Europe (Volkov allegedly controlled one account in Spain from which $500,000 had been paid to architects, interior designers and swimming pool contractors, but he still managed to deny owning any property in the country); the latter of laundering $38 million through the Bank of Boston and the notorious Bank of New York.[61]

Sheer spending power, and tight control of the mass media (see pages 198 and 269–70), were two reasons why Kuchma's winning 56% was more evenly spread through the Ukrainian regions than his 52% in 1994 (and of course Kravchuk's losing 45%). Another was the use and abuse of local state authority and pork-barrel politics to a much greater extent than had been possible in 1994. Several oblast governors were ruthlessly sacked between rounds for allowing Kuchma's opponents to win too many votes. Furthermore, this election was not polarised around ethnolinguistic issues, as both candidates had contrived to ensure that it was in 1994. The incumbent's main opponent this time was a Communist, not a would-be east Ukrainian everyman. Symonenko benefited from Russophone sympathy, but did not campaign as strongly on this issue as Kuchma had in 1994. The Communists, moreover, had inherent limits to their support, even in eastern Ukraine (which was precisely what Kuchma had banked on). Significantly, Kuchma caught up and even overtook Symonenko in several eastern oblasts between the rounds. Finally, Kuchma's highly eclectic approach to the national question (see pages 221–3), and the ease with which he said different things at different times and places, made him better able to consolidate votes across Ukraine than Kravchuk's narrow nationalising approach in 1994, albeit around a fairly soggy centre.

Kuchma's victory was well planned, but not preordained. Other possibilities enjoyed a brief existence during the campaign. Much media attention was devoted to the so-called Kaniv-4; after Moroz, former security chief and prime minister Yevhen Marchuk, parliamentary chairman Oleksandr Tkachenko and the relatively obscure major of Cherkasy Volodymyr Oliinyk signed a declaration in Kaniv on 24 August 1999 promising to decide on a common candidate. The date (the anniversary of independence) was obviously significant, as was the place (Shevchenko's grave) for Ukraine's new 'patriotic' left. The group eventually imploded in late October when an apparent agreement to support Marchuk was ratted on by Moroz (once again, presidential *kompromat* may have worked to ensure that one or other of them would make mischief). However, opinion polls indicated that none was necessarily a better replacement for the others.[62] The Kaniv-4 couldn't broaden their appeal to the right, as Rukh had been bought off, despite Marchuk putting out feelers to Yurii Kostenko, one of the leaders of the now divided Rukh, to join the group. Nor could Symonenko be easily added to their ranks (despite meeting them at least once for discussions on 13 October), as the expectation that the group would back the candidate with the highest poll rating would always have favoured him. In the end Marchuk played the role of Aleksandr Lebed in Russia-96, winning a handy 8.1% in the first round before suddenly accepting Kuchma's 'surprise' offer between the rounds to become secretary of the National Security Council. Whether his real job (transferring votes to Kuchma) finished on the day of his acceptance, or whether he would now be given a genuine free hand for an anti-corruption campaign, only time would tell. Significantly perhaps, unlike Lebed in 1996, Marchuk won no scalps on his arrival.

The second main counterfactual was the left unity scenario. In a belated declaration between the rounds, Symonenko issued an appeal backed by six other leftist candidates, including Tkachenko and Moroz (but not Vitrenko), in which the Communist leader surprised virtually everybody by suddenly comparing himself to Alexander Kwaśniewski, the reform leftist elected Polish president in 1995. Symonenko promised a coalition government, the rule of law, a voluntary renunciation of some presidential power, 'the equality of all forms of property, and [strikingly] the promotion and support of the development of private industry'. Equally striking was the statement that 'the aim of the programme is the building of a sovereign, independent, democratic and law-based state [and that we] will not join any union, which limits this sovereignty or draws it into military conflict'.[63] It was obviously too late to make such sweeping changes – or, at least, they did not carry the conviction or make the dramatic impact they would have earlier in the campaign. Symonenko won only 37.8% in the second round, less than the combined total of all the left candidates (45.1%) in the first.

The really interesting counterfactual would have been Symonenko's withdrawal in favour of Moroz, in truth of course the more likely Ukrainian version of Kwaśniewski. Intriguingly, Moroz paid a visit to Moscow in September 1999, where he met Gennadii Ziuganov, leader of the Russian Communists, mayor of Moscow Yurii Luzhkov, and Aleksii II, Patriarch of the Russian Orthodox Church. Several newspaper reports claimed that Ziuganov subsequently leant on Symonenko to consider the fact that a Communist was unlikely to become president of Ukraine, but that Communists could play a leading role in government in the light of a centre-left victory – although this was strongly denied by a leading Ukrainian Communist source interviewed by the author.[64] The Russian Communists had their own motives of course – namely, trying to create a bandwagon effect in advance of the Russian elections in December 1999 (parliamentary) and June, later March, 2000 (presidential) – but they probably understood the virtues of a 'popular front' strategy better than their Ukrainian counterparts.[65] Symonenko, however, stayed in the race and the opportunity was lost.

And With One Bound He Was Free?

Kuchma's strategists planned a Ukrainian version of Russia-96, and basically that is what they got, all rather too easily in fact. What next? Kuchma pledged to reinvent himself as 'Kuchma-2' and become a more determined advocate of reform. He simultaneously pressed for the formation of a 'new majority' in parliament, and sought to circumvent its blocking power in a controversial constitutional referendum in April 2000 (parliament was not due to be reelected until 2002, Kuchma's emergency decree powers ran out in June 1999). On the other hand, Kuchma had triumphed at the polls without necessarily securing popular endorsement of any positive strategy for change. If he had the wrong mandate in 1994, he missed the opportunity to press for the right one in 1999. Over 40% intended to vote for him as the 'lesser evil'.[66]

Nevertheless, after initially toying with reappointing Pustovoitenko, Kuchma surprised many with his radical choice in December 1999 for new prime minister: the former head of the National Bank and great liberal hope Viktor Yushchenko. Kuchma probably had a short-term tenure in mind – using Yushchenko to negotiate a resumption in IMF funding in a difficult repayment period – and was duly maneuvering to replace him once the normal year was up. However, Yushchenko, and Yuliia Tymoshenko, a surprise appointment as deputy premier in charge of the energy sector, proved rather more determined advocates of reform

Results of Ukrainian Elections, 1990–9
(i) Parliamentary (after initial faction formation)

	1990		1994		1998	
Groups						
Left	Communists'		Communists	84	Communists	122
	Group of 239		Socialists	25	Socialists/Agrarians	35
			Agrarians	36	Progressive Socialists	17
Centre			Interregional	25		
			Unity	25	Hromada	40
			Centre	38		
					Social Democrats	25
					Greens	29
	PDRU	28			National Democrats	93
			Reforms	27		
	Independents	61	Independents	23	Independents	37
Right	Rukh/DB	122	Rukh	27	Rukh	47
			Statehood	25		
Total		450		335		445

than Kuchma had expected. Yushchenko's popularity soared after a batch of relatively honest privatisations and a squeeze on the energy sector allowed him to pay off wage and pension arrears. Moreover, once in government, Tymoshenko began to reaccumulate resources and pose as patron of the opposition.

However, despite the hopes invested in Yushchenko, most of the factors that had constrained Kuchma's political choices in 1994–9 were still in operation. Most of his more questionable allies were still in office. The more depressing scenario was that his backers would begin calling in their chips, and a war over the further division of state assets was more likely to occupy their energies. Marchuk's role would therefore be as important as Yushchenko's. Unlike Lebed, Marchuk was a former local KGB head and master of kompromat, and was soon manoeuvring against his enemies. Either way, a variety of possibilities was now opening up, and Ukraine at least had some momentum to make a fresh start.

Conclusions

After eight years of what Dominique Arel has called 'the muddle way',[67] it seemed something had to give, unless it is a cathartic fallacy to assume that problems will always progress to a crisis point. Things, after all, *can* always get worse. Without some sudden defining event, however, Ukraine faced the real prospect of what Alexander Motyl has called 'Zaireisation' or 'Pakistanisation' – the creation of a self-cannibalising society where 'corrupt elites feed off their state, their society, and their economy, ultimately driving them all to possible perdition'.[68]

The alternatives to Zaireisation are not obvious. In Ukraine it has always been difficult to imagine the nationalist right governing alone. South-east Ukraine wouldn't wear it. Until 1999 it was also thought inconceivable that the left might win power. So long as Symonenko's Communists rather than Moroz's Socialists dominated any leftist coalition, Ukrainian nationalists would oppose them at any cost. The very stability of the state would be threatened if the national question were to be reopened, and the main geopolitical reasons for Western support for Ukraine would be undermined. The Ukrainian centre 'parties' have therefore governed by default and their long free ride has not been good for Ukraine. The centre has even come to prefer the maintenance of the left-wing bogey to keep the range of governing options narrow and disguise their own lack of will for real reform. Only after the Gongadze crisis in 2000–1 did a 'new centre' finally begin to emerge in opposition to Kuchma, albeit in a typically Ukrainian unexpected fashion. One part depended on Yushchenko's popularity, one on Tymoshenko's money, one on Oleksandr Moroz, as his Socialist Party attempted to leap-frog over the oligarchs to what in Ukraine would be called the centre-right. Only in Ukraine could such a bizarre troika be the main hope for a change of power in 2002 or 2004 (see epilogue).

Results of Ukrainian Elections 1990–9
(ii) Presidential (main candidates only)

1991	%	1994 (first round)	%	1994 (second round)	%
Kravchuk	61.6	Kravchuk	37.7	Kravchuk	45.1
Chornovil	23.3	Kuchma	31.2	Kuchma	52.1
Lukianenko	4.5	Moroz	13.1		
Hrynov	4.2	Lanovyi	9.4		
Yukhnovskyi	1.7				

1999 (first round)	%	1999 (second round)	%
Kuchma	36.5	Kuchma	56.2
Symonenko	22.2	Symonenko	37.8
Moroz	11.3		
Vitrenko	11.0		
Marchuk	8.1		
Kostenko	2.2		

Sources: Wilson, *Ukrainian Nationalism*, pp. 121 and 142; *Holos Ukraïny*, 2 June 1998; Taras, *Post-Communist Presidents*, pp. 97–9; *Vechirnii Kyïv*, 16 November 1999.

10

Imagining Ukrainians:
One Ukraine or Many?

The establishment of a successful democratic state would help to cement Ukrainians' relatively weak sense of national identity, but, unlike, say, Poland or Hungary, Ukraine does not yet possess many natural reserves of support for the national state, come what may. Modern Ukraine is not a homogeneous entity. Few states are, but Ukraine has inherited a set of ethnic, linguistic, religious and regional differences that are more complex than most – many of which divide the Ukrainians amongst themselves as much as they divide them from others. These divisions are not necessarily overlapping, and between the extremes of Galicia and the Crimea or Donbas there is a gradual gradation and merging of difference, rather than one all-encompassing divide along which the country might one day split.[1] Nevertheless, Ukraine has to live with diversity – to accommodate it or gradually overcome it, to deny or suppress it or to follow the American motto of *e pluribus unum*.

Ethnos or Lingos?

Any Ukrainian would accept that Ukraine is a multi-ethnic society. Ukrainians only make up 73% of the population. The key question for Ukrainians is the extent to which they conceive of *themselves* as a plural social group. The idea is foreign to most nationalists such as Pavlo Movchan, member of parliament and head of Prosvita, the society for the promotion of the Ukrainian language. He is a fervent adherent of the nineteenth-century idea that the Ukrainians are simultaneously an ethnic and a linguistic community. The two may not be coterminous in fact, but should be by nature: 'Language is the foundation of any national identity. It's impossible to imagine the French without the French language, or the English without the English language. Even the Irish and the Scots are trying to revive their language. It is just as impossible to imagine Ukraine without the Ukrainian language. Ukraine must speak in Ukrainian.'[2] To Ukrainian, or more precisely Ukrainophone, nationalists, any internal division of Ukrainian society is unnatural.[3] Ethnic Russians are either 'colonists' or, given that they have their own state over the border, not entitled to any special privileges in Ukraine. Russophone or Soviet Ukrainians are characterised as 'denationalised' Ukrainians, Lesia Ukraïnka's lost souls, 'memoryless Ivans',[4] who have been separated from their native tongue and culture by forcible policies of 'Russification'. According to a protest letter signed by leading Ukrainian cultural figures in 1999, for example, 'Russified Ukrainians are those who recoiled from their own ethnic community for the most part not from their own will, but as a consequence of deliberate colonial policies.'[5] Therefore, in the confident words of Kravchuk's deputy minister of education, Anatolii Pohribnyi, 'the Russification of such a large number of Ukrainians is only a superficial, exterior [and therefore] more or less *temporary* . . . phenomenon, not an internal one. At the level of ethnopsychology, in their depths these Russophones remain Ukrainians',[6] particularly because those who have defected to the (former) imperial culture have supposedly done so for basically material motives. The south and east of Ukraine may be superficially different from Galicia or Kiev, but only because of the relatively recent imposition of Soviet urban culture on historical Cossack territory.[7] This view of the Soviet (or historical 'Little Russian') Ukrainian is embodied in the nationalist cartoon shown in plate 16. The fat cat under the shadow of the Kremlin, dreaming of sausage in the shape of a Ukrainian trident, expresses the cosmopolitan materialist sentiment 'It's all the same to me whether it's *kovbasa* [the Ukrainian for sausage] or *kolbasa* [the Russian for sausage], so long as it's there.'

Ukrainophone nationalist thinking is reflected in the key clause (Article 10) on language adopted in the 1996 Ukrainian constitution, which declares unequivocally:

The state language in Ukraine is the Ukrainian language. The state guarantees the all-round development and functioning of the Ukrainian language in all spheres of social life on all the territory of Ukraine. In Ukraine the free development, use and protection of Russian, other languages of national minorities of Ukraine is guaranteed. The state promotes the study of languages of international communication.[8]

None of the above wording was left to chance. Deputies spent hours arguing over the comma in the phrase 'Russian, other languages of national minorities'. Bracketing Russian together with Bulgarian or Greek represented a huge diminution of its past status. Ukrainian nationalists were even concerned to omit an 'and' after 'Russian' – hence the rather ungrammatical sentence. Russian is of course not just the language of the 'national minority' (i.e. Russians only) in Ukraine.

Significantly, the state 'guarantees' the use of Ukrainian, but only 'promotes' languages of international communication (Soviet-speak for 'Russian'). It was also important to Ukrainophone nationalists that the state language function in 'all spheres of social life', not just in a few elite ministries in Kiev – and on 'all the territory of Ukraine' – that is, also in the east and south. When the author visited the east Ukrainian city of Kharkiv in summer 1996, just after the adoption of the constitution, it was significant that this last phrase occupied the most prominent place on the banners carried in a demonstration organised by Prosvita.

On the other hand, political reality has left these commitments suspended between Ukrainophone nationalists' desire for a statement of principle and leftists' and Russophones' assumptions that they would never actually be implemented. 'Ukrainianisation' has, on the whole, proceeded in fits and starts since 1994. Some would even claim that, particularly in popular publishing and the arts, the use of Ukrainian has actually diminished in that period.[9] Political and cultural elites may be switching to Ukrainian, but little has changed on the ground, where not only have patterns of language use barely shifted,[10] but there is also widespread support for some formal means of recognising the status of the Russian language in Ukraine.[11]

The Ukrainophone nationalist view of Ukrainian identity is only one amongst many. According to others, a Ukrainian is a Ukrainian, regardless of the language he or she speaks. Anybody 'can be a patriotic or law-abiding citizen of Ukraine, not just those who speak the Ukrainian language',[12] and not just those of Ukrainian ethnicity. Advocates of this approach have talked of building a 'Ukrainian political nation', although there are several different versions of this idea. Rukh too has given it support, but on the assumption that 'the core of this union is the Ukrainian people'.[13] There have also been suggestions that Ukrainians and others should retain their separate identities in such a project. According to a favourite formula of the Communist Party of Ukraine, 'Russians and Ukrainians are two branches of the one people of Ukraine', and so shall they remain. Alternatively, a 'Ukrainian political nation' will be a new identity transcending previous divides: Ukrainian citizens can come together through 'the formation of a Ukrainian political nation on the basis of the national blooming [*rastsvet*] of the Ukrainian people, as also of the blooming of all remaining ethnic groups'.[14] Other formulations have included the idea that centuries of Ukrainian–Russian interaction have created a fourth east Slavic nation that is a mixture of both (the *Rusichi*), as well as more familiar arguments about common Orthodoxy, 'Holy Rus' and pan-Slavic culture.[15]

Russophone activists have echoed the slogan adopted by Sri Lanka's Tamil minority after independence in 1948: 'One language, two nations. Two languages, one nation.' In other words, they claim that the imposition of only one official language in a bilingual society is dangerously divisive, whereas a stable civic nation can be built with both communities' equal participation. According to the 1998 election manifesto of Volodymyr Hrynov's Social–Liberal Union (SLOn), the idea of '"two languages, one people" is not a slogan, but a historical reality' . . . SLOn 'categorically rejects efforts to legalise the political separation of a united people into a so-called "titular nation" and "national minorities".'[16]

Elsewhere in the 1996 constitution there are clear signals of a delicate balancing act between these possibilities. The first line of the preamble refers to the constitution being enacted 'in the name of the Ukrainian people – citizens of Ukraine of all nationalities', a finely judged, if once again not necessarily grammatical, formulation. The phraseology was not consistently applied, however. In other parts, the constitution reverted to the formula of 'the Ukrainian nation' and 'national minorities', in particular Article 11: 'The State promotes the consolidation and development of the Ukrainian nation, its historical consciousness, traditions and culture, and also the development of the ethnic, cultural, linguistic and religious identity of all indigenous peoples and national minorities of Ukraine.'[17] Admirably liberal, but Russians in Ukraine do not like being called a 'national minority'. Nor would Russophones be entirely happy when identity is defined by reference to ethnicity only.

Opposition to Ukrainianisation is also overlain with the question of west Ukrainian and/or diaspora influence *within* Ukrainian culture. The 'Ukrainian question' is therefore actually three questions: the position of Ukrainophone culture within Ukraine as a whole; the influence of western Ukraine within Ukrainophone culture; and the influence of the diaspora on the west or on the whole. In Dnieper Ukraine Ukrainian language and culture have been marked by the centuries of Russian and Soviet influence, so that west Ukrainian and, even more so, diaspora speech are very different. According to the historian and parliamentary deputy Petro Tolochko:

> If the overhaul of the Ukrainian language creates definite difficulties for the Russian-speaking population today, then the introduction of a new orthography could create an analogous problem for Ukrainians tomorrow [if this includes] archaic Galician dialectisms that have long gone out of use in Galicia itself . . . What is being done today with language on the TV and in the periodical press is capable of repelling not just those who speak in the Russian language, but also those who were brought up on the classic Ukrainian language . . . of Kotliarevskyi, Shevchenko, Lesia Ukraïnka [and other writers from Dnieper Ukraine].[18]

Aside from accent and vocabulary, there are still considerable technical differences, even arguably 'linguistic-orthographic chaos' in modern

Ukraine, given the failed attempt to unify orthographies in 1928–9 (westerners tend to prefer 'i' for 'o', 't' for 'f' and use the special letter 'ґ').[19] There are even those who would like to revive the myth sometimes promoted in the Soviet period that Galician and Dnieper Ukrainian were really separate languages. Others have welcomed the difference, however broad, seeing diaspora and/or Galician influence as a means of linguistic deSovietisation. Others have not been so open. In the blunt words of a leading Socialist deputy from west-central Ukraine, Iosyp Vinskyi:

> Who is a better patriot of Ukraine – me or Slava Stetsko [the émigré leader of the Congress of Ukrainian Nationalists]?[20] Someone who has worked here all his life, or someone who has spent 50 years God knows where and then has the cheek to come back here and tell us how to speak, pronouncing 'narod' [people] 'narid' and other peculiar stuff?[21]

A 'Post-Colonial' Ukraine?

To many Ukrainians, Ukraine's current cultural plurality is an artificial reflection of the 'post-colonial' condition depicted by Edward Said, Franz Fanon, Homi Bhabha and others.[22] According to Ukrainian critics such as Roman Kis, Mykola Riabchuk and the diaspora author Marko Pavlyshyn, this has left Ukraine awkwardly *'in medias res'*,[23] with one eye on domestic culture and the other on Russia. Ukraine has yet to liberate itself from the spell of the former metropol and the inferiority complex of the forcibly provincialised (in the words of Natalka Bilotserkivets's poetic lament, 'we'll not die in Paris I now know for sure').[24] Ukrainian language and culture are still stigmatised by many Ukrainians (the writer Volodymyr Bazilevskyi has defined this as 'Ukrainophobia amongst Ukrainians'),[25] who still identify 'higher' or transcendent culture with Russia. Modern popular culture (pulp novels, pop music, game shows) is also more often obtained from Russian (or American) sources. According to Mykola Riabchuk, a form of 'creole nationalism' dominates amongst Russophone Ukrainians, which 'in political terms . . . is quite "Ukrainian", i.e. quite supportive of state independence, territorial integrity and many historical myths and symbols shared with Ukrainophones. In cultural and linguistic terms, however, it is rather "Russian" in nature, i.e. unsympathetic to Ukrainophones (with their alleged "western Ukrainian nationalistic obsession") and is thoroughly biased against the Ukrainian language and culture'[26] which it continues to regard as a low-status, peasant culture. Ukraine may be politically independent, but its psychological and cultural freedom can only be won by deconstructing the idea of empire, which still 'deforms our national space from within'.[27]

The tenacious grip of Russia on the Ukrainian psyche is the subject of the 1993 novel by Yurii Andrukhovych, *Moskoviada* (*The Last Days of Moscow*), which sought to continue the task begun by Shevchenko and Khvylovyi of deconstructing the myth of Moscow and its 'metropolitan discourse'. The narrative therefore has many deliberate and playful echoes of Shevchenko's poem *The Dream* (very postmodern – a parody of a parody, Shevchenko's work having been a rival to Pushkin's *The Bronze Horseman*). Whereas the 'New Literature' movement, founded by Yevhen Pashkovskyi with a similar purpose in 1993, attacked all Soviet Ukrainian art as imbued with a foreign spirit, Andrukhovych's novel is more honest about how this culture was internalised. His antihero symbolises Ukraine's 'post-colonial' malaise. Moscow is a dreadful place, but he is constantly drawn back to it and hates himself for the weakness in his character that allows him to be so fatally attracted.[28] Moscow the city still has a huge Ukrainian population – from artists to building workers – but the real point is that Moscow is also psychologically present in Ukraine. As in Chekhov's provincial study *Three Sisters*, 'To Moscow!' is still the dream.

Ukraine therefore still has a disoriented and profoundly split personality. Oksana Zabuzhko, in her novel *Field Notes on Ukrainian Sex* (1996), is constantly tired of her 'non-being in this world', of homelessness, of always being asked 'Ukraine – where is that?' She fears that only her children will finally be free of such complexes: 'slaves', she declares, 'should not have children'. The hero of Andrukhovych's novel *Perversion* (1997) – set in Venice, city of masks – has some forty names and identities. The Ukraine the two authors present 'is a pastiche . . . of peoples and cultures and narratives, that, like the phoenix, is still waiting to be born'.[29]

This theme of difficult disengagement, of Ukrainians still occupying 'two worlds', supposedly underlies many of Ukraine's more obviously political problems. According to Roman Kis:

> 'Ukraine on the border of two worlds' is [a] profoundly dangerous [idea], insofar as he who finds himself only on the border of two worlds has no powerful world of his own. The gradual neutralisation of Muscovitism . . . [and the danger of its] 'gangrenisation' of this part of Europe . . . is completely impossible without developing our own integral Ukrainian cultural-civilisational complex, with our own new Ukrainian urbanism, as the appropriate core of this complex. . . [as] in the large cities the subculture of Muscovite Eurasianism is still predominant.[30]

Significantly, Kis argues that a modern Ukrainian identity will eventually be found not in the rural romanticism of the nineteenth century or 'in endless chimerical fantasies about our ancient-remote-Aryan identity . . . but in our modern cities (and not in the graves of Shylov, the "etymological" fantasies of Chepurka or the "sacred Ukrainianess" of Berdnyk' (see pages 21–39).[31] In a similar fashion, the Russian writer Aleksandr

Prokhanov urged his own 'village prose' nationalists in the 1970s to embrace a modern urban nationalism of progress and technology, but he envisaged a convergence towards the Soviet identity; whereas a Ukrainian version must see its main task as the deconstruction of the Soviet identity in its urban redoubts. In part this could be achieved by mobilising the rural reserve – 32% of the population still live in the overwhelmingly Ukrainian countryside (87% of country-dwellers are Ukrainian, 40% of all Ukrainians still live in the countryside).[32] The first figure has remained stable through the economic difficulties of the last ten years, but can be expected to fall closer to the European norm in the longer term, especially if Ukraine's quasi-feudal collectivised agriculture is finally reformed. But renewed migration to the cities will not be enough in itself – Ukrainians may still move into low-status jobs.

The general idea that there was 'ethnic discrimination' in hiring practice in the USSR, which has carried over into the independence period, is difficult to sustain. There were plenty of opportunities at the top end of the scale for Ukrainians to make good in 'imperial' service; but at the bottom end it remains true that Ukrainians are still overconcentrated in collective farms and new-arrival labour (street cleaners, rubbish collection), which is a powerful factor contributing to the continued low status of Ukrainian culture.[33] The best commentary on this type of first-generation Ukrainian city life is still Viktor Ivanov's wonderful screen satire of social climbing and mis-elocution in late Tsarist Kiev, *Chasing Two Hares* or *Two Things at Once* (1961), in which both sides to a would-be marriage put on airs, graces and accents to impress the one they assume to be the richer party. All have left the village, but the village has not left them.

The new urban Ukrainians must therefore be attracted to (and help to create) a vibrant and modern Ukrainian culture that is capable of competing with nostalgia for the Soviet period, so that the towns and cities that Khvylovyi called 'non-Paris' can become proudly European. Mere success (!) in most spheres will suffice. Ukrainians will more readily associate themselves with the 'national idea', when it is more than just an idea – when it is itself associated with a stronger economy, a new rather than recycled culture and with sporting, musical and artistic success – when national heroes like Dynamo Kiev coach Valerii Lobanovskyi actually speak in Ukrainian. On the other hand, the trick is still in cultivating and modernising that which is nationally unique, as in the last analysis only this will displace Soviet-Russian culture and interest the jaded palates of the West – not pale imitations of themselves.[34] Ukraine should therefore stand up in its own right and 'not just [be] the West of the East or the East of the West',[35] but is not yet clear whether its unique selling point will be as a national-Ukrainian state or as a postmodern palimpsest.

'Post-colonialism' can, however, be distinguished from 'anti-colonialism'; decolonisation is not the same thing as the (re)construction of an imaginary pre-colonial reality. The latter tendencies, which encourage many Ukrainians to replace the myths of empire (the denigration of local cultures) with hyperbolic myths of their own (the exaggerated claim to an ancient past, the characterisation of the entire imperial period as a time of repression and 'cultural genocide'), can of course in part be excused as a reflection of and reaction to the distorting effects of past imperial control. They are, nonetheless, a potentially brittle basis for a new nation. 'Post-colonialism', on the other hand, can learn to subvert rather than just invert stereotypes, and avoid the Grand Narratives of either socialism or nationalism.[36] A truly post-colonial society would be one that no longer obsessively opposes the former imperial power.

Deconstruction, moreover, is a double-edged sword. Whereas Ukrainian nationalists have argued that Ukraine must 'understand the impossibility of living any longer *in medias res*' (between colonialism and independence, between Kiev and Moscow, between Europe and Eurasia),[37] for many other Ukrainians (and local Russians) that is precisely the point. The Ukrainophone nationalist version of Ukrainian identity can itself also be deconstructed. Different versions of Ukrainian identity can be defended and recovered. Nor, they would argue, is there any real dividing line between Ukrainian and Russian culture. The two shared so much in the past (according to the Kiev philosopher Myroslav Popovych, 'there is a huge difference between Mickiewicz and Pushkin – Pushkin is ours [*nash*], Mickiewicz is foreign [*chuzhyi*]')[38] and can still interpenetrate and overlap. Ukraine should not only recognise that it is a multicultural or multinational state and that this can be a potential source of strength; ethnic Ukrainians should acknowledge that their Ukrainian nation is itself multicultural.

The idea of a 'post-colonial' Ukraine is therefore deconstructed in turn by those who do not see themselves as colonial victims or Russia as an oppressor power. Volodymyr Hrynov has denied that 'Ukraine was ever a Russian colony, the Ukrainian people the people of a colonised country, or just the same, that the Russian people were ever the "conquerors" of Ukraine.'[39] 'Here [in Ukraine] the role of a metropol was never played by a geographic point [i.e. Moscow], but by the administrative-command system' – one set of Ukrainians oppressed another, rather than all being oppressed by Russia.[40] Ukraine, in short, was never a classic colony. Post-colonial theory can help shape our understanding of many aspects of modern Ukrainian life – but by no means all.

Russian Ukraine

This book is about the Ukrainians, but the more than 11 million Russians living in Ukraine still exert a powerful influence on Ukrainian identity and culture. Moreover, they are themselves influenced by the Ukrainian milieu. Depicting local Russians solely as 'colonists', a 'fifth column', even a 'diaspora', therefore does little justice to the variety of possible ways of being Russian in Ukraine.

A majority of Russians who live in Ukraine (57%) were born there.[41] A standard demand of Russian activists in Ukraine is therefore for the authorities 'to recognise Russians alongside Ukrainians as an indigenous people in Ukraine'.[42] As often, however, this demand has a variety of possible meanings. In part, it is a consequence of the privileging of Soviet-Russian culture under the USSR, and at the extreme an expression of the 'two cultures' theory of the 1920s, according to which the natural domain of the inferior Ukrainian culture was the countryside. It can also reflect the continuing popularity of myths of common east Slavic origin and subsequent joint endeavour. One such myth is that Ukraine was originally Rus; another is that its territory, or at least the east and south, was jointly settled by Russians and Ukrainians from the eighteenth century onwards. It is also symptomatic of the confusion about political borders and national boundaries in any type of modern Russian nationalism. One 1997 opinion survey revealed a fascinating pattern of layered identity in Ukraine. A relatively low 7.8% approved of the slogan 'There has been, is and will be Russian culture in Ukraine', less than the 1989 census figure for the ethnic Russian population in Ukraine (22%). A somewhat higher, if surprisingly low, 10.5% approved of a slogan on the need to 'preserve Russian-language Ukrainian culture', rising to 21.5% who supported the idea of 'One United Slav State' and finally 46.5% who approved of the slogan of 'Friendship and Partnership with Russia'.[43]

Russian nationalism, or Russo-Soviet nationalism, is therefore only one possibility in Ukraine. It has most appeal in Crimea, where the separatist 'Russian Bloc' and its would-be president Yurii Meshkov won convincing majorities in local elections in 1994. This was a dangerous moment for Ukraine, but was nevertheless fortuitously timed. Yeltsin had just shelled his nationalist opponents out of the White House[44] and offered Meshkov no practical support, refusing even to meet him on his first pilgrimage to Moscow (and this was before the first Chechen war broke out in December 1994). A different leader, a different time, who knows? Many Russians, including Aleksandr Solzhenitsyn, have bluntly expressed the view that the Chechen adventure was the wrong war. 'Without the bloody scheme in Chechnya', he bewailed in 1998, 'Moscow could perhaps (perhaps? . . .) have found the courage to support the lawful demands of the Crimeans, [instead] because of Chechnya – the hopes of Crimea were struck dumb and consigned to oblivion.'[45] As it was, Kiev was able to take advantage of Moscow's later entanglement in Chechnya to remove Meshkov from power, divide the 'Russia' movement and sharply reduce Crimean autonomy in 1995, but it has never been able to build up positive support on the peninsula.

In eastern Ukraine, however, local Russians are more likely to be Soviet-Russian in identity. East of Kiev and west of the Volga, centuries of interaction mean that it is difficult to identify who is a Ukrainian and who is a Russian (this also applies to Ukrainians on the Russian side of the border).[46] In the twentieth century, the Soviet 'melting pot' worked on some of its most promising material in eastern Ukraine. Russians in Ukraine are more likely than Ukrainians to be nostalgic for the USSR (in one 1997 survey, 44% of Ukrainian Russians agreed that 'the restoration of the USSR, if only in part, is possible in principle').[47] But not by much – 31% of Ukrainians agreed with the above statement. Soviet culture still crosses ethnic and linguistic boundaries. Many local Russians have been strongly influenced by Ukrainian culture and the Ukrainian habitus. Russians in Crimea might speak 'Moscow Russian', but in the cities of eastern Ukraine Russian is as likely to be influenced by Ukrainian as the other way around. In these areas, with millions of mixed families, many 'Russians' are just as much 'Russo-Ukrainians' as Ukrainians are 'Ukraino-Russians'.

The Russophile party SLOn (which means 'elephant' in Russian) was armed with this information in the 1998 election campaign,[48] but made the mistake of pitching its appeal at ethnic Russians rather than Russophones, and further narrowed its potential by trying to target the local Russian intelligentsia with the slogan 'Preserve Russian culture in Ukraine'. Its TV adverts used images of Russian poets and artists from Ukraine, including Mikhail Bulgakov and Maximilian Voloshyn (1877–1932), both born in Kiev, and Anna Akhmatova (1889–1966). However, SLOn's chosen archetypes were in fact very different from one another and not necessarily typical of Russian Ukraine. Bulgakov was something of a Ukrainophobe (see pages 86–7 and 126). Akhmatova (née Horenko) was born in Odesa, but in the Russian-Jewish Odessa beloved of Isaac Babel and Irina Ratushinskaia. In any case, Akhmatova soon left. SLOn would perhaps have built more bridges if it had shown more obviously Ukrainophile Russians, such as General Petro Grigorenko (1907–87, a Russian despite his Ukrainian surname), an active member of the Ukrainian Helsinki Group in the 1970s; or more popular Russian Ukrainian heroes – footballers, generals or astronauts. Its poor showing (0.84%) reflected the fact that the Russian Ukrainian intelligentsia largely disappeared in the 1930s and that the unadulterated 'Russian idea' is not popular in Ukraine.

Eastern Ukraine is also *terra incognita* for Ukrainian nationalism, but local Russians have tended to vote in much larger numbers for the Soviet patriotism of the Communist Party. Local politics is not therefore usually separatist. Because Russian is so dominant in such a large area of the east and south, there is no real logic in one small area like the Donbas seeking to secede. Rather, the idea is to make sure that the 'creole nationalists' in Kiev continue to look after the interests of both east and west. Nostalgia is for the lost unity of all of Ukraine and all of Russia. To date, Russian nationalists in Moscow have also played this game. A more limited project, a specific land-grab targeting Crimea and/or the Donbas, would upset everybody's calculations.

Russia's very separation from Ukraine may in time lead it to develop a more ethnically based understanding of what it means to be Russian, which could then be exported to Ukraine. On the whole, however, Russians in Ukraine tend to prefer 'pan-Slavic' versions of identity. They do not yet have the capacity either to think as, or act as, a specifically 'Russian' diaspora. Mobilising institutions, an ancillary civil society, do not really exist, now that the original Communist Party has gone. The Russian Orthodox Church and the Moscow patriarchate in Ukraine have limited appeal to a relatively atheistic or indifferent population; as yet independent trade unions are struggling to get off the ground.[49] Significantly, the increasingly standard term 'diaspora' is rejected amongst Ukrainian Russians, where the most typical sentiment is 'we haven't moved, the borders have'.

The 'Other Ukraine'

Whatever way one looks at it, a simple contrast between 'Ukrainian' and 'Russian' does not fully capture the reality of living in today's Ukraine. Clearly, there exists a third possibility, with its own culture of multiple influences. The group's loyalties are not yet clear. Nationalist Ukrainians tend to deny there is any such 'group' at all, assuming that 'Russophone' or 'Soviet' nationals are already 'rediscovering' their subterranean loyalties. More subtly, some have expressed the hope that the middle group is drawing ethnic Russians into their own blurred identity, as a half-way house for both to assimilation to the 'Ukrainian idea'. However, this would require a better understanding of the complex identities of these two groups. The vehemence of the hostility expressed towards Leonid Kuchma in the 1994 election and his demonisation as the 'pro-Russian' candidate showed that most nationalist Ukrainophones currently lack such an understanding.

Other scenarios for the 'other Ukraine' would include different possibilities for combination with ethnic Russians – the opposite of the Ukrainophone nationalist prediction. David Laitin has written of the possibility of the formation of a conglomerate identity for all Russian-speakers in Ukraine as an alternative to 'diasporisation', assimilation, protest or departure.[50] It has also been argued that the biggest inter-group difference in Ukraine is in fact that between west Ukrainians and the diapasonic majority of Russians and Dnieper Ukrainians. It is the westerners, the Galicians in particular, who are historically 'other' and culturally different.[51] It should be pointed out, however, that a self-proclaimed 'non-nationalist' majority would be unsure whom it was supposed to oppose – Galicia, the Greek Catholics, Habsburg Ukraine, the interwar west, Ukraine west of the Dnieper or all Ukrainophones.[52]

The third possibility is that the idea of an 'other Ukraine' captures what is likely to be a continuing reality in Ukrainian life. The 'other Ukrainians' will remain (as with Ukraine itself), in large measure because of sheer numbers, between two worlds. Ethnicity will impact on their identity, but so will language and culture. Insofar as the existence of the 'other Ukraine' is what keeps the extremes of Galician and Crimean nationalism apart, this may be no bad thing.

It is certainly true that there are problems with maintaining a mixed identity. The 'other Ukraine' has no fixed name – its members have been called Russophone Ukrainians, 'Little Russians', Soviet Ukrainians, Ukraino-Russians and, more pejoratively, 'Janissaries' 'mankurty' and 'sausage-heads' (like the cat in the earlier cartoon).[53] The 'other Ukraine' has no limits or clear boundaries: blurred boundaries are in fact the essence of this amorphous identity and are seen by the group itself as a valuable aspect of east Slavic identity as a whole. Such people are reluctant to be forced into a choice they see as largely artificial. As one activist put it, 'in terms of national-cultural identification we belong to a single Russian-Ukrainian cultural space' and should not be forced 'to choose between a mono- and a polycultural' identity.[54] The 'other Ukraine' has no obvious ideologue. 'Little Russian' thinkers of the nineteenth century such as Maksymovych or Drahomanov were explaining different realities, though perhaps Gogol would suffice as a symbol for the group. Less problematical, however, is a characteristic myth or narrative, a defensible justification to explain the group's existence. The myth of the common origin of the eastern Slavs is still propagated by historians like Petro Tolochko, and the idea of their continuing community of fate is still strong. In order to find existential ease with their identity, most members of the 'other Ukraine' are also likely to reject the Ukrainophone nationalist mythology which refuses to accept the very idea of their 'culture' and regards their existence as 'artificial' and 'the consequence of deliberate colonial policies'.

Boundaries Still Blurred

In 1989 the last Soviet census in Ukraine recorded 37.4 million ethnic Ukrainians and 11.4 million Russians out of a total population of 51.4 million. Soviet census practice was extremely questionable, however. Although the state was committed to building a supposedly supra-ethnic 'Soviet people', its authoritarian instincts got the better of it in the practice of fixed attribution of 'passport ethnicity', defined largely in unchangeable categories of patriarchal descent. Official Soviet figures therefore failed to capture the enormous degree of flexibility and crossover in terms of both language and ethnic identity in Soviet Ukraine, particularly in the 'new' regions of the urban south-east.[55]

Opinion polls since 1991 have tended to continue the Soviet practice of reifying ethnicity, producing fairly automatic responses. In a comprehensive survey undertaken in December 1997, when asked to give a definitive reply, 69% (73% in 1989) still considered themselves Ukrainian and 20% Russian (22% in 1989), although 6% now answered 'both Ukrainian and Russian'. However, when opinion polls are sensitive to the possibility of dual or situational identity and offer a broader choice of categories, the results can be very different. In the same 1997 survey, the largest ever carried out in Ukraine, respondents were asked the question a second time, with the following options. The answers were:

Ukrainian only	56%
Russian only	11%
Both Ukrainian and Russian	27%
including 'more Ukrainian than Russian' 7%	
'equally Ukrainian and Russian' 14%	
'more Russian than Ukrainian' 5%	

Large numbers of both Russians and Ukrainians, 27% of the whole population, saw themselves as having some kind of shared identity. In fact, an even higher proportion of Russians did so – only half (11%) of the 1989 census figure saw themselves as 'pure' Russians. Not surprisingly, the 'Ukraino-Russians' were concentrated in the urban centres of south-eastern Ukraine, where they were often the largest single group; 51% in the Donbas (Donetsk and Luhansk), 43% in Kharkiv, Dnipropetrovsk and Zaporizhzhia. In the three oblasts of southern Ukraine (Odesa, Kherson and Mykolaïv), with their higher rural population, the number of Ukraino-Russians was slightly lower, but still equal to the number of pure Ukrainians (both 38%, with 12% Russian). Only in Crimea did pure Russians (55%) outnumber both Ukrainians (10%) and Ukraino-Russians (21%).[56]

The idea of a blurred ethnic boundary between Ukrainians and Russians is common enough. Although nineteenth-century nationalists like Stepan Rudnytskyi and Khvedir Vovk believed that there were clear anthropological differences between north and south, the idea that the Ukrainians (or Russians) are somehow unique in their ethnic purity rather flies in the face of history. As Viacheslav Lypynskyi put it in the 1920s:

There is perhaps nothing more absurd and more bereft of all content than an expression such as a 'pure-blooded Ukrainian' in contrast to other local people – 'the impure in blood' . . . and there is nothing more comical or nationally dangerous than the monopolisation of this non-existent 'pure-blooded Ukrainian' by some particular local groups of the Ukrainian people – the most diverse in their origin.[57]

Language boundaries are also hard to draw. Although there was a strong linguistic influence from Ukraine to Russia in the eighteenth century (and to a limited extent in Gogol's day), since then the traffic has been overwhelmingly in the other direction, in terms of both language use and language content. The 1997 survey referred to above identified the language of *preference*,[58] of most (70%) of the Ukraino-Russian group and a significant minority even of self-identified Ukrainians (20%) as Russian, while only 3.5% of self-identified Russians were Ukrainophone. As a result, the number of Ukrainophones and Russophones in Ukraine is almost equal: 41% of the total 1997 survey were Ukrainophone, 44% Russophone and 14% equally happy in either language.[59] In other words, only a minority of the overall population, some 21 million, are actually Ukrainophone Ukrainians, that is Ukrainians who prefer to speak Ukrainian (and only half of those live in urban areas, where Russophones are a clear majority).

Patterns of actual language use are even more complex. In terms of competence, bilingualism is extremely widespread, in varying degrees in fact almost universal. 'Mutual understanding', however, is something of a misnomer. Virtually all Ukrainians can speak Russian, either because they were taught it at school or because they were taught *in* it (only after 1991 and then only in parts of western Ukraine will schoolchildren have grown up with no formal exposure to Russian). Russians, on the other hand, were only rarely taught Ukrainian. It is a safe bet that when many Russians claim an ability to speak Ukrainian they are most likely to be belittling its status and worth, assuming that it is so like Russian, or a mere dialect of Russian, that they possess a natural competence.

Functional bilingualism is nevertheless extremely common. People can move in and out of Russian and Ukrainian depending on context and audience. People may even use both in the same sentence; the linguistic boundary between the two is far from clear. Mixed Ukrainian and Russian is known as *surzhyk* (meaning a mixture of wheat and rye), but, although there may be common patterns of interaction, there is no such thing as a standard mixture, with fixed rules and grammar. Also, as pointed out above, Russian can be mixed with Ukrainian just as much as Ukrainian can be mixed with Russian. (The equivalent mixture of Belarusian and Russian is known as *trasianka*, 'hay and straw' – one underlying reason for the weakness of Belarusian nationalism is its prevalence in Belarus, where it is spoken by an estimated 35–40% of the population, compared to Russian, spoken by 45–50%, and pure Belarusian, spoken by less than 10% of the population).[60]

Ukraine badly needs a new census. More exactly, it needs a new census that asks the right questions, although at the time of writing it seemed that a planned survey in 2001 would fail to do that, given the political sensitivity of the exact size of the various ethnic and linguistic groups.

Jackdaw Nationalism

How successfully have Ukrainian leaders managed to combine these various elements? Most are ideological jackdaws, prepared to mix and match according to their particular purposes. Mykola Riabchuk has called this phenomenon 'creole nationalism' and rightly stressed its eclectic nature, although he perhaps overemphasises the legacy of 'empire'. 'Jackdaw nationalism' is my preferred term, as Riabchuk is describing a specific social sector, Ukrainian but Ukrainophobic. Whatever their origin, Ukrainian leaders are themselves still uncertain about which way to turn and have to appeal right across the spectrum, from Ukrainophone nationalists to creoles to Soviets to Russo-Ukrainians. They will, moreover, quite happily give out different signals to different audiences. I will try to illustrate this by discussing three concrete examples: the different ways in which the past is politicised in history texts and in public discourse; the use of public symbols such as monuments and banknotes in representing the self-image of the state; and, finally, some recent trends in the Ukrainian arts.

In a country with such a complicated past it is not surprising to find rival versions of that past – in particular the two opposing paradigms of common east Slavic origin and subsequent joint endeavour against the idea of Ukrainian distinction and separate development.[61] The struggle over which version to teach in the schools and celebrate on official occasions is still ongoing. Ukrainian nationalism tends to favour a unilinear variant of history as a morality play, celebrating Ukraine's ancient Trypillian past and depicting Rus as a more or less unequivocally Ukrainian state, whose ancient traditions were preserved in Galicia-Volhynia and Lithuania-Rus, revived in the Ukrainian Cossack state of the seventeenth century and then progressively dismantled by the upstart Russians after 1654. Dismantled, but never destroyed – Ukrainian nationalists take pride in the fact that there were no fewer than five declarations of Ukrainian independence in the twentieth century (1918 in Kiev and Lviv, 1939 in Transcarpathia, 1941 in Lviv and 1991 in Kiev) in the effort to resuscitate these traditions. In the words of the 1991 Declaration of Independence, therefore, Ukraine has a history of 'a thousand years of state-building' – rather more than a thousand for those who subscribe to the antiquity myths discussed in chapter two.

This is a potentially powerful mythology, although it ignores many of the complexities and counterfactuals that I have tried to address in previous chapters. It is also guilty of the existential fallacy of assuming that a given 'nation' is manifest at every stage in history. It is also assimilative of rival Ukrainian traditions based on the idea of some sort of cultural continuity between Ukraine and Russia. Alternative views of Ukrainian history are therefore still being propagated. The kind of Ukrainophobic Russian nationalism that denies any separate development at all to the Ukrainians can be found at the margins of Ukrainian life. Aleksandr Bazyliuk, a candidate for the presidency in 1999, not only helped to organise a reprint of the 1920 work by Russian émigré Count Aleksandr Volkonskii, *The Historical Truth and Ukrainophile Propaganda*, in Donetsk in 1998, but claimed in the introduction that the Ukrainian nation as such did not exist.[62] More importantly, the idea of the common origin and continuing community of fate of the three east Slavic peoples is still popular on the Ukrainian left, as is the idea that Ukrainian statehood, in its current form at least, is a twentieth-century Soviet creation. According to Kuchma, speaking on the fiftieth anniversary of Soviet liberation in 1994, 'Without the liberation of Ukraine in 1944, without the great Victory in May 1945, there would have been no state called Ukraine.'[63]

Different views obviously have different implications. Whereas Kravchuk eventually tended towards the unilinear Ukrainian nationalist view, Kuchma, despite becoming an equally ardent supporter of Ukrainian statehood, has tried to construct a more eclectic historiographical basis for it by integrating the heroic vitalism of the Soviet Ukrainian period with the national liberation struggle of the Ukrainophile paradigm. Like many modern Russian nationalists, Kuchma subscribes to a version of the 'two parties' theory of the Soviet past – the self-serving elite versus the mass of honest toiling citizens, victors in World War II and creators of a modern urban society. Kuchma has therefore called for the best bits of Soviet Ukrainian history to be combined with the best bits of the Ukrainophile version, shorn of awkward elements like the Purges or the OUN, to create a 'single national idea'.[64] As this task is not yet complete, Kuchma has roamed far and wide in his historical discourse, praising Hrushevskyi in Kiev one minute and tearfully pledging eternal friendship with Russia in Sevastopil the next.[65] Appealing to different audiences obviously, but also, again, to one particular audience – the 'other Ukraine', Russian-speaking Ukrainians, Soviet Ukrainians – the kind who see no contradiction in simultaneously supporting Ukrainian independence and east Slavic (re)integration. As one study of history writing in the Russian-language Ukrainian press concludes: 'A pantheon of cultural heroes is being built extremely eclectically: tsarist governor-generals coexist on the same level with the Cyrylo-Methodian Society, Bulgakov with Hrushevskyi, Sosiura with Stus, Chebykin with Ivan Marchuk, Petliura and Piłsudski with Soviet generals, submarine crews and tank builders.'[66]

A final example of this eclectic approach can be seen in Ukraine's choice of national holidays. Since independence, several Soviet holidays have been retained: 7 November is still around, albeit controversially and only referred to by the left as 'Revolution Day' (the Rada belatedly cancelled it in February 2000); more genuinely popular are International Women's Day on 8 March and Victory Day/Red Army Day on 9 May – in part because wives, husbands and lovers are fêted separately on these days rather than together on St Valentine's Day. Soviet holidays exist side by side with 24 August and 1 December as 'Independence' and 'Referendum' days (none of the other declarations of independence of the twentieth century is celebrated, least of all that of the OUN on 30 June 1941). There is a day of the Ukrainian armed forces on 6 December (the date on which the Ukrainian army was established in 1991), and one for the Soviet armed forces on 23 February (subtly renamed the 'Day of the Defenders of the [unnamed] Fatherland'). A 'Day of National Mourning' on 12 September was established by Kravchuk in 1993 to commemorate the 1932–3 Famine.[67] Easter and Christmas are also celebrated according to the Orthodox calendar. Ukraine, in short, now has a lot of holidays. Some work still gets done between times.

Sites and Symbols of Identity

'You can't be a real country unless you have a beer and an airline – it helps if you have some kind of football team, or some nuclear weapons, but at the very least you need a beer' – Frank Zappa

Ukraine has all but one of these. Obolon is the beer, which can now be bought in the West. Whereas the Yugoslav airforce destroyed Slovenia's planes on the tarmac of Ljubljana airport when it had the temerity to declare independence in 1991, Ukraine's fleet survived to become Air Ukraine International. Dynamo Kiev reached the semi-finals of the European Champions' League in 1999. Ukraine flirted with the idea of gaining control over the Soviet nuclear weapons left on its territory in 1991, but under intense international pressure agreed to give them up in 1994. In Frank Zappa's terms, then, Ukrainian identity ought to be quite firmly established. Other symbols, however – the politics of architecture and public space, the style of monuments old and new, the choice of faces on banknotes or stamps – can tell us much about the continued opacity of national identity in Ukraine.

The formal symbols of the state are those originally adopted by the Ukrainian People's Republic in 1917–20 (see page 123) – Volodymyr's trident, the azure and yellow flag and the national anthem 'Ukraine Has Not Yet Died'. Compromise proposals, such as including the crimson of the Soviet Ukrainian flag in the revived national version, have been rejected, although the controversial words of the national anthem (especially the call for 'our dear old enemies to perish, like dew in the sun') have been ditched and are to be replaced by public competition. Beneath the surface, however, Ukraine has been at least unconsciously 'postmodern', in that the public face of the new state is still an eclectic mixture of the Soviet, the national-Ukrainian and even the tsarist versions of the Ukrainian past.

In Kiev the physical evidence of Soviet rule remains ever-present.[68] President Kravchuk signed a decree on the dismantling of Soviet monuments in May 1992 in order to curry favour with the intelligentsia, but in typical Ukrainian fashion it was never implemented. Visitors to the capital, approaching from the airport and hoping to catch a glimpse of the golden domes of the Pechersk monastery, cannot fail to notice instead the massive and spectacularly hideous statue of the 'Mother of the Motherland', several hundred feet high, erected during the Brezhnev era in 1980. At its base is the Park of Eternal Glory, beside whose eternal flame and tomb to the unknown soldier (presumably known to be Red Army, not UPA) the Ukrainian Politburo would gather on Soviet holidays. The motherland Brezhnev had in mind was of course the USSR, but there are no plans to topple the statue into the Dnieper to join Perun.

Lenin still stands at one end of the main street, Kreshchatyk. Even more significantly Marshall Vatutin, the Soviet general who liberated Kiev in 1943 but died fighting against the UPA in 1944, still occupies pride of place opposite the parliament building. Parliament itself, and Kiev in general, still have plenty of monuments to *homo Sovieticus*, often in the classical triptych of worker, peasant and intellectual (see plate 8). The only significant Soviet monument to have been pulled down in Kiev since 1991 was the Lenin-and-workers ensemble that stood at the other end of Kreshchatyk opposite the main (Independence) square, but only because it was daubed with a swastika and the slogan 'hangman' during the August 1991 coup. Even then, it took months to demolish as it stood over one of the main underground stations. Compared to many other post-Communist capitals, especially Moscow with its rapid rebuilding of the cathedral of Christ the Saviour and Zurab Tsereteli's monumentally ugly statue of Peter the Great, Kiev's 'rebranding' has been rather low-key. A few streets have been renamed – parliament now stands on Hrushevskyi Street, Lenin Street is now Bohdan Khmelnytskyi Street – but change has been neither rapid nor wholesale.

Eclecticism is still the most notable feature, but so is the prominence of new buildings and monuments that relate to the time of Rus. This is logical enough, a simple reflection of Kiev's central role in the history of that era. However, it also offers a remarkable contrast with the nineteenth century, when Ukrainian symbolism concentrated overwhelmingly on the Cossack past. One explanation for this is a reaction against the manner in which the Soviet authorities coopted the Pereiaslav myth during the three hundredth anniversary in 1954 and converted it into a narrative of the reunion of fraternal peoples (Khmelnytskyi is also the symbol of the Civic Congress of Ukraine, a pan-Slavic party that had two deputies elected in 1994). The huge monument erected in Kiev for the occasion has been defaced; the enormous steel rainbow arch still stands, as do the two group monuments beneath it – one depicting seventeenth-century Ukrainians and Russians embracing one another, the other showing their twentieth-century equivalents doing the same (see plate 9). Someone has, however, chiselled away the reference to Russia's eternal future 'with Ukraine' at the foot of the second group. Similarly informal rebranding work has been carried out on a wall plaque to Khmelnytskyi in Lviv, in the square opposite St Yurii's, the headquarters of the Greek Catholic Church, which has had the reference to the Pereiaslav treaty removed from the bottom of the inscription (Shevchenko's lament that Khmelnytskyi had not been strangled at birth might be recalled in this context).

The new-found prominence of Rus in Ukrainian mythology also reflects the fact that Ukrainians and Russians are competing on much more equal terms than was the case in the nineteenth century. Then the Cossack myth was a useful means of carving out a local distinction within a broader imperial society: now Ukraine needs the precedent of past statehood to legitimise present-day independence. The myth of Rus also has a useful plasticity. An image of Volodymyr or Yaroslav can appeal to Ukrainian nationalists, who see them as the founders of Ukraine-Rus, to Russian nationalists, who believe that Vladimir was the founder of Russia, and to the middle ground, which looks to Rus as a time when present differences or disputes did not exist. In 1997, for example, visiting Russian prime minister Viktor Chernomyrdin declined to lay flowers at Kiev's Shevchenko monument and placed them at the new statue to Yaroslav instead (in 1993 Russia erected a rival statue to Yaroslav in the city he founded in 1010, Yaroslavl).[69] The famous figure of the Virgin Oranta above the altar in Kiev's St Sofiia's adorns one of the dreamy books about Ukraine's pagan past that were discussed in chapter two.[70] It was also featured heavily in official celebrations of a 'Thousand Years of Russian [sic] Christianity' in 1988 and is currently the advertising logo of a finance company in Kiev. The authorities wish to play things fairly safe in the capital and concentrate on symbols capable of appealing to Ukrainians' (and Russians') multilayered identity, although the erection of a new statue to Hrushevskyi opposite the Academy of Sciences in 1998 obviously, if obliquely, endorses his version of events (see plate 13).

This use of the myth of Rus in rebranding the capital can best be seen in the space stretching from Hrushevskyi along Volodymyr Street, past the old Golden Gates of the city, to St Sofiia's and the St Michael monastery. The new statue to Yaroslav the Wise was placed next to Musorgskii's 'Great Gates of Kiev' in 1997 and shows the ruler contemplating the plans to the nearby St Sofiia's – a reference to the original Byzantine statue to Constantine, holding in his left hand the spirit of his city (Tychē). Although Chernomyrdin did not notice, the implication is therefore of Yaroslav the (local Ukrainian) nation-builder (see plate 42). His calm is not reflected in his creation. St Sofiia's is still a state museum open to the public, but is being fought over by three rival Orthodox Churches. The former head of one, Patriarch Volodymyr, is still buried outside its bell tower after a violent confrontation at his funeral in 1995 (see next chapter), although the city council has at least provided some marble to give his makeshift grave some belated dignity.

At the other end of Volodymyr Street is a marble monument to the Rus saints, originally sculpted by Ivan Kavaleridze (1887–1978) in 1911, pulled down by the Communists in 1934 and restored in 1996 (Kavaleridze also designed the Shevchenko statue opposite Kiev University in 1918, the scene of nationalist demonstrations in the 1960s and 1980s, and the statue of the eighteenth-century humanist philosopher Hryhorii Skovoroda (1977) opposite the newly reopened Mohyla Academy in Podil). In the centre of Kavaleridze's statue is Olha, the 'first Christian ruler of Rus', alongside SS Cyril and Methodius, the inventors of the Slavic Cyrillic alphabet (Methodius never seems to get much credit for the achievement), and the apostle Andrew. The work therefore condenses several different eras' versions of the myth of Rus's long Christian pre-history before the 988 Baptism and is now a popular spot for wedding photographs. Andrew the apostle makes a second appearance as a new statue on Andriivskii Uzviz, a bustling shopping street dropping steeply from Rastrelli's St Andrew's church (round the corner from St Michael's) towards the river Dnieper. He is placed only yards from his name-church, near the site where he supposedly placed his cross on the hill in AD55 and a few hundred yards from the old tsarist statue of Volodymyr overlooking the Dnieper, erected in 1853. Once again, this is a plastic image. To Russians, Vladimir is gazing out on the vastness of the Russian steppe – to Vladivostok and the Pacific. To Ukrainians, Volodymyr is looking down at the river, the lifeblood of Ukraine. Ukrainians have clearly retained their sense of humour, however. The other new statue on the Uzviz is to Holokhvastov, the hero of *Two Things at Once*, on the exact spot where he was thrown down the steps of St Andrew's when he was exposed as a liar and a bankrupt (see plate 10).

Just as Vladimir is now normally Volodymyr, the city authorities have also rebranded or reclaimed the archangel Michael, a popular talisman in tsarist times, but also the symbol of the Zaporozhian Cossacks and more importantly the patron saint of Kiev since the time of Prince Volodymyr Sviatopolk (1108). A bronze statue of the archangel by Yurii Marchenko was erected in the main square in 1996 near the site where the wall of the central post office collapsed in the last days of the USSR, killing several bystanders. Some have criticised its neo-Roman style, but once again it is already a popular meeting point (see plate 14). Ironically, to Bulgakov the archangel was the force that would redeem the city from the godless Bolsheviks. The writer would be unlikely to appreciate the irony that the statue was put up by nationalist Ukrainian authorities.

There is less irony or ambiguity in the revival of several key sites of the Ukrainian Baroque. The most important to date is the reconstructed monastery of St Michael of the Golden Domes, originally built by Sviatopolk II in 1108–13 and destroyed by the Soviets in 1935–6,[71] but rebuilt in 1998 at the expense of Kiev city council and Metropolitan Filaret's mysteriously deep pockets (see plate 41). The new St Michael's is an obvious rival to Moscow's Cathedral of Christ the Saviour – its restored eighteenth-century appearance a more Ukrainian version of Rus.[72] It also restores an important symmetry to the area. The yellow ochre of its Baroque bell tower once again complements the blue of St Sofiia's tower on the other side of the two interconnecting squares, although the clock on St Michael's tower seems to be a modern addition and the paintings on the entrance walls could politely be called rushed. Other important symbols of the period have also been restored, some needing only a lick of paint, such as the bell tower in Pechersk, others reconstructed from scratch, for instance the Cathedral of the Assumption, Kiev's most prestigious architectural project, completed in the year 2000 (see page 243).

St Michael's and St Sofiia's were themselves originally highly eclectic Rus churches with Baroque additions, but the space around them pays even more eloquent testimony to Kiev's jackdaw nationalism (see plate 43). Halfway between them stands an old tsarist statue to Khmelnytskyi (finished by Mikhail Mikeshin in 1888). Khmelnytskyi's Hetman's mace still points towards Ukraine's destiny in Moscow, the city council having missed the opportunity to reposition it westwards when the square around him was pedestrianised in 1998 (the original plans for the monument would have had Khmelnytskyi's horse trampling a Polish landlord, a Jesuit and a Jewish leaseholder). A rather different symbolism is evoked by the monument to the 1932–3 Famine, erected after the state-sponsored sixtieth-anniversary commemorations in 1993. The central image of a mother and child is simple but plaintive, its message quiet but dignified (see plate 12). The monument is relatively small and was originally tucked away by the top of Kiev's small funicular railway, but the rebuilding of St Michael's now means that it occupies one of the city's central spaces. Next to it, and behind Kavaleridze's statue, is the high Stalinist ministry of foreign affairs, originally erected in the 1930s as the first of a series of planned encroachments on this space, albeit now pushed into the background by the pedestrianisation of most of the area.

A similarly eclectic but subtly nationalising approach has been taken to the hryvnia,[73] the new Ukrainian currency introduced in 1996. Volodymyr the Great adorns the one-hryvnia note, Yaroslav the Wise the two (see plate 45). The only controversial figure depicted is Mazepa, on the ten. The rest are fairly safe choices: Bohdan Khmelnytskyi (the five), Ivan Franko (the 20), Mykhailo Hrushevskyi (the 50) and Taras Shevchenko (the 100). Somewhat bizarrely, both Volodymyr and Yaroslav are depicted without beards but with moustaches, as if they were seventeenth-century Cossacks rather than early feudal monarchs. The architectural images on the reverse side of the notes are also relatively bland and/or plastic, including the ruins of the Greek Crimean city of Chersonessus, St Sofiia's and Lviv opera house. A similar choice of safe literary figures and, even safer, flora and fauna appears on Ukrainian stamps.

The city of Lviv, unsurprisingly, has been rather more active in erecting new monuments and in creating an urban symbolism that is more explicitly national. The most prominent new monument is to Shevchenko, near the site opposite the Habsburg opera house where Lenin was placed in Soviet times (see plate 15). The poet is flanked by a collage of other national figures, writers and Cossack heroes. A new statue of Hrushevskyi has been placed near the university (Ivan Franko still stands opposite), and a monument to the Prosvita society was erected in 1993. Evidence of Lviv's multi-ethnic past, on the other hand, can still be found. The old Polish statue to their national poet Adam Mickiewicz still stands only a few hundred yards from Shevchenko. A Holocaust memorial has been built by the route that members of the Lviv ghetto were forced to take out of town. Informal reminders are everywhere – Polish shop signs are still visible on faded walls, as are Habsburg manhole covers in German. Nevertheless, the public space of the city is being made more unambiguously Ukrainian. In comparison to Kiev, renaming practice has been both more comprehensive and more radical, with one street already named for, and a monument planned to, Stepan Bandera, wartime leader of the Organisation of Ukrainian Nationalists.

In the cities of the east and south, on the other hand, little has changed, in silent testimony to the survival of Soviet Ukrainian identity. Few monuments can better capture the spirit of a city or region than the massive miner that greets new arrivals from Donetsk railway station as they board overcrowded buses or try to hail infrequent cabs. The coal mines that once dominated the region may be slowly closing, but not as yet with indecent haste, and the statue embodies the identity of a city that traditionally sees itself as placing the virtues of labour before the complexities of ethnicity.

In Kharkiv the main square, the largest in Europe, is still dominated by a massive Lenin some 20 metres high. Behind him are the impressive Constructivist buildings put up for the Soviet Ukrainian government in the 1920s. The one exception to this remarkable lack of post-Soviet rebranding is Odesa, where the local authorities courted controversy by announcing plans to replace a statue to Catherine the Great in 1995. To Russophiles, she founded the region as 'New Russia'; to Ukrainophiles she only did so by destroying the traditional base of Cossack power in the region, the Zaporozhian Sich.

Art and Identity: Modernism or Post-Modernism?

My final example is the Ukrainian arts, where the nature of national identity has not surprisingly again been a key theme in the 1990s. Significantly, however, this has mainly been a debate *within* Ukrainian culture – as in the 1900s largely between nationalists and the politically disengaged. Russophone Ukrainians do not really have a cultural elite. Russians in Ukraine lost theirs in the 1930s, as the SLOn discovered in 1998. There has been little new Russian-language literature in Ukraine since 1991. Most significantly of all, there have been relatively few attempts to reassess Ukrainian identity in Russian. Other post-colonial societies have emerged from the imperial shadow by reinventing the former metropolitan language and reflecting it back at the centre – Yeats in Ireland, Claude McKay in the West Indies, Chinua Achebe in Nigeria. Precedents exist for Ukraine to follow this path: much nineteenth-century literature, Gogol in particular, the satires of Odesa natives Yevhen Petrov (1902–41) and Illia Ilf (1897–1937), *Twelve Chairs* (1928) and *The Golden Calf* (1931), whose lampooning of bunglers, bureaucrats and swindlers still strikes a chord in Ukraine's post-Soviet psyche (a statue to one of the novels' heroes, the con-man Panikovskyi, now stands just off Kreshchatyk). To date, however, Ukrainian nationalists have chosen to focus on the dangers of possible 'Irelandisation' – the marginalisation of the titular language – rather than on the potential opportunities provided when 'the empire writes back'.[74]

Although the fashionable term of self-description for Ukrainian writers is now 'postmodern', much of the contemporary artistic debate in fact covers the same ground as turn-of-the-century Modernism, picking up the unfinished agenda of the 1920s. In her book *Between East and West* Anne Applebaum quotes a Belarusian friend as saying: 'We are postmodernists . . . Belarus is the perfect postmodern country [ripe for] the revaluation of values . . . we young Belarusians can be like gods – we can create the world by inventing new names for things . . . we borrow from the past of others . . . [even] invent tradition afresh, if necessary, where we have forgotten it.'[75] The 'new wave' of Ukrainian writers, mostly in their thirties, has claimed a similar freedom. They have provided plenty of sex, of course (notably Oksana Zabuzhko, *Field Notes on Ukrainian Sex*), along with obscenity and subcultural weirdness (Yurii Andrukhovych, *Perversion*).[76] The young poets' movement Bu-Ba-Bu ('Burlesque, Farce, Buffoonery', harking back to the long Ukrainian tradition of Baroque irreverence and irony), founded by Andrukhovych and others, combined iconoclasm with a delight in novelty and invention in language that have helped to make Ukrainian a more flexible and fashionable tool.[77] The young have delighted in poking fun at the old, playing with the symbols of provincialism in the attempt to move away from the ethnocultural obsession with the 'national question' and develop a more reflective and self-critical culture. The artist, according to Zabuzhko, has been 'freed from the obligation to serve the nation'. As, again, in the 1900s, however, although in theory the whole point of the new eclecticism is to leave identity radically under-defined, in practice the new wave still write within the national tradition. Andrukhovych's richly comic novel *Recreations* (1992) tries to debunk the idea of the artist as the embodiment and progenitor of national revival. His heroes are writers, but they are also foul-mouthed drunks and philanderers who cobble together instant poetry to sell to gullible foreigners. Nevertheless, Andrukhovych is actually continuing the great tradition of artists writing about themselves and their own small world. The central event of the novel is a chaotic literary festival, but a literary festival nonetheless.[78]

Ukrainians working in the visual arts have been similarly eclectic (see plate 44). Some have sought inspiration in the recovery of national traditions, such as the marriage of folklorism with the primitivism of Henri Rousseau in the work of Oles Semernia, whose cartoon figures look like those in the American cartoon series *South Park* in sorochkas (embroidered shirts). Mariia Pryimachenko's (1908–97) colourful and exuberant naïve decorative art is still popular.[79] Icon-painters such as Nina Denysova and Petro Honchar have formed a 'Brotherhood of Alimpyi the Icon-Painter' in order to revive and redevelop the Ukrainian tradition of religious art. Others have gone back even further, to the Trypillians or Scythians or the pre-Christian culture of Rus, as with Natalia Rudiuk's beautifully ethereal pagan dolls. Much of this type of art is infected with the mystical musings of Sylenko and Kanyhin, but pagan gods and forest demons at least make interesting subjects. At the opposite extreme are the Ukrainian 'trans-avant-gardists' such as Oleksandr Soloviov and Kostiantyn Reunov of the 'Paris Commune' movement, who have embraced the 'radical eclecticism', 'anti-individualism', mytheotropism, shock tactics and 'aesthetics of ugliness' they have taken as characteristic of postmodernism. Like Bu-Ba-Bu, however, their *sharykovshchyna* (overplay, exaggeration, caricature) also draws on revised versions of local traditions such as the Baroque.[80]

Attentive readers will notice that little has been said about modern cinema. This is because, in truth, little of note has been produced since 1991. Partial rectification was due in autumn 1999, with the appearance of a new film version of Panteleimon Kulish's 1845 Cossack novel *The Black Council*, which aimed to be both a 'Ukrainian *Braveheart*' and a rival to *With Fire and Sword*, despite its minuscule budget of a little over $1 million.[81] Also worthy of mention are Vadym Kastelli's *Forward, to the Hetman's Treasures!* (1994), a burlesque and even 'anti-colonial' satire of contemporary nationalists who have taken seriously the myth of the 'lost gold' of eighteenth-century Hetman Pavlo Polubotok (1722–4), and *Mazepa* (2001), another myth-making historical epic.

Ukrainian music has also exhibited a variety of tendencies since independence.[82] Alongside the revival of traditional folk forms, there has been a veritable explosion of all things modern, with every Western style since the Beatles coming in a rush. Some groups, such as the *Snake Brothers* from western Ukraine, sing in a style that is self-consciously national, even didactic (their songs include 'Give Us Back our Language' and 'Don't Judge – We Have Forgotten Everything', that is language, culture etc). Others, such as *Mandry* and the long-standing Kiev favourite *V-V*, try to reproduce the pianos and accordians of European café society, singing mainly in Ukrainian interspersed with occasional Russian and French. The author's personal favourite is 'Tam, de nas nema' by *Okean Elzy* (Elza's Ocean, 1998), a modern refrain on the idea of Ukraine as 'non-Paris' and a reference to life, as in Griboedov's *Woe From Wit* (1825) always seeming better 'where we are not'. As throughout the former Communist world, however, many artists have leapfrogged over the national alternative in the enthusiastic embrace of modern American styles. *TNM Congo* for example produced 'the first real Ukrainian hip-hop' album in 1998.

Pop culture has at least been nationalised in form. Ukraine now hosts three national and many regional music festivals, countless talent shows, beauty contests and the like. There is, however, no dominant local style – the equivalent of Turbofolk in Belgrade or Disco-Polo in Warsaw. Torch singers such as Iryna Berlik and Taïsiia Povalii undoubtedly reach a wider audience than Oksana Zabuzhko or Yurii Andrukhovych, but their output usually has only a veneer of Ukrainian identity coating a core of undistinguished Euro-pap. Most Ukrainian groups, even in Kiev, sing in Russian – for instance, the *Brothers Karamazov* – and at the more popular level the Ukrainian market merges with the Russian. Ukraine is a huge market for Russian music (to some it is a 'dumping ground'), both for modern styles and for the nostalgia circuit from the 1970s. Many Ukrainians, such as Valerii Leontev and Natasha Kotalova, like their rather more distinguished eighteenth-century predecessors, continue to make a career in Russia.

Significantly, Ukraine's artistic avant-garde has been attacked by the old in terms starkly reminiscent of Serhii Yefremov's polemic against the Young Muse movement in the 1900s. In 1994 Yurii Mushketyk (born 1929), first secretary of the Writers' Union since 1986, wrote a long article in *Literary Ukraine* denouncing the 'modern Ukrainian post-avant-garde' for attempting to detach art from its national roots and

> create it on a wholly different basis – fanciful, abstract, self-willed, beyond ideals, beyond nationality . . . the 'pure', 'complete' avant-garde is supranational, anational. For them national problems (as with social problems) do not exist. . . . It is possible to allow a Frenchman or an Englishman to play around with literature, they have a strong state, a nation, prosperity in the country . . .

But, he argued, the 'post-colonial' Ukrainian case was entirely different. The parlous state of Ukrainian language and culture meant that now was no time for such games. As Yurii Mezhenko had complained in 1919, construction must logically precede deconstruction. As Andrukhovych has one of his conservative characters demand in *Recreations*, 'our poor nation needs courageous liberating words, not senseless playthings'.[83] It was the duty of every artist to defend his or her national culture, the very basis of their art:

> What would have happened with the nation, the people, if Shevchenko, Franko, Lesia Ukraïnka had played around with literature? For them, this [Ukrainian literature] was a 'fire in the clothes of a word', steel, a sword, but for the avant-garde it's a game, as if it were an abandoned child or some skittle pins. In the last analysis, the avant-garde would soon lose the very possibility of 'playing around' with the Ukrainian word, the Ukrainian language itself, if [other] people did not fight for it.[84]

Mushketyk has preferred to publish uplifting novels of Cossack heroism.[85]

In the future the arts may move beyond their obsession with the national question. Perhaps this would then be evidence that, in Yaroslav Hrytsak's words, Ukraine was a 'normal country'. Alternatively, if Ukraine does indeed move straight to a 'postmodern' phase, then navelgazing will be fashionable again. The centrality of the 'national question' is in any case perfectly 'normal', given its importance.

Conclusions

A Ukrainian nation is not yet fully 'made', in the sense of the clear and exclusive identities that nationalists tend to desire. Perhaps it would be more exact to say that a Ukrainian identity has yet to be fully 'unmade' or disentangled from the other histories in which Ukrainian lives have been caught up over the centuries – Russian, Soviet, Polish and Hungarian among others. The great contest between the Polish and Ukrainian 'national ideas' has been largely over since the 1940s, although vestiges of blurred identities remain in parts of south-east Poland. East Slavic interaction, on the other hand, is very much an ongoing process, albeit one in which the political borders between the three states now make an enormous difference.

Each of the three has influenced the others. Ukrainians and Belarusians still have much in common, although Ukrainian national identity has become much the stronger. As regards the main relationship, it would be churlish not to recognise that over the last two centuries Ukrainians have been more influenced by Russia, and by the Russian biases of Soviet culture, than vice versa. To take the most readily available, albeit rather rough, indicator, the number of Russophone Ukrainians in Ukraine is much higher (33% of the population) than the number of Ukrainophone Russians (just over 1%).[86] In the seventeenth and eighteenth centuries the flow was very much in the other direction, from Ukrainian and Belarusian Ruthenia to Moscow and St Petersburg, but recalling the history of mutual influence only serves to underline the closeness of the historical link between Ukraine and Russia.

In no way does this imply that Ukraine and Russia cannot be separate nations. Serbs and Croats, Germans and Austrians are now undoubtedly distinct, despite their closely intertwined pasts. Indeed, the Serb-Croat example indicates the possibility of what might be termed the fetishisation of small differences, at least in terms of language and history if not of religion, between two kindred peoples. Furthermore, history is only a starting point. Plenty of nations have emerged from another's shadow to forge a separate identity for themselves, such as the Slovaks in the middle of the twentieth century and the Moldovans at its end, even possibly one day the Rusyns in western Ukraine. However, a new national identity has to be built on secure foundations by working with the grain of the past. This is particularly true of Ukraine's need to relate to the Soviet legacy. Postmodernism may be fashionable in Ukraine – situated as it is at a crossroad of cultures, all making a return to myth as recent histories are retold in a rush – but Ukraine still has to live with the unfinished agenda of Modernism, which for most of the twentieth century meant participation in the Soviet experiment, as the Ukrainian variant of Modernism was never really able to develop on its own terms, even in the 1920s. Now that it can (potentially), Ukraine has to take care that the kind of uneven development that helped stimulate its own nationalism in the past does not lead to any kind of backlash on its own peripheries.

11

Angels and Pins: Ukrainian Religion

At various times in the past the distinctive characteristics of local religious faith have been a factor, sometimes the key factor, in creating a sense of distinct Ukrainian identity. The period since 1991 has not been one of those times. Divisions between Greek Catholic and Orthodox remain as sharp as ever, the Orthodox community has split into three factions and other 'fringe' religions, some traditional to Ukraine, some not, are on the rise. Nationalists have constantly bemoaned the failure to create a united national Church, without, however, stopping to think whether Ukraine really needs one. Others have argued that the religious sphere will be a test case for a new, more pluralistic Ukraine.

The Division of the Faiths

The current cacophony of churchmen was not foreseen when, in the run-up to the referendum on Ukrainian independence on 1 December 1991, the authorities convened a special 'All-Ukrainian Religious Forum' in Kiev to persuade members of all faiths they had nothing to fear from life in an independent Ukraine. Leonid Kravchuk stated clearly in his keynote speech:

> All religions, Churches and organisations of believers are equal. This means: no state, no privileged, no ruling religion or Church. Ours or another. All religions in which citizens of Ukraine believe are 'ours', because they are our people, who have the legal right to their own convictions and tastes . . . Calls to create a single national Church . . . originate with the romanticism of national revival . . . the objective tendencies of development in religious life are not towards any joining together, union or centralisation of religion, but the opposite . . . a pluralistic religious situation awaits us [after independence].[1]

Whether these were weasel words or a genuine statement of principle, the campaign to create 'an independent Church for an independent state' began almost immediately.[2] A Sobor (Council) of the Ukrainian Orthodox had already called for self-governance that very month, although by then there were already three main Churches in Ukraine. The Ukrainian branch of the Russian Orthodox Church, which had cosmetically renamed itself the Ukrainian Orthodox Church in October 1990, was rapidly losing the artificial monopoly it had enjoyed since the forcible dissolution of the Autocephalous Church in 1930 and the Greek Catholic Church in 1946. The Greek Catholics were *de facto* relegalised after the meeting between Gorbachev and Pope John Paul II in December 1989; the Autocephalous reestablished themselves at a special All-Ukrainian Sobor in Kiev in May 1990.

There were, however, many different ideas as to what autocephaly might mean. Kravchuk and his close ally the chairman of the Council of Religious Affairs, Arsenii Zinchenko, calculated that the quickest route to Church independence was the nationalisation of the existing Orthodox Church, and that a merger with the Autocephalous would serve as a short-cut to Ukrainianisation. The new Church was duly established at a Sobor in June 1992 and called the Ukrainian Orthodox Church (Kievan patriarchate), but the attempted forced marriage was not a success. The nationalisation campaign of 1992–4 resulted in the creation of not one, but three Churches (similar splits between the Autocephalous, the 'canonical' Conciliar-Episcopal and Renovationist Churches occurred in the 1920s and between 'Autocephalists' and 'Autonomists' in 1941–3). The old Orthodox Church in Ukraine had become one of the main carriers of Soviet-Russian culture, and most of its hierarchs were compromised by their links with the KGB. Genuine doubts about the canonical correctness of such a move were also important, and it did not help that the most prominent advocate of merger in Kiev was Filaret (Mykhailo Denysenko), exarch of Ukraine since 1966, but an ambitious turncoat, distrusted and despised in equal measure.[3]

The state supported the new Church, declaring that only its decisions had canonical effect,[4] but most parishes and bishops refused to support it, and those still loyal to Moscow christened themselves the Ukrainian Orthodox Church (Moscow patriarchate). Moscow recognised the authority of its rival Kharkiv Sobor convened in an attempt to head off the union in May 1992 (and which had removed Filaret). The Autocephalous, on the other hand, found Filaret's group rather less national and rather more compromised than they had hoped. Their émigré leader, Patriarch Mstyslav, appointed without his formal approval as head of the new Kievan patriarchate at the June Sobor, had considerable doubts about the merger. He was similarly dubious about Filaret's frequent violations of the original Autocephalous statute and the precipitate alienation of the Moscow patriarchate. Shortly before Mstyslav's death in

June 1993 he sanctioned the rebirth of the Autocephalous Church and Ukraine had, amazingly, three of the world's 17 Orthodox Churches.

The divisions were vividly highlighted in July 1995. Volodymyr, Mstyslav's successor as head of the Kievan patriarchate, died in suspicious circumstances after allegedly receiving threats against his life from agents of Filaret, then his deputy. Volodymyr had reportedly asked for police protection from Filaret in May 1995 and called for an investigation into money-laundering claims (Filaret having been awarded control of all the UOC's old accounts – several million in pre-inflation money – and 63 cars),[5] as well as Filaret's alleged funding of the paramilitary nationalist group UNA–UNSO. Filaret may also have opposed Volodymyr's ecumenical dialogue with the other Ukrainian Churches, as it threatened his own small fiefdom.[6] Volodymyr may even have tried to remove Filaret in May.[7]

Volodymyr's supporters sought to honour his short but historic tenure (and his 19 years spent in Soviet prison camps) by burying him in St Sofiia's. The cathedral, however, was still technically a state museum and its historic role as the primate ('metropolitan') church of Rus meant that it was coveted by all three Orthodox Churches, not to mention Aleksii of Moscow, who made a controversial visit there in October 1990 in the face of noisy nationalist protest. The Kiev authorities refused permission. Kuchma was now president and, having dissociated himself from Kravchuk's policy of favouring the Kievan patriarchate, declined to intervene. Volodymyr's cortege was headed by many prominent nationalists, including Kravchuk and Filaret, and flanked by paramilitaries from UNSO. OMON militia barred entry to the cathedral, resulting in violent clashes and eventual tactical retreat, which involved Volodymyr's unseemly burial under the pavement outside. Accusations flew as to who was to blame, but the upshot was that the would-be state Church, now headed by Filaret, clearly enjoyed no state support and its first patriarch was buried by a bus stop.[8]

It is not easy to determine which is the largest Church in Ukraine after the upheavals of the early 1990s. In part, this simply confirms the reality of religious pluralism in Ukraine. It is also a reflection of the fact that official figures (see Table 11.1 below) record the number of parishes, not the number of believers. Most of the Moscow patriarchate's parishes are in eastern and southern Ukraine, where levels of atheism or religious indifference are much higher and the number of believers per parish is much lower.

Opinion polls conducted since 1991 give a better idea of how widespread particular faiths are. According to the largest and most comprehensive poll undertaken in 1997, 65.7% of the sample considered themselves believers, and of these 62.5% expressed an allegiance to a particular Church. Of the latter, 12.3% declared themselves supporters of the UOC(MP) and a further 11.6% claimed to belong to the Russian

Table 11.1: Number of Parishes Belonging to the Main Ukrainian Churches, 1991–2001.*

	1991	1993	1997	1999	2001
UOC(MP)	5,031†	5,449	6,882	8,168	9,049
UOC(KP)		1,904	1,529	2,270	2,781
UAOC	811	–	1,167	1,049	1,015
Greek Catholic	1,912	2,807	3,098	3,315	3,317

* Information provided by the UOC (KP) and Verkhovna Rada Secretariat.
† Joint figure before the division of the Ukrainian Orthodox Church in 1992. The UAOC was deregistered in 1992–3 but made gains at the Kievan patriarchate's expense after its revival, until it too began to face problems of corruption and defecting bishops (*Ukrainian Weekly*, 19 January 1997). The Moscow patriarchate, significantly, has continued to grow.

Orthodox Church, although technically it no longer exists in Ukraine (its supporters can basically be grouped with those of the Moscow patriarchate). An impressive 43% named the UOC(KP) and only 4% the Autocephalous Orthodox. Greek Catholics accounted for 14.3%, concentrated overwhelmingly in the western regions of Galicia and Transcarpathia.[9]

Considerable differences were apparent between Ukraine east and west of the river Dnieper (the only regional breakdown available for the figures). Atheism and non-aligned belief were much more prominent in the east, where only 28% belonged to a particular Church, compared to 63% in the west. Of these, the west could count 12.9% belonging to the UOC(MP) and 1.4% to the Russian Orthodox Church. The UOC(KP) had more support, 46.7%, compared to 4.9% for the Autocephalous and 23.2% to the Greek Catholics. East of the river Dnieper, slightly more belonged to the Moscow patriarchate and the 'Russian Orthodox Church' (13.6% and 12.9%), and slightly fewer, 38.9%, belonged to the UOC(KP). Only 2.9% belonged to the Autocephalous Church and a minuscule 0.4% to the Greek Catholics.[10]

Ukraine is therefore still a state of many faiths. Even ethnic Ukrainians are divided in their loyalties. Many still belong to the Moscow patriarchate. The choice of religion therefore seems mainly to be a reflection of where people live and the historical differences between the Ukrainian regions rather than ethnicity or language *per se*.

In Search of a National Church

What, then, do the supporters of the various Churches believe in? Current divisions may have been sparked by politics and personalities, but real questions of faith and identity are also involved. The apostles of the Kievan patriarchate, the would-be national Ukrainian Orthodox

Church, such as the Rukh deputy Mykola Porovskyi, offer what is in the first place a political argument:

> A specific [problem] for Ukraine has been the fact that nearly always the religious centres under whose jurisdiction Ukrainian Churches have found themselves have been based beyond her borders, which has hampered the development of a state[-based] self-consciousness and encouraged the political dependency of the nation. Only an independent state can have an independent national Church. Hence the level of the development of the national Church is also a sign of the state-building strengths of the nation. National forms of spiritual and material culture – literature, science, art, architecture – also come under the formative influence of religion . . . state-nations everywhere form their own Churches, which become a powerful defender of the national state and vice-versa . . . the national Church in Ukraine can only be that Church which functions [by] resting on the deep ritual-cultural traditions of the people, promoting the progress of the ethnoculture, self-consciousness and state-building mentality of the nation.[11]

In short, both the new state and the fledgling Ukrainian nation needed their own Church. More reflective nationalists are well aware of the effect that the dissolution of the original Kievan Church in 1686 had on retarding the development of Ukrainian identity. Despite the existence of the Greek Catholics in the west, there was a clear and reasonably precise boundary between Ukrainians and Catholic Poles, whereas most Ukrainians and Russians spent most of the crucial early modern period as members of the same faith. As one commentator candidly admitted, 'the religious factor [has therefore] never played the role of a designated medium of national revival. The priority in this always belonged to the national idea.' Now, however, the Church could play such an instrumental role. There should be no surprise at 'the striving of the national-democratic forces of Ukraine to use the national Church itself in the role of a medium for the revival of the national spirit of Ukrainians and as a means of overcoming the processes of their denationalisation, which have lasted for centuries.'[12]

To this end, as in the 1920s, supporters of the Kievan patriarchate have consistently campaigned for the nationalisation of religion, for 'the rebirth of the historical memory of our people, the use of the Ukrainian language in church services [Church Slavonic being heavily infected with Russicisms], the formation of a national Church calendar, the translation and publication of the Holy Scripture and religious literature into our native language . . . and the manifestation of Christianity through national forms of ritual, also in the form of our national mentality.'[13] They have also sought the 'restoration' of sites of key symbolic value, in particular St Sofiia's and the Pechersk complex – to date without success.

It is not just that a new state needs a new Church. Supporters of the Kievan patriarchate have also argued that there is a specific type of Ukrainian Christianity that needs to be restored. As outlined in chapters one to three, Ukrainian historians have seen the local faith as long embodying forms of national exceptionalism, even before Volodymyr's baptism in AD988. The Ukrainian faith can therefore be easily distinguished from its Russian counterpart. According to Yevhen Sverstiuk:

> although the Ukrainian and Russian faiths are both Orthodox, they have a different spirit. Russian Orthodoxy concentrates on the external aspect of ritual, Ukrainian Orthodoxy is more spiritual. Because it grew out of folklore from the earliest times, it has preserved very deep popular traditions and an aesthetic based in popular belief . . . in Russia there was a much greater divorce between the official Church and popular belief; paradoxically the lack of an official state Ukrainian Church [after 1686] means that these customs were never controlled and were able to persist even into the twentieth century . . . the Ukrainian tradition is characterised by its openness – not exactly ecumenism, but a willingness to live with or alongside other faiths . . . this is why the Russians have so often falsely accused us of [excessive] intimacy with Protestantism or Latinism.[14]

The accusation of 'excessive intimacy' misses the point. Ukrainian identity lies in its specific version of Orthodoxy, in its relative openness to the West (as proved by the three 'unions' of 1246–7, 1448 and 1596 and by the reforms enacted under Mohyla in the seventeenth century and Lypkivskyi in the 1920s) and in the mutual influence of pre-Christian and Orthodox traditions, which is also expressed in the Greek Catholics' own unique synthesis. The 'popular tradition' and 'different spirit' of the Ukrainian faith are embodied in a rich variety of survivals from earlier, pagan ritual, such as offerings to the gods of the fields at harvest time (*obzhynky*), the festival of the fertility god Kupalo, the ritual kidnap and ransoming of the bride before marriage (*pereima*), New Year carolling (*shchedrivky*) and so on. In the words of one Ukrainian academic:

> The religiosity of Ukrainians is characterised by the retention of natural forms in the description and perception of the hypostasis of God and the saints, respect for the Bible as sacred along with an external knowledge of its contents, uniting respect towards the priesthood with a distinct anticlericalism, a lack of susceptibility to the orthodoxies of Christianity and freedom of religious thought and action. Also natural to the people is disdain for the preachings of Christian asceticism and a complete indifference to confessional differences and forms of expression of faith.[15]

Other myths of religious difference include the idea that the Ukrainians are more observant than the Russians and that their faith was therefore better able to survive Soviet rule.[16] Chapter five showed how the former myth featured in Lesia Ukraïnka's play *The Noble Woman*. Evidence for its corollary is provided by the oft-repeated claim that half of all churches in the USSR in 1991 were situated in Ukraine – which has the advantage of being more or less true.[17] Therefore, despite the local division into three separate Churches, it can still be argued that 'in terms of the number of parishes, Ukrainian Orthodoxy is now the biggest in the world'.[18] Hence, Moscow's tenacious fight to preserve Church unity has also been a fight to maintain its cherished former status as the world's largest Orthodox Church.

Ukrainian writers and churchmen have also argued that Moscow's 'Caesaropapist' brand of Orthodoxy has a long tradition of complicity in the defence of secular power, and indeed that the Church was infected with, and was a key contributor to, the ideology of Russian autocracy and imperialism. The Ukrainian Church kept faith with its flock, but the Russian compromised its original mission, which is why it is a Church in decline, the argument runs.

It is also claimed that the Kievan Church is the original Rus Church, from which the Moscow Church was but a later offshoot. At its October 1993 synod the Kievan patriarchate named itself the Church of 'Kiev and all Rus-Ukraine' to stress this link. 'The right of apostolic origin', it is claimed, therefore 'crosses over to the [restored] Ukrainian Church',[19] and Church leaders have continued to propagate the twin myths of 'the land of Rus-Ukraine, blessed by Andrew the apostle' and Kiev as the 'New Jerusalem'.[20] Supporters of the Kievan patriarchate have demanded swift recognition by the world Orthodox community – 'we would want the Church of Constantinople in the future to be a Holy Mother for us, not a stepmother' – as theirs was supposedly the Church originally under Constantinople's jurisdiction after 988. When, at a later date, Constantinople 'recognise[d] the Russian Orthodox Church in the borders of 1593, that was without Ukraine'.[21] Ukrainians claim that Constantinople has never formally accepted the takeover of the Kiev Church in 1686 (despite the issue of a formal writ by Dionysios IV, for which he was supposedly paid 200 guldens and 120 sable skins).[22] Constantinople's current patriarch, Bartholomeos I, has, however, been reluctant to involve himself directly in the dispute – as with his predecessors in the fifteenth century. A precondition for recognition would in any case be some kind of restored unity amongst the Orthodox of Ukraine. On the other hand, the Kievan patriarchate would claim that all the Orthodox Churches originally established their independence unilaterally – after all, it took Constantinople from 1448 to 1589 to recognise the Moscow Church. There is therefore nothing 'uncanonical' about their actions.[23]

The 'One True Church'

The nominally independent Ukrainian Orthodox Church of the Moscow patriarchate still claims to be the largest Church in Ukraine, at least institutionally if not in terms of popular sympathy. Its head, also Volodymyr (Viktor Sabodan), has claimed in public to support the eventual creation of a national Ukrainian Orthodox Church, so long as it is through a process that is both canonical and evolutionary. On the other hand, the UOC(MP) statute still declares that it 'forms [*sostavliaet*] . . . part of the Moscow patriarchate' (i.e. the parent Church in Moscow itself) and that it is obliged to 'put into practice the decisions of local councils of the Russian Orthodox Church'.[24] The August 2000 Synod of the ROC sharply narrowed Volodymyr's freedom of maneuvre by refusing to grant even autonomy, let alone autocephaly. Some have even sought its reregistration under the more 'honest' label of local branches of the Russian Orthodox Church.[25]

To its critics the UOC(MP) is therefore an artificial and 'politically anti-Ukrainian Church, created under pressure from Russia, that [is well known for its Ukrainophobic sentiments] and even denies the 1933 Famine. "Cooperation" would only be possible if they moved closer to the Ukrainian people, their language, their history. The issue of which Church is more truly "canonical" is a false question as people are more interested in practice.'[26] The 'canonical' question is important to many, however. The Moscow patriarchate has always claimed that it is the only properly established Church in Ukraine. Many of its adherents simply refer to themselves as the 'canonical Church', not the Moscow Church. This self-image as the one true faith can be seen in the picture on page 242, a copy of a poster obtained by the author at the Pochaïv monastery in western Ukraine (written in Ukrainian, not Russian). The 'one sacred united Apostolic Orthodox Church' is the central trunk of the oak, strong and true, the Church founded by Christ and the Ecumenical Councils of AD325–787. Subsequent splits are shown in the branches off to the right, the first being the Roman Catholic (1054), the second the various Protestant faiths – Anglicans can find themselves fourth from bottom (1534), Mennonites seventh from top (1895) and so on. The Greek Catholic Church created at the Union of Brest (1596) is depicted as the branch wrapping itself enthusiastically around the Catholics; the Kievan patriarchate is the final tiny and insignificant branch splitting from the main trunk in 1992.

As in the 1920s, therefore, Ukraine's would-be independent Church is attacked as an artificial creation of the 'self-consecrated'. The 1992–5 Sobors that created the Kievan patriarchate are condemned as unilateral acts of minorities, with essentially political motives and inadequate preparation in canon law. Lay participation in these Sobors (and in the Higher Church Council established in 1992), for the Kievan patriarchate a tradition dating back to the seventeenth century, is also attacked as

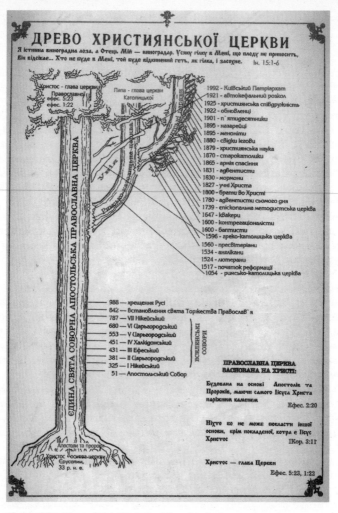

Ill. 14. 'The Tree of the Christian Church'. A view, written in Ukrainian, of the Orthodox Church (Moscow patriarchate) as 'The One Sacred United Apostolic Orthodox Church', as founded by Christ, the Apostles and the Ecumenical Councils of AD325–787.

'uncanonical'. Relations with the Kievan patriarchate therefore, 'a Church not built on Christian ideals, but on the "national idea" and on the personal ambitions of its leader' (Filaret), must be based on the idea of 'their return, not on the idea of "union" – it is they who left us, not the other way around.'[27]

The Moscow patriarchate argues that 'we already have sufficient marks of autocephaly – more than the Greek Catholics', who are supposedly dependent on Rome,[28] but claims that it would be a mistake to focus on political and statute issues alone. All the Eastern Orthodox remain united 'on the principle of their faith'. 'The Church cannot be completely independent. We cannot be independent from Christ'.[29] These traditions include the use of Church Slavonic for the liturgy (sermons still tend to be in Russian). 'Just as Latin was used in the West, this is the language of God in our Church, the language of conversation with our Lord. Believers must hear the word of God in the form they are used to, to understand His wisdom and His Grace' (an argument that has considerable appeal to conservative elderly Ukrainians). 'In this way, we can understand our fellow Orthodox from Serbia and Bulgaria . . . it is not our task to divide [people], but to bring [them] together.'[30] The Moscow patriarchate also claims that there are no 'good religious translations' in Ukrainian (by which they mean the main successor of Kulish's 1903 Bible, the 1963 diaspora version). It may be easier for people to read the Bible in their native language but, they would argue, this is not the point. Ukrainianisation would only bring about a narrowing of horizons and a loss of contact with tradition. Supporters of the Kievan patriarchate would of course observe that the Serbian and Bulgarian Churches are themselves already autocephalous. As Archbishop Adrian of Dnipropetrovsk has asked, 'Is our Ukraine any worse than Russia, Bulgaria, Romania, Serbia, Greece, Cyprus, Georgia or any other Orthodox countries which have their own local Orthodox Churches?'[31]

One pivotal symbol in these conflicts is the rebuilding of the Cathedral of the Assumption in Pechersk, which was decided on at the same time as the rebuilding of the monastery of St Michael of the Golden Domes but has been beset by much greater controversy. Whereas St Michael's has gone to the Kievan patriarchate, the Pechersk complex (upper half) is still a state museum, with the lower half under the control of the Moscow Church since 1988 (Pechersk had a strong tradition of Russian Orthodox nationalism in the nineteenth century; the Russian nationalist hero Petr Stolypin was buried there after his assassination in Kiev opera house in 1911). Kuchma's decision in 2000 to 'balance' church affairs in the capital by giving the Assumption to the Moscow patriarchate (and to invite Aleksii to the celebration of the 950th anniversary of Pechersk in August 2001, hot on the heels of the tenth anniversary of the decelaration of independence) therefore outraged Ukrainian nationalists. Architecturally, however, the church, like the St Michael's monastery, was re-created with the Baroque additions that adorned it when it was destroyed in 1941.[32]

The Moscow patriarchate has a definite Ukrainophobe wing, which has little or no understanding of Ukrainian Christianity as any kind of halfway house between the Latin and Orthodox worlds. They see in the Greek Catholics and the autocephaly movement only the 'threat of Catholicisation and decay in Union',[33] and point to the creeping

Latinisation of the Greek Catholics since 1720 as their own likely fate. Anti-Catholicism is also more apparent amongst the Moscow patriarchate. There are those who consider that 'the international ecumenical movement . . . has turned itself into an openly anti-Orthodox coalition'.[34] There are even many who accuse the Greek Catholics of being more anti-Orthodox than the Vatican, which since the Second Vatican Council (1962–5) and the opening of official dialogue in 1967 has seen the 'Russian Orthodox' as a 'sister Church'.[35] Although their ritual is still 'ours', the Greek Catholics are therefore *de facto* 'part of the Catholic world'.[36] This tendency may well gather strength as the parent Church in Moscow falls increasingly under the influence of Russian nationalism.

On the other hand, the Moscow patriarchate also contains many who view the Church as the joint property of both Ukrainians and Russians. They would also claim that 'our Church descends from Vladimir [Volodymyr] and Andrew the apostle',[37] but point out that 'when Orthodoxy began in Kiev, there was no Ukraine, no Russia, no Belarus – only Rus', which is of course true.[38] 'The Russian Orthodox Church' has always been 'a spiritual centre for many ethnoses and peoples. At present Ukraine, Russia and Belorussia are a common Slavic community which finds itself under the authority of a single Orthodox Church.'[39] Holy 'Kiev is neither a Russian nor a Ukrainian, but a Russo-Ukrainian city, which unites both elements in living combination.'[40] Or, as a 1998 election leaflet for the Party of Regional Revival put it, 'we must faithfully respect, preserve and augment that which our ancestors created at the price of great efforts over the centuries',[41] namely the united Church of all the eastern Slavs. This was the reasoning behind Moscow Patriarch Aleksii II's proposed millennial trip through all the 'nations of Rus' to Volodymyr's original place of baptism in Chernonessus, Crimea. Filaret of course was bitterly opposed to such 'provocation', as, in interesting contrast to 1995, was Kuchma's ally Volodymyr Horbulin, then secretary of the National Security Council.[42] The visit was banned.

It is significant that the Moscow patriarchate is therefore not just an east Ukrainian phenomenon. The kind of traditional conservative Orthodoxy represented by the Moscow Church also has its supporters on the western fringes of Ukrainian settlement, where the confrontation with Roman Catholicism has always been sharpest – particularly on the border that lasted for two centuries between the Russian empire and its Catholic neighbours. The Party of Regional Revival of Ukraine, supported by the Moscow patriarchate, despite its poor overall performance in the 1998 elections (0.9% in total, despite 14 sitting deputies having been party members), won its highest vote in the western oblasts of Volyn (1.8%) and Chernivtsi (4.8%) – in the latter case with the help of the local Romanian Orthodox population. A central symbol of this phenomenon is the Pochaïv monastery in Ternopil oblast. After a period under the control of the Greek Catholics between 1713 and 1831, when the spectacular ochre Cathedral of the Assumption was built, its strategic position on the edge of the Romanov/Habsburg border made Pochaïv a vital centre for proselytising the Orthodox message westwards in the nineteenth century, when, like Pechersk, it became famous as a stronghold of Russian nationalism.[43] Pochaïv may be in Galicia, but its priests are still resolutely Moscowphile.

The Persistent Autocephalous

The Autocephalous Orthodox Church began life in the 'Ukrainianising' 1920s, but, after its suppression in 1930, was forced to survive in the Ukrainian diaspora. In theory the Autocephalous ought therefore to share much common ground, at least with the principles if not the personalities, of the Kievan patriarchate. However, the shotgun 'merger' of 1992–3 was not a success. Bizarrely, at first the Autocephalous Church seemed to find more common ground with the Moscow patriarchate, opening formal negotiations in 1995. At least six meetings have since been held and a joint commission on dialogue now exists.

The cynical explanation of this strange turn of events would again look to politics. The Autocephalous Orthodox received state support as the lesser of two evils in the last days of the USSR to try and head off the Greek Catholic revival in Galicia. Now there have been persistent accusations that the Autocephalous are receiving covert support from the Moscow patriarchate in an attempt to undermine its Kievan rival. If the two were to link together, and Filaret's Church continued to wither on the vine, then the combined Church would easily be the largest in Ukraine, providing a possible incentive for final recognition by Constantinople.[44] The 1995 negotiations were supposedly also supported by elements in the Kuchma administration seeking to cut Filaret down to size, and even to explore the possibility of a new Ukrainian, but not militantly Ukrainian nationalist, Church taking the place of the Kievan patriarchate. A second, and simpler explanation of this coalition would be to blame Filaret. Many of the Autocephalous regard his violations of canon law as invalidating the 1992 merger.[45] Hostility towards him is so great on all sides that it is bound to create some strange bedfellows (on his death-bed in 1993, Mstyslav reportedly condemned the KGB-tainted Filaret).

In the long run, however, there is always likely to be a culture clash between the Autocephalous, who see themselves as a 'martyr Church' and have a strong nationalising agenda, and the Moscow patriarchate, which is just as tainted by the Soviet era as Filaret's Church and has a strong Ukrainophobic element. Former KGB clerics may feel close to the

Moscow patriarchate, but former diaspora clerics do not. Moreover, in Galicia and Volhynia at least, the Autocephalous now have a strong nationalist constituency and continue to represent the conciliar values of the 1920s better than Filaret's Kievan patriarchate. Tensions within the Church, including financial scandal, led to yet another split in 1996.

Since 2000, the Church has been led by a native Galician, Methodius (Kudriakov), who has encouraged a drift back towards the Kievan patriarchate. This development has been encouraged by president Kuchma, in his second term, who seems to have belatedly discovered the possible virtues of a single '*Pomesna*' (National) Church.

The Greek Catholics: Between Rus and Rome

The Greek Catholic Church also has considerable problems as it faces up to the new millennium. First, emerging from its long 'catacomb' period of 1946–89, it was disoriented to find that it had 'lost' much of what it regarded as its pre-1946 patrimony, thanks to 'poaching' by all the Orthodox factions, not just in traditionally Orthodox Volhynia, but in Galicia itself. After 50 years of persecution, it is understandably aggrieved. According to one Greek Catholic priest, 'even if the whole village is [now] Orthodox and one person is Greek Catholic, the church belongs to that Catholic because the church was built by his grandparents and great-grandparents'.[46] Greek Catholics tend to regard the Autocephalous Orthodox in particular as former Greek Catholics who are reluctant to take the risk of returning to a faith that they fear may have only temporarily returned, or as an artificial creation of the authorities in the late Soviet period.

The catacomb period has also revealed or exacerbated doctrinal differences. Greek Catholics from the diaspora, many of whom have returned since 1991 to play a key role in Church affairs, tend to emphasise the Rus origins of the Church and its roots both in original Byzantine and local Ukrainian culture. At a 1999 Synod it was even proposed to adopt the name 'Kievan Catholic Church'. Diaspora clerics were influential in securing the promises made at the Second Vatican Council to restore the traditional privileges of the eastern Churches (the decrees *Orientalium Ecclesiarum* and *Unitatis Redintergratio*) so that the Greek Catholics would again be subordinated to the Pope only in faith and morals, and would be administratively self-governing, as originally after the Union of Brest in 1596. The possibility of patriarchal status for the Church, first mentioned by the popes Gregory XVI (1831–46) and Pius IX (1846–78), has also been brought up again. It is only a superficial paradox that the westerners should be in favour of 'easternising' the Church, as this would help restore that which all the Ukrainian faithful shared before 1596 and make national ecumenicism easier. Ecumenical dialogue will be difficult, however, when the Church of 'Kiev and Halych' is also trying to expand territorially in the east, to 'regain' areas it lost in 1648 or 1839.

On the other hand, many local priests and faithful cherish the 'Latinised' traditions that have developed since 1720. When the Church was completely banned, from 1946 to 1989, what mattered most was maintaining the sense that they were not Orthodox, as Moscow proclaimed. Latinisms include devotional changes (the use of the rosary and the Stations of the Cross, the Sacred Heart of Jesus and the Immaculate Heart of Mary), dogma (the Filioque, the doctrines of papal infallibility and the Immaculate Conception) and even the physical appearance of churches (confessionals, organs, the absence of iconostases). Local Greek Catholics were understandably less subject to the influence of Vatican II and are often highly conservative, both in terms of faith and morals and in their view of the Orthodox Church as an enemy rather than a sister Church (the Vatican having tried to revive Catholic-Orthodox dialogue with John Paul II's *Slavorum Apostoli* epistle in 1985). Finally, the 'Latin party' is reluctant to get rid of traditions which have been seen as a bridge to Western culture and which explain why Galicia is more 'European' than the rest of Ukraine.

The dispute between, to put it crudely, Latinisers and Easternisers, is of course crucial to the possibility of ecumenical dialogue with the Ukrainian Orthodox. The Kievan patriarchate would obviously prefer partnership with the latter. According to Yevhen Sverstiuk, 'our ritual is basically the same, whether we are Orthodox or Greek Catholic. There is a Latin party in Lviv of course, but it has cut itself off from its national base and has, I hope, no perspective.'[47] Cardinal Liubachivskyi (born 1914), head of the Church, was perceived as being too attentive to Rome, but since 1996 practical power has been in the hands of his deputy, Liubomyr Huzar, who is more in favour of an ecumenical approach (Huzar formally succeeded in January 2001). However, the decision in 1991 to restore Church ritual to the forms established by the 1720 Zamość Synod, the high-water mark of Latin influence, means that fears of a drift to Rome will not be readily assuaged.

A further complication is added by relations with the separate branch of the Greek Catholic Church in Transcarpathia, which has its own agenda. The Transcarpathian Church owes its existence to the 1646 Union of Uzhhorod rather than the 1596 Union of Brest and, although Bishop Andrei Bachynskyi and others have periodically appeared to favour closer ties with Lviv, the Church in the 1990s and its head, Bishop Ivan Semedii of Mukachevo, have been seen, rightly or wrongly, as closely associated with the particularist Rusyn movement. Nor has the Lviv Church been able to restore links to its traditional eparchy in Peremyshl/Przemyśl, now over the border in Poland.

The Chimera of Church Unity

The 1993 Balamand Accord commits Catholic and Orthodox to refrain from proselytising amongst one another's flock. Attempts at conversion have nevertheless continued, as it is not always clear whose congregation is whose and all the Ukrainian Churches tend to promote myths of their 'captive' brethren under other denominations. The relative size of the main camps now seems fairly fixed, but the idea of combining forces is still on the agenda. In 1995 the Rukh deputy Liliia Hryhorovych established a parliamentary coordinating group working for Church unity entitled 'For One National Orthodox Church in Ukraine'.[48] Ecumenical dialogue really took off in 2000 with at least the Kievan patriarchate and the Autocephalous edging towards unity under the patronage of Bartholomeos I, the Ecumenical Patriarch of Constantinople.

Two historical models exist for establishing Church unity in Ukraine. One possible route would follow the teaching of Andrei Sheptytskyi (1865–1944), who did more than anyone to shape the modern Greek Catholic Church during his long tenure as metropolitan in Lviv from 1901 to 1944. Like Mohyla in the seventeenth century, Sheptytskyi sought unity between Ukraine's Churches in the context of broader Christian reconciliation and on the basis of the common Christian values of love, brotherhood and the sublimation of egoism. True religious unity could only be achieved by cultivating organic and canonical ties within a community of faith rather than relying on the ephemeral secular authority of the state – the latter, Sheptytskyi argued, being characteristic of the Russian messianic tradition. A true and lasting union would be built from below on the foundation of the individual's own conscience.[49] The German occupation of Ukraine in 1941–3 allowed Sheptytskyi to begin some ecumenical dialogue, but German hostility to any form of institutionalised Ukrainianism meant that the intriguing possibility was stillborn.

A second route might base itself on the teachings of one of the leading ideologues of Ukrainian autocephaly, the academic and churchman Ivan Ohiienko (1882–1972). Ohiienko served as minister first for education and then for religious affairs in the Ukrainian People's Republic in 1918–19, before emigrating via Poland to Canada in 1947, where he began a very different form of ministry as head of the local Ukrainian Orthodox Church, taking the name Metropolitan Ilarion. Ohiienko was instrumental in organising a unity conference amongst North America's three Ukrainian Orthodox Churches in 1960.

His approach to potential Church union differed not so much because of the fact that he based himself on the Orthodox tradition and Sheptytskyi on the Catholic, but in the fact that his starting premise was the common local roots of all Ukrainian religion. Ohiienko believed that 'a nation manifests itself first of all through its Church, in its ancient practice and in its ideology worked out through the ages'. The true Christian tradition was therefore the autocephalous, as each nation could best find God through its own language and tradition and 'the self-development of individual national-Church life'.[50] Ohiienko regarded this principle as 'the original apostolic' one, established at the Third Ecumenical Council (AD431) and elsewhere and exemplified by the original Church of 'Rus-Ukraine' (Ohiienko was an enthusiastic propagator of many of the nativist myths of the origins of Kievan Christianity mentioned in chapter two),[51] but 'Caesaropapist' Moscow had forgotten it, as had Rome, whom Ohiienko accused of campaigning from the fourth century onwards to create one 'international [Church], the same for all, even with one liturgical language', that is Latin. The restoration of original traditions would therefore only be possible through a thorough nativisation of the Church, 'through the use of the living Ukrainian language' and the cultivation of priests of 'Ukrainian nationality with a good knowledge of the Ukrainian language' dedicated to the evangelical principle that 'to serve one's people is to serve God'.[52]

Modern Ukraine seems to have ignored the advice of both Sheptytskyi and Ohiienko. Sheptytskyi's warnings against overreliance on the administrative methods of the secular state were obviously ignored in 1992–3, but so was Ohiienko's concern to build strong 'national-spiritual' foundations for any national Church. Sheptytskyi's organic approach would obviously be slow, Ohiienko's is more of a formula for unity amongst the already nationally conscious. Ukraine may therefore have to think of other approaches. One possibility is the Estonian or Moldovian model whereby Constantinople recognises two local Orthodox Churches – most probably an Autocephalous–Kievan patriarchate union in rivalry to the Moscow Church. After all, if Constantinople regained the territory it 'lost' in 1686, its relations with Moscow would be transformed.

Other Gods, Other Voices

Ukraine has many opponents of enforced religious unity, for whom 'the idea of a "state Church", of "one national Church" is medieval; it does not correspond to the demands of a modern democratic society, a law-based state, the priority of a free choice of world-view, the general principle of freedom of conscience.'[53] According to the historian Petro Tolochko, all of the proposed 'national' Churches are 'not national, but ethnographic-regional'; Christianity is better 'understood as an international and cosmopolitan phenomenon' and not in 'the unjustified assertion of national characteristics'.[54] Others have pointed out that even Orthodoxy is, in demographic terms, a 'minority' religion in Ukraine – 'the slogan of "To the Ukrainian State a National Church!"

is unscientific, all the more so because half of the population of Ukraine does not profess any religion, and the allegiance of the rest is far too differentiated.'[55]

Those who drafted the Ukrainian constitution, in part motivated by secular principles, in part by the desire to avoid taking sides in intra-Church disputes, have legally recognised this fact. As well as recognising that 'everyone has the right to freedom of personal philosophy or religion', Article 35 declares that 'the Church and religious organisations in Ukraine are separated from the state, and the school – from the Church. No religion shall be recognised by the state as mandatory.' It would therefore now be unconstitutional to set up an established Church, although that is unlikely to stop people from trying. At an 'All-Ukrainian International Christian Assembly' held in Kiev in February 1998 (in effect only for the Kievan patriarchate) Filaret once again bemoaned the fact that

up till now the process of state-building in Ukraine has lacked the necessary spiritual foundation, that is one United Ukrainian Orthodox Church . . . the development of Ukrainian society needs to have two mutually supportive elements: an independent state and an independent Church . . . is it really necessary to separate the Church from the state and the school from the Church so unconditionally, or should the law give some kind of priority to the traditional Church?[56]

However, as yet Ukraine has no equivalent of Russia's 1997 law on religion, which gives a privileged place to 'traditional' faiths. Ecumenism is therefore likely to be a slow societal process, with little political initiative coming from above, at least for the near future. This is not necessarily a bad thing at all. It is probably the best way of preserving a fragile social peace that would be severely tested if one Church were given privileged support.

Ukraine also has many 'minority' religions. The most numerous in parish terms were the more than 4,000 Protestant communities registered in Ukraine by 1998. Ukraine, unlike Russia, had a strong local Protestant tradition in the sixteenth century, and in the nineteenth-century temperance campaigners and prosperous Protestant German colonists (Mennonites, Lutherans) had some impact in alcohol-sodden rural Ukraine. Ukraine's 'traditional' Protestants are mainly Baptists, the Evangelical Union and Seventh-Day Adventists.[57] Many of the new communities, however, have been funded by American evangelists and, as in Russia, their giant football-stadium rallies have been much criticised by Orthodox traditionalists.

Ukraine's traditional Jewish community was devastated by the Holocaust. Some two-and-three-quarter million Jews lived in Habsburg and Romanov Ukraine at the turn of the nineteenth century, but only

486,000 remained in 1989, and up to half of these have since left for Israel. Kiev's central synagogue was until recently a children's puppet theatre. Nevertheless, there are some signs of life. Traffic between Kiev and Tel Aviv is not just one way and business links are strong. Podillia, the birthplace of the spiritual founder of Hassidism, Israel Ba'al Shem Tov, is now home to an annual festival attracting thousands of Jews from all over the world.

Ukraine also has its fair share of sects. Ukrainian neo-paganism and RUNVira were mentioned in chapter two. Lev Sylenko's disciples are well funded and have had considerable influence in fringe nationalist circles to whom the idea of Ukraine as originally a united community of pagan worship before the subsequent division of the faiths has obvious appeal. Similar organisations include the writer and former dissident Oles Berdnyk's 'Spiritual Republic' order established in 1989 (Berdnyk was briefly a candidate for the presidency in 1991).[58] There are also many supporters of the Russian New Age thinker Nicholas Roerich's Hindu-influenced 'Living Ethic' in Ukraine. Most notorious, however, was the apocalyptic 'White Brotherhood' cult which gathered in Kiev for the predicted end of the world and the promised self-immolation or crucifixion of its leaders on 24 November 1993. Analysing the eccentric ideology of the White Brotherhood is probably a waste of time. It paid lip service to several Ukrainian thinkers (Skovoroda, Franko) and shared some of Lev Sylenko's antiquarian mysticism (Umberto Eco reminds us in *Foucault's Pendulum* that 'the pharaoh Ahmose [I] established the Great White Fraternity, guardians of the antediluvian wisdom the Egyptians still retained'),[59] but this was only one element in a cultish mishmash of millenarian populism and onerous membership obligations. The Brotherhood's leader, 'Prophetess' Maria Devi Khristos, made the mistake of calling on her followers to destroy St Sofiia's, one of the Orthodox churches of the 'Emmanuel servants of Satan', allowing the authorities to arrest her on a simple criminal charge.

Conclusions

Religious divisions both reflect and reinforce other divisions in Ukrainian society. This is precisely why those who would like to see a more united Ukraine have attempted to build some form of overarching religious unity. There are, however, formidable obstacles to the creation of a 'national religion' in Ukraine. There are two, even three different 'national' Churches, all of which offer subtly different variations of the 'national idea'. The Greek Catholic version is synthetic, Western by recent tradition but Kievan in origin. The Kievan Orthodox version is ecumenical and Western-orientated, but is still marked by its local and 'Eastern' origins. Amongst the Moscow patriarchate outright Ukrainophobes coexist with those who still believe that Eastern

Orthodoxy is the common creation of Russians and Ukrainians. Welding such diversity together will be a difficult task. Nevertheless, the extent to which religious differences remain salient is likely to provide a good guide as to whether Ukrainian society is destined to ossify along current lines of division or is capable of more fluid development. The Pope's historic visit in June 2001 prompted some reconciliation, but also led to protests by the Moscow Patriarchate. Filaret's support, however, helped bring him back from the cold. The Moscow Patriarchate was heavily involved in the 2004 election, backing Yanukovych. Yushchenko, on the other hand, made Church unity a priority, without much practical success.

12

The IMF's Red Pencil: Ukraine's Economic Black Hole

> The dry cleaners left a shine on my trousers, and, er . . . my right lapel is slightly bent, and the laundry did *not* use enough starch in my shirt front. I mean, where *are* we – *the Ukraine*?! How can I get married if I look like a hobo?
>
> Kevin Kline, camp and flustered, playing Howard Brackett trying to get ready for a wedding he will eventually back out of, in the film *In and Out* (1998)

When the Ukrainian dissidents of the 1960s argued that their country would be better off economically outside the USSR, there was at least a partial case to be made. The economist Mykhailo Volobuiev (born 1900)[1] had first developed the argument that Ukraine was an exploited 'internal colony' of Russia/the USSR in the 1920s, ironically at a time when it was just about to benefit from strong inward investment during the first Five Year plan – the era of *Ivan* and the Dnieper dam. By the 1960s, however, the tide had definitely turned. Soviet planners switched their attention to Siberia and, as Volobuiev had predicted, without control over its own resources Ukraine could do precious little about its subsequent complaints – a substantial net withdrawal of national income, an aged and deteriorating capital base and many hidden losses through the underpricing of key Ukrainian products, food and ferrous metals in particular.[2] Independence, or in the language of the time economic sovereignty, it was argued, would allow better husbandry of Ukraine's considerable natural resources: fertile soil, a relatively well-educated workforce, substantial mineral reserves and a strategic trading position.

These arguments helped support for independence to reach the totally unexpected heights of 90.3% in the referendum of December 1991 – economic nationalism having reached those parts of Ukraine that Rukh's cultural nationalism decidedly could not. However, this early optimism soon dissipated as hare-brained schemes and economic mismanagement brought Ukraine to the brink of economic catastrophe. Inflation soared to a staggering 5,371% in 1993 (on a different basis of calculation 10,200%) – only war-torn Serbia's (rump Yugoslavia) was higher. For a brief period public phones were free as coinage became redundant and stamps were marked with the letters of the alphabet to represent various classes of delivery as the post office grew tired of constantly reprinting new prices. The cartoon opposite shows Ukraine's leaders of 1992 (Kravchuk is on the far left), in the style of the monument by the river Dnieper to the founders of Kiev (Kyi, Lybid and their brothers). Kravchuk is saying 'Now I understand why Vitold Pavlovych [Fokin, the prime minister] wanted to order the hryvnia [new currency] in Italy!' 'Why is that, Leonid Makarovych?' asks Ivan Pliushch, chairman of parliament. 'Because only there, Ivan Stepanovych, are they good at printing money with so many zeros!!!' replies Fokin.

From 1994 to 1996 a necessary stabilisation was achieved, culminating in the belated but successful introduction of a new national currency, the very same hryvnia, in September 1996 (the notes that finally arrived did indeed have '1992' printed on them, introduction having been repeatedly delayed). By then, however, official GDP was less than half that of 1991 (by 1998 it was only 41% – see the table on page 256 for figures). Every year since 1996 has been predicted to be the 'year of recovery', but official figures have continued to disappoint. Only in the first half of 2000 was real growth finally recorded. 'Recession' or 'depression' are hardly adequate words to describe this collapse. Nor could the loss of more than half of official GDP be explained as a cyclical phenomenon of supply adjusting to meet demand. The Soviet Ukrainian economy was so autarchic and *sui generis* that much of it simply collapsed when it was exposed to outsider competition and/or required to find markets of its own (post-Soviet, but commodity-based economies such as Uzbekistan have survived better). Whole sectors of production in areas most subject to quality competition (light industry, consumer goods like TVs or fridges) have basically disappeared. Investment has not so much declined as stopped.

Ukraine's trade performance has been patchy at best. Persistent deficits, mainly with the rest of the former USSR rather than the wider world, have drained Kiev's foreign reserves (never more than $2 or $3 billion, down to a low point of $482 million in February 1999) and led to the accumulation of $11.5 billion in foreign debt by the end of 1998 – only 38% of GDP, but a rapid rise from zero in 1991. Fiscal deficits have also been persistently large – usually at least twice the 3% of GDP limit of the Maastricht countries. After simply printing money to bridge the gap in 1992–4, a proper debt market began to function in 1995–8 (at its peak in 1997 Ukraine attracted a portfolio inflow of $1.6 billion), but quasi-default ('restructuring') in late 1998 all but closed this source of finance, and with persistent gaps in IMF funding there were real doubts that Ukraine could continue to pay its way.[3]

Economic reform began late (in October 1994), started well[4] and then stalled. Necessary structural reforms were avoided and the economy

Ill. 15. The Ukrainian way of inflation.

drifted into ever-higher levels of corruption and 'black' activity. Nevertheless, there were some improvements on the ground. At least in the big cities, the kind of service culture Kevin Kline's character in *In and Out* suspected did not exist was actually emerging. There were some signs of energy and prosperity. Every city seemed to be ringed by building sites for new dachas, often the gaudy homes of the nouveaux riches. Kiev began to experience the joys of the traffic jam. At the same time, whole sectors of the economy relapsed into barter (an estimated 40% of all activity – in 1998 it was still possible to meet people in the countryside who had not even *seen* the new currency) and real poverty was widespread. Official unemployment figures topped one million only in 1998, but these failed to account for the millions more in short-time or only nominal employment. The same official figures recorded a drop of 5,354,000 in total industrial employment since 1991.[5] Wage arrears of several months (6.3% of GDP in 1998) were the norm by the late 1990s.[6] The population actually declined from a peak of 52.2 million in 1992 to 49.3 million in 2000 – an astonishing phenomenon for a developed country (less than half the decline was due to net emigration). Theoretical official GDP per capita was a miserable $750 in 1998, down

Key Ukrainian Economic Indicators, 1991–2000

	1991	1992	1993	1994	1995
GDP (% change)*	−8.7	−9.9	−14.2	−22.9	−12.2
Investment (% change)	−7.1	−36.9	−10.4	−22.5	−35.1
Consumer prices (annual increase)	91.2	1210	5371	891	376.8
Budget deficit (% of GDP)		−12.5	−6.3	−9.5	−7.4
Current account balance ($ million)		−621	−854	−1163	−1152
Gross external debt ($ million)		3513	4214	7167	8217
Structural reform index**	0.1	0.23	0.13	0.33	0.53

	1996	1997	1998	1999	2000*
GDP (% change)*	−10	−3	−1.7	−0.4	+6.0
Investment (% change)	−22	−8.8	−6.1	2.9	11
Consumer prices (annual increase)	80.2	15.9	10.6	22.7	28.2
Budget deficit (% of GDP)	−4.4	−6.6	−1.9	−1.3	2.1
Current account balance ($ million)	−1185	−1335	−1296	1658	1481
Gross external debt ($ million)	8840	9555	11483	12437	11336
Structural reform index**	0.56	0.57	0.58		

Source*: Helen Boss, *Ukraine: Growth Continues Despite Political Morass* (Vienna: VIIW, June 2001); *The Ukrainian Economy at the Turn of the Century* (London: Royal Institute of International Affairs, 2000).
Source**: Alex Siedenberg and Lutz Hoffman (eds), *Ukraine at the Crossroads: Economic Reforms in International Perspective* (Heidelberg: Physica-Verlag, 1999), p. 16.

from $5,499 in 1990. If this were the whole story (it isn't, given the huge size of the 'unrecorded' economy), Ukraine's standard of living would be on a par with countries like Angola and Bolivia. The 1998 UN Human Development Report placed Ukraine 102nd out of 174 world states on a broad measure of standard of living (near Mongolia and down from eightieth in 1996). The Ukrainian authorities refuted many of its calculations, but were too embarrassed about the size of unofficial GDP to object to its non-inclusion.

Biznesmeni were regularly murdering one another, and members of the US Congress claimed in 1998 that Ukraine was one of the most corrupt countries in the world in which (to try) to do business. Powerful economic interest groups operated beyond the control of the state, or themselves controlled the state, and were robbing the country blind – left largely untouched by the 'Grand Bargain' negotiated during independence and Leonid Kravchuk's 'stability of cadres' policy. Nobody seemed to pay any taxes and huge holes were appearing in the system of social defence.

Groping towards an Economic Policy

In August 1998 prime minister Pustovoitenko tried to provide the smack of firm government by threatening an assembly of businessmen in Kiev's

Ukraïna Palace that nobody was leaving until they had paid their taxes, adding that 'the doors are locked, the toilets have been cleaned and are in good order'. Recalcitrants were sent to boot camp and had their cars impounded. It made good TV, but only served to remind observers that normal methods were not working. How did Ukraine get into such a state? Some have at least partially excused Ukraine's truly awful economic record under first president Kravchuk by arguing that his policies in fact laid the basis for subsequent improvement and that even simply conducting a national economic policy was impossible until the necessary state infrastructure (a central bank, a consolidated national budget, tax collection mechanisms and so on) had been established.[7] It has also been argued that Ukraine should not be unfairly compared with other 'post-Soviet' but economically more advanced states such as Poland and Hungary, or even with Russia, as the latter is energy-rich and inherited so many resources from the USSR.[8] Special-pleaders have also pointed to problems supposedly unique to Ukraine, in particular the legacy of over-industrialisation, a huge and precipitously redundant military sector, an unnatural and ahistorical trading structure, Ukraine's geographical and historical distance from the market systems of Europe and continued Chernobyl clean-up costs. Nationalists have blamed Russia for its unilateral price reforms in 1992, for burdening Ukraine with colossal energy bills from 1993–4 and for provoking a damaging trade war with the imposition of a 20% VAT on Ukrainian exports in 1996.

Blaming Russia is tempting, as trading relationships remain so lop-sided and most of the monopoly power resides with Russia.[9] Russia has not exploited the new situation as it might have, however. Elites on both sides of the border have an interest in keeping trade semi-commercialised (see pages 265–6). Nor is the defence of Kravchuk sustainable. Many of his policies, far from being neutral or transitional, incontrovertibly made things substantially worse. The attempt to underpin production by printing money hand over fist only served further to depress output by sending inflation expectations through the roof and promoting a flight from the currency. Second, economic policies were not necessarily consciously directed towards 'state-building'. Huge state hand-outs to maintain the loyalty of regional elites were not only grossly inflationary (the money printed by Kravchuk to settle the June 1993 miners' strike added a staggering 82% to nominal GDP),[10] they also created the capital base for Ukraine's emerging new parasitic rentier class. Only rarely did loans or subsidies actually help enterprises' cash-flow, more often they were taken as *ex gratia* windfalls to be stashed abroad. Third, the economic costs of leaving the USSR, however unfair the system may have been to Ukraine, were grossly underestimated. Levko Lukianenko, of all people, had warned before independence that 1991 was 'not 1917'. That is, Ukraine was no longer a self-sufficient rural economy relatively immune to trade disruption, and dismantling the highly integrated Soviet industrial economy would have to be a slow and careful process.[11] Above all, it was to say the least unrealistic to expect that Ukraine might escape scot-free from the systemic crisis that had gripped the Soviet economic order in the late 1980s.

The case for Kravchuk's defence also ignores key counterfactuals. First, Ukraine's economic weakness in 1991–4 would have left it extremely vulnerable to Russian pressure if a different kind of regime had been in power in the Kremlin. The kind of leverage Russia applied at the Massandra summit in September 1993 – when Russia demanded control of Ukraine's nuclear warheads and the Black Sea fleet, deliberately linking the question of Ukraine's debt with demands for political concessions – might have become the normal currency of relations between the two states. Second, in 1992–3 the Communist Party was still banned in Ukraine, and establishment elites – the potential rentiers – were still disoriented. A window of opportunity arguably existed to enact and implement radical reform (three privatisation laws were actually passed in early 1992 but left on the shelf).

Kuchma deserves credit for launching Ukraine's first real reform programme in October 1994, but also criticism for failing to press home its early successes. The reform package finally moved Ukraine into the grim world of fiscal and monetary discipline, or to be more precise of actually writing and sticking to an annual budget. The wilder excesses of inflation were then tamed. Most prices were freed, the foreign trade regime somewhat loosened (at least initially) and first steps were made towards microeconomic liberalisation. However, as pointed out in chapter nine, Kuchma was watering down the programme as early as mid-1995, when he was under no electoral pressure to do so. He was admittedly saddled with the left-leaning parliament elected before him in spring 1994, but governmental inaction, exemplified by the damp squib of Lazarenko's October 1996 reform 'relaunch', was as much to blame. Kuchma was able to take the initiative when it really mattered, as in the summer of 1998, when he issued a blitz of decrees in response to the new parliament's prolonged failure to elect a leadership and begin work, but by then the obvious question was, why not earlier?

The other key questions were: Did Ukrainian policy-makers know what they were doing? Were their policies misguided? Did self-interest simply take precedence? The answer is unfortunately yes to all three. Early economic 'policy-making' was simply incompetent. According to Yegor Gaidar, 'there wasn't a single crazy idea that the Russian opposition didn't toy with, and that the Ukrainians didn't attempt'. This was not Ukraine's fault. Talent drained away to Moscow (the Russian economist and politician Georgii Yavlinskii was born in Lviv); there was no Ukrainian equivalent of the think-tanks that produced the likes of Shatalin and Gaidar. Instead, as of 1998, Ukraine was left with the ill-qualified Stanislav Hurenko of all people as the chair of the key parliamentary committee on economic policy, property and investment. Nor was Kuchma, the great 'advocate' of market reforms, necessarily any better. Most of his reforms lacked systemic logic or were directed towards improving the position of his supporters. One of his 1998 decrees called for the use of 'administrative measures to reduce barter transactions by 5% each quarter' and for such barter to be replaced by trade at 'market prices defined by the Cabinet of Ministers' – an interesting melange of concepts. In November of that year Kuchma called for tighter state control over the national bank only a month after he had promised the IMF that he would sponsor a law on its independence. In the same speech he directed the government to increase its borrowing from the national bank to make up the economy's cash shortfall, at the same time as ordering the bank to maintain monetary growth at the previous year's level. He also called for an end to all tax loopholes and privileges and for a three-year tax moratorium for all agricultural producers – bar payments to the state-pension fund.[12] Playing to different audiences, successful mental compartmentalisation or simple ignorance? The reader is free to judge.

Under both Kravchuk and Kuchma, politicians continued to lace their speeches with references to a mythical Ukrainian 'third way' – not in the sense of an in-depth consideration of alternative models of political economy, but in simple denial of basic economic laws. A typical example was Kuchma's benchmark September 1995 speech on the economy, which warned against 'blindly copying foreign experience' and called instead for a policy 'based on the historical traditions, genetic roots, national identity and culture' of Ukraine. This 'Ukrainian way' seemed to boil down to an active 'industrial policy', maintaining a generous level of 'social protection', a distinct reluctance ever to let go definitively of traditional levers of control and the argument that Ukrainians would not bear the social costs of the kinds of shock-therapy programme introduced in Poland and elsewhere (though, as it often pointed out, they got the shock without the therapy).[13] Kuchma's 'Ukraine-2010' plan, the centrepiece of his 1999 reelection programme, was once again based on this idea of a Ukrainian 'third way' – a mixture of market, state regulation, national protection and the 'equality of all forms of ownership', with much wishful thinking about 'technology investment' as a motor for growth.[14]

Blat *and the State*

Ukraine is not genetically different. Nor is it immune to the basic laws of economics. Printing money causes inflation, price controls create shortages. On the other hand, the Ukrainian economy is 'different' in the sense that it does not yet operate like the neo-liberal model beloved of Harvard blackboards. Its constituent units and connecting relationships are different from those found in Western textbooks. Ukrainian firms are not market-shaping profit-maximisers; they are mini-communities, designed by the Soviet regime to distribute welfare and control workforces as much as actually to produce tanks and TVs. Households are not the rational independent consumers of *homo economicus* theory. How could they be, when incomes are rarely received and access to goods is still as much decided by favour and proximity to distribution systems as by purchasing power? Above all, the state is not a neutral nightwatchman or even a benign social arbiter, but is itself deeply involved in *blat*, the traditional Soviet favour system.[15] The interaction of money, business and politics is much more intimate than in the West. Free prices, IMF loans and open markets do not therefore necessarily affect the Ukrainian economy in a Western textbook fashion.

A second sense in which Ukraine might be considered a special case is that its new and relatively weak state apparatus has proven to be an easy prey for powerful vested interests. Without even the warped logic of the Soviet system of Communist Party oversight, powerful corporate empires have developed which are actually doing quite well out of Ukraine's semi-reformed economy and therefore make up a formidable lobby opposing further reform. Privatisation and economic liberalisation have proceeded extremely slowly in Ukraine and always in distorted forms – asset-stripping, sole tenders, rigged auctions that go to the applicant with the 'best business plan' but not necessarily the highest offer – despite the promises made in the 1994 programme (and in the 1992 legislation). Political insiders have been able to devolve control over Ukraine's highly corporatised and *étatist* economy to themselves and do not take kindly to outsiders muscling in on their territory. Massive short-term profits are easily secured by capturing and abusing the licensing, contract and control functions of a weak state, especially through export quotas, presidential 'import licences', arbitrage (securing goods artificially cheaply and selling them on), and 'tolling' (the practice of diverting a firm's output, at sub-market prices, to shell companies controlled by the bosses of the original enterprise). To many Ukrainians, this was what *biznes* actually meant – securing a tax holiday or a permit to export what somebody else had already produced. The politically connected are also guaranteed a flow of state subsidies, formal and informal, that prevent their enterprises having to harden their budgets. Formal subsidies are cash hand-outs and preferential credits; informal subsidies include acceptance of tax arrears and barter payments, along with the inevitable side payments, and maintaining energy supplies that are not interrupted by non-payment. All told, these subsidies still accounted for a massive 20% of GDP as of 1997.[16] The burden on the rest of the economy hardly needs elaborating. Such practices also explain why the well connected can make large personal profits at the same time as their firms post big losses.

Ukrainian elites have also sought to perpetuate what might otherwise have been only a series of one-off gains by creating a bubble of domestic and international credit. This meant Ukraine borrowing money at sky-high interest rates for very short terms, constantly rolled over – 95% of Ukrainian loans were for less than 12 months. Domestic interest rates' lowest level in 1998 was 29%, their highest 82%. This provided a tidy business for the new Ukrainian banks, but completely ruled out any kind of venture investment. Foreign loans became feasible after Kuchma's initial reforms helped construct a proper market in government debt, but for a high-risk country like Ukraine premiums were punitive – 16% for the 2001 Deutschmark Eurobond, 17.5% for the 1999 ING Barings bond.[17] Ukraine was soon paying the interest on the interest and flirting dangerously with trapping itself in the kind of pyramid schemes of limited duration familiar throughout the former Communist world.

For outsiders, doing business in Ukraine is a nightmare, as the same elites have retained infinitely irksome powers of regulation. The state either operates on your behalf or it has to be bought off. Even the smallest business must operate through a thicket of tax inspections, licensing procedures and 'safety' regulations. As of 1996, senior managers reportedly spent a massive 40% of their working time with state officials, trying to negotiate a way through the Byzantine bureaucracy.[18] The Ukrainian state was therefore simultaneously too weak and too powerful. Too weak to resist the penetration of special interests, too powerful in other people's lives – financially, bureaucratically and structurally. There were few other sources of support – certainly not the under-developed banking system, one of the smallest even in the post-Communist world. Private property is not yet widespread.

Few goods can be obtained directly, instead everyone is an intermediary or relies on a *vuiko* ('uncle' or padrone). Barter and the off-book economy flourish. One chilling statistic indicated the distorted nature of the official economy – not only was a huge amount of money kept outside the banking system, but the percentage actually went up from 25% in 1995 to 49% in 1998.[19] Another source suggested that the amount of (Ukrainian) money in the economy was only 16% of GDP.[20] Many measures of the 'non-official' economy ('black' economy would be too narrow a definition) estimate that it is possibly as large as official GDP. Optimists might take comfort from this, as real economic decline has therefore not been as catastrophic as official figures suggest. In truth, however, the huge size of the unofficial economy is an indication that the implicit social contract that underpins any modern state is in danger of breaking down. Taxes are counterproductively high, that much is obvious. Perfectly normal economic activities are forced off-book by over-regulation. More dangerously, neither the poor, who cannot afford to, nor the rich, who avoid it, pay tax. Ukraine's nascent middle class is overburdened instead. Moreover, payment cannot be given to the state in trust for social goods, when it is the state that is misallocating monies in the first place. Ukraine is in danger of falling into a black hole where the official tax base is not just too narrow, and not just declining, but where the state's very efforts to raise revenue are what is causing it to shrink in the first place.

Ukraine's self-proclaimed 'social market' state is therefore increasingly limited as to the services it can actually provide, especially since it tries to do too much and ends up doing too little. Government spending, at 42% of official GDP as of 1997, is still at one of the highest levels in the former Communist bloc,[21] but is badly targeted. The first call on expenditure remains the maintenance of the government's own sprawling bureaucracy. Then it must attempt to meet the sweeping promises of 'social protection' made in the 1996 constitution, which guarantees the individual's right to work, to rest, 'to an adequate standard of living for him/herself and family that includes adequate nutrition, clothing and housing', to free state education at all levels and access to 'the existing network of such [health] institutions [which] shall not be reduced'. The last pledge, if taken literally, would imply that no hospital or clinic could ever be closed – a promise that would shame Tony Blair's New Labour. None of these promises can in fact be met in full, and after trying to meet them in part there is too little money left over for state-funded investment or basic salary payments. Finally, of course, a state so stretched in resources has even more discretionary power in how they are allocated.

Then there is the fashionable term of moral hazard. Under Kravchuk, Ukraine had to rely on its own meagre resources, but the October 1994 reform programme unlocked a flow of Western credits. Since Ukraine took the IMF shilling, it has been locked into a rolling programme of conditional funding. IMF negotiators have imposed much tougher budgetary and monetary restraints than Ukraine would ever have established on its own. At times, Ukraine's recidivist economy ministers have been on monthly targets for key indicators such as inflation, interest rates, money emission and tax collection. In fact, the IMF has often seemed like the only real party of reform in Ukraine, albeit one imposing its own neo-liberal agenda without much regard for Ukrainian circumstance. There has been little to suggest that the Ukrainian authorities see IMF-mandated measures as valuable in themselves. Ukraine has always done the minimum to get by.

Increasingly, however, international lenders were trapped in a dilemma. Ukraine assumed it was too valuable to be allowed to fail (see pages 279–310). The West knew this, but continued to hand out money. The West also knew that its credits were helping to keep the existing elite in power. To a lesser extent (the Kuchma regime not being that sophisticated), Ukraine also knew that the West knew, and the West knew that Ukraine knew that they knew. The result was an elaborate game of Grandmother's Footsteps, with a predictable cycle of Ukrainian backsliding leading to IMF frustration, new negotiations and new promises, tougher conditions and an eventual return to reneging on those conditions. All the time this continued the IMF was bankrolling the corporate 'virtual economy'. Much money did get through on the ground, creating real investment (as also with World Bank and EBRD projects) that might assist eventual recovery in the real economy, but not enough. Nor did IMF assistance help to unlock significant amounts of foreign direct investment. As of the end of 1998, Ukraine had received an accumulated $2.6 billion in foreign investment since 1991, a tiny amount relative to the size of the country (it worked out at $51 per capita, compared to $1,672 in Hungary and $908 in the Czech Republic).[22]

A final and particularly frightening problem is that many Ukrainian elites do not see themselves as custodians of the national patrimony. Here, Ukrainian nationalists may for once have a point. Patriotism does act as a restraint on some forms of plunder. It is difficult to imagine Polish or Hungarian elites stripping state assets as ruthlessly as Ukraine's 'rootless cosmopolitans' have done. The sheer venality of Ukrainian elites defies belief. Corruption stories would regularly refer to tens, even hundreds of millions of dollars, not just the odd 50 in a brown envelope. In one notorious case in 1998 Vasyl Volha, general director of the International Union of Ukrainian Entrepreneurs, was visited by state 'enforcers'. When he questioned their patriotism, they replied, 'Nobody's going to save Ukraine, not now. If we do not take what we want today, someone else will tomorrow.'[23] The fact that this sort of thing has happened before in Ukraine – when Polonised magnates corralled hundreds of thousands of peasants into their latifundia in the sixteenth and seventeenth centuries, or when the new Cossack elite imposed serfdom on their less fortunate brethren in the late eighteenth century – is small consolation.

Creating a National Economy: Crony Capitalism in Ukraine

The Ukrainian economy is, of course, still evolving. In Soviet times, there was no 'Ukrainian' economy as such, Ukraine being a fully integrated part of the all-Union economy. A constant theme since 1991 has therefore been the need to create a truly 'national' economy. Much Ukrainian thinking on the subject is, in fact, distinctly old-fashioned. Many sincerely believe in the sort of autarchic 'national economy' that the new central European states strove to create in the 1920s and 1930s, an idea that has been given unwarranted after-life by the post-Marxist belief that Ukraine cannot be politically independent if it is not first economically independent. In the words of Ivan Drach, 'The economic subsoil of national interests is the creation of a Ukrainian internal market. We recall how this occurred to Volobuiev in the 1920s. On this level lies the solution to the objective and artificial contradictions [*superechnostei*] between the regions of Ukraine, which were [once] parts of different empires.'[24] Ukrainian nationalists have also expressed the hope that breaking economic ties with the USSR and with its Russian successor-state would in turn help people to sever cultural and emotional ties, undermining the economic basis of Ukraine's 'post-colonial' psychology.

Initial Ukrainian thinking on this subject was apparent in spring 1992, when two rival plans were drawn up for the post-independence period. The first, prepared by Kravchuk's fig-leaf liberal, Volodymyr Lanovyi, was presented to the IMF; the second, prepared by Kravchuk's old crony, one-time Gosplan stalwart Oleksandr Yemelianov, was discussed by a closed session of parliament.[25] The former talked the talk of open market economics, the latter called for an immediate departure from the rouble zone and the creation of a protectionist 'national market'. Given that Ukraine was so closely integrated into the former Soviet economy as to render talk of a 'Ukrainian economy' meaningless, the complete adoption of Yemelianov's programme would have been disastrous, but it nevertheless set the tone of much subsequent policy.

In essence, this amounted to the creation of a 'national capitalist' corporate economy – the establishment and protection of domestic monopolies, the attempt to create 'closed production cycles' from the Soviet debris and to confine incomes and expenditure within national channels. Unfortunately, it is precisely this strategy of 'the concentration of national capital' that has empowered Ukraine's venal elites.[26] As in Russia, political, business and media interests have begun slowly to coalesce. 'New capital has consolidated itself and entered into politics',[27] although most of Ukraine's new business groups do not actually produce anything. The majority are little more than private circles for the appropriation of public goods. This is also true of Russia, as is the predominance of energy interests in the new economy. Both countries are massive over-consumers of oil and gas. Ukraine does not, however, produce much energy of its own: it is a massive nett importer, so distribution rather than producer interests are to the fore. Ukraine does not have any equivalent of sprawling producer and/or raw material giants like Gazprom or Rosneft, and the new Ukrainian conglomerates do not enjoy the same concentration of power as Boris Berezovskii or Vladimir Gusinskii's notorious empires in Russia.[28]

Ukraine also made a late start on 'reform', so capital concentration is some three years behind Russia. A further difference is the insecurity of property rights and the faltering pace of privatisation in Ukraine. According to Vasyl Yurchyshyn of the Kiev International Centre for Policy Studies (as of 1998), 'there cannot be a Ukrainian Berezovskii', in the sense of a preeminent private-sector potentate, because even the most powerful economic interests are still semi-dependent on the state and on its still-wide range of administrative powers.[29] In Ukraine, power creates money, not the other way around. According to another Ukrainian analyst, 'in this sense, the Ukrainian type of oligarch is much closer to Indonesian than Russian or Latin American oligarchs.'[30] This was well illustrated in the 1998 elections, when the main government party, the National Democrats, originally won only 29 seats but soon expanded (temporarily) to a massive 93, as most 'independent' businessmen felt compelled to join in order to maintain good relations with the state. Since 1998 membership of one of the main successor 'centre' factions has been more or less compulsory.

Who are the new Ukrainian corporate capitalists? It is of course hard to tell, but some tentative connections can be established. As of 1999 the Ukrainian equivalent of Russia's 1996 'group of seven' was a 'group of five' – Oleksandr Volkov, Hryhorii Surkis, Ihor Bakai, Viktor Pinchuk and Vadym Rabinovych.[31] Particular individuals might come and go, of course, particularly in Ukraine's crony economy, with its insecure property rights and rampart short-termism, but a study of Ukraine's 'big five' at least reveals how Ukrainian business (and politics) was conducted at the time. A case in point would be Ukraine's most notorious original monopoly, United Energy Systems (UES) of Dnipropetrovsk. Ukrainian companies do not really give out annual reports and press packs, but the company's turnover is estimated to have been a mere $1.5 million before its main sponsor, Pavlo Lazarenko, became prime minister in 1996. In 1996–7 its turnover may have been as high $3 billion, insofar as the Russian giant Gazprom was estimated to owe Ukraine this amount in gas transit charges, but provided gas instead. UES, having been granted a privileged position as Ukraine's main wholesale buyer by Lazarenko, channelled its resale, but reportedly paid only $11,000 in taxes whilst Lazarenko accumulated $72 million in Swiss bank accounts. The company began to lose contacts, contracts and influence once Lazarenko went out of office in 1997 and his former bosses started to pursue him for alleged corruption. Lazarenko was arrested entering Switzerland with a Panamanian passport in November 1998 and, after losing a vote to suspend his parliamentary immunity, fled to the USA seeking political asylum in February 1999. Former Lazarenko ally Yuliia Tymoshenko had, however, made her peace with Kuchma in late 1998 and the company survived, albeit on a much-reduced scale.

Lazarenko's rise and fall showed that membership of the new Ukrainian elite was not granted on a permanent basis, access to political power being all-important. In June 1999 Rabinovych (an Israeli citizen) seemed likely to suffer a similar fate when the security services excluded him from the country for five years – probably for becoming too powerful in his own right and forgetting the rules about the division of the pie (and possibly for not contributing enough to Kuchma's reelection campaign).[32] His ouster also signalled, as did Rabinovych's ally Surkis's bruising defeat in the 1999 Kiev mayoral election, that the Ukrainian elite was not afraid to exploit the residual power of anti-Semitism in Ukraine (although it seems unlikely that Surkis will be similarly excluded from the corridors of power). Revolving doors were therefore more characteristic of Ukraine than the 'Russia–1996 model' of a united group of oligarchs combining to defeat the leftist threat to the presidency.

The important point, however, is that despite the fall of Lazarenko and (possibly) Rabinovych similar scams have continued. Energy consumers have limited funds and there has been no diversification in sources of state supply – a recipe for enriching middlemen. Nearly all the oil imported into Ukraine goes to private distribution monopolies – refineries have to buy from them. Gas is still distributed by regional monopolies. The Interhaz company, controlled by Ihor and Oleh Bakai and which stepped into UES's shoes, also won its position through state favour. Another Interhaz boss, Oleksii Kucherenko, was also head of Bari, Ukraine's biggest electricity trader and a leading light in the National Democratic Party until he and six other energy bosses left in November 1998, after a row with the party's (genuine) liberals, to found a new faction in parliament called 'Regional Revival' (a comic malapropism as the energy moguls were bleeding the regions dry). Funnily enough, Bari won a $500 million monopoly contract to supply state-owned factories with electricity in 1998. Ihor Bakai, former head of Bari and since 1997 first deputy head of the State Committee for Oil, Gas and Refining, heads yet another successor company to UES, Naftohaz Ukraïny (Oil and Gas of Ukraine), which controlled an estimated two-thirds of the gas market in 1998.[33] (Naftohaz was not afraid to play an overtly political role that would seem strange in the West: a special company congress endorsed Kuchma for reelection in 1999; Bakai sent Patriarch Filaret seventieth-birthday greetings in the same year.) Interhaz and Naftohaz have links with Kuchma dating from his days as head of the giant missile factory Pivdenmash, as does Spetzexport, Ukraine's arms export monopoly, which is largely under the control of the National Security Council.

Bakai has links with long-term Kuchma adviser, media magnate and head of the Regional Revival group Oleksandr Volkov, who runs Hravis TV (a major backer of Kuchma in the 1994 election) and, like Hryhorii Surkis, head of Dynamo Kiev, and Rabinovych, head of the Ukrainian Jewish Congress, made much of his early fortune from Ukrainian-Israeli trade. Volkov, who ran Kuchma's reelection campaign in 1999, is undoubtedly exceedingly rich. Frequent allegations of corruption against him have referred to a string of offshore companies in the Channel Islands, Bahamas and South-East Asia, an impressive 32 bank accounts in Belgium, a fleet of luxury cars almost as numerous, including a $262,000 Rolls-Royce Silver Seraph and a $349,000 Bentley Azure, which were impounded by local police in 1999, properties dotted all over Europe and a 100-seater TU-134 registered in the Caribbean.[34]

Another linked 'oil clan' is the Slavutych conglomerate controlled by Hryhorii Surkis, a holding company comprising Ukrainian Credit Bank, Dynamo-Atlantic, BIM International Law Firm and the 'Alternative' TV company, which also has links to other energy firms such as ITERA-

Ukraïna and Energy-plus and bankrolls the highly successful Dynamo Kiev football team. Slavutych delivers 10–15% of all commercial oil to Ukraine, especially to the Black Sea terminals of Odesa, Nikopol, Kherson, Kremenchuk and Lysychanskyi (rumour had it that the petrol shortage in Kiev in June 1999 was Surkis's revenge for his failure in the mayoral election). Surkis has admitted investing between $60 million and $70 million in Dynamo Kiev, but the real figure is no doubt much higher. Until 1999, when the team began to break up after narrowly failing to reach the final of the European Champion's League, he was able to turn down lucrative offers for star players like the forward Andrii Shevchenko (who eventually went to AC Milan for $25million). Much money still comes from the state, from circles close to Kuchma, some from circles close to another former prime minister, Yevhen Marchuk. The idea that Shevchenko's sale was delayed till an election year is of course far too cynical to be entertained.

Ferrous metals producers (tube steel, concrete reinforcement) are another powerful interest group in Ukraine (chemical exports are also high, but the industry has close links to gas interests). Ukraine has an estimated 5% of the world's mineral reserves, including its biggest supply of titanium. The giant arch erected in Kiev for the three hundredth anniversary of the Treaty of Pereiaslav in 1954 and Brezhnev's Mother of the Motherland are both made out of it – which is one way of using it up. Ukraine also has the world's third-biggest deposits of iron ore (over 200 billion tons plus), and 30% of the world's reserves of manganese ore. Crudely put, just as energy is energy, metal is metal, and Ukrainian producers have not had to face the problems of quality competition from former COMECON and East Asian states that have devastated domestic light manufacturing industry – in fact they have been accused of dumping abroad. Managers who can sell their metal for hard currency *and* avoid paying their workforces are amongst the richest of Ukraine's new rich.

Metals production has in fact been recovering since 1995, even growing by 12% in 1997, when Ukraine produced 25.2 million tons of steel (the eighth-highest world total). Metals are now the largest single sector of the economy, accounting for an estimated 20% of GDP and 28% of exports (42% by 2000).[35] Once again, however, production is dominated by the four members of the state cartel – Krivorihstal, Mariupol Illich (still touchingly named after Lenin), Azovstal and Zaporizhstal – which dominate the company towns in the south-centre of Ukraine after which they are named. All were still 51%-plus state-controlled until the sale of Zaporizhzhia's ferrous alloy plant for a pittance in 1998, with a key slice going to Slavutych in one of Ukraine's most notorious 'privatisations'. Also powerful is the industrial group Interpipe based in Dnipropetrovsk, whose former president Viktor Pinchuk was the main regional beneficiary of Lazarenko's fall and the inheritor of his local media empire (see below).

The agricultural sector is also dominated by a handful of semi-privatised monopsonists, especially Khlib Ukraïny (Bread of Ukraine), which has used the power of its state connections, including control of Ukraine's main grain elevators, to buy food cheaply and sell it on at market prices. The distributors' monopoly has therefore made it extremely difficult for Ukraine's brave but tiny private farming sector to get off the ground. The agricultural lobby has hedged its bets by maintaining links with both the state sector and the left-wing parties. Both Oleksandr Moroz, chairman of parliament from 1994 to 1998, and his successor, Oleksandr Tkachenko, were champions of the agricultural sector and long-standing opponents of agricultural reform, especially a free market in land. Tkachenko was also widely thought to be beholden to the authorities after they cancelled the debts of his agricultural firm Zemlia i liudy ('Land and People') and turned a blind eye to accusations that he had embezzled $70 million in funds earmarked for agricultural development, including money from the US Eximbank. Tkachenko also had links with Volkov (agriculture needs fuel) and the Slavutych group through Bohdan Hubskyi, United Social Democratic deputy and guiding light of the Ukrainian Agricultural Stock Exchange. Ukraine has two rural political parties – the older and more left wing Village Party, founded by Tkachenko in 1992, and the Agrarian Party, created by circles closer to Kuchma in 1996, of which Khlib Ukraïny boss Hryhorii Omelianenko was a leading member – but there is little to distinguish between them in policy terms.

It was testimony to the lobbying power of the agricultural sector that not only were collective farm chairmen repeatedly able to frustrate proposals for land privatisation, they were even able to prize more subsidies from the state at a time when the agricultural sector, once the mainstay of the Ukrainian economy but more or less a disaster zone since 1932–3, has been declining almost continuously, with output down a cumulative −39% between 1991 and 1998.[36] A further indicator of underperformance, and also of the prevalence of family subsistence agriculture, is that the 32% of the population who live on the land produce only 15% of (official) GDP, and the OECD estimates that 85% of food is produced on private plots. Nevertheless, the idea of a 'Ukrainian CAP' (Common Agricultural Policy) was taken seriously in some government circles, despite the massive potential burden of such an unproductive sector on the economy, and the theoretical liquidation of the collective farm system announced in Kuchma's December 1999 decree.

Finally, there is the handful of foreign players in the Ukrainian economy. Surprisingly perhaps, the direct influence of Russian capital in Ukraine is not as powerful as might be expected.[37] The same factors that have discouraged Western investment (limited privatisation, insecure property rights) have, at least initially, also discouraged new Russian capital. Magnates such as Berezovskii and Potanin are more likely to invest their money in the West or, after Russia's August 1998 crisis, to be preoccupied with defending their interests at home. Nevertheless, Berezovskii and Kuchma appear to be close – Kuchma nominated Berezovskii for his brief tenure as executive director of the CIS in 1998–9. Berezovskii also had dealings with Rabinovych, an initial investor in the TV channel 1+1 and an associate of both Surkis and Kuchma; and there were persistent rumours that Berezovskii was indirectly involved in marshalling TV support for Kuchma's reelection campaign in 1999.[38] Berezovskii's ORT was also an initial investor with Surkis in the Inter TV channel, Lukoil in STB. Gazprom has links to ITERA,[39] Ukrainian aluminium producers have links with Vladimir Potanin, the Trans World Group and the Chornyi brothers, Russian émigrés resident in Israel.[40] Informal channels also exist, of course. Much Russian capital has entered Ukraine via Cypriot banks. Many 'Ukrainian' banks were established with Russian capital. For almost a decade Kiev has sought to block big set-piece investments on 'strategic' grounds. However, Siberia Aluminium now controls 75% of Mykolaïv's MAP Aluminium plant through a front company cunningly disguised as 'Ukrainian Aluminium'. The Tiumen Oil Company (TNK) controls the Lysychanskyi oil refinery in the Donbas through 'TNK-Ukraine'.

The various clans have also been dividing up the Ukrainian media between them. Not surprisingly, Kuchma's supporters have a strong position in state TV and in the regional press (regional papers still tend to outsell national papers in Ukraine), but most of the major players also control their own papers. In the capital, Surkis's media interests include the newspapers *Law and Business*, *Alternative* and *Kiev News*; Bakai has *Today*; while Rabinovych controls (or controlled) *Capital News*, *Business Week*, the UNIAR news agency and the radio station Supernova – though none of the above made much impact on Surkis's election campaign for Kiev mayor in 1999. Pinchuk, Volkov and Bakai, with Alfa Kapital, have all been shareholders in the top-selling *Facts*; Yevhen Marchuk was associated with Ukraine's leading quality daily, *The Day*; the Socialist Party leader Oleksandr Moroz has close ties with the main rural paper, *Village News*, which is the closest thing to a national paper in Ukraine. Pavlo Lazarenko was able to use UES money to build a media empire after he left office in 1997, which at its peak included the newspapers *Truth of Ukraine*, *All-Ukraine News*, *Kiev News* and *Politics* (all Russian language) and the TV channel UTAR, although this impressive stable was dismantled almost as quickly in 1998 after the administration took fright at Hromada's success in the parliamentary elections.

In comparison to Russia, Ukrainian TV has been less subject to corporatisation. The state retains much more control over the main national companies, UT-1 and UT-2 and the semi-independent 1+1, which have over two-thirds of the national audience between them. Paradoxically, a truly national Ukrainian TV market was created under Kuchma rather than Kravchuk. Before 1994, UT-1's worthy coverage of folk-dancing and presidential visits to collective farms brought it an audience share of 7%, with many more viewers still watching Russian state TV (ORT). Russian TV's backing for Kuchma was a key factor in the 1994 presidential election. Since then the situation has been transformed by foreign investment in UT-1, the banning of direct foreign broadcasts in 1995, the launch of UT-2 to displace ORT in 1996 and the debut of the brasher 1+1 in 1997. Volkov, as well as controlling Hravis TV, has a strong influence on UT-1 and 1+1, underwrote *Era*, the main current affairs programme on UT-1, and has some interest with Bakai in ICTV and the New Channel. Surkis has most influence over Inter, the *de facto* UT-3, and after Lazarenko's fall Pinchuk inherited control over the powerful regional channel, '11' in Dnipropetrovsk. Ownership was coordinated behind the scenes by Volodymyr Horbulin, secretary of the National Security Council until 1999. His deputy Zinovii Kulyk kept an eye on programmes' political content.

The Kuchma administration was motivated mainly by a desire to control the 'national information market', however, and the state stranglehold on TV current affairs reporting has become notably tighter. State TV took on an unashamedly anti-Lazarenko stance in the 1998 elections, entertaining viewers with nightly showings of his snowbound and apparently empty country dacha (probably counterproductively, as it helped Lazarenko acquire an unwarranted 'outsider' image); left-wing firebrand Nataliia Vitrenko was on TV all the time when Kuchma was seeking to split the left-wing vote in 1998, less often once she rose uncomfortably high in the polls in late 1999. Oleksandr Moroz largely disappeared from the screens once he had lost his position as chairman of parliament. STB was harassed in 1999 – presumably because of its supposed links with Marchuk.

The final link in the chain of Ukrainian corporate power is the political parties that are backed by new business money (see also pages 186–7). As in Russia, business elites have sought seats in parliament partly to exercise influence and lobby for their interests, but also actually to conduct those interests in the corridors of power and enjoy the blanket immunity from criminal prosecution granted by the constitution. Once again, particular parties may come and go. Parties operating as fronts for business interests are inherently ephemeral, and Ukraine's would-be oligarchs are never likely to put all their eggs in one basket. Indeed, their ability to jump ship is remarkable – Surkis ally Viktor Medvedchuk served as an adviser to both Kravchuk and Kuchma as president – as did Kulyk; it was rumoured that a Tkachenko presidency would not, as it were, upset the key energy interests. Nevertheless, particular examples can help give some of the flavour of Ukrainian politics.

Most Ukrainian oligarchs were too lazy to start a party from scratch. It was far easier to join an existing one and then start chucking out its original members once they started complaining about changes in the party programme. In 1997 Lazarenko joined the tiny party Hromada ('Community') and spent a small fortune turning it into a national force.

Hromada had many celebrities such as the historian Petro Tolochko on its list for the 1998 elections, but this was not the reason why the party won 35% of the vote in United Energy Systems' home turf in Dnipropetrovsk and came sixth overall nationwide with 4.7% of the vote. UES money helped fuel the party's rise after the elections. At its high point (autumn 1998) Hromada controlled almost 10% of the seats in parliament, but as with UES itself the bubble soon burst. After Lazarenko's flight in early 1999 Tymoshenko formally split the party. As Hromada had also provided a temporary home for semi-independent businessmen like Kiev's Mykhailo Brodskyi, the original publisher of *Kiev News*, its demise was a double victory for the existing authorities

In a similar fashion Slavutych and Surkis parachuted themselves in 1997 into the Social Democratic Party (United), where they were joined by Anatolii Volkovskyi, head of ITERA, and by former premier Marchuk and former president Kravchuk, whose links with Dynamo Kiev date back to before 1990 and his days as Communist Party culture secretary ('culture' having a fairly broad definition in Communist days). On the eve of the 1998 elections the whole Dynamo team touchingly declared their loyalty to Surkis by joining the party. A 4-1 home defeat by Juventus two weeks before the vote prevented the Social Democrats free-riding too blatantly on the team's popularity, but the party still sneaked into parliament (4.01% overall) with a handy supply of votes from rural Transcarpathia. After the split in the National Democratic Party in late 1998, the Social Democrats were often Kuchma's most reliable supporters in parliament.

Apart, of course, from the new Regional Revival faction, whose membership was a veritable Who's Who of Ukrainian energy interests. Volkov, who also had links to the Agrarian Party, the Democratic Party and the Party of Regional Revival, was its head. Ihor Bakai was a member, as were former Donetsk mayor Volodymyr Rybak and the leader of the Agrarian Party, Kateryna Vashchuk. Another notable bad penny was former premier Yukhym Zviahilskyi, who, like Lazarenko, fled abroad after corruption charges were levelled against him in 1994 – his particular schemes having involved the resale of state-subsidised coal and a spectacular foreign currency scam that forced all enterprises to surrender half their hard currency earnings to his bank at one-quarter of the market rate – though he was forgiven and allowed to return in 1997. No doubt coincidentally, Viktor Razvadovskyi, former deputy head of the state tax militia, was also a member. Pinchuk and Andrii Derkach, son of the head of the Ukrainian security service, helped establish Labour Ukraine, a party not particularly noted for its left-wing idealism.

Then there was the Green Party, backed by bankers (Ukrinbank) and, once again, oil and gas traders (major polluters all), in particular the Shelton company, with Rabinovych reportedly a key background source of finance. Overall, an estimated 120 of Ukraine's 450 new parliamentary deputies in 1998 were backed by oil and gas interests. Even Rukh succumbed to the 'Trojan horse' effect, allowing businessmen onto its party list, in their case Oleksandr Slobodian, head of the Kiev brewery Obolon, although association with Ukraine's new national beer probably did not do Rukh too much electoral harm. The right-wing Republican Christian Party took money from Interhaz (Oleh Bakai, Ihor's brother, was on the party list), but then its ideological aim is quite specifically the creation of a new 'Ukrainian bourgeoisie'.

On the other hand, Ukraine's new oligarchs have not always spent their money wisely. A prime example was the so-called 'bankers' party' in the 1998 elections, the Party of National-Economic Development of Ukraine, stuffed with bigwigs from Prominvestbank (the country's largest), directors of the Malyshev tank factory in Kharkiv, the Kryvyi Rih steelworks, the Kherson shipyard and Poltava ore-enrichment plant – and Ihor Bakai. The party's big mistake was not to pretend they were someone else; unlike the Greens and the Social Democrats they stood under their own name and were humiliated at the polls with a mere 0.95%. A second example was the attempt by leading industrialists (Volkov, former prime minister Zviahilskyi) to free-ride into parliament on the back of the Democratic Party of Ukraine, whose anodyne name had long commanded high support in the polls. The party's old intelligentsia leaders were badly organised and made the disastrous decision to team up with discredited politicians in Crimea and subsume their popular name under a coalition label, NEP ('People's Power, Economy, Order', bizarrely evocative of the less than wonderful Soviet 1920s). NEP won only 1.3% of the vote and Volkov had to sneak into parliament via a repeat election in August 1998. Nor could money and the prestige of Dynamo Kiev buy Surkis victory in the 1999 Kiev mayoral election. Despite saturation coverage by his own media empire, he lost heavily to the incumbent Oleksandr Omelchenko (by 77% to 16%), after a campaign marked by hostility to Surkis's wealth and, rather more unfortunately, his Jewish background.

Hubris, Nemesis?

The bacchanalian behaviour of the new elite has been graphically documented (Roman-style orgies with chocolate-covered prostitutes popping out of cakes, country dachas the size of Southfork but not as tasteful – one just outside Kiev is in the shape of a medieval castle), their frenzied partying perhaps an indication that they know their days might be numbered.[41] Popular jokes about the vulgarity and conspicuous consumption of the 'New Ukrainians' abound, many simply recycled from mid-1990s Russia or 1980s Britain, poking fun at their gold bathtubs, $10,000 ties and the Rolex watches which they do not know how to work. Many oligarchs spent $1 million or more in the 1998 elections – Surkis spent an estimated $5 million on the 1999 race to be Kiev mayor and still lost.[42] Lazarenko's exile in the USA was not too uncomfortable once he had been granted the right to stay in his San Francisco mansion, formerly owned by Eddie Murphy, with its five swimming pools set in a dozen acres.

A serious restart to the economic reform process might help to spread economic power a bit more widely in Ukraine, but there is a very real danger that the country is already stuck in limbo. There has been sufficient change to create powerful new vested interests, but these are powerful enough to block further reform. A new government may initiate some high-profile prosecutions – as Primakov at least attempted to do in Russia. Bakai resigned in March 2000, citing 'international pressure'. A more likely threat to the oligarchs' power, however, is that elites may fall out amongst themselves. It is a simple but depressing truth that the theft of state assets in Ukraine is a competitive business, given the huge profits still to be made in insider privatisation deals and the continued abuse of state economic power. The general political temperature around the 1999 election was therefore much higher than in 1994, as outsider elites tried to win a share of the spoils and the existing clans tried to hang on to power. After all, in 1994 the main issue was only Ukrainian independence.

In fact, if the existing elite is not displaced from power there are worrying signs that inter-clan conflicts over the spoils of power might even jeopardise state security. Already several simple turf wars have threatened to get out of hand: for instance, the conflict between the Dnipropetrovsk and Donetsk clans in 1994–7 led to the contract killing of Donetsk 'boss' Yevhen Shcherban as he got off his plane at Donetsk airport; the bombing of a football stadium, Shaktiar Donetsk (the dead – team manager Oleksandr ('Alik the Greek') Brahin and five bodyguards – had allegedly creamed off £500,000 from the sale of winger Andrii Kanchelskis to English club Manchester United);[43] and an unsuccessful bomb attack on prime minister Lazarenko's car as he drove to Kiev airport to fly to Donetsk. Rumours that the prime minister may have staged the attempt on his own life, as François Mitterrand was alleged to have done in 1959, resurfaced as Lazarenko fell out of favour in 1998–9. Similar conflicts occurred in 1998 when state-backed Dnipropetrovsk elites tried to interfere in local disputes in Odesa and Crimea.

Odesa, the 'Ukrainian Chicago', has always had a tradition of organised crime. In 1918–20 it was basically run by gangsters, headed by the notorious Yaponchyk ('Wee Jap'). His predecessor was the equally ruthless Benia Krik, made famous by Isaac Babel's stories.[44] Their would-be modern equivalent, Karabas (real name Viktor Kulivar), was assassinated in 1997 – a year in which Odesa counted 312 murders.[45] Odesa also has a fine tradition of exporting gangsters, such as Semion

Mogilevich, currently resident in Budapest, who heads many countries' most-wanted lists after a decade of alleged money-laundering and arms-trading. Recent conflict back home has centred on the control of the lucrative trading networks that pass through the entrepôt port, producing a particularly bitter political struggle between the 'regional' clan, headed by the governor of the oblast council, Ruslan Bodelan, and more involved in international investment and agricultural purchase scams, and the 'city' clan, based around city mayor Eduard Hurvits. The latter is one of the largest groups with an international reach in the former USSR – the clan had an estimated 8,000 members in 1991, including muscle from the Olimp Athletic Association, long involved in local markets and the building trade.[46] The conflict came to a head when the two groups clashed over oil and shipping interests and stood against one another in the 1998 election for city mayor. Kiev eventually backed Bodelan – although his victory only came (again) after a nasty anti-Semitic campaign against his rival and the shooting of several other leading figures including the editor of *Odesa Evening News* and the head of the city election commission (there was also an abortive sniper attack on Hurvits).

In Crimea, on the other hand, rival gangs (the exotically named Basmachi and Seleim) have been allowed to conduct a particularly vicious war for the control of the hotels and sanatoria that make up the remnants of Crimea's once-proud tourist industry – the price that Kiev has been prepared to pay for devolving power to the peninsula in order to head off Russian nationalist separatism. When Kiev attempted to disrupt the local balance of power in the coastal resort of Yalta in February 1998, the relatively loyal Crimean deputy premier Alexander Safontsev was promptly murdered in a bomb attack. Kidnaps and contract killings have been frequent in Crimea. When one local deputy, Mykola Kotliarevskyi, was arrested in December 1998, the epic charge list included conspiracy to murder, assault and extortion with menaces.

One possible ground for optimism is that the very venality of the existing elite and their reluctance to open ranks could become factors encouraging the middling layers beneath them to coalesce in a genuine party of reform. Kuchma was able to put this off until after the 1999 election, so that his own reformist credentials would not be put to the test. The next privatisation round – that of oblast energy companies in particular (Surkis won key interests in five out of seven in the first round) – would be an indication of whether the old rules still applied.

Energy Geopolitics: A New Silk Road?

The key threat to the power of Ukraine's oligarchs, however, is the vexed question of energy supply. It is very much against their interests to see the existing distribution network broken up or supplanted, as it has made them so rich. Nevertheless, energy imports are the one area where the authorities are most serious about attempting to create a truly 'national economy'. Since 1991 Ukraine and Russia have waged a so-called 'energy war', with Ukrainian nationalists objecting vehemently to Ukraine's dependence on Russian sources of supply and an annual bill that peaked at $7–8 billion in the mid-1990s (only temporarily becoming affordable as oil prices collapsed towards $10 a barrel later in the decade – by 1999 the price was heading back to $25).[47] Russia has objected just as vehemently to Ukraine's lamentable payment record and habit of siphoning off supplies that cross its territory on their way to Western Europe.

It should immediately be noted that 'war' is not necessarily an appropriate term for the Mexican standoff that has developed since independence. There is nothing intrinsically anti-Ukrainian about Russia raising energy prices towards world levels, and the leftist parties in Ukraine have always pointed out that Russia has never really charged as much as it could and has been more forgiving of debt and late payment than more strictly commercial sources might have been. The left has therefore condemned alternative schemes as expensive white elephants. Moreover, continuing softness of budgets has allowed both Ukrainian and Russian elites to make money out of a seemingly one-way process. For obvious reasons, not much is known about these exchanges, but occasional clues have surfaced. Former Russian privatisation chief Alfred Kokh was sharing a car with Lazarenko when he was arrested in Switzerland in 1998; Berezovskii joked about applying for asylum in Ukraine when a warrant was temporarily issued for his arrest in 1999.

Ukraine's energy debt to Russia continued to spiral throughout the 1990s, reaching an estimated $4 billion in 1998 (energy imports account for 56% of all foreign debt), and the issue has begun to trouble Kiev's foreign policy establishment just as much as the nationalists, who have always fetishised the problem. However, it was a Ukrainian nationalist writing over 50 years ago who best described Ukraine's predicament – the relatively obscure geographer Yurii Lypa (1900–44) in two long-forgotten books: *The Division of Russia* (1941) and *Black Sea Doctrine* (1947).[48] Most of Lypa's arguments concerned Ukraine's geopolitical rivalry with Russia (see pages 294–5 and 308–9), but the strong economic element in his work was surprisingly prescient. In brief, he argues that Ukraine and Russia belong to two naturally different economic spaces, particularly in terms of energy and raw-material supply. Moscow's logical sources of supply are in the Urals and western Siberia, Kiev's are in Transcaucasia (see the map on page 276), although this truth was obscured when first Romanov Russia and then the Soviet Union artificially combined the two spaces (*The Division of Russia* appeared just as Hitler was about to launch his bid to seize Transcaucasian oil from Russia). To secure this supply Ukraine's natural

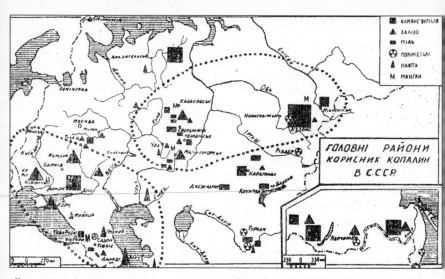

Ill. 16. Yurii Lypa's map (1941) purporting to show that Ukraine's natural source of energy supply lies in the Caucasus, Russia's in Siberia.

destiny therefore lay in an alliance with the Transcaucasian nations. Lypa's work could have been quietly forgotten and, to be honest, remains unknown to most Ukrainians (although a reprint of *The Division of Russia* appeared in Lviv in 1995), but this is more or less how Ukraine is currently thinking of extricating itself from its energy dependence on Russia.

After a false start in January 1997, when Ukraine created an (Energy) Diversification Agency only to disband it later that year, possibly as a result of Russian pressure,[49] Kiev finally seemed to endorse a Lypa-ite scheme, after years of indecision, in the summer of 1998 (significantly, the National Security Council was a prime mover behind the project).[50] The reason was the much-heralded prospect of large-scale Azerbaijani exports, possibly also supplemented by Kazakhstani supply. The USA preferred to see the oil come out through a new pipeline that would run via the eastern heel of Anatolia to the Turkish Mediterranean port of Çeyhan. Its priority was to rule out any route through Russia or Iran and, after the 1991 Gulf War, presumably to avoid committing itself to any putative defence of substantial overseas oil interests in a country like Ukraine rather than an existing NATO member like Turkey. Ukraine wanted the oil for itself, both to supply domestic needs and to earn lucrative transit fees. It therefore hoped that the consortium developing the Azerbaijani field (the Azerbaijani International Operating Company, led by BP-Amoco) would prefer to supply the more local destination rather than face Turkish hostility to greater tanker traffic through the Bosphorus, the extra transport costs of the Çeyhan pipeline or the final option of using the Romanian facilities at Constanţa.

The slump in world oil prices in 1998 seemed to work in Ukraine's favour by reducing international interest in the lengthy Baku–Ceyhan route, whose cost was estimated at between $3 and $4 billion. Ukraine has proposed instead that the developers concentrate on the route to Supsa on the Georgian coast and possibly then to Samsun in northern Turkey. From there the oil could go to Odesa, any other local market, or, eventually if necessary, down to Çeyhan – a shorter route than Baku–Çeyhan which would also have the advantage of bypassing areas of potential Kurdish unrest. Ankara has hinted that it sees the two routes as complementary. Ukraine has been gearing up accordingly. It has begun expanding the Pivdennyi ('Southern') oil terminal near Odesa to a handling capacity of 40 million tons (up from the projected 12 million), as well as modernising four oil refineries to create a combined processing potential of 20 million tons of crude. Ukraine also plans to construct a pipeline from Pivdennyi to Brody in western Ukraine with an extra 400km of pipe (in addition to some 250km already laid), boosting annual throughput capacity from 14 to 30 million tons. The total cost is estimated at $800 million.

A sweetheart landswap deal with Moldova in summer 1998 aimed to spread the benefits of the scheme by allowing Ukraine's neighbour to complete its own facilities by the Danube at Giurgiulesti. Eventual profitability, however, is likely to depend on Ukraine securing a role as a transit country to northern and central Europe. Poland might be brought into the plans by adding links from Brody to Adamova Zastawa and Gdańsk, as might Lithuania (Butinge) and even Hungary after the construction of a Transcarpathian pipeline. If the Ukrainian line linked up with the two branches of the old Soviet Druzhba pipeline, Ukraine could supply Germany and beyond, but Russia's influence over Druzhba makes this decidedly unlikely (Gazprom's $36 billion investment in the Yamal pipeline from Russia through Belarus to Poland is also a long-term threat to Ukraine, but its construction and expansion have been beset by difficulties). The other missing element is sea transport across the Black Sea to Odesa, which is potentially very vulnerable to Russian naval power in the region, although one little-noticed aspect of the Ukraine-EU summit in October 1998 was a promise of 15 million Ecu to help develop container transport from Poti to Odesa (the EU also recognised Ukraine as 'a main transit zone linking the Caucasus and Central Asia to Western Europe').

If any variant of the scheme does come off – and powerful vested interests in Ukraine as well as Russia are still strongly opposed to it – politics and economics in the region will be transformed. 'Geopolitical pluralism' in the post-Soviet space may become a reality – the term 'post-Soviet' may even begin to fade – and Ukraine would become a significant regional player, at the hub of a powerful non-Russian coalition of interests. Lypa may have the last laugh after all. If not, and if Yamal and an Uzbek trans-Caspian link to Turkey combine to undermine Ukraine's current transit status, its geopolitical influence will be severely reduced.

Conclusions

Ukraine was not hit as badly as Russia by the financial crisis in the summer of 1998 (the crisis was, after all, triggered by the falling oil price), but it was hit badly enough. A falling hryvnia and rising inflation threatened to undermine even the relative macroeconomic stability achieved in 1994–6, and the government's weak fiscal position meant that maintaining even the existing levels of 'social defence' would be increasingly difficult – particularly after the predictable splurge of expenditure in the run-up to the 1999 election. Rampant corruption, a semi-reformed economy and a weak rule of law burdened Ukrainians with a state that was both too weak and too strong – only a superficial paradox given the lack of countervailing powers elsewhere in Ukrainian society. Only in 2000–1 did a new dawn finally seem possible. New prime minister Yushchenko claimed credit for '(re)monitizing' the economy, clamping down on barter and opaque trading practice to produce an impressive hat-trick of a balanced budget, reduced foreign debt, and, politically most important, the elimination of all pension and wage arrears. The consequent boost to consumption produced an outturn for GDP growth in 2000 of +6%, against an original forecast of −0.5%. Another +7% was predicted for 2001. Others pointed to the delayed impact of the 1998 devaluation and the strong growth in the Russian market – still Ukraine's main export market – arguing that the sharp improvement in Ukraine's trade balance, from −$1.3 billion in 1998 to +$1.5 billion in 2000, was the real reason for GDP recovery (see the table on page 256). If Yushchenko was right, and his policies were continued, recovery might be sustained. If not, further stimuli would be necessary.

In the long term, Ukraine's one plus-point is that it is not lopsidedly dependent on raw-material and energy export, like Russia. Its big minus is that it has few sectors of obvious comparative advantage. Its major opportunity is to play a key role in the geo-economic restructuring of the Black Sea region and perhaps distance itself from Russia; its major constraint remains in the fact that the Ukrainian and Russian economies are still highly interdependent.

13

Imagining Ukraine: Towards a Theory of Ukrainian Geopolitics

What, then, should the rest of the world make of an independent Ukraine? In the first five years or so of independence, Ukrainian elites did not really want to over-define their country's place in the world. Politicians were distinctly reluctant to name names of potential friends and enemies – not even Russia. Nevertheless, the bland formula they inserted into the 1990 Declaration of Sovereignty, promising that Ukraine would be 'a permanently neutral state, taking no part in [any] military blocks',[1] served certain purposes, as did its successor slogan announcing a 'multi-vectored' foreign policy. It helped convince Western states that an independent Ukraine would not undermine Europe's delicate security architecture; it deflected unwelcome attempts to draw Ukraine into too close a relationship with Russia/the CIS; and, at home, it calmed fears amongst ardent Westernisers and Russophiles of too sharp a lurch in either direction. In the long run, however, Ukraine has to work out a real sense of geopolitics embedded in a practical calculation of national interests, given the 'geopolitical pluralism' increasingly characteristic of the post-Soviet space. In 1998 president Kuchma confirmed that need when he set up a research project entitled 'Ukraine 2010' to examine the nation's geostrategic needs for the new millennium.

This chapter aims to provide a background to that task by showing the different ways in which different groups have imagined Ukraine and its place in the world, and how rival visions of Ukraine have embodied different ideological and historical precepts.[2] Ukraine occupies a crucial space at the interface of two of the great geopolitical ideas of the twentieth century – 'Europe' and 'Eurasia' – and will have a crucial influence on how both of these ideas are being reconstructed at the beginning of the new millennium.

Ukrainian Visions

This chapter, then, does not provide a litany of diplomatic visits – it is about the geographical components of the 'national idea'. Although Ukrainian writers and politicians have long used geographical ideas, a specifically Ukrainian geopolitics only really began to develop in the first quarter of the twentieth century, its greatest exponent being Stepan Rudnytskyi (1877–1937).[3] The first challenge for the new discipline was the simple question of actually defining Ukraine. Superficially at least, the absence of state boundaries, a limited supply of natural borders and Ukraine's very size rendered it an amorphous and somewhat opaque entity. Indeed, Rudnytskyi rebuked his predecessors for 'failing to clarify for themselves even the size of Ukraine and its people'.[4] He himself proposed both a 'minimum' (where ethnic Ukrainians, that is members of his ascribed language group, made up an ethnographic majority) and a 'maximum' definition of Ukraine (where ethnic Ukrainians were the largest single group). As a further refinement, Rudnytskyi and his school believed in what has been termed the 'potato principle' – the idea that what counted in determining a given territory's ethnic status was the 'real' countryside, not the 'ephemeral' city. The peasantry were always the true 'indigenous' inhabitants. Thus, in Rudnytskyi's maximum definition, a given territory was defined as Ukrainian if a plurality of its rural inhabitants were deemed to be such. A similar argument was made by the ethnographer and linguist Stanislav Dnistrianskyi (1870–1935).[5]

This idea of 'ethnographic Ukraine' did not match any previous political boundaries, but Rudnytskyi also believed that the settlement patterns of the Ukrainian ethnolinguistic group were determined by, and coincided with, environmental criteria – the considerable natural difference between the Ukrainian and the Russian geographies helping to create and reinforce the difference between the two national groups. According to Rudnytskyi:

> The Ukrainian land forms a distinct geographical unit, independent of and separate from the neighbouring lands of Moldova, Hungary, Poland, Belarus and Muscovy. It rests upon the Black Sea, Carpathians and Caucasus in the south, and upon the marshes and forests of Polissia in the north. While Ukraine does not have good natural borders in the west, south-east and east, as the northern littoral country of the Black Sea it has important features of integrity . . . There is therefore no doubt that *the Ukrainian people has its own particular land, which forms a distinct and integral geographical unity.*[6]

Both Rudnytskyi and Yurii Lypa argued that Ukraine and Russia were defined by their different river networks. This was very much the fashion of the time, when drainage systems and the like were regarded as setting 'natural' frontiers.[7] Technological change in the twentieth century does not necessarily invalidate the argument that the two peoples developed in relative isolation in a period when river transport did indeed exert a key influence on the formation of cultures. According to Lypa:

If the geopolitical land-axis of Muscovy is the Upper Volga, then the land-axis of Ukraine is the north-eastern shore of the Black Sea. Whereas the majority of rivers in Muscovy flow to the north, in Ukraine they flow to the south, with the single exception of the Kuban. The most natural axis of expansion for Ukraine is the southern, just as the most natural for Muscovy is the northern axis. Muscovy is the North and Ukraine the South . . . Muscovy's [natural] trajectory is towards the Urals and Siberia, Ukraine's is towards the Don, the Lower Volga and the northern Caucasus.[8]

This attempt to fix the Ukrainian imagined community within a concrete geographical space has been hotly disputed, not least by Russian nationalists. The great advantage of Rudnytskyi and Lypa's schema, however, was its utility in refuting Russian attempts to deny or belittle Ukraine. Whereas Russian nationalists have tended to see Ukraine as part of Russia's vast, open 'continental space' on a line running east–west without natural geographical boundaries (apart from the Central Russian Uplands), Lypa's hydrographic conception imagines Ukraine in a north–south continuum. Southern Ukraine, to most Russians 'New Russia' – the lands conquered by Catherine the Great from the Ottomans in the eighteenth century, is thereby defined as a natural part of Ukraine: the littoral to Ukraine's river hinterland. Eastern Ukraine is also included, as the river set includes the Dniester, Dnieper, Donets and even the Don, all running on roughly the same north-south axis into the Black Sea. According to Rudnytskyi, 'outside of the [borderline] Don region, the Ukraine has no hydrographic connections with the Moscow country, which has always had different directions, different channels of traffic, and different centers of waterways.'[9] Once this mental rotation of Ukraine has been accomplished, it becomes more natural to focus on the Ukrainian river system as the defensive hinterland of Central Europe, rather than defining it in terms of the boundless steppe that marks the beginning of Eurasia. In modern strategic terms, Ukraine can be seen as the gateway to the Caucasus, a strategic point of entry to the northern European plain and a key staging point for Central Asia and the Near East.

It is instructive to compare the Ukrainian with the Belarusian national school of geography, preeminently associated with Arkadz Smolich (1891–1938), which has been much less successful in underpinning national identity with the idea of obvious geographical borders creating a natural Belarusian space. According to Smolich, Belarus was defined by its control of the watersheds of three great rivers, the Dnieper, Dvina and Neman, but not by control of the river systems themselves, let alone by control of their access to the sea (Ukraine was more successful in reaching 'its' sea – the Black Sea – than Belarus was in reaching the Baltic). Belarus, Smolich bemoaned, was a natural marchland, caught between the might of Russia and Poland, and too often the battleground for 'the eternal struggle between East and West'.[10] The closest Belarusians have to an idea of a unique national space is the idea of a protective forest culture, a geography that has allowed Belarusians to stay put as others have swept past. Clearly, the Ukrainian idea is much more resonant.

Three key tasks have followed on from Rudnytskyi's definition of Ukrainian geography. The first has been securing access to the Black Sea. According to Lypa, 'the Black Sea zone is Ukraine's lifeblood', which Ukrainians have 'sought to colonise since historical times'.[11] From their central Ukrainian heartland, they have expanded towards the sea in good times, retreated up their rivers in bad. The open border to the east and north-east (and south) has left Ukraine exposed to frequent waves of migration, from the (Royal) Scythians to the Russians, but the presence of the forest zone has always allowed the indigenous element to preserve itself and reemerge in better times. Russian attempts to minimise 'actual historical' Ukraine only show Ukraine at a low ebb in this cycle. When the cycle has waxed, as with the establishment of the Rus city of Tmutorokan in the tenth century or the settlement of the Kuban in the nineteenth, 'Ukraine' or Ukrainians have reached the far shores of the Black Sea and beyond (see the series of maps by Volodymyr Kubiiovych on page 283). Without access to the sea, Ukraine was artificially compressed into a hinterland where it was easy prey for neighbouring powers. With such access, Ukrainians' natural energy made them a significant local power, as with Rus's contacts with Byzantium (or Trypillia's supposed links with Egypt!) and the Cossacks' naval expeditions in the Black Sea.

Ukraine's second major geopolitical problem has therefore been settling a frontier to the south-east in order to keep these river routes open and end the threat from successive waves of invaders from the east. Until the steppe was secure, the Ukrainians could not afford to settle permanently in what is now south-eastern Ukraine and periodic invasions were always a factor hindering the development of Ukrainian society, urban life in particular. Ukraine's steppe frontier has also produced another major theme of Ukrainian political geography, shared with other peripheral European nations such as Poland, Hungary, Croatia, Romania and Georgia, namely the idea of Ukraine as an *antemurale*, a frontier nation playing, in Hrushevskyi's words, 'the honorable role of defenders of European civilisation against the Asian hordes'.[12] If Ukraine is an *antemurale*, then Europe does not stretch, as De Gaulle and Gorbachev would have it, 'from the Atlantic to the Urals' (in Gorbachev's case as far as Vladivostok), but only as far as the Don, where the Greek geographer Ptolemy first placed Europe's frontier. Some Ukrainians have depicted Ukraine and Russia as joint defenders of this frontier (see page 309), but the Ukrainian 'Occidentalist' tradition has mythologised Russia as an 'Asian' nation, or at least has noted the ambiguity of

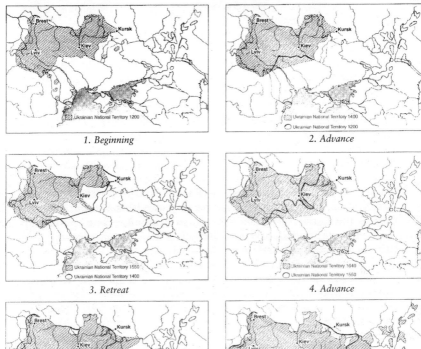

1. *Beginning*

2. *Advance*

3. *Retreat*

4. *Advance*

5. *Advance*

6. *Advance*

Ill. 17. *The Development of Ukrainian National Territory 1200–1910. Adapted from Volodymyr Kubiiovych's seven maps, 1941.*

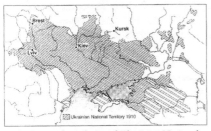

7. *Present boundaries of Ukrainian National Territories (1910)*

Russian attitudes to Europe and attacked the link with Russia for blurring this boundary and dragging Ukraine into 'Eurasia' or beyond.

According to the former dissident Mykhailo Horyn, 'Ukraine has saved European civilisation more than once from the onrush of eastern nomads, Tatar-Turkic expansion and Russo-Eurasian lust.'[13] In a modern refinement of this idea, former president Kravchuk, discussing the possibility of a Ziuganov victory in the 1996 Russian presidential election, argued that Ukraine, 'which occupies an exceptionally important geographical, strategic and geopolitical position, could become the force that defends the West from Communism' (ironically the old OUN myth), echoing the Rukh slogan of 'a Ukrainian state [as] the eastern forepost of democratic Europe!'[14] Readers will recall from chapter two that, according to Lev Sylenko and his followers, this Manichean struggle between European Ukraine and Asian Russia has lasted for millennia.[15] They will also recall the strength of the Communist Party of Ukraine, which out-polled its Russian equivalent in the roughly parallel elections of 1995 (Russia) and 1998 (Ukraine).

Following on from this theme is the idea that Ukraine is Russia's gateway from Asia to Europe and therefore its key to empire. Before 1654 Muscovy could only expand to the north and the east. After Pereiaslav, the real Russian imperial adventure began, Rudnytskyi argued. 'The natural borders of the Caucasus, the Black Sea and the Carpathians, necessary for any state which seeks to rule over the whole of Eastern Europe, can only be given by the possession of Ukraine.' Ukraine opened the way for Russia's drive to the south, and to the west 'domination over Ukraine [gave] the Russian world state *direct contact with Central Europe*' – to Poland and beyond. Without such control, Russia is only a distant threat and Central Europe will be freer to determine its own affairs.[16]

Ukraine's third traditional geopolitical problem has been using these pathways to reach out on its own and secure links to the wider world, the rest of Europe in particular. The first route was to the south. From Scythian times Ukraine's intermittent contact with the Black Sea littoral brought it access to the high culture of the Mediterranean, Near East and Byzantine worlds, although the link was never secure. This southern route was predominant until the rise of the Kingdom of Galicia-Volhynia and the establishment of the connection with Central Europe through Poland in the fourteenth century. In Rudnytskyi's words again, although Ukraine's river axes in the main point to the south-east, 'important borderlands of the Ukrainian territory – central Galicia, the region of Kholm, Pidlachia, western Volhynia – with their river system, belong to the Baltic slope',[17] providing a natural link to the Baltic littoral and the northern European plain. From the seventeenth century this began to be supplemented and, by the nineteenth century, ultimately replaced by a third route via St Petersburg and Moscow and participation in all-Russian access to European culture.

Mykhailo Drahomanov pointed out the paradox that Ukraine's first two geopolitical problems, namely access to the Black Sea and the problem of the open steppe, were solved on Ukraine's behalf by Russia's final victory against the Crimean Tatars and Ottoman Turks in the eighteenth century. 'Muscovite tsardom', he complained, had 'fulfilled Ukraine's elementary geographic-national task!' and seduced the Ukrainian Cossacks into their original Moscowphilia.[18] However, the link with Russia provided an ambiguous solution to the third problem, namely securing links to Europe and the wider world. As pointed out in chapters five and seven, Ukrainian elites could rise high in the Romanov and Soviet empires and gain a form of access to the West, but at the price of assimilation. Direct, unmediated access to European and eventually global culture was not possible on Ukraine's own terms.

Redefining Central Europe

It should be obvious by now that the idea that Ukraine is a natural part of Europe is a central component of the Ukrainian national idea. As to which part it belongs to, southern Europe has receded from the Ukrainian geographical imagination since the end of the Byzantine era. Western Europe would be pushing it a bit, although some Ukrainians have 'Atlanticist' ambitions (see pages 291–4). Eastern Europe is a currently unfashionable idea, although it still has some residual attraction for Ukrainian Slavophiles. It is too much on the margins of current centres of gravity in NATO or the EU and is still seen as code for a Russian sphere of interests. Indeed, it has almost disappeared from the political vocabulary in the rush to join the queue for European expansion, leaving 'Central Europe' as the only game in town, albeit sometimes as a region with a west but no east.

There are many different versions of the idea of Central Europe and of Ukraine's place within or outside it. In its original turn-of-the-nineteenth-century incarnation, *Mitteleuropa* or *Zwischeneuropa* was essentially a German idea, designed to delineate a new area of influence to the west of a redefined Russia. Ukraine did not always feature in such visions.[19] Friedrich Naumann, in his book *Mitteleuropa* (1915), concentrated on the region's supposed common 'economic character' (closer to that of Germany than work-shy Russia) and had little time for theories of cultural unity.[20] To Albrecht Penck in 1916, Ukraine up to the river Dnieper was *Mitteleuropisch*, but thereafter it belonged to the 'Varangian fringe' of *Hintereuropa*. On the other hand, the German philosopher Edward von Hartmann proposed as early as 1888 (possibly with Bismarck's approval) that Germany should work for the creation of a separate 'Kievan kingdom' out of a divided Russia, and that its borders should extend as far as the Volga. The historian Paul Rohrbach declared in 1897 that 'he who rules Kiev has the key to Russia'.[21]

Historians have differed as to what Germany intended when it actually occupied Ukraine in 1918. Some have seen German backing for the Hetmanate as part of a broad strategy to create a belt of new states stretching from the Baltic to the Caucasus. Others have seen Germany's purpose as little more than 'expansion under a cloak of self-determination',[22] with their priorities in Ukraine being the extraction of grain and raw materials and the maintenance of a stable military rear (the Pan-German League was at the time advocating the colonisation of Galicia and the Black Sea coast). Although the Hetmanate was cooperative enough, the possibility that a wholly independent Ukraine might have reverted to acting as a haven for left-wing forces had no part in the plans of the Reich (Austria-Hungary had swung during the course of the war from floating the idea of a Ukrainian 'Crownland' buffer state in 1915 to accepting a restored Poland with Galicia within its borders).[23]

German interest in Ukraine faded rapidly after 1918, despite the continuing concern of individuals such as Max Weber and the historian Hans Delbrück.[24] Ukraine played a key role in Alfred Rosenberg's tentative sketches for the region and in some of the schemes of Karl Haushofer's 'Geopolitik' school, but Nazi racial theorists saw it only in terms of a hinterland for their *Lebensraum*. During World War II, the Germans undoubtedly favoured the latter course in Ukraine, at unknown cost to their war effort. Nor has the revival of German interest after 1991 led to a restoration of the priorities of 1918 – that is, Ukraine before Russia.

The second version of 'Central Europe' was the product of the intellectuals of the Habsburg subject nations, working to undermine the idea of a pan-German *Mitteleuropa*. Their alternative vision looked forward to a self-sustaining community of states: in the words of Tomas Masaryk, the first president of Czechoslovakia, 'a peculiar zone of small nations extending from the North Cape to Cape Matapan' (the southern tip of Greece). Nevertheless, Masaryk and others were more certain about the western contours of their redefined Europe than those in the east. If the western border of their new Central Europe was to be an excluded Germany, most thought that the eastern border would be 'Russia', but were less sure what this 'Russia' might contain. Masaryk, although sympathetic to the Ukrainian cause, worried that an independent Ukraine would too easily fall under German influence and that Ukrainian statehood might undermine pan-Slavic solidarity.[25] To Hungarian scholars, Central or 'Inner' Europe has often meant, more or less, the Carpathian basin.[26] Romania, having occupied considerable Ukrainian territories in 1918, had an interest in the east, but only in terms of Ion Nistor's expanded vision of a Greater Romania.

Only Poland had a more differentiated attitude towards the 'east', in part because it still had ambitions in a region which, as in the Ukrainian vision, has often been defined as stretching from the Baltic to the Black

Seas (the area between the seas, or in Polish *Międzymorze*), rather than Masaryk's relatively narrow meridian or the Hungarian concentration on the Carpathian basin. Poland, however, has historically had an ambiguous attitude to Ukraine and to its role in the region. One tradition goes back to the 1658 Hadiach treaty and seeks constructive engagement with Ukraine and partnership in redefining Central and Eastern Europe – as with Josef Piłsudski's proposal in 1919 for an alliance of states from Finland to the Caucasus, to be led by Poland rather than Germany but with Ukraine as the linchpin. To other Poles, however, Ukraine remained invisible. Marshal Sikorski's alternative 1942 vision, like Masaryk's, looked forward to a postwar alliance of states on a more strictly north–south axis, starting again with Finland and ending with Greece, all within their prewar boundaries. Sikorski's putative alliance had no specific place for Ukraine. Poland was to be re-created within its borders of 1939.

Nor was Ukraine necessarily prominent when the idea of Central Europe began to be revived and refashioned for a third time, in the late 1980s.[27] Ukraine, to be frank, was simply not in the forefront of most people's minds. Indeed, as many intellectuals in Hungary, Poland and elsewhere were seeking to dismantle the standard Cold War bipolarity that posited only 'Western Europe' and an 'Eastern Europe' divided by the Iron Curtain, the implication was definitely that in the new tripartite Europe, Soviet Ukraine would be east of the 'centre', in the 'east' of Europe. Since 1991 many have welcomed the Ukrainians into the new Central Europe, but others have seen them as gatecrashers or at least as surprise candidates. The admission of Poland, Hungary and the Czech Republic into NATO in 1999 was made much easier by the groundwork of the 1980s, when dissident voices like Havel and Kundera prepared the intellectual basis for inclusion. Ukrainian voices, on the other hand, were not heard. Even those who have accepted Rudnytskyi's vision of a Ukrainian buffer as a great addition to their security have assumed that this implies some kind of intermediate status for Ukraine. Nor have the new Central Europeans much desire to help Ukraine escape from Russia's influence if this means, as Ukrainian nationalists have too often implied, the redefinition of their region as some kind of *cordon sanitaire*. President Kravchuk's idea of a special 'zone of stability and security' in east-central Europe met with little interest and much hostility when it was floated in 1993. Czech president Václav Havel, rather less ambiguously than his predecessor Masaryk, has declared that Ukraine should remain part of the 'Euro-Asian entity', not the 'Euro-Atlantic region'.[28] Poland, despite Lech Wałęsa's brief flirtation with the idea of a NATO-2, and the even more short-lived suggestion of a 'Brest Triangle' (Poland, Ukraine and Belarus) now looks to redefine itself in the West, not the East.

Central Europe, however, is a cartographic concept, not an absolute given. In the words of Oleksii Tolochko, 'Eastern' and 'Central' Europe are 'the same type of cultural project, which had a finite beginning and has its limits'.[29] Even the importance attached to 'determinant' environmental features is itself a form of cultural projection. Since 1991, therefore, Ukraine has been as much *redefining* itself as Central European as *returning* to Central Europe. Ukraine has been able to draw on important precedents for the idea of itself as *Mitteleuropisch*, but has also had to reinvent itself as such. In part, this can be done by appropriating some of the terminology of the new Central Europeans, such as the Hungarian writer György Konrád's definition, 'Central Europe exists today only as a cultural-political anti-hypothesis . . . to be a Central European is a *Weltanschauung*, not a *Staatsangehörigkeit*' ('nationality', more literally, 'state-kinship'), or Milan Kundera's formulation, 'the uncertain zone of small nations between Russia and Germany'.[30]

Can Ukraine reinvent itself as, in Kundera's words again, 'the Eastern border of the West'? Precedents exist. Some are of course Ukrainian, from the abortive Hadiach treaty through Heorhii Andruzkyi's plan for a Slavic federation to Drahomanov's sketch for a possible East European union in his essay 'Historical Poland and Great Russian Democracy' (1881).[31] The idea of a Baltic–Black Sea alliance has continued to resurface in Ukraine, despite the lack of enthusiasm of most would-be participants (it does, after all, follow on naturally from Rudnytskyi's definition of Ukrainian 'space'). Other advocates of a Central European Ukraine have included the Germanophile Swede Rudolf Kjellén (1864–1922), credited with coining the term 'geopolitics'. In his book *Political Problems of the World War* (1916), he identified a middle European or 'Critical Zone', whose western border ran from Trieste to Danzig (see A–B on the map on page 289) and whose eastern border (line C–D) began at Archangel on the shores of the White Sea and ended where the river Don flowed into the Black. Kjellén therefore placed Finland, the Baltic states, Belarus and Ukraine all in the 'Critical Zone' and Russia firmly beyond. Moreover, according to Kjellén, 'what is west of [the eastern border of the Critical Zone] belongs wholly to Europe, which is determined by culture, irrespective of race',[32] although he was somewhat vague as to what this common culture might be. Nevertheless, he confirmed the idea of a European cultural frontier or *limes* line on the Don and viewed Ukraine as being on the frontline in the defence of cultural Europe against 'Mongol-tainted Muscovite tsarism' and Russia's 'Asian unlimited will to power'.[33]

The British academic R.W. Seton-Watson also allocated Ukraine a central place on the list of emergent Central European states that he drew up in 1918. In part because of his contact in 1914 in Lviv with Hrushevskyi, Sheptytskyi and others, Seton-Watson drew Ukraine's western border largely as it would be after 1945 and proposed a much-reduced 'ethnographic' Poland. Belarus, on the other hand, was shown as part of Russia.[34]

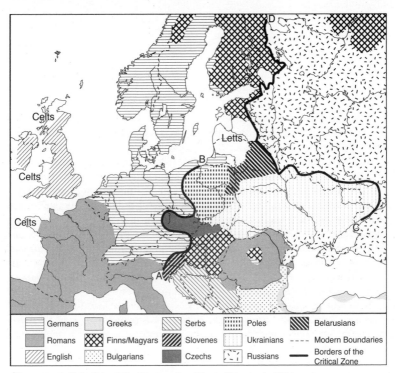

Germans · Greeks · Serbs · Poles · Belarusians
Romans · Finns/Magyars · Slovenes · Ukrainians · ---- Modern Boundaries
English · Bulgarians · Czechs · Russians · ▬ Borders of the Critical Zone

Ill. 18. Rudolf Kjellén, 'The Nationality Map of Europe', 1916.

Relying on redefined cultural boundaries to reposition Ukraine is a dangerous game, however. Ukraine could just as easily find itself on the edge or even the far side of such a boundary. The Ukrainian steppe, the 'wild field' and the Polish *kresy* have often been seen as the European 'edge'. So has the religious fault line between Catholicism and Orthodoxy, which runs through Ukraine.[35] Even 'the frontier between the Latin and the Cyrillic alphabet' and the eastern limits of Gothic architecture have been seen as barriers.[36] Just as dangerous is the absolutism of the Occidentalist claim that Ukrainians are definitively European and the Russian are not. A better strategy is the deconstruction of boundaries, not the construction of new ones. The very novelty of Ukrainian statehood can make a useful contribution towards rethinking the fossilised categorisations of both the Cold War and post-Cold War worlds. This applies equally to the idea of 'Central Europe'. It is not so long ago since the whole middle European region was seen as a geopolitical vacuum, little more than an 'in between', whose lack of real unity had sucked the surrounding powers into two world wars. As Halford Mackinder (1861–1947) argued in 1919, Central Europe's very marginality was likely to provoke a contest to control it.[37]

Engaging Europe: Myth and Reality

Under Kravchuk, Ukrainian foreign policy thinking about Europe, such as it was, was largely based on existential criteria. For Ukrainian nationalists, a 'return to Europe' was a means of reconfirming Ukraine's historical character and manifest destiny. Even a left-wing politician like Boris Oliinyk, a prominent leader of the Communist Party of Ukraine and chairman of the foreign affairs committee of the Ukrainian parliament after 1994, was moved to claim, 'It is not true that we are returning to Europe. This is not the case. We were always a part of Europe.'[38] Significantly, after an initial flirtation with 'Eurasianism', the Kuchma administration began if anything to push even harder than Kravchuk for 'inclusion' in Europe. At a deeper level, however, there is no consensus. The left remains opposed and public opinion divided on the issue.[39] Pan-Slavic sentiment is still alive and well. The conversion of Ukrainian elites demonstrates the *force majeure* of the economic, diplomatic and military attraction of the EU and NATO, rather than any fundamental shift in Ukraine's cultural *geopolitik*.

Nevertheless, the 'Fundamentals of National Security' passed by parliament in early 1997 dropped the pretence of 'equidistance' or a 'multi-vector policy' by providing for 'entry into extant and newly formed or emerging systems of universal and regional security',[40] as did the new formula of 'cooperation with the CIS, integration with Europe'.[41] The 'return to Europe', however, is only a slogan. It is necessary to grasp Ukraine's practical possibilities, of which there were at one time three. First was to redefine the expansion process. Although it proved impossible for Ukraine to catch up with the first and second waves of the expansion process for NATO and the EU – Ukraine was not even invited to the 1998 London expansion conference and was snubbed at the Helsinki summit in 1999, and was redefined as part of the 'European neighbourhood' after the big EU expansion in 2004. The Orange Revolution led to the signing of an 'Action Plan' with the EU in 2005 and the beginning of negotiations on an 'Association Agreement' in September 2008. But the hope for closer relations was simultaneously undermined by the French and Dutch 'no' votes against the European 'constitution' in the summer of 2005.

The second possibility is that this fresh round of expansion will indeed be limited to 10 or 11 states. Ukraine would then find itself in a new European 'Grey Zone'. Indeed, it would be the largest country in such a zone, which would actually be numerically rather small, consisting basically of Ukraine and Moldova, some Yugoslav remnants, the South Caucasus states and possibly one day Belarus (Turkey being a long-standing candidate for EU membership). Optimistic scenarios for Ukraine would then include 'the so-called Finnish model whereby Ukraine is oriented towards the West, [but] is politically and economically stable, and militarily neutral' or 'the signing of a joint treaty providing guarantees on the sovereignty, independence, territorial integrity and security of Ukraine similar to the one Austria signed in 1955'.[42] Pessimistic scenarios would be an isolated Ukraine turning in on itself or seeking *rapprochement* with Russia. Is this really what the West would want?

The third possibility would be for 'institutional Europe' to refashion its whole *Ostpolitik*. Post-Cold War Europe does not need a new border between Russia and Central Europe, nor does it need to be forced to choose one at the expense of the other. Nor are the current expansion limits politically, militarily or economically logical. For the moment NATO seems too concerned with Russia's possible reaction to any outreach to Ukraine, while the EU has barely thought about the exact contours of a post-expansion world.[43] Ukraine is the most important reason for rethinking the present narrow expansion trajectory and devising new overarching arrangements capable of accommodating a variety of definitions of 'Europe'. There is admittedly something of a chicken-and-egg dilemma. It might be argued that Europe, the EU in particular, cannot make any opening to Ukraine until its political and economic systems have been reformed in such a way as to bring them closer to the European norm. Alternatively, a clear political signal to Ukraine might be precisely the stimulus such reforms need. There is a real danger, however, that Ukraine will be left in the ante-room while a decision is made or constantly delayed. Europe can surely afford to be more generous than it has been: the costs of clearing up after a real 'Ukrainian problem' emerged would surely be much greater.

A Euro-Atlantic Ukraine?

Ukraine's key partner in Europe is, however paradoxically, America. By the time of President Clinton's reelection in 1996 Ukraine was the third-largest recipient of US foreign aid, behind only Egypt and Israel. This oft-quoted statistic represented a remarkable turnaround from George Bush's notorious 'Chicken Kiev' speech in 1991, when he lectured the Ukrainian parliament on the dangers of 'suicidal nationalism based on ethnic hatred' only a month before the failed Moscow coup led to the Declaration of Independence.

America's growing interest in Ukraine has been most clearly articulated by Zbigniew Brzezinski, Jimmy Carter's former National Security Adviser. Although Ukraine is not yet what Brzezinski calls a 'geostrategic player', he has argued that it is one of only five 'geopolitical pivots' which are the key to the balance of power in the whole Eurasian region, still 'the chessboard on which the struggle for global primacy continues to be played' (the others being Azerbaijan, South Korea, Turkey and Iran).[44] Ukraine is vital because (as with Rudnytskyi) its very existence determines Russia's terms of access from the Eurasian 'middle space' to the west and south, as well as denying Russia the resources for empire-building, 'drastically limit[ing its] geostrategic options', and acting as a defensive shield for Central Europe proper. Independent Ukraine has also had a 'catalytic effect' on other key players in the region, encouraging states such as Uzbekistan to resist Russian plans for a more centralised CIS.[45] And, rather more bluntly, in Henry Kissinger's words, 'it is a vital American interest to see to it that Eurasia not be controlled by a single power centre. In essence we have fought two world wars over this issue'.[46]

Ukraine is also important precisely because it could go either way. Its choice between integration with Europe or return to the Russian sphere will have a vital effect on the balance of power in the whole Eurasian region. Brzezinski is confident, assuming internal reforms go well, that Ukraine will choose Europe, becoming a serious candidate for full EU and NATO membership sometime between 2005 and 2015. Indeed, 'beyond 2010' Brzezinski predicts that Ukraine could link up with the three 'Weimar triangle' states (France, Germany and Poland) to establish a spinal partnership that will form 'the critical core of Europe's [future] security' and provide the eastern anchor of 'Atlanticist Europe' (see Brzezinski's map on page 293).[47]

Ukraine should therefore abandon any residual thoughts of a 'multi-vector' policy, facing as it does a much simpler choice between reintegration into the CIS or 'becoming in the foreseeable future a de facto Central European state . . . this orientation will give Ukraine its own geopolitical identity, one that separates it from its more traditional connection with Eurasia through Russia' and will enable it 'to strive to become indirectly, perhaps someday directly, an increasingly integral part of the Euro-Atlantic community'.[48] Many Americans are still distrustful of Moscow and have sought to reshape the postwar strategy of containing the Soviet Union along what Mackinder called the Eurasian 'rimlands' by shifting their definition inwards by a notch or two and seeking to 'contain' the new Russia on its own. Ukraine would basically be on the frontline, a new player in what Russian (and Ukrainian) Communists would call Atlanticist 'mondialism'. After the 1999 Kosovo war, it was entirely possible that disillusionment with Russia might tempt conservative 'Atlanticists' to back Ukraine even more strongly – even though Ukrainian public opinion sided with the Russians and Serbs – assuming America is not minded to give up on the region as a whole.

Before Kosovo, Brzezinski's arguments were beginning to find an echo in leading circles in Ukraine. One study by the National Institute of Strategic Studies in 1997 argued that 'as long as Ukraine adopts a pendulum politics of symmetrical manœuvre between the Russian and Western poles, it will experience pressure from the West, insofar as the

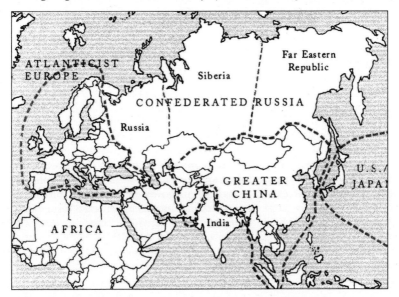

Ill. 19. Zbigniew Brzezinski, 'A Geostrategy for Eurasia', 1997.

latter is not interested in a strong Ukraine as a potential component part of Russia in the case of Ukrainian drift towards the Russian Federation.' Ukraine should therefore pursue an unambiguous course towards inclusion in the process 'of European and Euro-Atlantic integration, deepening relations with European countries and [beginning] a progressive departure from the Eurasian zone of Russian influence', while seeking 'relations with the USA on the level of a strategic partnership on the basis of a strengthening of the contradictions between Washington and Moscow'.[49]

Without American influence, the report continued, Europe would be more inclined to 'divide spheres of influence between the EU and Russia along a line south from the Baltic'. The Big Three of Europe are neither naturally united nor necessarily friendly in their policy towards Ukraine. The United Kingdom has most interest in a 'wider' Europe; the new Germany, with its capital in Berlin, most interest in a stable backyard; but France is unlikely to abandon its traditional policy of courting Russia to counterbalance Germany. Germany itself has looked to both Ukraine and Russia in the twentieth century, but the inertia of its postwar preference for the latter is still great.[50] With the addition of American influence, the report argues, Ukraine is more likely to be successful in shaping 'a Europe with a flexible geometry', one in which, moreover, the USA has a strategic interest in seeing 'Ukraine as a unifying link in the Baltic-Mediterranean arc' helping to join up the USA's other strategic partners, Poland and Turkey.[51]

The July 1997 'Charter on a Distinctive Partnership' signed between Ukraine and NATO at the Madrid summit gave Ukraine some hope of an 'Atlanticist' direction. Significantly, 'distinctive' is often mistranslated in Ukraine as 'special' (*osoblyvo*).[52] America has also been the main cheerleader for Ukraine in its rocky relations with the IMF (see pages 253–78), and its backing has allowed Ukraine to edge away from Russia much more quickly than would otherwise have been the case. A dramatic indication of how far this policy might take Ukraine came in June 1999 – when Kiev temporarily closed its airspace in response to the Russian attempt to reinforce its adventurous troop deployment at Pristina airport in Kosovo – and showed just how isolated Russia would be if Ukraine were 'lost' to the West. Bulgaria and Romania cooperating with NATO was one thing, Ukraine quite another. Kuchma instantly rescinded the decision in the face of Russian fury.

Ukrainian Eurasia

It would nevertheless be a mistake to equate Ukrainian geopolitics solely with the 'European', or increasingly the 'Euro-Atlantic idea'. Pan-(east) Slavism is still a powerful force and received a considerable boost from the fallout from the Kosovo war. More subtly, the need to build stable links with (the rest of) Europe was only one of Drahomanov's key geopolitical tasks and in recent years the question of a Ukrainian 'southern' or 'eastern' strategy has begun to return to the agenda. Although the problems of the open steppe have now lost all significance, energy politics in particular have taken their place. Nationalist as well as Russophile Ukrainians have therefore pointed out that, like Russia, 'we also have a Eurasia' and 'our own interests in the East'.[53] Yurii Lypa in particular built on the suggestions of Rudnytskyi, Hrushevskyi[54] and Khvylovyi (the 'Asiatic Renaissance') on the need for Ukraine to balance its interests in Europe by expanding its influence along equally natural channels to the east and south. Lypa's 'Black Sea Doctrine' was in part based on his prediction that Russia was an artificial state facing imminent collapse (see below), which would leave Transcaucasia as a natural sphere of Ukrainian influence and bridge to the east. While Russia was preoccupied with attempting to hold on to its Siberian 'colony', Ukraine could seek to expand its influence through the Caucasian 'gateway' to Turkey, Iran, India and even China ('Ukraine's one possible road to a great future'), having first secured control over the Crimean peninsula as a gateway to the gateway, as it were.[55] As argued in the previous chapter, Lypa also saw Transcaucasia as Ukraine's natural source of energy and raw-material supply. By weaning itself off a division of labour dictated by Moscow's imperial interests, a more natural husbandry of resources would allow Ukraine to emerge as an economic phoenix and leave Russia to its own affairs, which, Lypa dismissively predicted, would be mainly the 'export . . . of wood and oil' – a not too inaccurate forecast of Russia's economic strengths in the 1990s.[56]

Lypa is a particular favourite of the extreme nationalist group UNA–UNSO, which in 1996 established a Ukrainian Black Sea and National Geopolitics Institute in Odesa that was named after Lypa. UNA leader Dmytro Korchynskyi has declared that 'a small separatist Ukraine is not possible and not necessary. Ukraine can exist only as a dragon with its tail in the Far East, its heart in the Caucasus and its head in the Balkans.'[57] However, shorn of its more fantastical anti-Russian elements, Lypa's vision has overlapped to a surprising extent with the 'Ukrainian Eurasianism' periodically promoted by President Kuchma and several of his leading advisers. Their original version of Eurasianism, as developed in Kuchma's successful 1994 election campaign, was mainly cultural and historical, as exemplified by Kuchma's claim in his controversial inauguration speech that 'Ukraine is historically part of the [same] Eurasian economic and cultural space' as Russia and Belarus. Kuchma has since continued to object to the depiction of Ukrainian-Russian relations in Manichean terms, but in the furore that followed the speech his coterie redefined their Eurasianism in more pragmatic and more specifically Ukrainian terms. According to Kuchma's first chief of staff, Dmytro Tabachnyk, and political adviser Dmytro Vydrin, instead of 'Eurocentrism', 'isolationism and artificial hostility towards Russia' and the pointless pursuit of a chimerical Europe, where 'European conservative' capital was only interested in building an economic 'fortress Europe' in which Ukraine would play no constructive role, Ukraine should follow its historical traditions in the east and utilise the industrial strength of the former USSR as the only means by which it could hope to integrate itself 'into the world market as an equal partner'. Instead of 'Europe's backyard', Ukraine would then be at 'the heart of Eurasia'.[58]

It would be wrong 'to equate a new Eurasian zone with the former USSR' or with 'the reanimation of [the Russian] empire'. Ukraine, they argued, could build a second 'Eurasian zone', 'a new geoeconomic corridor' an alternative to Russian Eurasia, by uniting the interests of those 'states of the CIS which bridge the post-Soviet space with neighbouring geopolitical regions. This would be Kazakhstan (Asia), Azerbaijan (Asia and the Near East), Ukraine (the Asiatic-Near East region and Europe) and Belarus (Europe).' The Ukrainian version of 'Eurasia' would therefore link 'five strategic regions (the Pacific Basin, East Asia, the Eurasian region [proper], Europe and the Near East)'.[59] In other words, Ukraine should begin to mark out its own sphere of interests between 'Atlantic' Europe and Russia. Slavophile Eurasianism would be replaced by a realpolitik of post-Soviet economic interests, and future relations with Russia would be as much competitive as cooperative.[60] Even in areas where Russia was likely to dominate on a political level and cultural links were limited, Ukraine could establish significant economic relations, as with South Korea and China. Ukraine was unlikely to establish exclusive relations with such states, squeezing Russia out of the picture, but should at least make the most of the potential for competition.

The first concrete result of these ideas came in October 1997 when Ukraine was instrumental in establishing GUAM, a loose alliance of the four states of Georgia, Ukraine, Azerbaijan and Moldova.[61] Oil was the main motive, with Azerbaijan the producer, Georgia hoping to become the main transit state and Ukraine and Moldova the final market (see also pages 275–8). The alliance made broader geopolitical sense, however. Ukraine also hoped that GUAM would help to develop the TRACECA transport corridor from Central Asia through the Caucasus to the Black Sea. As Azerbaijan and Turkmenistan are competitors in energy production and Turkmenistan's current dependence on northerly out-routes through Russia for its exports has left it oriented towards the Iran-Armenia-Russia axis (albeit potentially resentful at this dependence), Ukraine has preferred to develop links with Uzbekistan, hoping that it could be persuaded to act as the eastern anchor for this new Eurasian 'corridor'. In any case, Ukraine and Uzbekistan are politically close – while Ukraine poses as the leader of the western flank of the more reluctant members of the CIS (Georgia, Moldova), Uzbekistan seeks to play the same role in Central Asia. Uzbekistan joined GUAM in 1999, creating the broader but less easily pronounceable GUUAM. By such means Ukraine seeks to present itself to NATO and the EU as the leading element in a clearing house or tidying-up operation in Europe's strategic rear, and as providing a strategic link to the countries of the 'Asiatic Renaissance', as illustrated in the following diagram.[62]

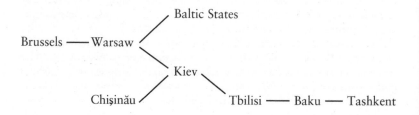

Turkey: A Key Missing Piece?

After the relative success of GUUAM, some Ukrainian strategists have talked of supplementing it with an 'Ankara-Kiev-Baku triangle', thereby creating a broader Black Sea alliance in opposition to the Russian-led axis of Bulgaria, Greece and Armenia.[63] However, while Ukraine has clearly been groping towards a 'southern strategy', there is as yet less evidence that Turkey is developing an explicit 'northern strategy' in response.

In the last days of the Ottoman empire there were some signs of a specific policy emerging towards Ukraine. A mission of Ukrainian nationalists (the 'Union for the Liberation of Ukraine') to Constantinople helped produce the November 1914 Talaat Bey Declaration, which, because it was the first international document to support the idea of an independent Ukrainian state, has been compared by some Ukrainians to the 1917 Balfour Declaration. According to the newspaper of the Young Turk movement, 'the interests of the Ukrainians are closely bound up with Turkey's. The Ukrainian state desired by Ukrainians would separate Russia from the Black Sea. The creation of a non-Russian Slavic state would free Turkey from the policy of intrigues pursued by Russia which strives to dominate Constantinople and the straits.'[64] A proposal was even floated for the émigré nationalists and the Ottoman army to make a joint landing in southern Ukraine or the Kuban. Ottoman military impotence prevented the relationship from flourishing, although the 1922 Friendship Treaty between Turkey and Soviet Ukraine indicated how things might have developed if the latter had been more able to implement a truly independent foreign policy. As Soviet Ukraine was somewhat cut off from Europe, Turkey accounted for a massive 45% of its trade by 1926–7.[65]

The Ottomans are gone. If Turkish history is deemed to begin with Ataturk in 1923, 'Ukrainian-Turkish relations do not have any past.'[66] Whereas Polish-Ukrainian *rapprochement* in the 1990s was as much the work of Poles as Ukrainians, modern Turkey has no real Ukrainian experts and few Ukrainophiles. Ukraine is now Turkey's main northern neighbour in geographical terms – the length of its Black Sea coastline is about twice that left to Russia – although Russia is still Turkey's more important economic partner, with an estimated annual $12 billion in 'suitcase trade' and around one million official tourists a year. The offer of EU membership made in 1999 is hardly likely to encourage it to edge closer to Ukraine. Nor does the Crimean Tatar issue necessarily promote warmer relations. Ankara, and Kiev, are well aware that direct engagement, over and above sympathy and material aid, could easily inflame the already volatile situation on the peninsula.

Russia Imagining Ukraine: Nationalist Visions

Ukraine's key foreign policy relationship is with Russia. This does not mean that an orientation towards Russia is Ukraine's only strategic option, or that success in Ukraine's other relationships is necessarily conditional on the state of its relationship with Russia. Nor is it to argue that Russia will always be central in this way. It is just that the two countries are still so often the other's *idée fixe*. Any serious Ukrainian engagement with Europe in the west or Eurasia in the south will always have to be balanced by a concern for a healthy relationship with Russia in the east, and by a regard for the pan-Slavism that remains a very real force in both Russia and Ukraine.

Even after almost a decade of independence for both states, the vast majority of Russian politicians and academics have yet to engage seriously with the reality of Ukraine's separate existence. Attitudes to Ukraine tend to be defined by reference to the unity of the territory and people of Rus, rather than by any consideration of subsequent history or the reality of a specifically Ukrainian geopolitics. Nor are Russian politicians particularly out of step with public opinion: in one Russian poll conducted in October 1997, 56% still considered that the 'Ukrainians and Russians were one people'.[67] Even amongst the minority who have addressed the question in depth, attitudes are still dismissive. Many Russians continue to argue that the very name 'Ukrainian' is a term invented in the chancelleries of Vienna and Berlin as a means of undermining the Russian state in the nineteenth century. Ukraine, in short, is (still) a natural part of Russia.

Most Russian nationalist visions share at least four features. First, the Russian space in whatever guise – tsarist, Soviet or neo-imperial – is conceived as continental, a 'Great Space' (*Bolshoe Prostranstvo*) or 'internal continental space' stretching, in the nineteenth-century phrase, 'from the Carpathians to the Pacific'. In the words of Gennadii Ziuganov, leader of the Russian Communist Party, 'the basis of Russia's material prosperity', the foundation of its cultural unity since the time of Kievan Rus and the central geopolitical fact in Russian life has always been 'control over [this] internal continental space' and war with the surrounding steppe.[68] The idea of a separate Ukrainian space or of any kind of natural border between Russia and Ukraine is ridiculed or simply ignored. According to two Russian émigré authors, Ukraine 'has only one natural frontier: the southern inclines of the western part of the Carpathians. We do not speak of the coasts of the Black Sea and the Sea of Azov which officially form its southern frontier, as this is above all the boundary of the Russian continent in its entirety.' In the east there is no boundary at all. And finally, 'we also do not notice anything, when going towards the north, between the Ukraine and Russia proper'.[69]

Second, this continental space is conceived as geopolitically, culturally and ethnically distinct – a separate Russian Europe, Eastern Europe or Eurasia ('not a synthesis of Europe and Asia', but 'a world of its own'),[70] and Ukraine is assumed to be a part of this space. Any attempt to (re)define Ukraine as Central European, let alone Euro-Atlantic is therefore emphatically rejected. Russians have reacted strongly against 'the attempts of some presumptuous circles in the Ukrainian political elite to draw a new de facto border between the West and the East – somewhere along the Don river, as the ancient Greeks did – thus remaking Ukraine into some kind of "front line" of Western civilisation.'[71] Putting these two ideas together, Russian nationalists have claimed that

> the Great Russian idea is a Grand Idea. The Ukrainian idea a small one . . . the choice between Moscow and Kiev is not an ethnic choice, but a choice of ideas, a choice of geopolitical Homeland . . . the Great Russians came into being as a *Eurasian integrating ethnos*, not just as the easternmost branch of the Slavs . . . the Great Russian (Muscovite) idea is not the idea of one nationality alone – as for example the Ukrainian idea.

Russia's mission is still to represent this idea and consolidate its historical space.[72]

Third, an exception is usually made for Galicia – the border of the Russian space is almost always imagined as passing through modern Ukraine, hopefully one day isolating the majority of Ukrainians from the unnatural influences to the west. There is a crucial difference in Russian nationalism between those who would seek to restore the Soviet or imperial Russian homeland and those who would target particular *irredenta*, which could become important if revanchist possibilities were open but limited, but reunion of the vast majority of 'Orthodox Ukraine' with Russia would be the preferred scenario for most. There are few Russian nationalists who would content themselves with just Crimea or the Donbas.

Fourth, the 'new' Russian geopolitics regards Ukraine as a crucial 'outlier', a gateway or link to the wider world. In a 1997 book prepared with the help of insiders on the Russian General Staff, Aleksandr Dugin, one of the doyens of the new Russian right, writing under the heading 'The Geopolitical Decomposition of Ukraine' caused a considerable stir in Kiev by loftily declaring that

> Ukraine as a state makes no geopolitical sense. It has no particular cultural message of global importance, no geographical uniqueness, no ethnic exceptionality . . . the independent existence of Ukraine (especially in its current borders) makes sense only as a *cordon sanitaire*, as elements with opposing geopolitical orientations [within

Ukraine] will not allow this country to adhere completely to either the Eastern or the Western bloc, that is to Russia-Eurasia or to Central Europe. All this dooms Ukraine to a puppet existence and to geopolitical service in the Talassocratic [i.e. the 'sea empire' or Altanticist] strategy for Europe.[73]

Ukraine, in other words, is an artificial buffer state with no prospect of long-term coherence. It cannot, in this particular Russian nationalist view, exist in and for itself, although at the beginning of the twenty-first century it is more likely to be a client state of America than Germany, as Masaryk had feared in 1918. According to Solzhenitsyn, 'Ukraine's anti-Russian position is just what America requires. The Ukrainian authorities, both under Kravchuk and under Kuchma, obligingly played into the hands of the American aim of weakening Russia . . . recalling willy-nilly the immortal Parvus plan of 1915: using Ukrainian separatism for the successful disintegration of Russia.'[74] The idea, popular among many Ukrainians, of Ukraine as a historical bridge for European influence to the whole of the east Slavic world, is precisely what makes many Russian nationalists see it as an 'Atlanticist Trojan Horse'.[75]

Dugin's map of Ukraine (see below) shows four regions 'with opposing geopolitical orientations': western Ukraine is shown cleaving towards Central Europe, Berlin in particular; eastern Ukraine is oriented towards Moscow, as is Crimea, although Dugin describes it as 'an independent pro-Eurasian geopolitical formation'; Right Bank Ukraine is left in limbo, but still 'gravitating towards Great Russia'. Dugin would allow western Ukraine to go its own way – 'Volhynia, Galicia and Transcarpathia could create a common "West Ukrainian Federation" ', but its openly proclaimed purpose would be to 'build a cultural-confessional

Ill. 20. Aleksandr Dugin's map of Ukraine, 1997

Ill. 21. Ukraine shown as a set of sub-ethnoses of the Great Russian people.

border between central Ukraine (the modern territory of Kiev) and western Ukraine, in order to avoid disruptive central European Catholic or Uniate influence on Orthodox territory.'[76]

Another typical Russian attempt to dismiss the very idea of geographical 'Ukraine' or a separate Ukrainian identity draws on the fashionable theory of ethnogenesis developed by the controversial Russian writer Lev Gumilev (see map above). According to this account there is no such thing as a Ukrainian 'ethnos'. Instead, the population of Ukraine is made up of at least four 'sub-ethnoses' of the Great Russian people. These are the 'Little Russians' in Ukraine's Cossack heartland, the 'New Russians' in the east and south, the Rusyns in the west and their neighbours the 'Red Russians' or Galicians. In the north-west many Ukrainians and Belarusians are more properly labelled 'Polessians'. The Ukrainians are therefore no more a 'nation' than any other subdivision of the Greater Russian whole, such as the 'South Russians' or the inhabitants of the region around Pskov. The Little Russians and Polessians are still in what Gumilev called the 'inert' phase of ethnic development and are likely to join the Rusyns as ethnographic 'relics'. They are therefore subject to the temporary leadership of the Galicians, who alone have passed to the higher, 'passionate' phase. In the immediate future, however, this leadership will pass to the 'New Russians' of southern and eastern Ukraine, whose ethnic consciousness is supposedly in the process of maturing to the same level as the Galicians'. This will naturally be in the form of a strengthened orientation towards Mother Russia, thus allowing the Galician tutelage to be rejected and a Ukrainian-Russian union to be reestablished, if necessary by excluding the Galicians, or possibly by a confederal link between Galicia and a new union of Little Russia, New Russia, Carpathian Rus and the Russian Federation.[77]

Similar views have been expressed by Alexei Mitrofanov, chairman of the Russian Duma's committee on geopolitics and an ally of Vladimir Zhirinovskii. According to Mitrofanov, Russia should not shrink from advocating independence both for Galicia (area 10 on his map, see page 303) and, more bizarrely, for a truncated 'Cossack Ukraine', defined as the belt of land at the historic boundary of the steppe zone 'from the south of Poltava to the Dnieper rapids' (area 8). (This last concession is most instructive. Even for those Russians who accept that Russian and 'Little Russian' culture diverged between the fourteenth and seventeenth centuries, the Cossack Hetmanate was supposedly much smaller than the fictional 'ethnographic' Ukraine invented by Ukrainian nationalists in the nineteenth century.)[78] Once again, the perfectly 'normal phenomenon' of Galician independence would then serve to isolate its pernicious influence from the rest of Ukraine.[79]

In Mitrofanov's vision of 'the world as it might be in the twenty-first century', an expanded Russia would include a 'Chernigov *guberniya*' covering most of eastern Ukraine (area 5), 'restored' Don Cossack territory in the Donbas (area 6), southern Ukraine and Crimea ('New Russia' – area 7), extended to take in a 'Dniester Republic' carved out of Moldova and a 'Russian [*Russkoe*] palatinate' around Kiev (area 9). Volhynia (area 11), because of 'its extreme closeness to the Belorussian dialect' and to 'Belorussian culture' (!), would be linked to Belarus, which would also be a part of the new Russia (with Vilnius restored on the Belarusians' behalf from Lithuania and Białystok from Poland). The new Russia would also control the region of Narva in north-east Estonia and that part of eastern Latvia that used to be the tsarist *guberniya* of Vitebsk, i.e. Latgalia.[80] Zhirinovskii's own vision of Russia restored, in his famous map sketched with a Biro for *Le Monde* in 1994, was similar, although the Lviv district was to be granted as compensation to a truncated Poland (Zhirinovskii's view of the world obviously could not cope with the complexities of 'Cossack Ukraine').[81]

A further argument made by the likes of Dugin and Ziuganov is that Ukraine and Russia still belong to the same 'civilisational space'. Both men have drawn on Samuel Huntington's claim that the 'new world order' will be dominated by the 'clash of civilisations' rather than economic or ideological struggle. According to Huntington, 'patterns of cohesion, disintegration and conflict in the post-Cold War world' will coincide with the persistent boundary-markers created by 'culture and cultural identities, which at the broadest levels are civilisational identities'.[82] According to Ziuganov, 'the main source of conflicts in the modern world will be cultural (civilisational) differences'. Ziuganov claims to disagree with Huntington in only advocating a 'balance of interests' between his 'Great Spaces', but much of his argument is drawn

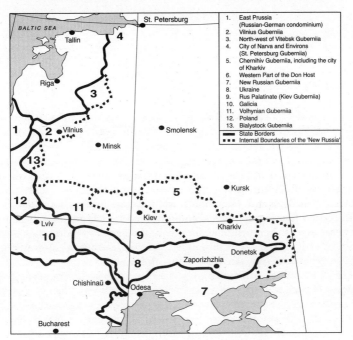

*Ill. 22. Alexei Mitrofanov, 'The West and South of European Russia [sic]',
1997*

The map legend reads:

1. East Prussia (Russian-German condominium)
2. Vilnius Guberniia
3. North-west of Vitebsk Guberniia
4. City of Narva and Environs (St. Petersburg Guberniia)
5. Chernihiv Guberniia, including the city of Kharkiv
6. Western Part of the Don Host
7. New Russian Guberniia
8. Ukraine
9. Rus Palatinate (Kiev Guberniia)
10. Galicia
11. Volhynian Guberniia
12. Poland
13. Bialystock Guberniia

━━━ State Borders
▪▪▪ Internal Boundaries of the 'New Russia'

from the Belgian neo-Fascist Jean Thiriart, who argued in the 1930s that
the destiny of Eurasia was to lead a spiritual struggle against the cosmopolitan and materialist Atlanticist order.[83] In Huntington's schema,
the eight major 'world civilisations' are the Western, Orthodox, Latin
American, Islamic, Sinic, Hindu, Japanese and, possibly, African. Dugin
and Ziuganov's lists are broadly similar.

Modern Russian 'Eurasianists' (not to be confused with the Ukrainian
version) have therefore sought to revive the ideas first propagated in the
1920s about the natural 'symphonic' unity of the geopolitical and civilisational space occupied by Russia and Ukraine, and their natural partnership in the 'global confrontation between the Atlantic (USA and
Western Europe) and Eurasian ([former] USSR and Eastern Europe)
Great Spaces' – in particular during Ziuganov's 1996 Russian election
campaign.[84] In Ziuganov's characteristically opaque terminology, the
essence of the east Slavic 'civilisation' and 'the pivot of Eurasianism' is
an 'intricate ethnic commonality . . . the powerful national core of the
Great Russians, Little Russians and White Russians',[85] who are simultaneously united by a 'geographical and geopolitical outlook', a 'unique
cultural-historical type' centred around the ideas of 'corporate unity'
(*sobornost*), spiritual hierarchy and 'autonomous economic organism',
and a 'superethnic [form of] self-sufficiency and self-development'.

Eurasian Russia is based on the east Slavic 'core', but also includes outer layers of other kindred peoples: 'the basis of the Eurasian super-ethnos [key terms are once again derived from Lev Gumilev] is the peaceful coexistence and cooperation of Slavic, Finno-Ugric and Turkic peoples, attained on the basis of their mutual complementarity (sympathy) and settlement into different ecological niches' (for the Russians this was 'river valleys and fields [*opolia*]', for the Ukrainians 'watersheds'). Ziuganov and his supporters have therefore claimed to be promoting 'not Russian nationalism, but general-Eurasian nationalism . . . the basis of which is the tolerance and indifference to ethnicity of the Russian people'.[86]

Both Ziuganov and Huntington have a view of the world in which cultural borders never change. Huntington, for example, is extremely sceptical about the possibility of 'civilisational shifts'. Although Kemal Ataturk sought to create a new 'Western' and 'European' Turkey in the 1920s, the rise of the Islamicist Refah and Welfare parties in the 1990s demonstrates that Turkey is simply reverting to type. Ukraine will therefore, in Huntington's terms, always be a 'kin country' to Russia even if it is a separate state or even nation. Huntington himself places most, but not all, of Ukraine in the same 'Orthodox' civilisational camp as Russia, presumably in likely joint opposition to the West. Although his demarcation line is drawn in several different places, he is basically making the same point as Dugin and Mitrofanov that Galicia is 'European' and the rest of Ukraine is not.[87] Ukraine will therefore never be able to leave the Eurasian space or redefine itself outside it.

Previous chapters, however, have sought to demonstrate both the complexity of Ukraine's actual cultural history and the dangers of assuming that identities are historically predetermined. In any case, Huntington relies too much on religion as a defining feature of cultural identity. Just because a majority of the population uses the Byzantine liturgy, it hardly follows that Ukraine will always be a part of the same 'civilisation' as Russia. The fact that Huntington's views coincide with those of extreme Russian nationalists should make one wary of both.

Finally the 'new Russian geopolitics' has also raided the work of other Western theorists, in particular Halford Mackinder and Karl Haushofer (1869–1946). Writing in 1904, Mackinder famously argued that control of the great natural land fortress of the Eurasian 'heartland' would be the key to world power in the twentieth century. Once its internal communications were developed, the heartland would dominate the 'world island' of Europe, Africa and Asia, leaving the declining sea powers on the coastal periphery which Mackinder termed the 'rimlands'.[88] In his original formulation, this 'heartland', 'the geographical pivot of world history' from the age of the Mongols to the Russian empire, corresponded roughly to the area from the Volga to Mongolia. In his revised definition of 1919, Eastern Europe, including Ukraine, was the key to the 'heartland'.

Russian nationalists have tried to use Mackinder's work to argue that Ukraine is an essential part of the geographical core of their Eurasian 'heartland' or 'internal continental space' and a vital means of access to the rimlands. An 'Atlantic' Ukraine would therefore be a massive blow to Russian security.[89] Ironically, this Russian view is only the inverse of Brzezinski's argument that Ukraine is one of Eurasia's five key 'geopolitical pivots'. The space that Brzezinski wishes to enter is the space that Dugin wishes to defend. Many Ukrainians are therefore understandably critical of Dugin's version of Mackinder.[90] They are presumably unaware that Mackinder actually visited 'South Russia' in 1919–20 and that in a scheme laid before the British cabinet in 1920 he included an independent Ukraine as one of the key pivots of a new Europe (see the map below). The cabinet's grounds for declining to support Mackinder's proposals (although H.A.L. Fisher called them 'absurd' and left early) were simply that they had come too late and the British had no appetite for a further war.[91]

Ill. 23. Halford Mackinder's plan for a new Eastern Europe, 1919–20.

Dugin and Zhirinovskii have also flirted with the works of Karl Haushofer. This latter's 1920s vision of a global 'New Order' envisaged three 'panregions' or 'continental blocks', dividing Africa-Eurasia into respective zones of influence along meridional axes to their south. The three blocks would be based in Berlin, Moscow and Tokyo, with Germany dominating Europe and potentially Africa (Anglo-Saxon sea power permitting), Moscow hegemonic in the continental core of Eurasia and Japan building an 'Indo-Pacific sphere', although India and other parts of the Anglo-Saxon colonial world might pass into the Soviet orbit. Haushofer's scheme suits modern Russian nationalist thinking because, like Mackinder's vision, it offers Moscow a reserved domain of influence, this time because of its emphasis on a *southerly* projection of power.[92] In the modern 'New World Order', the western power is America and the east is dominated by the emergent Pacific powers. Once again, Russia will have to dominate the space in between if it is to survive and prosper. Control of Ukraine, as the traditional 'gateway to the south' and the Mediterranean world, is the vital first step in such a task.

Russia Imagining Ukraine: Moderate Voices

The schemes of Dugin, Zhirinovskii and Mitrofanov can all too easily be dismissed as fantastical. However, because they are deeply rooted in Russia's existential view of itself, these fantasies are likely to recur. On the other hand, not all Russians are nationalists. Nor has nationalist rhetoric towards Ukraine always been matched by Russia's actions. In fact, the most important feature of Ukrainian-Russian relations since 1991 has been a gradual, if often crab-like, groping towards some sort of coexistence. As Russian deputy premier Oleg Soskovets remarked in 1995, 'it is high time to get used to the fact that Ukraine is a sovereign state and that it is entitled to decide on its internal issues independently.'[93] The problem is that there is no real underlying geopolitical or historiographical articulation of this attitude; its very essence is that it has yet to be properly expressed. This leaves the field clear for the noisy voices of the right. It is significant that Russia's liberal and centrist parties have in the main been deafeningly silent on the Ukrainian issue.

The lacunae in the pragmatists' approach were well exposed in a November 1997 radio address given by Yeltsin on relations with Ukraine. Yeltsin built his talk around a typically folksy reference to one of Gogol's short stories, *The Tale of How Ivan Ivanovich Quarrelled with Ivan Nikiforovich* (1835) or 'The Two Ivans' for short, about a dispute between two dim-witted friends that begins over an imagined insult, but is sustained through litigation and failed attempts at reconciliation until old age. Gogol, Yeltsin stressed, was 'our common legacy . . . both our peoples are equally proud of him'. 'It is not for us [Ukraine and Russia] to imitate Gogol's famous heroes. Remember how Ivan Ivanovich quarrelled with Ivan Nikiforovich and how easily they destroyed their old friendship over a trifle.'

Yeltsin's moral is clear, if confused. Sibling peoples like Ukraine and Russia are too close to fight. In the same address, Yeltsin spoke of how 'Russians and Ukrainians lived in a communal flat, so to speak. Our separation was painful. We had to divide the indivisible and test the resistance of normal human, even family, links. Some even took it into their heads to divide our common historical legacy . . . we cannot get it out of our systems that the Ukrainians are the same as we are. That is our destiny, our common destiny.'[94] One author has seen in this a characteristic Russian tendency to over-'intimatise' relations with Ukraine (the use of metaphors of love, painful divorce, family, brotherhood) and a fixation with the 'Siamese twin' complex (neither can exist without the other).[95] The point of Gogol's story, however, is that quarrels can become self-sustaining. In any case, in the original story both men were Ukrainian (though neither is portrayed particularly sympathetically) and one of the original causes of their dispute was about noble status, in essence about who was the truer Cossack.

The keystone 1997 Russia-Ukraine treaty is also illustrative of Russia's continued underlying confusion. On the one hand, by signing the treaty (eventually) Russia gave an unequivocal recognition of Ukrainian *statehood*, if only for ten years. The treaty described Ukraine and Russia unambiguously as 'equal sovereign states . . . building relations on the basis of the principles of mutual respect for sovereign equality, territorial integrity, inviolability of borders, peaceful regulation of disputes, the non-use of force or the threat of force, including economic and other forms of pressure, the right of peoples freely to control their fate, non-interference in internal affairs.' On the other hand, many Russians still seem reluctant to let go of their doubts as to the underlying existence of a Ukrainian *nation* and insisted on a reference in the preamble to the treaty stating that it was based 'on the close links which have historically developed, the relations of friendship and cooperation between the people of Ukraine and Russia'.[96] While this may be existentially satisfying, it is meaningless in terms of international law. The Russians may find that they have agreed to more than they thought. Significantly, the agreement took almost a year to be ratified by the Russian Duma after passing through the Ukrainian Rada with relative ease.[97]

Moderate Russians have yet to develop an appropriate vision of Ukrainian space. Moreover, since around 1993, pragmatists have been steadily losing ground to nationalists in their influence on Russia's overall foreign policy vision. Herein lies many Ukrainians' justifiable fear that recent *rapprochement* is built on shaky foundations.

Ukraine Imagining Russia

As in the nineteenth century, there is a much greater diversity of visions on the Ukrainian side in contrast to the relative consensus in Russian nationalism. These visions range from rabid Russophobia in western Ukraine to equally Ukrainophobic Russian nationalism in Crimea. The former has built on the myth developed in the nineteenth and early twentieth centuries of Russia as an 'anti-Occidental' power, the antithesis of European civilisation (or sometimes even as an 'anti-civilisational' or 'civilisationally marginal' power). According to one recent book published in Lviv by the writer Roman Kis, Russia's impressive list of sins includes the following: 'Messianism, chiliasm, utopianism, "ideokratiia", universalism, "symphonism", charismatism, "prophetism", hegemonism, expansionism, militarism, ethnocentrism, xenophobia, Aesopianism [given Lenin's advice to the Bolsheviks to say one thing and mean another], "vaalism" [idol-worship], soteriolism [salvationism], Gnosticism [the belief in the reality of their own privileged transcendental knowledge], eschatologism and a statism "deprived of all individuality".'[98] This is a vision shared at least in part with many other Central and East European intellectuals and mythologists (and many Atlanticists), such as Milan Kundera and Richard Pipes. The cover of a second Ukrainian book called *The Mentality of the Horde*,[99] assembles many of the same myths in its montage. The road to Moscow, the 'third Rome', the capital of anti-European 'Eurasia' or 'Azopa', is paved with skulls; dark clouds and ravens hover above its barren land; the tsarist eagle is crowned with the symbol of the Communist Party to stress that Russian imperialism comes in many guises (the other double-headed eagle on the signpost to the 'third Rome' is made to look like a Nazi crest), but all have governed through the noose and the axe (see also the nationalist cartoons on page 180).

Yurii Lypa liked to argue that Russia's natural authoritarianism was a direct consequence of its artificial nature as a state. Russia's superficial 'ethnic unity was only an outer skin, the result of the strident centralisation of its government', which would collapse as soon as the latter was removed.[100] The Russian phrase may have it that *Russkoe bol'she Rossii*, best translated as '[that which is] Russian is more than [that which is] Russia', but Lypa argued the truth was the other way around. Russia, not Ukraine, 'makes no geopolitical sense'. In his book *The Division of Russia* (1941) Lypa predicted that Russia would eventually collapse into four parts along two axes, one running north–south through the Ural mountains and the other east–west from Vladivostok to the Ukrainian-Belarusian border (see the map on page 309). In the north–west quadrant, Russia proper, or 'Muscovy', would be reduced to its boundaries at the time of Ivan the Terrible's conquest of Kazan (according to Lypa, 'the borders of 1553 are the natural borders of

Ill. 24. Yurii Lypa, The Division of Russia, 1941.

Muscovy').[101] Siberia would go its own way in the north-east, as would Central Asia in the south-east, leaving the south-west quadrant to Ukraine as a natural 'zone of influence'. In other words, the whole of Russia's 'soft underbelly' in the lower Volga and Caucasus regions was a natural space for the expansion of Ukrainian power. Ukraine should therefore work to speed up Russia's collapse, from which it stands to be one of the prime beneficiaries. Radical or not, Lypa's vision is not too dissimilar to Brzezinski's prediction of a future Russia collapsing into a decentralised confederation of European Russia (Muscovy), Siberia and a Far Eastern Republic (see page 293).[102]

At the other extreme lie the Communist Party of Ukraine (CPU), the biggest party at the 1990, 1994 and 1998 elections, and smaller Russophile groups such as the Civic Congress or SLOn, who advocate views that are little different from those of modern-day Russian 'Eurasian nationalists' and of course are the polar opposite of those of Ukrainian 'Occidentalists'. Amongst the leadership of the CPU, Borys Oliinyk for example has argued that in a world still dominated by 'civil-isational' divides, Ukraine and Russia are jointly part of Orthodox rather than European civilisation, in potential conflict with both the lib-eral West and the Islamic South.[103] The idea of common enemies is still a powerful factor for many. Pan-Slavic analysts in Crimea have echoed Russian nationalist fears of the threat of 'the formation of an unbroken belt of Turkic states along the line Ankara-Baku-Ashkabad-Tashkent-Alma-Aty with the potential to spread along the territory of the High Altai, Tuva and Buriat-Mongolia', eventually reaching the Far East and creeping up the Russian spine via Tatarstan.[104] In an extraordinary open letter to Solzhenitsyn published in the summer of 1998, Ukraine's former prime minister Pavlo Lazarenko argued from his home base in the eastern city of Dnipropetrovsk that Ukraine and Russia should unite in the struggle against both the West (international finance) and the South (Islam).[105] Others have echoed Ziuganov's neo-Marxist sentiment that the new 'global *bandokratiia*' (the ruling bandit class) in the West is seeking a form of colonial hegemony over both Ukraine and Russia for the purposes of raw-material and energy extraction, even the 'de-industrialisation' of Ukraine.[106]

Although Russian nationalist parties are not very popular in Ukraine, this kind of popular pan-(east) Slavism is still a significant social force. The official policy of the Communist Party of Ukraine, even as late as the 1998/9 elections, was 'the voluntary creation of an equal Union of fraternal peoples' on the territory of the former USSR – and the Communists remain Ukraine's largest party by far.[107] Even the Ukrainian Socialists have cited Huntington in support of a call to defend 'Orthodox Slavic civilisation' through the creation of a local equivalent of the Organisation of African Unity.[108] A potent reminder of this sentiment was provided in March 1999, when the Ukrainian parliament summoned up an unexpectedly large majority of 231 to 46 to condemn NATO action in Kosovo. As the war unfolded, Kuchma tried to create a more balanced policy, but the residual strength of popular pan-Slavism was a surprise to many who had noted only the conversion of Ukrainian elites to the 'European idea'.[109]

Conclusions

In the 1920s Mykola Khylovyi argued that Ukraine could choose 'psychological Europe' through an act of will alone. Given Ukraine's complex historical past, this would be an impressive feat. Galicia may be more or less unambiguously Central European, but the rest of Ukraine is not. Many Ukrainians continue to look east, or at least simultaneously east and west. Ukraine is unquestionably being pulled towards Europe at the moment, but this is largely a function of the current imbalance of power between Moscow and the West and of the predominance of elite over mass opinion in Ukraine. Pro-European attitudes are more widespread than they were, but Ukraine is still a culturally divided country, and differences of geopolitical vision retain their potential to influence politics at all levels.

Ukraine would like to reshape current ideas of 'Europe' to allow for its inclusion, but it is unable to press for this as unambiguously as it might. Russian calls for 'reintegration' still find an echo in Ukraine, though echoes of course fade in time. After 1994 discussion of Ukraine's 'eastern option' largely moved into opposition circles, but it revived in 1999, largely because the underlying cultural divisions are little changed. Ukraine's final choice is even more important to the New Europe, although the possibility that it might never be able to make a definite decision also remains very real.

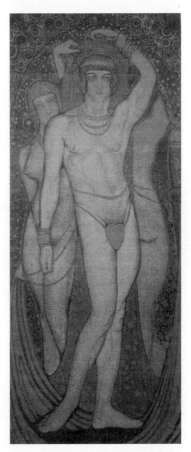

Plate 28 (*right*). The Ukrainian Beardsley: Vsevolod Maksymovych's *The Two*, 1913.

Plate 29. Anatolii Petrytskyi, *Young Woman in the Catacombs*, 1921 – notable for its vibrant 'Ukrainian' colours.

Plate 30 (*right*). Mariia Syniakova (a follower of Boichuk), *Bomb*, 1916.

Plate 31. David Burliuk (another 'Boichukist'), *Carousel*, 1921.

Plate 32 (*left*). Vasyl Yermelov, *A* (for Avant-garde), 1928.

Plate 33. The joys of labour: Ivan Pashchyn's *The Smiths*, 1930.

Plate 34. Kasimir Malevich's haunting *The Running Man*, 1933–4, here interpreted as an indictment of the Great Famine.

Plate 35. The finest hour of the 'Soviet nation': Mykhailo Khmelko's, *Triumph of the Conquering People*, 1949.

Plate 36. Khmelko's vision of east Slavic 'Eternal Unity', 1954.

Plate 37 (*above*). Wartime posters attempt a broad appeal: the Soviet army is urged, 'Forward, Brave Successors of Bohdan!' with Kiev's statue to Khmelnytskyi in the background, 1944.

Plate 38. An appeal: 'To Battle – O Slavs!', 1942, a sharp contrast to Stalin's 1945 victory toast to the 'Great Russian people'.

Plate 39 (*right*). 'Ukraine is Free!', 1944. A Soviet, not a Ukrainian, nationalist force is depicted uniting Ukrainian territory and marching onwards to Berlin. The borders shown are those of 1939–41, not those settled in 1944–5.

Plate 40. A classic of Ukrainian Socialist Realism: Tetiana Yablonska's *Bread*, 1949 – awarded the Stalin Prize in 1950 as a reward for abandoning earlier 'Impressionist' tendencies.

Plate 43. Khmelnytskyi Square, Kiev, including the Tsarist statue to the Cossack leader and the belltower of St Sofiia's.

facing page

Plate 41. The rebuilt monastery of St Michael of the Golden Domes, Kiev, the centrepiece of Kuchma's election broadcasts in 1999.

Plate 42. A new version of Yaroslav the Wise, Ukrainian nation-builder, Kiev.

Plate 44. Oles Semerniia, *My Town*, 1982.

Plate 45. Another version of Yaroslav the Wise, with 'Cossack moustache', on the two-hryvnia note introduced in 1996.

Plate 46. The barricades in Kyiv during the 'Revolution of Dignity', February 2014

Plate 47. Jamala wins the Eurovision Song Contest for Ukraine in 2016 with her song '1944', about the Soviet Deportation of the Crimean Tatars. In 2021 Ukraine passed a law recognising the Crimean Tatars as the indigenous people of Crimea.

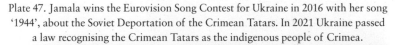

Plate 48. President Poroshenko looks on as the new Orthodox Church of Ukraine is established at a Sobor in St Sofiia, Kyiv in December 2018.

Plate 49. New monument to Kyiv's protector the Archangel Michael, showing the city as a constellation of churches.

Plate 50. An explosion over Maidan during the opening hours of the Russian invasion in February 2022.

Plate 51. President Zelenskyi makes a characteristic online video on Kyiv's empty main street Khreshchatyk, approaching the Maidan.

Plate 52. St George depicted as a Cossack, fighting off the Russian double-headed eagle in east Ukraine, 2015.

Plate 53. The 1954 Friendship Monument is dismantled in 2022 (for the original, see Plate 9).

14

The Orange Revolution and its Aftermath

The Gongadze Scandal, 2000–1

Leonid Kuchma achieved at least a semblance of economic order on taking office in 1994, and a new currency and constitution by 1996. However his second term (1999–2004) was marked by political drift and a reversion to semi-authoritarianism and corruption at the highest levels. Most notorious was the 'Gongadze scandal', after the headless body of an opposition journalist (Hryhorii Gongadze, the editor of Ukraine's first campaigning internet site, 'Ukrainian Truth') was discovered in a forest outside Kiev in November 2000. The scandal multiplied with the release of tapes supposedly secretly recorded in Kuchma's presidential office by one of his own security guards, Major Mykola Melnychenko, who claimed to have used a personal recorder hidden under a settee. On the tapes Kuchma was heard ordering Gongadze's beating or kidnapping – if not his actual murder – amidst hours of other dialogue full of obscenities, threats, corruption and general sleaze. Kuchma calls one opponent a 'fucking Yiddish sprout' and demands that another be 'hung by the balls'. His attitude to the rule of law was revealed succinctly: 'judges, in general, are fuckers'.[1]

Melnychenko fled to the West with his treasure trove some time between Gongadze's disappearance on 16 September and the body's discovery on 3 November. His exact schedule and role in precipitating the scandal is still unclear. Melnychenko originally claimed to have acted alone, but from his peripatetic exile in first the Czech Republic and then the USA he increasingly hinted at the involvement of rival 'oligarchs'. Sadly, he soon got caught up in their schemes, accepting money from Boris Berezovskii for transcribing the tapes, allegedly concocting some new releases,[2] and ultimately making an inglorious return to Ukraine in November 2005.

The revelations were highly damaging. The affair led to Ukraine's de facto diplomatic isolation by the West. The USA took particular exception to the 'Kolchuha' tapes released in September 2002, which appeared to show that Kuchma had secretly approved the sale of a sophisticated radar system to Iraq on the eve of the 2003 war (Kolchuha means 'chainmail' – the system was never found). At a NATO summit in 2002, countries had to be labelled in French so that Kuchma for Ukraine would not sit next to Bush for the USA or Blair for the UK. The new Russian President Vladimir Putin, on the other hand, became Kuchma's best friend, skilfully exploiting Ukraine's weakness to extend Russia's diplomatic and economic influence.

A protest campaign dubbed 'Ukraine without Kuchma' was organised over the winter of 2000–1, but it began from a low ebb. The demonstrations in Kiev never topped more than 30,000, perhaps due to the coldness of that winter. The authorities organised a cover-up, demonised the opposition in the mass media, and infiltrated its ranks with agents provocateurs to provide the necessary scenes of violent protest at the last demonstrations in March 2001, providing them with the justification they needed for a crackdown. So Ukraine was stuck with Kuchma – though in the long run the campaign would empower a new opposition. Lessons were learnt, and many of the same leaders would be prominent in the protest campaign that became the Orange Revolution in 2004.

Economic Recovery

Another paradox was that a reformist government had been in office since December 1999, although the leaders of the street protests were disappointed at the lack of support from the new Prime Minister Viktor Yushchenko. As a former head of the National Bank, Yushchenko saw his priority as reforming the economy rather than the political system, hoping to undermine or win over some of Ukraine's 'oligarchs' even after the Gongadze scandal broke. According to the arguments advanced by his more articulate supporters, the suddenly spectacularly rich post-Soviet elite had corrupted the political system to such an extent that they would simply crush any revolutionary challenge to their rule. Normal politics would never be possible until Ukraine developed normal business practice. Yushchenko's critics argued that this approach would have the opposite effect. The new elite was acquiring the power to reproduce itself, and would swallow up any challengers who were not politically strong enough to change the rules of the game. Hence his controversial decision to appoint none other than Yuliia Tymoshenko as Deputy Prime Minister, the 'gas princess' who had once worked hand in glove with the notorious Pavlo Lazarenko, with a brief to clean up the energy sector. Tymoshenko, in short, knew exactly how the system worked, and could dismantle it from inside.

Economic recovery was clearly long overdue. Not only did Ukraine lose 60% of official GDP in the 1990s, but it was also one of the last east European states to resume growth. Russia had done so in 1997 (before another short-term collapse in 1998), Belarus in 1996. Ukraine had to wait until 2000, but then there were eight long years of boom, despite a dip in 2005.

Not surprisingly, the Yushchenko-Tymoshenko tandem claimed credit for the initial turnaround, attributing it to reforms concentrated on the domestic economy. An attack on tax breaks and payment in kind, and a new round of more transparent privatisations, were both laudable in themselves and, by 'remonetising' the state budget, provided the funds to pay off wage and pension arrears. Tymoshenko's energy sector reforms removed an estimated $4 billion of rent-seeking from gas and electricity trading. Deregulation eased, though did not end, the administrative and harassment burdens on small and medium businesses. A ground-breaking agricultural reform, albeit one that stopped short of allowing the full trading of land, promised to unlock the long-neglected potential of the Ukrainian 'black earth'.

Consumption duly recovered and GDP figures swung dramatically from −0.2% in 1999 to +5.9% in 2000. Growth averaged 7.5% over the next eight years – more than both Russia and Poland. Critics claimed recovery was due to trading improvements: the devaluation of the Ukrainian currency in 1998, a local export boom as markets recovered in neighbouring markets after their own parallel devaluations and rising world demand for key Ukrainian products such as steel. The Ukrainian boom, in other words, was made in Russia and China.

Change in Ukrainian GDP, 1999–2009, as a percentage

1999	−0.2
2000	+5.9
2001	+9.1
2002	+5.2
2003	+9.6
2004	+12.1
2005	+2.7
2006	+7.3
2007	+7.6
2008	+1.8
2009	−5.0 to −12 forecast

Source: http://www.bank.gov.ua/Engl/Macro/

But it was undoubtedly a boom, at least in the major cities. It had to be, as many of the pathologies, inefficiencies and corrupt practices of the 1990s remained. In some areas they got worse, with those clans that emerged strongest from the property wars of the 1990s seeking to impose victors' justice and scoop up all the spoils. Ongoing insider privatisation led to the creation of new empires in the 2000s, particularly in the steel industry. Growth was also lopsided, with too much reliance on quantitative exports such as steel and chemicals, a credit boom and property bubble in the big cities and not enough investment or product diversification. External debt rose from $29 billion to $105.4 billion in 2008, with Ukrainian banks' share rising from $2.4 billion to $42 billion. There was widespread privatisation in the small business and service sector, but Soviet company towns simply swapped dictatorial party bosses for dictatorial 'oligarchs' – often the same man in a nicer suit. Agriculture, however, forged ahead – by 2008 the annual grain harvest was 46 million tonnes, up from 26 million in 1999 – and a middle class began to appear. Ukrainians learned to love to shop as huge new malls appeared overnight, often underground. But the dispossessed of the 1990s and the late Soviet era were still around. Total economic growth between 2000–8 barely took Ukraine back to its initial starting point in 1991. Nevertheless compared with the military domination of the old Soviet economy for many and its consumer shortages and value-subtracting absurdities, real standards of living were undoubtedly higher for many.

But for almost a decade the strength of growth floated many of these problems along. The hybrid Ukrainian economy, however, increasingly supported three types of politics: one was based in the patronage and dependency networks of the old Soviet system; another in the populism that appealed mainly, if not exclusively, to economic 'losers'; while the third appealed to the nascent middle class. The elite politics of the 'oligarchs' was harder to predict. Many hoped that in time they would seek respectability and the rule of law, but this was based on the assumption that they had grabbed all that they could and that others had no incentive to grab it off them.

The 2002 Elections

Yushchenko's cautious tactics also reflected a specifically Ukrainian problem, namely his desire to break out of the ghetto of the traditional 'national-democratic' opposition, which had never won an election, peaking at around 25% of the vote in the Gorbachev era before declining to about 10% in 1994 and 1998, and less than 5% in 1999. Hence his new model pragmatism was designed to transcend traditional cultural and linguistic nationalism (which is why Yushchenko ultimately chose orange, rather than the blue and yellow of the national flag, for his campaign colours in 2004). Yushchenko campaigned vaguely on social issues and the old favourite of 'time for change'. In other words, before he became leader of the Orange Revolution, Yushchenko wasn't exactly proposing revolution.

Many in the old regime assumed his quiet style meant he would quietly fit in with their plans. They forced him out of office in April 2001. The more dangerous Tymoshenko was fired from government three months earlier and was even briefly imprisoned in February to prevent her short-lived 'National Salvation Committee' taking over the leadership of the street protests.

Yushchenko launched a new party, dubbed 'Our Ukraine', for the parliamentary elections due in March 2002. He brought on board as many turncoats and financiers as he could, some from businesses alienated from the regime and others that soon found themselves in the same position once the government punished their desertion. Other defectors such as the former komsomol businessman Oleksandr Zinchenko, Yushchneko's new campaign chief, brought with them too much of the political culture of the old regime. For a while it was even possible to think that Our Ukraine could become the local version of Russia's 'Unity' (set up by Yeltsin's courtiers to storm the elections on the eve of his departure in 1999) – the designated successor party that Kuchma had yet to create. Nevertheless, Our Ukraine topped the poll with 23.6%.

Tymoshenko, on the other hand, radicalised by her two-month spell in Kiev's less-than-glamorous Lukianivska prison where 'Iron' Felix Dzerzhinsky (founder of the Cheka) had once also served time, set up a much more personal party, the 'Block of Yuliia Tymoshenko', whose Ukrainian acronym 'BYuT' or 'BYT' was supposed to remind voters of her undoubted glamour. BYT won 7.3%. The Socialist Party won another 6.9%, led by Oleksandr Moroz, who, as the biggest loser from the 1999 election, had been all too willing to publicise Melnychenko's initial revelations. On the other side of the fence, the two main pro-Kuchma parties, 'For a United Ukraine', which elbowed aside Our Ukraine to become the new 'party of power', and the 'Social-Democratic Party (united)', a brazenly fake name for the party of the corrupt Kiev business elite, won only 11.8% and 6.3% – a pretty poor performance as neither won many voluntary votes.

However, the opposition was unable to take control of parliament. The Communist Party was still showing some signs of life and won 20%, but it was under the influence of pro-government parties based in east Ukraine. The government parties used 'administrative resources' and outright vote-buying to win the vast majority of the local constituencies, and then bought up most of the 83 originally elected as independents (at a slightly higher price). As this was still not enough, bribery and intimidation were used to thin the opposition's ranks as well. Too many of Yushchenko's invitees immediately jumped ship. If his party was supposed to be a 'reserve aerodrome' (*zapasnyi aerodrom*) for potential defectors from the ruling elite, heavy government bombardment meant that it was hardly a safe haven, and there was too much flight in the other direction. Others stayed put but dictated their terms, like Petro Poroshenko, Ukraine's 'chocolate king'. For the next two years Yushchenko's poll ratings were steady but unspectacular.

The regime therefore controlled parliament, even though it had lost the election. Thus they also expected to win the key presidential election due in 2004, regardless of whether they actually won it or not, but it was clear the real contest would be close.

The Orange Revolution

The authorities toyed with various options in the run-up to the election. In December 2003 the Constitutional Court was persuaded to rule on a spurious technicality that Kuchma could stand for a third term. But he was always too unpopular and often too ill to run. The authorities tried to fix the constitution in April 2004, so that any incoming president would have much less power. The attempt fell only six votes short of the two-thirds majority required in parliament, with 294 votes out of 450, rather than the 300 needed.

The third option for the regime was to impose a single candidate on its disunited supporters. The choice fell on the sitting prime minister Viktor Yanukovych who represented the strongest regional clan, the Party of Regions from Donetsk. Since the fall of Lazarenko in 1999 (who came from Dnipropetrovsk), the Donetsk group had restored the pre-eminence it briefly enjoyed in 1993–4, assisted by the prominent role of their steel exports in Ukraine's recovering economy. The Donetsk group were also Ukraine's toughest tough guys, having honed their skills in the gangster wars of the 1990s, which were particularly vicious in Ukraine's 'wild east', home to both the Soviet Union's model worker Aleksei Stakhanov and those who preferred brute force to brute strength. The Donetsk group simply imposed Yanukovych on a weakened Kuchma in November 2002, after a brief caretaker premiership by Yushchenko's technocratic successor Anatolii Kinakh.

However, the Donbas's considerable financial resources and thuggish political culture alienated many in the ruling elite. For the broader public, they also turned Yushchenko's vices into virtues. Neutral voters clearly preferred his quiet and pragmatic style, especially after Tymoshenko's decision not to stand (at least not this time). The two signed a public agreement to form a coalition they dubbed the 'Force of the People' in July 2004. Yanukovych also made the mistake of trying to act tough in public, posing as the 'Ukrainian Putin'. Apart from physically, the relatively short Putin, the former chekist, looked down on the burly Yanukovych, a former 'zek' (the Soviet term for camp inmate – Yanukovych had served time for robbery and serious bodily harm in his wayward youth). Ukraine does not have the same cult of authority as Russia, as Ukrainians are too used to power being exercised elsewhere. Nevertheless, although relatively late to enter in the campaign, Putin endorsed a populist Russophile operation: a doubling of pensions, promises to upgrade the status of the Russian language and attacks on the USA and NATO, backed up by Russian promises of VAT waivers on Ukrainian exports and easier travel to Russia for work. This was all designed to appeal to voters in east Ukraine, which it did, but voter intimidation, manipulation and fraud embedded in Donetsk political culture were losing votes elsewhere.

The Yanukovych campaign also used 'political technology'. No less than thirteen candidates in the election were fakes: four were faux-extreme nationalists designed to blacken Yushchenko by campaigning in unsolicited support; three were leftist 'locomotives' designed to mobilise voters in east Ukraine in the first round of the election and then pass their votes on to Yanukovych in the second round; six were 'technical candidates', whose campaigns did not really exist, but whose presence on the ballot created a solid block of Yanukovych supporters on local election committees, primed to overlook any fraud in his favour.

Most worryingly, the authorities seemed to be toying with a 'strategy of tension' to swing the poll. On 12 August 2004, during a campaign trip in southern Ukraine, Yushchenko's campaign car was almost forced off the road by a truck. A bomb went off on 20 August in a market on the edge of Kiev, killing one person and injuring eleven, and was immediately blamed on 'extremist supporters' of Yushchenko. Most mysteriously, late on the evening of 5 September, Yushchenko went to a secret meeting with the heads of the Security Service of Ukraine (SBU). The circumstances were murky, but the aim was clear – to persuade the SBU to stay out of the authorities' manipulative schemes. One strange thing about the meeting is that Yushchenko seems to have got what he wanted – and more. By election time, one faction in the SBU was actually feeding his camp with secret information on voting fraud. The September meeting, which was held at the private dacha of Volodymyr Satsiuk, deputy head of the SBU, was apparently also jovial, at least judging by the amount of alcohol consumed: beer, vodka and a final round of cognac. But Yushchenko rapidly fell ill. He was rushed to Austria on 9 September for the first of several visits to a private clinic, where dioxin poisoning was eventually diagnosed. This was not before the local media had poured scorn on Yushchenko's 'hangover', 'herpes', botched 'botox' or self-inflicted stunt. But dioxin it certainly was: Yushchenko's once handsome face was terribly disfigured and he had apparently come close to death. His dramatic return from Austria led to a surge of public support.

The authorities had expected one or more of their tactics to deliver a knockout blow, but they had grown used to the relatively easy election fixes of 1999 and 2002. They now made the hubristic calculation that they simply needed more fraud. The counting of the first round vote lasted for ten days and was suspended twice as the Election Commission tried to manipulate the books. But Yushchenko still ended up officially ahead, by 39.9% compared to Yanukovych's 39.3% (see table E.1). Socialist leader Oleksandr Moroz came third and agreed to back Yushchenko, but only if the latter agreed to support Moroz's pet project of constitutional reform. Anatolii Kinakh, the former prime minister and leader of the centrist 'Industrialists' Party', also climbed on board. The perennial trouble-maker Nataliia Vitrenko supported Yanukovych, as did the fake version of the Communist Party, backed by the Party of Regions and led by Oleksandr Yakovenko. The 'official' Communist Party led by Petro Symonenko did so with more reluctance, as it claimed Yanukovych had stolen votes from them all over east Ukraine.

The run-off three weeks later on 20 November was therefore always going to be close. Yanukovych had briefly led the polls in October, but most surveys now put Yushchenko about five points ahead in a straight fight. On the other hand, the authorities had decided that Yanukovych was going to win. The opposition and the youth movement Pora had decided to protest. Pora had already set up a tent camp in downtown Kiev, outside the main private university. Something had to give.

The authorities attempted a display of *force majeure*. Instead of the ten days for the first count, the second one was conducted in less than ten hours. Over a million extra votes were added to the count overnight, mainly in Donetsk, where turnout supposedly soared from 78% to 97%. When people went to bed, they were told 78.7% had voted nationally; when they woke up it was 80.7%. The corrupted Election Commission attempted to declare Yanukovych the winner by 49.5% to 46.6%. But a massive exit poll, with 15,000 interviewees and therefore a minimal margin of error, indicated that Yushchenko had won by 53.7% to 43.3%.

However, even the opposition did not expect the torrent of protest unleashed by the crudity of the fraud. Many in the regime were already uneasy about the aggressive tactics used by the Donetsk group, but the potential hard-liners were out-manoeuvred by the sheer numbers who poured on to the streets of Kiev and elsewhere the next morning (21 November) – over 100,000 by the end of the day, and more than 500,000 by day three. Radical repressive measures were apparently not considered until a week into the protests.

Frustration had been building up for years. The protest organisers had also learnt the lessons of the failure of the 'Ukraine without Kuchma'

Table E.1: Ukrainian Presidential Election, 2004

First Round, 31 October 2004		Second Round, 20 November 2004		Third Round, 26 December 2004	
Viktor Yushchenko	39.9%	Yushchenko	46.6%	Yushchenko	51.2%
Viktor Yanukovych	39.3%	Yanukovych	49.5%	Yanukovych	44.2%
Oleksandr Moroz	5.8%				
Petro Symonenko	5%				
Nataliia Vitrenko	1.5%				
Anatolii Kinakh	0.9%				
Oleksandr Yakovenko	0.8%				
Others	1.7%				
Against all	2%	Against all	2.3%	Against all	2.3%
Invalid Votes	3%	Invalid Votes	1.6%	Invalid Votes	1.5%

campaign in 2001. Not only was protest strictly non-violent, there was also a deliberate attempt to create a carnival atmosphere once the protest epicentre moved to Kiev's main square, 'the Maidan'. There was music and coordinated colour, with hundreds of thousands decked in Yushchenko's orange campaign scarves and hats and waving a sea of orange flags. Tymoshenko, who had not run in the election, was now in her element. Despite her rabble-rousing glamour, Yushchenko was then seen as an electable moderate, but she was not. During the protests, however, she was carried away by her own rhetoric and frequently urged radical missteps, such as the storming of parliament or the presidential administration, which might have caused a bloodbath. Such plans were also unrealistic. According to Taras Stetskiv, who was in charge on the ground, 'The most absurd plan called for the placing of ladders on the cordon of police, and that way, scale the ladders into the building, like they stormed castles during medieval times.'[3] The revolution, cast in Yushchenko's image, was not supposed to be revolutionary. Tymoshenko's incautious rhetoric led to constant rows with Stetskiv and the young Socialist leader Yurii Lutsenko (later interior minister), who had to use their contacts with the police and armed forces to assure them that no one was planning to attack them. Yushchenko, on the other hand, felt honour-bound to avert a violent crackdown, even if Kuchma was again playing with the much darker intentions of those behind him, such as his strong-arm chief-of-staff Viktor Medvedchuk.

With the authorities caught off guard, the sheer number of people on the Maidan became an immovable force, but they were difficult to direct as an active agent of a more ambitious revolution. Violent dispersal was contemplated after a week of protests, on the night of Sunday, 27 November, but it was already too late. The costs of repression were now too high and protest ensued all down the chain of command, although a flurry of private phone calls was still necessary to make sure troops returned to barracks.

The authorities therefore sought countervailing power elsewhere. On 28 November, east Ukrainian leaders gathered at a special conference in the Donbas mining town of Severodonetsk, and made radical noises about not recognising an 'orange coup', demanding a federal Ukraine, and threatening to split the country in two. In retrospect this was a blatant ploy to gain leverage, but at the time many treated the threat seriously. It seems to have spooked Yushchenko back towards the negotiating table.

Compromise was also facilitated by Polish-led international mediation. By most accounts, the idea of an international mission was proposed by the Polish President Aleksander Kwaśnicwski and his Lithuanian counterpart Valdas Adamkus, who then persuaded Javier Solana to join in, semi-officially, for the EU. The Poles also caught the Russians unawares. Although Putin sent Boris Gryzlov, the Chair of the Duma, Russia was still reeling from the shock of the protests. The mission also arrived relatively early, on 25 November, when the initial protests might otherwise have been losing momentum. They created a 'round table' process that kept both sides talking, though by early December they were talking in circles.

The final track was the Supreme Court, which began a review of the elections on 29 November. Yanukovych's lawyers made a reasonably strong case that Yushchenko was exploiting the vast crowds to prevent due process – there was a sort of revolution taking place after all. The former jailbird's lawyers argued that the televised hearings meant the judges were influenced by the atmosphere on the streets. But the Court also heard incontrovertible evidence of election fraud, some of it allegedly supplied by the SBU. However, the authorities expected a long hearing. Instead, the Supreme Court suddenly broke the deadlock on 3 December by condemning the fraudulent second round and ordering a repeat vote, which was eventually settled for 26 December. (Optimists hoped that this would be Ukraine's *Marbury v Madison* moment – a landmark decision enshrining a tradition of judicial independence. They would be disappointed.)

The decision completely changed the political game. The authorities' hand was drastically weakened. But the 'Revolution' now moved into its most controversial phase. From a position of strength, Yushchenko accepted a compromise 'package' adopted by parliament on 8 December. The authorities agreed to a new election law and Election Commission to facilitate a free and fair repeat vote on 26 December, but only in return for constitutional reforms very similar to those that had narrowly failed to pass in April. The reforms were to take effect after a year's delay, on 1 January 2006. To critics, Yushchenko gave away the fruits of victory. He could be confident of becoming president in the repeat election, but he would only have one year of full power. From 2006 Ukraine would become a hybrid republic. Parliament would now sit for five years rather than four and dissolution would in theory only be possible if it failed to fulfil its functions, for example, by failing to assemble. All seats would be elected by proportional representation to strengthen the role of parties (though the barrier for entry was reduced from 4% to 3%). Deputies would serve a so-called 'imperative mandate' – if they left their party, as had happened so often in the past, they would cease to serve. The parties would have to form a formal 'majority' which would select the Prime Minister and government, though the president still directly appointed the ministers of defence and foreign affairs and the head of the Security Service, the SBU.

Yushchenko is alleged to have made more far-reaching compromises in private, promising immunity for Kuchma and his entourage if they put the 'separatist' genie back in the bottle – after they themselves had released it. Sviatoslav Piskun, whose only previous achievement was to cover up the Gongadze scandal during his previous term of office in 2002–3, was reappointed as procurator on 10 December 2004: on a spurious technicality, but more importantly on a private understanding that he would not actually prosecute anybody (the constitutional changes absurdly gave more power to this controversial hangover from the Soviet era). On a tape made during the Orange Revolution and released in June 2005, Piskun is apparently heard promising to defend one oligarch as if he were 'family'.[4]

The crowds on the streets outside now thinned. Yushchenko and Yanukovych returned to formal campaign mode, but no one doubted the eventual result. Both sides squabbled over the voting rules, but the 'third round' vote was remarkably similar to the pollsters' estimate of the real vote in the second round, with Yushchenko now beating Yanukovych by 51.2% to 44.2%. Despite all the turmoil of the Orange Revolution, voting patterns had barely changed – this helped confirm the original allegations of fraud. There was no landslide of votes in Yushchenko's favour.

Tymoshenko urged the crowds to stay on until Yushchenko's inauguration day on 23 January 2005, ostensibly to guard against the authorities ratting on the transition deal, but some saw it as blackmail to push her name forward as prime minister. Yushchenko's supporters also allege that on inauguration day itself Tymoshenko packed the crowd with activists primed or paid to chant her name. Yushchenko allegedly tried to back out of appointing her, but his hesitation was trumped by a secret part to the 'Force of the People' agreement signed by the two back in July 2004, which promised Tymoshenko first shot at the premiership. Tymoshenko formed the first 'Orange government' in February 2005.

———

Retrospective radicals have argued that the real revolutionary opportunity was missed in December 2004, when Yushchenko's constitutional compromises snatched defeat out of the jaws of victory. The 'Orange Revolution' can be understood more exactly as a drama in three acts. In Act One, hundreds of thousands of protesters packed the streets of Kiev and other cities. The crowd became a revolutionary actor, trumping the calculations of all sides. In Act Two the story moved on to an agreed settlement between elites, the 'package' agreed behind semi-closed doors on 8 December. In Act Three, the aftermath, Yushchenko made a disastrous decision to avoid 'revolutionary justice'. However, 'bandits to prison' was more than just a slogan. A few key prosecutions, involving at a minimum the perpetrators of the election fraud, Gongadze's killers, and Yushchenko's own mysteriously under-investigated poisoning, would have changed the rules of the game – and were definitely expected at the time by the panicky old guard, several of whom ended up dead in mysterious circumstances.

In December 2004 Heorhii Kirpa, the boss of the Ukrainian railways who had provided trains for Yanukovych voters to travel the country in 'repeat voting', was found dead in a Kiev sauna. Neighbours heard several shots. The chosen method of suicide of Yurii Liakh, head of the Ukrainian Credit Bank, was stabbing himself several times in the neck with a letter opener. In March 2005 the former Interior Minister, Yurii Kravchenko, the key witness in the Gongadze affair, shot himself twice, on the morning he was due to give evidence. Yushchenko bizarrely declared the Gongadze case 'solved', but the only people to be put on trial were three members of his kidnap squad. Their boss, Interior Ministry 'Head of Surveillance' Oleksii Pukach, was allowed to flee to Israel. In June, Ihor Pluzhnykov of the SDPU(o) was found dead in a Czech health spa, aged 46. Several businessmen fled to Russia; the steel baron Rinat Akhmetov spent much of 2005 in comfortable exile in Moscow and the south of France.

Together, Acts Two and Three made a disastrous combination. The package agreement on its own, without the informal amnesty, would not necessarily have strengthened parliament's role as a crook's haven. The informal amnesty on its own would have been less of a problem if the system had been reshaped. Taken together, the old guard survived, returned and prospered. Despite a universal agreement on non-violent protest in 2004, many came to regret that the Orange Revolution was not a bit more revolutionary.

It was not that nothing had changed: Ukraine now had a vibrant civil society. In subsequent years, Russia would do everything it could to prevent the growth of similar 'technologies' at home and elsewhere in the former USSR. Subsequent elections would be free and fair. Ukraine now enjoyed unprecedented media pluralism, to the extent that it became the best place to look for news about Russia. Psychologically, 'people power' mattered too, if only in the sense that the new authorities would spend the next few years paying the price for ignoring it.

Don't Cry for Me Ukraïna: Yuliia and Viktor – Evita and Perón?

However, the Orange Revolution was rotting from within. The role of the crowd made the Revolution potentially revolutionary. The energy and political capital were there in early 2005, but they were wasted. And the story of how they were wasted is probably better told by a play-wright or novelist than a political scientist. (In fact, local writers have tried. In 2006 Yurii Rohoza published a delightfully trashy *roman à clef*, *Kill Yuliia*, featuring a glamorous Prime Minister, called Yuliia, and her thinly disguised enemies, such as 'Pincheruk' the oligarch). It was hubris, human frailty and a clash of personalities that threw the Revolution off course, not social trends or voting patterns. The stage was crowded by the sheer number of clashing egos and corrupt bit-players, though increasingly politics would boil down to the clash between the two very different personalities at the top.

Tymoshenko had sex- and brand-appeal, with the trademark east-European chic and braided hairstyle that Jean-Paul Gaultier plundered for his 2005 fashion show. Yushchenko was branded in a different way, better known for the poisoning that made him instantly recognisable around the world. The dioxin he unwittingly consumed in 2004, accord-ing to yet another secret tape recording of a conversation between a Russian and a Ukrainian secret serviceman, helped 'to disfigure the Messiah, and to brand him with the mark of the beast'.[5]

Tymoshenko had personality in spades. Critics used to accuse Yushchenko of having the personality of a bank manager – at least while that was his job, running the National Bank of Ukraine from 1993 to 1999 (and when bank managers, before the global credit crunch, were still thought of as staid). Yushchenko also tended to think like a post-Marxist banker, assuming that political economy was more important than politics.

Tymoshenko, on the other hand, had lived her whole life as a per-formance, compared to the boring desk jobs Yushchenko had laboured at in his early career. She therefore played the politics of the personality with more natural ease. The fact that she was universally referred to as 'Yuliia' or even the diminutive 'Yulka' was an advantage in itself. But Tymoshenko was also an inveterate intriguer. Born into relative poverty and deserted by her father at the age of two, she had to fight her way to the top – and never stopped fighting. She also had to battle with sexism in its particularly toxic post-Soviet form, where high-profile women are expected to be either high-octane or high-maintenance. She always expected to be number one. In 2005 her cabinet meetings lasted all day, like the old Soviet Politburo. Delegation was not her greatest strength.

Tymoshenko's previous life as a 'gas princess' was well-known. A fortuitous marriage to the son of a local Communist Party boss helped her make starter capital in a video business. But she made her real fortune from two expanded 'family' companies – first the Ukrainian Oil Corporation and then the United Energy Systems of Ukraine. The latter was given the monopoly right to supply Ukraine's energy-thirsty eastern regions around Tymoshenko's hometown of Dnipropetrovsk, when local strongman, Pavlo Lazarenko, became prime minister in the mid-1990s (see pages 197–8). There is little information about just how much of United Energy System's windfall wealth ended up in Tymoshenko's pocket. On the Melnychenko tapes, during a conversation between Kuchma and Poroshenko in June 2000, Kuchma claims that 'in 1996–7 alone, in Cyprus alone she [Tymoshenko] transferred $350 million dollars, from Energy Systems'.[6]

On the other hand, when Tymoshenko was prime minister in 2005, she filed an official income declaration of just UAH 65,667 (then just under $13,000), plus a mere UAH 900 in the bank. She was forced to sit through an embarrassing press conference while a brave journalist read out the price of her stylish outfits and handbags – a Manhattan PM Louis Vuitton at $1,280 and a Le Talentueux at $2,140 – proof, at least, that Ukraine now had a relatively free press. And Tymoshenko's wealth was not just a question of personal style: she needed money to campaign, and was in permanent campaign mode.

Tymoshenko had, however, grasped a truth under-appreciated in the West, that Putin's anti-oligarch campaign in Russia, whether fake or not, was enormously popular throughout the region. The average Russian thought that the former Yukos boss Mikhail Khodorkovskii, despite sitting in a former Gulag camp in Siberia, got off lightly. So did the average Ukrainian. Given her past, it seemed incredible that this card could be best played by Tymoshenko, but the volte-face came more naturally to her. She made her money, and then hid it. Yushchenko, on the other hand, made a more public courtship of business and money. And if anyone were to take on the system from the inside, poacher-turned-gamekeeper was the natural role to play.

Could Ukraine get the balance right? Yushchenko was too complacent about the old guard while Tymoshenko was too broad-brush. While Yushchenko was too trusting, Tymoshenko was often too rash. Yushchenko constructed the first electoral coalition capable of winning a national election, but he was not apparently capable of challenging the post-Soviet system of power. Corruption scandals tainted his aides, his brother and his son (and his American-born wife was alleged to be fond of the odd fur coat), if not Yushchenko himself. He did little to heal Ukraine's internal divisions after 2004, whereas Tymoshenko could reach the parts of east Ukraine that Yushchenko could not. Yushchenko developed an obsession with historical issues: collecting Trypillian artefacts, securing recognition of the Stalinist Famine as genocide, and rehabilitating the OUN-UPA. On his first visit to Donetsk after the election, Yushchenko harangued his audience for corruption and political thuggery. While this was fair comment, he built no bridges, compared to Tymoshenko taking hostile questions on local TV wearing the soccer shirt of the local team Shakhtar (meaning 'miner') Donetsk. (Ironically the Donetsk club play in orange, while their rivals Dynamo Kiev play in Yanukovych's campaign colours of blue and white.) Tymoshenko was a populist, but she was an effective populist.

If Tymoshenko was turning into the East European Evita, the best-dressed friend of the poor, Yushchenko was becoming the Ukrainian Perón, who, as president of Argentina from 1946 to 1955, proved to be a lazy under-achiever. The spirit of the Orange Revolution was still there (though Yushchenko's teenage son Andrii bizarrely tried to copyright it, or at least the T-shirt and souvenir mug part), and the two were locked in a struggle to reclaim it, although it could just as easily slip out of both of their grasps. A cross-breed of the two might at one stage have been ideal, but instead a war of mutual destruction soon beckoned.

The First Orange Government

Yushchenko was finally inaugurated on 23 January 2005. The old parliament endorsed Tymoshenko as Prime Minister in an unconvincing display of consensus by 373 votes to 0 on 4 February; Yushchenko sought to balance her power by installing one of his business allies, Petro Poroshenko, as head of an expanded National Security Council – a de facto parallel government. The two were soon at loggerheads. Arguments also raged over Tymoshenko's allegedly populist economic policy, including her promise to fulfil both Yushchenko's and Yanukovych's campaign pledges (the former on welfare payments and state salaries, the latter on pensions), a massive increase in maternity benefits from the new 'mother of the nation', and misguided attempts to control the price of meat and energy that resulted in queues and shortages. But Tymoshenko's most controversial campaign was to right some of the wrongs of the Kuchma era by 'reprivatisation' – first the nationalisation, and then the resale, of industries that had been corruptly privatised. As the list was open-ended, business confidence was severely affected and domestic investment collapsed. Although, in the end, only one full reprivatisation was conducted – in October 2005 just after Tymoshenko had left office. The Kryvorizhstal steel mill, sold to two of Ukraine's biggest oligarchs (Viktor Pinchuk, then close to Kuchma, and Rinat Akhmetov, then close to Yanukovych) for $800 million in 2004, was now resold for $4.8 billion to Mittal Steel, indicating that the original price may have been a little low.

Meanwhile, Yushchenko was hamstrung by the campaign favours he thought he had to repay. His campaign had spent less than a tenth of his opponent's orgy of palm greasing and largesse, which, according to a leaked tape of a secret meeting between Medvedchuk and his Russian counterpart Aleksandr Voloshin, amounted to $600 million, divided 50-50 between Russian (Gazprom) and Ukrainian sources (mainly Akhmetov).[7] But Yushchenko had still spent an estimated $46 million, or according to another key business supporter, Davyd Zhvaniia, $150 million, over two years.[8] If his financiers expected payback, some of his aides were corrupted by the system, tempted by the goods they found were still in the candy store. The energy sector was the most potent symbol that one group of bandits had simply replaced another. Yushchenko's chief of staff, Oleksandr Tretiakov, who made money in the mid-1990s through the gas station chain Tiko and his links to Russia's Lukoil, was reputed to have demanded control of energy policy himself – much to the new prime minister's surprise. Tretiakov levered himself on to the board of state monopolies such as Oshchadbank and Ukrtelekom, and allegedly appointed his man Oleksii Ivchenko as head of Oil and Gas of Ukraine, making sure that it still reported directly to the president.

The key bauble inherited from the old regime was 'RosUkrEnergo', in essence a scheme for creaming off massive payments for nominal services in the transport of gas to Ukraine from Turkmenistan, worth an estimated $350 million a year for *both* sides.[9] Later estimates were that the company's gas was worth $4.35 billion a year at 2007 prices.[10] The sheer amount of money involved was arguably the biggest single factor in forcing the Orange Revolution off track.[11] The scheme was originally launched at a meeting between Kuchma and Putin in the summer of 2004. By 2006 the press was able to publicise the main shareholder on the Ukrainian side as Dmytro Firtash, though it was not clear when he took control. The other main Ukrainian players were said to be Ivchenko's predecessor Yurii Boiko, sacked by Yushchenko in February 2005, and his deputy Ihor Voronin, sacked by Tymoshenko on the eve of her own departure in September 2005, but then mysteriously reinstated a month later. In January 2006 Voronin supposedly orchestrated the government's approval of a new gas deal, although, as he was not formally a member of the Cabinet of Ministers, he set up camp in the gents' toilets next to the office where the deal was being done. Money was also allegedly finding its way back to Tretiakov and the energy minister Ivan Plachkov. Even the president's older brother Petro Yushchenko was allegedly involved.

In June 2005 Tymoshenko ordered an investigation, and by the end of summer the Security Services were supposedly close to arresting Boiko and Voronin – when Yushchenko ordered Tymoshenko to lay off 'his boys'.[12] The trail also led back to Russia. Yushchenko allegedly stopped the investigation after he came under pressure from the Russian controllers of the deal: Igor Sechin, deputy head of the presidential administration and boss of Rosneft, Aleksandr Riazanov, one of the *siloviki*'s men at Gazprom, and allegedly from Putin himself. Also on the Russian side was Oleg Palchikov who, like Firtash, was accused of longstanding links to the mobster Semion Mogilevich. (The notorious Mogilevich was born in Kiev in 1946. His economics degree from Lviv University had earned him the nickname, in admittedly unimpressive company, of 'the brainy don'. He operated mainly in Israel and Hungary, earning a place on the FBI's most wanted list in 2003, before his eventual arrest by the Russians during an unexplained sojourn in Moscow in January 2008.) Tymoshenko claimed that after the president warned her off, she thought to herself that 'RosUkrEnergo had found itself a new *krisha*', (a mafia term for 'protective roof').

Other new ministers had obvious conflicts of interest. Yevhen Chervonenko, who ran a freight company, was made minister of transport. Zhvaniia's role as minister for emergency situations gave him influence over fuel supply for the atomic energy monopoly Enerhoatom, in which the Brinkford concern he ran with Mykola Martynenko, the head of the Our Ukraine group in parliament, had won interests while Yushchenko was prime minister. Yushchenko had a particular blindspot for Petro Poroshenko, who is godfather to one of his children. Poroshenko (whose estimated wealth was $350 million), had hoped to be prime minister and was soon running his own after-hours government instead. He would wheel and deal in the day before arriving at work in the evening, ready to undo any good work anyone had done elsewhere. Poroshenko even managed to sabotage Ukrainian foreign policy. On an official visit to Teheran in July, he spent a couple of hours discussing diversification of energy supply with his hosts before moving on to more lengthy personal negotiations on the caviar trade. His proposals for solving Moldova's problems with the separatist 'Transnistrian Republic' were thought to favour the Russian-backed enclave. He was therefore accused by agencies linked to the Moldovan security services of being more interested in promoting his investments in the capital Chişinău, including its main department store, and shadier activities in the Transnistrian Republic.

Another scandal involved the exiled Russian tycoon Boris Berezovskii, who claimed to have given $15 or $21 million (someone was keeping loose accounts) to the Yushchenko campaign for the 'development of democracy' in Ukraine, via Tretiakov and the part-Georgian Zhvaniia Berezovskii claimed to have met Zhvaniia through his Georgian business partner Badri Patarkatsishvili, who died of a heart attack in February 2008, aged 52. (Foreign financing of parties and election campaign is illegal under Ukrainian law.) In February 2006 Berezovskii refined the figure to $22.85 million, supposedly paid between 1 August 2003 and 12 November 2004 to two front companies nominated by Yushchenko's men, and he threatened to sue if they couldn't tell him where the money had gone. One defence proposed by the Yushchenko side was that it was actually Tymoshenko who took the money.[13]

Equally damaging were the stories about Tymoshenko and so-called 'orange oligarchs'. As in Russia, the suspicion rapidly grew that the state was not acting against oligarchs in general, but simply redistributing property from one group to another. Tymoshenko allegedly wanted to win control of Ukraine's second-most popular TV channel, 1+1, in the run-up to the 2006 elections. The complicated plan was for Ihor Kolomoiskyi's Privat group, based in Dnipropetrovsk, to buy a 40% stake (half of which was owned by Boris Fuchsmann, an alleged Mafioso and gold smuggler) and pass it over to a shell company. In exchange the government would take the Nikopol Ferroalloys plant, Europe's largest producer of ferroalloys, from rival oligarch Viktor Pinchuk, and pass it on to Privat. The government would also block Pinchuk's attempts to arrange a preemptive sale to two Russian oligarchs, Aleksandr Abramov and Viktor Vekselberg (Pinchuk and Tymoshenko had bad blood going back to the collapse of a putative joint venture, ironically entitled 'Friendship', in 1995). Pinchuk and Kolomoiskyi ultimately settled out of court.

The constant feuding and escalating war of allegation continued throughout the summer of 2005. The economy first slowed down and then in August actually contracted. In Ukraine trouble often comes to a head when politicians return from holiday in September, and so it proved on this occasion. Oleksandr Zinchenko, who had run the 2004 campaign and helped organise the protests on the Maidan, first brought the war of allegation and insinuation to the surface with a dramatic press conference. Yushchenko decided to fire almost everybody, including Tymoshenko and Tretiakov. He even finally removed the do-nothing procurator Piskun. As Yushchenko's right-hand man, Oleh Rybachuk commented sarcastically: 'we have probably saved Piskun from having to open a case against himself', and from 'investigat[ing] it in one day' and then declaring it closed.[14] Piskun's sudden flurry of activity during his last month included his claim that he was only removed in order to halt his investigation into a £155,000 bill to fly the first lady's family to Kiev on inauguration day, supposedly paid for by Dmytro Firtash. Piskun also claimed he had refused to reopen the file on Tymoshenko, closed in February. Reporters should have perhaps filtered this particular story through the rumours that Piskun was preparing to sell his services to the highest bidder, eventually leaving office with several suitcases full of kompromat. In the 2006 elections, Piskun ended up on the Party of Regions' list.

As the dust settled, however, it became clear that Yushchenko had taken sides. The president denied that those he had sacked on his side had done anything wrong, and allowed them to continue dominating his party as it sank in the polls. The blasé comments of the then deputy prime minister, Roman Bezsmertnyi, about Berezovskii's useful 'cooperation ... on public campaigns', betrayed a woeful ignorance of the effectiveness of yet another propaganda hit. Tymoshenko therefore emerged from the war of kompromat an initial winner.

Tymoshenko also had enough votes in parliament to block Yushchenko's first attempt to appoint a new government, headed by Yurii Yekhanurov, who had masterminded Ukraine's privatisation programme in the 1990s and had good links with the 'oligarchs'. The attempt fell just three votes short of success on 20 September. Yushchenko then showed his characteristic failing of excessive compromise (he needed only three votes more, but did not look elsewhere) by doing a deal with none other than Viktor Yanukovych, his bitter opponent in 2004. The deal declared 'the impermissibility of political repressions against the opposition' – in other words making the immunity promise for the old regime public knowledge – and even included a specific amnesty for election fraud. Yekhanurov won 289 votes at the second attempt on 22 September 2005, but the price for 'stability' seemed overly high.

A brief period of 'business-friendly' pragmatism ensued, but the fragile unity of the new arrangement did not last long. In January 2006 Russia suddenly reduced gas supplies to Ukraine in the depth of midwinter. Before the Orange Revolution, Russia had agreed to sell Ukraine gas for $50 per 1000 m^3 until 2010, but now it wanted $230. The timing of Russia's move seemed blatantly political, to punish the Orange parties and reward the Party of Regions at the forthcoming elections (Belarus was then paying $46.68). Yanukovych proclaimed loudly that the price would not go up if he was in charge. But just as European consumers downstream were complaining loudly enough potentially to force Moscow to back down, Ukraine signed a curious deal which promised a headline price of $95, but locked it into importing gas from Central Asia with a massive 20% payment in kind going to RosUkrEnergo. In the deal RosUkrEnergo also mysteriously gained control of Ukraine's vast underground gas storage reserves. The Yekhanurov government was formally censured but limped on. Disillusioned Orange voters switched to the Tymoshenko camp.

The 2006 Elections: The Return of Yanukovych

In the immediate aftermath of the Orange Revolution, none of Ukraine's new leaders expected the next elections to be a problem. In early 2005, Ukraine effectively had a one-and-a-half party system, with the united Orange forces confidently expecting to crush the discredited remnants of the old regime at the next scheduled votes in March 2006. After September 2005, Ukraine suddenly had a three-party system: the Orange camp split in two after Yushchenko sacked Tymoshenko, while the strongest clan party of the Kuchma era, the Party of Regions, reinvented itself as a party representing all of eastern and southern Ukraine. The stakes were increased by the constitutional changes that took effect on 1 January 2006, which transferred many powers to parliament.

Yushchenko's Our Ukraine party maintained its links to the businessmen that Tymoshenko now sarcastically called the 'dear friends'. Petro Poroshenko may barely have spoken to Yushchenko since September, but he controlled at least eight places on the party list. The Ukrainian press commented sarcastically that it had no photo to print of Dmytro Firtash, as he had deputised two managers from his Kiev basketball club to stand. Our Ukraine's campaign looked tired and retrospective. Its main slogan 'Don't Betray the Maidan' made no positive promises, and served to remind voters of exactly what they thought the 'dear friends' were guilty of.

Tymoshenko had been happy to welcome all comers to her eponymous faction in parliament in 2005, and it more than doubled in size (as Prime Minister, she needed the numbers: she started 2005 with only 19, but by June she had 37). However, after September 2005, some of her more unlikely allies, such as former Kuchma oligarch Oleksandr Volkov (see pages 269–72), began to attract bad publicity, stirred up by Yushchenko's supporters. Her eventual election list therefore left him out, and also excluded a now disillusioned Zinchenko. The list did include other controversial figures such as Bohdan Hubskyi, one of Kiev's not-so-magnificent seven business oligarchs, and the wealthy 'minigarch' Kostiantyn Zhevaho (the Ukrainian spelling of 'Zhivago', though the oligarch bore more of a resemblance to Joe Pesci than to Omar Sherif), and Vasyl Khmelnytskyi, who owned another steel giant Zaporizhstal and several oblenergos, and was previously notorious for helping Kuchma to set up fake opposition parties to compete with the real 'orange' opposition.

The other main Orange party was the Socialists – but their surprise shadowy sponsors included Zhevaho (again), another Dnipropetrovsk oligarch Andrii Derkach, boss of Era TV, and Volodymyr Boiko, boss of the giant Illich factory in Mariupol. As with Tymoshenko, the Socialists' choice of partners led to the loss of one of their most prominent and principled members: Interior Minister Yurii Lutsenko.

Even the Communists were involved in the game of 'chase the sponsor', chiefly the Russian energy magnate Konstantin Grigorishin. The

'Progressive Socialist Party' was covertly sponsored by Russia and by business interests in the Party of Regions. Finally, the People's Party, led by parliamentary speaker Volodymyr Lytvyn, was an expensively packaged life raft for insiders from the old regime. It was a team of last resort for misfits and bad guys, such as the Oakland Raiders in the NFL or Blackburn Rovers in the English soccer league.

Something was clearly amiss. Politics is always expensive and politicians the world over cultivate business sponsors. But Ukraine needed business-friendly government, not government that was in the pockets of business. The oligarchs were now everywhere: their rearguard action in December 2004 seemed to have worked.

The renewed prominence of old guard businessmen was most obvious in Viktor Yanukovych's Party of the Regions – more accurately the party of Ukraine's richest man, Rinat Akhmetov, whose estimated fortune of $2.5 billion was temporarily (but still disappointingly) down from $3.5 billion in 2004. Previously a secretive man, not only did Akhmetov now return from his lengthy holidays, but he also put himself at number seven on the list, followed by no less than thirty-seven of his employees. The organisers of the voting fraud in 2004 were also on the list, including the supposedly disgraced ex-head of the Central Election Commission, Serhii Kivalov.

On the other hand, some oligarchs were apparently cleaning up their act. Viktor Pinchuk (estimated wealth of $1.5 billion in 2005), controller of a vast empire based on his Interpipe company and three of Ukraine's main TV channels, plus a half share in Kryvorizhstal that he lost and another in the Nikopol Ferroalloys Plant, was not standing in the elections. Nor was his counterpart in Kharkiv, Oleksandr Yaroslavskyi ($650 million), thinking of taking a direct role in the new parliament – allegedly the price of BNP Paribas buying 51% of the shares in his UkrSibBank in December 2005. Ihor Kolomoiskyi's Privat group (despite, or possibly because of, his wealth rising to an estimated $2.8 billion) kept its distance and did not attempt to enter parliament via Tymoshenko's list.

The political crisis that had been ongoing since September, and Russia's favour during the January gas crisis, allowed Yanukovych's Party of the Regions to make a strong comeback (see table E.2). The disparate eastern Ukrainian elite parties of the Kuchma era had now become one, though not without tensions between the Donetsk group and the rest. However, perhaps surprisingly, voters in central and western Ukraine were prepared to give the three Orange parties a second chance. Yushchenko's Our Ukraine block came a poor third, but Tymoshenko's surprisingly strong second place meant that a new Orange coalition was possible, even likely. Together Tymoshenko's Block, Our Ukraine and the Socialists had 243 out of 450 seats. Several attempts by Kuchma-era politicians to convince voters they had changed their spots were failures: the People's Party led by parliamentary chair Volodymyr Lytvyn, the 'liberal' party Viche, the Social-Democrats reinventing themselves as Ne Tak! (bizarrely meaning 'No to Yes!', 'Yes!' having been Yushchenko's positive feel-good slogan in 2004). Smaller Orange parties – the remnants of Rukh led by Yurii Kostenko and Ivan Pliushch, and the youth protest movement Pora – were also squeezed out.

Nevertheless, negotiations dragged on for over three months. Our Ukraine's business wing was reluctant to see the return of Tymoshenko as Prime Minister, and began to contemplate a shock deal with the Party of Regions instead, despite the message from their voters. A fallback position was a 50-50 coalition between Our Ukraine and Regions, with Yekhanurov remaining as prime minister, which was within a whisker of being signed in June. However, Yushchenko's insistence on pushing Poroshenko as chair of parliament provoked a crisis in July, when the Socialists sensationally defected to form an alternative 'anti-crisis coalition' with Regions and the Communists. Allegations that the Socialists had been bought (for a surely implausible $300 million) surfaced soon enough,[15] but personal ambition also played a part. The deal ensured that Socialist leader Oleksandr Moroz would return to the position of chair of parliament that he had so much enjoyed in 1994–8, while Regions insisted on Yanukovych as prime minister. Hopelessly outmanoeuvred, Yushchenko's one crumb of comfort was the 'Universal of National Unity' signed in August, which nominally committed the new government to maintaining Ukraine's post-2004 course towards democracy and European integration. Six Our Ukraine ministers joined the

Table E.2: Ukrainian Parliamentary Elections, March 2006

Party of Regions	32.1%	186 seats
Tymoshenko Block (BYT)	22.3%	129
Our Ukraine	13.9%	81
Socialists	5.7%	33
Communists	3.7%	21
People's Opposition (Vitrenko)	2.9%	
Lytvyn Block	2.4%	
Kostenko/Pliushch	1.9%	
Viche	1.7%	
Pora/Reforms and Order	1.5%	
Ne Tak!	1%	
Others	7%	
Against All	1.8%	
Invalid votes	1.9%	

(3% was the barrier for representation)

new coalition, although only 30 out of 81 Our Ukraine deputies could bear to vote for Yanukovych.

Our Ukraine ministers who joined the new coalition soon regretted their choice: four out of six quit by October, while Yanukovych tested his new constitutional powers to the limit. The Party of Regions failed to maintain the spirit of the 'Universal' once in office, running a sustained campaign to curtail Yushchenko's power, questioning his right to appoint local governors, challenging his every decree, forcing out his favourite ministers, ramming through a self-aggrandising 'Law on Government' in January 2007 (in which Tymoshenko was shamefully complicit), and even conducting a shadow foreign policy.

Regions had enjoyed an extensive PR makeover, ironically this time from US political consultants, since many of its leading members tried to rig the 2004 election; but at heart it was still a clientelistic and authoritarian organisation. In order to function as such, it needed to reward its friends and punish its enemies, and show both who was now back in charge – and it needed to do this semi-publically. To use the local euphemism, 'administrative resources' were used increasingly blatantly and partially. Notorious crooks such as Volodymyr Shcherban, one time 'boss of bosses' in Donetsk, returned home; the Prosecutor's Office was taken over by Donetsk 'enforcers'. Donetsk enterprises such as Azovstal and the Yelnakievo Metal Factory received preferential VAT refunds of UAH 696 million (over $120 million) instead of the UAH 313 million originally proposed, while other payments were sharply cut back. Even Oschadbank, traditionally the savings bank of first choice for the average Ukrainian (a kind of glorified Post Office), was not safe from a blatantly political takeover.

2007: Another Year, Another Crisis. The Return of Tymoshenko

Ultimately however, members of the Party of Regions over-reached themselves, as their aggrandisement seemed never-ending. Yushchenko felt he had to stop them somewhere, somehow, and he began adopting similar methods to his opponents to try and compete. He promoted 'his' tough guy to head the Presidential Administration in September 2006, Viktor Baloha, a thuggish Machiavellian from Transcarpathia in Ukraine's wild west and former protégé of Viktor Medvedchuk; and he appointed 'his' businessmen to compete with Yanukovych's businessmen, such as Vitalii Haiduk of the Industrial Union of the Donbas, a local rival to Akhmetov, and Valerii Khoroshkovskyi, president of the Russian steel giant Evraz since 2004. Yushchenko hoped to use their clout to bolster the National Security and Defence Council as a rival power-base, and their money to help finance a relaunch of Our Ukraine. In private, Yushchenko supped closer to the devil, negotiating with odious figures such as President Kuchma's former strong-arm Chief of Staff Viktor Medvedchuk over the control of many of the judges he helped appoint back in 2002–4.

The final straw came in April 2007 when eleven parliamentary deputies, allegedly after suitable financial encouragement, defected from the Orange parties to the Yanukovych coalition. Regions boasted vaingloriously that it would control a constitutional majority, 300 deputies out of 450, by the summer, which would give it an almost complete free hand. After eight months of accumulating political humiliation, Yushchenko finally acted on 2 April 2007 by dramatically ordering the dissolution of parliament and scheduling new elections for 27 May. Not surprisingly, Yanukovych's government and its majority in the 'old' parliament, which was only one year into its five-year term, refused to cooperate. Yushchenko's decree was legally shaky. Originally, he cited the defection of the unmagnificent eleven as his main reason for dissolving parliament, as contrary to the 'imperative mandate'. This was a fair point, but not mentioned in Article 90 of the Constitution which lays out the grounds for dissolution. The Constitutional Court was asked to arbitrate, but the judge acting as self-appointed rapporteur was accused of taking $12 million in bribes, and in a general atmosphere of legal nihilism the Court avoided making a definitive decision, to avoid the opprobrium of the losing side. So Yushchenko flailed: a second decree on April 26 revised the election date and the grounds for dissolution; Constitutional Court judges were sacked then reinstated; the Orange parties colluded in a dangerous precedent, withdrawing their 210 deputies so that parliament was no longer quorate; Kiev came close to becoming a theatre of violence (if not quite close as it had come in November 2004) on 26 May in a stand-off between rival troops over the control of the Interior Ministry and Procurator's office.

But the intrigues of the Yanukovych government had also worried some of its supporters. The threat of violence concentrated minds – as did UEFA's unexpected decision to award the Euro 2012 soccer finals jointly to Ukraine and Poland (the final would be in Kiev). The crisis was finally solved on 27 May, when one set of businessmen grouped around the presidential administration reached a compromise with another set grouped around Akhmetov, both of whom were big soccer fans, based on an assumed eventual 'grand coalition' involving both. Tymoshenko was not a party to the agreement, which was designed to shut her out.

The one flaw in this plan was that Tymoshenko had always been a much better public performer and campaigner than the president, and so it proved. Tymoshenko roared ahead in the campaign from 22.3% to 30.7%, winning not just redistributed 'Orange' votes (two Orange parties not running this time won 3.4% in 2006) but new votes as well. A second surprise was that the president's party had to reconnect with all things orange and sideline its business wing merely to tread water in the polls. Our Ukraine (NU) entered an awkward alliance with the new People's Self-Defence (NS) party set up by the popular former Interior Minister and former Socialist Yurii Lutsenko (popular because he had actually done something in office to reform his notoriously corrupt ministry). By polling day the president was forced to play an obvious double game, with one half of his entourage working hard to prevent a renewed Orange alliance just as hard as the other worked to build it up.

The Party of Regions shot itself in the foot by swallowing most of the smaller parties on its side of the fence. Its vote only went up from 32.2% in 2006 to 34.4% in 2007, and it ended up with fewer allies to form a potential coalition on its own. Among the smaller parties, the Socialists dropped out and the Communists sneaked back in. The former result at least showed that Ukrainian democracy had its virtues, as Moroz's party was punished by the electorate for abandoning the position it was elected on in 2006. Lytvyn's Block, having narrowly missed out in 2006, made it this time, with twenty seats.

The major oligarchs played musical chairs: Akhmetov's group in Regions actually went up from around sixty deputies to around ninety, but the party's main financier was now alleged to be Firtash. The IUD and Privat swapped places, with Privat now supporting Yushchenko and the IUD supporting Tymoshenko, as her other sponsors such as Zhevaho took a big hit from the global economic crisis. Vasyl Khmelnytskyi invested an alleged $30 million in Lytvyn.[16]

One half of the electorate showed extraordinary patience in once again voting Orange – arguably for the fourth time, if the 2002 election can be counted alongside 2004, as well as the 'second chance' vote of 2006 and the 'third chance' vote of 2007. Other possibilities were only narrowly excluded, however. The parties to the original May agreement had expected to join together in a government of all the businessmen, but that now looked like political suicide for Our Ukraine. Nor could Regions govern on their own, or even in alliance with smaller partners. The Socialists were gone. The former chair of parliament Volodymyr Lytvyn had planned to sell himself to both sides, but the maths didn't

Table E.3: Ukrainian Parliamentary Elections, September 2007

Party of Regions	34.4%	175 seats (−11)
Tymoshenko Block (BYT)	30.7%	156 (+27)
Our Ukraine-People's Self Defence (NUNS)	14.1%	72 (−9)
Communists	5.4%	27 (+6)
Lytvyn Block	4.0%	20 (+20)
Socialists	2.86%	−
Progressive Socialists (Vitrenko)	1.3%	−

add up. The Party of Regions plus the Communists plus the supposedly 'neutral' Lytvyn Block would still make only 222 seats out of 450. The Orange parties did not need him at this stage: NUNS and BYT could govern on their own with a majority of two.

Typically, Yushchenko still tried to have it both ways. The default option of a new Orange coalition was put together a week before Christmas with Tymoshenko once again prime minister, but at the same time the president tried to run a businessmen's coalition through the Presidential Administration and National Security Council. The one new face was Rada Chair Arsenii Yatseniuk, then a youthful thirty-three, and nicknamed the 'kinder surprise' – though in fact he was nearly bald. As with its predecessor in 2005, the second Orange government was soon undermined by constant feuding, though this time coming mainly from the weaker party, as Baloha and his henchmen constantly sought to undermine the prime minister. Tymoshenko's key populist move this time around was partial recompense for those who had lost their Soviet era savings in the great hyperinflation of the early 1990s. Yushchenko's own grand initiative was to send a letter to NATO in January 2008 asking for a Membership Action Plan (MAP) only three months before the key summit in Bucharest in April. Most NATO members were understandably reluctant to be bounced by a divided Ukrainian leadership, and Ukraine was offered the disastrous half-way house of membership in principle, but no MAP any time soon.

The second Orange government was more quietly professional than the first, but its wafer-thin majority meant that it had few legislative achievements to its name. Moreover, by April 2008 Yushchenko and Tymoshenko had switched the roles they had had in 2005: the president was so determined to frustrate the prime minister at every turn that he now took his turn to act the populist, blocking privatisation and an attempt to end the moratorium on the sale of land. Ukraine finally joined the WTO in May 2008, ahead of Russia, and began uncertain preparations to host Euro 2012 (the award was made in April 2007). Ukraine had the opposite problems to Poland – several new stadia, but woeful infrastructure. But scheming seemed more important than actually governing or getting things built. Ukraine narrowly escaped censure by UEFA in September 2008.

The Georgia Crisis

The war in Georgia in August 2008 led to yet another crisis over yet another spiteful summer. Ukrainians, as often, took different sides. In a poll taken shortly after the war, 38.4% blamed Georgia for starting the conflict, compared to 20% who blamed Russia.[17] After some initial hesitation, Yushchenko expressed strong solidarity with Georgia and with his fellow democratic poster boy, Georgian President Mikheil Saakashvili. Tymoshenko, on the other hand, stayed uncharacteristically quiet. The Party of Regions was divided: Yanukovych called for the recognition of Abkhazia and South Ossetia (not a good precedent for Crimea), but the main paper controlled by Akhmetov urged Ukrainians to stay out of the conflict.[18]

Baloha's attack dogs promptly accused Tymoshenko of plotting with leading Russians and old Kuchma-ites to unseat Yushchenko in 2009 or 2010 in return for shifting to a more Russia-friendly line. The plot was allegedly hatched during summer cruises off Sardinia and funded to the tune of almost a billion dollars. The word 'treason' was used,[19] and a massive 'dossier', several hundred pages long but short on actual evidence apart from some names of yachts, was sent to an unimpressed procurator. On 2 September, Tymoshenko retaliated by collaborating with Regions on a technical vote to reduce the president's powers. A furious Yushchenko then ordered Our Ukraine to pull the plug on the government coalition – only a week before a crucial EU-Ukraine summit on 9 September and amidst much speculation about whether Ukraine might be 'next' in Russia's sights. Ukrainian politicians' addiction to the mortal combat of internal politics had never looked more myopic.

If that was not bad enough, Ukraine was badly hit by the global financial crisis of autumn 2008. Beforehand, the economy had been seriously over-heating: with inflation peaking at 31% in May 2008, and the current account deficit ballooning from 3.7% of GDP in 2007 to a massive 6.7% in 2008. The IMF promised an emergency loan of $16.4 billion, but rightly complained it did not know whom to talk to, and only made a preliminary dispersal of $4.5 billion. The initial package – a virtual freeze on bank lending and the creation of a 'stabilisation fund' that would receive all receipts from privatisation and government bond sales – seemed characteristic sleight of hand by Tymoshenko. By February she was negotiating with Russia as well, for a $5 billion loan.

But Yushchenko and Baloha were determined to bring the coalition down, although only 39 out of 64 NUNS deputies voted to leave it on 2 September, and de facto it reassembled itself to pass the economic package on 29 October (with Lytvyn's votes). The alternative idea of reviving a coalition between Our Ukraine and Regions, which was mooted in 2006 and again in 2007, seemed passed its sell-by-date, after the two parties had taken such different lines on Georgia. Another option was for BYT to ally with Regions. This would have had some logic. Such a 'grand alliance' might have a grand agenda, using a two-thirds' constitutional majority to force through many long-delayed reforms (such as the budget and judicial reform), but it might also be grubby, and use that power to entrench the interests of both parties' business supporters. It was the one combination of the big three parties that hadn't yet been tried, which risked exposing the fact that none of Ukraine's politicians could actually work together.

Tymoshenko's manoeuvre was stunning but cynical, and therefore only partly successful. It was a clear attempt to position herself as more friendly to Ukraine's Russian-speaking population and the pivotal electoral middle ground. It might persuade Russia to go easy on ongoing gas price negotiations. But the volte-face was a leap too far for the Western powers, and threatened to alienate voters in western Ukraine.

For two months Yushchenko was apparently serious about ordering yet another dissolution of parliament and scheduling early elections in December 2008. This was delusional. His constitutional powers in this respect were limited. Yushchenko had dissolved the last parliament in 2007 on shaky legal grounds, but the West and much of the Ukrainian public had bought the utilitarian argument that new elections were necessary to 'reboot' the political system. The idea of new elections, scarcely more than a year later for narrow partisan advantage, quite rightly tried everyone's patience.

They were also suicidal, as NUNS was polling at 5% or less, and rapidly falling apart, with increasing numbers gravitating towards BYT. Yet more elections risked the wrath of Ukrainians, who were rightly disillusioned with all their politicians. Yushchenko's advisers were suggesting that he reinvent himself as a Ukrainian nationalist, after his relatively strong stance on Georgia gave him a brief bump up in the polls. But this is never a winning strategy in an Ukrainian election, as such a large percentage of the population speaks Russian and lives east of the river Dnieper. It also rested on Ukraine's residual, but fast-fading, hopes of being granted a NATO Membership Action Plan.

Yushchenko's chief of staff, Viktor Baloha, had an interest in new elections, as he had set up a new party, United Centre, which he hoped would control a key block of seats in a new parliament. But there would be little strategic point if this came at the expense of a collapse in support for Our Ukraine. The Presidential Administration also rested its hopes on a 'many-layered pie' of old-style political technology parties: the block led by Kiev's eccentric mayor Leonid Chernovetskyi, the embryonic party led by Yanukovych's former deputy Raïsa Bohatyrova that was designed to take votes from Regions in the east, and the veteran provocateur Oleh Tiahnybok's Freedom Party to tap nationalist votes in the west. Perhaps Yushchenko could then hide behind the new parties as a bridge to a new coalition with Regions.

The January 2009 Gas Crisis

The lack of viable alternatives meant that the idea of new parliamentary elections was quietly dropped, and an 'Orange+' or 'Orange-' coalition was stitched back together on 10 December 2008. This time forty NUNS deputies voted to rejoin BYT by replacing the youthful Yatseniuk with the veteran Volodymyr Lytvyn as Chair of the Rada. It was assumed the twenty votes of the 'Lytvyn Block' would now support a new coalition, though the position of the twenty-seven Communists who also backed Lytvyn was not clear.

Tymoshenko was once again secure in the prime minister's chair, but this merely sparked yet another round of political manoeuvring, this time unfortunately on the eve of the annual gas row with Russia and one of the coldest Januaries in years. On 1 January 2009, Russia reduced the gas pressure, despite an agreement apparently having been on the table the previous day. Thus far, all was normal and Russia even claimed it had finely calibrated the reduction so that only Ukraine should suffer, rather than any customers further downstream. But the stakes were dramatically raised on 7 January, when Russia cut off all supply. Gazprom, via a new PR web site www.gazpromukrainefacts.com, claimed that Ukraine had been stealing gas, although Kiev was well-known to have built up good reserves. Unlike the short dispute in 2006, when Europe had fretted about the potential energy security threat, it was now very real: Europe lost 23–30% of its gas imports overnight. Large parts of the old 'eastern Europe', the new EU states that had been connected to the Soviet gas network under Communism, suddenly faced severe shortages. Bulgaria struggled to secure heating for schools and hospitals as thousands of households were left without heating during temperatures of −20C. With the notable exception of Hungary, few EU states were revealed to have kept the promises they had made to invest in energy security back in 2006. Bulgaria and Slovakia threatened to restart recently closed Soviet-era nuclear reactors to keep warm. An EU monitor scheme to check the flow of gas through Ukraine never got off the ground – as no gas was flowing. And the sheer length of the crisis – two weeks, compared to three days in 2006 – was a factor in itself, as Europeans recoiled at the myopic selfishness of both Russia and Ukraine.

As in 2006, the final deal negotiated tête-à-tête between Putin and Tymoshenko on 18 January, after Putin deliberately cut Yushchenko out of the process, had a disturbing sub-text. It at least promised to get rid of RosUkrEnergo, but that was also in Tymoshenko's narrow political interest if the company was indeed financing both the President and the Party of Regions. The key short-term drama was now the fight between Tymoshenko and Firtash. His new role in the Party of Regions was causing increasing controversy: but even if he were to be forced out, he was also alleged to be backing Yatseniuk, along with Khmelnytskyi, whom Tymoshenko sacked as head of the customs service in January 2009 only for Yushchenko to make him deputy head of the SBU. Tymoshenko agreed that RosUkrEnergo's debt to Gazprom would be paid by its rival

Naftohaz Ukraïny, with advance transit payments from Gazprom; in effect RosUkrEnergo now owed Naftohaz money. The customs and security services were dragged into a fight over who owned 11 billion m^3 of gas in underground storage that Natfohaz claimed from RosUkrEnergo, worth $1.7 billion.

The promise of a 20% discount on (actually widely variable) European prices for a year seemed an obvious political gift to Tymoshenko, and rendered the whole dispute seemingly meaningless, as it implied an average price of $228 per 1,000 m^3 in 2009 (other estimates went up to $360, Tymoshenko's calculations may have been based on the underground gas). At the beginning of the dispute Ukraine had been offering $235 (after incremental yearly increases since 2006, Ukraine had been paying $179.50 in 2008). One version of events was that RosUkrEnergo had sabotaged an earlier deal, by offering $285 to try and maintain its own profit margin on imports from Central Asia – as the Central Asian price had been heading up towards the European price, their potential for arbitrage had been disappearing. In both 2006 and 2009, European consumers were too relieved to baulk at the absurdity of what had been agreed: in 2006 this was the barely concealed venality of a price and supply mix set up for the sole benefit of RosUkrEnergo, while in 2009 it was an unclear price and a monthly payment schedule Ukraine could not afford. By spring the 'annual gas crisis' had become monthly.

Towards the Next Election

Tymoshenko was still many people's favourite for the next presidential election, scheduled for January 2010. There is still talk of new parliamentary elections, though the ideal scenario would be a 'big bang': simultaneous parliamentary and presidential elections, together with a referendum on a new constitution. Then Ukraine might finally free itself from the logjam that had existed since the first Orange coalition collapsed in September 2005. Without it, the ongoing stalemate would suit Russia well. The economic crisis, with forecasts for Ukrainian GDP in 2009 as dire as -12%, might also lead to some shakeout amongst the Ukrainian oligarchs.[20] But it could also lead to default. Ukraine was harder hit than almost all its neighbours. Its foreign exchange reserves were down from $38.1 billion to $28.8 billion by the end of January: government and government-secured debt was, it is to be hoped, manageable, but the corporate sector was thought to owe over $40 billion. Unlike Russia, where the oligarchs fought over handouts, Ukraine did not have the funds for too many bailouts. Several major corporate bankruptcies loomed, especially in the steel sector.

Yushchenko, meanwhile, was fast becoming Saakashvili-2. Both men's unique selling point had been their image as young leaders of young democracies. Saakashvili fatally damaged that image by introducing a temporary state of emergency in November 2007, even before his misadventure in South Ossetia in August 2008. Yushchenko's equivalent mistake (his controversial dissolution of parliament in 2007 did not help) was his appointment of Baloha, who turned the president into 'Kuchma-lite' by reverting to strong-arm tactics, the abuse of judiciary and of 'administrative resources'. Yushchenko seemed likely to lose the next elections in whatever form they took, a victim of the forces he had helped unleash in 2004. At best Ukrainian democracy remained immature. President Yuliia seemed a real possibility, but so, amazingly, did President Yanukovych unless the political landscape was to be drastically changed by the shift to a new generation. In 2009 the name most often mentioned was Yatseniuk, but Ukrainian politics had come to be defined by its surprises. Many more undoubtedly lay ahead.

15

Yanukovych's Disastrous Presidency: Another Attempt at Revolution Ends in War

Tymoshenko didn't become president, Yanukovych did. Tymoshenko's main problem was simply incumbency, presiding over a 15% collapse of GDP in 2009 without offering a coherent programme for recovery. Yushchenko's final stab in the front was not just to refuse to back her in the run-off, but to make a series of moves that could only help Yanukovych, most notably a last-minute decree making Stepan Bandera a 'Hero of Ukraine', which did nothing but mobilise voters in the east to tilt at the usual windmills (Yanukovych reversed the award a year later). Yushchenko and his family, and his family's businesses, duly enjoyed a comfortable retirement once Yanukovych was president.

Tymoshenko also undermined her cause by negotiating a 'power-sharing' deal with Yanukovych in April 2009. Although the deal collapsed at the last minute, it showed contempt for democratic choice, plotting a proportional carve-up of all key jobs in central and local government, the two swapping jobs until 2029, delaying parliamentary elections and impeaching Yushchenko. When Tymoshenko resumed her attacks on Yanukovych they therefore lacked credibility, as did her story that the deal would have tamed his instincts and left him free to play golf and tennis, which contradicted her constant warnings that Yanukovych would install an 'openly criminal regime'.[1] Her tragedy was that she was unable to convince enough voters the threat was real.

Yanukovych hid behind expensive US advisers, who dressed him in less expensive suits (but were unable to veto expensive hair treatments) and coached him, with some success, to replace gaffes with soundbites and pose as an East Ukrainian everyman. Even his dark past, it was hinted, made him more 'normal'. Yanukovych promised stability, but little in policy terms.

All the main candidates were supported by oligarchs, playing the local version of musical chairs. Anti-corruption rhetoric was therefore both universal and meaningless. Tymoshenko was backed by Zhevaho, Poroshenko, Serhii Taruta and Vitalii Haiduk. Yushchenko was helped by Kolomoiskyi and even Pinchuk, though more to smooth his exit strategy than as a serious investment in a second term. Yushchenko's backers hedged their bets more than most.[2] Yanukovych was again backed by Akhmetov, Ukraine's richest man. But this time Firtash was just as important, after Tymoshenko had tried to take RosUkrEnergo away from him in 2009. Once Yanukovych won the election, Firtash got 'his gas' back after the new Ukrainian authorities failed to put up any defence against two cases at the Stockholm International Arbitration Tribunal. But Firtash also had much closer ties to Russia. Cheap Russian credit and gas worth up to $11 billion channelled through yet another new company, OSTCHEM, allowed him to buy up much of the Ukrainian chemical and fertiliser industry after 2010.[3]

Yanukovych won, but with only 48.9% of the vote. In yet another polarised election, his vote was nearly all in the east and south. Tymoshenko was close behind with 45.5%, leading in the west and centre, but was not close enough for her claims of marginal fraud to have enough traction. Yushchenko was eliminated in the first round with only 5.5% – a humiliation, but still enough to have tipped the scales the other way.

The uninspiring choice led a record number, 4.4% or 1.1 million, to vote 'against all'. The election was also fertile ground for anyone claiming to be a 'third force', such as the youthful former foreign minister Arsenii Yatseniuk – at least until he switched to a disastrous attempt to portray himself as a Putin clone after hiring some Russian political technologists, limping home with only 7%. The former Yanukovych adviser turned banker Serhii Tihipko won 13%, mainly the votes of the new middle class in Kiev and east Ukrainian cities, for whom Yanukovych was a little too proletarian – though Tihipko eventually joined his new government. The rest were mainly the usual suspects: the Communist leader Petro Symonenko on 3.5%; the perennial 'centrist' and plagiarist academic Volodymyr Lytvyn on 2.4%; and the discredited Socialist Party leader Oleksandr Moroz on 0.4%. One new face, the right-wing firebrand Oleh Tiahnybok, came from nowhere to win 1.4%.

Yanukovych as President

Given how Yanukovych's presidency ended, it is important to remember that there were some positive possibilities at the start of his rule, even if the apparent optimism was mainly a function of 'Ukraine fatigue', or more exactly 'Orange fatigue'. Many were simply glad that the long feuds between Ukraine's big three seemed finally over; although Tymoshenko appeared unable to recognise the fact, concentrating all her energies on attacking the new president rather than on formulating her own survival strategy.

A more balanced foreign policy was a possibility at the start of Yanukovych's presidency. In fact, some commentators, myself included, initially toyed with a local version of the 'Nixon in China' theory – that Yanukovych, because he represented the east of Ukraine, might be better placed to do a historic deal with Europe. His first symbolic visit was to Brussels; but his first substantive deal was with Russia. Cravenly cynical horse-trading produced the Kharkiv Pact, signed in April 2010, which gave Russia a twenty-five year extension on the lease of its Black Sea Fleet in Sevastopil, in return for a fleeting gas discount.

There were some early economic reforms in Yanukovych's first six months as well. The budget was cut and a 50% hike in gas prices agreed. Relations with the IMF briefly re-started, with Ukraine receiving the first two tranches of a $15 billion loan, making Ukraine the world's third largest borrower. But once the economy recovered, albeit weakly (GDP rose by 4% in 2010), the pressure to reform was off. A business-friendly tax reform became the opposite, lining the pockets of the oligarchs and causing protests, dubbed the 'Tax Maidan' by SME leaders in December 2010.

Pressure to reform was further reduced by Yanukovych's elimination of all rival centres of power, which was also largely done in six months, by October 2010. One reason Yanukovych was elected was that Tymoshenko was still prime minister; some kind of power sharing was much more likely this way around. Moreover, according to the constitutional changes agreed in 2004, Tymoshenko was prime minister for the lifetime of the parliament elected in 2007, which was not due to be re-elected until 2012, so long as the party-based majority that elected her remained intact. 'Political tourism', or individual deputies changing sides because of cynicism or bribery, had been banned for good reasons. Tymoshenko's star was on the wane, but all these rules had to be broken to oust her as prime minister in March, with twenty-eight of her deputies and seventeen from Yushchenko's Our Ukraine Party abandoning her, along with Lytvyn as chair of the Rada. Yanukovych replaced her with his loyal ally Mykola Azarov, so he now controlled both parliament and government. In the summer a draconian legal reform, imposing executive control over pay and appointments and creating new loyalist courts or bypassing residually independent ones, ensured he had control over the judiciary too. In October 2010 the Constitutional Court voted to restore the much more presidential pre-2004 constitution, without much in the way of actual legal argument.

Yanukovych Retreats to Mezhyhyriia

These moves were not just unconstitutional, they arguably amounted to a *coup d'état*. But because he was now both all-powerful and incompetent, Yanukovych produced a disaster a year, at least in PR terms. In 2011 he orchestrated a string of 'political prosecutions', including that of

Tymoshenko. In 2012, he presided over the European Championship football finals, which Ukraine co-hosted with Poland. The national team did OK, and the Ukrainians were magnificent hosts; but Yanukovych used the finals to unleash a tidal wave of corruption in public procurement. Ukraine received football stadia and airports, but the new national stadium in Kiev somehow cost almost $600 million. In 2013 Yanukovych provoked mass protests by rejecting a key deal with Europe. In 2014 he ran away to Russia.

This way of telling the story implies constant upheaval, but although the protests of 2013–14 didn't come of out of nowhere, they were unexpected at the time. By November 2013 Yanukovych was three years into a process of hollowing out Ukrainian democracy in advance of the next elections due in 2015. Ukrainians seemed to lack the capacity to protest; or rather protest was now part of the political technology industry. One of the few growth sectors in the Ukrainian economy consisted of the companies that would organise a crowd to order.[4]

Yanukovych increasingly leant on Russian courtiers. Secret parallel agreements to the Kharkiv Pact meant a massive expansion of Russian intelligence activity in Ukraine, and the penetration of the Defence Ministry and SBU by native Russians, including even the ministers at the top. Ukraine's external forces were effectively hollowed out, while the internal ones thrived; Yanukovych spent unprecedented sums on the militia to defend himself and his regime, but ran the army into the ground.

The other change in the elite was the rise of the Yanukovych family. His elder son Oleksandr Yanukovych joined the ranks of the oligarchs, in part to hide the fact that Yanukovych senior was increasingly number one oligarch himself. Oleksandr organised a network of *smotriashchi* (a local mafia term for 'overseer') to target and take over all profitable parts of industry and the state – some of the front men being implausibly young, such as Serhii Kurchenko, born in 1985, and tax boss Oleksandr Klymenko, born in 1980. The energy business, trade and procurement scams were the new favourite schemes. The Ukrainian language has a great word, *shkematolog*, meaning someone whose idea of business is just constant scheming – Oleksandr Yanukovych was in theory a *stomatolog* (dentist), but he was also in charge of the notorious *kopanky*, open-cast mines in the Donbas where desperate locals worked in extremely hazardous conditions to extract illegal coal, which was then marked up and mixed in with official mines' output – making a nonsense of the family's claim to be a friend of its home region. Older scams like VAT rebate bribes were expanded. A giant pyramid of corruption supposedly netted $100 billion over four years.[5]

All of this increasingly personalised power was symbolised by Yanukovych's vast estate at Mezhyhyriia, north of Kiev. Like the Sun King and his nobles, Yanukovych liked to gather a narrowing circle of oligarchs to pay homage at his hunting club at this Ukrainian Versailles. But its ostentatious architecture was not the competitive Baroque of

Louis XIV, just the Soviet kitsch of Yanukovych's *khamokratiia* ('rule of ill-mannered thugs'). Mezhyhyriia had a restaurant inside a Spanish galleon and a zoo full of kangaroos that failed to survive the Ukrainian winter. It was also illegally privatised property, run through a complex network of offshore companies.

The 2012 Rada Elections

The rise of Yanukovych's family really took off after the Rada elections in October 2012. But its rise also meant the economy's fall. Much of Europe was making a faltering recovery, but Ukraine was strangled by corruption. Economic growth ended in the second half of 2012, once the boost of Euro 2012 had faded. Overall GDP grew by only 0.2% in 2012, and 0.4% in 2013. The greedy elite took more and more of a shrinking pie, and were losing popularity even in eastern and southern Ukraine.

This meant fixing the rules for the 2012 elections, mainly by restoring the system last used in 2002: only half of the Rada would be elected by the party lists system and half in territorial constituencies, where the power of money, administrative pressure and patronage was easier to deploy. The Party of Regions duly won only 30% of the party list vote, but half (113 out 225) of the territorial seats, and would sweep up most of the forty-three local 'independents'. The Communists (thirty-two seats) were tame allies, albeit increasingly under Russian influence. But the opposition did surprisingly well. In fact, as in 2002, it technically won, but was denied victory by the system.

A broad coalition was organised around Tymoshenko's old Fatherland Party, which won an impressive 25.6% of the vote. Tymoshenko remained in prison, but Fatherland was still 'her' party, although not all of her colleagues who remained at liberty thought so; the coalition was led by Arsenii Yatseniuk, who was now more 'centrist' than in his ill-fated 2010 campaign. A new centrist party led by the boxer Vitalii Klitschko, named UDAR ('Punch'), won 14%. The elections' big surprise was the far-right Freedom Party, which won 10%. With the old PR system, the opposition troika would therefore have had a majority.

As in 2002, and helped by an increasing clampdown on media freedom, the revival of 'political technology' also distorted the results. The Freedom Party was secretly financed by regime oligarchs and was suddenly ubiquitous on oligarch-controlled TV (the plan being to promote it as an unelectable opposition in 2015). Fatherland (Zhevaho, Pinchuk) and UDAR (Firtash, Kolomoiskyi) took the oligarchs' money too. But, as the newest party, Freedom claimed to be outside the system, and also represented real grievances and economic frustrations, as well as benefiting from being the most radical apparent opposition to Yanukovych, which is why it did so well in Kiev.

That said, the most obviously fake party, Forward Ukraine!, won only 1.6%. The $80 million spent on its campaign (mainly by Akhmetov) was counter-productive. It smelt too plainly of money, despite being named after a football chant and featuring Ukraine's most famous footballer, Andrii Shevchenko, who hung up his boots after scoring twice at Euro 2012.

Ukraine and Europe

Euro 2012, which was won by Spain, was followed by a long year of negotiations with the EU. One of Yushchenko's few achievements had been to launch trade negotiations with Brussels back in 2008, which were supplemented by the launch of the EU's 'Eastern Partnership' in 2009. Two waves of EU expansion in 2004 and 2007 had taken the EU to the borders of Ukraine, though it was never clear whether the new 'Partnership' – aimed at six states in total, Belarus and Moldova alongside Ukraine, plus Georgia, Armenia and Azerbaijan – was a clearing house (a kind of training scheme for eventual membership) or a substitute.

But Ukraine's negotiations were initially the most advanced among the six (Moldova caught up later). In EU jargon, an 'Association Agreement', including a 'Deep and Comprehensive Trade Agreement', was ready to sign by December 2011. However, Tymoshenko was in prison by then, charged with 'abuse of office' over the January 2009 gas agreements with Russia. Her actual crime was far from clear, as was the reason why she was sentenced in October 2011 to seven years in prison and fined a bizarre $188 million.

The EU put the agreements on ice and made them conditional; though it was never explicitly stated whether the key condition was Tymoshenko's release or legal reform to prevent the same thing happening again. (Georgian president Mikheil Saakashvili later revealed how Yanukovych would boast in private meetings 'very loudly about how he had corrupted senior officials, in the supreme court and the constitutional court'.[6]) By 2013 summer, it seemed the EU was getting confused and/or softening its stance, as it needed a political success at the key Eastern Partnership summit in Vilnius in November 2013. Rumours circulated that Tymoshenko's freedom was no longer a prerequisite. This was bad for Ukraine, threatening as it did to give Yanukovych a free pass to entrench himself further in power. Russia could perhaps have been more relaxed, as it looked as though the agreement might be watered down or take years of implementation. But it reacted instead to the increased possibility of Ukraine's mere signature, and unleashed a trade war in August, using much bigger sticks and carrots than the EU. Yanukovych was allegedly threatened with the loss of Crimea,[7] while a $15 billion loan that was agreed in December, most of the first instalment of which instantly disappeared into the family's pockets, seems to have been promised in private earlier.

The Euromaidan

But it was still a shock when Ukraine simply stopped all negotiations with the EU on 21 November, a week before the Vilnius summit. On the same day, parliament gave up on the pretence of legal reform or freeing Tymoshenko. Also on the same day, small demonstrations began on the Kiev Maidan, born of frustration that the Yanukovych regime would now consolidate itself under Russian protection. He continued to string EU leaders along until the very last minute, blatantly trading with both Brussels and Moscow. But once the Vilnius summit ended in disarray, a brutal attempt was made to disperse the protestors in the small hours of 30 November, while Yanukovych went hunting. But the threat of Yanukovych winning the 2015 elections and surviving beyond made for a new resolve. Even on the official figures, seventy-nine protestors were badly injured; but thousands more flooded into the Maidan and began a permanent occupation – the same location as in 2004, but in a very different style.

This time, the protests would last for three months. They were dubbed the 'Euromaidan', but this was something of a misnomer, as general opposition to the regime was the driving force. Unlike 2004, the authorities vacillated, but only between taking a hard line and a harder line. Andrii Kliuiev, the head of Yanukovych's presidential administration, said in private, 'this is war, and in war all means are good'.[8] The local militia, the *Berkut*, were toughened up and reportedly trained by Russians to regard the protestors as paid sub-human representatives of *gayropa* ('Gay Europe').[9] They were supplemented by gangs of local thugs, dubbed *titushki*, recruited from sports clubs, the unemployed and Russian nationalist fight-clubs like Oplot.

But the threat of Western sanctions worried many of the regime's oligarchic supporters. Periodic repression and violence was usually followed by relative calm; the regime could not go all out, but shifted much of its repression 'off screen' – organising kidnappings and beatings of protesters away from the Maidan and therefore away from the world's cameras and smart phones.

In response, the protesters dug in; the Maidan looked more and more like a fortress. The crowds grew younger and more radical at the sharp end, as conflict escalated. But at the same time, they were backed by a much stronger civil society than in 2004. Activists raised money, cooked meals, provided cars, recorded regime violence and rebuffed Russian propaganda online. Whenever the regime threatened the protestors, they could count on a hinterland of hundreds of thousands of ordinary citizens of Kiev in support.

On the other hand, there was even more frustration than in 2004. One of the key arguments for non-violent protest is not giving the authorities the excuse or narrative they need to crack down. But what if they are going to invent that narrative and crack down anyway? Ukrainian and Russian media tried to pretend all the protestors were Nazis. After a secret trip by Yanukovych to confer with Putin, notorious 'Dictatorship Laws' were rammed through parliament without a real vote on 16 January 2014, criminalising everything the protestors had been doing and more. Confrontation escalated and four protestors were killed on 22 January. The protestors fought back with cobblestones, Molotov cocktails and improvised weapons.

On 28 January an apparent compromise led to the resignation of Prime Minister Azarov, who showed his confidence in Yanukovych's future by fleeing to Austria, and the repeal of some of the Dictatorship Laws. But then Yanukovych disappeared for four days, so his 'illness' would prevent him signing or negotiating anything. This only left an unfinished agenda for political change. On 18 February a mass march on parliament to demand revisions to the constitution and new elections led to renewed confrontation and another sixteen dead. The final showdown came on 20 February, when seventy protestors were shot dead by snipers. The total recorded number of dead kept changing due to the chaotic conditions and chilling number of the 'disappeared' (272 as of March 2014);[10] but 103 were eventually listed as dead, plus thirteen militia, and dubbed the 'Heavenly Hundred'.

Only after such violence, and with the prospect of the tables turning if a reported 1,200 weapons seized in west Ukraine were to reach Kiev, did the regime begin to show real cracks. Some 5,000 militia evacuated Kiev on the 21 February.[11] Nevertheless, a deal was still negotiated and signed that afternoon by EU envoys. The 2004 constitution would be restored, and there would be a national unity government and new elections in December. Many baulked at the prospect of Yanukovych remaining president until then, but he didn't stay long, fleeing Kiev in the small hours of 22 February.

Russia Invades

Yanukovych and Russia may well have hoped events in Kiev would look more like a *coup d'état* after he fled, but the Maidan forces were too restrained. There was no 'revolutionary justice', in fact the opposite. The snipers and their political bosses escaped; though Russia carried on claiming there was mass disorder and discrimination against ethnic Russians anyway. But the euphoria in Kiev lasted only a week, before Russia first seized Crimea and then fomented a war in east Ukraine.

Some have used underlying grievances and alienation in Crimea and east Ukraine to explain the events after February 2014.[12] Others have argued that the crisis showed the inherent flaws in the Ukrainian project ever since 1991.[13] But although this book has argued that the Ukrainian nation-building project was indeed 'unexpected' and capable of fraying around the edges, things were always more complicated than a simple binary split between a nationalist and pro-European half of Ukraine and its pro-Russian rival. Ukraine had not lost Crimea or the Donbas in 1994 and had not split in 2004; things were not necessarily any worse this time around.

Pro-Russian sentiments clearly existed, but were everywhere a minority. Even in Crimea one reliable opinion poll taken in the second week of February showed 41% of voters supporting union with Russia; compared to 33% in Donetsk, 24% in Luhansk and a national average of 12%.[14] And much of this sentiment was self-inflicted. Ten years of polarising prop-aganda since 2004 had gone into overdrive during the Maidan. Eastern and southern Ukraine were also disaffected by decades of bad government and by Yanukovych's gesture politics and failure to deliver economic recovery. Another opinion poll in April 2014, after his flight to Russia, showed that only 19.6% in the east and south still thought that Yanukovych was, or more or less was, the legitimate president; but they weren't that keen on the new authorities either, with only 30–33% backing his succes-sors (see below). Popular opinion was also split on the Maidan: 41.7% in the south and east saw the events as a 'citizens' protest against corruption and the arbitrary dictatorship of Yanukovych'; but 46% saw an 'armed *coup d'état*, organised by the opposition with the help of the West'.[15]

But it is important to emphasise just how much of the local rebellions was artifice. Russia and pro-Russian forces did what was now ingrained, and cloned what they thought they had seen on the Maidan, but so-called *Putingi* (pro-Putin *mitingi* or meetings) were a pale imitation. So in Crimea they opted for a *coup d'état*, which was much more effective. The Russian move was so rapid, it was clearly pre-planned, most prob-ably drawn up at the time of Russia's war with Georgia in 2008; though some say 2006,[16] and former Putin adviser Andrei Illarionov says 2003.[17] Yanukovych was reportedly threatened with the loss of Crimea to help him change his mind over the EU Agreements in 2013, as was Yushchenko over his attempts to veto Russia's use of the Black Sea Fleet in the war with Georgia in 2008.

Armed men took over the local Crimean assembly and forced a change of government on 27 February. The new Crimean prime minister was a former gangster known as 'Goblin', Sergei Aksionov, whose Russian nationalist party had won only 4% at the 2012 Crimean elections. Even the notorious rebel commander sent from Russia, Igor Strelkov, later admitted that the operation had been a coup. 'I did not see any support from the (Crimean) state authorities in Simferopol where I was. It was militants who collected deputies and forced them to vote [for Aksionov]. Yes, I was one of the commanders of those militants'. But they were backed by Russian forces, both in the Black Sea Fleet based in Sevastopil and new arrivals.[18] An infamous Russian medal, 'For the Return of Crimea', was dated 'from 20 February to 18 March'. In March 2015 a hubristic Putin appeared in a Russian TV documentary in which he boasted about ordering the invasion overnight on 22–23 February.[19] The coup that changed the Crimean government was therefore precisely that, the local militias were really Russian armed forces, and the referendum they organised in March with a 96.7% vote for union with Russia was both fake and irrelevant.

Things didn't work out the same in eastern Ukraine. A few noisy locals conducted unsuccessful demonstrations in March. So Strelkov led a stealth invasion in April. But even this produced only a local spark, not a conflagration. Russia clearly expected some sort of general uprising throughout Novorossiia, the idea endorsed by Putin that the whole of Russian-speaking eastern and southern Ukraine was just an extension of Russia; but this didn't happen. Strelkov admitted, 'the only factor that was missing' was 'the presence of the Russian army'.[20] His point was to claim that annexation could also have been possible in the Donbas, but his argument clearly underscored the artificial side of the protests.

In Crimea Russian troops were already in place, though more were quickly sent. Now they were massed on the east Ukrainian border. NATO counted 40,000: Ukrainian sources claim that the figure was 146,000 in April 2014, in three separate groups poised for an all-out invasion; one at the Belarus–Russian border to seize Kiev, one around Kursk to invade Kharkiv, and one to attack the Donbas from Rostov-on-Don; while amphibious forces could attack Odesa from Crimea. Half of the higher figure were claimed to be paramilitary forces of the Russian Interior and Emergency Situations Ministries – the type you would need for a full occupation.[21]

The Russian troops also had an indirect role, encouraging revolt and limiting Ukraine's options, while Russian-armed proxies took power. Ultimately, however, so-called 'hybrid war' didn't look so clever or effective in the Donbas as in Crimea: the main initial result was anarchy. Russia could deny its involvement, but if it wanted to preserve deniability then its involvement had to be limited. (Ukraine won limited concessions in September 2014 after it threatened to reveal hundreds of captured dog tags, Russian soldiers' IDs, to the world media.[22]) The number of Russian dead, 800 by early 2015 according to one source, was also a constraint.[23] Plus the Kremlin and the GRU (Main Intelligence Directorate) had little to work with on the ground. Strelkov stood out for his ascetic nationalism; most of the local foot soldiers were drawn from the same social circles as the *titushki*. Many were drunks or criminals.

But a consistent Russian modus operandi soon emerged. A few hundred special forces and GRU in command-and-control functions were ever present, along with volunteers from Russia and specialist crews for advanced weaponry.[24] Chechen special forces were already stationed in the rear, east of Donetsk city, in case any fighters proved less than enthusiastic. The number of regular troops varied with the task in hand. Whole battalion tactical groups were committed for the big battles, meaning 10,000 regular Russian troops in Ukraine by the end of 2014. No less than 117 units were involved, 104 of which saw fighting, which meant 42,000 men in total, rotated in and out across the border, to keep frontline troops fresh and Ukraine and the West confused. There were also 26,000 to 28,000 Russian troops in the now heavily militarised Crimea. The number of Russian nationalist volunteers from Russia was several hundred.[25] Local fighters also numbered around 10,000, with proper uniforms by June 2014, Russian kit from the time of the Chechen and Georgia wars. Wages of $350 a month and $500 for officers produced a steady stream of volunteers; though according to one commentator at least, 'rebel formations in essence have been used as cannon fodder'.[26]

There was a regular routine of fight-pause-resume. What looked like or were claimed to be ceasefires were in fact re-supply periods. The rebels used a lot of ordinance, as the simplest way of defeating the Ukrainians was overwhelming force, and Russia used a series of 'humanitarian convoys' to smuggle in supplies. Temporary withdrawals or demilitarised zones at the front-line meant little, as the rebels were supplied with fast tanks and (armoured personnel carriers).

After simply not fighting in Crimea, the Ukrainian armed forces, reinforced with new volunteer battalions, many of them veterans from the Maidan, put up a better than expected fight. By the summer the rebels were on the defensive, and Russia may have thought of abandoning them, until they were saved by a conventional Russian attack in late August. The Ukrainians sued for peace; but the Minsk agreement signed in September failed to stop the rebels from fighting, and another 1,500 were killed by late January 2015.[27] The second Minsk agreement in February 2015 was even worse. The rebels ignored both, or, as they were so inured to telling lies, claimed they allowed them to do what they wanted, like holding 'elections' in November 2014 or taking the key town of Debaltseve in February 2015. The rebel 'republics' were now 'like a modern-day Sparta, armed with prodigious amounts of artillery and more than 500 Russian tanks' – which if accurate, was twice as many as the British army.[28] The rebels also had escalation bias: Russia would allow them to keep any territory they gained, and bail them out if they suffered losses. Fighting was almost all the rebel leaders were any good at, and they needed victories to divert attention from an economic and humanitarian disaster in the region.

But most importantly, the rebels didn't have what they wanted; as of March 2015 neither the whole of Donetsk and Luhansk nor even the territory they originally occupied in June 2014, still less the whole of Novorossiia. Some rebels, and their supporters in Russia now led by the exiled Strelkov, argued Russia was holding them back.

The conflict therefore seemed far from over in spring 2015, by which time the number of dead was more than 6,000 and Ukraine had to cope with 1.3 million IDPs (internally displaced persons), while around 700,000 had moved to Russia.[29]

The New Ukraine

Even as he set about trying to destroy Ukraine, Putin was paradoxically helping to reinvent it. Like Stalin, whose armed forces had done what the UPA could not and 'liberated' west Ukraine from the Poles in the 1940s, Putin was actually a Ukrainian nation-builder. Many commentators claimed to detect the 'birth of a new political nation', which was technically exact, but the infant was still vulnerable. A new civic patriotism was no longer defined by language disputes (even the extremist Right Sector now argued that only the cause mattered, not what language you spoke). Elections and opinion polls showed greater unity across Ukraine, minus Crimea and half the Donbas; although there was a strong contrary trend, especially in Galicia, to demonise the Donbas as too Soviet, too criminal, too corrupt and too disloyal. Many argued that Ukraine would be better off without it – which was a strange argument to others when Ukraine was fighting to keep it.[30] Civil society groups such as *Dopomoha Dnipro* (Help on the Dnieper), which had previously found life precarious in eastern and southern Ukraine, now mushroomed, focused on supporting the army and helping IDPs. Dnipropetrovsk, previously such a Soviet city, emerged as the capital of the new patriotism. The idea of the east and south as an alternative Ukraine, with its neo-soviet, localist or hybrid identities, seemed to be in decline, as a new bilingual, multiethnic and state-centred patriotism took hold. The border between Russia and Ukraine, which in the 1990s was often seen as an artificial impediment, at least in eastern Ukraine, was now increasingly seen as a security issue. Russia was doing its best to prove that Drahomanov and Lypynskyi were right (see page 94): the core difference between Ukraine and Russia was not language but political culture. The Ukrainians might not be ideal democrats and Europeans, but the difference between an imperfect Ukrainian democracy and authoritarian Russia's sudden recidivist imperial spasm was clear enough.

The role of nationalism in the Maidan protests was also misunderstood. It was a motivating factor for some, but for most cause and effect was the other way round. The protests came first and led to a 'revolution of values' – not just the photogenic but belated dismantling of Soviet monuments that caught world headlines, but also the reappropriation of nationalist symbols. 'Glory to the heroes!' used to be a UPA slogan, a relic of the past. Now it was universal, as there were current-day heroes to celebrate. National flags and symbols, once controversial, were also more universal, as a symbol of support for a state under siege rather than a particular historiography. In other words, a lot of what looked like nationalism in Kiev, especially as depicted in Russian propaganda, wasn't what it seemed. Ukrainians themselves, including those on the right, preferred to call the events the 'Revolution of Dignity', depicted not in terms of ethnicity or class, but in simple civic black and white – a revolution of the people against Yanukovych's 'Mordor' and his 'Orcs'.

The Maidan had also been supported by most of Ukraine's religions. But there was a sense that religion needed to be more religious and less corrupt, as part of the revolution of values. There was a surge in support for the Kievan Patriarchate over its discredited Moscow rival. But the new Ukraine was multi-faith as much as it was multi-lingual. Jews and Crimean Tatars could be Ukrainian patriots, and Protestants were prominent in NGOs supporting IDPs – in sharp contrast to the intolerant brand of Russian Orthodox Messianism fuelling the separatist conflict in the Donbas.

But most of this freshly minted Ukrainian unity was horizontal. Vertical linkage between the new Ukrainians and their old rulers was still a problem. Politics-as-usual proved surprisingly resilient. The oligarchy did not fall. Even the Yanukovych family continued to operate its many businesses from exile in Russia. Entrenched corruption and bad government remained endemic. 'Lustration' therefore became the buzzword.

Rebooting the Political System

Given that Russia depicted the situation after the uprising in Kiev as 'a *coup d'état* supported by external forces' leading to 'continuing anarchy', 'real threats to life and the safety of people, everyday cases of violence, gross and mass violation of human rights',[31] it is important to note that government was ineffective but not absent in the immediate aftermath. The three opposition parties who thought they were the real winners of the 2012 elections simply formed an 'acting government', including the Freedom Party, which was a calamitous free gift to Russian propaganda about Nazis in Kiev. Tymoshenko's Fatherland Party took most positions; Yatseniuk became the prime minister and Oleksandr Turchynov acting president. Tymoshenko herself was freed on 22 February, but took no formal position. Unfortunately there was no attempt to form a national unity government with representatives of eastern and southern Ukraine. There was disdain for the old Party of Regions and those who had voted for the January Dictatorship Laws, but there was also a pressing need to consolidate power east of Kiev, where many local elites were hedging their bets, and some were playing with fire.

Ukraine's most important achievement was to hold new elections; though they only partially succeeded, in the words of the new local cliché, in 'rebooting' the political system. The new president was from the old elite, but in the new parliament 236 out of 423 MPs (56%) were first-timers.[32] But at the least, the simple fact of fresh elections exposed the absurdity of Russian propaganda about illegitimate power in Kiev. In fact, an authoritarian state was attacking a democratic one. That said, politics took something of a back seat while the war was on.

Presidential elections were fast-forwarded to May. After something resembling a revolution in February, Ukrainians were now at war and already looking for a safe pair of hands. Tymoshenko had failed to adjust to new political realities since her release from prison. Having been a symbol of the old regime's repression for so long, she had hoped for more of a hero's welcome; but for many she simply represented the old style of politics before 2014. She stood for president again, but won only 12.8%. On the other hand, May was too early for any new Maidan politicians to emerge, and most of them were 'anti-political' anyway. On the right, Tiahnybok won just 1.2% and the leader of Right Sector Dmytro Yarosh 0.7%. Their fake populist rival Oleh Liashko (backed by many of the oligarchs to replace the Freedom Party) did better, with 8.3%. The remnants of the Party of Regions, various centrist projects and old hands like the Communist leader Symonenko scrambled for votes.

The field was therefore surprisingly clear for Petro Poroshenko. He was a businessman or oligarch, depending on your definition, and hardly a neophyte, having rowed with Tymoshenko during her 2005 premiership, backed her in 2010 and then ended up in Yanukovych's government in 2012, if only for nine months. When the protests began he was 'independent'. His overwhelming win, with 54.7%, was mainly due to a desire to avoid risks, consolidate the political system against Russia's attacks, close ranks between the regions – Poroshenko was ahead in every one, a remarkable change since the many polarised elections between 2004 and 2012 – and avoid a potentially dangerous second round. It also helped that Crimea and a considerable portion of the Donbas could not or would not vote.

Poroshenko's election slogan was 'Living the New Way'. He represented the idea of the 'Ukraine of the Centre', proposed back in 2010 by a Kiev-based Russian-speaking intellectual Mykhail Dubynianskii, namely a new Ukraine free of both the authoritarian Yanukovych and 'Galician and Donbas tribalists'.[33] But Poroshenko also represented rather too much of politics-as-usual.

New Rada elections were held in October 2014. The precarious ceasefire signed in east Ukraine in September fuelled a desire to re-launch the reform projects largely sidelined since the coup in Crimea. Even Poroshenko talked of 'rebooting' the political system; but unlike the presidential election, a big majority for his newly formed Poroshenko Block seemed counter-productive. It would allow too much of politics-as-usual to survive as his coalition of centrists and turncoats took over as much of the old regime as possible. The civic activists who joined the party, like the crusading journalist Mustafa Nayiem who started the Euromaidan protests with a famous tweet (to do more than 'like' his protests and go to the Maidan), underestimated the mood for change.

Poroshenko caused much controversy by not pushing harder to change the election rules adopted in 2012. Voters sought out the newest and freshest-looking party: the cleverly named Self-Help, which surged from nowhere into third place with 11%. The Poroshenko Block also lost ground to the newly formed Popular Front led by Yatseniuk, which initially campaigned for a tougher line with Russia, but realised that most Ukrainians were war-weary; and those who weren't were likely to vote for even more radical parties. So the Front switched tactics in the last week to call for 'Yatseniuk in his proper place', meaning to remain as prime minister rather than allow Poroshenko to monopolise power. It came first in the PR vote, with 22.2% against 21.8% for the Poroshenko Block. The fact that the latter finished with more seats because of the territorial constituencies also marked it out as an 'old-style' party. Tymoshenko was left even further behind. The new mantra of 'self-help' now conflicted with her self-appointed role as national saviour, and her Fatherland Party only just won the necessary 5%.

As in May, Right Sector won only 2%; though more than twenty veterans and army commanders were elected, including Andrii Biletskyi, the commander of the Azov battalion of right-wing activists. But the veterans' role in the new parliament was ambiguous: some wanted to 'cleanse' the system, like the civic activists; some wanted more resources for national defence, regardless of where they came from. The idea that they might lead a 'third Maidan' was overdone. Any new protests might be more violent, which would only play into Russia's hands.

The Freedom Party had lost its niche as the most radical opponent of President Yanukovych to those who actually fought and died on the Maidan. It won only 4.7% and failed to enter the new Rada, which at least deprived Russia of one source of propaganda. Once again, voters preferred the fake populist bluster of Liashko (7.4%) to real hard-line nationalists.

A new Opposition Block was cobbled together at the last minute after the old ruling party, the Party of Regions, decided not to stand, but it was an obvious life raft for Yanukovych supporters, many of whom were accused of running solely to benefit from deputies' constitutional immunity from prosecution. Poroshenko was accused of a secret deal with Putin to allow some of them to stand unopposed in the Donbas. The Block was organised by Viktor Medvedchuk, whose daughter has President Putin for a godfather. It was even more pro-Russian than the Party of Regions, which, when in office, had concentrated on doing favours for itself more than the Kremlin. As in the presidential election, Ukraine was less regionally divided than in previous elections, but the

Opposition Block still won 9.4% of the vote, mainly in the east. According to Oleksii Haran, the point was not the mere existence of a Russian fifth column in Ukraine: 'Putin [was] interested in seeing how big a Fifth Column he [could] get',[34] and hoped to see it grow under the stress of the military and economic challenges he himself had imposed.

There was only one real coalition option: a new government made up of the Popular Front, Poroshenko Block and Self-Help. All three were pro-European, which was a first in Ukrainian history; and their comfortable majority meant the new government had no excuse for not getting things done, except the war in the east. Liashko and Tymoshenko have also joined, but they most likely won't stay for long. They behave as if they are in opposition anyway.

Challenges Ahead

The economy remained Ukraine's weak spot. Even in the 2000s growth had never been stellar, followed by one of Europe's worst recessions in 2009 and a weak recovery in 2010–11 – even before the Yanukovych regime emptied the coffers and the costs of war with Russia and its proxies piled up. Ukraine's GDP fell by 6.9% in 2014. The reform plans of the new government that took office after the October 2014 elections could also have been more convincing. Headlines were made by the appointment of foreign-born ministers to repeat reforms that had been successful in Georgia (traffic police and health), Estonia (e-government) and Lithuania (cutting spending and bureaucracy to emerge from the 2009 recession); but they were overshadowed by the fear that the government was playing a giant game of chicken with the West, doing only the minimum to induce new lending in the hope that the EU and US would not allow a country under attack from Russia to go under. It was even rumoured the foreign parachutists would be replaced once funding was secured. Ukraine launched a so-called 'de-oligarchisation' campaign, but it really amounted to a few forced adjustments to the rules of oligarchy. The new government was so desperate for money it had to close off some of the most egregious examples of leaching the state budget. Ihor Kolomoiskyi was forced to step down as governor of Dnipropetrovsk; Naftohaz Ukraïny was partially reformed. But the oligarchy, and the individual oligarchs, remained.

Nevertheless, a new IMF deal for $17.5 billion was agreed on 12 February, the same day as the second Minsk agreement, leading to a four-year programme with all lenders of around $40 billion. Just in time, as the currency, the Hryvnia, had fallen by 70%. A package of laws passed in March promised to begin the difficult work of slashing the budget and bloated bureaucracy, raising energy prices to remove the main source of corruption (cheap energy meant for households diverted to industry or sale at world prices) and cut the pensions bill.

One poll showed that a more patriotic public was more prepared to make sacrifices: 10% for 'as long as it takes' and 33% for up to a year, but that left 48% unprepared or too sceptical.[35] Putin clearly hoped for the opposite and that the new government would soon collapse, once the public mood turned sour. In the first quarter of 2015, with a real war and a trade war both raging. Ukrainian GDP fell by 17.6%. Russia was suffering from international sanctions and a lower oil price: as in 2009, its famously huge international reserves had fallen by a third in a year, so could be used up in another two. But Russian GDP 'only' fell by 2.2% in the first quarter. It looked like Russia could last longer.

The war in the Donbas was far from over. Crimea was annexed but isolated. Sanctions and the collapse of tourism hit its economy hard. The 270,000 Crimean Tatars were stranded and oppressed. The risk of problems spilling over into the rest of the region was ever present.

Ukraine's future lay in the balance, but this time, unlike so many other occasions since 1991, largely because of external pressure. The consequences of a second failed revolution in ten years would be catastrophic, but Russia seems determined to make it happen.

16

Poroshenko and Zelenskyi

Ukraine's first task after 2014 was to survive. Despite the defeats at Ilovaisk and Debaltseve, the military turnaround in 2014–15 was remarkable. With only 6,000 battle-ready soldiers in February 2014,[1] there was within two years a regular army of 250,000. The volunteer battalions were incorporated into the regular army. Conscription for men aged 18 to 27 was reintroduced in May 2014. By 2020 Ukraine was spending over 4% of GDP on defence, twice the NATO target; but not counting the huge ongoing civil society effort to mobilise and maintain the army. The war in the east never became a 'frozen' conflict. It remained a proper war, as Russia and the rebel 'Republics' sought to bleed Ukraine of men and materials. The OHCHR estimated 14,200 to 14,400 casualties by January 2022, including 3,404 civilians.[2] Ukraine was in a weaker position diplomatically. Western governments led by France and Germany pressured Ukraine to move on its parts of the Minsk 'agreements' specifying internal political concessions, before Russia completed its parts, especially troop withdrawal and the restoration of border control to Kyiv. The Ukrainian parliament passed a constitutional reform bill at first reading with 265 votes in August 2015; three police were killed in riots outside. A provisional special status bill for the Donbas was passed annually. But Russia's real goal, disguised as 'federalisation', was a second version of Bosnia-Herzegovina – a minimal central Ukrainian state, with the Donbas having veto powers over the whole.

The war and Russia's additional ongoing trade war put enormous strain on the Ukrainian economy. In 2014–15 GDP fell by 17% from peak to trough. The currency collapsed; foreign exchange reserves were below $5 billion; GDP per capita hit a low of $2,200. With a steep recession added to the cost of war, there were many voices saying now was not the time to reform. Maidan activists, however, argued that this was precisely why Putin had annexed Crimea and fomented unrest in east Ukraine – to prevent Ukraine becoming a successful counter-example to Russia. Ukraine's military won eventual success precisely because it was reformed. Ukraine's new leaders rushed to tie up the EU Association

Agreement that Yanukovych had abandoned. It was split into two parts to help, with the political half signed in March 2014 and the economic half in June. The EU then set up a wholly unnecessary year's 'consultation' with Russia; so the Agreement, with its Deep and Comprehensive Free Trade Agreement, belatedly came into force in January 2016. Russia's share of Ukraine's trade fell from one-third to under 10%; the EU share went up; but so did Ukrainian trade to the south and the developing world. Ukraine remained heavily dependent on metal exports; because of the EU Common Agricultural Policy, grain went mainly to the Middle East. But the EU Agreements also helped reshape politics: the 'sandwich' of the EU and domestic civil society often pressed a reluctant government towards reform; particularly because there were enough reformist ministers in the first post-Maidan government to do their own thing or add to the pressure on the old guard.

Reform efforts were paying off by the third quarter of 2015. Thereafter the economy grew by an average of 3% a year. Government spending as a proportion of GDP was cut from 44.8% to 40.6%. A fiscal deficit of –10% of GDP became a small surplus. The highly corrupt banking system was cleaned up: over ninety 'pocket banks' (for oligarchs to lend to themselves) were closed. The biggest, Ihor Kolomoiskyi's PrivatBank was nationalised in 2016, with $5.5 billion missing. Many SOEs were reformed, particularly Naftohaz, whose massive annual deficit of –5.5% of GDP was turned into a small surplus. Gas prices were increased to cut down on corruption, and reduce consumption of Russian imports. In return, household gas subsidies went up from 1% to 1.7% of GDP. Domestic gas production was increased; there were consumption economies; reverse gas supply meant an end to Russian imports. The gas import bill was cut from a maximum of $12 billion in 2009 to $2 billion. According to one think-tank analysis of 'Ukraine's Fight Against Corruption', $6 billion a year was saved from closing down various schemes and scams.[3] Ukraine improved in the global Ease of Doing Business Index from 140th in 2012 to 64th in 2019. A debt deal on $18 billion with foreign creditors was reached in August 2015.

Anti-corruption reforms included the online procurement system ProZorro (Ukrainian for 'transparent') and E-liky for health care. A National Anti-Corruption Bureau (NABU) was set up in 2015. But all-important legal reform was constantly frustrated by entrenched corruption. NABU could only investigate crime, not prosecute. The necessary complement, the High Anti-Corruption Court of Ukraine, was not established until September 2019. An embryonic public broadcaster, eventually called Suspilne ('Public', a would-be 'Ukrainian BBC'), was set up, although under-funded.

Once military and economic survival seemed assured, the post-Maidan authorities abandoned their early caution on cultural policy. The attempted repeal of the 2012 Language Law in February 2014 had been widely seen as a mistake. But an Education Law in 2017 made Ukrainian the language of instruction after the fifth grade, a policy to be phased in by 2023, although allowing for minority languages. In the last weeks of the Poroshenko presidency a law on 'Supporting the Functioning of the Ukrainian Language as the State Language' made Ukrainian the language of state administration. 90% of TV and film content should be in Ukrainian, 50% for printed media and books. In 2015 four Decommunisation Laws banned the use of Soviet symbols, mandated the removal and substitution of Soviet-era place names and the removal of statues, and renamed the Soviet Great Patriotic War as World War Two.

Remembrance was Europeanised, with a new emphasis on sacrifice rather than victory. Ukraine adopted the poppy symbol, and Victory Day was shifted from 9 to 8 May. The law on the 'Legal Status and Honouring of the Memory of the Fighters for the Independence of Ukraine in the 20th Century' created a pantheon stretching from the UNR to the OUN and UPA to Rukh. But it only included nationalists and dissidents; no mention was made of Ukrainian Communists. By 2022 public opinion in Ukraine was markedly divergent to Russia. Only 11% regretted the fall of the USSR, compared to 63% in Russia. 80% saw the holiday as a day for 'remembrance of war victims', 15% saw it as 'Victory Day'. All 'fighters for independence' were now seen as positive, including Khmelnytskyi and Hrushevskyi, but now also Ivan Mazepa (up from 44% in 2012 to 76% in 2022), Petliura (26% in 2012 to 49% in 2022) and even Stepan Bandera (22% in 2012 to 74% in 2022).[4] In February 2019 the constitution was changed to assert 'the European identity of the Ukrainian people and the irreversibility of the European and Euro-Atlantic course of Ukraine'. Cultural and attitudinal change after the Maidan was huge. Solid majorities now wanted membership of the EU and NATO, even if both seemed a long way off. On the other hand, economic recovery after 2015 was uneven; and a fixed majority of 70% thought the country was headed in the wrong direction,[5] even though they also reported slowly improving personal and family circumstances.[6]

'Sistema' Also Survives

It was illogical that this scepticism was little changed by economic, political or military events. But Ukrainians were right to be wary that the 'Revolution of Dignity' had been more revolutionary on a societal than on a political level. After a quarter century of patchy reform, vested post-Communist interests were entrenched. What Ukrainians called 'sistema' also survived after 2014. Reforms were not radical or comprehensive enough to dismantle Old Corruption and its complex networks, informal practices and defence mechanisms. The main oligarchs did not lose much property, though their wealth was trimmed by recession. According to research by David Dalton, 'the domestic business wealth of the 100 richest Ukrainians' as a percentage of GDP 'fell from a peak of 18% in 2010 to around 9% in 2017'.[7] The decline was important, but didn't affect the way that politics worked. The oligarchs still dominated Ukrainian media: the main oligarch-owned TV channels had a 70% market share.[8] Which they used to exercise political influence via political technology parties. Most bought influence in the new administration – and protection in the judiciary and Procurator's Office. Some like Ihor Kolomoiskyi reinvented themselves as bulwarks against separatism.

Reformers in government, known as 'white crows' (black sheep), were picked off one by one. In February 2016 the government fell. Prime Minister Yatseniuk was replaced by a Poroshenko loyalist and stability-first administrator Volodymyr Groisman. Poroshenko expanded his business from beer and chocolate into areas like banking and energy,[9] where profits depended on informal connections. He and other oligarchs featured in the Panama Papers in 2016. They protected themselves with a so-called 'sweet counter-revolution' ('sweet' because it was not full-on revanche, but also a reference to Poroshenko's chocolate company Roshen,[10] whose shops now occupied the best spots on Ukrainian high streets). The most outspoken NGO activists, such as the heads of the Anti-Corruption Centre (AntAC) found themselves harassed. IMF relations stalled in 2017–18, meaning yet another uncompleted programme, despite a new bridging loan in December 2018.

The authorities found it difficult to sell the success of their reforms. A narrative set in that politicians enriched themselves, while ordinary people paid the price. In Ukrainian, this was #zrada ('betrayal') interpreting any event in a negative light. #pogana vlada or 'bad power' was personified by Poroshenko, the #baryga or 'huckster'. The elite were #torgivlia na krovi, 'making money on blood' – i.e. the war in the east – while for everyone else there was only #zubozhinnia or 'impoverishment'. #zrada was not shifted by economic recovery or by political reforms.

Russia also changed tactics. As the chimera of Novorossiia disappeared, Russia shifted much of its military efforts to Syria in September 2015. But at the same time it reinvented its propaganda in Ukraine. Most Russian TV was banned in 2014. Measures against some social media like VKontakte followed in 2017. Trust in Russian mass media was anyway only 4%.[11] But Russia rebuilt an audience by using Ukrainian proxy owners for new media projects, particularly Viktor Medvedchuk, who by 2019 had indirect control over three TV stations: 112, NewsOne and ZIK. Russia also used social media; populist sites like strana.ua, launched in 2016, echoed many Russian propaganda points. They attacked the Maidan; Ukrainian reforms had failed; Ukraine was 'country 404' – 'country not found'.[12] Shock jock vlogger Anatolii Sharyi set up a party which won 2.2% in the 2019 elections. Churnalism and junk news sites could be easily fed. Ukraine was more united and patriotic; but still vulnerable to what Russians called 'shadow technology'.

The New Orthodox Church of Ukraine

The Moscow Church was one of Russia's biggest channels of influence. At the time of the Maidan Revolution, Ukraine still had the three rival Orthodox Churches from the 1990s (see pages 235–6). President Yushchenko pushed for Orthodox unity when Ecumenical Patriarch Bartholomeos visited Kyiv in 2008; but failed because he was basically pushing for a bigger version of Filaret's narrowly nationalist Ukrainian Orthodox Church, the UOC(KP). The Maidan Revolution changed perspectives entirely. Only the Moscow Church failed to endorse the protestors. In Kyiv, UOC(KP) churches provided physical shelter. The Greek Catholics also strongly backed the protests, in both Kyiv and Lviv; as did Jewish and Crimean Tatar leaders and activists. The conflict was often framed in religious terms: Yanukovych was Herod, the cruel tyrant servant of empire,[13] the Ukrainians needed their Moses.[14] Many UOC(MP) priests supported the rebels in the east, while framing the Maidan protestors for *besnovanie*, meaning 'possession' by ethnophyletism (putting nation before God) or foreign forces.[15] Two of Ukraine's Churches also gained new leaders in 2014. Metropolitan Makarii of the UAOC had been part of the autocephalous movement since 1989. For the UOC(MP), on the other hand, Metropolitan Volodymyr died after a long illness, and was replaced by Onufrii, a more militant supporter of the 'Russian World'. The UOC(KP) was still led by the controversial Filaret. So two Orthodox Churches were closer together; but further apart from the UOC(MP). In parliament, however, there was a new political consensus: two votes in June 2016 (245 MPs) and April 2018 (268 MPs) asked the Ecumenical Patriarch to grant autocephaly to Ukraine. According to Rostyslav Pavlenko, who was then the deputy head of the presidential administration in charge of the negotiations: 'there were three reasons for Phanar's agreement [the site of the Patriarch's residence in Istanbul]. The new elite consensus. The fact that opinion polls had changed since 2014 [towards autocephaly]. And Russian behaviour.'[16] The Russian Church had failed to attend the all-Orthodox Council in Crete in 2016, despite years of planning by the Ecumenical Patriarch, and then condemned its decisions afterwards.

By 2018 Poroshenko added his strong support. In October a Synod of the Ecumenical Patriarchate decided to lift the anathema against Patriarch Filaret of the UOC(KP). In a huge historical move, the decision of Bartholomeos's predecessor to accept the dissolution of the Kyivan Church in 1686 was overturned and the Kyivan Metropolitanate restored. The idea was then that all three Orthodox Churches would unite under its banner. Filaret was therefore encouraged to step aside. At a special Unity Sobor held in Kyiv's St Sofiia's in December 2018, the UAOC and UOC(KP) dissolved themselves and created a new Church, the Orthodox Church of Ukraine (OCU). Ten bishops out of ninety in the UOC(MP) had signed the original appeal for autocephaly, but ultimately only two attended the Unity Sobor – and were promptly expelled from the UOC(MP). Financial and political pressure from Russia and from local Ukrainian oligarchs kept the numbers low.[17] Epifanii, a protégé of Filaret's from the UOC(KP), was chosen as head of the new Church: his title was Metropolitan of Kyiv and all Ukraine. A Tomos, a formal letter from the Ecumenical Patriarch granting autocephaly, was presented in Kyiv on Orthodox Christmas Day, 7 January 2019.

This was a seismic event. Instead of being popular but 'uncanonical', the Orthodox Church of Ukraine was now Ukraine's officially recognised first Church. The Russian Church was reminded that the Ecumenical Patriarch, the Archbishop of Constantinople, was first among equals in the Orthodox world, not them. In a letter to Onufrii of the UOC(MP), the Patriarch said that it was Russia that 'unilaterally cut itself off from canonical authority, i.e. the Holy Great Church of Christ (1448)', while 'other metropolitans in the city of Kyiv, being lawful and canonical' remained under the authority of his predecessors.[18] Without its parishes in Ukraine, the Russian Church risked losing its position as the biggest world Orthodox Church. The reactions of the Russian Church and state were extreme. They encouraged the UOC(MP) to have nothing to do with the new Church. Relations with the Ecumenical Patriarch, condemned as the 'Istanbul Patriarchy',[19] were cut off. Moscow campaigned to undermine or overthrow his decision or the Patriarch personally. Notwithstanding, a rival gathering in Amman in February 2020 could only muster four primates: from Russia, Jerusalem, Serbia, Czech Republic and Slovakia, plus Onufrii of the UOC(MP). Other Orthodox Churches were pressured not to recognise the Orthodox Church of Ukraine. At the time of writing in 2022, only Greece, Cyprus and Alexandria had done so. Russia supported unsuccessful attempts by the still ambitious Filaret to revive the UOC(KP). An initial flurry of parishes transferring to the Orthodox Church of Ukraine slowed once Zelenskyi became president in April 2019 and took a more neutral line than Poroshenko. But one opinion poll in 2020 showed that 62.3% of Ukrainians considered themselves Orthodox. Of these, 32.2% were adherents of the new Orthodox Church of Ukraine, outnumbering 21.9% for the UOC(MP) and 0.8% for others, including the old UOC(KP). The highest number, 43.1%, described themselves as 'just Orthodox', however.[20]

The Orthodox Church of Ukraine saw itself as completing the work begun under Petro Mohyla in the seventeenth century (see pages 54–5) and the UAOC in the 1920s (page 139). 'Ten Theses' published by supporters in 2019 stressed the importance of reviving Kyivan

Christianity, rival to Russian Messianism and Caesaropapism.[21] The key guiding principles for the new Church should be religiosity and separation from the state, lay participation and conciliar democracy.[22] According to OCU spokesperson Archbishop Yevstratii Zoria, we should 'use a modern, understandable language for sermons. And find good in other traditions. [. . .] We have thirty million believers, the Greeks have 9.5 million, the Georgians, Bulgarians and Serbs have less. The Ukrainian historical tradition is much more open to Europe than Russian Orthodoxy. [. . .] Sooner or later Kyiv as a centre of the Orthodoxy communion will play, not the same role as in the time of Mohyla, but a much more important role than we have now. The Ukrainian Church can replace Moscow as a centre of Slavonic Orthodox tradition.'[23]

The 2019 Elections

Poroshenko was not expected to win the 2019 election, even though he toured the country with the Tomos. Only one Ukrainian president has ever won reelection, Leonid Kuchma in 1999, albeit with the use of questionable political technology (see pages 200–202). At least that made Ukraine's imperfect democracy crudely capable of leadership change. The campaign was another of Ukraine's mini-revolutions: a vote for change and revolt against the political class. Adding to the negative public mood was a rash of corruption stories, the most damaging about circles close to Poroshenko benefiting from military procurement schemes.

The political class, on the other hand, were also well used to this cycle, and adept at protecting and reinventing themselves. Poroshenko had promised in 2014 to 'live in a new way'. Now his slogan was the nationalist appeal of 'Army! Language! Faith!' The other candidates fought to own the label of the 'new'. At first, this seemed to be the obviously old politician Yuliia Tymoshenko, whose slick PR promises of a 'New Course' and 'New Deal' pushed her to the top of the polls in 2018. There were many warnings of vote-buying. Its Ukrainian variant, the distribution of food or cash at elections, is called *grechka* – 'buckwheat'. Interior Minister Mykola Azarov, an unlikely democrat, claimed to have prevented mass fraud; but just as important were the calculations of local elites – why help Poroshenko when he didn't look likely to win anyway? Less noticed was the election's main political technology of 'close marking'. Poroshenko was able to come second with only 15.9% of the vote, because each of his main opponents was shadowed by a 'clone', or candidate with a similar profile, to reduce their vote. Yuliia Tymoshenko won 13.4%, with her main clones Yurii Tymoshenko (same name) taking 0.6% and Oleh Liashko (the same populist tactics) 5.5%. The Party of Regions' much reduced electorate was targeted by both Yurii Boiko on 11.7% and Oleksandr Vilkul on 4.2%. The liberal and pro-Western

Anatolii Hrytsenko's 6.9% was almost beaten by his rival Ihor Smeshko on 6.0%.

Tymoshenko had at least set the demand for the 'new'; but her fake newness was soon eclipsed by the more radical version offered by Volodymyr Zelenskyi. He is often described as (just a) comedian. But the key to his success was that he clearly stood outside the political system; and because he was so well-known as a comedian, actor, the winner of Ukraine's Dancing with the Stars, and the voice of Paddington Bear in the Ukrainian version of the movie. It was like Tom Hanks running for president. Zelenskyi's newness also came from his doubly virtual campaign. First, it was all online: where he could use bots, which some commentators have suggested might have spread misinformation about Poroshenko[24] (surpassing the Poroshenko team's efforts to do the same), but where he could also enlist genuine popular enthusiasm for change. As a veteran performer, Zelenskyi was way ahead of any opponent in using visual social media like YouTube, Instagram and TikTok. Second, Zelenskyi's campaign was a fantasy, in that it carefully echoed the themes of his popular TV show *Servant of the People*, whose third series was playing in real time during the election. In the show Zelenskyi played an ordinary guy who becomes president after his rant against corruption goes viral; and then slays the demons of Old Corruption.

Zelenskyi had more prosaic advantages. He was not entirely 'new'. He was supported by traditional media, mainly Ukraine's biggest TV channel 1+1. There were question marks over his links to its owner, the oligarch Ihor Kolomoiskyi, who had prospered in the first two years after the Maidan Revolution, but then lost control of his PrivatBank. Finally, there was no one to 'close mark' Zelenskyi. This might have been the rock singer Sviatoslav Vakarchuk; but his long tease of voters reflected his own reluctance to run. Vakarchuk was from west Ukraine and would likely take votes of Poroshenko. His newly-formed party Voice ran in the parliamentary elections instead.

Zelenskyi won the first round of the election by 30.2% to Poroshenko's 15.9%. In the second round he soared to victory by 73.2% to 24.4%. Zelenskyi won everywhere apart from Galicia in the west and in more prosperous parts of Kyiv. Superficially, this looked like the elections of 1990 and 1991 (see pages 147, 160–1, 164–5 and 169). Many of Poroshenko's 24% claimed they were the only 'real' Ukrainians: true patriots could not vote for a comedian at a time of war. But the philosopher Volodymyr Yermolenko argued that Zelenskyi's victory also reflected the fact that there were still many types of Ukrainian; and Zelenskyi won the votes of Russian-speaking patriots and those who 'after Russian aggression . . . no longer have illusions about Moscow', but 'cannot identify with the Ukrainian cultural project' or only with parts of it.[25] Zelenskyi also won on pocket-book issues: the 70% who thought the country was heading in the wrong direction. Opinion polls also showed the war in the east was at the top of voters' concerns after five years, as was the economic and humanitarian cost.[26]

Zelenskyi as Pre-War President

As befitted a performer, Zelenskyi's early presidency got mixed reviews, despite his landslide election victory. No one thought of his presidency as 'pre-war' – given how inconceivable Russian invasion was at the time. But it was very different to his later wartime presidency, and very much a mixed picture. Some saw his election as a conspiracy,[27] particularly because of his ties to Kolomoiskyi. Some saw Zelenskyi as naïve: with the right skill set for PR but not for an executive presidency. Some saw him as too much from a Russian milieu – he had built his career as much on Russian as on Ukrainian TV. Some saw him as too lax on, or unobservant of, the stealth return of figures from the Yanukovych era. Zelenskyi saw himself as a new broom, the 'sentence' (*vyrok*) pronounced against the old system. His neophyte Servant of the People party, hastily assembled from business, the IT sector, NGOs and non-politicians – like Emmanuel Macron's En Marche! in France – won another landslide in early parliamentary elections, 254 seats out of 424 in July 2019 (26 seats from the Donbas and Crimea were empty).

Some saw the old cycle of change and disappointment. But Zelenskyi's many faces were his very essence. In government, in action, he was many things at once. There was no real party government. There was government by pronouncement, as in Macron's France. There was government by social media. According to his opponent, now opposition MP Rostyslav Pavlenko, 'it seems that Zelenskyi and his entourage are running a television show, which has its episodes and series. If they see their ratings go down, they invent a new plot, new characters, new heroes and enemies. If that helps the political situation, all the better; but that's not the main reason.'[28] There were some substantial achievements, such as providing government services via the 'state-in-a-smart-phone' app Diia. There were some good ministers, some bad. Undoubtedly, Zelenskyi's first government under Prime Minister Oleksii Honcharuk was better than his second under Denys Shmyhal – with many seeing no reason for the hasty change in March 2020 when Honcharuk was doing relatively well.

Zelenskyi himself was not pro-Russian. But his narrative on pushing for peace and the Poroshenko elite profiteering from the war overlapped with Russia's. Zelenskyi pushed to reactivate the Minsk Process and win humanitarian improvements, notably prisoner exchanges after a summit in Paris in December 2019. But this did not prompt Russia to shift. In July 2020 an experiment on 'Additional Measures to Strengthen the Ceasefire' envisaged *de facto* dialogue with the rebel 'Republics'. The idea was dropped by

September; Zelenskyi was learning that Russia did not negotiate. In fact, Russia only increased its domestic interference. Russia-friendly voices like Viktor Medvedchuk and vlogger Anatolii Sharyi expanded their media presence. Legal 'curators' like Andrii Portnov returned.

To make things worse, Ukraine also faced information war from Trump's America. In July 2019, in a now notorious telephone conversation, President Trump asked Zelenskyi, 'I would like you to do us a favour'.[29] Trump was searching for what Rudy Giuliani called 'evidence of Ukrainian collusion, not Russian collusion'[30] in the 2016 election, and for dirt on his likely opponent in the 2020 election, Joe Biden – all tied to the threat to withhold around $400 million of military aid. Trump's pressure on Zelenskyi got him impeached in December 2019. But Kyiv remained at the centre of a murky network of conspiracy entrepreneurs: Giuliani for Trump, Russian operatives selling dodgy 'peace deals', Ukrainian legal officials who 'knew what would interest Giuliani',[31] and oligarchs like Kolomoiskyi, Firtash and Andrii Derkach trying to leverage themselves out of legal troubles. In May 2020 edited tapes emerged featuring Biden telling President Poroshenko that Ukraine would not get $1 billion in assistance unless the Prosecutor General was fired; this was framed as Biden protecting his son from investigation.[32] In a complicated web, as Medvedchuk's and Ihor Kolomoiskyi's media attacked #demokoruptsiia, US authorities were also investigating Kolomoiskyi. His media attacked reformists in Prime Minister Honcharuk's government, so-called Sorosiata (George Soros's piglets),[33] and played a part in his downfall. Shmyhal presided over a purge of most reformist ministers and of senior figures at the highly respected National Bank of Ukraine. The Prosecutor General's Office under the newly installed Iryna Venediktova began what looked like vindictive and selective prosecutions against Poroshenko, his associates from Investment Capital of Ukraine bank, and former managers of the National Bank. At one stage, Poroshenko faced no fewer than twenty-one charges. The Constitutional Court began striking down many post-Maidan reforms. Ukraine, like the rest of the world, was hit by the coronavirus pandemic from the spring of 2020; but unlike the developed West, it didn't have the resources for furloughs or business support, and had no vaccines until February 2021. Medvedchuk and Kolomoiskyi media also peddled virus disinformation.

By early 2021 something had to be done. Ukraine needed to write itself back into Washington's good books, after Biden won the 2020 election. In March 2021 Kolomoiskyi was 'designated' by the US for corruption. Seven other Ukrainians were sanctioned by America for supplying Giuliani with dirt. In internal politics, much of the reform agenda was stalled. Medvedchuk and other media pushed the Opposition Platform – the main successor party to the Party of Regions, which had been rebranded from 'pro-Russian' to 'pro-peace' – to the top of the opinion polls.

Zelenskyi declared that 'Ukraine fights back', characteristically in a YouTube video. Medvedchuk was sanctioned and his media channels closed. Zelenskyi tried firing the head of the Constitutional Court. The powerful Interior Minister Arsen Avakov was forced out in July. A Banking Law prevented the return of banks to former owners – blocking Kolomoiskyi's campaign for the return of PrivatBank. A land reform promised to create a private market in land, to boost agricultural production. An 'anti-oligarch' law was signed in November. It defined an oligarch as anyone meeting three out of four criteria: net worth of 2.4 billion Ukrainian hryvnias ($91 million), control of a business monopoly, media control, and 'participation in political life'. Anyone meeting the definition would be forced onto an official register and banned from financing political parties. In typical Zelenskyi style, the move was good PR, but it was unclear how it would work in practice.

Zelenskyi consolidated in the polls, but cast the net wide. Both the anti-Russian and anti-oligarch campaigns were channelled through the National Security and Defence Council, not parliament or the courts. The NSDC sanctioned customs officials, a Chinese company targeting aeroplane manufacturer Motor Sich, French MEPs who visited Crimea and ten 'traitor generals' for failing to prevent the annexation of Crimea in 2014. In January 2022 former president Poroshenko was charged with treason: supposedly for the sale of coal that helped finance the rebel Donbas 'Republics'. Half-way through his first term, Zelenskyi was at least attempting relaunch; but his critics saw only rebranding.

17

Putin and War

Putin's Ukraine Obsession

In March 2021 Russia began massing troops on the Ukrainian border. Some interpreted Putin's move as directly motivated by the moves against Medvedchuk,[1] who since the Kuchma era had served as Russia's main point man in Ukraine. Putin was godfather to his daughter and Godfather to Medvedchuk. But Putin had also decided for himself that there was 'unfinished business' since 2014. More generally, the radical turn in Russia's Ukrainian policy since 2012 had had eight more years to mature. Previous chapters have shown that Russian-Ukrainian hostility is not a constant. There was, if not a Golden Age, a pragmatic age in Russian-Ukrainian relations from the signing of the State Treaty in 1997 (see page 307) to the Orange Revolution in 2004. As it turned out, the Orange Revolution changed Russia even more than it changed Ukraine. Russia was no longer a democracy by 2004. It was a political technology and propaganda state, increasingly locked into a narrative of 'fortress Russia' under threat from the West, as exemplified by Putin's 2007 Munich Speech, pre-dating the 2008 war in Georgia. Chapter fifteen described Russia's aggression in 2014. Putin basked in the 'Crimean consensus' from 2014 to his reelection as president in 2018. But this was notable for its radical nothingness. There was no campaign, no mandate, nothing of what Russians call a *dramaturgiia* (a carefully scripted drama). Putin was free to do what he wanted; but his popularity was on the slide. There was no recognition of over-reach; or that the Novorossiia project had been a failure.

Propaganda metastasised instead. The geopolitical fantasists of chapter thirteen were now mainstream – as was *pobedobesie* ('victory frenzy', the obsession with 1945), Putin's retooling of the Great Patriotic War that turned the wartime Allies into the mythical West, the collective enemy. Not (just) because of the expansion of NATO, but because the West was not just anti-Russian but 'Russophobic'. TV propaganda easily shape-shifted when necessary. In 2015 Syria briefly took centre stage; but the

West and Ukraine remained the main targets. The real danger of Europe was the safe and prosperous life that many Russians coveted. The top propaganda subjects were therefore not NATO, but the 'horrors of life' in Europe (22%), 'decaying Europe' (22%), then protests (19%), terrorism (12%) and the refugee crisis (8%).[2] Four years after the annexation of Crimea, in 2018, 30% of Russian TV news was still about Ukraine.[3] Russian TV was full of fake Ukrainians, fighting w ith e ach o ther a nd playing the parts of the incompetent and corrupt. Russian films dehumanised Ukrainians as traitors and collaborators, and as barely literate defective Russians.[4] Russia's narrative of 'Nazi Ukraine' was well-established by 2022, not invented on the eve of invasion. Even before the 2022 invasion, Cold War taboos about nuclear war were cast aside. TV regularly used Putin quotes like 'Why do we need such a world, if Russia will not be in it?'[5] and 'If they start a nuclear war, we will respond. But we, being righteous people, will go straight to Heaven, while they will just croak.'[6]

In July 2021 Putin published an extraordinary 'essay' denying Ukraine's independent history. It was bad history, and badly ahistorical. 'Russians, Ukrainians and Belarusians are all descendants of Ancient Rus', he declared, which meant they were all Russian.[7] There were no other possibilities; and nothing else had happened since to change this founding 'fact'. There was no room in Putin's analysis for change over time, for choice, for culture, for ordinary people at all. Ukraine was nothing but an 'anti-Russia project' created by foreign intrigue. But Putin led a virtual chorus. The rest of the elite had to agree. That was how the Russian system worked. Former President Dmitry Medvedev followed up with an open letter, using undiplomatic language to brand Ukrainians as 'people who do not have any stable self-identification', 'prey to rabid nationalist forces', and 'absolutely dependent people'. 'It makes no sense for us to deal with these vassals', Medvedev concluded.[8] Putin would no doubt regard Ukrainians' own opinions as irrelevant; but national identity is all about subjective belonging. In an opinion poll taken just after Putin's article came out, 70% of Ukrainians disagreed with Putin, saying that the Ukrainians and Russians were not one people.[9] The reverse proportion, 64% of Russians, said yes they were.[10]

Why 2022?

But there is still the question of why Putin chose to invade, and why he did so in 2022? Putin clearly thought new president Zelenskyi was inexperienced and exploitable. When that proved only partially true, Russia bizarrely decided that Zelenskyi's populist overthrow of the Poroshenko presidency in 2019 made no difference: the 'Maidan regime' was still in place. The Orthodox Church of Ukraine, about which Putin was particularly obsessed, was also created in 2019. Russia intensified its efforts to rebuild and reinvent its influence networks in Zelenskyi's first two years, assuming it could manoeuvre through them to replace him if necessary. But also that they should do so before Zelenskyi's 'anti-oligarch' measures of 2021 took effect. Events in Belarus also played their part. After another rigged election in August 2020, there were three months of unprecedented protests. Aliaksandr Lukashenka called on Russian help to repress them and survive. More than 30,000 were initially arrested.[11] There were 1,200 political prisoners.[12] The Russian bailout left Lukashenka haggling with Putin over the price of survival. Lukashenka wanted to keep his power system intact; he wanted to avoid selling profitable assets to Russian oligarchs. But he could concede on security. In the autumn of 2021 Belarus hosted 30,000 Russian troops for *Zapad* ('West') exercises, just as Russia began a second military build-up on Ukraine's borders. On 21 February 2022 it was announced the Russian troops in Belarus would stay. It was not clear if Lukashenka had been asked or just informed. This gave Russia the ability to threaten Kyiv from the north. The Kremlin also drew the lesson from the crackdown in Belarus that it could be more repressive at home. Russia was already getting more authoritarian after 2018; but it dealt severely with protests after the arrest of Aleksei Navalny in January–February 2021. The elections to the Duma in September 2021 were safely fixed. Putin therefore felt more secure at home, but still needed some formula for the next presidential election in 2024.

Other international factors may also have caused Putin to act precipitously. Joe Biden was now US president – but presided over the debacle of withdrawal from Afghanistan in August 2021. Merkel was on her way out in Germany; France faced a presidential election; the UK was still consumed by Brexit. Russia had, for Putin, banked its gains in Syria. Maybe it was time to bank other advantages while China was on the rise.

And post-Maidan Ukraine had many weaknesses. Significantly, Putin's *casus belli* speech on 24 February,[13] the beginning of the 2022 invasion, seemed in part to be based on polling data about Ukraine, no doubt distorted upwards by his intelligence staff.[14] He talked a lot about Ukraine's domestic problems. He expected that Ukrainians were too disgruntled with their everyday lives to fight. He expected that no one would fight for the corrupt elite, which would either capitulate or run away. If its *raison d'être* was manipulation by foreign powers, it would simply shift to Russia. But Putin was totally blind to cultural and civil society factors. Ukrainians were consolidated horizontally. They were fighting for each other and for their native land, not for their political leaders (Zelenskyi's wartime success was to reflect this). They also valued the improvements that had been made since 2004 and 2014 and wanted more. In December 2021, even before the invasion started, 50.2% of Ukrainians declared they would resist, 33.3% with arms.[15] In December 2021 Rating Group asked their usual question about whether the country was headed in the right or wrong direction. Apart from a brief surge of optimism when Zelenskyi was first elected, Ukrainians remained generally pessimistic. The question was also a proxy for generally low opinion about the country's leadership. 67% thought the country was headed in the wrong direction.[16] In March 2022 when Rating asked the same question, a massive 76% said the country was headed in the right direction.[17] This was not about the economy or social conditions. The war had started; both were dire. It was not about Zelenskyi. It was an existential statement: Ukrainians thought they were doing the right thing by fighting.

Ultimately, however, Putin put his own propaganda before public opinion. As he complained to an invited Western audience in October 2021, 'One gets the impression that the Ukrainian people are not allowed and will not be allowed to legally form the bodies of power that would uphold their interests. The people there are even afraid to respond to polls. They are scared, because the small group that has appropriated the victory in the fight for independence holds radical political views. And that group actually runs the country, regardless of the name of the current head of state.'[18]

But whatever Russia's tactical calculations were, they were wrapped in strategic miscalculations. These included bad history and a failure to understand Ukrainian identity, no real invasion plan that made military sense, no real occupation plan, and no real post-war plan.

The War

Russia clearly assumed victory within days. Captured documents showed plans for fifteen days maximum.[19] Ukrainians alleged that captured Russians had uniforms with them for their victory parade.[20] The calculation was that the Ukrainian army would collapse, the leadership would flee, and the West would not have time to help. According to Mark Galeotti, it would be like Hungary in 1956 or Czechoslovakia in 1968, with Europe and the USA confined to expressing anguish from afar.[21] Russia thought from experience in 2008 and 2014 that sanctions would be limited and survivable. Rising energy prices were filling up Russia's reserves. There was allegedly a fund to bribe the Ukrainian army not to fight, at least partially embezzled,[22] although most of the bribeable parts of Yanukovych's hollowed-out army were long gone. Most importantly, Russia's assumption of a short war was based on its own propaganda. Ukraine was an artificial state and a fake nation, so would collapse. It could not fight on its own, and its Western 'curators' would not be able to supply it in time. Conversely, Russia had built up its military might since the war in Georgia in 2008; but this proved to be partly propaganda too.

By late 2021 US and UK intelligence was clear on plans for a mass invasion in February 2022.[23] That said, it was still hard to imagine all-out war. Russia had stayed below many thresholds in 2014. Its pressure was working on Western diplomats, who flocked to Moscow. Despite Ukraine's insistence on the principle of 'Nothing about Ukraine without Ukraine' (from the old slogan in the Polish Commonwealth, 'Nothing about us without us'), this is precisely what the West was doing. US and European leaders seemed ready to give Putin what he wanted on European security, on Ukrainian neutrality and on arms control. Putin could have got all of this without war. But he thought he was risking little. But Western intelligence release made it difficult to construct a cover story. There was no declaration of war on 24 February. The 'special military operation' was supposed to prevent Nazi genocide against the Donbas – the lamest of *legendas* or cover stories. Full-on invasion was hard to disguise. Again, the only explanation is that Russia expected a quick victory, and that a story would emerge from the victorious pro-Russian side after regime change.

Ukrainian resistance destroyed the plans. The army was a completely different entity to 2014. The political leadership survived Russian special forces' attempts to kill or capture them in the first hours of the war.[24] Zelenskyi proved to be a much better war leader than pre-war president. His rating soared to 93%. The armed forces were backed by 98%, while 86% of Ukrainians now wanted to join the EU and 76% to join NATO.[25] In part this was because Zelenskyi's old skills now came into their own. His short online videos were masterpieces of communication, combining bravery, defiance, hope and a sense of location – the places that Ukrainians were dying to defend. Zelenskyi also discovered new skills. He learned how to address foreign audiences, pushing their own memory and culture buttons. Above all, though, Zelenskyi was popular because he was a mirror for ordinary Ukrainians. He wore green T-shirts and looked like he had just emerged from a bunker, because that was how so many Ukrainians were living their lives. In contrast to Putin's foul-mouthed machismo, Zelenskyi talked openly about his fears, which was much more plausible to ordinary Ukrainians. He broadcast from Kyiv's main street Khreshchatyk and the Maidan; it was hard to imagine Putin leaving home, let alone visiting real or potential battlefields.

Leadership makes a difference. But Ukraine's main strengths were horizontal. The armed forces were effective and popular. They benefited from massive civil society and NGO support, and from a general population versed in the Maidan paradigm of passive resistance. Ukrainians were fighting for their homeland; Russian soldiers were fed propaganda that either curdled on contact with reality, or fuelled war crimes against dehumanised Ukrainians. Ukraine launched a general mobilisation in March – which Russia could not do.

Russia clearly had maximalist goals compared to 2014, starting with regime change and the *de facto* division or 'Bosniafication' of Ukraine.

Commentators rightly mocked Russia's absurd slogan of 'denazification'. The number of real extremists was lower in Ukraine than in most European states, and a lot lower than in Russia. Zelenskyi was Jewish. His great-grandfather and three brothers perished in the Holocaust. But there was a warped logic. Timothy Snyder called this 'schizofascism'.[26] Ukrainians call it 'ruscism'. Both meant the absurdity of transposing your faults on to the enemy. But in Putin's Russia, Nazism was defined by its hostility to the USSR; little else was mentioned in official history, not the Holocaust, not Nazism as an ideology. And Ukraine was hostile to Russia. According to former President Medvedev, 'Deep Ukrainianism, fuelled by anti-Russian poison and all-consuming lies about its identity, is one big fake.'[27] One chilling article, necessarily quoted at length, declared that 'Denazification is necessary when a considerable number of population (very likely most of it) has been subjected to the Nazi regime and engaged into its agenda. That is, when the "good people – bad government" hypothesis does not apply. [. . .] Those Nazis who took up arms must be destroyed on the battlefield, as many of them as possible. [. . .] A total lustration must be conducted. All organizations involved in Nazi actions must be eliminated and prohibited . . . besides the highest ranks, a significant number of common people are also guilty of being passive Nazis and Nazi accomplices.[. . .] The further denazification of this bulk of the population will take the form of re-education through ideological repressions (suppression) of Nazi paradigms and a harsh censorship not only in the political sphere but also in the spheres of culture and education.[. . .]Denazification will inevitably also be a de-Ukrainization – a rejection of the large-scale artificial inflating of the ethnic component of self-identification of the population of the territories of historical Malorossiia and Novorossiia, begun by the Soviet authorities.'[28] Typically for Putin's Russia, the author of these words was Timofei Sergeitsev, not a real expert on anything, but a Russian political technologist, who had worked for Ukrainian President Kuchma's cynical reelection campaign in 1999 (see page 200). Kuchma won by playing up a largely non-existent 'Communist threat'. For Sergeitsev, no doubt, 2022 was just another campaign against the *khokhly* ('hicks'). Sergeitsev also wrote the screenplay for a truly terrible Russian movie *Match* in 2012, about the infamous 'death match' between Ukrainian footballers and German occupiers in Kyiv in 1942. In his version, the heroes are all Russian.

This was genocidal language – confirmed on the ground in areas liberated by Ukraine after initial Russian occupation. In May the Ukrainian Ombudswoman Liudmyla Denysova cited a figure of 1.2 million individuals kidnapped and taken to Russia.[29] In late April Russia's Ministry of Defence admitted 951,000.[30] Children were forcibly separated from families. Ukrainian culture was deliberately targeted in occupied areas. The threat to everyone, elites and masses alike, meant that Ukrainians had to fight. The revelations of war crimes in occupied areas only added to the sense of existential danger.

Russian propaganda at home led many to buy the Kremlin line. But it could not prepare ordinary Russian soldiers to fight for a lie. Despite years of rising tension, Putin's war seemed last-minute. Military preparations were inadequate. Arms and equipment were less modernised than claimed. Training, tactics and battlefield leadership were poor. At the time of writing, in May 2022, it would be foolish to speculate on outcomes, particularly the military situation. Russia failed in its original multi-pronged invasion. It failed to take Kyiv. Its only successful assault was in the south, allowing it to create the land-bridge to Crimea. Once Ukraine had survived more than a few days, Western sympathy and assistance kicked in. International sanctions against Russia were much tougher than expected. Many things previously dismissed as impossible were now suddenly deemed possible. Half of Russia's reserves were frozen, SWIFT sanctions were imposed on many banks, Russian oligarchs had their property seized, countries talked of reducing imports of Russian energy, a bond default loomed in the summer of 2022. US support under Biden was much more solid and professional than who-knows-what under Trump, Ukraine having benefited from the bridges rebuilt since 2020. By May Ukraine was getting the heavy weaponry it needed to assist with limited but strategic counter-attacks. Ukraine still had 80% of its territory, but risked losing access to the Black Sea. Even if Odesa was not attacked, trade via Ukraine's south-western ports still faced a naval blockade. After early Russian setbacks, there were rightly fears of further Russian escalation. Extra conventional force was tried first, but Russia's basic problem was with troop quality and morale. By late May Russia had suffered an estimated 20,000 dead and 40,000 wounded; for Ukraine the figures were 5,000 to 8,000 dead and 20,000 wounded.[31] Russia had few volunteer fighters, unlike in 2014. Belarusians, Chechens, Syrians, even Africans were mooted. Tanks and APCs were taken from the Belarusian army as Russian losses mounted. Russia therefore shifted from infantry to firepower, artillery especially; but a summer stalemate loomed. Putin seemed afraid of a formal declaration of war and a general mobilisation. Barely disguised threats to use chemical or nuclear weapons were, it was hoped, compensation for conventional weakness, or part of Russian 'honey badger' strategy (the super-aggressive animal that others then avoid).[32] But a failing or cornered Putin, or even a Putin threatened with removal, had different calculations.

Post-War

It was also premature to talk about Ukraine's future when its very existence was under mortal threat. But in April 2022 Zelenskyi talked of

Ukraine becoming 'a big Israel, with our own face' after the war.[33] He meant that Ukraine would overcome the threat to its very existence, like Israel in 1948, 1967 and 1973. He also meant securitisation: 'post-war' Ukraine would still face mortal threats. Soldiers in 'cinemas, supermarkets, and people with weapons' would be the new normal. Assuming the survival test was passed, this was indeed likely. The elite would still be targeted by Russian special forces. There might be domestic atrocities.

But Ukraine was not Israel. Ukraine had no real internal enemy, real or created, to protect itself against, like Israel and the Arabs and Palestinians. To say that local Russians might be such was just Russian propaganda. A Law on Collaboration was passed in March 2022. This allowed for further arrests, such as vlogger Anatolii Sharyi in Spain. According to the chair of parliament, 'around ten' MPs fled.[34] If Russia won the war, the Orthodox Church of Ukraine would be eliminated. If Ukraine won or there was a respectable peace, the UOC(MP) would come under huge pressure to cut ties with Russia and develop a relationship with the OCU. In May 2022 the UOC(MP) declared 'independence' but not full autocephaly to try and avoid this fate. It now wished to be known as the 'Ukrainian Orthodox Church'.[35]

A securitised post-war Ukraine was one possible outcome. According to Zelenskyi, this Ukraine might not be 'exactly what we wanted from the very start', and not *liberal'shchyna* ('general liberalism').[36] But Ukraine could also emerge as the 'anti-Russia' in a much more positive sense: a more united and cohesive nation, with stronger vertical bonds between leadership and people in addition to its strong civil society. The Ukrainian oligarchy could end up weaker, after seeing many of its physical assets destroyed. A post-war Marshall-style was mooted at $1 trillion – partly to be paid for with seized Russian assets. Ukraine, along with Moldova and Georgia, made a triple application to join the EU. Candidate status for Ukraine was possible, but candidacy could take a long time. A possible eventual peace would also test which bad habits were ingrained in Ukraine, especially the selective persecution of enemies and the lack of a rule of law.

Ukraine's fate also depends on what happens in Russia. Ukrainians argued that Putin did not need an 'off-ramp'. He needed to be defeated and his armed forces degraded, or Russia would simply attack again. Ukraine also had to hope for regime change in Russia. It would not be truly safe until the Big Lie was deconstructed, and the state propaganda machine no longer pushed the line that Ukraine did not exist.

Conclusion

Ukraine's successive refoundations since the end of the USSR have been cumulative. Each was a further step towards the consolidation of the 'unexpected nation'. For those who saw Ukraine as politically but not fully psychologically independent in 1991 (see page 211), there had been two revolutions, in 2004 and 2014, with the second 'Revolution of Dignity' much more explicitly anti-colonial than the first. Two Russian invasions – the first using proxies in 2014, the second in 2022 with no pretence – refounded Ukraine yet again, proving that war is a great driver of identity consolidation and change. Whenever the end, and whatever the outcome, of the war that began in February 2022, Putin had not destroyed Ukraine as the 'anti-Russia'. Ukrainian resistance was strong enough to reverberate globally. The unexpected nation had come of age.

Bibliographical Essay

As this book is largely for a Western audience, recommendations are in English or other Western languages, although I have included a few key Ukrainian works at the end. There are two standard histories of Ukraine, more comprehensive in their approach than I wished to be. Orest Subtelny's *Ukraine: A History* (Toronto: University of Toronto Press, 1988; 3rd edn 2000) has also been published in large print runs in Ukraine. Paul Robert Magocsi's *A History of Ukraine* (Toronto: University of Toronto Press, 1996) seeks to provide a more multi-ethnic and variegated approach. A third is Andreas Kappeler's concise and reliable *Kleine Geschichte der Ukraine* (Munich: C.H. Beck, 1994), which has been translated into French as *Petite histoire de l'Ukraine* (Paris: Institut d'études slaves (1997), but not yet, alas, into English.

There are several entertaining accounts by journalists of time spent in Ukraine, in particular Anna Reid's *Borderland: A Journey through the History of Ukraine* (London: Wiedenfeld & Nicolson, 1997). Anne Applebaum's travelogue *Between East and West: Across the Borderlands of Europe* (London: Papermac, 1994) takes her down through western Ukraine. Michael Ignatieff's *Blood and Belonging: Journeys into the New Nationalism* (London: Vintage, 1994) contains a chapter on Ukraine – home to his Russian ancestors. Neal Ascherson's *Black Sea* (London: Jonathan Cape, 1995) contains much on Ukraine's steppe heritage.

As regards particular historical periods, there is little in English on the pre-Rus era that deals with Ukrainian historical theories, but the Canadian Institute of Ukrainian Studies has begun printing Mykhailo Hrushevskyi's monumental ten-volume *History of Ukraine-Rus'* (Edmonton: CIUS, vol. one 1997). With Rus history a good place to start would be Simon Franklin and Jonathan Shepard, *The Emergence of Rus 750–1200* (London: Longman, 1996). Two stimulating collections of essays on the subsequent medieval period are Ihor Ševčenko, *Ukraine between East and West: Essays on Cultural History to the Early Eighteenth Century* (Edmonton: CIUS, 1996) and Jaroslaw Pelenski,

The Contest for the Legacy of Kievan Rus' (Boulder: East European Monographs, 1998). Borys A. Gudziak's *Crisis and Reform: The Kyivan Metropolitanate, the Patriarchate of Constantinople, and the Genesis of the Union of Brest* (Cambridge, Mass.: Harvard Ukrainian Studies, 1999) is a detailed study of the watershed religious and cultural changes of the sixteenth and early seventeenth centuries. Highly recommended is Serhii Plokhy, *The Cossacks and Religion in Early Modern Ukraine* (Oxford: Oxford University Press, 2001). Michel Cadot and Emile Kruba (eds), *Les Cosaques de l'Ukraine* (Paris: Nouvelle Sorbonne, 1995) is an interesting collection of essays on the Cossacks.

An excellent introduction to Ukrainian life under the Romanovs and Habsburgs is Roman Szporluk's article 'Ukraine: From an Imperial Periphery to a Sovereign State', *Daedalus*, 126, 3 (summer 1997), pp. 86–119. Szporluk is currently preparing a book-length treatment of the subject. David Saunders, *The Ukrainian Impact on Russian Culture 1750–1850* (Edmonton: CIUS, 1985) looks at the period when influences from south to north were still strong. Ivan L. Rudnytsky, *Essays in Modern Ukrainian History* (Edmonton: CIUS, 1987) mainly covers the nineteenth and twentieth centuries and is particularly strong on intellectual history. Those interested in the latter can also find a collection of original sources in Ralph Lindheim and George S.N. Luckyj (eds), *Towards an Intellectual History of Ukraine: An Anthology of Ukrainian Thought from 1710 to 1995* (Toronto: University of Toronto Press, 1996), although the selection is biased towards conscious Ukrainophilism. On literary politics, see George S.N. Luckyj, *Between Gogol and Sevcenko: Polarity in Literary Ukraine 1798–1847* (Munich, 1971) and the same author's *The Anguish of Mykola Hohol, a.k.a. Nikolai Gogol* (Toronto: Canadian Scholars' Press, 1998). There are four chapters on the development of nineteenth-century Ukrainian history writing in Thomas Sanders (ed.), *Historiography in Imperial Russia: The Profession and Writing of History in a Multinational State* (Armonk, New York: M.E. Sharpe, 1999). On the issue of Russia as an empire and the Ukrainians' place therein, try Dominic Lieven, *Empire. The Russian Empire and its Rivals* (London: John Murray, 2000), Geoffrey Hosking, *Russia: People and Empire, 1552–1917* (London: HarperCollins, 1997) and Olga Andriewsky, *The Politics of National Identity. The Ukrainian Question in Russia, 1904–1918* (forthcoming).

The best recent study of the Habsburg Ruthenians is John-Paul Himka's essay, 'The Construction of Nationality in Galician Rus': Icarian Flights in Almost All Directions', in Michael D. Kennedy and Ronald G. Sumy (eds), *Intellectuals and the Articulation of the Nation* (Ann Arbor: University of Michigan Press, 1999) pp. 109–64. See also the collected essays in Andrei S. Markovits and Frank E. Sysyn (eds), *Nationbuilding and the Politics of Nationalism: Essays on Austrian Galicia* (Cambridge, Mass.: Harvard Ukrainian Research Institute,

1984) and Himka's *Religion and Nationality in Western Ukraine: The Greek Catholic Church and the Ruthenian National Movement in Galicia, 1867–1900* (Quebec: McGill, 1999).

On the period 1917–20 the standard works are still Taras Hunczak (ed.), *The Ukraine, 1917–1921: A Study in Revolution* (Cambridge, Mass.: Harvard Ukrainian Research Institute, 1977) and John Reshetar, *The Ukrainian Revolution, 1917–1920: A study in Nationalism* (Princeton: Princeton University Press, 1952). There is no real study of the Soviet Ukrainian period in its entirety, although Bohdan Krawchenko, *Social Change and National Consciousness in Twentieth-Century Ukraine* (Basingstoke: Macmillan, 1985) offers a confident and provocative sociological thesis about the emergence of modern Ukrainian national identity. James Mace, *Communism and the Dilemmas of National Liberation: National Communism in Soviet Ukraine, 1918–1933* (Cambridge, Mass.: Harvard Ukrainian Research Institute, 1983) looks at the key decade of the 1920s. On western Ukraine, the best book treating the radical Ukrainian movement that developed in the 1920s and 1930s is still John A. Armstrong, *Ukrainian Nationalism* (1st edn, 1963; 3rd edn, Englewood, Colorado: Ukrainian Academic Press, 1990), while Alexander J. Motyl, *Turn to the Right: The Ideological Origins and Development of Ukrainian Nationalism 1919–1929* (Boulder: East European Monographs, 1980) is a more detailed study of the movement's origins.

On the period leading up to independence, there is Taras Kuzio and Andrew Wilson, *Ukraine: Perestroika to Independence* (Basingstoke: Macmillan, 1994) and Bohdan Nahaylo's more detailed narrative *The Ukrainian Resurgence* (London: Hurst, 1999), whose later chapters also cover the period up to 1996 – as will Robert S. Kravchuk, *Ukrainian Politics, Economics and Governance, 1991–96* (Basingstoke: Palgrave, 2002). More wide-ranging is Roman Szporluk's excellent *Russia, Ukraine and the Breakup of the Soviet Union* (Stanford: Hoover Institution Press, 2000). See also Solomea Pavlychko, *Letters from Kiev* (New York: St Martin's Press, 1992) – a memoir of the period 1990–1. The first book on politics after independence was Alexander J. Motyl's theoretical *mise-en-scène Dilemmas of Independence: Ukraine after Totalitarianism* (New York: Council on Foreign Relations Press, 1993). Taras Kuzio and Paul D'Anieri (eds), *State- and Institution-Building in Ukraine* (New York: St Martin's Press, 1999) and Kuzio (ed.), *Contemporary Ukraine: Dynamics of Post-Soviet Transformation* (Armonk: M.E. Sharpe, 1998) contain much that is useful.

Anatol Lieven's short book *Ukraine and Russia: A Fraternal Rivalry* (Washington, DC: Institute of Peace Press, 1999) is full of common sense and says much that is interesting about the complex interrelationship between the two nations. Ilya Prizel, *National Identity and Foreign Policy: Nationalism and Leadership in Poland, Russia, and Ukraine*

(Cambridge, UK: Cambridge University Press, 1998), Sherman W. Garnett, *Keystone in the Arch: Ukraine in the Emerging Security Environment of Central and Eastern Europe* (Washington, DC: Carnegie Endowment for International Peace, 1997) and Tor Bukkvoll, *Ukraine and European Security* (London: Royal Institute of International Affairs, 1997) all deal with the relationship between domestic and foreign politics. Garnett's book in particular is an excellent short introduction to Ukrainian politics. Yaroslav Bilinsky, *Endgame in NATO's Enlargement: The Baltic States and Ukraine* (Westport: Praeger, 1999) makes the case for Ukraine's entry into NATO. Lubomyr Hajda (ed.), *Ukraine in the World* (Cambridge, Mass.: Harvard Ukrainian Research Institute, 1999) is a special issue of Harvard Ukrainian Studies looking at Ukrainian foreign policy.

My own *Ukrainian Nationalism in the 1990s: A Minority Faith* (Cambridge, UK: Cambridge University Press, 1997) seeks to explain why the appeal of narrow ethnonationalism in Ukraine is limited not just by geopolitics and the presence of Ukraine's large Russian minority, but also by the existence of the 'other Ukraine' and its more porous version of Ukrainian national identity. Catherine Wanner, *Burden of Dreams: History and Identity in Post-Soviet Ukraine* (Pennsylvania: Pennsylvania State University Press, 1998) has many interesting things to say about the persistence of 'Soviet Ukraine' and about post-Soviet Ukrainian culture. Paul D'Anieri, Robert Kravchuk and Taras Kuzio, *Politics and Society in Ukraine* (Boulder: Westview, 1999) is actually mainly about politics and economics. Sharon L. Wolchik and Volodymyr Zviglyanich (eds), *Ukraine: The Search for a National Identity* (Lanham, MA: Rowman & Littlefield, 2000), came out as this book was going to press.

There are several works specifically on the Ukrainian economy, namely Axel Siedenberg and Lutz Hoffmann (eds), *Ukraine at the Crossroads: Economic Reforms in International Perspective* (Heidelberg: Physica-Verlag, 1999), Hans van Zon, *The Political Economy of Independent Ukraine* (Basingstoke: Macmillan, 2000), King Banaian, *The Ukrainian Economy Since Independence* (Aldershot: Edward Elgar, 1999), and Andrew Wilson and Igor Burakovsky, *The Ukrainian Economy under Kuchma* (London: Royal Institute of International Affairs, 1996). Alan Robinson (ed.), *Ukraine: Restructuring for Growth* (London: Euromoney Books, 1998) is a glossy publication for optimistic investors.

There are several good local histories of Ukrainian cities or regions. Theodore H. Friedgut's two-volume history *Iuzovka and Revolution* (Princeton: Princeton University Press, 1989 and 1994) looks at the Donbas between 1869 and 1924. Hiroaki Kuromiya, *Freedom and Terror in the Donbas: A Ukrainian-Russian Borderland, 1870s–1990s* (Cambridge, UK: Cambridge University Press, 1998) is livelier, but both books help explain why the Donbas has so often been a law unto itself. Patricia Herlihy, *Odessa: A History 1794–1914* (Cambridge, Mass.: Harvard Ukrainian Research Institute, 1986) focuses on the period when Odesa was still a Russian/Jewish city. Michael F. Hamm, *Kiev: A Portrait, 1800–1917* (Princeton: Princeton University Press, 1993) looks at Kiev's multi-ethnic nineteenth century. Gwendolyn Sasse is writing a political history of Crimea (London: Hurst) that might be out in 2000 or 2001. This book's theme and title have prevented me from writing about the Crimean Tatars. Interested readers should try Edward Allworth (ed.), *The Tatars of Crimea: Return to the Homeland* (Durham, NC: Duke University Press, 1998), which includes a chapter on modern politics by myself; and for history, Alan Fisher, *The Crimean Tatars* (Stanford: Hoover Institution Press, 1978). On Transcarpathia, the standard history is Paul Robert Magocsi, *The Shaping of a National Identity: Subcarpathian Rus', 1848–1948* (Cambridge, Mass.: Harvard University Press, 1978). Readers will be entertained by Timothy Garton Ash's essay 'Long Live Ruthenia!' in his *History of the Present: Essays, Sketches and Despatches from Europe in the 1990s* (London: Allen Lane/Penguin, 1999), pp. 376–81, although the author adds some comic-opera, Ruritanian overtones which he normally (and wisely) advises others to avoid in their coverage of Central and Eastern Europe.

Works on modern Ukrainian culture are in limited supply, apart from Marko Pavlyshyn and J.E.M. Clarke (eds), *Ukraine in the 1990s* (Melbourne: Monash University, Slavic Section, 1992). The hard-to-find *1900–2000: Mystetstvo Ukraïny XX stolittia/The Art of Ukraine of the Twentieth Century* (Kiev: Art Galleries Association of Ukraine/NIGMA, 1998) was published to coincide with the hundredth anniversary of the Kiev Museum of Ukrainian Art and a major reorganisation of its contents and has an English text of sorts, although the selection of works is sometimes limited. On the same subject, with a wider view of more contemporary work, there is *Ukrainian Avant-Garde and Contemporary Art* (Odense: Art Galleries Association of Ukraine, 1996). More historical is Myroslova Mudrak, *The New Generation and Artistic Modernism in Ukraine* (Ann Arbor: UMI Research, 1986). *100 Films of the Ukrainian Cinema* (Kiev: Spalakh, 1996) was published with the help of UNESCO to celebrate another centenary: 100 years of world cinema from 1895 to 1995. *This Is Ukraine* (Kiev: Computer Systems Publishing House, 1995) has sections on art, music, architecture etc. Volume thirteen of the journal *Glas*, Ed Hogan (ed.), *From Three Worlds: New Writing from Ukraine*, was reprinted by the Harvard Ukrainian Research Institute in 1996. Pat Simpson and Grygory Shyshko, *Borderlands – Impressionist and Realist Paintings from Ukraine* (University of Hertfordshire, 1999) is an interesting short study.

Three Ukrainian books ought to be mentioned. First are the companion volumes that together form the best recent survey of Ukrainian history: Yaroslav Hrytsak, *Narys istoriï Ukraïny: formuvannia modernoï ukraïns'koï natsiï XIX–XX stolittia* ('Outline of a History of Ukraine: The Formation of a Modern Ukrainian Nation in the Nineteenth to Twentieth Centuries') (Kiev: Heneza, 1996) and Natalia Yakovenko, *Narys istoriï Ukraïny: z naidavnishykh chasiv do kintsia XVIII stolittia* ('Outline of a History of Ukraine: From the Most Ancient Times to the End of the Eighteenth Century' – though Yakovenko does not think that 'Ukrainian history' can actually be traced back as far as the title might suggest) (Kiev: Heneza, 1997). Second is Myroslav Popovych's *Narys istoriï kul'tury Ukraïny* ('Outline of a History of the Culture of Ukraine') (Kiev: ArtEk, 1998), which covers some of the same ground as I have.

On the Orange Revolution and subsequent developments, see Andrew Wilson, *Ukraine's Orange Revolution*, (London and New Haven: Yale University Press, 2005); Michael McFaul and Anders Åslund (eds), *Revolution in Orange: The Origins of Ukraine's Democratic Breakthrough*, (Washington, DC: Carnegie Endowment, 2006); Paul D'Anieri, *Understanding Ukrainian Politics: Power, Politics and Institutional Design*, (New York: M.E. Sharpe, 2006); Anders Åslund, *How Ukraine Became a Market Economy and Democracy*, (Washington, DC: Peterson Institute, 2009); Ingmar Bredies, Andreas Umland and Valentin Yakushik (eds), *Aspects of the Orange Revolution*, (series, vols. 1–6) (Stuttgart: Ibidem-Verlag, 2007 onwards); Michael McFaul, 'Ukraine Imports Democracy: External Influences on the Orange Revolution', *International Security*, vol. 32, no. 2 (Fall 2007), pp. 45–83. On the events of 2014, see my *Ukraine Crisis: What the West Needs to Know* (New Haven and London: Yale University Press, 2014); and Anders Åslund, *Ukraine: What Went Wrong and How to Fix It* (Washington DC: Peterson Institute, 2015).

Important recent works covering earlier periods include Serhii Plokhy, *The Origins of the Slavic Nations: Premodern Identities in Russia, Ukraine and Belarus* (Cambridge: Cambridge University Press, 2006); Paul Kubicek, *The History of Ukraine*, (Westport: Greenwood Press, 2008); Serhy Yekelchyk, *Ukraine: Birth of a Modern Nation*, (Oxford: Oxford University Press, 2007); Peter Rodgers, *Nation, Region and History in Post-Communist Transitions: Identity Politics in Ukraine, 1991–2006*, (Ibidem-Verlag, 2008); Timothy Snyder, *Bloodlands: Europe Between Hitler and Stalin* (New York: Basic Books, 2010); Serhii Plokhy, *The Last Empire: The Final Days of the Soviet Union* (New York: Basic Books, 2014); Faith Hillis, *Children of Rus': Right Bank Ukraine and the Invention of a Russian Nation* (Ithaca: Cornell University Press, 2013); and Mara Kozelsky, *Christianizing Crimea: Shaping Sacred Space in the Russian Empire and Beyond* (Dekalb: Northern Illinois University Press, 2009). See also Serhii Plokhy, *Gates of Europe: A History of Ukraine* (New York: Basic Books, 2017); Paul D'Anieri, *Ukraine and Russia: From Civilized Divorce to the Uncivil War* (Cambridge: Cambridge University Press, 2019).

Notes

Preface

1   Maria Todorova, *Imagining the Balkans* (Oxford and New York: Oxford University Press, 1997).

2   Ernest Renan, *Qu'est-ce que c'est, une nation?* (Paris: Calmann-Levy, 1882), pp. 7–8.

3   Yaroslav Hrytsak, *Narys istoriï Ukraïny: formuvannia modernoï ukraïns'koï natsiï XIX–XX stolittia* (Kiev: Heneza, 1996), p. 3.

Chapter 1

1   Adapted from the translation by Vladimir Nabokov, *The Song of Igor's Campaign* (London: Weidenfeld & Nicolson, 1961), lines 39–50, at p. 31.

2   'Kievan Rus' is a common enough term nowadays, but was little used at the time. Moreover, it conveys the assumption that Rus was always centred on Kiev. As this is a controversial but largely justified claim, I have used both terms, 'Kievan Rus' and 'Rus'.

3   O.P. Motsia, 'Kyïvs'ka Rus': rezul'taty ta perspektyvy doslidzhen'', *Ukraïns'kyi istorychnyi zhurnal*, 4 (1996), pp. 41–9, at p. 41.

4   Petro Tolochko, *Kyïvs'ka Rus'* (Kiev: Abrys, 1996), p. 248.

5   *The Song of Igor's Campaign*, lines 67–70, at p. 32. The extract parodies an earlier style, but can still be taken as descriptive.

6   The Kazakh author Olzhas Suleimenov caused a considerable stir in the 1970s by developing a theory of the Turkic/Asian/Polovtsian cultural and linguistic influence on the writing of *The Lay*; see Suleimenov, *Az-i-Ya* (Alma-Ata: Zhazushi, 1975).

7   *The Song of Igor's Campaign*, lines 276–9, at p. 43.

8   Petro Tolochko, *Litopysy Kyïvs'koï Rusi* (Kiev: Eurobusiness Academy, 1994), pp. 35–9.

9   Pierre Brégy and Prince Serge Obolensky, *The Ukraine – A Russian Land* (London: Selwyn & Blount, 1940), p. 33.

10 *The Song of Igor's Campaign*, lines 147–50, at p. 36, and lines 857–9, at p. 72.

11 Ihor Ševčenko, 'Byzantine Elements in Early Ukrainian Culture', in his *Byzantium and the Slavs in Letters and Culture* (Cambridge, Mass.: Harvard Ukrainian Research Institute, 1991), pp. 163–72.

12 Petro Tolochko, *Volodymyr Sviatyi. Yaroslav Mudryi* (Kiev: ArtEk, 1996), pp. 76–122; *Kyïvs'ka Rus'*, pp. 257–303.

13 Dmytro Stepovyk, *Istoriia ukraïns'koï ikony X–XX stolit'* (Kiev: Lybid', 1996), p. 161, classifies the *Annunciation* as 'Kiev school'.

14 Helen G. Evans and William D. Wixom (eds), *The Glory of Byzantium: Art and Culture in the Middle Byzantine Era, A.D. 843–1261* (New York: Metropolitan Museum of Art, 1997), p. 298.

15 For a discussion of this question, see Horace G. Lunt, 'The Language of Rus' in the Eleventh Century: Some Observations about Facts and Theories', *Harvard Ukrainian Studies*, 12–13 (1988–9), pp. 276–313.

16 Author's interview with Petro Tolochko, 24 June 1997.

17 Yurii Zaitsev et al., *Istoriia Ukraïny* (L'viv: Svit, 1996), p. 67.

18 Simon Franklin (trans. and ed.), *Sermons and Rhetoric of Kievan Rus'* (Cambridge, Mass.: Harvard Ukrainian Research Institute, 1991), p. 4.

19 Tolochko, *Kyïvs'ka Rus'*, p. 250.

20 Author's interview with Petro Tolochko, 24 June 1997.

21 See Anthony D. Smith, *The Ethnic Origins of Nations* (Oxford: Basil Blackwell, 1986), on 'pre-modern' identities.

22 Raïsa Ivanchenko, *Kyïvs'ka Rus': pochatky Ukraïns'koï derzhavy: Posibnyk z istoriï* (Kiev: Prosvita, 1995), p. 60, quoting from the *Hypatian Codex*. Cf. the translation in Ševčenko, *Ukraine between East and West* (Edmonton: CIUS, 1996), p. 61.

23 Author's interview with Petro Tolochko, 24 June 1997.

24 Uladzimir Arloŭ, *Taiamnitsy polatskai historyi* (Minsk: Belarus', 1994), p. 27.

25 Author's interview with the Belarusian historians Anatol' and Valentin Hrytskevich, 2 September 1995.

26 Igor' Froianov, *Kievskaia Rus'* (Leningrad: Leningrad University Press, 1980); and (with Andrei Dvornichenko), *Gorodagosudarstva Dreveni Rusi* (Leningrad: Leningrad University Press, 1988). See also Igor' Froianov, *Drevniaia Rus'* (Moscow: Zlatoust, 1995).

27 S.H. Cross and O.P. Sherbowitz-Wetzor (trans and eds), *The Russian [i.e. Rus] Primary Chronicle: Laurentian Text* (Cambridge, Mass.: Medieval Academy of America, 1953), pp. 56–7.

28 Hermann Pálsson and Paul Edwards, *Vikings in Russia. Yngvar's Saga and Eymund's Saga* (Edinburgh: Edinburgh University Press, 1989), pp. 71 and 38. The author is grateful to Vera Rich for pointing out this source. See also Dmytro Nalyvaiko, *Ochyma Zakhodu: Retseptsiia Ukraïny v Zakhidnii Yevropi XI–XVIII st.* (Kiev: Osnovy, 1998), pp. 517 and 43–51.

29 Stephen Rudnitsky (Stepan Rudnyts'kyi), *Ukraine: The Land and its People* (New York: Rand McNally/Ukrainian Alliance of America, 1918), p. 242.

30 Pálsson and Edwards, *Vikings in Russia*, pp. 50 and 54–8.

31 Dmytro Doroshenko, *Narys istoriï Ukraïny*, vol. 1 (Kiev: Globus, 1991), a reprint of the 1932 edn, pp. 55–68.

32 Mykhailo Hrushevs'kyi, *History of Ukraine-Rus': Volume One* (Edmonton: CIUS, 1997), p. 291.

33 Ivan Yushchuk, 'Status rosiis'koï movy', *Slovo Prosvity*, 2 (February 1998).

34 See for example Alexander Issatchenko, *Geschichte der Russichen Sprache* (Heidelberg: Karl Winter, 1980), 2 vols.

35 Zaitsev et al., *Istoriia Ukraïny*, p. 65.

36 'Sofiinyi kharakter kyïvs'koho khrystyianstva', in Yurii Kalinin and Yevhen Khar'kovshchenko, *Relihiieznavstvo* (Kiev: Naukova dumka, 1997), pp. 116–45, at p. 131.

37 Author's interview with Yevhen Sverstiuk, 24 March 1998.

38 P. Yarots'kyi et al. (eds) *Istoriia pravoslavnoï tserkvy v Ukraïni* (Kiev: Chetverta khvylia, 1997), p. 10.

39 Author's interview with Yevhen Sverstiuk.

40 Kalinin and Khar'kovshchenko, 'Sofiinyi kharakter kyïvs'koho khrystyianstva', pp. 132–3, 138, 135 and 133.

41 Franklin, *Sermons and Rhetoric of Kievan Rus'*, pp. 7 and 22–3.

42 John Fennell, *A History of the Russian Church to 1448* (London: Longman, 1995), p. 59.

43 Jaroslaw Pelenski, *The Contest for the Legacy of Kievan Rus'* (Boulder: East European Monographs, 1998), p. 33.

44 Some Ukrainian historians argue that Poland's great national icon, the *Black Madonna* of Częstochowa, was also originally from Rus before it was plundered by the Poles from Galicia.

45 Ihor Ševčenko, 'Rival and Epigone of Kiev: The Vladimir-Suzdal' Principality', in *Ukraine between East and West*, pp. 56–67.

46 Tolochko, *Kyïvs'ka Rus'*, p. 303.

47 Stepovyk, *Istoriia ukraïns'koï ikony*, p. 127. Stepovyk is a leading supporter of the new 'national' Ukrainian Orthodox Church of the Kievan patriarchate – see chapter twelve. See also Sviatoslav Hordynsky, *The Ukrainian Icon of the XIIth to XVIIIth Centuries* (Philadelphia: Providence Association, 1973).

48 Stepovyk, *Istoriia ukraïns'koï ikony*, pp. 12–13.

49 Igor' Grabar', *O drevnerusskom iskusstve* (Moscow: Nauka, 1966).

50 Myroslav Popovych, *Narys istoriï kul'tury Ukraïny* (Kiev: ArtEk, 1998), p. 102.

51 Nadezhda Nikitenko, *Rus' i Vizantiia v monumental'nom komplekse Sofii Kievskoi* (Kiev: Institute of Ukrainian

Archaeology, 1999) argues that building was in fact begun under Volodymyr.

52 Olexa Powstenko, *The Cathedral of St. Sophia in Kiev* (New Jersey: Special Edition of the Annals of the Ukrainian Academy of Arts and Sciences in the US, 1954), pp. 33–41.

53 Ivanchenko, *Kyïvs'ka Rus'*, p. 71.

54 Stefan Tomashivs'kyi, *Ukraïns'ka istoriia. Starynni i seredni viky* (L'viv: Vchora i nyni, 1919), vol. 1, book 4, pp. 85–112, at p. 89. See also his *Halychyna: politchyno-istorychnyi narys z pryvodu svitovoï viiny* (2nd edn; L'viv: Polïtychna Biblïoteka, 1915).

55 Richard Pipes, *Russia under the Old Regime* (London: Weidenfeld & Nicolson, 1974), pp. 1–21 and 199.

56 Leonid Zalizniak, 'Ukraïna i Rosiia: rizni istorychni doli', *Starozhytnosti*, 19 (1991).

57 Mykola Chubatyi, *Istoriia khrystyianstva na Rusi-Ukraïny*, vol. 1 (Rome and New York: Neo Eboraci, 1965), pp. 625–42. It is just as likely that fear of provoking the Horde prevented Danylo from taking any such measure.

58 V.A. Potul'nyts'kyi, *Istoriia ukraïns'koï politolohïï* (Kiev: Lybid', 1992), p. 125.

59 See also Andreas Kappeler, *Petite histoire de l'Ukraine* (Paris: Institut d'études slaves, 1997), pp. 44–5, and Simon Franklin and Jonathan Shepard, *The Emergence of Rus 750–1200* (London: Longman, 1996), p. xvii.

60 A good guide to Gumilev's views is Bruno Naarden, '"I Am a Genius, But No More Than That." Lev Gumilëv (1912–1992), Ethnogenesis, the Russian Past and World History', *Jahrbücher für Geschichte Osteuropas*, 44, 1 (1996), pp. 54–82.

61 Lev Gumilev, *Ot Rusi k Rossii* (Moscow: Ekopros, 1992), pp. 137–94.

62 Vera Tolz, 'Forging the Nation: National Identity and Nation-Building in Post-Communist Russia', *Europe-Asia Studies*, 50, 6 (September 1998), pp. 993–1022, at p. 1001; remarks made by Maureen Perrie at the University of Birmingham, 26 February 1998.

Chapter 2

1 Edward S. Reisman, 'The Absence of a Common-Descent Myth for Rus", *Russian History/Histoire Russe*, 15, 1 (1988), pp. 9–19.

2 For an antidote, try Petro Tolochko et al., *Davnia istoriia Ukraïny*, 3 vols planned (Kiev: Naukova dumka, first 1997, second 1998), or even the popular rebuttal (written in Russian) by S. Kruk et al., *Po sledam 'Puti Ariev'* (Khmel'nyts'kyi: Podillia Skovoroda Society, 1998).

3 For Kravchuk's foreword, see Yurii Kanyhin and Zenovii Tkachuk, *Ukraïns'ka mriia* (Kiev: Leksykon, 1996), pp. 3–5. Kanyhin, *Put' ariev/ Shliakh arïïv* was published in *Visnyk NAN Ukraïny* 1–6 (1995); Oleksii Bratko-Kutyns'kyi, *Fenomen Ukraïny* (Kiev: Vechirnii Kyïv, 1996).

4 Yurii Kanyhin, *Shliakh arïïv: Ukraïna v dukhovnii istorïï liudstva* (Kiev: Ukraïna, 1997), p. 182. See also Yurii Kanyhin, *Vekhi Sviashchennoi istorii: Rus'-Ukraina* (Kiev: Ukraïna, 1999).

5 Kanyhin and Tkachuk, *Ukraïns'ka mriia*, p. 25. Most biblical scholars would place Tubal, insofar as this is possible at all, in Asia Minor.

6 Kanyhin and Tkachuk, *Ukraïns'ka mriia*, p. 144.

7 Ibid., p. 26.

8 Neal Ascherson, *Black Sea* (London: Jonathan Cape, 1995), pp. 49–50 and 60–1.

9 The careful reader will note that they are joined by a king and a bishop in the very front of the right foreground – Martin sensibly thought that position alone was no guarantee of entrance into the Kingdom of Heaven.

10 Cross and Sherbowitz-Wetzor *The Russian Primary Chronicle: Laurentian Text*, p. 51.

11 Quoted in Ihor Ševčenko, *Ukraine between East and West*, p. 143.

12 See also A.S. Myl'nikov, *Kartina slavianskogo mira: vzgliad iz Vostochnoi Yevropy: Etnogeneticheskie legendy, dogadki, protogipotezy XVI–nachala XVII veka* (St Petersburg: Peterburgskoe Vostokovedenie, 1996).

13 Zviad Gamsakhurdia, *Ts'erilebi, esseebi* (Tbilisi: Khelovneba, 1991).

14 On the idea of an *Ursprache*, see Maurice Olender, *The Languages of Paradise: Race, Religion and Philology in the Nineteenth Century* (Cambridge, Mass.: Harvard University Press, 1992). See also Hrushevs'kyi's sensible scepticism on this question, *History of Ukraine-Rus': Volume One*, p. 48.

15 Serhii Plachynda, *Slovnyk davn'o-ukraïns'koï mifolohïï* (Kiev: Ukraïns'kyi pys'mennyk, 1993), p. 6. See also

Velesova knyha. Skryzhali buttia ukraïns'koho narodu (Kiev, 1995).

16 Lev Sylenko, *Maha Vira* (New York: RUNVira, 1979), pp. 27 and 58.

17 Most famously V. Gordon Childe, *The Aryans: A Study of Indo-European Origins* (London: Kegan Paul, Trench & Trübner, 1925), pp. 183–200. See also J.P. Mallory, *In Search of the Indo-Europeans: Language, Archaeology and Myth* (London: Thames & Hudson, 1989), p. 144; and G. M. Bongard-Levin, *The Origins of the Aryans: From Scythia to India* (New Delhi: Arnold-Heinemann, 1980).

18 Colin Renfrew, *Archaeology and Language: The Puzzle of Indo-European Origins* (London: Pimlico, 1998).

19 Kanyhin, *Shliakh ariïv*, pp. 251–70.

20 Kanyhin and Tkachuk, *Ukraïns'ka mriia*, p. 15.

21 Bratko-Kutyns'kyi, *Fenomen Ukraïny*, p. 197.

22 Kanyhin and Tkachuk, *Ukraïns'ka mriia*, p. 30.

23 Mykola Dmytrenko et al., *Ukraïns'ki symvoly* (Kiev: Narodoznavstvo, 1994).

24 For example Vitalii Dovhych (ed.), *Onuky Dazhbozhi*, issue 1–2 *Indo-Yevropa* (Kiev: Taki spravy, 1995–6 or, in their system, 'the year 7504').

25 For one amongst many examples see Aleksandr Dugin, *Misterii Yevrazii* (Moscow: Arktogeia, 1996).

26 Kanyhin and Tkachuk, *Ukraïns'ka mriia*, p. 25.

27 Viktor Petrov, *Pokhodzhennia ukraïns'koho narodu* (Kiev, 1992).

28 Vadym Mytsyk, *Mista sontsia* (Tal'ne: n.p. 1993).

29 Kanyhin, *Shliakh ariïv*, p. 89.

30 Kanyhin and Tkachuk, *Ukraïns'ka mriia*, p. 36.

31 Lev Sylenko, *Hist' z Khramu Predkiv* (Kiev: Oberehi, 1996), p. 20.

32 Bratko-Kutyns'kyi, *Fenomen Ukraïny*, p. 197.

33 Kanyhin and Tkachuk, *Ukraïns'ka mriia*, pp. 36–7 and 43.

34 Stepan Mishko, *Narys rann'oï istoriï Rusy-Ukraïny* (New York, Toronto and Munich: Ukrainian Historical Association, 1981), p. 171.

35 Volodymyr Kyrychuk, 'Istorychni koreni ukraïns'koho narodu: do pytannia etnohenezu ukraïntsiv', *Heneza*, 1 (1994), pp. 142–9, at p. 143.

36 Kanyhin, *Shliakh ariïv*, p. 91.

37 R.D. Liakh and N.R. Temirova, *Istoriia Ukraïny. Z naidavnishykh chasiv do seredyny XIV stolittia* (Kiev: Heneza, 1995), p. 18. This is an official history text for 12-year-old pupils.

38 Kanyhin, *Shliakh ariïv*, p. 89.

39 See Mykola Susloparov, 'Rozshyfruvannia naidavnishoï pysemnosti z berehiv dnipra', a postscript to Ivanchenko, *Kyïvs'ka Rus'*, pp. 77–94, at p. 92.

40 Kanyhin, *Shliakh ariïv*, p. 90.

41 Sylenko, *Hist' z Khramu Predkiv*, pp. 20–1. See also the early maps in the atlas produced with the help of the supposedly respectable Shevchenko Scientific Society in Canada: Volodymyr Païk, *Ukraïna v mynulomu i s'ohodni (istorychni i heohrafichni karty)* (Edmonton, 1982; L'viv, 1998).

42 Sylenko, *Maha Vira*, p. 60.

43 Bratko-Kutyns'kyi, *Fenomen Ukraïny*, p. 197.

44 Homer, *Odyssey*, 11.14; as quoted in Hrushevsky, *History of Ukraine-Rus': Volume One*, p. 79.

45 Leonid Zalizniak, *Narysy starodavn'oï istoriï Ukraïny* (Kiev: Abrys, 1994), p. 116. The words 'tsar', 'caesar' and 'Kaiser' are supposedly derived from the Ukrainian root '-ksai', from the Sanskrit 'kshatra', meaning 'power'.

46 Yaroslav Malyk, Borys Vol and Vasyl' Chupryna, *Istoriia ukraïns'koï derzhavnosti* (L'viv: Svit, 1995), p. 11.

47 Mishko, *Narys rann'oï istoriï Rusy-Ukraïny*, p. 76.

48 A.D. Godley (trans.), *Herodotus: The Histories*, 2nd of 4 vols (London: William Heineman, 1921), bk IV, chaps 108–9, p. 309 and chap. 100, p. 303; Païk, *Ukraïna v mynulomu i s'ohodni*, p. A-7.

49 Bratko-Kutyns'kyi, *Fenomen Ukraïny*, p. 208.

50 Sylenko, *Hist' z Khramu Predkiv*, vol. 2, pp. 26 and 25.

51 Godley, *Herodotus: The Histories*, vol. 2, bk IV, chap. 82, p. 285, chap. 52, p. 253, chap. 2, p. 201, chapter 127, p. 327 and chap. 46, p. 247.

52 Ibid., chaps 64–6, pp. 261–5.

53 Ibid., chap. 62, p. 261.

54 From Ovid's *Tristia*, V, VII, 46; as quoted by Liah Greenfeld in her *Nationalism: Five Roads to Modernity* (Cambridge, Mass.: Harvard University Press, 1992), p. 273.

55 Peter Conrad, *Modern Times, Modern Places: Life and Art in the 20th Century* (London: Thames & Hudson, 1998), pp. 362–4.

56 See I. Desnians'kyi, *Ukraïna–Skyto–Roksolianiia* (London: Ukrainian Publishers Ltd, 1964).

57 Hrushevsky, *History of Ukraine-Rus: Volume One*, p. 133. Hrushevskyi wisely made few claims about earlier periods.

58 Yurii Zaitsev et al., *Istoriia Ukraïny* (L'viv: Svit, 1996), p. 58.

59 Mishko, *Narys rann'oï istoriï Rusy-Ukraïny*. Alternatively, see Alexander Vasiliev, *The Goths in Crimea* (Cambridge, Mass: Mediaeval Academy of America, 1936). Elements of Gothic civilisation survived into the fifteenth century and beyond.

60 Païk, *Ukraïna v mynulomu i s'ohodni*, p. A-9.

61 Kanyhin and Tkachuk, *Ukraïns'ka mriia*, p. 34.

62 Ivanchenko, *Kyïvs'ka Rus'*, p. 70.

63 Sviatoslav Hordynsky, *The Ukrainian Icon of the XIIth to XVIIIth Centuries*, p. 9; Kost' Panas, *Istoriia ukraïns'koï tserkvy* (L'viv: Transintekh, 1992), p. 13.

64 Zaitsev et al., *Istoriia Ukraïny*, p. 66.

65 Bratko-Kutyns'kyi, *Fenomen Ukraïny*, p. 219.

66 For a useful corrective, see Sophia Senyk, *A History of the Church in Ukraine. Volume 1: To the End of the Thirteenth Century* (Rome: Pontificio Instituto Orientale, 1993).

67 Panas, *Istoriia ukraïns'koï tserkvy*, p. 12, points out that the legend of Andrew may have been a later invention designed to boost the Ukrainian Church's claim to autocephaly as an original 'apostolic' foundation.

68 O.S. Onyshchenko et al. (eds), *Istoriia khrystyians'koï tserkvy na Ukraïni* (Kiev: Naukova dumka, 1992), p. 5.

69 Zaitsev et al., *Istoriia Ukraïny*, p. 261.

70 Ivan Ohiienko, *Ukraïns'ka tserkva*, vol. 1 (Kiev: Ukraïna, 1993), a reprint of the 1942 Prague edn, pp. 5 and 8. See also the short reprint under the title Metropolitan Ilarion, *Ukraïnsk'a tserkva* (Zhytomyr: Demokrat, 1992), p. 4.

71 Fennell, *A History of the Russian Church*, p. 22.

72 Panas, *Istoriia ukraïns'koï tserkvy*, p. 13.

73 From Cross and Sherbowitz-Wetzor, *The Russian Primary Chronicle: Laurentian Text*, p. 77.

74 Ibid., p. 137.

75 Metropolitan Ilarion, *Dokhrystyians'ki viruvannia ukraïns'koho narodu* (Kiev: Oberehy, 1994), a reprint of the edition

first published in Winnipeg in 1965.

76 Boris Rybakov, *Yazychestvo drevnei Rusi* (Moscow: Nauka, 1987).

77 Franklin, *Sermons and Rhetoric of Kievan Rus'*, p. lx.

78 Olenka Z. Pevny, 'Kievan Rus', in Evans and Wixom, *The Glory of Byzantium*, p. 281.

79 Halyna Lozko, *Ukraïns'ke yazychnytstvo* (Kiev: Ukrainian Centre of Spiritual Culture, 1994), p. 79.

80 Bratko-Kutyns'kyi, *Fenomen Ukraïny*, pp. 218–19. See also the pictures on p. 237.

81 Lozko, *Ukraïns'ke yazychnytstvo*, p. 19; Païk, *Ukraïna v mynulomu i s'ohodni*, p. A-6.

82 Kanyhin, *Shliakh ariïv*, p. 97.

83 *The Song of Igor's Campaign*, lines 304–5, at p. 44, and 258, at p. 42.

84 Valerii Shevchuk, *Myslene derevo* (Kiev: Molod', 1989). A similar argument is made by the supporters of an original Celtic, popular and humanistic Druidic faith that supposedly existed before the arrival of 'institutional religion' in the British Isles. See, amongst others, Shirley Toulson, *The Celtic Alternative: A Reminder of the Religion We Have Lost* (London: Rider, 1987).

85 Mishko, *Narys rann'oï istoriï Rusy-Ukraïny*, p. 50.

86 Lozko, *Ukraïns'ke yazychnytstvo*. For a more scholarly analysis, see V.M. Zubar' and Yu.V. Pavlenko, *Khersones Tavricheskii i rasprostranenie khristianstva na Rusi* (Kiev: Naukova dumka, 1988), pp. 86–108.

87 Bratko-Kutyns'kyi, *Fenomen Ukraïny*, p. 53.

88 Godley, *Herodotus: The Histories*, vol. 2, chaps 110–17, pp. 309–17.

89 Vasyl' Khytruk, 'Ukraïns'ka Troaia', in Vitalii Dovhych (ed.), *Kosmos drevn'oï Ukraïny* (Kiev: Knyha, 1992), pp. 146–53. This particular claim is bizarre enough to be attacked even by Kanyhin, who admits that, despite the 'Scythian influence' on Troy, it was probably where Heinrich Schliemann found it in the nineteenth century. See Kanyhin, *Shliakh ariïv*, p. 140. Païk, *Ukraïna v mynulomu i s'ohodni*, p. A-7, places Troy in the Dardanelles, where it was 'built by émigrés from Oriiana at the beginning of the third millenium BC'.

90 Kanyhin, *Shliakh ariïv*, p. 152.

91 Hryhorii Vasylenko, *Velyka Skifiia* (Kiev: Znannia, 1991).

92 Norman Davies, *Europe: A History* (Oxford: Oxford University Press, 1996), p. 232.

93 Anthony Smith, 'The "Golden Age" and National Revival', in Geoffrey Hosking and George Schöpflin (eds), *Myths and Nationhood* (London: Hurst, 1997), pp. 36–59, at p. 56.

94 Dmytro Korchyns'kyi, *Vyklykaiu vohon' na sebe!* (Kiev: n.p., 1998), p. 4.

Chapter 3

1 Chubatyi, *Istoriia khrystyianstva na Rusi-Ukraïny*, vol. 1.

2 Stepan Tomashivs'kyi, *Istoriia tserkvy na Ukraïni* (Zhovkva: Zapysok Chyna Sv. Vasyliia Velykoho, 1932).

3 Kalinin and Khar'kovshchenko, 'Sofiinyi kharakter kyïvs'koho khrystyianstva', p. 134.

4 Natalia Polonska-Vasylenko, *Ukraine-Rus and Western Europe in 10th–13th Centuries* (London: Association of Ukrainians in Great Britain, 1964), p. 12.

5 Panas, *Istoriia ukraïns'koï tserkvy*, p. 14.

6 Cross and Sherbowitz-Wetzor, *The Russian Primary Chronicle: Laurentian Text*, p. 97. There is little other documentary evidence for the idea of Muslim contact with Rus. See Tolochko, *Kyïvs'ka Rus'*, p. 277.

7 Volodymyr's predecessor Sviatoslav (ruled 962–72) even proposed moving the Rus' capital to Pereiaslavets' on the Danube in order to strengthen the link with Byzantium.

8 Cross and Sherbowitz-Wetzor, *The Russian Primary Chronicle: Laurentian Text*, p. 97.

9 Polonska-Vasylenko, *Ukraine-Rus*, pp. 17–18 and 28.

10 Compare the examples discussed in Simon Forde, Lesley Johnson and Alan V. Murray (eds), *Concepts of National Identity in the Middle Ages* (Leeds: Leeds Texts and Monographs, 1995).

11 For a guide to the frequently daunting complexities of the period, see Fennell, *A History of the Russian Church to 1448*, pp. 132–88.

12 Ihor Ševčenko, 'The Policy of the Byzantine Patriarchate in Eastern Europe in the Fourteenth Century', in his *Ukraine between East and West*, pp. 69–91.

13 Constantinople's reaction to Kazimierz's threat was probably a simple defensive act rather than a response to local ethnic self-assertion.

14 N.I. Kochan, 'Florentiis'ka uniia i Kyïvs'ka mytropoliia: do kharakterystyky rozvytku ta vtilennia ideï uniï tserkov', *Ukraïns'kyi istorychnyi zhurnal*, 1 (1996), pp. 28–44.

15 Païk, *Ukraïna v mynulomu i s'ohodni*, p. A-11.

16 Anatol' Hrytskevich, 'Historyia heapalityki Belarusi. III. Heapalitychnae stanovishcha Belarusi u XIX–XX stst.', *Spadchyna*, 4 (1994), pp. 48–61; Jan Zaprudnik, *Belarus: At a Crossroads in History* (Boulder: Westview, 1993), p. 48; Yakovenko, *Narys istoriï Ukraïny*, p. 248.

17 V.A. Smolii and V.S. Stepanov, *Ukraïns'ka derzhavna ideia XVII–XVIII stolit': problemy formuvannia, evoliutsiï, realizatsiï* (Kiev: Al'ternatyvy, 1997), p. 12.

18 As quoted in Ševčenko, *Ukraine between East and West*, p. 118.

19 Natalia Yakovenko, *Ukraïns'ka shliakhta z kintsia XIV do seredyny XVII st. (Volyn' i Tsentral'na Ukraïna)*, (Kiev: Naukova dumka, 1993).

20 Quoted in Andrej Kaminski, 'The Cossack Experiment in *Szlachta* Democracy in the Polish-Lithuanian Commonwealth: The Hadiach (*Hadziacz*) Union', *Harvard Ukrainian Studies*, 1, 2 (June 1977), pp. 178–97, at p. 180, note 4.

21 Quoted in Natalia Yakovenko, *Narys istoriï Ukraïny z naidavnishykh chasiv do kintsia XVIII stolittia* (Kiev: Heneza, 1997), p. 173.

22 For a detailed study of this period, see Borys A. Gudziak, *Crisis and Reform: The Kyivan Metropolitanate, the Patriarchate of Constantinople, and the Genesis of the Union of Brest* (Cambridge, Mass.: Harvard Ukrainian Studies, 1999).

23 Some Ukrainian sources claim that attacks on the Uniates were inspired by Moscow. See for example His Beatitude Myroslav Ivan Cardinal Lubachivsky, *Was It Really Russia That Was Christianised in 988?* (London and Rome: Ukrainian Publishers Ltd, 1986), p. 30.

24 Ivan Paslavs'kyi, *Mizh Skhodom i Zakhodom. Narysy z kul'turno-politychnoï istoriï Ukraïns'koï Tserkvy* (L'viv: Strim, 1994).

25 Anatol' Hrytskevich, 'Uniiatskiia tendentsyi i ŭniiatskaia tsarkva na Belarusi ŭ XV–XVIII stst.', *Khrys'tsiianskaia Dumka*, 1 (1993), pp. 162–72.

26 The Peresopnytsia Gospel (1556–61), on which the Ukrainian president now swears his inauguration oath, translated four books of the New Testament into the west Ukrainian vernacular, likewise the Krekhiv *Apostol* (1560) translated Acts and Epistles; but neither enjoyed wide circulation.

27 According to Georges Florovsky, the Ostrih and Novgorod Bibles were tainted by their imports from the Latin Vulgate, although he blamed Gennadii for beginning this process of 'slipping away into the Latin channel' and the Ostrih Bible was notable for its reexamination of original Greek sources: *Aspects of Church History* (Belmont, Mass.: Nordland Publishing Co. distributed by Notable and Academic Books, 1987), pp. 159–60.

28 Adrian Hastings, *The Construction of Nationhood: Ethnicity, Religion and Nationalism* (Cambridge, UK: Cambridge University Press, 1997).

29 As quoted in Frank E. Sysyn's survey of the question, 'Concepts of Nationhood in Ukrainian History Writing, 1620–1690', *Harvard Ukrainian Studies*, 10, 3–4 (December 1986), pp. 393–421, at p. 408.

30 Ihor Ševčenko, 'The Rebirth of the Rus' Faith', in his *Ukraine between East and West*, pp. 131–48, at p. 143.

31 D.S. Likhachev has argued that this 'new historicism' developed as early as the fourteenth century; this is disputed by Yaroslaw Pelenski – see chapters four and five in *The Contest for the Legacy of Kievan Rus*.

32 Edward Keenan, 'On Certain Mythical Beliefs and Russian Behaviours', in S. Frederick Starr (ed.), *The Legacy of History in Russia and the New States of Eurasia* (New York: M.E. Sharpe, 1994), pp. 123–45.

33 See the commentary by Stephen Velychenko in his *National History as Cultural Process* (Edmonton: CIUS, 1992), pp. 80–8.

34 Simon Franklin, 'The Invention of Rus(sia)(s): Some Remarks on Medieval and Modern Perceptions of Continuity and Discontinuity', in Alfred P. Smyth (ed.), *Medieval Europeans: Studies in Ethnic Identity and National Perspectives in Medieval Europe* (London: Macmillan, 1998), pp. 180–95. See also

Geoffrey Hosking, 'The Russian National Myth Repudiated', in *Myths and Nationhood*, pp. 198–210.

35 David A. Frick, 'Misrepresentations, Misunderstandings and Silences: Problems of Seventeenth-Century Ruthenian and Muscovite Cultural History', in Samuel H. Baron and Nancy Shields Kollman (eds), *Religion and Culture in Early Modern Russia and Ukraine* (Dekalb: Northern Illinois University Press, 1997), pp. 149–68, at p. 160.

36 See P.M. Sas's illuminating study, *Politychna kul'tura ukraïns'koho suspil'stva (kinets' XVI-persha polovyna XVII st.)* (Kiev: Lybid', 1998).

37 Author's interview with Natalia Yakovenko, 30 March 1998.

38 Zbigniew Wójcik, *Dzikie Pola w ogniu* (Warsaw, 1968).

39 Popovych, *Narys istoriï kul'tury Ukraïny*, p. 197.

40 Quoted in Ihor Ševčenko's informative article on the subject, 'The Many Worlds of Peter Mohyla', *Harvard Ukrainian Studies*, 8, 1–2 (June 1984), pp. 9–44, at p. 13.

41 Arkadii Zhukovs'kyi, *Petro Mohyla i pytannia yednosty tserkov* (Kiev: Mystetstvo, 1997), a reprint of the 1969 Paris edition.

42 Ševčenko, *Ukraine between East and West*, p. 143.

43 Ibid., p. 183. See also p. 191 and Magocsi, *A History of Ukraine*, p. 188.

44 Velychenko, *National History as Cultural Process*, p. 145. For the text, see Hans Rothe (ed.), *Sinopsis, Kiev 1681: Facsimile mit einer Einleitung* (Cologne: Böhlau Verlag, 1983).

45 Father Georges Florovsky, *Puti russkogo bogosloviia* (Paris: YMCA Press, 1937).

46 As quoted by Lindsey Hughes in her *Russia in the Age of Peter the Great* (New Haven and London: Yale University Press, 1998), p. 333.

47 Lev Gumilev, *Ot Rusi k Rossii* (Moscow: Ekopros, 1992), p. 254.

48 Teresa Chynczewska-Hennel, 'The National Consciousness of Ukrainian Nobles and Cossacks from the End of the Sixteenth to the Mid-Seventeenth Century', *Harvard Ukrainian Studies*, 10, 3–4 (December 1986), pp. 377–92.

49 David A. Frick, *Meletij Smotryc'kyj* (Cambridge, Mass.: Harvard Ukrainian Research Institute, 1995).

50 Frank E. Sysyn, *Between Poland and Ukraine: The Dilemma of Adam Kysil', 1600–1653* (Cambridge, Mass.: Harvard Ukrainian Research Institute, 1985).

Chapter 4

1 The title of a book edited by V.A. Smolii, *Ukraïns'ka kozats'ka derzhava* (Kiev and Cherkasy: Institute of History, 1994).

2 Viktor Brexunenko, 'Les relations entre la Cosaquerie ukrainienne et celle du Don aux XVIe et XVIIe siècles', in Michel Cadot and Emile Kruba (eds), *Les Cosaques de l'Ukraine* (Paris: Nouvelle Sorbonne, 1995), pp. 75–83.

3 Jurij Koc'ubej, 'Les éléments orientaux dans la culture et dans la vie quotidienne des Cosaques ukrainiens', in Cadot and Kruba, *Les Cosaques de l'Ukraine*, pp. 117–24.

4 This at least was the popular image of Nalyvaiko – his origins may in fact not have been all that humble.

5 Andrej Kaminski, 'The Cossack Experiment in *Szlachta* Democracy in the Polish-Lithuanian Commonwealth: The Hadiach (*Hadziacz*) Union', p. 178.

6 Magocsi, *A History of Ukraine*, p. 203.

7 Ševčenko, *Ukraine between East and West*, p. 192. Khmelnyts'kyi's original 'hurt and harm' was the loss of his estates and possibly his sweetheart Helena to a Polish neighbour.

8 Yurii Lypa, *Chornomors'ka doktryna* (Geneva: Ukrainian Naval Institute, 1947), p. 14.

9 See for example Mykola Vinhranovs'kyi, *Severyn Nalyvaiko – roman* (Kiev: Veselka, 1996).

10 Supposedly this was a real historical letter, addressed to the 'Turkish demon, brother and fellow to accursed Satan and secretary to Lucifer himself'. Yevhen Shabliovsky, *Ukrainian Literature through the Ages* (Kiev: Mystetstvo, 1970), p. 19.

11 On the four hundredth anniversary of Khmelnyts'kyi's birth in 1995 the official newspaper of the Ukrainian parliament used Ivasiuk's painting to frame its celebrations: *Holos Ukraïny*, 23 September 1995.

12 Vladislav Zubok and Constantine Pleshakov, *Inside the Kremlin's Cold War: From Stalin to Krushchev* (Cambridge, Mass.: Harvard University Press, 1996), p. 23.

13 Yakovenko, *Narys istoriï Ukraïny*, pp. 242–53.

14 See also Kaléna Uhryn, *La notion de 'Russie' dans la cartographie occidentale (XVIe–XVIIIe siècle)* (Paris: Institut ukrainien des Sciences économiques, 1975).

15 V.A. Smolii (ed.), *Istoriia Ukraïny*, (Kiev: Al'ternatyvy, 1997), p. 92; as also quoted in Philip Longworth, 'Ukraine: History and Nationality', *Slavonic and East European Review*, 78, 1 (2000) – a useful review of recent historiography.

16 For a discussion, see Ivan Rudnytsky, 'Pereiaslav: History and Myth', in his *Essays in Modern Ukrainian History*, pp. 77–89; and John Basarab, *Pereiaslav 1654: A Historiographical Study* (Edmonton: CIUS, 1982).

17 George Vernadsky (ed.), *A Source Book for Russian History from Early Times to 1917*, vol. 1 (New Haven and London: Yale University Press, 1972), p. 296.

18 Kaminski, 'The Cossack Experiment'; Magocsi, *A History of Ukraine*, pp. 220–5; Yakovenko, *Narys istoriï Ukraïny*, pp. 211–13.

19 'Mazeppa [sic]', in *Lord Byron: Selected Poems* (London: Penguin Classics, 1996), pp. 602–26, lines 97–106, at p. 605.

20 Hubert F. Babinski, *The Mazeppa Legend in European Romanticism* (New York: Columbia University Press, 1974).

21 Figures from Magocsi, *A History of Ukraine*, p. 245.

22 Frank E. Sysyn, 'The Changing Image of the Hetman: On the 350th Anniversary of the Khmel'nyts'kyi Uprising', *Jahrbücher für Geschichte Osteuropas*, 46 (1998), pp. 531–45.

23 See also Volodymyr Aleksandrovych, *L'vivs'ki maliari kintsia XVI stolittia* (L'viv: Misioner, 1998).

24 Stepovyk, *Istoriia ukraïns'koï ikony*, pp. 44–5.

25 T.I. Ulevich (ed.), *Ikanapis Belarusi XV–XVII stahoddziaŭ* (Minsk: Belarus', 1998), p. 19.

26 Dimitri Obolensky, *The Byzantine Commonwealth: Eastern Europe, 500–1453* (London: Sphere, 1974), p. 464, quoting from C.R. Morey, *Medieval Art* (New York, 1942), p. 167.

27 Engelina S. Smirnova, 'Simon Ushakov – "Historicism" and "Byzantinism". On the Interpretation of Russian Painting from the Second Half of the Seventeenth Century', in Baron and Kollman (eds), *Religion and Culture*, pp. 169–83, at p. 179.

28 Volodymyr Ovsiichuk, *Maistry ukraïns'koho barokko* (Kiev: Naukova dumka, 1991).

29 Larysa Skoryk, 'Natsional'nyi svitohliad i spetsyfika ukraïns'koho barokko v arkhitekturi', in Oleksa Myshanych

(ed.), *Ukraïns'ke barokko* (Kiev: Academy of Sciences, 1993), pp. 220–5.

30 Author's interview with Petro Tolochko, 24 June 1997.

31 Anatolii Zheleznyi, *Proiskhozhdenie russko-ukrainskogo dvuiazychiia v Ukraine* (Kiev: Fund for the Support of Russian Culture in Ukraine, 1998).

32 Quoted in Jurij Šerech, 'Stefan Yavorsky and the Conflict of Ideologies in the Age of Peter I', *Slavonic and East European Review*, 30, 74 (December 1951–2), pp. 40–62, at p. 75.

33 Some support for this view can be found in George Fedotov, *The Russian Religious Mind* (2nd edn; Cambridge, Mass.: Harvard University Press, 1966), who agrees that the 'nationalised, and thus corrupted, Byzantism' (p. x) that eventually triumphed in Muscovy was a considerable departure from the original Rus faith, although he would not trace this development back to Bogoliubskii.

Chapter 5

1 Roman Szporluk's essay 'Ukraine: From an Imperial Periphery to a Sovereign State', in *Daedalus*, 126, 3 (summer 1997), pp. 85–119, provides an excellent analysis of the process of 'nation-unmaking' whereby Ukraine disentangled itself from Russia, Poland and Austria, but says less about the factors leading to assimilation.

2 Stephen Velychenko, 'Empire Loyalism and Minority Nationalism in Great Britain and Imperial Russia, 1707 to 1914: Institutions, Law, and Nationality in Scotland and Ukraine', *Comparative Study of Society and History*, 39, 3 (July 1997), pp. 413–41; Dominic Lieven, *Empire. The Russian Empire and its Rivals*, (London: John Murray, 2000) pp. 280–1.

3 Linda Colley, *Britons: Forging the Nation, 1707–1839* (New Haven and London: Yale University Press, 1992).

4 See also Liah Greenfeld on the prominence of Ukrainians in building the eighteenth-century Russian identity, *Nationalism: Five Roads to Modernity* (Cambridge, Mass.: Harvard University Press, 1992), pp. 238–9 and 245.

5 Magocsi, *A History of Ukraine*, p. 289.

6 Oleksandr Hrytsenko, *"Svoia mudrist'"*: *Natsiolal'ni mifolohiï ta "hromadians'ka relihiia"v Ukraïni* (Kiev: Ukrainian Centre for Cultural Research, 1998), p. 33.

7 See for example the article by Petro Kravchuk in *Vechirnii Kyïv*, 4 March 1993.

8 Vladimir Morosan, *Choral Performance in Pre-Revolutionary Russia* (UMI Research Press, 1984).

9 See also Igor' Losievskii, *Russkaia lira s Ukrainy: Russkie pisateli Ukrainy pervoi chetverti XIX veka* (Kharkiv: Oko, 1993).

10 Nikolai Trubetskoy, 'The Ukrainian Problem', in his *The Legacy of Genghis Khan and Other Essays on Russia's Identity* (Ann Arbor: Michigan Slavic Publications, 1991), pp. 245–67, at pp. 248 and 251.

11 Alexander Riasanovsky, *Nicholas I and Official Nationality in Russia, 1825–1855* (Berkeley: University of California Press, 1967), p. 139.

12 David Saunders, *The Ukrainian Impact on Russian Culture, 1750–1850* (Edmonton: CIUS, 1985), p. 67.

13 Ibid., pp. 111 and 107.

14 See also Aleksei Miller, *'Ukrainskii vopros' v politike vlastei: russkom obshchestvennom mnenii (utoraia polovina XIX v)* (St Petersburg: Ateleiia 2000).

15 Theodore R. Weeks, *Nation and State in Late Imperial Russia: Nationalism and Russification on the Western Frontier, 1863–1914* (DeKalb: Northern Illinois University Press, 1996); Alfred J. Rieber, 'Struggle over the Borderlands', in S. Frederick Starr (ed.), *The Legacy of History in Russia and the New States of Eurasia*, pp. 61–90; Geoffrey Hosking, *Russia: People and Empire, 1552–1917* (London: HarperCollins, 1997), pp. 367–97.

16 Szporluk, *Ukraine: From an Imperial Periphery to a Sovereign State*; Andreas Kappeler, *Russland als Vielvolkerreich: Entstehung, Geschichte, Zerfall* (Munich: C.H. Beck, 1992).

17 Ernest Gellner, *Nations and Nationalism* (Oxford: Basil Blackwell, 1983).

18 Overall literacy was on the rise before 1914, to somewhere between 30% and 40%, but was concentrated in urban areas where the Ukrainian presence was weak. See Jeffrey Brooks, *When Russia Learnt to Read: Literacy and Popular*

Culture, 1861–1917 (Princeton: Princeton University Press, 1985).

19 Szporluk, *Nationalism after Communism* , pp. 307–8, which refers in turn to Rieber, 'Struggle over the Borderlands', p. 81.

20 Robert J. Kaiser, *The Geography of Nationalism in Russia and the USSR* (Princeton: Princeton University Press, 1994), pp. 43–82, argues that 'social communication' was beginning to spread.

21 Andreas Kappeler, 'Mazepintsy, malorossy, khokhly: ukraintsy v etnicheskoi ierarkhii rossiiskoi imperii', in Miller et al. (eds), *Rossiia-Ukraina* , pp. 125–44.

22 Vasyl' Lyzanchuk, *Navicho kaidany kuvaly: fakty, dokumenty, komentari pro rusyfikatsiiu v Ukraïni* (L'viv: Academy of Sciences, 1995), pp. 17–19.

23 Volodymyr Hryn'ov, *Nova Ukraïna, yakoiu ya ïï bachu* (Kiev: Abrys, 1995), p. 60, refers to 'natural processes ... of mutual assimilation and mutual influence'.

24 Hubertas F. Jahn, *Patriotic Culture in Russia during World War I* (Ithaca and London: Cornell University Press, 1995) argues that war propaganda was attractive to many, if somewhat diffuse in focus; although he makes no real specific reference to Ukraine.

25 Eugene Weber, *Peasants into Frenchmen: The Modernization of Rural France, 1870–1914* (London: Chatto & Windus, 1979).

26 Don C. Rawson, *Russian Rightists and the Revolution of 1905* (Cambridge, UK: Cambridge University Press, 1995), pp. 92–5.

27 Witold Rodkiewicz, 'Russian Nationality Policy in the Western provinces of the Empire during the Reign of Nicholas II, 1894–1905' (Harvard PhD thesis, 1996), pp. 317–52.

28 For a modern restatement of this view from eastern Ukraine, see Valentin Mamutov, 'Dikoe pole – ne terra-inkognita', *Donetskii kriazh*, 35 (8–14 October 1993).

29 Andrea Rutherford, 'Vissarion Belinskii and the Ukrainian National Question', *The Russian Review*, 54, 4 (October 1995), pp. 500–15.

30 Rodkiewicz, 'Russian Nationality Policy', pp. 369–70 and 447–9

31 Greenfeld, *Nationalism: Five Roads to Modernity*, pp. 260–74; Iver B. Neumann, *Russia and the Idea of Europe* (London: Routledge, 1996), pp. 28–60.

32 A.I. Savenko in *Kievlianin*, 17 November 1911, as quoted by Jurij Borys in *The Sovietisation of Ukraine, 1917–23* (Edmonton: CIUS, 1980), p. 383, and Roman Szporluk, 'The Ukraine and Russia', in Robert Conquest (ed.), *The Last Empire* (Stanford: Hoover Institution Press, 1986), pp. 151–82, at p. 155.

33 Michael F. Hamm, *Kiev: A Portrait, 1800–1917* (Princeton: Princeton University Press, 1993), p. 103.

34 See Yakov Soroker's interesting study *Ukrainian Musical Elements in Classical Music* (Edmonton: CIUS, 1995), although it is in fact largely about the use of Ukrainian forms and melodies in the classical canon.

35 From the Penguin edition of *Chekhov: Plays* (London, 1983), pp. 341–2. A similar point is made in Ernest Gellner, *Nationalism* (London: Wiedenfeld & Nicolson, 1997), p. 55.

36 Irina Ratushinskaya, *The Odessans* (London: Sceptre, 1996), p. 26.

37 Key parts of the opera, including much of its admittedly weak dramatic structure, were finished by Rimskii-Korsakov and Alexander Glazunov.

38 Jaqueline Decter, *Nicholas Roerich: The Life and Art of a Russian Master* (London: Thames & Hudson, 1989), p. 89.

39 From the Methuen edition of *Bulgakov: Six Plays* (London, 1991), p. 9. Readers may also care to look at Anna Reid's entertaining account in *Borderland: A Journey through the History of Ukraine* (London: Weidenfeld & Nicolson, 1997), pp. 20–2.

40 *Bulgakov: Six Plays*, p. 28.

41 Paul Robert Magocsi, 'The Ukrainian National Revival: A New Analytical Framework', *Canadian Review of Studies in Nationalism*, XVI, 1–2 (1989), pp. 45–62.

42 See also Volodymyr Potul'nyts'kyi, *Teoriia ukraïns'koï politolohiï* (Kiev: Lybid', 1993), pp. 56–72; *Istoriia ukraïns'koï politolohiï* (Kiev: Lybid', 1992), pp. 75–107: and his excellent essay 'The Image of Russia and the Russians in Ukrainian Political Thought (1860–1945)', in Koichi Inoue and Tomohiko Uyama (eds), *Quests for*

Models of Coexistence: National and Ethnic Dimensions of Change in the Slavic Eurasian World (Sapporo: Slavic Research Centre, Hokkaido University, 1998), pp. 163–95.

43 See the reprint of Drahomanov's 'Lysty na Naddniprians'ku Ukraïnu', in A. Zhukovs'kyi (ed.), *B. Hrinchenko – M. Drahomanov. Dialohy pro ukraïns'ku natsional'nu spravu* (Kiev: Academy of Sciences, 1994), pp. 149–271.

44 Mykhailo Drahomanov, 'Literatura rosiis'ka, velykorus'ka, ukraïns'ka i halyts'ka', in his *Literaturno-publit-systychni pratsi* (Kiev: Naukova dumka, 1970), vol. 1, pp. 80–220, at p. 113.

45 N.I. Kostomarov, 'Dve russkie narod-nosti', *Osnova*, 3, 1861 (reprinted in Kiev by Maidan, 1991); 'Mysli o federa-tivnom nachale drevnei Rusi', *Osnova*, 1, 1861; and Hrytsenko, 'Svoia mud-rist' ', pp. 113–20.

46 Yevhen Malaniuk, 'Hohol-Gogol', *Ukrainian Review*, 14, 3 (1967), pp. 55–69.

47 Yevhen Sverstiuk, *Bludni syny Ukraïny* (Kiev: Znannia, 1993), pp. 16–18.

48 See George S.N. Luckyj, *Between Gogol' and Shevchenko: Polarity in the Literary Ukraine, 1798–1847* (Munich, 1971); and *The Anguish of Mykola Hohol, a.k.a. Nikolai Gogol* (Toronto: Canadian Scholars' Press, 1998). See also David Saunders, 'Contemporary Critics of Gogol's *Vechera* and the Debate about Russian *narodnost'* (1831–1832)', *Harvard Ukrainian Studies*, 5, 1 (March 1981), pp. 66–82.

49 Letter from Gogol to his long-time friend Alexandra Smirnova, also born in Ukraine, 24 December 1844, in N.V. Gogol', *Sobranie sochinenii*, vol. 10 – collected letters (Moscow: Russkaia kniga, 1994), p. 276.

50 Panteleimon Kulish, 'Ob otnoshenii malorossiiskoi slovesnosti k obshcher-usskoi' (Epilogue to the Black Council), *Tvory v dvokh tomakh*, vol. 2 (Kiev: Dnipro, 1989), pp. 458-76. An English version can be found in Lindheim and Luckyj, *Towards an Intellectual History of Ukraine*, pp. 105–21.

51 Luckyj, *Between Gogol' and Shev-chenko*, p. 127.

52 Ibid., p. 126

53 Nikolai Gogol, *Dead Souls*, translated by Richard Pevear and Larissa Volokhonsky (New York: Pantheon, 1996), pp. 252–3.

54 Luckyj, *Between Gogol' and Shev-chenko*, p. 194.

55 See also George Grabowicz, *The Poet as Mythmaker. A Study of Symbolic Meaning in Taras Ševčenko* (Cambridge Mass.: Harvard University Press, 1982); George Grabowicz, 'Three Perspectives on the Cossack Past: Gogol', Ševčenko, Kuliš', *Harvard Ukrainian Studies*, 5, 2 (June 1981), pp. 171–94, and compare Judith Deutsch Kornblatt, *The Cossack Hero in Russian Literature: A Study in Cultural Mythology* (Wisconsin: University of Wisconsin Press, 1992).

56 Oksana Zabuzhko, *Shevchenkiv mif Ukraïny. Sproba filosofs'koho analizu* (Kiev: Abrys, 1997), pp. 42 and 45.

57 From 'The Night of Taras', lines 15–20, as translated by Vera Rich, *Taras Shevchenko: Song out of Darkness* (London: Mitre Press, 1961), p. 11,

58 From 'Chyhyryn', lines 17–25; ibid., p. 23.

59 Ibid., p. 23.

60 From 'To my Fellow-Countrymen', lines 256–9; ibid., p. 80.

61 Ibid., lines 31–2, ibid., p. 74.

62 From 'The Dream', lines 275–8; in Rich, *Song out of Darkness*, p. 32.

63 Ibid., lines 420, 438–45 and 416–19, slightly adapted, p. 36.

64 From 'O my Thoughts, my Heartfelt Thoughts', lines 60–1, ibid., p. 9; and 'The Great Vault', lines 175–370, pp. 45–51.

65 Yevhen Hutsalo, *Mental'nist' ordy* (Kiev: Prosvita, 1996), pp. 108–25.

66 Adapted from 'Kateryna', lines 1–6; in *Taras Shevchenko: Selected Works* (Moscow: Progress, 1970), p. 37.

67 From 'The Plundered Grave', lines 25–36; in Rich, *Song out of Darkness*, p. 21.

68 From 'The Night of Taras', lines 37–8; in ibid., p. 12.

69 From 'To the Poles', lines 1–3; in *Kobzar* (Kiev: Prosvita, 1993), p. 304.

70 From 'Haidamaki', in *Taras Shev-chenko: Selected Works*, pp. 92 and 98–9.

71 His biographer Thomas Prymak argues that 'there can be no doubt that the his-torian would have taken a very different position [on the national question] if he had been free to do so', although this rather takes the historian out of the con-text of his time. *Mykola Kostomarov: A Biography* (Toronto: University of Toronto Press, 1996), p. 181.

72 Lypyns'kyi, *Lysty do brativ-khliborobiv*, p. xxv.

73 Natalie Kononenko, *Ukrainian Minstrels: And the Blind Shall Sing* (New York: M.E. Sharpe, 1998).

74 Ivan Lysiak-Rudnytsky, 'The Intellectual Origins of Modern Ukraine', in his *Essays in Modern Ukrainian History* (Edmonton: CIUS, 1987), pp. 123–41, at p. 139.

75 *Dialohy pro ukraïns'ku natsional'nu spravu*, p. 14.

76 Ibid., pp. 11 and 93. See also Borys Hrinchenko, *Tiazhkym shliakhom* (two editions, 1906 and 1912).

77 Lesia Ukraïnka, *Boiarynia* (Toronto: Organisation of Ukrainian Women of Canada, 1971), p. 14.

78 Ibid., pp. 39, 13 and 20.

79 Ibid., pp. 24, 40, 27, 37, 29 and 54. Emphasis added. See also Olha Witochynska, 'La noblesse cosaque dans le drame *Boyarynia* de Lessia Oukraïnka', in *Les Cosaques de l'Ukraine*, pp. 239–45.

80 From the edition of Ukraïnka's works with a foreword by Clarence Manning, *Spirit of Flame* (New York: Bookman, 1950), pp. 107 and 110.

81 See Mykola Riabchuk's interesting essay 'The Nativist-Westernizer Controversy in Ukraine: The End or the Beginning?', *Journal of Ukrainian Studies*, 21, 1–2 (summer–winter 1996), pp. 27–54, at pp. 38 and 48–9.

82 I. Bashtovy (Nechui-Levyts'kyi), *Ukrainstvo na literaturnykh pozvakh z Moskovshchyvnoiu* (L'viv: Dilo, 1891).

83 Riabchuk, 'The Nativist–Westernizer Controversy', pp. 51.

84 *Dialohy pro ukraïns'ku natsional'nu spravu*, p. 162.

85 Riabchuk, 'The Nativist–Westernizer Controversy', p. 50. See also Oksana Zabuzhko, *Filosofilia ukraïns'koï ideï ta yevropeis'kyi kontekst: Frankivs'kyi period* (Kiev: Osnova, 1993).

86 P.S. Sokhan' et al. (eds), *Kyrylo-Mefodiïvs'ke Tovarystvo*, vol. 2 (Kiev: Naukova dumka, 1990), p. 570.

87 See Peter Duncan, *Russian Messianism* (London: Routledge, 2000).

88 Nikolai Gogol, 'Vzgliad na sostavlenie Malorossii', in Gogol', *Sobranie sochinenii* , vol. 7, pp. 152–60; Robert A. Maguire, *Exploring Gogol* (Stanford: Stanford University Press, 1994), pp. 282–4. Gogol was a better writer than a historian. He spent two unhappy years

as a history professor at St Petersburg university.

89 Gogol, 'Vzgliad na sostavlenie Malorossii', p. 157.

90 See also Hrytsak, *Narys istoriï Ukraïny:* p. 11.

91 Significantly, a collection of anti-Ukrainian tracts from the turn of the century was republished in 1998 as M.B. Smolina (ed.), *Ukrainskii separatizm v Rosii. Ideologiia natsional'nogo raskola* (Moscow: Moskva), thereby saving Russian nationalists the trouble of updating their views.

92 R.W. Seton-Watson, 'The Ukraine Problem', in his *Europe in the Melting-Pot* (London: Macmillan, 1919), pp. 365–76, at pp. 372–3.

93 Rodkiewicz, 'Russian Nationality Policy', pp. 334 and 352.

Chapter 6

1 See also John-Paul Himka's excellent essay 'The Construction of Nationality in Galician Rus': Icarian Flights in Almost All Directions', in Michael D. Kennedy and Ronald G. Sumy (eds), *Intellectuals and the Articulation of the Nation* (Ann Arbor: University of Michigan Press, 1999), pp. 109–64.

2 The requirement was temporarily abolished in 1812, though by then the network was established. See also Gary B. Cohen, *Education and Middle-Class Society in Imperial Austria, 1848–1918* (West Lafayette, Indiana: Purdue University Press, 1996).

3 Szporluk, *Ukraine: From an Imperial Periphery to a Sovereign State*, pp. 100 and 108.

4 Hrytsak, *Narys istoriï Ukraïny*, p. 46.

5 Andrzej Walicki, *Poland between East and West: The Controversies over Self-Definition and Modernization in Partitioned Poland* (Cambridge, Mass.: Harvard University Ukrainian Research Institute, 1994).

6 Hrytsak, *Narys istoriï Ukraïny*, p. 52.

7 Yuliian Bachyns'kyi, *Podil Halychyny* (L'viv, 1897).

8 Henryk Sienkiewicz, *With Fire and Sword*, translation by W.S. Kuniczak (New York: Hippocrene Books, 1991), pp. 33–4; see also Myroslav Trukhan, *Negatyvnyi stereotyp ukraïntsia v pol's'kii povoienii literaturi* (Munich/L'viv, 1992).

9 See the essays by Solomon Wank in Karen Dawisha and Bruce Parrot (eds), *The End of Empire? The Transformation of the USSR in Comparative Perspective* (New York: M.E. Sharpe, 1997), and Karen Barkey and Mark von Hagen (eds), *The End of Empire: Causes and Consequences* (Boulder: Westview, 1997).

10 Hrytsak, *Narys istoriï Ukraïny*, p. 52.

11 Ibid., p. 75.

12 Ibid., p. 76.

13 Magocsi, *A History of Ukraine*, p. 448.

14 Mykola Kostomarov, 'Mysli o federativnom nachale v drevnei Rusi', *Osnova*, 1 (1861); Prymak, *Mykola Kostomarov*, pp. 104–6.

15 Franciszek Duchiński, *Peuples Aryâs et Tourans, agriculteurs et nomades* (Paris, 1864).

16 The Austrians tried to avoid offending the Poles by insisting that the chair was in 'Universal History' with reference to 'Eastern Europe'. Hrushevs'kyi was born in Kholm and spent most of his early years in tsarist Ukraine; he was able to return there with increasing frequency after the 1905 revolution (his application for a chair at Kiev University was, however, refused in 1908).

17 Hrushevs'kyi's famous 1904 essay 'The Traditional Scheme of "Russian" History and the Problem of a Rational Organisation of the History of the Eastern Slavs' is reprinted in English in *From Kievan Rus' to Modern Ukraine: Formation of the Ukrainian Nation* (Cambridge, Mass.: Ukrainian Studies Fund, 1984). The first volume in Hrushevs'kyi's magnum opus *History of Ukraine-Rus'*, was published by the Canadian Institute of Ukrainian Studies in 1997. Nine more will follow.

18 It is nevertheless conceivable, in extremis, that a 'European Galicia' could have been counterposed to an 'Asian Russia-Ukraine', if circumstances had been *very* different.

19 The term 'Ukraine' can be found in chronicles from the twelfth century, although as a commonplace it is a late nineteenth-century coinage.

20 Khvedir Vovk, *Studiï z ukraïns'koï etnohrafiï ta antropolohiï* (Kiev: Mystetstvo, 1995).

21 Ihor Zhuk, *Istoryko-arkhitekturnyi atlas L'vova* (L'viv: Tsentr Yevropy, 1996).

22 Konrad Sadkowski, 'From Ethnic Borderland to Catholic Fatherland: The Church, Christian Orthodox, and State Administration in the Chełm Region, 1918–1939', *Slavic Review*, 57, 4 (winter 1998), pp. 813–39, and the following article by Chris Hann on Peremyshl. See also Ihor Vynnychenko, *Ukraïntsi Beresteishchyny, Pidliashshia i Kholmshchyny v pershiï polovyni XX stolittia: Khronika podii* (Kiev: Ukraïna, 1997) for a Ukrainian version of the history of these regions.

23 See Alexei L. Petrov, *Medieval Carpathian Rus': The Oldest Documentation about the Carpatho-Rusyn Church and Eparchy* (New York: Columbia University Press/East European Monographs, 1998), and Athanasius B. Pekar, *The History of the Church in Carpathian Rus'* (New York: East European Monographs, 1992).

24 The standard work on the region's history is Paul Robert Magocsi, *The Shaping of a National Identity: Subcarpathian Rus', 1848–1948* (Cambridge, Mass.: Harvard University Press, 1978). On the historiography of the region, see pp. 105–29.

25 Oleksandr Maiboroda, *Politychne Rusynstvo'. Zakarpats'ka versiia pereferiinoho natsionalizmu* (Kiev: Kiev-Mohyla Academy, 1999), pp. 14–15.

26 Magocsi, *The Shaping of a National Identity*, p. 27.

27 Magocsi, *A History of Ukraine*, p. 456. Thirty-five bilingual schools remained.

28 See also Maria Mayer, *The Rusyns of Hungary: Political and Social Developments, 1860–1914* (New York: Columbia University Press/East European Monographs, 1998).

29 Grigore Nandriş, *Bessarabia and Bucovina: The Trojan Horse of Russian Colonial Expansion to the Mediterranean* (London: Society for Romanian Culture 1968), pp. 14, 27 and 66. See also Ion Nistor, *La Bessarabie et la Bucovine* (Bucharest: Academy of Sciences, 1937) and Ion Nistor, *Românii şi rutenii în Bucovina: Studiu istorie şi statistic* (Bucharest: Librăriile Socec, 1915).

30 Raimund Kaindl, *Geschichte der Bukowina* (Chernivtsi: 1896–9).

31 Denys Kvitkovs'kyi, Teofil' Bryndzan and Arkadii Zhukovs'kyi, *Bukovyna: ïï mynule i suchasne* (Paris/Philadelphia/Detroit: Zelena Bukovyna, 1956), pp. 115, 141, 200, 725 and 435. See also the end-map.

32 See Irina Livezeanu, *Cultural Politics in Greater Romania: Regionalism, Nation-Building and Ethnic Struggle, 1918–1930* (Ithaca: Cornell University Press, 1995), chap. 2.

33 Ann Lencyk Pawliczko (ed.), *Ukraine and Ukrainians throughut the world: A Demographic and Sociological Guide to the Homeland and its Diaspora* (Toronto: University of Toronto Press, 1994), pp. 328 and 358. This is the main work on the diaspora.

34 There are many works specifically on the west Ukrainian diaspora, whose publishing activity is highly organised. Try Orest Subtelny, *Ukrainians in North America: An Illusrated History* (Toronto: University of Toronto Press, 1991).

35 See Andrew Wilson, 'Ukraine: Engaging the Eastern Diaspora', in Charles King and Neil J. Melvin (eds), *Nations Abroad: Diaspora Politics and International Relations in the Former Soviet Union* (Boulder: Westview, 1998), pp. 103–31.

36 Mykhailo Hrushevs'kyi, 'Halychyna i Ukraina', *Literaturno-naukovyi vistnyk*, 36 (1906). Emphasis added.

37 Ihor Ševčenko, *Ukraine between East and West* , p. 5.

38 Ibid.

39 Mykhailo Hrushevs'kyi, 'Ukrainskii P'emont', *Ukrainskii vestnik*, 2 (1906).

Chapter 7

1 Yaroslav Hrytsak, *Narys istoriï Ukraïny: formuvannia modernoï ukraïns'koï natsiï XIX–XX stolittia* (Kiev: Heneza, 1996).

2 Vasyl' Kremen', Dmytro Tabachnyk and Vasyl' Tkachenko, *Ukraïna: al'ternatyvy postupu (krytyka istorychnoho dosvidu)* (Kiev: ARC-Ukraine, 1996), p. 198.

3 Smolii et al., *Istoriia Ukraïny*, p. 177.

4 See Oleksii Holobuts'kyi and Vitalii Kulyk, *Ukraïns'kyi politychnyi rukh na Naddniprianshchyni kintsia XIX pochatku XX stolittia* (Kiev: Smoloskyp, 1996), pp. 92–3.

5 Smolii et al., *Istoriia Ukraïny*, p. 182.

6 John-Paul Himka, 'Ukrainians, Russians, and Alexander Solzhenitsyn', *Cross-Currents: A Yearbook of Central European Culture*, 11 (1992) pp. 193–204.

7 Aleksandr Solzhenitsyn, *The Russian Question at the End of the 20th Century*

(London: Harvill Press, 1995), p. 38.

8 Ibid.

9 As quoted in Hrytsak, *Narys istoriï Ukraïny*, p. 129.

10 See the programmes of the Ukrainian parties in V.F. Shevchenko (ed.), *Ukraïns'ki politychni partiï kintsia XIX – pochatku XX stolittia: prohramovi i dovidkovi materialy* (Kiev: Feniks, 1993), pp. 95, 123 and 152

11 V.M. Boiko, 'Uchast' ukraïns'kykh partii u munitsypal'nii kampaniï 1917 r.', *Ukraïns'kyi istorychnyi zhurnal*, 5 (September–October 1997), pp. 25–40, at p. 37.

12 As quoted in Oleksandr Derhachov (ed.), *Ukrainian Statehood in the Twentieth Century* (Kiev: Political Thought, 1996), p. 5.

13 Mark Baker, 'Beyond the National: Peasants, Power and Revolution in Ukraine', *Journal of Ukrainian Studies*, 24, 1 (June 1999), pp. 39–67, at p. 49. Baker's article emphasises the peasants' localism and 'their unwillingness to sacrifice for larger ideas of community' (p. 66).

14 Arthur E. Adams, 'The Great Ukrainian Jacquerie', in Taras Hunczak (ed.), *The Ukraine 1917–21: A Study in Revolution* (Cambridge, Mass.: Harvard Ukrainian Research Institute, 1977), pp. 247–70.

15 Magocsi, *A History of Ukraine*, p. 499.

16 Evan Ostryzniuk, 'The Ukrainian Countryside during the Russian Revolution, 1917–19: The Limits of Peasant Mobilisation', *The Ukrainian Review*, 44, 1 (spring 1997), pp. 54–63; and Ostryzniuk, 'Revolution in the Ukrainian Village: The Trans-Dnipro Countryside of Ukraine during the Russian Revolution from Spring 1917 to Spring 1919' (University of Cambridge PhD, 1999); Graham Tan, 'Peasant Action and Village Social Organisation: The Peasantry of Right Bank Ukraine during the Revolution, 1917–1923' (University of London PhD, 1999).

17 Wherever the ranks of Ukrainian activists also included more nationally conscious village elements (the occasional schoolteacher, cooperative heads, some priests), then the Ukrainian movement was much stronger. This question, however, has been little researched, although see Andreas Kappeler, 'The Ukrainians of the Russian Empire, 1860–1914', in

Kappeler et al. (eds), *The Formation of National Elites*, vol. 6 (Dartmouth: New York University Press, 1992), pp. 114–20; and Heorhii Kas'ianov, *Ukraïns'ka intelihentsiia na rubezhi XIX–XX stolit': sotsial'no-politychnyi portret* (Kiev: Lybid', 1993), pp. 27–44.

18   *Bulgakov: Six Plays*, p. 27.

19   Ibid., p. 39.

20   Hrytsak, *Narys istoriï Ukraïny*, p. 128.

21   Ibid., pp. 127–34, quotation at p. 129.

22   Pavlo Skoropads'kyi, *Spohady* (Kiev/Philadelphia: V.K. Lypyns'kyi East European Research Institute et al., 1995), p. 48.

23   Jaroslaw Pelenski, 'Hetman Pavlo Skoropadsky and Germany (1917–18) as Reflected in his Memoirs', in Hans-Joachim Torke and John-Paul Himka (eds), *German-Ukrainian Relations in Historical Perspective* (Edmonton: CIUS, 1994), pp. 69–83, at p. 77.

24   The largely peasant armies that restored the UNR in December 1918 soon melted away. With Skoropads'kyi's army gone, Ukraine had to build its defences from scratch and could never match the Bolsheviks or Whites.

25   For a recent, rather romanticised history of the West Ukrainian People's Republic, see Mykola Lytvyn and Kim Naumenko, *Istoriia ZUNR* (L'viv: Academy of Sciences/OLIP, 1995).

26   Correspondence of the Austrian Consul in L'viv Urbas, as quoted in Derhachov (ed.), *Ukrainian Statehood in the Twentieth Century*, p. 223.

27   Magocsi, *A History of Ukraine*, p. 485; Michael Palij, *The Ukrainian-Polish Defensive Alliance, 1919–1921: An aspect of the Ukrainian Revolution* (Edmonton: CIUS, 1995).

28   Yevhen Onats'kyi, *Shliakhom na Rotterdam* (Buenos Aires: Yuliiana Serelinka, 1983); *Zhyttia i smert' Polkovnyky Konoval'tsia* (L'viv: Chervona kalyna, 1993).

29   Mykhailo Sosnovs'kyi, *Dmytro Dontsov. Politychnyi portret* (New York and Toronto: Trident International, 1974), pp. 205 and 207.

30   See the English translation of Malaniuk's essay 'Little Russianism', in Lindheim and Luckyj, *Towards an Intellectual History of Ukraine: An Anthology of Ukrainian Thought from 1710 to 1995*, pp. 316–29.

31   From the translation in Lindheim and Luckyj, *Towards an Intellectual History of Ukraine*, pp. 260–8. Dontsov's main

work, *Natsionalizm* (1926), is available in many modern reprints.

32   'Materiialy druhoho velykhoho Zboru Ukraïns'kykh Natsionalistiv', in Taras Hunchak and Roman Sol'chanyk (eds), *Ukraïns'ka suspil'no-politychna dumka v 20 stolitti*, vol. 2 (Munich: Suchasnist', 1983), pp. 399–402.

33   'Postanovy II (krakivs'koho) Velykoho Zboru Orhanizatsiï Ukraïns'kykh Natsionalistiv', ibid., vol. 3, pp. 7–22, at p. 15.

34   Information provided by the Kiev historian Heorhii Kas'ianov from his study of the Ukrainian Section in the Central State Archives in Prague. See also Onats'kyi, *Shliakhom na Rotterdam*.

35   Serhy Yekelchyk, 'Nationalisme ukrainien, biélorusse et slovaque', in Chantal Delsol and Michel Maslowski, *Histoire des idées politiques de l'Europe Centrale* (Paris: Presses Universitaires de France, 1998), pp. 377–93, at pp. 380–1.

36   See Alexander J. Motyl's study *The Turn to the Right: The Ideological Origins and Development of Ukrainian Nationalism, 1919–1929* (Boulder: East European Monographs, 1980).

37   Derhachov (ed.), *Ukrainian Statehood in the Twentieth Century*, p. 240, retranslated from the Ukrainian original, quoting from 'Resolution No. 1 of the National Assembly of Ukrainians', Ukrainian State Archive: f. 3833, op. 1, sprava 5, arkush 3.

38   Rosenberg's 'Memorandum No. 2', prepared in April 1941, envisaged an independent Ukraine stretching as far as the Volga and in alliance witrh a federation of new Caucasian states and a Volga German republic.

39   Józef Darski, *Ukraina. Historia, Współczesność, Konflikty Narodowe* (Warsaw: Polish Policy Institute, 1993), p. 28.

40   *OUN v svitli postanov Velykykh Zboriv, Konferentsii ta inshykh dokumentiv z borot'by 1929–1955 r.* (N.p. Library of the Ukrainian Underground, 1955), pp. 128 and 145.

41   As quoted in Sosnovs'kyi, *Dmytro Dontsov*, p. 97.

42   As quoted in Serhy Yekelchyk's fascinating study 'The Body and National Myth: Motifs from the Ukrainian National Revival in the Nineteenth Century', *Australian Slavonic and East European Studies*, 7, 2 (1993), pp. 31–59, at p. 34

43 Panas Myrnyi, 'Naroduliubets', *Zibrannia tvoriv u semy tomakh* (Kiev: Naukova dumka, 1970) vol. 4, pp. 85–108, at p. 107.

44 Grabowicz, *The Poet as Mythmaker*, p. 162.

45 Oleh S. Ilnytzkyj, *Ukrainian Futurism, 1914–1930: A Historical and Critical Study* (Cambridge, Mass.: Harvard Ukrainian Research Institute, 1997), pp. 337 and xii.

46 Steven Mansbach, *The Emergence of Modern Art in Eastern Europe* (Cambridge, UK: Cambridge University Press, 1999); N. Aseeva, *Ukrainskoe iskusstro i europeiskse khudozhestvennye tsentry* (Kiev: Naukova dumka, 1989).

47 Ivan T. Berend, *Decades of Crisis: Central and Eastern Europe before World War II* (London and Berkeley: University of California Press, 1998).

48 See Jo-Anne Birnie Danzker et al., *Avant-Garde and Ukraine* (Munich: Klinkhardt and Biermann, 1993); and Dmytro Horbachov (ed.), *Ukraïns'kyi avanhard 1910–1930 rokiv* (Kiev: Mystetstvo, 1996).

49 Horbachov, *Ukraïns'kyi avanhard*, p. 380.

50 Murashko and Maksymovych were confirmed as the progenitors of Ukrainian modernism when each was granted a separate room in the Kiev National Museum of Fine Art in 1999.

51 Popovych, *Narys istoriï kul'tury Ukraïny*, p. 521.

52 Mykhailo Semenko, as quoted in Ilnytzkyj, *Ukrainian Futurism*, p. 336.

53 Lutsky, quoted in Cyzevs'kyj, *A History of Ukrainian Literature*, p. 689.

54 V. Revutsky, 'Mykola Kulish in the Modern Ukrainian Theatre', *Slavonic and East European Review*, 49, 116 (July 1971), pp. 355–64, at pp. 359–60.

55 As quoted in Ilnytzkyj, *Ukrainian Futurism*, p. xiv.

56 See also Solomiia Pavlychko, *Dyskurs modernizmu v ukraïns'kii literaturi* (Kiev: Lybid', 1997).

57 As quoted in Myroslav Shkandrij, *Modernists, Marxists and the Nation: The Ukrainian Literary Discussion of the 1920s* (Edmonton: CIUS, 1992), p. 76.

58 Mykola Khvyl'ovyi, 'Ukraïna chy malorosiia?', and 'Psykholohichna Yevropa', in his 'Dumky proty techiï', first written in 1926, as reprinted in the collection *Ukraïna chy malorosiia?* (Kiev: Smoloskyp, 1993), pp. 241 and 106–8.

59 Ilya Prizel, *National Identity and Foreign Policy: Nationalism and Leadership in Poland, Russia, and Ukraine* (Cambridge, UK: Cambridge University Press, 1998), p. 328, referring to George S.N. Luckyj, *Literary Politics in the Soviet Ukraine 1917–1934* (Freeport: reprint of original Columbia University Press edition, 1971), pp. 94–111.

60 See also Andre Partykevich, *Between Kyiv and Constantinople: Oleksander Lototsky and the Quest for Ukrainian Autocephaly* (Edmonton: CIUS, 1998).

61 Mark Mazower, *Dark Continent: Europe's Twentieth Century* (London: Penguin, 1998), pp. 117–28 and 281–6; Ronald Grigor Sumy, *The Soviet Experiment: Russia, the USSR, and the Successor States* (New York and Oxford: Oxford University Press, 1998).

62 See for example George Luckyj's essay at the end of the second edition of Dmytro Cyzevs'kyj, *A History of Ukrainian Literature (from the 11th to the End of the 19th Century)* (New York: Ukrainian Academic Press, 1997), pp. 731–40.

63 See also Kenneth C. Farmer's prescient study *Ukrainian Nationalism in the Post-Stalin Era: Myths, Symbols and Ideology in Soviet Nationality Policy* (The Hague: Martinus Nijhoff, 1980).

64 Interested readers may consult Marco Carynnyk (ed.), *Alexander Dovzhenko: The Poet as Filmmaker* (Cambridge, Mass.: MIT Press, 1974); Vance Kepley, Jr, *In the Service of the State: The Cinema of Alexander Dovzhenko* (Wisconsin: University of Wisconsin Press, 1986); and the special edition of the *Journal of Ukrainian Studies* (summer 1994), or watch the films. George Liber of the University of Alabama is currently working on a new biography of Dovzhenko.

65 Tychyna's 1934 novel *The Party Leads* can be taken as the central text in the Sovietisation of Ukrainian literature.

66 As Dovzhenko was out of official favour by 1943, the film was credited to his wife, Yuliia Solntseva.

67 Some estimates go as high as 4 million; I.T. Mukovs'kyi and O.Ye. Lysenko, *Zvytiaha i zhertovnist'. Ukraïntsi na frontakh druhoï svitovoi viiny* (Kiev, 1997), p. 401.

68 Matthew Cullerne Bown, *Socialist Realist Painting* (London: Yale University Press, 1998), p. 288.

69 Yurii Maniichuck et al., *Realizm ta sotsialistychnyi realizm v ukrains'komu zhyvopysu radians'koho chasu* (Kiev: Polihrafknyha 1998); Bown, *Socialist Realist Painting*, p. 356.

70 See Stanislav Kul'chyts'kyi (ed.), *Kolektyvizatsiia i holod na Ukraini, 1929–1933. Zbirnyk dokumentiv i materialiv* (Kiev: Naukova dumka, 1992). The key Western sources are Robert Conquest's justifiably polemical *The Harvest of Sorrow: Soviet Collectivisation and the Terror-Famine* (London: Hutchinson, 1986); and James Mace, *Famine in the Soviet Ukraine, 1931–1933*, (Cambridge, Mass.: Harvard Ukrainian Institute, 1986). See also Yaroslav Hyrtsak's balanced commentary in *Narys istorii Ukraïny*, pp. 203–4.

71 This is the interpretation of the painting given in Horbachov, *Ukraïns'kyi avanhard*, p. 383.

72 Ivan Drach, 'Chy pokaiet'sia Rosiia? Vystup na mizhnarodnii naukovii konferentsiï "Holod 1932–1933 rr. v Ukraïni"', in Ivan Drach, *Polityka* (Kiev: Ukraïna, 1997), pp. 354–8, at pp. 354 and 357.

73 James Mace, 'Politchni prychyny holodomoru v Ukraïni', *Ukraïns'kyi istorychnyi zhurnal*, 1 (1995), pp. 34–48, at p. 46.

74 See for example Colm Tóibín's bibliographical essay on the Irish famine, 'Erasure', in the *London Review of Books*, 30 July 1998.

75 The review of 80 years of history produced by the Communist Party of the Ukraine in 1998, *Tezy do 80-richchia Komunistychnoï partiï Ukraïny (1918–1998 rr.)* (Kiev: Central Committee of the Communist Party of Ukraine, 1998), still fails to mention the Famine.

76 See the map of the affected areas in Magocsi, A *History of Ukraine*, p. 562.

77 See Ziuganov's claim that Communist values 'are in tune with the age-old Russian traditions of community and collectivism' (*Sovetskaia Rossiia*, 19 March 1996). Ziuganov's definition of Russia is somewhat blurry, however, and the myth of opposition between 'collectivist' Russians and 'family-farming' Ukrainians has been criticised. See Tan, *Village Social Organization*, p. 285.

78 Hrytsak, *Narys istorii Ukraïny*, pp. 177–8 and 184–6. See also Serhii

Pirozhkov, 'Population Loss in Ukraine in the 1930s and 1940s', in Bohdan Krawchenko (ed.), *Ukrainian Past, Ukrainian Present* (Basingstoke: Macmillan, 1993), pp. 84–96.

79 *Memoirs: Andrei Sakharov* (London: Hutchinson, 1990), p. 164.

80 Heorhii Kas'ianov, *Ukraïns'ka intelihentsiia 1920-kh – 30-kh rokiv: sotsial'nyi portret ta istorychna dolia* (Kiev: Hlobus, 1992), p. 172.

81 Mikhail Epstein, *After the Future: The Paradoxes of Postmodernism and Contemporary Russian Culture* (Amherst: University of Massachusetts Press, 1995), pp. 194–7.

82 Serhy Yekelchyk, 'The Making of a "Proletarian Capital": Patterns of Stalinist Social Policy in Kiev in the Mid-1930s', *Europe–Asia Studies*, 50, 7 (November 1998), pp. 1229–44.

83 Dominique Arel, *Language and the Politics of Ethnicity: The Case of Ukraine* (University of Illinois at Urbana-Champaign PhD, 1993), pp. 160 and 178.

84 Kenneth C. Farmer, *Ukrainian Nationalism in the Post-Stalin Era* (The Hague: Martinus Nijhoff, 1980), p. 30; Prizel, *National Identity and Foreign Policy*, p. 366; Hrytsenko, 'Svoia mudrist' ', p. 154.

85 See also Paul Pirie, 'National Identity and Politics in Southern and Eastern Ukraine', *Europe-Asia Studies*, 48, 7 (November 1996), pp. 1079–1104.

86 John A. Armstrong, 'The Ethnic Scene in the Soviet Union: The View of the Dictatorship', in Eric Goldhagen (ed.), *Ethnic Minorities in the Soviet Union* (New York: Praeger, 1968), pp. 3–49.

87 Bohdan R. Bociurkiw, *The Ukrainian Greek Catholic Church and the Soviet State (1939–1950)* (Edmonton: CIUS, 1996), p. 164.

88 Zhores and Roy Medvedev, *N.S. Khrushchev: The 'Secret' Speech* (Nottingham: Spokesman Books/Bertrand Russell Peace Foundation, 1976), p. 58.

89 Magocsi, A *History of Ukraine*, p. 642; Subtelny, *Ukraine: A History*, p. 483.

90 Even when presidents Kuchma and Kwaśniewski attempted mutual forgiveness in 1998, finding the right language proved difficult. For modern interpretations of these events, see Yaroslav Isaievych et al., *Ukraïna-Pol'shcha* (Kiev: Lybid', 1993); Ryszard Torzecki, *Polacy i Ukraińcy Sprawa ukraińska w czasie II wojny światowej na terenie II*

Rzeczypospolitej (Warsaw: Naukowe PWN, 1993); and Tadeusz Piotrowski, *Polish–Ukrainian Relations during World War II* (Toronto: Adam Mickiewicz Foundation, 1995).

91 Lubomyr Y. Luciuk and Bohdan S. Kordan, *Anglo-American Perspectives on the Ukrainian Question 1938–1951* (Kingston, Ontario: Limestone Press, 1987), especially pp. 137–43, 156–8 and 202–3. Britain still felt that any 'Ukrainian population in Poland must be so small' as to prevent the Bolsheviks using them as a 'fifth column'; see at p. 139.

92 See for example Prof. Vasyl' Dubrovs'kyi, *Ukraïna i Krym v istorychnykh vzaiemynakh* (Geneva: Ukrainian Naval Institute, 1946).

93 For a recent Ukrainian view of Crimean history, see Vasyl' Chumak, *Ukraïna i Krym: spil'nist' istorychnoï doli* (Kiev: Biblioteka Ukraïntsia, no. 2–3, 1993); for a Russian view see Sergei Kiselev and Natal'ia Kiseleva, *Razmyshlennia o Kryme i geopolitike* (Simferopil': Krymskii arkhiv, 1994); and for a Crimean Tatar view, Ye. Kudusov, *Istoriia formirovannia Krymskotatarskoi natsii* (Simferopil': n.p., 1996).

Chapter 8

1 'Ukraïns'kyi patriotychnyi rukh pro dekolonizatsiiu SRSR', in Taras Hunchak and Roman Sol'chanyk (eds), *Ukraïns'ka suspil'no-politychna dumka v 20 stolitti*, vol. 3 (Munich: Suchasnist', 1983), pp. 377–8.

2 Yurii Badz'o, *Pravo zhyty* (Kiev: Takson, 1996), p. 110.

3 See also Roman Szporluk's prescient article on the dual nature of Ukrainian identity, 'Russians in Ukraine and Problems of Ukrainian Identity in the USSR', in Peter J. Potichnyj (ed.), *Ukraine in the Seventies* (Oakville: Mosaic Press, 1975), pp. 195–217.

4 Seamus Dean, as quoted by Colm Tóibín in *The Irish Famine* (London: Profile, 1999), p. 67–8.

5 Bohdan Krawchenko and Jim A. Carter, 'Dissidents in Ukraine before 1972: A Summary Statistical Profile', *Journal of Ukrainian Studies*, 8, 2 (winter 1983), pp. 85–8; Heorhii Kas'ianov, *Nezhodni: ukraïns'ka intelihentsiia v rusi oporu 1960–80-kh rokiv* (Kiev: Lybid', 1995),

pp. 191–2.

6 Hrytsak, *Narys istoriï Ukraïny*, p. 295. See also Anatolii Rusnachenko's detailed study, *Natsional'no-vyzvol'nyi rukh v Ukraïni: seredyna 1950-kh – pochatok 1990-kh rokiv* (Kiev: Oleny Telihy, 1998).

7 Ivan Dzyuba, *Internationalism or Russification?* (London: Weidenfeld & Nicolson, 1968).

8 From the programme of Levko Luk"ianenko's Ukrainian Worker-Peasants' Union, Rusnachenko, *Natsional'no-vyzvol'nyi rukh*, p. 406.

9 Ibid.

10 D. Shakhai (the pseudonym of Yosyp Pozycheniuk), 'Our Tactics with Regard to the Russian People', in Peter J. Potichnyj and Yevhen Shtendera (eds), *Political Thought of the Ukrainian Underground, 1943–1951* (Edmonton: CIUS, 1986), p. 284. See also p. 322.

11 Levko Luk"ianenko, 'Do istoriï ukraïns'koho pravozakhysnoho rukhu', *Vyzvolennia* '91, no. 2.

12 Hrytsak, *Narys istoriï Ukraïny*, p. 292.

13 Rusnachenko, *Natsional'no-vyzvol'nyi rukh*, p. 564.

14 Krawchenko and Carter, 'Dissidents in Ukraine before 1972', p. 87.

15 Yaroslav Bihun (ed.), *Boomerang: The Works of Valentyn Moroz* (Baltimore: Smoloskyp, 1974).

16 This milieu is well evoked by a recent *Festschrift* for the writer Ivan Svitlychnyi (1929–92): Valerii Shevchuk et al. (eds), *Dobrookyi. Spohady pro Ivana Svitlychnoho* (Kiev: Chas, 1998).

17 Pavlychko, *Dyskurs modernizmu v ukraïns'kii literaturi* (2nd edn; 1999), chap. 6.

18 *Mystetstvo Ukraïny XX stolittia* (Kiev: Art Galleries Association of Ukraine/ NIGMA, 1998), p. 119.

19 See Marko Pavlyshyn's many works, including 'Mythological, Religious and Philosophical Topoi in the Prose of Valerii Shevchuk', *Slavic Review*, 50, 4 (winter 1991), pp. 905–13.

20 Robert Lakatosh, 'Tradytsiia i novatorstvo v strukturuvanni zobrazhennia u fil'makh Serhiia Paradzhanova', *Kino-teatr*, 4 (1999), pp. 2–4.

21 See Derhachov (ed.), *Ukrainian Statehood in the Twentieth Century*, pp. 111–14.

22 Central State Archive of Civic Organisations of Ukraine: f. 1, op. 11, delo 2023 (Ukrainian Politburo resolution concerning 'counteraction' against

'anti-social elements', dated 27 February 1989).

23 *Literaturna Ukraïna*, 13 February 1986, as quoted in Kulyk, 'Pys'mennyts'ke vidrodzhennia', p. 57.

24 See Hiroaki Kuromiya, *Freedom and Terror in the Donbas: A Ukrainian-Russian Borderland, 1870s–1990s* (Cambridge, UK: Cambridge University Press, 1998).

25 Anatolii Rusnachenko, *Probudzhennia. Robitnychyi rukh na Ukraïni v 1989–1993 rokakh* (Kiev: KM Akademia, 1995), 2 vols.

26 Wilson, *Ukrainian Nationalism in the 1990s*, p. 69. The original document, entitled 'Pro stan i tendentsiï rozvytku robitnychnoho rukhu v respublitsi', is in the Central State Archive of Civic Organisations of Ukraine: f. 1, op. 11, delo 2279, pp. 157–62.

27 Wilson, *Ukrainian Nationalism in the 1990s*, pp. 64–8. See also Hryhorii Honcharuk, *Narodnyi Rukh Ukraïny. Istoriia* (Odesa: Astroprynt, 1997).

28 Volodymyr Kulyk, 'Pys'mennyts'ke vidrodzhennia: ukraïns'ka derzhavna ideia v dyskursi "opozytsiï vseredyni rezhymu" pershykh rokiv perebudovy', *Suchasnist'*, 1 (1998), pp. 54–79.

29 Wilson, *Ukrainian Nationalism in the 1990s*, p. 66; Oleksii Haran', *Ubyty drakona: z istoriï Rukhu ta novykh partii Ukraïny* (Kiev: Lybid', 1993), p. 58.

30 Vladimir Paniotto, 'The Ukrainian Movement for Perestroika – "Rukh": A Sociological Survey', *Soviet Studies*, 43, 1 (1991), pp. 177–81, at pp. 178–9.

31 *Visnyk Rukhu*, 7 (1990), p. 33.

32 Oleksa Haran', 'Do voli – cherez Natsional'nyi kongres', *Moloda hvardiia*, 12 October 1990.

33 In the Baltic states, by contrast, the diaspora has already provided at least one president (Valdas Adamkus in Lithuania) and one foreign minister (Toomas Ilves in Estonia) since 1991.

34 Rukh was actually prevented from standing directly in the elections and masqueraded as the 'Democratic Bloc', but this made little practical difference.

35 Mykola Riabchuk, 'Posuvannia na Zakhid i ozyrannia na Skhid: proi-evropeis'ki oriientatsiï ukraïns'kykh elit ta ambivalentna svidomist' naselennia', in Mariia Zubryts'ka (ed.), *Nova Ukraïna i nova Yevropa: chas zblyzhennia* (L'viv: Litopys, 1997), pp. 64–8, at p. 65. See also the most detailed survey of Ukraine undertaken to date, Mikhail

Pogrebinskii (ed.), *Politicheskie nastroeniia nakanune vyborov* (Kiev: Centre for Political Research and Conflictology, 1998). Stephen Rapawy, *Ethnic Reidentification in Ukraine* (Washington, DC: IPC Staff Paper No. 90, 1997), p. 19, records 46.3% of Ukrainians identifying their homeland as Ukraine, 20.4% as the USSR, 29.5% as 'the region I live in/grew up in'.

36 See Michael Cox (ed.), *Rethinking the Soviet Collapse: Sovietology, the Death of Communism and the New Russia* (London and New York: Pinter, 1998)

37 A point well made by John-Paul Himka in *Krytyka*, 7–8 (1998), p. 20. See also Alexander J. Motyl, *Will the Non-Russians Rebel? State, Ethnicity and Stability in the USSR* (Ithaca, NY: Cornell University Press, 1987), chap. 4.

38 Roman Szporluk, 'Nationalism after Communism: reflections on Russia, Ukraine, Belarus and Poland', *Nations and Nationalism*, vol. 4, no. 3 (1998), pp. 301–20.

39 See his rather turgid homily *Ukraïno, nasha radians'ka* (Kiev: Politvydav Ukraïny, 1970).

40 Vitalii Vrublevskii, *Vladimir Shcherbitskii: pravda i vymysly* (Kiev: Dovira, 1993).

41 Oleksandr Moroz, *Kudy idemo?* (Kiev: Postup, 1993), pp. 111 and 115.

42 Volodymyr Kulyk, *Ukraïns'kyi natsionalizm u nezalezhnii Ukraïni* (Kiev: Kiev-Mohyla Academy, 1999), pp. 13 and 27.

43 See my *Ukrainian Nationalism in the 1990s*, p. 108.

44 Ibid. Also from material in the Central State Archive: f. 1, op. 11, delo 2061 (reports from local party branches), p. 10.

45 Bohdan Nahaylo, *The Ukrainian Resurgence* (London: Hurst, 1999), pp. 178, 182 and 210–11.

46 Central State Archive: f. 1, op. 11, delo 2202 (Ukrainian Politburo meeting, 5 November 1990), p. 12.

47 Remarks made by Kravchuk at the 24 August session of parliament; *Pozacherhova sesiia Verkhovnoï Rady Ukraïns'koï RSR: Dvanadtsiatoho sklykannia*, Bulletin no. 1, p. 21; Valentin Varennikov, *Sud'ba i sovest'* (Moscow: Paleia, 1993), p. 32.

48 Author's conversations with leaders of the Ukrainian Republican Party, 19 and 20 August 1991.

49 Serhii Holovatyi, speaking in parliament on 24 August, *Pozacherhova sesiia Verkhovnoï Rady*, Bulletin No. 1, p. 37;

V.M. Litvin, *Ukraina: politika, polityky, vlast'* (Kiev: Al'ternatyvy, 1997), p. 212.

50 Stanislav Hurenko et al. (eds.), *Kommunisticheskaia partiia Ukrainy. Khronika zapreta* (Donets'k: Interbuk, 1992), pp. 12 and 8.

51 'Speech of L. Kravchuk on Ukrainian TV (19 August 1991)', in Les' Taniuk (ed.), *Khronika oporu* (Kiev: Vik-Dnipro, 1991), pp. 102–3

52 Roman Solchanyk, 'Ukraine: Kravchuk's Role', *Report on the USSR*, 3, 36 (6 September 1991), which is a detailed account of Kravchuk's words and actions. See also Litvin, *Ukraina: politika, polityky, vlast'*, pp. 209–19.

53 Ihor Yukhnovs'kyi, speaking in parliament on 24 August, *Pozacherhova sesiia Verkhovnoï Rady*, Bulletin No. 1, pp. 90–1.

54 Central State Archive: f. 1, op. 11, delo 2280 (protocol of the Politburo meeting), p. 2, and delo 2069, pp. 1–2. See also Volodymyr Lytvyn (Litvin), *Politychna arena Ukraïny* (Kiev: Abrys, 1994), p. 272; and Litvin, *Ukraina: politika, polityky, vlast'*, p. 215, quoting a participant. Kravchuk's signature, however, is not on the order of the day.

55 Hurenko et al., *Khronika zapreta*, pp. 22–3.

56 Levko Luk"ianenko, 'Ne dai smiiatys' voroham nad ridnym kraiem', *Holos Ukraïny*, 13 September 1995.

57 The one vote against was cast by Al'bert Kornieiev from Donets'k, on the grounds that the resolution was prepared in haste, imprecisely phrased and undemocratically imposed and that the preamble referring to Ukraine being in 'mortal danger' and the culmination of 'a thousand years of state-building' was absurd; interviewed by the author and Dominique Arel, 8 July 1993.

58 'Yak komunisty zaboronialy Komunistychnu partiiu Ukraïny', *Komunist*, 1 (February 1994), p. 7.

59 Volodymyr Hryn'ov, *Pozacherhova sesiia Verkhovnoï Rady*, Bulletin No. 2, p. 24.

60 *Literaturna Ukraïna*, 19 September 1991.

61 The main Ukrainian sources for the events of 7–8 December 1991 are the two collections of reminiscences by Leonid Kravchuk, interviewed by Serhii Kychyhin in *Ostanni dni imperiï ... pershi roky nadiï* (Kiev: Dovira, 1994) and Valentyn Chemerys in *Prezydent. Roman-ese* (Kiev: Svenas, 1994).

Kravchuk's words do not always tally in the two texts – he seems to be summarising the gist of conversations as reported speech. Yeltsin's memoir in *The View from the Kremlin* (London: Harper Collins, 1994), pp. 111–16, lacks real detail. Shushkevich's version can be found in Liudmila Klaskoŭskaia and Aliaksandr Klaskoŭsk, *Stanislaŭ Shushkevich: putsiavina liosu* (Minsk: Polymia, 1994), pp. 78–99, and confirms some aspects of Kravchuk's account.

62 Kychyhin, in *Ustanni dni imperiï* pp. 17 and 20; Chemerys, *Prezydent*, p. 267.

63 Yeltsin's reported incredulity is in Kychyhin, *Ostanni dni imperiï* at p. 21.

64 Chemerys, *Prezydent*; pp. 269 and 268.

65 James A. Baker III (with Thomas DeFrank), *The Politics of Diplomacy: Revolution, War, and Peace, 1989–1992* (New York: G.P. Putnam's Sons, 1995), pp. 560–2, 582–3; Michael R. Beschloss and Strobe Talbott, *At the Highest Levels: The Inside Story of the End of the Cold War* (Boston: Little Brown, 1993), pp. 448–9.

66 Chemerys, *Prezydent*, p. 269; Kychyhin, *Ostanni dni imperiï* p. 32.

67 Kychyhin, *Ostanni dni imperiï* pp. 23–6.

68 Chemerys, *Prezydent*, pp. 270–1.

69 Kychyhin, *Ostanni dni imperiï* p. 30.

Chapter 9

1 R.W. Johnson, *The Long March of the French Left* (London: Macmillan, 1981).

2 Speech at the third congress of the Ukrainian Republican Party, *Samostiina Ukraïna*, 20 (May 1992).

3 Levko Lukïanenko, 'URP na suchasnomu etapi', *Samostiina Ukraïna*, 5 (January 1992).

4 *Samostiina Ukraïna*, 31 (August 1992). The passage is taken from the original – Lypyns'kyi, *Lysty do brativkhliborobiv*, pp. xli–xlii – as Skoryk slightly misquoted it.

5 Yurii Badz'o, *Vlada-opozytsiia-derzhava v Ukraïni s'ohodni. Dumky proty techiï* (Kiev: Smoloskyp, 1994), p. 12.

6 V"iacheslav Chornovil, 'Shcho dali?', *Za vil'nu Ukraïnu*, 24 January 1992.

7 Rukh election leaflet, March 1998. The translation tails off in the wistful manner of the original.

8 From resolutions passed at the founding conference of the Ukrainian Conservative Republican Party in June 1992,

Materialy nadzvychainoï konferentsiï UKRP (Kiev: Party brochure, 1992).

9 Luk"ianenko's speech to the third congress of the Ukrainian Republican Party, *Samostiina Ukraïna*, 20 (May 1992), p. 3.

10 'Manifest Ukraïns'koï Intelihentsiï', *Literaturna Ukraïna*, 12 October 1995.

11 Lypyns'kyi, *Lysty do brativkhliborobiv*, p. xli.

12 Dmytro Pavlychko, 'Chomu ya holosuvav za Leonida Kravchuka', *Literaturna Ukraïna*, 30 June 1994.

13 From the collection of interviews and articles, Leonid Kravchuk, *Ye taka derzhava – Ukraïna* (Kiev: Hlobus, 1992), p. 174.

14 Remarks made by V"iacheslav Chornovil at the British East-West Centre, 26 January 1998.

15 *III Vseukraïns'ki Zbory Narodnoho Rukhu Ukraïny* (Kiev: Rukh, 1995), pp. 28 and 32–3; *Narodna hazeta*, 8 (March 1992).

16 From the author's notes at the congress. The stenographic report proceedings, *III Vseukraïns'ki Zbory*, gives a surprisingly full account. See especially pp. 244–7.

17 This argument is developed at length in my *Ukrainian Nationalism in the 1990s*.

18 Author's interview with Yurii Badz'o, 29 April 1992.

19 Anatolii Svidzyns'kyi, 'Meta i tsinnosti suchasnoï OUN', *Rozbudova derzhavy*, 1–2 (January–February 1996), pp. 4–5, no. 1.

20 *Materiïaly Pershoho Zboru kongresu Ukraïns'kykh Natsionalistiv* (Kiev: KUN, 1995), pp. 300–1.

21 Valentyn Yakushyk (ed.), *Politychni partiï Ukraïny* (Kiev: Kobza, 1996), p. 109.

22 Ibid., p. 119.

23 See also *Ukrainian Nationalism in the 1990s*, pp. 68–80 and 179–80.

24 See my chapter in Ray Taras (ed.), *Post-Communist Presidents* (Cambridge, UK: Cambridge University Press, 1997), pp. 67–105, or Alexander J. Motyl, 'The Conceptual President: Leonid Kravchuk and the Politics of Surrealism', in Timothy J. Colton and Robert C. Tucker (eds), *Patterns in Post-Soviet Leadership* (Boulder: Westview, 1995), pp. 103–21; and Robert S. Kravchuk, *Ukrainian Politics, Economics and Governance, 1991–96* (Basingstoke: Palgrave, 2002).

25 A valid result required a 50% turnout and 50% of the vote going to one particular individual.

26 See Dominique Arel and Valeri Khmelko, 'The Russian Factor and Territorial Polarization in Ukraine', *Harriman Institute Review*, 9, 1–2 (March 1996), pp. 81–91.

27 Author's interview with Yurii Badz'o, 29 April 1992.

28 Remarks made by V"iacheslav Chornovil at the British East-West Centre, 26 January 1998.

29 Author's conversations with Valerii Khmel'ko, leader of the PDRU in 1990–2, at various times in 1998.

30 For more detail, see my 'The Ukrainian Left: In Transition to Social Democracy or Still in Thrall to the USSR?', *Europe-Asia Studies*, 49, 7 (November 1997), pp. 1293–1316.

31 From the election programme of the Communist Party in *Vybory '98: politychnyi kompas vybortsia* (Kiev: KIS, 1998), p. 10.

32 Yakushyk (ed.), *Politychni partiï Ukraïny*, p. 53.

33 Communist Party programme, *Vybory '98*, p. 10.

34 Speech of Oleksandr Moroz at the sixth congress of the Socialist Party, June 1998; *Novyi kurs Ukraïny* (Kiev: Socialist Party brochure, 1998), p. 7.

35 Declaration of the Progressive Socialist faction in parliament, *Holos Ukraïny*, 22 September 1998.

36 Moroz, *Novyi kurs Ukraïny*, p. 6.

37 Election programme of the Communist Party, *Vybory '98*, p. 10; material from the second CPU congress, *Komunist*, 11–12 (March 1995).

38 *Komunist*, 18 (April 1998), p. 3.

39 See also Serhii Hrabovs'kyi, 'Petro Symonenko oholosyv v Ukraïni rekonkistu', *Den'*, 22 May 1997. On Ziuganov's party, see Joan Barth Urban and Valerii D. Solovei, *Russia's Communists at the Crossroads* (Boulder: Westview, 1997).

40 In the long term, evolution towards pan(East)-Slavic nationalism may prove the best way of preserving the party's core constituency. See for example Petro Symonenko, 'Komunisty pro tserkvu ta ïï rol'u zhytti suchasnoï Ukraïny', *Holos Ukraïny*, 26 May 1999.

41 *Tezy do 80-richchia Kommunistychnoï partiï Ukraïny (1918–1998 rr.)*.

42 Wilson, 'The Ukrainian Left'; Vasilii Sekachev, 'Sotsialisticheskaia partiia Ukrainy i osobennosti ukrainskoi parti-

inoi sistemy', in Dmitrii Furman (ed.), *Ukraina i Rossiia: obshchestva i gosudarstva* (Moscow: Prava cheloveka, 1997), pp. 205–23.

43 Oleksandr Moroz, *Vybir* (Kiev: Postup, 1994), p. 101.

44 As quoted in *Nezavisimaia gazeta*, 25 June 1994, p. 3.

45 Yakushyk (ed.), *Politychni partiï Ukraïny*, p. 55.

46 See the sceptical discussion in Oleksii Haran' and Oleksandr Maiboroda, *Ideini zasady livoho rukhu v Ukraïni: chy vidbuvaiet'sia dreif do sotsial-demokratiï?* (Kiev: University of the Kiev-Mohyla Academy, 1999), p. 12.

47 In 1995 the Russian Communists proposed turning the group into a looser 'Communist International', but were defeated by 270 votes to 125, thanks in large part to the Ukrainians' opposition, including that of the ultra-radical Union of Communists of Ukraine: Yakushyk (ed.), *Politychni partiï Ukraïny*, p. 48. The Socialists' 'Eurasian Congress' was based in Kiev and was supported by parties from Spain (the United Left) and Greece (PASOK) as well as Russia, Kazakhstan etc.

48 Moroz entered, and won 13.1% in the first round. The Communist leader Symonenko declined to run.

49 Charles Clover, 'Questions over Kuchma's Adviser Cast Shadows', *The Financial Times*, 29 October 1999.

50 His speech is in *Holos Ukraïny*, 21 July 1994.

51 *OSCE/ODIHR Election Observation, Republic of Ukraine Parliamentary Elections 29 March 1998*, p. 17.

52 Rukh was an obvious potential rival to the former Communist establishment in 1992; the Republican Party's new strategy of right-wing economic populism presented a different kind of threat in 1996.

53 Roman Kis', *Final Tret'oho Rymu: rosiis'ka mesiians'ka ideia na zlami tysiacholit'* (L'viv: Institute of Popular Sciences, 1998).

54 William L. Miller, Stephen White and Paul Heywood, *Values and Political Change in Postcommunist Europe* (Basingstoke: Macmillan, 1998), pp. 140–76. If anything, the reverse was true.

55 Mykola Riabchuk, 'Ukraïns'ka intelihentsiia v poshukakh "menshoho zla" ', *Krytyka*, 10 (October 1999), pp. 6–9.

56 Nataliia Vitrenko, *Spasti Ukrainu* (Kharkiv: Prapor, 1997).

57 *Pravda*, 26 December 1997–2 January 1998; *Den'*, 5 December 1997; *Nezavisimaia gazeta*, 12 and 24 December 1997.

58 *RFE/RL Daily Report*, 27 October 1999.

59 *Vedomosti*, 12 October 1999.

60 Ibid.; Irinia Dubrova, 'Kharizmatiki i ortodoksy', *Novoe vremia*, 26 (July 1999). Russian sources were often able to say more about such things.

61 *Kyiv Post*, 10 June 1999; *Nezavisimaia gazeta*, 24 and 30 September 1999; *Le Soir*, 24 September 1999, and *Holos Ukraïny*, 13 November 1999.

62 Oleksandr Vyshniak, 'Prezydents'ki vybory: ostannii prohnoz 1 turu holosuvannia', *Vybory-99*, 1 (October 1999), pp. 20–1.

63 'Do hromadian Ukraïny. Zvernennia kandydativ u Prezydenty Ukraïny', *Komunist*, 45, 11 November 1999, p. 1.

64 *Kommersant'-Daily*, 26 October 1999; *Nezavisimaia gazeta*, 27 August 1999. Comments by Valerii Mishura, editor of the Communist Party paper *Komunist*, in an interview with the author and Sarah Birch on 12 November 1999.

65 See in particular Ziuganov's implicit support for the Ukrainian Socialist Party's line in their party journal *Tovarysh*, 10 (March 1999).

66 Information provided at two round-tables of Ukrainian sociologists organised by the Democratic Initiatives Foundation, Kiev, 10 and 12 November 1999. See also the analysis in the Foundation's bulletin *Vybory-99*, 1 and 2 (October 1999).

67 Dominique Arel, 'The Muddle Way', *Current History*, 621 (October 1998), pp. 342–6.

68 Alexander J. Motyl, 'State, Nation and Elites in Independent Ukraine', in Taras Kuzio (ed.), *Soviet to Independent Ukraine: Dynamics of Post-Soviet Transformation* (New York: M.E. Sharpe, 1998), pp. 3–16, at p. 11.

Chapter 10

1 Sherman W. Garnett, *Keystone in the Arch: Ukraine in the Emerging Security Architecture of Central and Eastern Europe* (Washington, DC; Carnegie

Endowment for International Peace, 1997), pp. 18–21.

2 Author's interview with Pavlo Movchan, 18 March 1998.

3 See Anatolii Pohribnyi, *Yakby my vchylys' tak, yak treba . . . Rozmovy pro nabolile* (Kiev: Prosvita, 1999); and Larysa Masenko, *Mova i polityka* (Kiev: Soniashnyk, 1999).

4 As quoted in Kulyk, 'Pys'mennyts'ke vidrodzhennia', p. 60.

5 Open letter signed by Ivan Drach, Pavlo Movchan, Yurii Mushketyk and 14 others, *Literaturna Ukraïna*, 2 March 1999.

6 Pohribnyi, *Yakby my vchylys' tak, yak treba*, p. 238. Emphasis in original.

7 The most detailed statements of this view are by Petro Lavriv. See his *Istoriia pivdenno-skhidnoï Ukraïny* (L'viv: Slovo, 1992); and *Kolonizatsiia ukraïns' kykh i sumizhnykh stepiv* (Kiev: Prosvita, 1994).

8 Adapted from the English-language version of the constitution in *The Ukrainian Review*, 43, 4 (winter 1996), pp. 4–5.

9 Pohribnyi, *Yakby my vchylys' tak, yak treba*, passim.

10 There have been two major changes. In Galicia Russian has been almost forced out of the official sphere altogether, and in Kiev there has been a considerable switch, although Russian is still often the language of first conversation. In the east and south, Ukrainianisation has yet to go much beyond street signs and official notepaper.

11 In the poll undertaken by Pogrebinskii's Institute, 35.4% favoured making Russian 'a second official language in those areas where the majority of the population wishes it', 25.5% 'a second official language in all of Ukraine' and 21.1% 'making it a second state language', although these figures were high even by Ukrainian standards. Pogrebinskii (ed.), *Politicheskie nastroeniia nakanune vyborov*, p. 199.

12 Petro Tolochko, *Vid Rusi do Ukraïny*, (Kiev: Abrys, 1997), p. 331.

13 *Prohrama i statut Narodnoho Rukhu Ukraïny* (Kiev: Rukh 1992), p. 13.

14 V. Yakovlev, 'Obshchenatsional'nye idei sovremennoi Ukrainy', *Tovarysh*, 2 (January 1996).

15 Interested readers can also consult my chapter (6) in Graham Smith et al., *Nation-Building in the Post-Soviet Borderlands: The Politics of National*

16 *Vybory '98: politychnyi kompas vybortsia* (Kiev: KIS, 1998), p. 61.

17 In *Ukrainian Review*, 43, 4 (winter 1996), p. 5.

18 Tolochko, *Vid Rusi do Ukraïny*, pp. 329 and 338.

19 Petro Tolochko, *Shcho abo khto zahrozuie ukraïns'kii movi?* (Kiev: Oriiany, 1998), pp. 13 and 10.

20 The 1996 constitution gives the oldest deputy the right to make the first address at the opening of a new parliament. Stetsko, then 75, earned this right in 1998, only to be loudly barracked by the Communists throughout.

21 Interviewed by the author and Sarah Birch, 25 March 1998.

22 Mykola Pavlyshyn, 'Postkolonial'na krytyka i teoriia', in Mariia Zubryts'ka (ed.), *Antolohiia svitovoï literaturno-krytychnoï dumky XX st.* (L'viv: Litopys, 1996).

23 Roman Kis', *Final Tret'oho Rymu*, p. 15.

24 See also her discussion with Pavlyshyn in *Krytyka*, 2, 4 April 1998.

25 Nahaylo, *The Ukrainian Resurgence*, p. 111. See also the two articles by Mykola Riabchuk in *Den*, 18 September 1997 and 8 December 1998.

26 Mykola Riabchuk, 'A Future Ukraine: One Nation, Two Languages, Three Cultures?', *The Ukrainian Weekly*, 6 June 1999.

27 Kis', *Final Tret'oho Rymu*, p. 14.

28 On this theme in Ukrainian literature, see Volodymyr Dibrova, 'Contemporary Ukrainian Literature. The Problem of Decolonization', in Endre Bojtár (ed.), *The Comparable and the Incomparable* (Budapest: Central European University, 1996), pp. 199–239.

29 Oksana Zabuzhko, *Pol'ovi doslidzhennia z ukraïnst'koho seksu* (Kiev: Fakt, 1998), pp. 31, 111 and 114 ('Pol' is a pun on 'gender'); Yurii Andrukhovych, *Perverziia* (Ivano-Frankivs'k: Lileia-NV, 1997); Michael M. Naydan 'National Identity for the Ukrainian Writer: Writing into the New Millennium', in Theofil Kis and Irena Makaryk (eds), *Towards a New Ukraine II* (Ottawa: Chair of Ukrainian Studies, 1999), pp. 143–52, at p. 152.

30 Kis', *Final Tret'oho Rymu* , pp. 741 and 7.

31 Ibid., p. 9.

32 Vsevolod Naulko, *Khto i vidkoly zhyve*

v Ukraïni (Kiev: National Minorities' Publishers, 1998), p. 63.

33 The latter point is frequently made by Mykola Riabchuk. See, *inter alia*, his article 'A Future Ukraine: One Nation, Two Languages, Three Cultures?' The difference between the percentage of Ukrainians who were classed as 'white collar' (*sluzhbovtsi*) in the 1989 Soviet census and the percentage of Russians (24% to 36%) is significant, but hardly comparable with apartheid South Africa or even Soviet Central Asia. The difference between the percentage of collective farmers (Ukrainians 22%, Russians 5%) is much more indicative. See Naulko, *Khto i vidkoly zhyve v Ukraïni*, p. 61.

34 Natalka Bilotserkivets', 'Kryven'ka kachechka, abo Shche raz pro trahediiu Tsentral'no-Skhidnoï Yevropy', *Krytyka*, 2 (February 1998).

35 Kis', *Final Tret'oho Rymu*, p. 6.

36 See Marko Pavlyshyn, 'Post-Colonial Themes in Contemporary Ukrainian Culture', *Australian Slavonic and East European Studies*, 6, 2 (1992), pp. 41–55.

37 Kis', *Final Tret'oho Rymu*, p. 14.

38 Author's interview with Myroslav Popovych, 27 June 1997.

39 Volodymyr Hryn'ov, *Nova Ukraïna: yakoiu ya ïï bachu* (Kiev: Abrys, 1995), p. 61.

40 Yakushyk (ed.), *Politychni partiï Ukraïny*, p. 68.

41 Nikolai A. Shulga, 'Ethnicity in Ukrainian Society as a Possible Source of Conflict', in Hans-Georg Ehrhart and Oliver Thränert (eds), *European Conflicts and International Institutions: Cooperating with Ukraine* (Baden-Baden: Nomos Verlagsgesellschaft, 1998), pp. 125–33, at p. 126.

42 From the draft of a project for a law on the 'Use of the Russian language as a language of one of the indigenous peoples of Ukraine', prepared by the Congress of Russian Communities of Ukraine in 1996.

43 Pogrebinskii (ed.), *Politicheskie nastroeniia nakanune vyborov*, p. 201. Respondents were asked which slogans they would like to see local candidates use and could name up to three from a list of ten.

44 Local Crimean politicians had made much of their support for the motley crew in the Moscow White House; author's interview with Leonid Hrach,

last leader of the Communist Party in Crimea before August 1991 and chairman of the Crimean Assembly after March 1998, 30 September 1993.

45 Aleksandr Solzhenitsyn, *Rossiia v obvale* (Moscow: Russkii put', 1998), p. 81.

46 Ludmilla Chizhikova, *Russko-ukrainskoe pogranich'e: istoriia i sud'by traditsionno-bytovoi kul'tury (XIX–XX vv.)* (Moscow: Nauka, 1988).

47 *Russkie v Ukraine* (Moscow: Centre for the Study of Russian Minorities in the Countries of the Near Abroad, 1997), p. 21.

48 Author's private information.

49 See also Graham Smith and Andrew Wilson, 'Rethinking Russia's Post-Soviet Diaspora: The Potential for Political Mobilisation in Eastern Ukraine and North-East Estonia', *Europe-Asia Studies*, 49, 5 (1997), pp. 845–64; and Lieven, *Chechnya*, chap. 7.

50 David D. Laitin, *Identity in Formation: The Russian-Speaking Populations in the Near Abroad* (Ithaca, NY and London: Cornell University Press, 1998), pp. 190–8 and 265–8.

51 Dmitrii Kornilov, *Dve Ukrainy* (unpublished manuscript, 1998).

52 One example of this confusion can be found in Samuel Huntington, *The Clash of Civilizations and the Remaking of World Order* (New York: Simon & Schuster, 1996), pp. 159 and 166. Huntington draws one 'line of cleavage' between the Greek Catholic and Orthodox worlds (inaccurately – the traditionally Orthodox region of Volhynia is on the wrong side of the divide) and then another along the river Dnieper.

53 The term 'mankurt' (literally 'worm-brain' – a mindless automaton) comes from the popular Soviet novel by the Kirgiz author Chingiz Aitmatov, *Burannyi Polustanok* (Moscow: Molodaia gvardiia, 1981).

54 Yu.G. Morozov, 'Russkie Ukrainy – nositeli dvukh yazykovykh kul'tur – russkoi i ukrainskoi . . .', *Vidrodzhennia*, 1 (1994). See also Smith et al., *Nation-Building in the Post-Soviet Borderlands*, p. 134.

55 In fact the practice of ascriptive but *chosen* nationality (teenagers could choose their own passport nationality on gaining maturity) may have increased regional divisions. In mixed families in western Ukraine, 'Ukrainian' was the more likely choice, 'Russian' in eastern

Ukraine ('Soviet' was not an option), but with some overall bias to the titular nationality perhaps strongest in central Ukraine.

56 Pogrebinskii (ed.) *Politicheskie nastroeniia nakanune vyborov*, p. 211. Rapawy, *Ethnic Reidentification in Ukraine*, p. 16, reports a lower figure of 15.8% 'Ukraine-Russians', from a 1995 survey.

57 Lypyns'kyi, *Lysty do brativkhliborobiv*, p. 425.

58 Interviewees were offered a choice of Ukrainian or Russian questionnaires by bilingual interviewers.

59 Pogrebinskii (ed.), *Politicheskie nastroeniia nakanune vyborov*, pp. 17–18 and 194–5.

60 The estimates are in the article by Andrii Dyn'ko, 'Bilorusomovni suproty kvaziderzhavy i kvaziburzhuaziï', *Heneza*, special issue (1999), pp. 56–8, at p. 56.

61 Interested readers might care to consult my 'Myths of National History in Belarus and Ukraine', in Geoffrey Hosking and George Schöpflin (eds), *Myths and Nationhood* (London: Hurst, 1997), pp. 182–97; and 'National History and National Identity in Ukraine and Belarus', in Smith et al., *Nation-Building in the Post-Soviet Borderlands*, pp. 23-47.

62 A. Volkonskii, *Istoricheskaia pravda i ukrainofilskaia propaganda* (Donets'k: Donetsk Booklovers' Society, 1998).

63 *Holos Ukraïny*, 11 October 1994. See also the claim by Socialist deputy Ivan Chyzh, speaking on the fifth anniversary of independence in 1996, 'the first lesson of independence: as a state Ukraine existed thanks to the Soviet period of its history', 'P"iat' urokiv nezalezhnosti', *Tovarysh*, 34 (August 1996).

64 See his speech in *Uriadovyi kur"ier*, 29 August 1996.

65 *Reuters*, 8 May 1999.

66 Mykola Riabchuk, 'Ukraïns'ka presa: mizh prosvitnytstvom i maskul'tom', *Krytyka*, 5 (May 1999) pp. 8–16, at p. 16.

67 See also Catherine Wanner, *Burden of Dreams: History and Identity in Post-Soviet Ukraine* (Pennsylvania: Pennsylvania State University Press, 1998), chap. 6; and Mykola Riabchuk, 'Parad u porozhnechi', *Den'*, 21 August 1999.

68 See also Wanner, *Burden of Dreams*, chap. 7.

69 Blair A. Ruble, *Money Sings: The Changing Politics of Urban Space in*

Post-Soviet Yaroslavl (Washington, DC, and Cambridge: Woodrow Wilson Center Press and Cambridge University Press, 1995), has a photograph of the monument on p. 128.

70 Kanyhin and Tkachuk, *Ukraïns'ka mriia*.

71 On Kiev's lost churches and other buildings, see Titus D. Hewryk, *The Lost Architecture of Kiev* (New York: The Ukrainian Museum, 1982); and K.O. Tretiak, *Kyïv: Putivnyk po zruinovanomy mistu* (Kiev: Kyivs'kyi universytet, 1998).

72 Russian nationalists have felt they have a right to criticise the style of the reconstruction. It featured prominently in Kuchma's TV adverts during the 1999 election campaign.

73 The *hryvna* was the original monetary unit of Rus'. When the Ukrainian People's Republic adopted its own currency in 1917–20, notes were printed with the word *hryvn-ia*, not *hryvn-a*, a Galician dialectism, which remained when the currency was reintroduced in 1996.

74 Yurii Badz'o, 'Ukraïna i Malorosiia – spivisnuvannia nemozhlyve', *Suchasnist'*, 2 (February 1999), pp. 62–73, at p. 73; Bill Ashcroft, Gareth Griffiths and Helen Tiffin, *The Empire Writes Back: Theory and Practice in Post-Colonial Literature* (London: Routledge, 1989).

75 Anne Applebaum, *Between East and West: Across the Borderlands of Europe* (London: Papermac, 1994), pp. 167–9.

76 See also Volodymyr Yeshkilev and Oleh Hutsuliak, *Adept, abo svidotstvo Oleksiia Sklavina pro skhodzhennia do tr'okh imen* (Ivano-Frankivs'k: Lileia-NV, 1997).

77 Yurii Andrukhovych et al., *Bu-Ba-Bu* (L'viv: Kameniar, 1995).

78 Yurii Andrukhovych, *Rekreatsiï. Romany* (Kiev: Chas, 1997). This novel was published by CIUS in an English translation (*Recreations*) by Mykola Pavlyshyn in 1998; Zabuzhko's novel is being translated by Halyna Hryn.

79 Mariia Pryimachenko, *Al'bom* (Kiev: Mystetstvo, 1994).

80 See *Mystetstvo Ukraïny XX stolittia* (Kiev: Art Galleries Association of Ukraine/NIGMA, 1998), pp. 116ff.

81 *Polityka i kul'tura*, 7 (1999).

82 See Romana Bahry, 'Rock Culture and Rock Music in Ukraine', in Sabrina Petra Ramet (ed.), *Rocking the State: Rock Music and Politics in Eastern*

Europe and Russia (Boulder: Westview, 1994), pp. 243–96.

83 Andrukhovych, *Recreations*, p. 97.

84 Yurii Mushketyk, 'Koleso. Kil'ka dumok z pryvodu suchasnoho ukraïns'koho postavanhardu', *Literaturna Ukraïna*, 27 October 1994. See also Mykola Pavlyshyn, 'From Osadchy to the "Koleso" Controversy: Modernity and its Meanings in Ukrainian Culture since the 1960s', *Journal of Ukrainian Studies*, forthcoming.

85 See the whole series of 'Ukrainian historical novels' published by the Ukrainian Centre of Spiritual Culture in 1996–8.

86 Reliable figures do not exist for the 4.4 million Ukrainians recorded by the 1989 Soviet census as living in Russia (Ukrainian nationalists would claim the real figure is as many as 20 million). One survey in 1992 indicated that only 36% could speak Ukrainian freely. See *The Ukrainian Weekly*, 12 December 1993.

Chapter 11

1 From Kravchuk's speech at the forum, 'Vil'na tserkva – u vil'nii derzhavi', *Holos Ukraïny*, 21 November 1991.

2 Sabrina P. Ramet, *Nihil Obstat: Religion, Politics and Social Change in East-Central Europe and Russia* (Durham, NC: Duke University Press, 1998), p. 255. Chapter ten is a good guide to Ukraine's complex religious politics.

3 Filaret's critics pointed to his links with the KGB, his original ambition to head the Russian Orthodox Church before the election of Patriarch Aleksii II in June 1990 and the fact that he had a common-law wife and three children.

4 *Holos Ukraïny*, 2 June 1992.

5 For a critique of Filaret, see Oleksa Novak, *Ternystyi shliakh ukraïns'koho pravoslav"ia u dobu suchasnosti* (Rivne: n.p. 1995), especially pp. 13 and 20.

6 *Holos Ukraïny*, 29 November 1994 records Volodymyr's meeting with Oleksandr Moroz, then chairman of parliament.

7 *Nezavisimost'*, 28 July 1995 carried a detailed report on the allegations.

8 Two years later Volodymyr's grave was at least given the dignity of added marble, while the opening of the bell tower to St Sofiia's and the pedestrianisation of the outside square in 1998 improved its surroundings.

9 According to another Sosis-Gallup poll in February 1998, 41% claimed no religion, 20.4% backed the UOC(KP), 7.5% the UOC(MP), 1.8% the UAOC and 6.3% the Greek Catholics, with the drop in KP support probably accounted for by the 16% who saw themselves as Orthodox, but of no particular branch: *Den'*, 26 February 1998.

10 Pogrebinskii (ed.), *Politicheskie nastroeniia nakanune vyborov*, pp. 196–7 and 40–1.

11 Mykola Porovs'kyi, 'Rol' Tserkvy v stanovlenni natsiï i derzhavy', in his *Zabutyi zapovit bortsiam za Ukraïnu* (Kolomiia: Vik, 1996), pp. 19–25, at pp. 23 and 25.

12 Anatolii Kolodnyi, 'Pravoslav'ia v konteksti natsional'noho vidrodzhennia Ukraïny', *Pravoslavnyi visnyk*, 1–2 (January–February 1998), pp. 28 and 26.

13 Kolodnyi, 'Pravoslav'ia v konteksti', pp. 27–8.

14 Author's interview with Yevhen Sverstiuk, 24 March 1998.

15 Anatolii Kolodnyi, 'Relihiini vyiavy natsional'noho buttia ukraïntsiv', in V. Shynkaruk and Ye. Bystryts'kyi (eds), *Fenomen ukraïns'koï kul'tury* (Kiev: Feniks, 1996), pp. 373–84, at p. 380.

16 Porovs'kyi, 'Rol' Tserkvy v stanovlenni natsiï i derzhavy', p. 19.

17 *The Millennium of the Holy Baptism of the Kievan Rus' 988–1988* (Leuven: Ukrainian House, 1987–8), pp. 81–3.

18 Kolodnyi, 'Pravoslav'ia v konteksti', p. 26.

19 Ibid.

20 Remarks by Patriarch Volodymyr, *Pravoslavnyi visnyk*, 10–11 (1993); speech of L'viv metropolitan Andrii, 'On the Road to the New Jerusalem', *Pravoslavnyi visnyk*, 1–2 (1999), pp. 4–11.

21 Kolodnyi, 'Pravoslav'ia v konteksti', p. 26–7.

22 Cardinal Lubachivsky, *Was It Really Russia That Was Christianised in 988?*, p. 31.

23 Abbot Dymytrii (ed.) *Nepravda moskovs'kykh anafem* (Kiev: Kievan patriarchate, 1999).

24 Section 1, Article 4. See also Kolodnyi, 'Pravoslav'ia v konteksti', p. 26.

25 Open letter by Archbishop Adrian of Dnipropetrovs'k, in author's possession, dated April 1998, p. 1.

26 Author's interview with Sverstiuk.

27 Author's interview with Tsaromonakh Yevlogii, Lecturer in the Kiev Spiritual Academy of the UOC(MP), 24 September 1998.

28 Author's interview with Archpriest Father Vasilii (Zaiev), adviser to the UOC(MP) Metropolitanate on Religious Affairs, 23 September 1998.

29 Author's interview with Valentin Lukianyk, head of the council of the Orthodox Brotherhoods of Ukraine, 23 September 1998.

30 Author's interview with Father Vasilii.

31 Open letter by Adrian, p. 1.

32 Author's interview with Yablons'kyi, 23 September 1998.

33 *Ukraïns'ka Avtokefal'na Tserkva: istorychnyi narys pro tserkovnyi rozkol na Ukraïni* (Pochaïv: Pochaïv Lavra, 1995), p. 31.

34 N.Ya. Arestova, 'Relihiï Ukraïny v konteksti svitovoho relihiinoho protsesu', in *Fenomen ukraïns'koï kul'tury*, pp. 431–43, at p. 435.

35 *Na puti k pravoslavno-greko-katolicheskomu dialogu*, document supplied to the author by Father Vasilii, 1998.

36 Author's interview with Tsaromonakh Yevlogii.

37 Author's interview with Father Vasilii.

38 Author's interview with Tsaromonakh Yevlogii.

39 Remarks made by Archpriest Viktor (Petliuchenko), the Moscow patriarchate official responsible for links with Ukraine: *Nezavisimaia gazeta-Religii*, 7 April 1999, p. 2.

40 Zen'kovskii, *Piat' mesiatsev u vlasti*, p. 218.

41 Election leaflet of the Party of Regional Revival of Ukraine, March 1998.

42 *Parlamentskaia gazeta* (Moscow), 4 June and 29 July 1999.

43 Rawson, *Russian Rightists and the Revolution of 1905*, pp. 92–5. See also the two rival histories of Pochaïv: *Istoriia Sviato Uspenskoi Pochaevskoi lavry* (Pochaïv, 1996); and S. Antonovych, *Korotkyi istorychnyi narys Pochaïvs'koï Uspens'koï lavry* (Ternopil': Vil'ne zhyttia, 1997). Although Pochaïv was traditionally a part of Volhynia, the surrounding

Kremianets' district was transferred to Galicia in 1939, so that the monastery could serve as a Trojan horse for dismantling the Greek Catholic Church. During World War II, when the Autocephalous Church was briefly revived in Ukraine, Pochaïv was the site of the rival, more pro-Moscow Ukrainian Autonomous Orthodox Church.

44 Ramet, *Nihil Obstat*, p. 261; Oleh W. Gerus, 'Church Politics in Ukraine', *Ukrainian Quarterly*, 52 (spring 1996).

45 Novak, *Ternystyi shliakh ukraïns'koho pravoslav"ia*, pp. 9–11 and 16.

46 As quoted in Prelec, 'Where Orthodox and Catholic Meet', p. 25.

47 Author's interview with Sverstiuk.

48 See her book *Stratehiia i taktyka stvorennia yedynoï pomisnoï Pravoslavnoï Tserkvy v Ukraïni* (Kiev, 1997).

49 Andrii Kravchuk, *Christian Social Ethics in Ukraine: The Legacy of Andrei Sheptysky* (Edmonton: CIUS, 1997), pp. 118–19 and 219–23.

50 Zynovii Timenuk, *Ivan Ohiienko (Mytropolyt Ilarion) 1882–1972. Zhyttiepysno-bibliohrafichnyi narys* (L'viv: Shevchenko Society, 1997), pp. 105–6.

51 Ohiienko, *Ukraïns'ka tserkva*; Ilarion, *Dokhrystyians'ki viruvannia ukraïns'koho narodu*.

52 Timenyk, *Ivan Ohiienko*, pp. 102–13.

53 P. Yarots'kyi et al. (eds), *Istoriia pravoslavnoï tserkvy v Ukraïni* (Kiev: Academy of Sciences/Chetverta khvylia, 1997), p. 294.

54 Petro Tolochko, 'Chy potribna Ukraïna natsional'na tserkva?', in his *Vid Rusi do Ukraïny*, pp. 364–72, at p. 369.

55 Arestova, 'Relihiï Ukraïny', p. 434.

56 *Vseukraïns'ka Mizhnarodna Khrystyians'ka Asambleia (Zbirnyk ofitsiinykh materialiv)* (Kiev, 1998), pp. 36 and 39. The last quotation is from one of the Assembly's official appeals.

57 V. Liubashchenko, *Istoriia protestantyzmu v Ukraïni* (L'viv: Prosvita, 1995).

58 Oles' Berdnyk, 'Na porozi novoho svitannia', *Zoloti vorota*, 1 (1991), pp. 111–20.

59 Włodzimierz Pawluczuk, *Ukraina. Polityka i Mistyka* (Kraków: Nomos, 1998), p. 223, referring to Umberto Eco, *Foucault's Pendulum* (London: Secker & Warburg, 1989), p. 203.

Chapter 12

1 Volobuiev was probably shot in 1938, but some versions of his life have him living out his days in Rostov-on-Don.

2 See I.S. Koropeckyj (ed.), *The Ukraine within the USSR: An Economic Balance Sheet* (London and New York: Praeger, 1977); and *The Ukrainian Economy. Achievements, Problems, Challenges* (Cambridge, Mass.: Harvard Ukrainian Research Institute, 1992).

3 Timothy Ash, *WestLB Research Country Profile – Ukraine* (London: August 1999).

4 Andrew Wilson and Igor Burakovsky, *The Ukrainian Economy under Kuchma* (London: Royal Institute for International Affairs, 1996).

5 Helen Boss, *Domestic Inactions, Russian Connections: An Analysis of Slow Economic Reform in Ukraine, 1991–1999* (Vienna: WIIW, 1999), pp. 18–19.

6 In November 1998, Kuchma quoted a figure of 8 billion hryvnia, or just under $3 billion; *Literaturna Ukraïna*, 26 November 1998.

7 Alexander J. Motyl, 'The Conceptual President: Leonid Kravchuk and the Politics of Surrealism', in Timothy J. Colton and Robert C. Tucker (eds), *Patterns in Post-Soviet Leadership* (Boulder: Westview, 1995), pp. 103–21; and his 'State, Nation, and Elites in Independent Ukraine', in Kuzio (ed.), *Contemporary Ukraine*, pp. 3–16.

8 Alexander Motyl, 'Yak zrozumity Ukraïnu', *Krytyka*, 1 (January 1998).

9 See Paul D'Anieri, *Economic Interdependence in Ukrainian-Russian Relations* (Albany: SUNY Press, 1999).

10 Economist Intelligence Unit Country Report, *Ukraine, Belarus, Moldova* (third quarter 1993), p. 20.

11 From Luk"ianenko's speech at the second Republican congress in 1991: *II z'izd ukraïns'koï respublikans'koï partiï* (Kiev: URP, 1991), pp. 7–28. See especially pp. 14–15.

12 Katya Gorchinskaya, 'Kuchma Veers from West's Reform Path', *Kyiv Post*, 20 November 1998. Gaidar, *Defeat and Victory* (Seattle: University of Washington Press, 1999), p. 156.

13 Leonid Kuchma, 'Ekonomika Ukraïny: aktual'ni pytannia ïï suchasnoho rozvytku', *Ekonomika Ukraïny*, 11 (November 1995), pp. 4–16, at p. 5. See also Volodymyr Zviglianich's essay

'Ethnic Economics: Is a "Ukrainian Economic Model" Possible?', *The Ukrainian Weekly*, 24 December 1995, or *Prism*, 1, 23 (November 1995).

14 See Kuchma's speech in *Uraidovyi kur"ier*, 10 March 1999.

15 See Alena V. Ledeneva's excellent study *Russia's Economy of Favours: 'Blat', Networking and Informal Exchange* (Cambridge, UK: Cambridge University Press, 1998).

16 Inna Lunina and Volkhart Vincentz, 'The Subsidisation of Enterprises in Ukraine', in Axel Siedenberg and Lutz Hoffmann (eds), *Ukraine at the Crossroads: Economic Reforms in International Perspective* (Heidelberg: Physica-Verlag, 1999), pp. 119–30.

17 *The Financial Times*, 24 June 1999.

18 Daniel Kaufman, 'Why Is Ukraine's Economy – and Russia's – Not Growing?', *Transition*, 8, 2 (1997), p. 7.

19 Viktor Pynzenyk, *Koni ne vynni, abo Reformy chy ïkh imitatsiia* (Kiev: Akademiia, 1998), p. 56.

20 *Ukrainian Economic Trends*, January 1998, p. 4 (ratio of Broad Money to GDP).

21 Siedenberg and Hoffmann, *Ukraine at the Crossroads*, p. 15.

22 *EBRD Transition Report*, 1998, p. 230; Ash, *WestLB Research Country Profile – Ukraine*, p. 5.

23 Interviewed in *Den'*, 22 December 1998.

24 Ivan Drach, *Polityka* (Kiev: Ukraïna, 1997), p. 364.

25 *Holos Ukraïny*, 1 May 1992.

26 The phrase was in Kuchma's 1994 election programme. See his 1999 election brochure *1999 rik. Prezydent Ukraïny L.D. Kuchma*, p. 11.

27 Author's interview with Vasyl' Yurchyshyn, 25 September 1998.

28 See Anatol Lieven's analysis in *Chechnya: Tombstone of Russian Power* (New Haven and London: Yale University Press, 1998), chap. 4.

29 Author's interview with Yurchyshyn.

30 Viacheslav Pikhovshik, "Oligarkhovedenie", *Zerkalo nedeli*, 5 June 1999.

31 The article 'Surkis, Lazarenko i drugie. "Khit-parad" politicheskikh oligarkhov v Ukraine', *Stolichnaia gazeta*, 25 May 1999, came out after this was written, but confirms the basic analysis.

32 Rabinovych quarrelled with Horbulin over control of the TV station 1+1; *Nezavisimaia gazeta*, 3 July 1999.

33 *The Financial Times*, 9 December 1998; *Kyiv Post*, 10 December 1998.

34 Katya Gorchinskaya, 'Top Officials Accused of Corruption', *Kyiv Post*, 17 June 1999.

35 *The Financial Times*, 5 May 1998.

36 Boss, *Domestic Inactions, Russian Connections*, p. 15.

37 Author's interview with Yurchyshyn.

38 *Den'*, 6 and 26 June 1999.

39 *Halyts'ki kontrakty*, 49 (December 1997).

40 Tetiana Metel'ova, 'Vybir iz preventyvnymy zakhodamy', *Krytyka*, 3 (March 1999), p. 8.

41 'Ukraine's New Rich Squander Wealth on Vice and Luxury', *Agence France Presse*, 20 November 1998.

42 Mykola Tomenko, 'Osoblyvosti natsional'noï vyborchoï kampaniï', *Politychnyi portret Ukraïny*, 21 (1998), pp. 6–17, at p. 7; *Vechirnii Kyïv*, 25 June 1999.

43 See the report in *The Independent*, 7 August 1999.

44 Two local authors, Viktor Faitel'berg-Blank and Valerii Shestachenko, have written a history of crime in the city, *Banditskaia Odessa* (Odesa: Astroprint, 1999). A second volume, due in 2000, will cover the period up to 1999.

45 See the article 'Odes'ke Chykago', in *Polityka i kul'tura*, 13 (1999).

46 A detailed account can be found in *Ukraïna moloda*, 19 August 1998.

47 Boss, *Domestic Inactions, Russian Connections*, p. 20.

48 Yurii Lypa, *Rozpodil' Rossiï* (L'viv: Academy of Sciences, 1995), a reprint of the original 1941 edition published in New York by Hoverlia in 1954; and *Chornomors'ka doktryna* (Geneva: Ukrainian Naval Institute, 1947).

49 This may have been a quid pro quo for Russia signing the long-awaited interstate treaty with Ukraine in May of that year – see page 307.

50 See Bohdan Klid, 'Caspian Sea Oil and Ukraine's Quest for Energy Autonomy', *Geopolitics of Energy*, 20, 10 (October 1998); and Manabu Shimizu (ed.), *The Caspian Basin Oil and its Impact on Eurasian Power Games* (Tokyo: Institute of Developing Economies, 1998), especially pp. 43–6 on Ukraine.

Chapter 13

1 The text of the Declaration can be found in Charles F. Furtado, Jr. and Andrea Chandler (eds), *Perestroika and the Soviet Republics: Documents on the National Question* (Boulder: Westview, 1992), pp. 237–41.

2 Jeremy Black, *Maps and History: Constructing Images of the Past* (New Haven and London: Yale University Press, 1997).

3 For a commentary on Rudnyts'kyi's life and work, see Oleh Shablii, *Akademik Stepan Rudnyts'kyi – fundator ukraïns'koï heohrafiï* (L'viv: L'viv State University, 1993).

4 Stepan Rudnyts'kyi, 'Ukraïns'ka sprava zi stanovyshcha politychnoï heohrafiï', from the 1923 Berlin edition reprinted in *Chomu my khochemo samostiinoï Ukraïny* (L'viv: Svit, 1994), p. 94.

5 Stanislav Dnistrians'kyi, *Natsional'na statystyka. Mova yak kryterii narodnosti* (Lviv, 1910).

6 Stepan Rudnyts'kyi, 'Chomu my khochemo samostiinoï Ukraïny', from the collection with the same title (1994), pp. 35–92, at pp. 78–9, emphasis in original.

7 See for example Maxime-Auguste Denaix, *Atlas physique, politique et historique de l'Europe* (Paris, 1829).

8 Lypa, *Rozpodil' Rossiï*, pp. 70 and 83.

9 Stephen Rudnitsky (Stepan Rudnyts'kyi), *Ukraine: The Land and its People*, p. 231.

10 Arkadz' Smolich, *Heohrafiia Belarusi* (3rd edn; Vilnius: B.A. Kletskina, 1923), pp. 113–16 and 148–51, quotation at p. 116. A fourth edition was published in Minsk in 1993.

11 Lypa, *Chornomors'ka doktryna*, p. 9 and *Rozpodil' Rossiï*, p. 76.

12 Hrushevsky, *History of Ukraine-Rus': Volume One*, p. 11.

13 Mykhailo Horyn', 'Ukraïns'kyi shliakh do Yevropy', in his *Zapalyty svichu u pit'mi* (Kiev: Ukrainian Republican Party, 1994), pp. 56–61, at p. 57.

14 Kravchuk quoted in *Novosti*, 29 April 1996; V"iacheslav Chornovil, 'Shcho dali?', *Za vil'nu Ukraïnu*, 24 January 1992.

15 Kanyhin and Tkachuk, *Ukraïns'ka mriia*, p. 144.

16 Stepan Rudnyts'kyi, 'Ukraïns'ka sprava zi stanovyshcha politychnoï heohrafiï', pp. 155–7, emphasis in original.

17 Rudnitsky (Rudnyts'kyi), *Ukraine: The Land and its People*, p. 231.

18 Mykhailo Drahomanov, 'Lysty na Naddniprians'ku Ukraïnu', in *M.P.*

Drahomanov. Literaturno-publitsysty-chni pratsi, vol. 1 (Kiev: Naukova dumka, 1970), p. 446. Ukrainian historians would argue that this victory was largely achieved by local Cossacks, but it is also true that the Cossacks were somewhat ambivalent about the definitive removal of a threat that provided their main *raison d'être*.

19 See Jörg Brechtefeld, *Mitteleuropa and German Politics: 1848 to the Present* (London: Macmillan, 1996), especially the maps on pp. 98–102.

20 Friedrich Naumann, *Mitteleuropa*, as translated by Christabel Meredith under the title *Central Europe*, (London: P.S. King & Son, 1917), pp. 123–5.

21 Dmytro Doroschenko, *Die Ukraine und das Reich* (Liepzig: S. Hirzel, 1942), pp. 154–5; Hrytsak, *Narys istorii Ukraïny*, pp. 77 and 103. See also Rohrbach, *Russland und mir* (Stuttgart, 1915), pp. 16–18.

22 David Stevenson, *The First World War and International Politics* (Oxford: Oxford University Press, 1988), p. 199.

23 Ihor Kamenet'skyi, 'Nimets'ka polityka suproty Ukraïnu v 1918-mu rotsi ta ïï istorychna heneza', *Ukraïns'kyi istoryk*, 1–4 (1968), pp. 5–18, at p. 12.

24 Michael Burleigh, *Germany Turns Eastwards: A Study of 'Ostforschung' in the Third Reich* (Cambridge, UK: Cambridge University Press, 1988); Derhachov et al., *Ukrainian Statehood*, pp. 135–7.

25 Thomas G. Masaryk, *The New Europe (The Slav Standpoint)* (2nd edn; London: Eyre & Spottiswoode, 1918), pp. 43–4 (on p. 43 Masaryk refers to the 'politically unripe body of the Ukraine'); O.I. Bochkovs'kyi, *T.G. Masaryk, natsional'na problema ta ukraïns'ke pytannia* (Podebrady/ Prague, 1930), pp. 223–32.

26 See András Rónai, *Atlas of Central Europe* (Budapest: Institute of Political Sciences, 1945; and Püski, 1993).

27 George Schöpflin and Nancy Wood (eds), *In Search of Central Europe* (Oxford: Polity Press, 1989).

28 Oleksandr Pavliuk, 'Ukraine and Regional Cooperation in Central and Eastern Europe', *Security Dialogue*, 28, 3 (1997), pp. 347–61, at p. 355. On the traditional attitudes of Poland, Hungary, historical Czechoslovakia and Romania towards Ukraine, see Derhachov et al., *Ukrainian Statehood*, pp. 143–205.

29 Oleksii Tolochko, 'The Good, the Bad and the Ugly', *Krytyka*, 7–8 (1998), pp. 24–31, at p. 29. See also Yaroslav Hrytsak, 'Skhidna Yevropa yak intelektual'na konstruktsiia', *Krytyka*, 11 (November 1998), pp. 17–21.

30 Timothy Garton Ash, *The Uses of Adversity* (Cambridge, UK: Granta/ Penguin, 1988), p. 170; Milan Kundera, 'The Tragedy of Central Europe', *New York Review of Books*, 26 April 1984.

31 Reprinted in Drahomanov, *Sobranie polytycheskykh sochinenii*, vol. 1 (Paris: Société nouvelle de librairie et d'édition, 1905).

32 Rudolf Kjellén, *Die politischen Probleme des Weltkrieges* (Leipzig, 1916), p. 98. Kjellén's map is also notable for his assumption that Scandinavians as well as Austrians are 'German', that Croats and Bosnians are all 'Serbs' and for his omission of Slovaks and Lithuanians. Careful observers will also note that Kjellén classified Crimea and parts of southern Ukraine as 'Russian'.

33 Quoted in Derhachov et al., *Ukrainian Statehood*, pp. 122–4.

34 R.W. Seton-Watson, 'Our Peace Terms (October 1918)', *Europe in the Melting-Pot* (London: Macmillan, 1919), p. 183.

35 See Samuel Huntington, *The Clash of Civilisations*, pp. 165–8 for a modern perpetuation of this stereotype.

36 See chapter six in Todorova, *Imagining the Balkans*, which can stand on its own as an essay on this question, pp. 148 and 156. See also Heikki Mikelli, *Europe as an Idea and an Identity* (London: Macmillan, 1998).

37 Halford Mackinder, *Democratic Ideals and Reality* (London: Constable, 1919).

38 *Ukraïns'ka hazeta*, 26 September 1996.

39 See the special issue of *Politychnyi portret Ukraïny*, 18 (1997) on foreign policy issues.

40 Volodymyr Horbulin, 'National Security of Ukraine and International Security', *Political Thought* (Kiev), 1 (1997), pp. 80–93, at p. 84.

41 Oleksandr Kupchyshyn, 'Spivrobitny-tstvo z SND, intehratsiia z Yevropoiu', *Polityka i chas*, 7 (1996), pp. 13–16.

42 Volodymyr Horbulin, 'Ukraine's Place in Today's Europe', *Politics and the Times*, 1 (October–December 1995), pp. 10–15, at p. 14.

43 Ukraine signed a Partnership and Cooperation Agreement with the EU in May 1994, but it only came into operation in March 1998.

44 Zbigniew Brzezinski, *The Grand Chessboard: American Primacy and its Geostrategic Imperatives* (New York: Basic Books, 1997), pp. 31, 40–1 and 46–7.

45 Ibid., pp. 34, 46 and 92–3.

46 Quoted in Yuri Shcherbak, *The Strategic Role of Ukraine* (Cambridge, Mass.: Harvard Papers in Ukrainian Studies, 1998), p. 63.

47 Brzezinski, *The Grand Chessboard*, pp. 39, 84–5 and 121–2; Brzezinski, 'A Geostrategy for Eurasia', *Foreign Affairs*, 76, 5 (September–October 1997), pp. 50–64, at p. 60.

48 Zbigniew Brzezinski, 'Ukraine's Critical Role in the Post-Soviet Space', *Politics and the Times*, 2–3 (1997), pp. 16–23, at pp. 21–2.

49 O. F. Belov et al., *Natsional'na bezpeka Ukraïny, 1994–1996 rr.* (Kiev: National Institute of Strategic Studies, 1997), pp. 117 and 112.

50 Yaroslav Bilinsky quotes Jim Hoagland's opinion that both France and Germany 'believe [NATO expansion] should stop at the frontiers of the former Soviet Union'; *Endgame in NATO's Enlargement: The Baltic States and Ukraine* (Westport: Praeger, 1999), p. 92.

51 Belov, *Natsional'na bezpeka Ukraïny*, p. 119.

52 The full text is in Bilinsky, *Endgame in NATO's Enlargement*, appendix II, and Lubomyr Hajda (ed.), *Ukraine in the World* (Cambridge, Mass.: Harvard Ukrainian Research Institute, 1999), appendix I.

53 Roman Koval', 'Evraziistvo: ukraïns'ka versiia', in his *Z kym i proty koho* (Kiev: DSU, 1992), pp. 21 and 23.

54 Mykhailo Hrushevs'kyi, *Na porozi novoï Ukraïny* (Kiev: 1918). See the reprint edited by Lubomyr R. Wynar, *On the Threshold of the New Ukraine* (New York: Ukrainian Historical Association, 1992), pp. 18–20.

55 Lypa, *Rozpodil Rosiï*, p. 80.

56 Ibid. p. 65.

57 Dmytro Korchyns'kyi, *Vyklykaiu vohon' na sebe!* (Kiev: n.p., 1998), p. 26.

58 Hryn'ov, *Nova Ukraïna: yakoiu ya ïï bachu*, p. 83; and Dmytro Vydrin and Dmytro Tabachnyk, *Ukraïna na porozi*

XXI stolittia: politychnyi aspekt (Kiev: Lybid', 1995), pp. 37 and 126.

59 Vydrin and Tabachnyk, *Ukraïna na porozi XXI stolittia*, pp. 136 and 130.

60 See also O.L. Valevs'kyi and M.M. Honchar, *Struktura heopolitychnykh interesiv Ukraïny: Monohrafiia* (Kiev: National Institute of Strategic Research, 1995) on the importance of the south-eastern vector in Ukrainian foreign policy.

61 In 1919 UNR diplomats floated the idea of a 'Black Sea Union' involving Ukraine, Georgia, Azerbaijan, Armenia and the embryonic Ukrainian Republic in the Kuban; Volodymyr Serhiichuk, 'Do istoriï stvorennia Chornomors'ko-Baltiis'koho soiuzu', *Rozbudova derzhavy*, 9 (September 1994), pp. 36–8, at p. 36.

62 Hryhorii Perepelytsia, *Bez"iadernyi status i natsional'na bezpeka Ukraïny* (Kiev: National Institute of Strategic Research, 1998), p. 79.

63 Belov et al., *Natsional'na bezpeka Ukraïny*, p. 120.

64 The Young Turk paper *Jeune Turque*, as quoted in Derhachov, *Ukrainian Statehood*, p. 209.

65 Derhachov, *Ukrainian Statehood*, p. 213.

66 Author's interview with Hüseyin Bagci, of the Middle East Technical University, Ankara, 20 March 1998.

67 'Stavlennia rosiian do Ukraïny ta ukraïntsiv', *Politychnyi kalendar* (Kiev: Institute of Post-Communist Society, issue 3, November 1997), p. 34.

68 Gennadii Ziuganov, *Veriu v Rossiiu* (Voronezh: Voronezh, 1995), pp. 37–8.

69 Brégy and Obolensky, *The Ukraine – A Russian Land*, pp. 19–20.

70 Gennadii Ziuganov (ed.), *Sovremennaia Russkaia Ideia i Gosudarstvo* (Moscow, 1995), p. 28.

71 Vladimir P. Lukhin, 'Our Security Predicament', *Foreign Policy*, 88 (fall 1992), pp. 57–75, at p. 63.

72 Aleksandr Dugin, *Osnovy geopolitiki. Geopoliticheskoe budushchee Rossii* (Moscow: Artogeia, 2nd edn, 1999), pp. 800–1. Emphasis in original.

73 Aleksandr Dugin, *Osnovy geopolitiki.* (Moscow: Arktogeia, 1st edn, 1997), pp. 377 and 379.

74 Solzhenitsyn, *Rossiia v obvale*, p. 78.

75 Dugin, *Osnovy geopolitiki*, 2nd edn, p. 799.

76 Dugin, *Osnovy geopolitiki*, 1st edn, p. 382.

77 E.F. Morozov, 'Bol'shoi Evraziiskii Proekt', *Russkii Geopoliticheskii Sbornik*, 2 (1997), pp. 14–26, at pp. 22–3. The author is grateful to Dominique Arel for providing this source.

78 Wolkonsky, *The Ukraine Question*, pp. 136–8, 121 and the map on p. 236.

79 Alexei Mitrofanov, *Shagi novoi geopolitiki* (Moscow: Russkii vestnik, 1997), pp. 274 and 173.

80 Mitrofanov, *Shagi novoi geopolitiki*, pp. 273–5. Amongst Mitrofanov's other views was the suggestion that the floods that struck Poland and the Czech Republic in late 1997 were a direct consequence of the decision to expand NATO 'negatively reflecting on the state of Europe's weather': ibid., p. 267.

81 *Le Monde*, 29 January 1994, p. 7.

82 Huntington, *The Clash of Civilizations*, p. 20.

83 Ziuganov (ed.), *Sovremennaia Russkaia Ideia i Gosudarstvo*, p. 29.

84 Gennadii Ziuganov, *Za Gorizontom* (Moscow: Informpechat, 1995), p. 30.

85 Ziuganov likes this phrase so much it can be found in *Rossiia i sovremennyi mir* (Moscow: Obozrevatel', 1995), p. 20; *Veriu v Rossiiu*, p. 73; and in *Rossiia – Rodina moia. Ideologiia gosudarstvennogo patriotizma* (Moscow: Informpechat', 1996), p. 50.

86 Ziuganov (ed.), *Sovremennaia Russkaia Ideia i Gosudarstvo*, pp. 26–31.

87 For Huntington's views on Ukraine, see *The Clash of Civilizations*, pp. 37, 165–8 and the map on p. 159.

88 See Milan Hauner, *What is Asia to Us? Russia's Asian Heartland Yesterday and Today* (London: Routledge, 1992).

89 Dugin, *Osnovy geopolitiki*, 1st edn, p. 382; Ziuganov, *Veriu v Rossiiu*, p. 45.

90 See the critical reply to Dugin by Arsenii Zinchenko in *Polityka i chas*, 1 (1998).

91 Brian W. Blouet, 'Sir Halford Mackinder as British High Commissioner to South Russia, 1919–1920', *The Geographical Journal*, 142, 2 (July 1976), pp. 228–36, at p. 234. See also Blouet's *Halford Mackinder: A Biography* (College Station: Texas A&M University Press, 1987), pp. 163 and 172–7.

92 Gennadii Ziuganov, *Geografiia pobedy. Osnovy rossiiskoi geopolitiki* (Moscow: n.p. 1998), p. 283; Dugin, *Osnovy geopolitiki*, 1st edn, pp. 68–72.

93 As quoted in the collection *Rosiia, yaku my . . .* (Kiev: Ukrainian Centre for Independent Political Research, 1996), p. 22.

94 Radio Russia, SWB SU 3083, 22 November 1997, pp. 14–15.

95 Ihor Losiev, 'Ukraïns'ki kompleksy rosiis'koï svidomosti', *Heneza*, special issue (1999), pp. 48–54.

96 *Uriadovyi kur"ier*, 3 June 1997.

97 The Ukrainian Rada approved the treaty by 317 votes to 27 in January 1998. The Russian Duma did so by 244 votes to 30 on 25 December 1998, the seventh anniversary of Gorbachev's resignation as Soviet president, seeming to think that it actually promoted 'reintegration'.

98 Kis', *Final Tret'oho Rymu*, pp. 11 and 726. On Russia's 'civilisational marginalism', see ibid., p. 6.

99 Yevhen Hutsalo, *Mental'nist' ordy* (Kiev: Prosvita, 1996). For some similar views, see Oleh Hyrniv, *Ukraïna i Rosiia: partnerstvo chy protystoiannia? Etnopolitychnyi analiz* (L'viv: Institute of Popular Sciences, 1997); and the work by the émigré author Petro Holubenko, *Ukraïna i Rosiia u svitli kul'turnykh vzaiemyn* (Kiev: Dnipro, 1993).

100 Lypa, *Rozpodil Rosiï*, p. 57.

101 Ibid., p. 59. Lypa further subdivided the 'Muscovites' into Novgorodians, Suzdalians, 'south-easterners' (from Riazan) etc.

102 Zbigniew Brzezinski, 'A Geostrategy for Eurasia', *Foreign Affairs*, 76, 5 (September–October 1997), pp. 50–64, at p. 60.

103 Author's interview with Borys Oliinyk, 17 June 1997.

104 Sergei Kiselev and Natal'ia Kiseleva, *Razmyshleniia o Kryme i geopolitike* (Simferopil': Krymskii Arkhiv, 1994), pp. 20–1.

105 Pavlo Lazarenko, 'Optimisticheskaia tragediia vostochnykh slavian', *Dniprovskaia pravda*, 29 June 1998.

106 Author's interview with Yevhen Marmazov, 18 June 1997.

107 From the election programme of the Communist Party, *Vybory '98*, p. 10.

108 Valerii Safonov, 'Chto stroit'? (Slavianskii proekt)', *Tovarysh*, 36 (September 1998).

109 See for example Borys Oliinyk's polemic, *Khto nastupnyi?* ('Who's Next?') (Kiev: Oriiany, 1999).

Chapter 14

1 Jaroslaw Koshiw, *Beheaded: The Killing of a Journalist*, (Reading: Artemia Press, 2003), pp. 58 and 235; Nikolai [Mykola] Mel'nichenko, *Kto est' kto. Na divane prezidenta Kuchmy*, (Kiev: No pub, 2002), p. 10.

2 See Koshiw, 'Kuchma's "Parallel Cabinet": The center of President Kuchma's authoritarian rule based on the Melnychenko recordings', at http://www.uottawa.ca/academic/gradetudesup/ukr/pdf/P_Koshiw_Danyliw07.pdf

3 http://www.uottawa.ca/academic/gradetudesup/ukr/ukraine_list/ukl354_11.html

4 Yaroslav Koshiv (Jaroslaw Koshiw), *Gongadze. Ubiistvo, kotoroe izmenilo Ukrainu*, (Moscow: Prava cheloveka, 2005), p. 225.

5 Adapted from the translation at http://eng.maidanua.org/node/137. The original broadcast of the tape on Channel 5 was at http://5tv.com.ua/pr_archiv/136/0/265/.

6 Jaroslaw Koshiw, The Politics of Kuchma – the Melnychenko Recordings.

7 Anders Åslund, *How Ukraine Became a Market Economy and Democracy*, (Washington, DC: Peterson Institute, 2009), pp. 180 and 182–3.

8 See http://www.eerc.kiev.ua/news/Materials/Aslund/AslundR1.pdf.

9 See 'It's a Gas: Funny Business in the Turkmen-Ukraine Gas Trade', April 2006, http://www.globalwitness.org/reports/show.php/en.00088.html. Since 2007 at www.globalwitness.org/media_library_detail.php/479/en/its_a_gas._funny_business_in_the_turkmen_ukraine_g.

10 Edward Chow and Jonathan Elkind, 'Where East Meets West: European Gas and Ukrainian Reality, *The Washington Quarterly*, vol. 32, no. 1 (January 2009), pp. 77–92.

11 This argument is made by Margarita Balmaceda, *Energy Dependency, Politics, and Corruption in the Former Soviet Union: Russia's power, oligarchs' profits and Ukraine's missing energy policy, 1995–2006*, (London: Routledge, 2008).

12 Yuliia Mostova, 'Pro butony, kvitochky ta yahidky', *Dzerkalo tyzhnia*, no. 2, 2006, http://www.dt.ua/ 1000/1030/52384/. See also Mostova, 'HAZOVA FIRTASHka', *Dzerkalo tyzhnia*, no. 17, http://www.dt.ua/1000/1030/53328/.

13 Oleg Varfolomeyev, 'Did Berezovsky Finance Ukraine's Orange Revolution?', *Eurasia Daily Monitor*, vol. 2, no. 173, 19 September 2005.

14 See 'Ukrainian president fires prosecutor', 15 October 2005, www.ua-reporter.com/eng/13932.

15 'S'ohodni BYuT opryliudnyt' zapysy, shcho svidchat' pro pidkup Moroza', *Hazeta po-ukraïns'ky*, 15 September 2006, http://gpu-ua.info/index.php?&id=130312.

16 Åslund, *How Ukraine Became a Market Economy and Democracy*, p. 221.

17 See www.kiis.com.ua.

18 Elena Tribushnaia, 'Rossiia i Zapad: voina na poroge', *Segodnia*, 26 August 2008, http://www.segodnya.ua/news/12059037.html.

19 See www.president.gov.ua/news/10989.html.

20 See Åslund, *How Ukraine Became a Market Economy and Democracy*, chapters 8 and 9.

Chapter 15

1. Interview with Hryhorii Nemeriia, 15 January 2010.

2. Stefan Wagstyl and Roman Oleachyk, 'Ukraine Election Divides Oligarchs', *Financial Times*, 15 January 2010.

3. Stephen Grey, Tom Bergin, Sevgil Musaieva and Roman Anin, 'Putin's Allies Channelled Billions to Ukraine Oligarch', *Reuters*, 26 November 2014; www.reuters.com/article/2014/11/26/russia-capitalism-gas-special-report-pix-idUSL3N0TF4QD20141126.

4. Richard Boudreaux, 'Bucks Populi', *Wall Street Journal*, 5 February 2010.

5. Guy Faulconbridge, Anna Dabrowska and Stephen Grey, 'Toppled "Mafia" President cost Ukraine up to $100 Billion, Prosecutor Says', *Reuters*, 30 April 2014; www.reuters.com/article/2014/04/30/us-ukraine-crisis-yanukovich-idUSBREA3T0K820140430.

6. 'Viktor Yanukovych Boasted of Ukraine Corruption, Says Mikheil Saakashvili', *Guardian*, 25 February 2014.

7. See http://www.politico.com/magazine/story/2014/10/vladimir-putins-coup-112025_Page3.html#.VPibBvmG9J8.

8. 'Inadequate Yanukovych Promised to Bury Us All – Turchynov', *Gazeta.ua*, 21 November 2014; http://gazeta.ua/articles/politics/_neadekvatnij-anukovich-obicyav-nas-usih-zakopati-turchinov/594135.

9. See http://news.eizvestia.com/news_politics/full/756-chto-i-kto-stoit-za-zhestokostyu-berkuta-ili-kak-rabotal-rossijskij-omon-na-majdane.

10. C. J. Chivers, 'A Kiev Question: What Became of the Missing?', *The New York Times*, 9 March 2014; www.nytimes.com/2014/03/10/world/europe/a-kiev-question-what-became-of-the-missing.html?_r=0.

11. Andrew Higgins and Andrew E. Kramer, 'Ukraine Leader Was Defeated Even Before He Was Ousted', *New York Times*, 3 January 2015; www.nytimes.com/2015/01/04/world/europe/ukraine-leader-was-defeated-even-before-he-was-ousted.html?_r=0.

12. Serhiy Kudelia, 'Domestic Sources of the Donbas Insurgency', *PONARS Eurasia Policy Memo*, no. 351, September 2014; www.ponarseurasia.org/memo/domestic-sources-donbas-insurgency.

13. Richard Sakwa, *Frontline Ukraine: Crisis in the Borderlands* (London and New York: I.B. Tauris, 2015), talks of 'two models of Ukrainian statehood', caricatured as 'monist nationalism' and 'Malorussianism'.

14. 'How Relations Between Ukraine and Russia Should Look Like? Public Opinion polls' Results', Kiev International Institute of Sociology website, 4 March 2014; http://kiis.com.ua/?lang=eng&cat=reports&id=236&page=1.

15. 'The Views and Opinions of Residents of South-Eastern Ukraine: April 2014', Zn.ua website, 18 April 2014; http://zn.ua/UKRAINE/mneniya-i-vzglyady-zhiteley-yugo-vostoka-ukrainy-aprel-2014-143598_.html.

16. See http://zn.ua/UKRAINE/koval-rossiya-nachala-podgotovku-k-gibridnoy-voyne-v-ukraine-kak-minimum-let-8-nazad-148949_.html.

17. See http://www.lithuaniatribune.com/69155/speech-by-andrei-illarionov-at-nato-pa-session-in-vilnius-201469155/.

18. 'Girkin: "We Forcibly Herded Crimean Deputies to Vote for a Referendum on Secession from Ukraine"', *YouTube*, 25 January 2015; www.youtube.com/watch?v=aelwn_UfeN0. See also http://zavtra.ru/content/view/kto-tyi-strelok/.

19. Lucian Kim, 'Kremlin TV', *Slate*, 19 March 2015; www.slate.com/articles/news_and_politics/foreigners/2015/03/vladimir_putin_s_documentary_is_trying_to_rewrite_history_crimea_the_way.html.

20. 'Girkin: "We Forcibly Herded Crimean Deputies"', *YouTube*.

21. 'Russia Planned Invasion Through Sumy and Chernihiv – Malomuzh', *TVi*, 5 March 2015; http://tvi.ua/new/2015/03/05/rosiya_planuvala_vtorhnennya_cherez_sumy_ta_chernihiv__malomuzh.

22. 'Battle for Ukraine: How a Diplomatic Success Unravelled', *Financial Times*, 3 February 2015; www.ft.com/cms/s/2/7cfc8ac6-ab17-11e4-91d2-00144feab7de.html#axzz3UBUUWmHz.

23. Igor Sutyagin, 'Russian Troops in Ukraine', Royal United Services Institute Briefing Paper, March 2015; www.rusi.org/downloads/assets/201503_BP_Russian_Forces_in_Ukraine_FINAL.pdf.

24. Ibid.

25. See http://www.sova-center.ru/racism-xenophobia/publications/2014/09/d30505/.

26. Sutyagin, 'Russian Troops in Ukraine', p. 7.

27. 'Death Toll in Ukraine Conflict Exceeds 5,000, May Be "Considerably Higher" – UN', United Nations website, 23 January 2015; www.un.org/apps/news/story.asp?NewsID=49882#.VMKQSmTF9FA.

28. Adrian Karatnycky, 'Making the Most Of Minsk', *New York Times*, 19 February 2015. Another source in December 2014 counted 350 tanks; http://zik.ua/en/news/2014/12/14/rebels_have_700_tanks_and_apcs_in_donbas_549013.

29. 'Ukraine Death Toll Hits 6,000 Amid Ongoing Fighting – UN', *UN News Centre*, 2 March 2015; www.un.org/apps/news/story.asp?NewsID=50215.

30. Andriy Portnov, 'Ukraine's "far east": on the effects and genealogy of Ukrainian Galician reductionism', *NYU Jordan Center*, translated 15 August 2014; http://jordanrussiacenter.org/news/ukraines-far-east-effects-genealogy-ukrainian-galician-reductionism/.

31. Speech of Russian foreign minister Sergei Lavrov to the Russian Duma, 20 March 2014; www.mid.ru/brp_4.nsf/0/94D6676508BC6C4844257CA2005B0613.

32. See http://chesno.org/media/gallery/2014/10/30/parl_results.jpg.

33. Mykhail Dubynianskyii, 'Zolota sere-dyna', *Ukraïns'ka pravda*, 28 June 2010; www.pravda.com.ua/articles/2010/06/28/5173726.

34. Author's interview, 25 October 2014.

35. See www.dif.org.ua/ua/polls/2014_polls/jjorjojkpkhpkp.html.

Chapter 16

1   Anna Shamanska, 'Behind Closed Doors: Ukraine's Panicked Meeting Ahead Of Crimean Seizure', *RFE/RL*, 23 February 2016; www.rferl.org/a/ukraine-crimea-seizure-panicked-meeting/27569836.html.

2   'Conflict-Related Civilian Casualties in Ukraine', Office of the UN High Commissioner for Human Rights (OHCHR), 27 January 2022; https://ukraine.un.org/sites/default/files/2022-02/Conflict-related%20civilian%20casualties%20as%20of%2031%20December%202021%20%28rev%2027%20January%202022%29%29%20corr%20EN_0.pdf.

3   Ihor Burakovskyi, 'Ukraine's Fight Against Corruption: The Economic Front. Economic Assessment of Anticorruption Measures Implemented 2014–2018. Research Report', Institute for Economic Research and Policy Consulting, 13 July 2018; www.ier.com.ua/en/publications/reports?pid=5993.

4   'The Tenth National Survey: Ideological Markers of the War (27 April 2022)', *Rating*, 3 May 2022; https://ratinggroup.ua/en/research/ukraine/desyatyy_obschenacionalnyy_opros_ideologicheskie_markery_voyny_27_aprelya_2022.html.

5   'Public Opinion Survey of Residents of Ukraine', *IRI*, 13–27 December 2018; www.iri.org/wp-content/uploads/legacy/iri.org/2019.1.30_ukraine_poll.pdf.

6   'Perception of Own Wellbeing by the Residents of Ukraine in May 2018', *KIIS*, 13 July 2018; www.kiis.com.ua/?lang=eng&cat=reports&id=773&t=7&page=1.

7   David Dalton, 'How Did the Ukrainian Oligarchy Keep Going after Euromaidan?', *Vox Ukraine*, 22 February 2021; https://voxukraine.org/en/how-did-the-ukrainian-oligarchy-keep-going-after-euromaidan/.

8   Oleksiy Sorokin, 'Screen Masters: TV Stations Guard Interests of Oligarchs', *Kyiv Post,* 5 March 2021; www.kyivpost.com/ukraine-politics/screen-masters-tv-stations-guard-the-interests-of-oligarchs.html.

9   Graham Stack, Sergei Kuznetsov and Ben Aris, 'Poroshenko's Empire – the Business of Being Ukraine's President', *BNE Intellinews*, 29 August 2016; www.intellinews.com/long-read-poroshenkos-empire-the-business-of-being-ukraines-president-103790/.

10 Yaroslav Hrytsak, 'Sladkaia kontrrevolyutsiia', *Novoe Vremya*, 11 June 2017; http://nv.ua/opinion/grytsak/sladkaja-kontrrevoljutsija-1288921.html.

11 Volodymyr Paniotto, 'Trust to Social Institutes [sic], December 2018', *KIIS*, 29 January 2019; www.kiis.com.ua/?lang=eng&cat=reports&id=817&page=2.

12 dastin18, 'Strana 404 – chto eto znachit?', *pikabu*, 2017; https://pikabu.ru/story/strana_404__chto_yeto_znachit__4433793.

13 'Christmas and Revolution: The Study of Religious Rhetoric and Imagery During the Revolution of Dignity in Ukraine 2013–2014', *Journal of Religion in Europe.*

14 'Ukraïna 30 rokiv ne maie svoho Moiseia, – Pankevych', Original on Espreso TV, *YouTube*, 25 August 2021; www.youtube.com/watch?v=5pTWh3RikY8.

15 Artem Skoropadskii, ' "O sotsial'noi psikhoterapii" ', *Den'*, 14 January 2014; https://day.kyiv.ua/ru/article/podrobnosti/o-socialnoy-psihoterapii.

16 Interview with Rostyslav Pavlenko, 25 June 2019.

17 Oleksandr Zhelizniak, 'Ob"iednavchyi sobor: rozkryto intryhu obrannia Epifaniia mytropolytom', *Narodna Pravda*, 16 December 2018; https://narodna-pravda.ua/2018/12/16/ob-yednavchij-sobor-rozkrito-intrigu-obrannya-epifaniya-mitropolitom/.

18 'Patriarch Bartholomew Explains Metropolitan Onufriy Reasons for Ukraine Church's Autocephaly (Letter)', *UNIAN*, 7 December 2018; www.unian.info/politics/10367883-patriarch-bartholomew-explains-metropolitan-onufriy-reasons-for-ukraine-church-s-autocephaly-letter.html.

19 'Tserkovnaia Ukraina stanovitsia zavisimoi ot islamskogo Stambula?', *Regnum.ru*, 12 October 2018; https://regnum.ru/news/2499499.html.

20 'Osoblyvosti relihiinoho i tserkovno-relihiinoho samovyznachennia hromadian Ukraïny: tendentsiï 2000–2020 rr.', *Razumkov Centre*, 25 November 2020; https://razumkov.org.ua/uploads/article/2020_religiya.pdf.

21 'Sign Petition: Ten Theses for the Orthodox Church of Ukraine', *RISU*, 12 February 2019; https://risu.ua/en/sign-petition-ten-theses-for-the-orthodox-church-of-ukraine_n96394.

22 Vitaliy Klos, *Avtokefaliia Ukraïns'koï Tserkvy: Ohliad vid Khreshchennia do Synodal'noho Tomosu* (Kiev, 2019), p. 63.

23 Interview with Zevstratii, 27 June 2019.

24 Bukvy's editorial, 'How "Bot Farms" Use Smear Campaigns on Social Media to Attack Political Opponents of Zelensky', *Bukvy*, 15 February 2021; https://bykvu.com/eng/thoughts/how-bot-farms-use-smear-campaigns-on-social-media-to-attack-political-opponents-of-zelensky/.

25 Volodymyr Yermolenko, 'What Does Comedian's Big Win Mean for Ukraine?', *Atlantic Council*, 2 April 2019; www.atlanticcouncil.org/blogs/ukrainealert/what-does-comedian-s-big-win-mean-for-ukraine.

26 'New Ukraine Poll Reveals Increased Concern over Military Conflict in Donbas', *International Republican Institute*, 20 August 2018; https://www.iri.org/resources/new-ukraine-poll-reveals-increased-concern-over-military-conflict-in-donbas/. 'Yak zminylasia dumka ukraïntsiv pro rosiis'ko-ukraïns'ku viinu za dva roky prezydentsva Zelens'koho', *Democratic Initiatives Foundation*, 9 June 2021; https://dif.org.ua/article/yak-zminil-asya-dumka-ukraintsiv-pro-rosiysko-ukrainsku-viynu-za-dva-roki-prezidenst-va-zelenskogo?fbclid=IwAR0lNd-9cWOYeD-4eApezo7FtMYb2lPD9jmr-0PRZelrmE573aZeB1fr7Z6aI.

27 'Concluding Remarks #ksf2019. Oksana Zabuzhko, Writer, Philosopher, Shevchenko Prize Laureate of 2019', *Kyiv Security Forum*, 17 April 2019; http://ksf.openukraine.org/en/photo-video/video/79-pidsumki-ksf2019-oksana-zabuzhko-pysymennicya-filosof-laureat-shevchenkivsykoji-premiji-2019-roku.

28 Interview with Rostyslav Pavlenko, 9 April 2021.

29 'Read Trump's Phone Conversation with Volodymyr Zelensky', *CNN*, 26 September 2019; https://edition.cnn.com/2019/09/25/politics/donald-trump-ukraine-transcript-call/index.html.

30 Ian Schwarz, 'Giuliani: I Have Documents Showing Ukrainian Collusion With Top Democrats', *RealClearPolitics*, 3 October 2019; www.realclearpolitics.com/video/2019/10/03/giuliani_i_have_documents_showing_ukrainian_collusion_with_top_democrats.html.

31 Adam Entous, 'The Man in the Middle', *New Yorker*, 23 December 2019, p. 54.

32 Andrew Roth, 'Ukraine to Investigate Leaked Calls between Joe Biden and Ex-President', *The Guardian*, 20 May 2020; www.theguardian.com/world/2020/may/20/ukraine-joe-biden-petro-porosh-enko-recordings-investigation.

33 'Who is behind the Media Campaign against George Soros?', *Ukraine Crisis Media Center*, 4 May 2020; https://medium.com/@hwagaucmc/who-is-behind-the-media-campaign-against-george-soros-b51be92dc0c9.

Chapter 17

1 Simon Shuster, 'The Untold Story of the Ukraine Crisis', *Time*, 2 February 2022; https://time.com/6144109/russia-ukraine-vladimir-putin-viktor-medvedchuk/.

2 'UCMC, How Russian Media Foments Hostility Towards the West', *UCMC*; https://disinfoportal.org/how-russian-media-foments-hostility-toward-the-west/. See also Olga Smirnova, 'Russian TV: Contesting European Values', *Reuters Institute Fellow's Paper*, 2016; https://reutersinstitute.politics.ox.ac.uk/our-research/russian-tv-contesting-european-values.

3 UCMC, 'War Narratives on Russian TV', *YouTube*, 20 September 2018; http://uacrisis.org/66976-grupa-z-analizu-gi-bridnih-zagroz-ucmc.

4 Illia Gladshtein, 'How Russian Cinema Dehumanized Ukrainians and Laid the Ground for Today's War Crimes', *Ukraine World*, 19 May 2022; https://ukraineworld.org/articles/russian-aggression/how-russian-cinema-dehumanized-ukrainians?fbclid=IwAR1f2CZJFpQeW6itLkNVvil0RoVNvbZmixKrLjL3iOATtv3j4kfnN-L9zPzk.

5 Vladimir Solov'ev, ' "Zachem nam takoi mir, esli tam ne budet Rossii?" Putin – o global'noi katastrofe posle yadernogo udara', *Meduza*, 7 March 2018; https://meduza.io/news/2018/03/07/zachem-nam-takoy-mir-esli-tam-ne-budet-rossii-putin-o-globalnoy-katastrofe-posle-yader-nogo-udara.

6 Masha Gessen, 'Inside Putin's Propaganda Machine', *New Yorker*, 18 May 2022; www.newyorker.com/news/annals-of-communications/inside-putins-propaganda-machine.

7 'Article by Vladimir Putin "On the Historical Unity of Russians and Ukrainians" ', *Kremlin.ru*, 12 July 2021; http://en.kremlin.ru/events/president/news/66181.

8 'Pochemu bessmysllenny kontakty s nyneshmim ukrainskim rukovodstvom', *Kommersant*, 11 October 2021; www.kommersant.ru/doc/5028300.

9 'Citizens' Assessment of the Main Theses of Putin's Article "On the Historical Unity of Russians and Ukrainians" (July–August 2021)', *Razumkov Centre*, 11 August 2021; https://razumkov.org.ua/napriamky/sotsiologichni-doslidzhennia/otsinka-gromadianamy-ukrainy-golovnykh-tez-statti-v-putina-pro-istorychnu-iednist-rosiian-ta-ukraintsiv.

10 Richard Allen Greene and the Visuals Team, 'Half of Russians Say It Would Be Right to Use Military Force to keep Ukraine out of NATO', *CNN*, 23 February 2022; https://edition.cnn.com/interactive/2022/02/europe/russia-ukraine-crisis-poll-intl/index.html.

11 Olga Kapustina, 'Belarus Incarcerates Anti-Lukashenko Protesters en Masse', *DW*, 11 December 2020; www.dw.com/en/belarus-incarcerates-anti-lukashenko-protesters-en-masse/a-55912923.

12 See the data from the human rights organisation Viasna at https://prisoners.spring96.org/en.

13 'Transcript: Vladimir Putin's Televised Address on Ukraine', *Bloomberg*, 24 February 2022; www.bloomberg.com/news/articles/2022-02-24/full-transcript-vladimir-putin-s-televised-address-to-russia-on-ukraine-feb-24.

14 Nick Reynolds and Dr Jack Watling, 'Ukraine Through Russia's Eyes', *RUSI*, 25 February 2022; https://rusi.org/explore-our-research/publications/commentary/ukraine-through-russias-eyes.

15 'Chy budut' Ukraïntsi chynyty opir rosiis'kii interventsii: rezul'taty telefonnoho opytuvannia, provedenoho 3–11 hrudnia 2021 roku', *KIIS*, 17 December 2021; www.kiis.com.ua/?lang=ukr&cat=reports&id=1079&page=1&fbclid=IwAR3akv1dZbaMZmKbgFTAEEZXNsb0OsB82xdQ5z2cIsijLVoTVa-DID5R1MeM.

16 'Suspil'no-politychni nastroï naselennia (14–16 hrudnia 2021)', *Rating*, 20 December 2021; https://ratinggroup.ua/research/ukraine/obschestvenno-politicheskie_nastroeniya_naseleniya_14-16_dekabrya_2021.html.

17 'Chetverte zahal'nonatsional'ne opytuvannia ukraïntsiv v umovakh viiny (12–13 bereznia 2022)', *Rating*, 15 March 2022; https://ratinggroup.ua/research/ukraine/chetvertyy_obschenacionalnyy_opros_ukraincev_v_usloviyah_voyny_12-13_marta_2022_goda.html.

18 'Vladimir Putin Meets with Members of the Valdai Discussion Club. Transcript of the Plenary Session of the 18th Annual Meeting', *Valdai Club*, 22 October 2021; https://valdaiclub.com/events/posts/articles/vladimir-putin-meets-with-members-of-the-valdai-discussion-club-transcript-of-the-18th-plenary-session/.

19 Yuri Zoria, 'Captured Docs Reveal Date When Russia Greenlit Ukraine Invasion', *Euromaidan Press*, 2 March 2022; https://euromaidanpress.com/2022/03/02/captured-docs-reveal-date-when-russia-greenlit-ukraine-invasion/.

20 Sinéad Baker, 'Ukraine Said Russian Troops Brought Parade Uniforms to Kyiv, Expecting a Quick Triumph that Never Came', *Business Insider*, 7 April 2022; www.businessinsider.com/ukraine-said-found-russian-parade-uniforms-left-behind-in-kyiv-2022-4?r=US&IR=T.

21 Author's conversation with Mark Galeotti, 10 May 2022.

22 Irina Borogan and Andrei Soldatov, 'Putin Places Spies Under House Arrest', *CEPA*, 11 March 2022; https://cepa.org/putin-places-spies-under-house-arrest/. Soldatov and Borogan, 'Vicious Blame Game Erupts Among Putin's Security Forces', *CEPA*, 25 April 2022; https://cepa.org/vicious-blame-game-erupts-among-putins-security-forces/.

23 Gordon Corera, 'Ukraine: Inside the Spies' Attempts to Stop the War', *BBC*, 9 April 2022; www.bbc.co.uk/news/world-europe-61044063.

24 Simon Shuster, 'Inside Zelensky's World', *Time*, 28 April 2022; https://time.com/6171277/volodymyr-zelensky-interview-ukraine-war.

25 'Zahal'nonatsional'ne opytuvannia: Ukraïna v umovakh viiny (1 bereznia 2022)', *Rating*, 1 March 2022; https://ratinggroup.ua/research/ukraine/obschenacionalnyy_opros_ukraina_v_usloviyah_voyny_1_marta_2022.html.

26 Timothy Snyder, 'We Should Say It. Russia Is Fascist', *New York Times*, 19 May 2022; www.nytimes.com/2022/05/19/opinion/russia-fascism-ukraine-putin.html.

27 https://t.me/medvedev_telegram/34, *Telegram*, 5 April 2022.

28 Timofei Sergeitsev, 'Chto Rossiia dolzhna sdelat' s Ukrainoi', *RIA Novosti*, 3 April 2022; https://ria.ru/20220403/ukraina-1781469605.html.

29 'Porushennia prav liudyny na okupovanykh terytoriia'. Press conference of Liudmyla Denysova at UNIAN, *YouTube*, 9 May 2022; www.youtube.com/watch?v=nRiu05hFGc8.

30 'V Minoborony RF zaiavili ob evakuatsii v Rossiiu bolee 950 tysiach zhitelei Ukrainy, DNR i LNR', *Interfaks*, 23 April 2022; www.interfax.ru/russia/837576.

31 Information from military expert Gustav Gressel, 24 May 2022.

32 Mikhail Korostikov, 'Russia Is the Honey Badger of International Relations', *Buzzfeed*, 14 December 2017; www.buzzfeednews.com/article/mikhailkorostikov/the-honey-badger-doctrine.

33 Daniel B. Shapiro, 'Zelenskyy Wants Ukraine to Be "a Big Israel"'. Here's a Road Map', *Atlantic Council*, 6 April 2022; www.atlanticcouncil.org/blogs/new-atlanticist/zelenskyy-wants-ukraine-to-be-a-big-israel-heres-a-road-map/.

34 'Ruslan Stefanchuk: Shansiv u bud'-yakoï prorosiis'koï partiï bil'she ne bude', *RBK Ukraïna*, 25 April 2022; www.rbc.ua/ukr/news/ruslan-stefanchuk-shansov-lyuboy-prorossiyskoy-1650837541.html.

35 'Postanova Soboru Ukraïns'koï Pravoslavnoï Tserkvy vid 27 travnia 2022 roku', *news.church.ua*, 27 May 2022; https://news.church.ua/2022/05/27/postanova-soboru-ukrajinskoji-pravoslavnoji-cerkvi-vid-27-travnya-2022-roku/.

36 'Zelens'kyi – pro Ukraïnu mriï: My mozhemo staty velykym Izraïlem, ale zi svoïm oblychchiam', *UNIAN*, 5 April 2022; www.ukrinform.ua/rubric-uarazom/3449109-zelenskij-pro-ukrainu-mrii-mimozemo-stati-velikim-izrailem-ale-zi-svoim-obliccam.html.

Index